Frommer's®

Switzerland

12th Edition

by Darwin Porter & Danforth Prince

Here's what the critics say about Frommer's:

"Amazingly easy to use. Very portable, very complete."

—*Booklist*

"Detailed, accurate, and easy-to-read information for all price ranges."
—*Glamour Magazine*

"Hotel information is close to encyclopedic."

—*Des Moines Sunday Register*

"Frommer's Guides have a way of giving you a real feel for a place."
—*Knight Ridder Newspapers*

WILEY

Wiley Publishing, Inc.

About the Authors

A team of veteran travel writers, **Darwin Porter** and **Danforth Prince** have produced numerous titles for Frommer's, including best-selling guides to Italy, France, the Caribbean, England, and Germany. Porter is also a noted Hollywood biographer, his most recent releases (2005) being *Howard Hughes: Hell's Angel* and *Brando Unzipped.* He is a noted radio commentator and columnist on popular culture with broadcasts heard in all 50 states. Prince, formerly of the *New York Times* Paris bureau, is the president of Blood Moon Productions and other media-related firms.

Published by:

Wiley Publishing, Inc.

111 River St.
Hoboken, NJ 07030-5774

ISBN-13: 978-0-471-77123-4
ISBN-10: 0-471-77123-6

Editor: Michael Kelly
Production Editor: Bethany J. André
Cartographer: Tim Lohnes
Photo Editor: Richard Fox
Production by Wiley Indianapolis Composition Services

For information on our other products and services or to obtain technical support, please contact our Customer Care Department within the U.S. at 800/762-2974, outside the U.S. at 317/572-3993 or fax 317/572-4002.

Wiley also publishes its books in a variety of electronic formats. Some content that appears in print may not be available in electronic formats.

Manufactured in the United States of America

5   4   3   2

Contents

List of Maps

An Invitation to the Reader

In researching this book, we discovered many wonderful places—hotels, restaurants, shops, and more. We're sure you'll find others. Please tell us about them, so we can share the information with your fellow travelers in upcoming editions. If you were disappointed with a recommendation, we'd love to know that, too. Please write to:

Frommer's Switzerland, 12th Edition
Wiley Publishing, Inc. • 111 River St. • Hoboken, NJ 07030-5774

An Additional Note

Please be advised that travel information is subject to change at any time—and this is especially true of prices. We therefore suggest that you write or call ahead for confirmation when making your travel plans. The authors, editors, and publisher cannot be held responsible for the experiences of readers while traveling. Your safety is important to us, however, so we encourage you to stay alert and be aware of your surroundings. Keep a close eye on cameras, purses, and wallets, all favorite targets of thieves and pickpockets.

Other Great Guides for Your Trip:

Frommer's Europe
Frommer's Europe by Rail
Frommer's Road Atlas Europe

Frommer's Star Ratings, Icons & Abbreviations

Every hotel, restaurant, and attraction listing in this guide has been ranked for quality, value, service, amenities, and special features using a **star-rating system.** In country, state, and regional guides, we also rate towns and regions to help you narrow down your choices and budget your time accordingly. Hotels and restaurants are rated on a scale of zero (recommended) to three stars (exceptional). Attractions, shopping, nightlife, towns, and regions are rated according to the following scale: zero stars (recommended), one star (highly recommended), two stars (very highly recommended), and three stars (must-see).

In addition to the star-rating system, we also use **seven feature icons** that point you to the great deals, in-the-know advice, and unique experiences that separate travelers from tourists. Throughout the book, look for:

Finds	Special finds—those places only insiders know about
Fun Fact	Fun facts—details that make travelers more informed and their trips more fun
Kids	Best bets for kids and advice for the whole family
Moments	Special moments—those experiences that memories are made of
Overrated	Places or experiences not worth your time or money
Tips	Insider tips—great ways to save time and money
Value	Great values—where to get the best deals

The following **abbreviations** are used for credit cards:

AE	American Express	DISC	Discover	V	Visa
DC	Diners Club	MC	MasterCard		

Frommers.com

Now that you have the guidebook to a great trip, visit our website at **www.frommers.com** for travel information on more than 3,000 destinations. With features updated regularly, we give you instant access to the most current trip-planning information available. At Frommers.com, you'll also find the best prices on airfares, accommodations, and car rentals—and you can even book travel online through our travel booking partners. At Frommers.com, you'll also find the following:

- Online updates to our most popular guidebooks
- Vacation sweepstakes and contest giveaways
- Newsletter highlighting the hottest travel trends
- Online travel message boards with featured travel discussions

What's New in Switzerland

Faced with the majestic mountain scenery of Switzerland, you at first think that it is eternal. But there are always changes—a new resort opening up or an old favorite shutting down. The roster of what's hot in dining can shift from year to year. Here are some highlights of the latest developments in Switzerland.

ZURICH This urban bed-and-breakfast hotel, former home of a German-speaking, Broadway-style theater, **Hotel du Theatre**, Seilergraben 69 (© **044/267-26-70**), is truly a find. Just a short walk from the city center and 5 minutes on foot from the Bahnhof, the hotel has comfortable accommodations in an eccentric environment.

Those Italian wine moguls, the Antinori family, have invaded Zurich with their fine wines and sublime Florentine cuisine served at **Cantinetta Antinori**, Augustinergasse 25 (© **044/211-72-10**). Almost overnight the restaurant has become a staple in the local dining picture. The wine tavern is known for its generous portions, high-quality ingredients (often from Antinori farms), and a traditional yet inventive cuisine. See chapter 4.

BASEL The headquarters of the *Evangelische Missionswerk* (Protestant Mission) has emerged as one of the best-value hotels in a superexpensive city. **BildungsZentrum 21**, Missionsstrasse 21 (© **061/260-21-21**), attracts with its central location, its garden, its comfortable rooms, and certainly those affordable prices.

Locals and visitors alike are heading to **Brauerei Fischerstube**, Rheingasse 45 (© **061/692-66-35**), boasting the best beer in a town known for the brew. Its house ale, Ueli Bier, is served in 5-liter portions. Reasonably priced pub grub is also served. See chapter 6.

BERN Gathering rave reviews and an impressive amount of devotees, **Mille Sens,** Markethalle Bubenbergplatz 9 (© **031/329-29-29**), has brought European fusion cuisine to the Swiss capital. The old factory building converted into a restaurant has a warm and inviting ambience to match the culinary creations turned out by the kitchen. See chapter 7.

INTERLAKEN For cozy quarters in an inviting atmosphere **Hotel Alphorn,** Rugenaustrasse 8 (© **033/822-30-51**), is gaining a large and devoted following. It is a favorite for families because of its comfortable bedrooms and reasonable prices.

Fans of Indian food are raving about **Spice India,** Postgasse 6 (© **033/821-00-91**). A vast array of curry dishes, prepared to perfection, await you at this restaurant, and the vegetarian will also find a happy home here. See chapter 8.

LAUSANNE The most visited city museum has gone through a rejuvenation period, evoking the cliché "out with the old, in with the new." **Musée Cantonal des Beaux-Arts,** in the Palais de Rumine, 6, place de la Riponne (© **021/316-34-45**), has placed all artwork from the baroque period and the Renoir collection, among other works of grand masters, into storage. The new focus of the museum is on Swiss artists of the 18th and 19th centuries. See chapter 10.

GENEVA   This French-speaking city has either restored, improved, expanded, or inaugurated new exhibits in a trio of museums. **Fondation Martin Bodmer,** 19-21 route de Guignard (© 022/707-44-33), houses first-printed versions of classics by Dante Alighieri and handwritten texts by Homer. The collection of more than 160,000 books, manuscripts, autographs, and artwork is a highlight for many visitors.

Art lovers have started coming in hordes to see the private collection of one of the world's best-ever art collectors, Josef Mueller. **Musée Barbier-Mueller,** rue Jean-Calvin 10 (© 022/312-02-70), is a place where visitors can see everything from Renoir paintings to primitive pieces from Oceania.

One of the world's best collections of timepieces is causing quite a stir among residents and sightseers alike. The **Patek Philippe Museum,** rue de Vieux Grenadiers 7 (© 022/807-09-10), has antique and historical pieces along with a collection displaying 160 years of Patek Philippe watches. See chapter 11.

LUCERNE   The central location of **Magic Hotel,** Brandgässli (© 041/417-12-20), is only part of the attraction. The hotel, living up to its name, offers the most whimsical decor in town, every room and suite a different statement. Since its opening, families have discovered its theme suites (one is devoted to pirates), and couples warm to its Victorian elegance. See chapter 12.

AROSA   The discerning few are abandoning the highly touted government-rated five-star hotels and checking in to this informal suite hotel: **BelArosa,** Prätschilstrasse (© 081/378-89-99), with spacious living areas—often with a tiled stove and a kitchenette—has become a family favorite. See chapter 13.

KLOSTERS   Originally launched in 1890, **Hotel Vereina,** Highway 179 (© 081/410-27-27), has made a comeback in the 21st century. Ultrachic and elegant, and lying only a short drive from the resort's center, it now reigns as the queen of Klosters, having knocked the Pardenn off its pedestal. See chapter 13.

ST. MORITZ   Internationally renowned sushi chef Nobuyuki "Nobu" Matsuhisa has nourished celebrities and royalty in cities such as London, New York, Los Angeles, and Tokyo for years. Now his namesake restaurant, **Nobu,** is in the Badrutt's Palace Hotel (© 081/837-10-00), along with his long lines of clientele and delectable dishes. See chapter 14.

LOCARNO   The little hotel **Camelia,** Via G.G. Nessi 9 (© 091/743-00-21), has a romantic early-20th-century architecture. It lies in the Muralto section of Locarno, with a shuttle that takes guests to and from the train station. See p. 453.

By all accounts, **Navegna,** via alla Riva 2 (© 091/743-22-22), is gaining a reputation as one of the best restaurants in the area. Almost all the food comes fresh from the owner's farm. The harmony of flavors is rare at a combination hotel/restaurant. See chapter 15.

LUGANO   Just a block away from the lakefront is **San Carlo Garni,** via Nassa 28 (© 091/922-71-07). The hotel's modern decor, comfortable rooms, and low prices made it a huge hit with visitors in 2005.

When the late Baron von Thyssen-Bornemisza sold his astounding collection of modern art to Spain, it looked like a death knell for the **Villa Favorita,** via Rivbera 14 (© 091/972-17-41). That assessment has turned out to be premature. In restored surroundings, the 17th-century mansion, though its collection has been reduced in scope, is still a grand gallery of the works of modern artists such as Jackson Pollock. More and more visitors are discovering it. See chapter 15.

The Best of Switzerland

You're visiting Switzerland to relax and have a good time, and you don't want to waste precious vacation hours searching for the best deals and experiences. So take us along and we'll do the work for you. Throughout our years traveling in Switzerland, we've tested the best lakeshores, reviewed countless restaurants, inspected hotels ranging from remote alpine inns to luxurious city palaces, and sampled the best skiing, mountain climbing, and hiking. We've even learned where to get away from it all when you want to escape the crowds. The following is a very personal, opinionated list of what we consider to be the best Switzerland has to offer.

1 The Best Travel Experiences

- **Hiking the Swiss Mountains:** From the time the snows melt in spring until the late autumn winds blow too powerfully, visitors head for the country's alpine chain to hike its beautiful expanses. Well-trodden footpaths through the valleys and up the mountains are found in all the resorts of Switzerland. Hiking is especially enjoyable in the Ticino and the Engadine, but quite wonderful almost anywhere in the country. You'll find fewer visitors in some of the less-inhabited valleys such as those in the Valais. Every major tourist office in Switzerland has a free list of the best trails in their area. If you go to one of the area's local bookstores, you can purchase topographical maps of wilderness trails.

- **Viewing Castles & Cathedrals:** There is so much emphasis on outdoor sports in Switzerland that many visitors forget that it is rich in history and filled with landmarks from the Middle Ages. Explore at random. Visit the castle at Chillon where Lord Byron wrote *The Prisoner of Chillon*. Everyone knows Gruyères for the cheese, but it's also the

most craggy castle village of Switzerland, complete with dungeon and spectacular panoramic views. Both Bern and Basel have historic Münsters of cathedrals—the one in Bern dates from the 14th century. Among the great cathedrals, St. Nicholas's Cathedral, in the ancient city of Fribourg near Bern, dominates the medieval quarter, and Schloss Thun, on Lake Thun in the Bernese Oberland, was built by the dukes of Zähtingen at the end of the 12th century.

- **Joining the Revelers at Fasnacht (Basel):** Believe it or not, Switzerland has its own safe and very appealing version of Carnaval, with origins dating back to the Middle Ages. It begins the Monday after Ash Wednesday (usually in late Feb or early Mar). The aesthetic is heathen (or pagan), with a touch of existentialist absurdity. The horse-drawn and motorized parades are appropriately flamboyant, and the cacophonous music that accompanies the spectacle includes the sounds of fifes, drums, trumpets, and trombones. Sometimes as many as 20,000 people participate in the raucous festivities, which may change your image of straight-laced Switzerland. See "Basel" in chapter 6.

- **Summiting Mount Pilatus:** The steepest cogwheel train in the world—with a 48-degree gradient—takes you to the top of Mount Pilatus, a 2,132m (6,993-ft.) summit overlooking Lucerne. Once at the top you'll have a panoramic sweep that stretches all the way to Italy. Until the 1600s it was forbidden to climb this mountain because locals feared that Pontius Pilate's angry ghost would provide trouble. His body, or so the legend says, was brought here by the devil. Queen Victoria made the trip in 1868 and did much to dispel this long-held myth. You can follow in the queen's footsteps. See "Lucerne" in chapter 12.

- **Discovering the Lakes of Central Switzerland:** Experience the country's sparkling lakes with a tour through central Switzerland on the William Tell Express. Begin in Lucerne on a historic paddle-wheel steamer that chugs across the lake while you have lunch. Before the tour is over, you'll have boarded a train on the lake's most distant shore, traversed one of the most forbidding mountain ranges in central Europe (through the relative safety of the St. Gotthard Tunnel), and descended into the lush lowlands of the Italian-speaking Ticino district. See chapter 12.

- **Wandering the Waterfront Promenades:** One of the greatest summer pleasures of Switzerland is wandering the palm-lined promenades in the Ticino, the Italian-speaking southern section of the country. The best resorts—and the best promenades—are found at Ascona, Locarno, and Lugano. You'll have not only lake scenery but also the rugged Italian Alps as a backdrop on your stroll. Of course, you can do more than just walk. There's swimming, boating, cafe sitting, people-watching, and even shopping. At night, when the harbor lights shine, you can join the Ticinese in their evening stroll. See chapter 15.

2 The Best Scenic Drives

- **The Road over the Great St. Bernard Pass:** Of the many mountain passes of alpine Europe, this is the most famous. Since the days of the Roman Empire, much of the commerce between northern Italy and the rest of Europe has navigated this low point in one of the most forbidding mountain ridges in the world. Modern-day pilgrims follow in the steps of Napoleon and his armies, who traversed the perilous pass in 1800 to invade Italy. Since 1964, a tunnel beneath the mountains has allowed traffic to move unhindered for at least half of every year. Technically, the Swiss section of the pass road begins in French-speaking Martigny and ends in Italian-speaking San Bernardino, 56km (35 miles) away. In reality, most motorists use the pass road as a slow but scenic midsummer diversion with long drives that begin near Basel or Zurich and end in the Italian cities of Aosta or Milan. See "Verbier" in chapter 9.

- **The Road over the Furka Pass:** Traveling in a southwest-to-northeast line for only 32km (20 miles), from the hamlet of Gletsch, northeast of Brig, to the mountain resort of Andermatt, the road follows the high-altitude frontier between German-speaking and Italian-speaking Switzerland. En route you'll see the frozen mass of the glacier that feeds the Rhône and scenery that's absolutely magnificent.

Any number of scenic highlights radiate out from here. See "Andermatt" in chapter 12.

- **St. Gotthard Pass Road:** One of the most vital roads in Europe stretches for 64km (40 miles) between German-speaking Andermatt and the Italian-speaking village of Biasca. It shares many characteristics of the above-mentioned St. Bernard Pass, which lies about 40 almost-impassable kilometers (25 miles) to the east. Some historians have suggested that the tolls collected since the 1300s along this road helped finance the continued independence of Switzerland itself. Since 1980, a 16km (10-mile) tunnel has allowed motorists to travel the route year-round. Traffic on the high road, however, remains clogged with summer vacationers who come for the stunning views. The landscape is mournful and bleak throughout much of this adventure, a testimony to the savage climactic conditions that exist at these high altitudes. See "Andermatt" in chapter 12.

- **The Road over the Bernina Pass:** During the Middle Ages, merchants led horse- and donkey-drawn caravans over this pass, risking their lives to carry supplies between what are now the German-speaking and Italian-speaking regions of Switzerland. Frostbite was commonplace, and many died in the snows en route. Today cars can navigate the pass as part of a 2-hour,

55km (34-mile) drive between St. Moritz and Tirano. Be warned, this drive is never problem-free. The road is winding, and ice patches have a way of surfacing even in summertime. Snow usually closes the pass completely between mid-October and late April, although trains can usually get through except during the worst midwinter blizzards. But the views are truly spectacular. See "Pontresina" in chapter 14.

- **The Simplon Pass Road:** Unlike the St. Gotthard Pass Road, which is interspersed with artfully engineered bridges, hairpin turns, and retaining walls, the Simplon Pass Road gracefully conforms to the natural topography of some of the most scenic mountainsides in Europe. It stretches about 64km (40 miles), from German-speaking Brig over the Italian border to Domodossola. Napoleon demanded a low-altitude pass for his artillery, and the present road follows the 1805 plan designs. Napoleon's grip on power, ironically, crumbled before his armies could ever use the pass. Despite the best efforts of the Swiss Department of Highways, the road is often closed between December and early May, with automobiles diverted onto flatbed trains instead. These are rather awkwardly carried through one of the longest railway tunnels in the world, the Simplon Tunnel. See chapter 15.

3 The Best Train Trips

- **The *Glacier Express:*** It's advertised as the slowest express train in the world, requiring more than 7½ hours to pass through southeastern Switzerland. Despite that, its 274km (170 miles) of track are an awesome triumph of engineering (of which Switzerland is justifiably proud). Beginning every day in Zermatt, in

southwest Switzerland, and ending in St. Moritz, in Switzerland's east, it crosses more than 291 bridges and goes through 91 tunnels, traversing some of the country's most inaccessible mountains with an ease that medieval pilgrims would have considered an act of God. You can also take the train from St. Moritz to Zermatt.

Naturally, the scenery is breathtaking. The windows are large enough to allow clear views, and a dining car serves lunch with civilized efficiency. Advance reservations are required; for more information, call **Rail Europe** (© **877/257-2887**). See chapters 9 and 14.

- **The *Palm Express:*** This 2-day itinerary of bus and rail routes takes travelers from St. Moritz (in the rugged Engadine district, near Switzerland's eastern frontier) to either Brig or (for a supplemental fee) Zermatt, in Switzerland's southwest. More leisurely than either of the two rail routes described here, it includes a hotel night en route. The scenery is spectacular. For more information, call **Rail Europe** (© **877/257-2887**). See chapter 14.

- *Bernina Express:* Like the *Glacier Express,* this railway excursion offers sweeping views of otherwise inaccessible alpine landscapes. A 4-hour trip (each way), it begins in the German-speaking capital of Zurich, traverses isolated regions where the native tongue is the ancient Romansh language, and ends in Italian-speaking Lugano. The rugged, high-altitude landscapes near Chur give way to the verdant, palm-lined lake districts near Tirano. It's the only train route in Switzerland that crosses the Alps without the benefit of tunnels en route. (It also travels some of the steepest railway lines in the world, negotiated without the benefit of racks and pinions.) Consider extending this trip with bus connections from Tirano—the end of the rail line—to the resort town of Lugano. For more information, call **Rail Europe** (© **877/257-2887**). See chapter 15.

4 The Best Walks

- **Mount Säntis:** At 2,502m (8,207 ft.), Säntis is the northern outpost of the Alps and the most towering peak in the Alpstein massif. The quaint village of Appenzell is a good place to base yourself. The walk itself begins in the village of Wasserrauen, which is linked to Appenzell by hourly trains. After 8.9km (5½ miles)—4½ to 5½ hours, depending on your stamina—it ends at the village of Schwägalp, from which you can take a cable car to the viewing platform overlooking the summit of Säntis. Schwägalp is the terminus of the roads coming in from Urnäsch and Neu-St-Johann. See "Appenzell" in chapter 5.

- **Grosse Scheidegg:** This popular walk ("The great watershed" in English) takes you through some of the most dramatic scenery in the Jungfrau region of central Switzerland, known for stunning white glaciers and soaring summits. One of the highlights of the walk is the awesome beauty of the Wetterhorn's massive gray rock walls. Setting out from the village of Meiringen, the walk ends 21km (13 miles) away (6½–9 hr.) in the resort of Grindelwald. If you get tired, take advantage of the bus stops along the way. See "Grindelwald" in chapter 8 for more details.

- **The Bürgenstock Felsenweg:** In the Lake Lucerne area, this dramatic hike passes through one of the beauty spots of Switzerland, filled with numerous vistas and alpine foothills. From the ritzy resort of Bürgenstock, it is a 7km (4½-mile), 2½-hour walk to Ennetbürgen, one of the most scenic resorts along Lake Lucerne. Along the way you'll come upon spectacular views of Mount Pilatus and serene Lake Lucerne. See "Bürgenstock" in chapter 12.

- **The Upper Engadine Lakes:** The four highland lakes of the Upper Engadine are 1,771m (5,809 ft.) above sea level, but as you walk along, it's like traversing the floor of a valley. Craggy ranges and scenic lake vistas greet you at every turn as you make your way along the 14km (8½-mile), 3- to 3½-hour walk from Maloja to the resort of Silvaplana. You'll pass through the enchanting village of Segl-Maria, one of the most charming of the Romanesque-style villages in eastern Switzerland, eventually arriving at the western edge of Lej da Silvaplana, a lake of unsurpassed beauty. See chapter 14.

5 The Best Bike Trips

- **Around the Katzensee:** If you're in Zurich on a hot summer day and you're longing for the perfect place to swim, try cycling from Seebach station through the shaded woods to Katzenruti (picnic spot) and then on to the Katzensee, a lake with a beach and Waldhaus restaurant. Return via Affoltern. Duration: 1½ hours, 13km (8 miles). See "Attractions" in chapter 4.

- **Around the Lake of Murten:** Start out at the small medieval town of Murten (stroll down the main street and visit the castle). Carry on to Faoug, Salavaux, Bellerive (a perfect lookout point), and Vully. Duration: 4 hours, 40km (25 miles). See "Murten" in chapter 6.

- **In the Rhône Valley, Lower Valais:** Cyclists on this route through the Valais set off from Martigny station then cross the Rhône River to the villages of Fully, Chataigner, Mazembroz, and Saillon. The cable-car ride to Iserables from the terminus of Riddes is well worth the trip. Duration: 1½ hours, 20km (12 miles). See chapter 9.

- **Through the Lake Geneva Vineyards:** Before leaving from the station at Morges, take a look at the castle (military museum). The route then leads up to Lully and, via Bussy and Ballens, to Biere. Continuing down a small valley to Begnins and Fechy (a scenic lookout point), you'll find yourself in Aubonne. Finally, take the second-class road, via Lavigny, Villars-sous-Yens, and Lully, back to Morges. Duration: 5½ hours, 56km (35 miles). See "Attractions" in chapter 11.

- **Along the Shore of Lake Lucerne:** This trip can last a whole day, as there are so many spots worth stopping at along the way. Set off from Lucerne station and head for St. Niklausen and Kastanienbaum in the direction of Tribschen (location of the Richard Wagner Museum). The most beautiful stretch is along the lake to Winkel-Horw Beach. Return to Lucerne. Duration: 1½ hours, 13km (8 miles). See "Lucerne" in chapter 12.

- **Lugano's Hinterland:** To discover the small villages around Lugano, set off from the station for the nature reserve at Origlio Lake, and then proceed to Ponte Capriasca (a parish church with a well-preserved copy of da Vinci's *The Last Supper*). Continue to Tesserete and Colla, along the left valley side of Cassarate, through the woods to Sonvico, and then on to Dino, Ponte di Valle, and Lugano. Duration: 4 hours, 37km (23 miles). See "Lugano" in chapter 15.

6 The Best Small Towns & Villages

- **Appenzell:** Nowhere is folkloric Switzerland as well preserved as at the base of the green foothills of the Alpstein, where this old-fashioned country town still has cowmen in yellow breeches and scarlet waistcoats walking its streets. People in other parts of Switzerland tend to call the locals "hillbillies"; and for many Americans attracted to the quirky and the quaint, it evokes the Ozarks. As you wander its centuries-old streets, sampling pear bread and honey cakes while in pursuit of local embroidery, you'll know why Appenzell is called the most authentic of Swiss villages. See "Appenzell" in chapter 5.

- **Wengen:** On a sheltered terrace high above the Lauterbrunnen Valley, this ski resort is one of the gems of the Bernese Oberland. No cars are allowed in this idyllic village, and from its streets (cleared of snow even in winter) and hotel windows, magnificent panoramic views greet you at every turn. The sunsets—over crags and waterfalls—are the most memorable we've ever seen in Switzerland. The village is best known for hosting the Ski World Cup, with the longest and most dangerous downhill race staged every January. See "Wengen" in chapter 8.

- **Sion:** Although it's the small capital of the Valais, this old Roman town with a French-speaking population is often neglected by those rushing to sample the pleasures of Zermatt and Verbier.

But sleepy Sion has its own rewards. The town is dominated by the castles of Valère and Tourbillon, and, in its greater days, Sion's bishops were big players on the medieval stage. The moody, melancholy look of the town has inspired such luminaries as Rilke, Goethe, and Rousseau. See "Sion" in chapter 9.

- **Andermatt:** At the crossroads of the Alps, in the Urseren Valley, this picture-postcard town lies at the junction of two alpine roads—the St. Gotthard highway and the road to Oberalp and Furka. From the top of Gemstock, reached by cable car, you can see 600 alpine peaks. Hikers, cross-country skiers, and mountain bikers are attracted to this little backwater. The life of the town is centered on the main street, some sections of which are still paved with granite stones. See "Andermatt" in chapter 12.

- **Morcote:** At the southernmost tip of the Ceresio peninsula, 11km (7 miles) south of Lugano, stands Switzerland's most idyllic village. Built in the Lombard style familiar to those who have toured Milan, Morcote's arcaded houses, often clay-colored, open directly on the water, with everything set against a backdrop of vineyards and cypresses. For the best view of this cliché of Ticino charm, climb the 400 steps to the Chiesa di Madonna del Sasso, which dates from the 13th century. See "Morcote" in chapter 15.

7 The Best Romantic Getaways

- **Mürren:** It's so isolated that you can only get here by cog railway or cable car. Set on a rocky, high-altitude ledge hundreds of feet above the Lauterbrunnen Valley, Mürren has a handful of chalet-style hotels, excellent ski and hiking trails, and sweeping views over

the mountains of the Bernese Oberland. It's as picture-perfect a Swiss village as you'll find. See "Mürren" in chapter 8.

- **Gstaad:** Lying at the junction of four alpine valleys midway between the Bernese Oberland and the Vaud Alps,

Gstaad is a winter capital of the European glitterati. You can't get any more stylish, and the skiing is good too. Regardless of their price range, all the hotels seem to have cozy bedrooms, blazing fireplaces, and enough schnapps to set the mood. See "Gstaad" in chapter 8.

- **Verbier:** It lies at the bottom of an enormous alpine bowl ringed with spectacular ski slopes. Although many British travelers appreciate Verbier's charms, the language and atmosphere of the resort are unpretentious and very, very French. You can have a lot of fun in Verbier, and if you didn't happen to import your own romance, you're likely to find some here. See "Verbier" in chapter 9.

- **Bürgenstock:** The only road leading here is so treacherous that almost everyone opts to travel by cog railway or cable car. The town, set on a densely forested limestone ridge high above Lake Lucerne, shelters some of the most luxurious hotels in Switzerland. Reserve part of every day here for climbs along the well-maintained hiking paths, at least one of which skirts the edge of a very steep and panoramic cliff. See "Bürgenstock" in chapter 12.

- **Arosa:** One of the highest (1,800m/ 5,904 ft.) ski resorts in Switzerland, Arosa is less expensive and less forbiddingly elegant than its nearest competitor, St. Moritz. Although the skiing here is excellent, you may consider a romantic getaway in midsummer, when a network of hiking trails leads to lush forests and small lakes. When you tire of these, cable cars can carry you and your companion to alpine heights and sublime vistas. See "Arosa" in chapter 13.

8 The Best Skiing

The jagged borders of Switzerland contain dozens of worthwhile ski resorts; the most popular are described in detail in the chapters that follow. But before heading off to the mountains for a bit of downhill racing, ask yourself some important questions: Do you prefer to schuss down a Swiss mountainside in relative isolation or accompanied by many other skiers? How chic and how expensive do you want your vacation to be? Do you pursue sports other than skiing (perhaps hang-gliding, curling, ice-skating, or tobogganing)? And after a day in the great outdoors, do you prefer to retire early to a simple mountain hut with a view of the stars, or do you yearn for late nights with the glittering demimonde of Europe?

- **Grindelwald:** This is one of the few resorts in the Bernese Oberland that occasionally mistakes itself for a genuine city rather than an artificial tourist creation. It offers a healthy dose of restaurants, bars, discos, and, unfortunately, traffic. There are a lot of affordable accommodations here—it's not nearly as snobby as some of the other resorts. Many skiers use it as a base camp for long-haul excursions to the slopes of First, Männlichen, and Kleine Scheidegg. From Grindelwald, the resorts of Wengen and Mürren are accessible by cog railway and/or cable car (no traffic!). See "Grindelwald" in chapter 8.

- **Gstaad/Saanenland:** Gstaad is the most elegant pearl in the larger ski region of Saanenland, on the western edge of the Bernese Oberland. Although you can find a few inexpensive lodgings if you're lucky, don't count on it. The jet set comes here to see and be seen, and there's a lot to do off the slopes: music festivals, shopping, people-watching. The architecture is stubbornly alpine, and the interior decorations range from baronial and woodsy in the most expensive hotels to kitschy in the cheaper ones. Opportunities for skiing are widespread, but the slopes are hardly the most difficult in Switzerland. Skiing is best for beginners and intermediates. See "Gstaad" in chapter 8.

- **Mürren:** One of the most oddly positioned resorts in Switzerland, Mürren sits on a rock ledge high above the Lauterbrunnen Valley of the Bernese Oberland. Accessible only by cable car, it's among the most picture-perfect resorts, full of chalet-style architecture and completely free of traffic. Though its isolation makes it charming, it also tends to make the cost of staying here somewhat higher. Mürren is closer than any other resort to the demanding slopes of the Schilthorn. From here, experienced skiers are offered nearly 32km (20 miles) of some of the finest powder in Europe—and eagle-eyed panoramas over some of the most dramatically beautiful landscapes in Europe. See "Mürren" in chapter 8.

- **Verbier:** This is the premier ski resort of French-speaking Switzerland, with an unpretentious panache and a fun-filled atmosphere. Its restaurants serve some of the finest creative cuisine in the region; others make do with simple alpine fare for hearty appetites. If you don't speak French, you won't feel uncomfortable—many of the resort's nightlife options cater to Brits. (Throughout the town, English-style pubs compete cheerfully with French cafes.) Verbier lies at the heart of a sprawling, high-tech network of cable cars and gondolas that will connect you to such relatively unknown satellite resorts as Veysonnaz and La Tzoumaz. The resort is favored by world-class athletes for the difficulty of many of its slopes. See "Verbier" in chapter 9.

- **Zermatt:** It's the most southwesterly of the great Swiss ski resorts, occupying a high-altitude plateau at the foot of Switzerland's highest and most-photographed mountain, the Matterhorn. Much of the resort's charm derives from its strict building codes—you'll rarely see a modern-looking building here—and its almost complete lack of traffic. Access from the valley below is via cog railway only. Known for over a century as the party town of the Alps, Zermatt has always been a place where the beer-drinking and hedonistic—sometimes raunchy—revelry last into the early-morning hours. The skiing, incidentally, is superb. A complicated network of chairlifts, cog railways, and gondolas carries skiers to such peaks as Stockhorn, Rothorn, Riffelberg, Trockner Steg, and Testa Grigia. See "Zermatt & the Matterhorn" in chapter 9.

- **Arosa:** One of the most isolated of eastern Switzerland's resorts, Arosa is a relative newcomer to the country's ski scene. Drawing a young crowd, it's filled with contemporary buildings rather than traditional, chalet-inspired architecture. Ample annual snowfall, vast alpine meadows, and only one steeply inclined road into town make Arosa ideal for escapists and nature lovers. Families with children usually like the place too. Not as stratospherically expensive or pretentious as St. Moritz, Arosa offers lots of runs for intermediate skiers. Some of the resort's most dramatic slopes, which drop more than 1,000m (3,280 ft.) from beginning to end, are only for very experienced athletes. See "Arosa" in chapter 13.

- **Davos:** It's larger, with many more hotels, restaurants, après-ski bars, and discos than its neighbor, Klosters (see below), with which it shares access to a sweeping network of ski lifts and

Impressions

A Swiss artist living in the south of France said it: "Switzerland does not exist."
This made some Swiss upset. Though Switzerland doesn't exist, every Swiss cit-
izen has his assault rifle at home (with ammo). Of course they very rarely use
their rifle to attack a bank or to hurt their wives. The Swiss used to be merce-
naries, but today they don't want to get involved in other countries' feuds.
Although they use migrant workers, they don't like foreigners (tourists are
okay). Switzerland is this Disneyland of order and social harmony. It is a secure
and peaceful place. It is not part of Europe. It might not even really be part of
the world. This, I guess, should be good for the banking business.

—Olivier Mosset, 1994

slopes. Davos attracts a sometimes-curious mixture of the very wealthy and the more modest. It has slopes that appeal to advanced skiers, intermediates, and beginners. One of the most challenging runs descends from Weissflühgipfel at 2,844m (9,328 ft.) to Küblis at 810m (2,657 ft.). See "Davos" in chapter 13.

- **Klosters:** Named after a 13th-century cloister founded on the site, this resort is smaller, more intimate, and less urban than its nearest major competitor, Davos (see above). A favorite of the royal families of both Sweden and Britain, it offers at least two easily accessible ski zones, the snowfields of the Gotschna-Parsenn and the Madrisa. There's a wide range of trails and facilities, offering challenges to all skill levels. See "Klosters" in chapter 13.

- **St. Moritz:** The premier ski and social resort of eastern Switzerland, St. Moritz draws a lot of folks familiar with the art of conspicuous consumption. This is as close as you'll get to Hollywood in Switzerland. It's more distinctly Austrian than French in its flavor. Although only one or two authentic buildings remain from the town's medieval origins, vast amounts of money have been spent installing folkloric fixtures, carved paneling, and accents of local granite in the public and private areas of most hotels. Skiing in the region is divided into distinctly different areas, the most popular of which is Corviglia, on the mountains above St. Moritz. Adventurers seeking diversion farther afield head for the slopes above the satellite resort of Sils Maria (Corvatsch) and the slopes above the nearby village of Pontresina (Diavolezza). There are plenty of difficult slopes in the region if you seek them out, but intermediate-level skiers enjoy taking a cable car from St. Moritz-Dorf to the top of Piz Corvatsch, almost 3,451m (11,319 ft.) above sea level. From here, with only one cable-car connection en route, you can ski a network of intermediate-level trails all the way back down to the resort's lake. St. Moritz boasts some of the most dependable annual snowfalls in Switzerland. See "St. Moritz" in chapter 14.

9 The Best Festivals

- **L'Escalade:** Way back on December 11, 1602, the city of Geneva was attacked by Savoyard soldiers trying to scale its ramparts. The duke of Savoy had lost his former possession and wanted it back. Alas, it was not to be. The denizens of Geneva valiantly held out, and one brave Amazon, Mère Royaume, scaled the ramparts and poured a pot of hot soup on the head of a Savoyard soldier. For 3 days and nights beginning December 11, normally staid Geneva becomes virtually Rabelaisian, staging torchlight marches, country markets, and fife-and-drum parades, as a festive crowd in period costumes marches through the streets of the old city. Many present-day Mère Royaumes—armed with soup pots, of course—can be seen. See "When to Go" in chapter 2.

• **Vogel Gryff Volksfest:** This colorful tradition has a griffin, a lion, and a "wild man of the woods" floating down the Rhine followed by dancing in the streets. It occurs alternately on January 13, 20, or 27 (changes every year). On a wintry day in January, a raft, laden with two drummers, two men with large flags, and two cannoneers, who repeatedly fire gun salutes, floats down the Rhine. The principal figure is a savage masked man carrying an uprooted pine tree. At Mittlerebrücke (the middle bridge), he's met by a lion and a bird with an awesome beak. At noon the three figures dance on the bridge to the sound of drums. The Wilder Mann (savage man), the Leu (lion), and the Vogel Gryff (griffin) are old symbols for three Basel societies that could be called neighborhoods today. Throughout the afternoon and evening, street dancing in Basel honors the occasion, which originated in the 16th century. The purpose of all this madness? Ostensibly, to strengthen community ties. See "Basel" in chapter 6.

• **Celebrating the Onion:** If your favorite sandwich consists of only bread, mayonnaise, and onions, or your idea of humor is to poke fun at buffoons disguised as onions, you'll love the Swiss capital's celebration of Zibelemärit, held annually on the fourth Monday of November. During the festival, huge sections of the city's historic center are filled with vegetable stalls featuring plaited strings of onions (more than 100 tons may be sold in a day here) and other winter vegetables. The barrels of confetti thrown by competing camps of high-spirited students offer endless photo ops. Facetiously dressed jesters appear in bars and restaurants to poke fun (usually in Swiss-German) at the sometimes-pompous political posturing of their governmental elders. See the introduction to chapter 7 for more information.

10 The Best Museums

• **Museum Rietberg (Zurich):** Some of Europe's most interesting collections were amassed by gifted amateurs with enough money to pursue their hobbies. This museum honors the acquisitive skill of Baron von der Heydt, who donated his collection to the city of Zurich in 1952. It includes sculptures and artworks from the Americas and North and South Asia, archaic Buddhist art, carpets from Armenia, and masks from Africa and Oceania. See p. 107.

• **Landesmuseum (Swiss National Museum, Zurich):** This museum traces the growth and development of Swiss civilization from prehistory to the modern age. The collections include prehistoric artifacts, mementos from the Roman and Carolingian empires, and artworks from Romanesque, Gothic, and Renaissance periods. There are also unusual collections of Swiss clocks, Swiss armor and weapons, and folkloric costumes and artifacts from each of the country's cantons. See p. 107.

- **Kunstmuseum (Fine Arts Museum, Basel):** Its first acquisition goes back to 1662. Since then, the bulk of the museum's 3,000 artworks have included works by Swiss and German artists from the 15th and 16th centuries. Despite the excellence of its old-master paintings, the museum is especially known for its large collections of modern works, only a fraction of which can ever be exhibited at the same time. See p. 153.

- **Kunstmuseum (Fine Arts Museum, Bern):** Bern's premier museum, this civic showcase contains everything from 13th-century Italian primitives to one of the most complete collections of works by Paul Klee anywhere. See p. 193.

- **Musée d'Art et d'Histoire (Art and History Museum, Geneva):** Geneva's premier museum devotes equal space to exhibits on the history of civilization, the civic history of Geneva, archaeology, and world-class painting—everything from medieval to modern art. See p. 334.

- **Verkehrshaus der Schweiz (Swiss Transport Museum, Lucerne):** One of Switzerland's newer museums, founded in 1959, this collection pays homage to the railway, auto, and airplane industries that helped propel Europe into the modern age. It contains more than 60 historic locomotives, 40 automobiles, 50 motorcycles, and dozens of other conveyances. Other exhibitions are devoted to cable cars, steamships, and spaceships. There's even a planetarium. See p. 362.

11 The Best Luxury Hotels

- **Baur au Lac** (Zurich; © 044/220-50-20; www.bauraulac.ch): Prestigious and historic, it's one of the country's grandest hotels, welcoming prosperous guests since 1844. Richard Wagner, Franz Liszt, and John Lennon are some of the artists who have experienced its charms. Today the international business community considers it a favorite. See p. 84.

- **Widder Hotel** (Zurich; © 044/224-25-26; www.widderhotel.ch): In the heart of the city's Old Town, 10 historic buildings dating from the 15th century have been transformed into an intimate luxury inn. Massive wooden beams and 16th-century frescoes still exist from the days when these buildings were part of the butchers' guild, but now they're juxtaposed with glass elevators and stainless-steel furniture. It's an offbeat, fun choice in a staid city, made especially inviting because of the live jazz in the bar. See p. 85.

- **Hotel Drei Könige** (Basel; © 061/260-50-50; www.drei-koenigebasel.ch): Claiming to be the oldest hotel in Europe, the Hotel Drei Könige has operated continuously as an inn since 1026. It was the site of a meeting between two Holy Roman emperors and a Burgundian king that eventually established the southwestern borders of present-day Switzerland. Voltaire, Queen Victoria, and Kaiser Wilhelm II were only a few of this hotel's famous guests. Today there's live jazz in the bar and a cosmopolitanism that permeates every part of this very comfortable hotel. See p. 156.

- **Hotel Schweizerhof** (Bern; © 031/326-80-80; www.schweizerhof-bern.ch): A favorite of diplomats, this grand hotel, built in 1859, is filled with antiques and offers great comfort in its state-of-the-art bedrooms. Richly accessorized, it evokes grand luxury in the style of the 19th century. See p. 184.

- **Royal Park Hotel** (Kandersteg; ℂ 033/675-88-88; www.royal kandersteg.com): Guests wear dinner jackets or semiformal gowns every night at dinner at this very discreet and upper-class hotel. The same family has maintained solidly impeccable standards for at least three generations, and the decor, which has lots of chiseled stone and timbers, seems as solid as the Central Bank of Switzerland itself. Although guests can have a very good time here, this is a seriously elegant hotel known for perfect manners and an utter lack of frivolity. See p. 236.

- **Palace Hotel Gstaad** (Gstaad; ℂ 033/748-50-50; www.palace.ch): Every winter this becomes one of the most sought-after hotels in the world, attracting the chic and fabulous who create what's been called the most amusing and expensive annual house party in Europe. Built in 1912, the hotel sits on a promontory above Gstaad (not exactly a village unfamiliar with luxury). Everything is very, very luxurious. See p. 240.

- **Beau-Rivage Palace** (Lausanne; ℂ 021/613-33-33; www.brp.ch): This is the most prestigious hotel in Lausanne. Undeniably beautiful, it's a Beaux Arts masterpiece richly associated with the city's cultural and social elite. Service is impeccable. Although it has long catered to wealthy and conservative French-speaking Swiss,

it has made great efforts in recent years to attract a younger, more international clientele. See p. 281.

- **Le Richemond** (Geneva; ℂ 022/715-70-00; www.roccofortehotels.ch): Built in 1875 in the style of a neoclassical palace, Le Richemond drips with Gobelin tapestries, French antiques, and a sophisticated, hardworking staff for whom absolutely nothing is a surprise. It also has the most fascinating bar in town; but if you decide to have a drink here, don't even think of showing up in torn jeans. See p. 313.

- **The Bürgenstock Hotels** (Bürgenstock; ℂ 041/612-90-10; www.buergenstock-hotels.ch): If you're tired of waiting in lines at museums to admire paintings by Rubens and Tintoretto, try this hotel. Composed of three different buildings placed behind the trees of a 4.8-hectare (12-acre) park, it shelters the world-class art collection of the present owner's father. Plush and comfortable, the hotel has elaborate gardens, lots of blazing fireplaces, and very good service. See p. 380.

- **Kulm Hotel** (St. Moritz; ℂ 081/836-80-00; www.kulmhotel-stmoritz.ch): This is the great bastion of luxury of the Engadine, rivaling even Suvretta House and Badrutt's Palace Hotel for supremacy. The greats and near-greats of the world have found refuge from the snows here in this trio of buildings, the oldest of which dates from 1760. See p. 431.

12 The Most Charming Small Hotels

- **Hotel Romantik Florhof** (Zurich; ℂ 044/250-26-26; www.florhof.ch): The most charming of the little boutique hotels of Zurich, this was originally the home of a wealthy 15th-century merchant before its transformation. At the edge of Old

Town, the hotel represents superb value. See p. 88.

- **Hotel Appenzell** (Appenzell; ℂ 071/788-15-15; www.hotel-appenzell.ch): Set on the main square of the most folkloric town in Switzerland, this hotel is outfitted in a rustic country-Swiss theme with touches of marble and walnut in the bedrooms. Check out the elaborate antique paneling in one of the dining rooms, rescued from a much older building just before it was demolished. See p. 135.

- **Hotel-Restaurant Adler** (Stein-am-Rhein; ✆ 052/742-61-61; www.adlersteinamrhein.ch): Although its bedrooms are comfortable and clean, the location, in one of the most colorful cities on the Rhine, is what gets our vote. We love the hotel's frescoed facade, which depicts characters and plots derived from medieval Rhenish legends. See p. 143.

- **Hotel Krafft** (Basel; ✆ 061/690-91-30; www.hotelkrafft.ch): It's inexpensive and conveniently located a short walk from the historic core of the city. Its outdoor terrace overlooks the river, the town hall, and the cathedral. The bedrooms have the kind of worn but decent early-20th-century furnishings that remind us of these old-fashioned family-run pensions of postwar Europe. See p. 158.

- **Hostellerie des Chevaliers** (Gruyéres; ✆ 026/921-19-33; www.gruyeres-hotels.ch): This atmospheric inn stands conveniently aloof from the overrun tourist center but offers the same panoramic views as the châteaux at Gruyères. The decor is the warmest and most old-fashioned in town, rich with antiques, woodwork, and ceramic stoves. See p. 171.

- **Belle Epoque** (Bern; ✆ 031/311-43-36; www.belle-epoque.ch): The most sophisticated small-scale hotel in the Swiss capital was created out of two historic town houses from the Middle Ages. The hotel celebrates Jugendstil or a Teutonic Art Nouveau. The place is a jewel. See p. 184.

- **Hotel Olden** (Gstaad; ✆ 033/748-49-50; www.hotelolden.ch): Set on the town's main thoroughfare, the Olden is a great deal compared to other Gstaad hotels. It enjoys a solid reputation, especially among the many skiers and mountain guides who patronize the restaurant and cafe on the hotel's ground floor. The rooms are cozy and a bit cramped, but comfortable—perfect if you're planning to spend your time out and about. See p. 241.

- **Hotel Antika** (Zermatt; ✆ 027/967-21-51; www.antika.ch): It's one of the few hotels in Zermatt that won't gobble up most of your travel budget. You wouldn't really guess that it's an affordable option at first glance: Each room has its own covered loggia, and the lobby is carefully paneled with weathered planks. This is a good choice for exploring the most famous resort town of Switzerland's Valais district. See p. 267.

- **The Hotel** (Lucerne; ✆ 041/226-86-86; www.the-hotel.ch): This is central Switzerland's most charming boutique hotel. Designed by Jean Nouvel, France's most famous architect, it is exclusive and elegant, luxury personified yet artfully simple at the same time. See p. 366.

- **Hotel Drei Könige und Post** (Andermatt; ✆ 041/887-00-01; www.3koenige.ch): Located directly north of the St. Gotthard Pass at 2,109m (6,918 ft.), this hotel was built on the site of an inn that has been showing wayfarers hospitality since 1234. Even Goethe spent a night at this family-run place in 1775. Some of the rooms open onto balconies, and the hotel's regional Swiss cuisine attracts both locals and visitors. See p. 390.

- **Hotel Drei Könige** (Chur; ✆ 081/252-17-58; www.dreikoenige.com): Its foundations were laid in the 1300s, and the same hardworking family has owned and managed the place since 1911. It provides a note of cheer in an industrialized, high-altitude town where the temperatures can sometimes plummet. Of special note is its restaurant, one of the most consistently popular in town. See p. 395.

13 The Best Restaurants

- **Kronenhalle** (Zurich; ℂ 044/251-66-69): It has a hearty, rustic alpine theme, but a glance at its menu, its clientele, and its artwork will quickly convince you that this is a supremely distinctive restaurant. Enjoy paintings by such luminaries as Kandinsky, Matisse, Klee, and Braque as you dine. See p. 96.

- **Peter's Kunststuben** (Küsnacht; ℂ 044/910-07-15): Come here for the sublime cuisine of chef Horst Petermann. Since he opened this acclaimed restaurant south of Zurich, demanding diners have been heading here to partake of the constantly changing specialties. After you've sampled his herby Tuscan dove with pine nuts or his lobster with artichoke and almond oil, you'll know that this is as good as it gets in the Zurich area. See p. 99.

- **Restaurant Stucki Bruderholz** (Basel; ℂ 061/361-82-22): There's a garden, a collection of upscale antique furniture, a clientele speaking every conceivable European language, and some of the best cuisine in northwestern Switzerland, all based on modern interpretations of French and German recipes. See p. 161.

- **Le Restaurant Pierroz** (Verbier; ℂ 027/771-63-23): You'd never know that the simple chalet-style facade of this place shelters one of the most legendary restaurants in the Valais. One of the finest meals we've ever had in Switzerland was served here on a snowy night. It included a platter of sea bass with sea urchins, followed by couscous of crawfish and pigeon with truffles. Gourmets and epicures will cross any number of national borders to sample the creative cuisine of Roland Pierroz. See p. 251.

- **Hotel de Ville** (Crissier; ℂ 021/634-05-05): Philippe Rochat is the chef of the moment in Switzerland, having taken over from Alfred (Frédy) Girardet, who some hailed as the world's greatest chef. That was some chef's toque for Rochat to wear, but he has succeeded in retaining the international acclaim that Girardet enjoyed. Occupying a building originally designed as the town hall of a village outside Lausanne, the master continues to please the hundreds of devoted gastronomes who often travel great distances at great expense to dine here. See p. 324.

- **Le Pont de Brent** (Brent; ℂ 021/964-52-30): No one had even heard of Brent until this restaurant opened in a late-19th-century house in the heart of the village. Today the restaurant has put the village on the map, in part because of the excellence of such dishes as mussel-and-leek soup and roast rabbit with mustard sauce. See p. 300.

- **Le Chat-Botté** (Geneva; ℂ 022/716-69-20): Richly sheathed with tapestries and accented with the kind of art and accessories that would have made Louis XVI feel right at home, this restaurant attracts some of the wealthiest and most jaded clients in the world. Everything works smoothly, with nary a glitch, but you can only imagine how hard the staff labors to maintain its position as one of the best restaurants in Switzerland. See p. 322.

- **Le Cygne** (Geneva; ℂ **022/908-90-85**): When the Noga Hilton decided to open a restaurant in its lakefront hotel, neither expense nor effort was spared to make it the best in Geneva. This is no small feat, considering the tough local competition. In a plush, upholstered setting of lacquered wood and deep banquettes, attended by a well-trained army of waiters, you can enjoy a cuisine that ranks among the most sophisticated in Europe. The desserts are a triumph of the pastry maker's art. See p. 322.

- **La Favola** (Geneva; ℂ **022/311-74-37**): This is the best Italian restaurant in Geneva, and possibly the city's best restaurant of any kind. The chefs' tender pillows of tortellini would be hard to find this side of Bologna. The cuisine has authentic flavor, the service is skilled and smooth, and only the freshest ingredients go into the kitchen's skillets and stewpots. See p. 326.

- **Chesa Grischuna** (Klosters; ℂ **081/42222-22**): This restaurant succeeds every evening at creating a genuine sense of unpretentious, old-fashioned warmth. Over the years it has hosted such showbiz and political types of yesterday as Winston Churchill, the Aga Khan, Truman Capote, and Audrey Hepburn. The food is hearty and nourishing—perfect for the cold-weather climate of Klosters. See p. 406.

- **Chadafo Grill, in the Chesa Veglia** (Dorf; ℂ **081/837-28-00**): This business is located in what's said to be the only authentic Engadine-style house—built in 1658—that remains in all of St. Moritz. It contains three different dining rooms, one of which is an informal pizzeria. The other two are rustically elegant hideaways, redolent with warmth and comfort, which cater to an international and very prosperous clientele. See p. 434.

2

Planning Your Trip to Switzerland

This chapter is devoted to the where, when, and how of your trip—the advance planning required to get it together and take it on the road. Browse through this section before you hit the road to ensure you've covered all the bases.

1 The Regions in Brief

The Swiss landscape has been shaped by glaciation. Glaciers hollowed out the valleys and led to the creation of a multitude of magnificent lakes, a large part of Switzerland's beautiful scenery.

The Swiss plateau, set between the Jura and Alps mountain chains and extending from Lake Geneva in the southwest to Lake Constance in the northeast, represents about 30% of the country's surface area. The main cities and industries are concentrated on this plateau, making Switzerland one of the world's most densely populated countries. Most of the Swiss live in this zone, with half the population based in the urban areas of Geneva, Lausanne, Basel, Bern, Olten, Aarau, Zurich, and Baden. The plateau is also the country's center of agricultural production.

Within its borders Switzerland has nearly every variety of landscape, vegetation, and climatic condition known in Europe. Only a few dozen miles, as the crow flies, separate the lowest point in Switzerland, the shores of Lake Maggiore (where palm trees thrive in a Mediterranean climate), from the highest, the Dufourspitze (where the climate is one of eternal snow and ice).

Of course, the Alps are the main tourist attraction of Switzerland, with about 100 peaks above 3,600m (about 12,000 ft.).

Some 1,800 glaciers offer the sight of an awesome and sometimes-savage nature. The view south from the Jungfraujoch, the highest rail station in Europe, is one of windswept rock and ice, majestic and dramatic.

The Swiss Alps form the centerpiece of Europe's alpine range. They're broken by the great valleys of the Rhône in the canton of the Valais and the Rhine in the canton of the Graubünden, as well as by many lateral valleys. (A canton is a division similar to a U.S. state.) To the north, the chain ends in the Bernese Alps (Finsteraarhorn) and to the south in the Valais Alps (the Monte Rosa range). To the east the Alps end at Piz Bernina. In the canton of Ticino, which on the map looks like a triangular section of northern Italy, Switzerland possesses part of the southern face of the Alps as well.

Zurich Close to the northern border of Switzerland, Zurich is the country's largest city, spreading across 93 sq. km (36 sq. miles), with a population of around 400,000. The fiscal and business center of the country, it was also the political capital until 1848, when that honor was transferred to Bern.

The Bernese Oberland Switzerland's best-known alpine region is named after its largest city, Bern, the Swiss capital.

Known for the beauty of its mountains, it includes many famous resorts, the largest of which is Interlaken, popular mainly in the summer. At its higher altitudes, where the snowfall is more consistent, are such chic ski resorts as Gstaad, Grindelwald, Kandersteg, Mürren, and Wengen.

Northeastern Switzerland Relatively neglected by tourists, this region is separated from southern Germany and Austria by the waters of the Rhine and Lake Constance. Its highlights include St. Gallen, a lace-making center and the economic center of the region, certain sections of the Rhine valley, and the Rhine Falls, near Neuhausen.

Basel & the Jura In northwestern Switzerland, Basel, the capital of the region, is an ancient university town and trading center on the Rhine, set midway between French Alsace and the Jura canton in Switzerland. The Jura is a range of "folded" limestone ridges between two great rivers, the Rhône and the Rhine.

The Valais This rugged valley of the upper Rhône offers such geographic attractions as the Matterhorn and the Great St. Bernard Pass. Equally divided between French- and German-speaking residents, it's rich in alpine folklore. Its most frequented ski resort is Zermatt.

Lausanne & the Shores of Lake Geneva Called Lac Léman by the Swiss, Lake Geneva is the largest freshwater body in central Europe, covering some 583 sq. km (225 sq. miles). It's partially fed by the alpine waters of the Rhône and is emptied by a continuation of the same river, which eventually pours into the Mediterranean. Lausanne, the cultural center of the area, is the second-largest city on Lake Geneva and the fifth largest in Switzerland.

Geneva Geneva, Switzerland's second-largest city, is distinctly different from the rest of Switzerland and culturally more attuned to France. It's built on the Rhône, at the lower end of Lake Geneva, and is bordered on three sides by French territory. This center of world banking and commerce—and the site of many world organizations, such as the Red Cross—is celebrated for its prosperity, elegance, and sophistication.

Lucerne & Central Switzerland The heartland of Switzerland, this region takes in four different cantons: Lucerne, Uri, Unterwalden, and Schwyz, from which the country's name is derived. The region's only major city is Lucerne, a medieval town made famous as a resort in the 19th century. It sits at the northern edge of the lake that bears its name. Despite Switzerland's wealth of attractions, Lucerne is the Swiss city that most North Americans prefer to visit.

The Grisons & the Engadine This area is the largest and most easterly of the cantons of Switzerland. It's also one of the least populated, taking in about 363 sq. km (140 sq. miles) of glaciers and legions of jagged, windswept mountain peaks. Its capital is Chur, the oldest town in Switzerland, but most visitors bypass it en route to the ski resorts of Arosa, Klosters, and Davos. The Engadine stretches for 97km (60 miles), from the Maloja Plateau to Finstermünz. The region's chief attraction is the glamorous winter resort of St. Moritz.

The Ticino The Italian-speaking part of Switzerland, the Ticino is the most southerly—and warmest—region of the country. Not surprisingly, it's the retirement dream for many residents in the northern cantons. The region includes the major cities of Lugano and Locarno, which share, respectively, the lakes of Lugano and Maggiore with Italy. The Italian influence is most strongly felt in the region's relaxed tempo.

Switzerland & Liechtenstein

2 Visitor Information

SWITZERLAND TOURISM OFFICE
You can get the latest tourist information before leaving home from the nearest branch of the Swiss tourism office. In the **United States** the center now has an office only at 608 Fifth Ave., New York, NY 10020 (© **877/794-8037;** www. myswitzerland.com). In **Great Britain** contact the Swiss Centre, Swiss Court, New Coventry Street, London W1V 8EE (© **020/7720-4900**). In **Australia** you have to contact the Embassy of Switzerland, 7 Melbourne Ave., Forrest (Canberra), ACT 2903 (© **02-61-62-84-00**).

3 Entry Requirements & Customs

ENTRY REQUIREMENTS

Every traveler entering Switzerland must have a valid passport, although it's not necessary for North Americans to have a visa if they don't stay longer than 3 continuous months. For information on permanent residence in Switzerland and work permits, contact the nearest Swiss consulate.

For information on how to get a passport, go to the Fast Facts section of this chapter—the websites listed provide downloadable passport applications as well as the current fees for processing passport applications. For an up-to-date country-by-country listing of passport requirements around the world, go to the "Foreign Entry Requirement" Web page of the U.S. State Department at **http://travel.state.gov/foreignentryreqs.html**.

WHAT YOU CAN BRING INTO SWITZERLAND

You can take personal effects into Switzerland, such as clothing, toilet articles, sports gear, photographic and amateur movie or video cameras (including film), musical instruments, and camping equipment. Medicine must be for your personal use only. You can also take 2 liters of alcohol (up to 15% proof) or 1 liter of more than 15% proof. You are also allowed 400 cigarettes, 100 cigars, or 500 grams of tobacco if you're flying in from outside Europe. Those entering from other European countries are allowed 200 cigarettes, 50 cigars, or 250 grams of tobacco.

WHAT YOU CAN TAKE HOME FROM SWITZERLAND

Returning **U.S. citizens** who have been away for at least 48 hours are allowed to bring back, once every 30 days, $800 worth of merchandise duty-free. You'll be charged a flat rate of 4% duty on the next $1,000 worth of purchases. Be sure to have your receipts handy. On mailed gifts, the duty-free limit is $100. With some exceptions, you cannot bring fresh fruits and vegetables into the United States. For specifics on what you can bring

---

Tips Passport Savvy

Allow plenty of time before your trip to apply for a passport; processing normally takes 3 weeks but can take longer during busy periods (especially spring). And keep in mind that if you need a passport in a hurry, you'll pay a higher processing fee. When traveling, safeguard your passport in an inconspicuous, inaccessible place like a money belt and keep a copy of the critical pages with your passport number in a separate place. If you lose your passport, visit the nearest consulate of your native country as soon as possible for a replacement.

back, download the invaluable free pamphlet *Know Before You Go* online at **www. cbp.gov** (click on "Publications" and then "Know Before You Go"). Or contact the **U.S. Customs and Border Protection (CBP),** 1300 Pennsylvania Ave. NW, Washington, DC 20229 (✆ **877/287-8667**), and request the pamphlet.

For a clear summary of **Canadian** rules, write for the booklet *I Declare,* issued by the **Canada Border Services Agency** (✆ **800/461-9999** in Canada or 204/983-3500; www.cbsa-asfc.gc.ca). Canada allows its citizens a C$750 exemption, and you're allowed to bring back duty-free one carton of cigarettes, one can of tobacco, 40 imperial ounces of liquor, and 50 cigars. In addition, you're allowed to mail gifts to Canada valued at less than C$60 a day, provided they're unsolicited and don't contain alcohol or tobacco (write on the package "Unsolicited gift, under $60 value"). All valuables should be declared on the Y-38 form before departure from Canada, including serial numbers of valuables you already own, such as expensive foreign cameras. *Note:* The C$750 exemption can only be used once a year and only after an absence of 7 days.

Citizens of the U.K. who are **returning from a European Union (E.U.) country** will go through a separate Customs exit (called the "Blue Exit") especially for E.U. travelers. In essence, there is no limit on what you can bring back from an E.U. country, as long as the items are for personal use (this includes gifts), and you have already paid the necessary duty and tax. However, Customs law sets out guidance levels. If you bring in more than these levels, you may be asked to prove that the goods are for your own use. Guidance levels on goods bought in the E.U. for your own use are

3,200 cigarettes, 200 cigars, 400 cigarillos, 3 kilograms of smoking tobacco, 10 liters of spirits, 90 liters of wine, 20 liters of fortified wine (such as port or sherry), 110 liters of beer.

For more information, contact **HM Customs & Excise** at ✆ **0845/010-9000** (from outside the U.K., ✆ 020/8929-0152), or consult their website at www.hmce.gov.uk.

The duty-free allowance in **Australia** is A$400 or, for those under 18, A$200. Citizens can bring in 250 cigarettes or 250 grams of loose tobacco, and 1,125 milliliters of alcohol. If you're returning with valuables you already own, such as foreign-made cameras, you should file form B263. A helpful brochure available from Australian consulates or Customs offices is *Know Before You Go.* For more information, call the **Australian Customs Service** at ✆ **1300/363-263,** or log on to www.customs.gov.au.

The duty-free allowance for **New Zealand** is NZ$700. Citizens over 17 can bring in 200 cigarettes, 50 cigars, or 250 grams of tobacco (or a mixture of all three if their combined weight doesn't exceed 250g); plus 4.5 liters of wine and beer, or 1.125 milliliters of liquor. New Zealand currency does not carry import or export restrictions. Fill out a certificate of export, listing the valuables you are taking out of the country; that way, you can bring them back without paying duty. Most questions are answered in a free pamphlet available at New Zealand consulates and Customs offices: *New Zealand Customs Guide for Travellers, Notice no. 4.* For more information, contact **New Zealand Customs Service**, The Customhouse, 17-21 Whitmore St., Box 2218, Wellington (✆ **04/473-6099,** or 0800/428-786 in New Zealand; www.customs.govt.nz).

4 Money

The prices in Switzerland are often higher than those found in the United States and Canada. Nevertheless, this book will try to help you stretch your national

The Swiss Franc, U.S. Dollar, British Pound & the Euro

For American Readers At this writing, $1 = approximately 1.21 Swiss francs (or 1F = approximately 82¢), and this was the rate of exchange used to calculate the dollar values given in this guidebook.

For British Readers At this writing, £1 = approximately 2.317 Swiss francs (or 1F = approximately 0.43 pence), and this was the rate of exchange used to calculate the pound values in the chart below.

Regarding the Euro Despite the willingness of many countries within Europe to adopt the euro as their currency of choice, Switzerland, at press time, remained resolutely committed to maintaining the Swiss franc as their currency of choice. As a benchmark indicator, however, the rate of exchange between the euro and the Swiss franc, at this writing, was 1€ = 1.54F (stated differently, 1F = approximately 65 eurocents).

Note: Although the Swiss franc is relatively stable, international exchange rates fluctuate frequently, and this may not be the same rate when you travel to Switzerland. Therefore, please use this table only as a reflection of approximate, rather than current, values. For the latest on exchange rates, you can go online to **www.xe.com**.

SF	US$	UK£	Euro	SF	US$	UK£	Euro
1.00	0.82	0.43	0.65	75.00	61.50	32.25	48.75
2.00	1.64	0.86	1.30	100.00	82.00	43.00	65.00
3.00	2.46	1.29	1.95	125.00	102.50	53.75	81.25
4.00	3.28	1.72	2.60	150.00	123.00	64.50	97.50
5.00	4.10	2.15	3.25	175.00	143.50	75.25	113.75
6.00	4.92	2.58	3.90	200.00	164.00	86.00	130.00
7.00	5.74	3.01	4.55	225.00	184.50	96.75	146.25
8.00	6.56	3.44	5.20	250.00	205.00	107.50	162.50
9.00	7.38	3.87	5.85	275.00	225.50	118.25	178.75
10.00	8.20	4.30	6.50	300.00	246.00	129.00	195.00
15.00	12.30	6.45	9.75	350.00	287.00	150.50	227.50
20.00	16.40	8.60	13.00	400.00	328.00	172.00	260.00
25.00	20.50	10.75	16.25	500.00	410.00	215.00	325.00
50.00	41.00	21.50	32.50	1000.00	820.00	430.00	650.00

currency. There are many good-value hotels and restaurants, but don't expect to find them in the expensive cities of Zurich and Geneva or in such chic resorts as St. Moritz and Arosa. If you're watching your budget, try to stay in small villages, such as Klosters, on the periphery of celebrated resorts.

The basic unit of Swiss currency is the Swiss franc (F), which is made up of 100 centimes. Banknotes are issued in denominations of 10, 20, 50, 100, 500, and 1,000 francs, and coins are minted as 5, 10, 20, and 50 centimes, and 1, 2, and 5 francs.

ATMs

The easiest and best way to get cash away from home is from an ATM (automated teller machine). The **Cirrus** (© **800/424-7787;** www.mastercard.com) and **PLUS**

(✆ **800/843-7587;** www.visa.com) networks span the globe; look at the back of your bank card to see which network you're on, then call or check online for ATM locations at your destination. Be sure you know your personal identification number (PIN) before you leave home and be sure to find out your daily withdrawal limit before you depart. Also keep in mind that many banks impose a fee every time a card is used at a different bank's ATM, and that fee can be higher for international transactions (up to $5 or more) than for domestic ones (where they're rarely more than $1.50). On top of this, the bank from which you withdraw cash may charge its own fee. To compare banks' ATM fees within the U.S., use www.bankrate.com. Ask your bank about international withdrawal fees.

You can also get cash advances on your credit card at an ATM. Keep in mind that credit card companies try to protect themselves from theft by limiting the funds someone can withdraw outside their home country, so call your credit card company before you leave home. Also keep in mind that you pay interest from the moment of your withdrawal, even if you pay your monthly bills on time.

TRAVELER'S CHECKS

Traveler's checks are something of an anachronism from the days before the ATM made cash accessible at any time. Traveler's checks used to be the only sound alternative to traveling with dangerously large amounts of cash. They are as reliable as currency, but, unlike cash, can be replaced if lost or stolen.

These days, traveler's checks are less necessary because most cities have 24-hour ATMs that allow you to withdraw small amounts of cash as needed. However, keep in mind that you will likely be charged an ATM withdrawal fee if the bank is not your own, so if you're withdrawing money every day, you may be better off with traveler's checks—provided that you don't mind showing identification every time you want to cash one.

You can get traveler's checks at almost any bank. **American Express** offers denominations of $20, $50, $100, $500, and (for cardholders only) $1,000. You'll pay a service charge ranging from 1% to 4%. You can also get American Express traveler's checks over the phone by calling ✆ **800/221-7282;** Amex gold and platinum cardholders who use this number are exempt from the 1% fee.

Visa offers traveler's checks at Citibank locations nationwide, as well as at several other banks. The service charge ranges between 1.5% and 2%; checks come in denominations of $20, $50, $100, $500, and $1,000. Call ✆ **800/732-1322** for information. AAA members can obtain Visa checks without a fee at most AAA offices or by calling ✆ **866/339-3378.** **MasterCard** also offers traveler's checks. Call ✆ **800/223-9920** for a location near you.

Foreign-currency traveler's checks are useful if you're traveling to one country, or to the euro zone; they're accepted at locations such as bed-and-breakfasts where dollar checks may not be, and they minimize the amount of math you have to do at your destination. **American Express, Thomas Cook, Visa,** and **MasterCard** offer foreign-currency traveler's checks. You'll pay the rate of exchange at the time of purchase, so monitor the rate before you take the plunge. Most companies charge a transaction fee per order and a shipping fee if you order online.

If you choose to carry traveler's checks, be sure to keep a record of their serial numbers separate from your checks in the event that they are stolen or lost. You'll get a refund faster if you know the numbers.

CREDIT CARDS

Credit cards are a safe way to carry money, they provide a convenient record

Tips Dear Visa: I'm Off to Zermatt!

Some credit card companies recommend that you notify them of any impending trip abroad so that they don't become suspicious when the card is used numerous times in a foreign destination and block your charges. Even if you don't call your credit card company in advance, you can always call the card's toll-free emergency number if a charge is refused—a good reason to carry the phone number with you. But perhaps the most important lesson here is to carry more than one card with you on your trip; a card might not work for any number of reasons, so having a backup is the smart way to go.

of all your expenses, and they generally offer good exchange rates. You can also withdraw cash advances from your credit cards at banks or ATMs, provided you know your PIN. If you've forgotten yours, or didn't even know you had one, call the number on the back of your credit card and ask the bank to send it to you. It usually takes 5 to 7 business days, though some banks will provide the number over the phone if you tell them your mother's maiden name or some other personal information. Keep in mind that when you use your credit card abroad, most banks assess a 2% fee above the 1% fee charged by Visa, MasterCard, or American Express for currency conversion on credit charges. But credit cards still may be the smart way to go when you factor in things like exorbitant ATM fees and higher traveler's check exchange rates (and service fees).

5 When to Go

THE WEATHER

The temperature range is about the same as in the northern United States, but without the extremes of hot and cold. Summer temperatures seldom rise above 80°F (26°C) in the cities, and humidity is low. Because of clear air and lack of wind in the high alpine regions, sunbathing is sometimes possible even in winter. In southern Switzerland the temperature remains mild year-round, allowing subtropical vegetation to grow.

June is the ideal month for a tour of Switzerland, followed by either September or October, when the mountain passes are still open. During summer the country is usually overrun with tourist traffic.

HOLIDAYS

The legal holidays in Switzerland are New Year's (Jan 1–2), Good Friday, Easter Monday, Ascension Day, Whit Monday, Bundesfeier (the Swiss National Holiday; Aug 1), and Christmas (Dec 25–26).

Low-season airfares are usually offered from November 1 to December 14 and from December 25 to March 31. Fares are slightly higher during shoulder season (during Apr and May, and from Sept 16 to the end of Oct). High-season fares apply the rest of the year (June 1–Sept 15), presumably when Switzerland and its landscapes are at their most hospitable and most beautiful.

Keep in mind that it's most expensive to visit Swiss ski resorts in winter, and slightly less so during the rest of the year. Conversely, it's cheaper to visit lakeside towns and the Ticino in winter. Cities such as Geneva, Zurich, and Bern don't depend on tourism as a major source of capital, so prices in these cities tend to remain the same all year.

Switzerland's Average Temperatures (°F/°C)

		Jan	Feb	Mar	Apr	May	June	July	Aug	Sept	Oct	Nov	Dec
Geneva	High	40/4	43/6	50/10	59/15	67/19	74/23	77/25	76/24	70/21	58/14	47/8	40/4
	Low	29/–2	31/–1	36/2	41/5	49/9	56/13	59/15	58/14	54/12	45/7	38/3	32/0
Lugano	High	43/6	49/9	56/13	63/17	70/21	77/25	81/27	81/27	74/23	61/16	52/11	45/7
	Low	29/–2	31/–1	38/3	45/7	50/10	58/14	61/16	59/15	56/13	47/8	38/3	32/0
Zermatt	High	26/–3	26/–3	27/–3	36/2	46/7	52/11	58/14	53/12	52/11	38/3	33/1	26/–3
	Low	20/–7	19/–7	19/–7	28/–2	36/2	42/6	48/9	44/7	42/6	32/0	27/–3	20/–7
Zurich	High	36/2	41/4	50/10	59/15	67/19	74/23	77/25	76/24	68/20	58/14	45/7	38/3
	Low	27/–3	2/–29	34/1	40/4	47/8	54/12	58/14	56/13	52/11	43/61	36/2	29/–2

SWITZERLAND CALENDAR OF EVENTS

The festivals mentioned in this section, unless otherwise specified, fall on different dates every year. Inquire at the Swiss National Tourist Office or local tourist offices for an updated calendar. See "The Best Festivals" in chapter 1 for more information.

January

Vogel Gryff Festival (The Feast of the Griffin), Basel. The "Wild Man of the Woods" appears on a boat, followed by a mummers' parade. For more information, call ☏ **061/268-68-68.** Mid-January.

February

Basler Fasnacht, Basel. Called "the wildest of carnivals," with a parade of "cliques" (clubs and associations). For more information, call ☏ **061/268-68-68;** www.fasnacht.ch. First Monday after Ash Wednesday.

March

Hornussen ("Meeting on the Snow"), Maloja. A traditional sport of rural Switzerland. For information, call ☏ **081/824-31-81.** For a description of the sport, see the box "Hornussen, Schwingen & Waffenlaufen," later in this chapter. Mid-March.

April

Primavera Concertistica, Locarno. April marks the beginning of a festival of music concerts that lasts through October. For information, call ☏ **091/791-00-91.** Mid-April.

Sechseläuten ("Six O'Clock Chimes"), Zurich. Members of all the guilds dress in costumes and celebrate the arrival of spring, which is climaxed by the burning of Böögg, a straw figure symbolizing winter. There are also children's parades. The **Zurich Tourist Office** (☏ **044/215-40-00**) shows the parade route on a map. (Böögg is burned at 6pm on Sechseläutenplatz, near Bellevueplatz.) Third Monday of April.

May

Corpus Christi. Solemn processions in the Roman Catholic regions and towns of Switzerland. End of May.

June

Fête de Lausanne, Lausanne. Beginning of an international festival, showcasing weeks of music and ballet. For information, call ☏ **021/613-73-73;** www.fetedelausanne.ch. End of June.

William Tell Festival Play, Interlaken. Performances of the famous play by Schiller. For more information, call ☏ **033/822-37-32;** www.tellspiele.ch. End of June through September.

July

Montreux International Jazz Festival, Montreux. More than jazz, this festival features everything from reggae bands to African tribal chanters. Monster dance-fests also break out nightly. The festival concludes with a 12-hour marathon of world music. For more information, call ℂ **021/963-82-82;** www.montreuxjazz.com. Lasts 2½ weeks and is held in the beginning of July.

Züri Fäscht, Zurich. This summertime citywide festival takes over Zurich with fairground revelry. Held every 3 years in early July; the next one will take place in 2007.

August

Fêtes de Genève, Geneva. Highlights are flower parades, fireworks, and live music all over the city. For more information, call ℂ **022/909-70-11;** www. fetes-de-geneve.ch. Early August.

Lucerne Festival, Lucerne. Concerts, theater, art exhibitions, and street musicians. For more information, call ℂ **041/226-44-80;** http://e.lucerne festival.ch. Mid-August through mid-September.

Zurich Sreet Parade. Visitors flock to Zurich for a daylong techno/dance party and parade that takes over the entire city. You'll either want to book a hotel far in advance or avoid this at all costs. Visit www.streetparade.ch. See detailed box on p. 106. Early to mid-August.

September

Fribourg Braderie, Fribourg. A popular festival and onion market with a citywide sidewalk sale and folk entertainment. Call ℂ **026/350-33-00** for more information. Late September.

October

Wine Growers' Festival, Lugano. A parade and other festivities mark harvest

time. Little girls throw flowers from blossom-covered floats and oxen pull festooned wagons in a colorful procession. For information, call ℂ **091/913-32-32.** Early October.

Aelplerchilbi, Kerns and other villages of the Unterwalden Canton. Dairymen and pasture owners join villagers in a traditional festival to mark the end of an alpine summer. For more information, call the **Saren Tourismus,** Hofstrasse 2 (ℂ **041/666-50-40**). Late September or October.

November

Zibelemärit, Bern. The famous "onion market" fair. Call ℂ **031/328-12-12** for more information. Mid-November.

December

Christmas Festivities. Ancient St. Nicholas parades and traditional markets are staged throughout the country to mark the beginning of Christmas observances, with the major one at Fribourg. Mid-December.

L'Escalade, Geneva. A festival commemorating the failure of the duke of Savoy's armies to take Geneva by surprise on the night of December 11–12, 1602. Brigades on horseback in period costumes, country markets, and folk music are interspersed with Rabelaisian banquets, fife-and-drum parades, and torch-lit marches. Geneva's Old Town provides the best vantage point. Call ℂ **022/909-70-11** for more information. Three days and nights (nonstop) in mid-December.

6 Travel Insurance

Since Switzerland for most of us is far from home, and a number of things could go wrong—lost luggage, trip cancellation, a medical emergency—consider the following types of insurance.

Check your existing insurance policies and credit card coverage before you buy travel insurance. You may already be covered for lost luggage, canceled tickets, and/or medical expenses. The cost of travel insurance varies widely, depending on the cost and length of your trip, your age, health, and the type of trip you're taking, but expect to pay between 5% and 8% of the vacation itself.

TRIP-CANCELLATION INSURANCE

Trip-cancellation insurance helps you get your money back if you have to back out of a trip, if you have to go home early, or if your travel supplier goes bankrupt. Allowed reasons for cancellation can range from sickness to natural disasters to the State Department declaring your destination unsafe for travel. (Insurers usually won't cover vague fears, though, as many travelers discovered who tried to cancel their trips in Oct 2001 because they were wary of flying.) In this unstable world, trip-cancellation insurance is a good buy if you're getting tickets well in advance—who knows what the state of the world, or of your airline, will be in 9 months? Insurance policy details vary, so read the fine print—and especially make sure that your airline or cruise line is on the list of carriers covered in case of bankruptcy. A good resource is **"Travel Guard Alerts,"** a list of companies considered high-risk by Travel Guard International (see website below). Protect yourself further by paying for the insurance with a credit card—by law, consumers can get their money back on goods and services not received if they report the loss within 60 days after the charge is listed on their credit card statement.

Note: Many tour operators, particularly those offering trips to remote or high-risk areas, include insurance in the cost of the trip or can arrange insurance policies through a partnering provider, a convenient and often cost-effective way for the traveler to obtain insurance. Make sure the tour company is a reputable one, however: Some experts suggest you avoid buying insurance from the tour company you're traveling with, saying it's better to buy from a "third party" insurer than to put all your money in one place.

For information, contact one of the following recommended insurers: **Access America** (✆ 800/729-6021; www.accessamerica.com); **Travel Guard International** (✆ 800/826-4919; www.travelguard.com); **Travel Insured International** (✆ 800/243-3174; www.travelinsured.com); or **Travelex Insurance Services** (✆ 888/457-4602; www.travelex-insurance.com).

MEDICAL INSURANCE For travel overseas, most health plans (including Medicare and Medicaid) do not provide coverage, and the ones that do often require you to pay for services upfront and reimburse you only after you return home. Even if your plan does cover overseas treatment, most out-of-country hospitals make you pay your bills upfront, and send you a refund only after you've returned home and filed the necessary paperwork with your insurance company. As a safety net, you may want to buy travel medical insurance, particularly if you're traveling to a remote or high-risk area where emergency evacuation is a possible scenario. If you require additional medical insurance, try **MEDEX Assistance** (✆ 410/453-6300; www.medexassist.com) or **Travel Assistance International** (✆ 800/821-2828; www.travelassistance.com; for general information on services, call the company's **Worldwide Assistance Services, Inc.** at ✆ 800/777-8710; www.worldwideassistance.com).

LOST-LUGGAGE INSURANCE On international flights (including U.S. portions of international trips) baggage is limited to approximately $9.07 per pound, up to approximately $635 per checked bag. If you plan to check items more valuable than the standard liability, see if your valuables are covered by your homeowner's policy, get baggage insurance as part of your comprehensive travel-insurance package, or buy Travel Guard's "BagTrak" product. Don't buy insurance at the airport, as it's usually overpriced. Be sure to take any valuables or irreplaceable items with you in your carry-on luggage, as many valuables (including books, money, and electronics) aren't covered by airline policies.

If your luggage is lost, immediately file a lost-luggage claim at the airport, detailing the luggage contents. For most airlines, you must report delayed, damaged, or lost baggage within 4 hours of arrival. The airlines are required to deliver luggage, once found, directly to your house or destination free of charge.

7 Health & Safety

STAYING HEALTHY

Medical care and health facilities in Switzerland are among the best in the world. As a result, no endemic contagious diseases exist. Swiss authorities, however, require immunization against contagious diseases if you have been in an infected area during the 14-day period immediately preceding your arrival in Switzerland. Take along an adequate supply of any prescription drugs that you'll need, as well as a written prescription that uses the generic name—rather than the brand name—of the drugs (in general, French and German, not U.S., drugs are available in Switzerland). You may want to include some motion-sickness medicine as well. Be sure to carry your vital medicines and drugs in your carry-on luggage, in case your checked luggage is lost.

WHAT TO DO IF YOU GET SICK AWAY FROM HOME

Any foreign consulate can provide a list of area doctors who speak English. Nearly all of them do. If you get sick, consider asking your hotel concierge to recommend a local doctor—even his or her own. You can also try the emergency room at a local hospital. Many hospitals also have walk-in clinics for emergency cases that are not life-threatening; you may not get immediate attention, but you won't pay the high price of an emergency-room visit. We list hospital and emergency contact numbers under "Fast Facts," later in this chapter and in chapters 4, 7, and 11.

If you suffer from a chronic illness, consult your doctor before your departure. For conditions like epilepsy, diabetes, or heart problems, wear a **MedicAlert Identification Tag** (© **888/633-4298;** www.medic alert.org), which will immediately alert doctors to your condition and give them access to your records through MedicAlert's 24-hour hot line.

Pack **prescription medications** in your carry-on luggage, and carry prescription medications in their original containers, with pharmacy labels—otherwise they won't make it through airport security. Also bring copies of your prescriptions in case you lose your pills or run out. Don't forget an extra pair of contact lenses or prescription glasses. Carry the generic name of prescription medicines, in case a local pharmacist is unfamiliar with the brand name.

Contact the **International Association for Medical Assistance to Travellers (IAMAT)** (© **716/754-4883** or 416/652-0137; www.iamat.org) for tips on travel and health concerns in the countries you're visiting, and lists of local, English-speaking doctors. The United States **Centers for Disease Control and Prevention** (© **800/ 311-3435;** www.cdc.gov) provides up-to-date information on necessary vaccines and health hazards by region or country.

STAYING SAFE

The potential for specific threats or acts of violence involving American citizens in Switzerland is remote; nonetheless, travelers should always review their security practices and be alert to their surroundings. The Consular Agencies in Zurich and Geneva may close periodically to assess their security situations. Americans are encouraged to check the Consular Affairs home page for updated travel and security information.

Switzerland has a low rate of violent crime. However, pickpocketing and purse snatching do occur in the vicinity of train and bus stations, airports, and some public parks, especially during peak tourist periods (such as summer and Christmas) and when conferences, shows, or exhibits are scheduled in major cities. Liechtenstein has a low crime rate. Travelers may wish to exercise caution on trains, especially on overnight trains to neighboring countries. Even locked sleeping compartments can be entered by thieves, who steal from passengers while they sleep. The loss or theft abroad of a U.S. passport should be reported immediately to the local police and the nearest U.S. embassy or consulate. U.S. citizens may refer to the Department of State's pamphlet *A Safe Trip Abroad* to promote a trouble-free journey. The pamphlet is available from the Superintendent of Documents, U.S. Government Printing Office, Washington, DC 20402, and via the Internet at www.gpoaccess.gov or via the Bureau of Consular Affairs home page at http://travel.state.gov.

If you are a victim of a crime overseas, in addition to reporting to local police, contact the nearest U.S. embassy or consulate for assistance. The embassy/consulate staff can, for example, assist you in finding appropriate medical care, contact family members or friends, and explain how funds could be transferred. Although the investigation and prosecution of a crime is solely the responsibility of local authorities, consular officers can help you to understand the local criminal process and to find an attorney if needed.

8 Specialized Travel Resources

TRAVELERS WITH DISABILITIES

Most disabilities shouldn't stop anyone from traveling. There are more options and resources out there than ever before. A few helpful tips:

- A fact sheet and special hotel guide for persons with disabilities is available from the Swiss National Tourist Office.
- On Swiss trains, wheelchair passengers travel in a special section of the passenger car. Certain trains cannot accommodate them there, in which case they travel in a specified area of the luggage car.
- Hertz rents minibuses accessible to wheelchair passengers. Arrangements should be made well in advance with **Hertz AG,** Morgartenstrasse 5, Zurich (© **044/298-8484;** www.hertz.ch).

Because of Switzerland's many hills and endless mountains, visitors with disabilities may have difficulty getting around the country, but conditions are slowly improving. Newer hotels are more sensitive to the needs of those with disabilities, and the more expensive restaurants, in general, are wheelchair-accessible. However, because most places have limited, if any, facilities for people with disabilities, you may want to consider taking an organized tour specifically designed to accommodate travelers with disabilities.

Many travel agencies offer customized tours and itineraries for travelers with disabilities. **Flying Wheels Travel** (© **507/451-5005;** www.flyingwheelstravel.com) offers escorted tours and cruises that emphasize sports and private tours in minivans with lifts. **Access-Able Travel Source** (© **303/232-2979;** www.accessable.com) offers extensive access information and advice for traveling around the world with disabilities. **Accessible Journeys** (© **800/846-4537** or 610/521-0339; www.disabilitytravel.com) caters specifically to slow walkers and wheelchair travelers and their families and friends.

Organizations that offer assistance to travelers with disabilities include **MossRehab** (www.mossresourcenet.org), which provides a library of accessible-travel resources online; **SATH (Society for Accessible Travel & Hospitality;** ✆ **212/447-7284;** www.sath.org; annual membership fees: $45 adults, $30 seniors and students), which offers a wealth of resources for all types of disabilities and recommendations on destinations, access guides, travel agents, tour operators, vehicle rentals, and companion services; and the **American Foundation for the Blind (AFB)** (✆ **800/232-5463;** www.afb.org), a referral resource for the blind and visually impaired that includes information on traveling with Seeing Eye dogs.

For more information specifically targeted to travelers with disabilities, the website **iCan** (www.icanonline.net/channels/travel/index.cfm) has destination guides and columns on accessible travel. Also check out the quarterly magazine *Emerging Horizons* ($15 per year, $20 outside the U.S.; www.emerginghorizons.com); and *Open World Magazine,* published by the Society for Accessible Travel & Hospitality (see above; subscription: $13 per year, $21 outside the U.S.).

GAY & LESBIAN TRAVELERS

Basel, Zurich, and Geneva are the centers of gay life in Switzerland, although such chic resorts as Gstaad, St. Moritz, and Arosa are also popular destinations for gay and lesbian travelers (mostly in winter). The national organization for gays in Switzerland is **Pink Cross,** Zinggstrasse 16, P.O. Box 7512, 3001 Bern (✆ **031/372-33-00;** www.pinkcross.ch).

Before you go you might pick up the latest edition of *Frommer's Gay & Lesbian Europe* (www.frommers.com). Although Switzerland is not specifically included in this guide, it will be helpful if you're planning to combine a visit to Switzerland with stopovers in such gay meccas as London or Paris.

The International Gay and Lesbian Travel Association (IGLTA) (✆ **800/448-8550** or 954/776-2626; www.iglta.org) is the trade association for the gay and lesbian travel industry, and offers an online directory of gay- and lesbian-friendly travel businesses.

Many agencies offer tours and travel itineraries specifically for gay and lesbian travelers. **Above and Beyond Tours** (✆ **800/397-2681;** www.abovebeyondtours.com) is the exclusive gay and lesbian tour operator for United Airlines. **Now, Voyager** (✆ **800/255-6951;** www.nowvoyager.com) is a well-known San Francisco–based gay-owned and -operated travel service. **Olivia Cruises & Resorts** (✆ **800/631-6277;** www.olivia.com) charters entire resorts and ships for exclusive lesbian vacations and offers smaller group experiences for both gay and lesbian travelers.

The following travel guides are available at most travel bookstores and gay and lesbian bookstores, or you can order them from **Giovanni's Room** bookstore, 1145 Pine St., Philadelphia, PA 19107 (✆ **215/923-2960;** www.giovannisroom.com): *Out and About* (✆ **800/929-2268;** www.outandabout.com), which offers guidebooks and a newsletter 10 times a year packed with solid information on the global gay and lesbian scene; *Spartacus International Gay Guide* (Bruno Gmünder Verlag; www.spartacusworld.com/gayguide) and *Odysseus: The International Gay Travel Planner* (Odysseus Enterprises Ltd.), both good, annual English-language guidebooks focused on gay men; the **Damron** guides (www.damron.com), with separate, annual books for gay men and lesbians; and *Gay Travel A to Z: The World of Gay & Lesbian Travel Options* *at Your Fingertips,* by Marianne Ferrari (Ferrari International; Box 35575, Phoenix, AZ 85069), a very good gay and lesbian guidebook series.

SENIOR TRAVELERS

Many discounts are available for seniors (women over age 62 and men over 65). Be advised, however, that you often have to be a member of an association to obtain certain discounts.

Members of **AARP** (formerly known as the American Association of Retired Persons), 601 E St. NW, Washington, DC 20049 (© **800/424-3410** or 202/434-2277; www.aarp.org), get discounts on hotels, airfares, and car rentals. AARP offers members a wide range of benefits, including *AARP: The Magazine* and a monthly newsletter. Anyone over 50 can join.

Many reliable agencies and organizations target the 50-plus market. **Elderhostel** (© **877/426-8056;** www.elderhostel. org) arranges study programs for those age 55 or over (and a spouse or companion of any age) in the U.S. and in more than 80 countries around the world. Most courses last 5 to 7 days in the U.S. (2–4 weeks abroad), and many include airfare, accommodations in university dormitories or modest inns, meals, and tuition. **ElderTreks** (© **800/741-7956;** www. eldertreks.com) offers small-group tours to off-the-beaten-path or adventure-travel locations, restricted to travelers 50 and older.

Recommended publications offering travel resources and discounts for seniors include: the quarterly magazine *Travel 50 & Beyond* (www.travel50andbeyond. com); *Travel Unlimited: Uncommon Adventures for the Mature Traveler* (Avalon); *101 Tips for Mature Travelers,* available from Grand Circle Travel (© **800/221-2610** or 617/350-7500; www.gct.com); *The 50+ Traveler's Guidebook* (St. Martin's Press); and *Unbelievably Good Deals and Great Adventures That You Absolutely Can't Get Unless You're Over 50* (McGraw-Hill).

FAMILY TRAVELERS

If you have enough trouble getting your kids out of the house in the morning, dragging them thousands of miles away may seem like an insurmountable challenge. But family travel can be immensely rewarding, giving you new ways of seeing the world through smaller pairs of eyes.

Traveling with Minors

It's always wise to have plenty of documentation when traveling with children in today's world. For changing details on entry requirements for children traveling abroad, keep up-to-date by going to the U.S. State Department website: **http://travel.state.gov/foreignentryreqs.html**.

To prevent international child abduction, E.U. governments have initiated procedures at entry and exit points. These often (but not always) include requiring documentary evidence of relationship and permission for the child's travel from the parent or legal guardian not present. Having such documentation on hand, even if not required, facilitates entries and exits. All children must have their own passports. To obtain a passport, the child **must** be present—that is, in person—at the center issuing the passport. Both parents must be present as well. If not, then a notarized statement from the parents is required. Any questions parents or guardians might have can be answered by calling the **National Passport Information Center** at © **877/487-2778** Monday to Friday 8am to 8pm Eastern Standard Time.

Tips Rail Bargains

In Switzerland children under age 16—if accompanied by at least one adult—travel free on national rail lines. This family travel plan is valid for the purchase of Swiss Passes, Swiss Flexi Passes, Swiss Cards, and point-to-point tickets (see "By Train" in "Getting Around," later in this chapter).

On airlines, you must request a special menu for children at least 24 hours in advance. If baby food is required, however, bring your own and ask a flight attendant to warm it to the right temperature.

Arrange ahead of time for such necessities as a crib, bottle warmer, and a car seat (in England, small children aren't allowed to ride in the front seat).

The University of New Hampshire runs **Familyhostel** (© **800/733-9753;** www. learn.unh.edu), an intergenerational alternative to standard guided tours. You live on a European college campus for the 2- or 3-week program, attend lectures and seminars, go on lots of field trips, and do all the sightseeing—all of it guided by a team of experts and academics. It's designed for children (ages 8–15), parents, and grandparents.

Look also for our "Kids" icon, indicating attractions, restaurants, or hotels and resorts that are especially family-friendly.

Remember that for people 15 and under, a passport is valid for only 5 years, costing $40, whereas for those 16 and up, a passport is valid for 10 years, costing $60.

Recommended family travel Internet sites include **Family Travel Forum** (www. familytravelforum.com), a comprehensive site that offers customized trip planning; **Family Travel Network** (www.familytravel network.com), an award-winning site that offers travel features, deals, and tips; **Traveling Internationally with Your Kids** (www.travelwithyourkids.com), a comprehensive site offering sound advice for long-distance and international travel with children; and **Family Travel Files** (www. thefamilytravelfiles.com), which offers an online magazine and a directory of off-the-beaten-path tours and tour operators for families.

9 Planning Your Trip Online

SURFING FOR AIRFARES

The "big three" online travel agencies, **Expedia.com, Travelocity.com,** and **Orbitz.com,** sell most of the air tickets bought on the Internet. (Canadian travelers should try Expedia.ca and Travelocity.ca; U.K. residents can go to Expedia. co.uk and Opodo.co.uk.) Each has different business deals with the airlines and may offer different fares on the same flights, so it's wise to shop around. Expedia and Travelocity also send **e-mail notification** when a cheap fare becomes available to your favorite destination. Of the smaller travel agency websites, **SideStep** (www.sidestep. com) has gotten the best reviews from Frommer's authors. This browser add-on purports to "search 140 sites at once," but in reality only beats competitors' fares as often as other sites do.

Also remember to check **airline websites,** especially those for low-fare carriers whose fares are often misreported or simply missing from travel agency websites. Even with major airlines, you can often shave a few bucks from a fare by booking directly through the airline and avoiding a travel agency's transaction fee. But you'll get these discounts only by **booking online:** Most airlines now offer online-only fares that even their phone agents know nothing about. For the websites of airlines that fly to and from your destination, go to "Getting There," later in this chapter.

Great **last-minute deals** are available through free weekly e-mails provided directly by the airlines. Most of these are announced on Tuesday or Wednesday and must be purchased online. Most are only valid for travel that weekend, but some can be booked weeks or months in advance. Sign up for e-mail alerts at airline websites or check megasites that compile comprehensive lists of last-minute specials, such as **Smarter Living** (http://smarterliving. com). For last-minute trips, **site59.com** and **lastminute.com** in Europe often have better air-and-hotel package deals than the major-label sites. A website listing numerous bargain sites and airlines around the world is **www.itravelnet.com.**

If you're willing to give up some control over your flight details, use an **"opaque" fare service** like **Priceline** (www.priceline. com; www.priceline.co.uk for Europeans) or its smaller competitor **Hotwire** (www. hotwire.com). Both offer rock-bottom prices in exchange for travel on a "mystery airline" at a mysterious time of day, often with a change of planes en route. The airlines are all major carriers. Hotwire tells you flight prices before you buy; Priceline usually has better deals than Hotwire, but you have to play their "name our price" game. If you're new at this, the helpful folks at **BiddingForTravel** (www.biddingfor travel.com) do a good job of demystifying Priceline's prices and strategies. Priceline and Hotwire are great for flights between the U.S. and Europe. Priceline has added nonopaque service to its roster. You now have the option to pick exact flights, times, and airlines from a list of offers—or opt to bid on opaque fares as before.

For much more about airfares and savvy air-travel tips and advice, pick up a copy of *Frommer's Fly Safe, Fly Smart* (Wiley Publishing, Inc.).

SURFING FOR HOTELS

Expedia offers a long list of special deals and "virtual tours," or photos of available rooms, so you can see what you're paying for (a feature that helps counter claims that the best rooms are often held back from bargain-booking websites). **Travelocity** posts unvarnished customer reviews and ranks its properties according to the AAA rating system. Also reliable are **Hotels. com** and **Quikbook.com.** An excellent free program, **TravelAxe** (www.travelaxe. net), searches multiple hotel sites at once, even ones you may never have heard of— and conveniently lists the total price of the room, including taxes and service charges. Another site, **Travelweb** (www.travelweb. com), is partly owned by the hotels it represents (including the Hilton, Hyatt, and Starwood chains) and is plugged directly into the hotels' reservations systems— unlike independent online agencies, which have to fax or e-mail reservation requests to the hotel, a good portion of which get misplaced in the shuffle. More than once, travelers have arrived at the hotel only to be told that they have no reservation. To be fair, many of the major sites are undergoing improvements in service and ease of use, and Expedia will soon be able to plug directly into the reservations systems of many hotel chains—none of which can be bad news for consumers. In the meantime it's a good idea to **get a confirmation number** and **make a printout** of any online booking transaction.

SURFING FOR RENTAL CARS

For booking rental cars online, the best deals are usually found at rental-car-company websites, although all the major online travel agencies also offer rental-car reservations services. Priceline and

Frommers.com: The Complete Travel Resource

For an excellent travel-planning resource, we highly recommend **Frommers. com** (www.frommers.com), voted Best Travel Site by *PC Magazine*. We're a little biased, of course, but we guarantee that you'll find the travel tips, reviews, monthly vacation giveaways, bookstore, and online-booking capabilities thoroughly indispensable. Among the special features are our popular **Destinations** section, where you'll get expert travel tips, hotel and dining recommendations, and advice on the sights to see for more than 3,000 destinations around the globe; the **Frommers.com** Newsletter, with the latest deals, travel trends, and money-saving secrets; our **Community** area featuring **Message Boards,** where Frommer's readers post queries and share advice (sometimes even our authors show up to answer questions); and our **Photo Center,** where you can post and share vacation tips. When your research is done, the **Online Reservations System** (www.frommers.com/book_a_trip) takes you to Frommer's preferred online partners for booking your vacation at affordable prices.

Hotwire work well for rental cars too; the only "mystery" is which major rental company you get, and for most travelers the difference between Hertz, Avis, and Budget is negligible.

10 The 21st-Century Traveler

INTERNET ACCESS AWAY FROM HOME

Travelers have any number of ways to check their e-mail and access the Internet on the road. Of course, using your own laptop—or even a PDA (personal desk assistant) or electronic organizer with a modem—gives you the most flexibility. But even if you don't have a computer, you can still access your e-mail and even your office computer from cybercafes.

WITHOUT YOUR OWN COMPUTER

It's hard nowadays to find a city that *doesn't* have a few cybercafes. Although there's no definitive directory for cybercafes—these are independent businesses, after all—three places to start looking are at **www. cybercaptive.com**, **www.netcafeguide. com**, and **www.cybercafe.com**.

Most major airports now have **Internet kiosks** scattered throughout their gates. These kiosks, which you'll also see in shopping malls, hotel lobbies, and tourist information offices around the world, give you basic Web access for a per-minute fee that's usually higher than cybercafe prices. The kiosks' clunkiness and high prices means they should be avoided whenever possible.

To retrieve your e-mail, ask your **Internet service provider (ISP)** if it has a Web-based interface tied to your existing e-mail account. If your ISP doesn't have such an interface, you can use the free **mail2web** service (www.mail2web.com) to view (but not reply to) your home e-mail. For more flexibility, you may want to open a free, Web-based e-mail account with **Yahoo! Mail** (mail.yahoo. com). (Microsoft's Hotmail is another popular option, but Hotmail has severe spam problems.) Your home ISP may be able to forward your e-mail to the Web-based account automatically.

If you need to access files on your office computer, look into a service called **GoToMyPC** (www.gotomypc.com). The service provides a Web-based interface for you to access and manipulate a distant PC from anywhere—even a cybercafe—provided your "target" PC is on and has an always-on connection to the Internet (such as with Road Runner cable). The service offers top-quality security, but if you're worried about hackers, use your own laptop rather than a cybercafe to access the GoToMyPC system.

WITH YOUR OWN COMPUTER

Wi-Fi (wireless fidelity) is the buzzword in computer access, and more and more hotels, cafes, and retailers are signing on as wireless "hotspots" from where you can get high-speed connection without cable wires, networking hardware, or a phone line (see below). You can establish a Wi-Fi connection in several ways. Many laptops sold in the last few years have built-in Wi-Fi capability (an 802.11b wireless Ethernet connection). Mac owners have their own networking technology, Apple AirPort. For older computers, an 802.11b/**Wi-Fi card** (around $50) can plug into your laptop.

You sign up for wireless access service much as you do for cellphone service, through a plan offered by one of several commercial companies that have made wireless service available in airports, hotel lobbies, and coffee shops, primarily in the U.S. (followed by the U.K. and Japan). **T-Mobile Hotspot** (www.t-mobile.com/hotspot) offers wireless connections at more than 1,000 Starbucks coffee shops in the U.S. **Boingo** (www.boingo.com) and **Wayport** (www.wayport.com) have networks in airports and high-class hotel lobbies. IPass providers (see below) also give you access to a few hundred wireless hotel-lobby setups. Best of all, you don't need

to be staying at the Four Seasons to use the hotel's network; just set yourself up on a nice couch in the lobby. The companies' pricing policies can be Byzantine, with a variety of monthly, per-connection, and per-minute plans, but in general you pay around $30 a month for limited access—and as more and more companies jump on the wireless bandwagon, prices are likely to get even more competitive.

There are also places that provide **free wireless networks** in cities around the world. To locate these free hotspots, go to **www.personaltelco.net/index.cgi/WirelessCommunities**.

If Wi-Fi is not available at your destination, most business-class hotels throughout the world offer dataports for laptop modems, and a few thousand hotels in the U.S. and Europe now offer free high-speed Internet access using an Ethernet network cable. You can bring your own cables, but most hotels rent them for around $10. **Call your hotel in advance** to see what your options are.

In addition, major Internet service providers (ISPs) have **local access numbers** around the world, allowing you to go online with a local call. Check with your ISP to find out how you can use your account away from home, and how much it will cost.

If you're traveling outside the reach of your ISP, the **iPass** network has dial-up numbers in most of the world's countries. You'll have to sign up with an iPass provider, who will then tell you how to set up your computer for your destination(s). For a list of iPass providers, go to www.ipass.com and click on "Individual Purchase." One solid provider is **i2roam** (www.i2roam.com; © **866/811-6209** or 920/235-0475).

Wherever you go, bring a **connection kit** with the right power and phone adapters, a spare phone cord, and a spare

Online Traveler's Toolbox

Veteran travelers usually carry some essential items to make their trips easier. Following is a selection of online tools to bookmark and use.

- **Visa ATM Locator** (www.visa.com) for locations of PLUS ATMs worldwide, or **MasterCard ATM Locator** (www.mastercard.com) for locations of Cirrus ATMs worldwide.
- **Foreign Languages for Travelers** (www.travlang.com). Learn basic terms in more than 70 languages and click on any underlined phrase to hear what it sounds like.
- **Intellicast** (www.intellicast.com) and **Weather.com** (www.weather.com). Provide weather forecasts for all 50 states and for cities around the world.
- **Mapquest** (www.mapquest.com). This best of the mapping sites lets you choose a specific address or destination, and in seconds it will return a map and detailed directions.
- **Universal Currency Converter** (www.xe.com/ucc). See what your dollar or pound is worth in more than 100 other countries.

Ethernet network cable—or find out if your hotel supplies them to guests.

USING A CELLPHONE

The three letters that define much of the world's **wireless capabilities** are GSM (Global System for Mobiles), a big, seamless network that makes for easy crossborder cellphone use throughout Europe and in dozens of other countries. In the U.S., T-Mobile, AT&T Wireless, and Cingular use this quasiuniversal system; in Canada, Microcell and some Rogers customers are GSM.

If your cellphone is on a GSM system and you have a world-capable multiband phone—such as many Sony Ericsson, Motorola, or Samsung models—you can make and receive calls almost anywhere. Just ask your wireless operator to activate "international roaming" on your account. Unfortunately, per-minute charges can be high—usually $1 to $1.50 in western Europe.

That's why it's important to buy an "unlocked" world phone from the get-go.

Many cellphone operators sell "locked" phones that restrict you from using any removable computer memory phone chip (called a **SIM card**) other than the ones they supply. Having an unlocked phone allows you to install a cheap, prepaid SIM card (found at a local retailer) in your destination country. (Show your phone to the salesperson; not all phones work on all networks.) You'll get a local phone number—and much, much lower calling rates. Getting an already-locked phone unlocked can be a complicated process, but it can be done; just call your cellular operator and say you'll be going abroad for several months and want to use the phone with a local provider.

For many, **renting** a phone is a good idea. We suggest renting the phone before you leave home. That way you can give loved ones and business associates your new number, make sure the phone works, and take the phone wherever you go. This is especially helpful for overseas trips through several countries, where local phone-rental agencies often bill in local currency and may not let you take the phone to another country.

Phone rental isn't cheap. You'll usually pay $40 to $50 per week, plus airtime fees of at least a dollar a minute. If you're traveling to Europe, local rental companies often offer free incoming calls within their home country, which can save you big bucks. The bottom line: Shop around.

11 Getting There

BY PLANE

Switzerland is situated at the center of Europe and thus is a focal point for international air traffic. The busy intercontinental airports of Zurich and Geneva can be reached in about 8 hours from the east coast of North America and in less than 2 hours from London or Paris. The country is also the crossroads of Europe—all rail lines, road passes, and mountain tunnels lead to it. Similarly, the main European route for east-west travel passes through Switzerland, between Lake Constance and Geneva.

FROM NORTH AMERICA

From New York, it takes about 7 hours to fly to either Geneva or Zurich; from Chicago, about 10 hours; and from the West Coast, about 14 hours.

Swiss International Air Lines Ltd. (simply called **Swiss**) has taken over as the major carrier for Switzerland in the wake of the famous Swissair going belly up. For information, contact Swiss at © **877/ FLY-SWISS** in the U.S., 0848/85-20-00 in Switzerland, or 0845/601-90-56 in London. Or else search out www.swiss.com.

From North America, the most popular Swiss routes are daily flights from New York's JFK Airport to either Zurich or Geneva. There is also a daily Newark, New Jersey–Zurich flight, as well as a daily flight from Boston, Los Angeles, Miami, Chicago, and Dallas (in partnership with American Airlines).

From Montreal, Swiss flies to Zurich daily; from London, there are three daily Swiss flights to Basel, four to Geneva, and six to Zurich.

American Airlines (© **800/433-7300;** www.aa.com) makes one daily nonstop flight from Dallas/Fort Worth (DFW) to Zurich, one direct flight from DFW through Chicago, one direct flight from DFW through Miami, one direct flight each from DFW through New York's JFK and La Guardia, and one direct flight from Newark.

Delta Airlines (© **800/221-1212;** www.delta.com) has one daily nonstop to Zurich from both Newark and Atlanta.

Air Canada (© **888/247-2262;** www.aircanada.com) flies nonstop daily from Toronto to Zurich. Flight time from Toronto is about 8 hours.

FROM BRITAIN

From London's Heathrow Airport, **British Airways (BA)** (© **0870/850-9850;** www.britishairways.com) offers three daily nonstop flights to Zurich; on Saturday there are four flights. The airline also provides between three and five daily flights from Heathrow to Geneva. From Gatwick, BA offers at least three daily nonstops to Geneva.

You can also check for flights by **Aer Lingus** (© **800/IRISH-AIR;** www.aerlingus.com) from Manchester, and flights from London on **easyJet** (© **0870/600-0000;** www.easyjet.com).

British newspapers are always full of classified advertisements touting bargain airfare. Although competition is fierce, one well-recommended company that consolidates bulk ticket purchases and then passes the savings on to its consumers is **Trailfinders** (© **020/7937-5400** in London; www.trailfinders.com), which offers discounted tickets on major airlines.

GETTING THROUGH THE AIRPORT

With the federalization of airport security, security procedures at U.S. airports are more stable and consistent than ever. Generally, you'll be fine if you arrive at the airport **2 hours** before an international flight; if you show up late, tell an airline employee and you'll probably be taken to the front of the line.

Bring a **current, government-issued photo ID** such as a driver's license or passport. Keep your ID ready to show at check-in, the security checkpoint, and sometimes even the gate. Children under 18 do not need government-issued photo IDs for domestic flights, but they do for international flights to most countries.

In 2003 the TSA phased out **gate check-in** at all U.S. airports. And **e-tickets** have made paper tickets nearly obsolete. Passengers with e-tickets can beat the ticket-counter lines by using airport **electronic kiosks** or even **online check-in** from their home computers. Online check-in involves logging on to your airline's website, gaining access to your reservation, and printing out your boarding pass—and the airline may even offer you bonus miles to do so! If you're using a kiosk at the airport, bring the credit card you used to book the ticket or your frequent-flier card. Print out your boarding pass from the kiosk and simply proceed to the security checkpoint with your pass and a photo ID. If you're checking bags or looking to snag an exit-row seat, you will be able to do so using most airline kiosks. Even the smaller airlines are employing the kiosk system, but always call your airline to make sure these alternatives are available. **Curbside check-in** is also a good way to avoid lines, although a few airlines still ban curbside check-in; call before you go.

Security lines are getting shorter than they were between 2001 and 2003, but some doozies remain. If you have trouble standing for long periods of time, tell an airline employee; the airline will provide a wheelchair. Speed up security by **not wearing metal objects** such as big belt buckles or clanky earrings. If you've got metallic body parts, a note from your doctor can prevent a long chat with the security screeners. Keep in mind that only **ticketed passengers** are allowed past security, except for folks escorting passengers with disabilities or children.

Federalization has stabilized **what you can carry on** and **what you can't.** The general rule is that sharp things are out, nail clippers are okay, but lighters of any kind may not be carried, nor may they be checked in your luggage. Food and beverages must be passed through the X-ray machine—but security screeners can't make you drink from your coffee cup. Bring food in your carry-on rather than checking it, as explosive-detection machines used on checked luggage have been known to mistake food (especially chocolate, for some reason) for bombs. Travelers in the U.S. are allowed one carry-on bag, plus a "personal item" such as a purse, briefcase, or laptop bag. Carry-on hoarders can stuff all sorts of things into a laptop bag; as long as it has a laptop in it, it's still considered a personal item. The Transportation Security Administration (TSA) has issued a list of restricted items (www.tsa.gov/public/index.jsp).

Airport screeners may decide that your checked luggage needs to be searched by hand. You can now purchase luggage locks that allow screeners to open and relock a checked bag if hand-searching is necessary. Look for Travel Sentry certified locks at luggage or travel shops and Brookstone stores (you can buy them online at www.brookstone.com). Luggage inspectors can open these TSA-approved locks with a special code or key. For more information on the locks, visit www.travelsentry.org.

If you use something other than TSA-approved locks, your lock will be cut off your suitcase if a TSA agent needs to hand-search your luggage.

FLYING FOR LESS: TIPS FOR GETTING THE BEST AIRFARE

Passengers sharing the same airplane cabin rarely pay the same fare. Travelers who need to purchase tickets at the last minute, change their itinerary at a moment's notice, or fly one-way often get stuck paying the premium rate. Here are some ways to keep your airfare down:

- Passengers who can book their ticket **long in advance,** who can **stay over Saturday night,** or who **fly midweek** or **at less-trafficked hours** will pay a fraction of the full fare. If your schedule is flexible, say so, and ask if you can secure a cheaper fare by changing your flight plans.
- You can also save on airfares by keeping an eye out in local newspapers for **promotional specials** or **fare wars,** when airlines lower prices on their most popular routes. You rarely see fare wars offered for peak travel times, but if you can travel in the off-months, you may snag a bargain.
- Search **the Internet** for cheap fares (see "Planning Your Trip Online," earlier in this chapter).
- **Consolidators,** also known as bucket shops, are great sources for international tickets, although they usually can't beat the Internet on fares within North America. Start by looking in Sunday newspaper travel sections; U.S. travelers should focus on the *New York Times,* the *Los Angeles Times,* and the *Miami Herald.* For less-developed destinations, small travel agents who cater to immigrant communities in large cities often have the best deals. *Beware:* Bucket shop tickets are usually nonrefundable or rigged with stiff cancellation penalties, often as high as 50% to 75% of the ticket price, and some put you on charter airlines, which may leave at inconvenient times and experience delays. Several reliable consolidators are worldwide and available on the Net. **STA Travel** is now the world's leader in student travel, thanks to their purchase of Council Travel. It also offers good fares for travelers of all ages. **ELTExpress (Flights.com)** (✆ **800/ TRAV-800;** www.eltexpress.com) started in Europe and has excellent fares worldwide, but particularly to that continent. It also has "local" websites in 12 countries. **FlyCheap** (✆ **800/FLY-CHEAP;** www.1800fly cheap.com) is owned by package-holiday megalith MyTravel and has especially good fares to sunny destinations. **Air Tickets Direct** (✆ **800/ 778-3447;** www.airticketsdirect.com) is based in Montreal.
- Join **frequent-flier clubs.** Accrue enough miles and you'll be rewarded with free flights and elite status. It's free, and you'll get the best choice of seats, faster response to phone inquiries, and prompter service if your luggage is stolen, your flight is canceled or delayed, or if you want to change your seat. You don't need to fly to build frequent-flier miles—**frequent-flier credit cards** can provide thousands of miles for doing your everyday shopping.

BY TRAIN
FROM PARIS

One of the busiest rail links in Europe stretches from Paris to Geneva and Lausanne. Almost as busy are the rail routes between Paris and Zurich. Most of the trains assigned to these routes are part of Europe's network of high-speed trains. (The French refer to them as *trains à grande vitesse,* or TGV). From Paris's Gare de Lyon, about four trains a day depart, respectively, for both Geneva and Lausanne. Travel time to Geneva is about 4 hours; travel time to Lausanne is about 4½ hours.

Trains from Paris to Zurich depart three times a day from Paris's Gare de l'Est. Ironically, kilometers traveled by train within Switzerland are proportionately more expensive than equivalent distances within France, so ongoing fares from Zurich or Geneva to other points within Switzerland may come as an unpleasant surprise. Travelers who anticipate lots of rail travel are well advised to consider the purchase of any of Rail Europe's passes, or one of the Swiss Passes.

Schedules, prices, departure times, and confirmed reservations can be arranged before you leave North America through **Rail Europe, Inc.** (ⓒ **877/257-2887;** www.raileurope.com).

FROM LONDON
Rail links are also convenient between London and Switzerland. Both the following routes are easy, but the route through France is considerably more scenic (plus, you'll get the thrill of crossing the Chunnel—one of the world's engineering marvels).

VIA THE HOOK OF HOLLAND
The standard EuroCity express route sets out from London's Liverpool Street Station, sails from Harwick to the Hook of Holland, and then proceeds by train via Cologne, Germany, to either Basel or Zurich. Once here, it's easy to find rail links to the rest of Switzerland.

ACROSS OR UNDER THE CHANNEL THROUGH PARIS   It's also possible to take the rail link from London across or under the English Channel to Paris, where you can make ongoing rail connections to Switzerland. If you depart London

at 10am, you can arrive in Geneva or Lausanne before 10pm the same day.

One of the most convenient ways to reach Paris from London is the Citylink rail-hovercraft-rail service. English trains originate at London's Victoria Station and chug through the English countryside to the port of Folkestone. Passengers disembark and board a hovercraft or, in some cases, a conventional ferryboat, and continue across the channel to the French port of Boulogne. Once you reach the Continent, you'll proceed south on a waiting train through France into Paris's Gare du Nord. In Paris passengers must travel by taxi or metro (subway) across town to either the Gare de Lyon, for ongoing transfers to Geneva and Lausanne, or the Gare de l'Est, for Basel and Zurich. Trains then depart for Switzerland at regular intervals.

For information, timetables, and confirmed reservations (which are required on certain segments of these routes), contact **Rail Europe, Inc.** (ⓒ **877/257-2887**).

In 1994 the *Eurostar Express* began twice-daily passenger service between London and both Paris and Brussels. The $15-billion Channel tunnel, one of the great engineering feats of all time, is the first link between Britain and the Continent since the Ice Age. The 50km (31-mile) journey between Great Britain and France takes 35 minutes, although actual Chunnel time is only 19 minutes.

Eurostar offers a round-trip first-class fare between London and Paris costs $570, $410 in regular second class. You can make reservations for **Eurostar** at ⓒ **0870/584-8848** in the United Kingdom; in France at ⓒ **01-55-31-54-54;** in the United States at ⓒ **800/EUROSTAR;** or online at www.eurostar.com.

Chunnel train traffic is roughly competitive with air travel, if you calculate door-to-door travel time. Trains leave from London's Waterloo Station and arrive in

Paris at Gare du Nord, where fast rail connections can be made to whatever Swiss city you want.

The tunnel trains also accommodate passenger cars, charter buses, taxis, and motorcycles under the English Channel from Folkestone, England, to Calais, France. They operate 24 hours a day, 365 days a year, running every 15 minutes during peak travel times and at least once hourly at night. Tickets may be purchased at the toll booth. With Le Shuttle, gone are weather-related delays, seasickness, and a need for reservations.

You'll drive onto a half-mile-long train and travel through an impermeable underground tunnel.

Before boarding Le Shuttle, you must stop at a tollbooth and pass through Immigration for both countries at one time. During the ride you'll stay in bright, air-conditioned carriages, remaining inside your car or stepping outside to stretch your legs. When the trip is completed, simply drive off toward your destination—in our case, heading southeast to Switzerland.

BY CAR

Situated in the middle of the continent, Switzerland has a network of express highways linking it to other European countries. You can drive all the way from Britain to Switzerland by taking a northerly route through Belgium or the Netherlands and then Germany. British motorists tend to prefer this express auto route, which is free, to going through France and paying expensive toll charges.

The route through France is also much slower. It begins a few miles south of Calais and leads directly to the Périphérique (ring road around Paris), where you can pick up the Autoroute du Soleil to Switzerland. In Britain the best connection for a road link across France is from Portsmouth to Le Havre.

From the south of Germany, Autobahn E35 leads directly into Basel. From Basel, head east to Zurich on E60.

BY BUS

Because of its location at the crossroads of Europe, Switzerland is on several important bus routes. **Eurolines, Ltd.,** 52 Grosvenor Gardens, London SW1W 0AU, U.K. (© **0870/514-32-19** or 020/7730-8235; www.eurolines.com), offers routes into Switzerland from several major European cities, including London. Departing from London's Victoria Coach Station, buses have toilets, air-conditioning, and reclining seats, and maintain a strict nonsmoking policy. They stop about every 4 hours for a brief rest and refreshments. Other buses depart 2 nights a week for Zurich at 8pm, arriving the next day at 1:15pm. One-way fares from London to Zurich go for £65 ($124) one-way and £95 ($181) round-trip. Persons under 26 pay £59 ($112) each way and £89 ($169) round-trip.

12 Package Tours for the Independent Traveler

Before you start your search for the lowest airfare, you may want to consider booking your flight as part of a travel package. Package tours are not the same thing as escorted tours. Package tours are simply a way to buy the airfare, accommodations, and other elements of your trip (such as car rentals, airport transfers, and sometimes even activities) at the same time and often at discounted prices—kind of like one-stop shopping. Packages are sold in bulk to tour operators—who resell them to the public at a cost that usually undercuts standard rates.

One good source of package deals is the airlines themselves. Most major airlines offer air/land packages, including **American Airlines Vacations** (© 800/321-2121; www.aavacations.com), and **Delta Vacations** (© 800/221-6666; www.delta vacations.com).

13 Escorted General Interest Tours

Escorted tours are structured group tours, with a group leader. The price usually includes everything from airfare to hotels, meals, tours, admission costs, and local transportation.

There are many escorted-tour companies to choose from, each offering transportation to and within Switzerland, prearranged hotel space, and such extras as bilingual tour guides and lectures.

U.S. TOUR OPERATORS   There are many different tour operators eager for a share of your business, but one of the most unusual is **Abercrombie & Kent International, Inc.**, 1520 Kensington Rd., Oak Brook, IL 60521 (© 800/554-7016; www.abercrombiekent.com), a Chicago-based company established more than 30 years ago. It specializes in deluxe 10-day train tours of Switzerland, which, despite all the extras they offer, still cost less than any personally arranged tour.

Other well-recommended tour operators include outfits endorsed and approved by two of North America's largest airlines. These include **Delta Vacations** (© 800/221-6666; www.deltavacations.com) and **American Airlines Vacations** (© 800/321-2121; www.aavacations.com). Both outfits factor inexpensive airfare into land or hotel packages that can save substantial amounts of money over what you'd have paid if you'd booked the arrangements yourself.

Consider contacting one of the world's largest travel organizers, **American Express Vacations** (© 800/346-3607; www.americanexpress.com). Favored treatment and special discounts are usually offered to holders of gold or platinum American Express cards (if you have one of these, call © 800/525-3355); but a wide array of interesting and unusual tours are offered to the general public as well.

Other organizations that offer both escorted and package tours are: **Trafalgar Tours** (© 800/854-0103; www.trafalgar tours.com); **Globus & Cosmos** (© 800/276-7092; www.globusandcosmos.com); **Grand Circle Travel** (© 800/959-0405; www.gct.com); **Switzerland Tours** (www.switzerlandtours.net); and **Connection Tours** (© 877/449-4652 in the U.S. or 416/449-4652; www.connection tours.com).

For river cruises (also barge tours), the most reliable agency, for both Switzerland and Germany, is **KD River Cruises of Europe** (© 973/605-2442).

BRITISH TOUR OPERATORS   **HF Holidays,** Imperial House, Edgware Road, Colindale, London NW9 5AL (© 020/8905-9556; www.hfholidays. co.uk for a brochure), offers a range of 1- to 2-week packages to Switzerland and an array of some 150 special-interest offerings throughout Europe.

One of the best purveyors of Swiss vacations in England is **Waymark Holidays,** 44 Windsor Rd., Slough, SL1 2EJ (© 01753/516-477; www.waymark holidays.com). Walking and cross-country skiing are primarily featured, with destinations including the Engadine, Kandersteg, S-Chanf, and Santa Maria.

14 Special-Interest Trips

The destination chapters in this book are full of specific details on local ski trails, hiking trails, boating, fishing, and more. But here we've assembled a roundup of sports highlights—some of the very best ways to get outdoors and enjoy Switzerland's magnificent scenery. Most activities can be enjoyed independently, but if you like to have someone else sweat the details, we've also listed some of the region's best outfitters.

BALLOONING Balloon rides over Switzerland are even more spectacular than those in France. Contact **Buddy Bombard's Private Europe,** 333 Pershing Way, West Palm Beach, FL 33401 (© **800/862-8537** or 561/837-6610; www.bombardsociety.com).

BIKING Biking is a great way to see the Swiss countryside. You can rent a bike for a small fee at one railroad station and return it at another. In addition, bikes can be transported on passenger trains for a nominal fee. You should reserve your bike a day or so in advance at the station from which you plan to start.

Touring Club Swiss (TCS) maintains 10 cycling centers that rent bicycles and offer brochures and maps of nearby bike routes. The club will direct you along the least-congested routes, taking you through villages and past castles and manor houses that you would not otherwise discover. Even in remote areas, you can usually find someone who speaks English to help you if you have a problem or get lost. The central information office of the touring club is in a suburb of

---

⌐Fun Fact Hornussen, Schwingen & Waffenlaufen

For the majority of the Swiss, the sport of choice is walking, followed by swimming, and only then, skiing. The Swiss are fond of some uniquely Swiss sports as well: "Hornussen," "Schwingen," and "Waffenlaufen." And while these sports may not be seen in the Olympics, they do call for a certain amount of athletic prowess.

One of Switzerland's greatest writers, Jeremias Gotthelf, praised "Hornuss" in 1840. He wrote, "There is not any game which calls for as much strength, agility, and coordination between hand, foot, and eye as 'Hornuss.'" The sport was first practiced in the 17th century and stems from war games that had the objective of avoiding projectiles sent flying in the air. Today Hornuss can be most accurately described as a cross between lacrosse and cricket. The whistling sound the disk makes as it flies through the air is similar to the sound of a hornet. The German word for hornet is *Hornuss,* hence the name of the game. The opposing team must try to stop the flying disk as quickly as possible with heavy wooden bats.

In the wrestling game "Schwingen," strength counts above all. Two wrestlers, or "Schwingers," face each other in the middle of a pit with the goal of grabbing the adversary's oversized shorts, to unbalance him, and bringing both his shoulders down to touch the ground. This sport of attack and defense was once a training technique for soldiers preparing for war.

One sport that exists exclusively in Switzerland is called "Waffenlaufen." Runners in military uniform must carry a mountain rucksack to which a rifle is fixed. Together, the rucksack and rifle must not weigh less than 7.5 kilograms (17 lb.). Thus equipped, thousands of Swiss race along courses ranging from 26km to 28km (16–17 miles) each year.

Geneva at 4, rue Blandonnet, 1214 Vernier (© **022/417-27-27;** fax 022/417-20-20; www.tcs.ch).

Erickson Cycle Tours, 6119 Brooklyn Ave. NE, Seattle, WA 98115 (© **888/ 972-0140;** www.ecycletours.com), offers some of the best bike tours in Switzerland, through the Alps, past lakes and valleys, for groups limited in size to some 20 riders. Included are the mountain venues of Zermatt, Grindelwald, Bernina, and the San Bernardino passes.

CURLING & SKATING   Curling is currently a hot team sport in Switzerland, particularly popular in Davos, Villars, Gstaad, and Zermatt. Curling, of course, is a game played by sliding a large, smooth stone along the ice at a mark (called the tee) 35m (115 ft.) away.

Ice-skating is one of the leading winter sports of Switzerland, and nearly all major resorts have natural ice rinks. Also, there are dozens of artificial ones, of which Davos has the best.

FISHING   In this relatively small country, there are at least 32,000km (20,000 miles) of rivers and streams, as well as 1,349 sq. km (521 sq. miles) of lakes. These waters are situated at heights between 210m and 1,965m (689 and 6,445 ft.) above sea level, and vary in configuration and fauna as much as in altitude. Such a wide choice of conditions certainly puts anglers on their mettle, for they're presented with a fascinating range of challenges. For those who know how to adapt themselves, there is excellent sport in store. Angling techniques and bait must be suited to the particular water one happens to be fishing. With few exceptions, fly-fishing, spinning, and ground fishing, with natural or artificial bait, are permitted in most waters. Trout can be found in most waters up to altitudes of 1,800m (5,904 ft.), and lake trout have been known to weigh up to 10 kilograms (22 lb.). You need a license to fish, but they're easily acquired through

municipal authorities, beginning at 50F ($41) per day. Regulations vary from place to place, so to be sure you're legal; inquire at a hotel or local tourist office.

GOLF   There are more than 30 golf courses in Switzerland, 24 of them with 18 holes. Not a lot for a whole country, you may think, but they're located so strategically that, wherever you happen to be in Switzerland, you're likely to find a course nearby—and one within a wide range of altitudes: The lowest course is in Ascona, which lies a mere 210m (689 ft.) above sea level; among the highest are St. Moritz, at 1,692m (5,550 ft.), and Riederalp, at 1,920m (6,297 ft.). All the local clubs cater to visitors, who, incidentally, have the advantage of being able to play on weekdays while the locals earn their daily bread. If you left your clubs at home, a set can be rented locally. Should you want to improve your swing, "pros" are available too.

For more information, contact the **Swiss Golf Association,** 19, place de la Croix-Blanche, CH-1066, Epalinges VD, Switzerland (© **021/784-35-31;** www. asg.ch). Another tool for computer-savvy golfers is the Swiss Golf Network (www. swissgolfnetwork.ch), which includes information on all major golf courses in Switzerland.

Some of the top courses include **Golf Club Davos** at Davos Dorf (© 081/416-56-34; www.golfdavos.ch); **Golf Club de Verbier,** Verbier (© 027/771-53-14; www. verbiergolf.com); and **Golf Club Interlaken-Unterseen** at Interlaken (© 033/823-60-16; www.interlakengolf.ch).

HIKING   With 48,000km (30,000 miles) of well-marked and well-maintained walking paths, Switzerland is a Valhalla for hikers. The paths lead through alpine valleys, over lowlands, up hills to meadows, and into the heart of the Alps. Whether you choose a gentle walk or a rigorous trek, you're sure to see miles and miles of unspoiled beauty.

Many hotels offer walking or hiking excursions, with a serious hiking tour possibly entailing 4 to 7 hours of hiking each day.

Topographic maps, hiking maps, and books can be ordered from such outlets as Amazon.com and various bookstores. These include *Walking Switzerland—The Swiss Way,* which describes numerous hikes and a selection of inn-to-inn tours in the mountain areas. Also of interest is *100 Hikes in the Alps,* containing an interesting section on Switzerland. *Walking Easy in the Swiss Alps* is a 192-page book featuring day walks in six alpine villages, including Zermatt, Saas-Fee, Champex, Kandersteg, Lauterbrunnen, and Samedan/St. Moritz.

HIKING TOURS A specialist in walking and hiking tours is **Mountain Travel Sobek,** 1266 66 St., Suite 4, Emeryville, CA 94608 (© **888/687-6235;** www.mt sobek.com). You can wander with this adventure company across the full landscape of Switzerland, from alpine mountains of the Bernese Oberland to lakeside vistas in Mediterranean-like Ticino. Most nights are spent in old-fashioned hotels or hikers' lodges, and at least 1 night is in an alpine refuge. Hikes are ranked as easy, moderate, or strenuous; one of the most challenging tours, the "Mount Blanc Circuit," is a 13-day hike that covers parts of Switzerland along with areas of Italy and France. The company will provide complete details about all tours.

HORSEBACK RIDING Both St. Moritz and Arosa are good places for horseback riding. Switzerland has 230 riding centers that will rent horses. The only riding stable in St. Moritz, but one of the country's finest, is **Reithalle,** via Ludains 3 (© **079/432-60-22**), a 10-minute walk from the town center. Rides are conducted either in the rink or in the nearby forests. For more information, refer to St. Moritz in chapter 14. Another large concentration of top riding horses is in and around Arosa at **Fuhrhalterei,** Wierhof (© **081/377-41-96**). Rain or snow, these horses take visitors for scenic rides year-round. For more information, refer to Arosa in chapter 13.

MOUNTAINEERING Recognizing the allures (and the very real dangers) of climbing up the rocky crags that dot the surface of Switzerland, the 86,000-member Swiss Alpine Club (SAC), founded in 1863, promotes mountaineering and ski tours in the high Alps. Although its primary function is to organize alpine rescue services, it also lobbies politically to protect the alpine ecology. Working closely with equivalent associations in Austria, Germany, France, and Italy, the club has built mountain huts at strategic spots throughout the country, often hauling in building supplies by helicopter during the short summer season when construction is possible. The huts are modest, with bunk rooms sleeping 10 to 20 people. The average rate for a night's lodging (without food) for members of the club is from 35F ($29) per person per night. You can write the club and reserve space.

Applicants for membership in the club must be at least 10 years of age and should mail their applications, along with a passport-size photo and a check covering membership fees, to whatever branch of the club interests them the most. (Membership in any regional club grants the right to discounted accommodations at huts throughout the country). To learn of branch offices, contact the organization's headquarters in Bern: the **Swiss Alpine Club,** Mombionstrasse 61, P.O. Box 3000, Bern, Switzerland 23 (© **031/370-18-18;** www. sac-cas.ch). If you're looking for a particularly active regional branch, consider joining the group in Zermatt. Their address is Swiss Alpine Club, Sektion Zermatt, c/o Herr Kreiger, Haus Golomit, CH-3920 Zermatt, Switzerland (© **027/967-26-10**). Membership fees range from 75F to 130F

($62–$107), depending on the individual branch you join. Checks should be drawn on a Swiss bank. Membership includes a subscription to the organization's German- or French-language magazine, *Die Alpen,* and the above-mentioned discounted accommodations at the mountain shelters maintained by the club.

The organization is affiliated with mountain-climbing schools throughout the country, including branches in Andermatt, Champéry, Crans, Davos, Les Diablerets, Fiesch, La Fouly, Glarus, Grindelwald, Kandersteg, Klosters, Meiringen, Pontresina, Riederalp, Saas-Fee, Saas-Grund, Schwende, Tasch, Zermatt, and Zinal. Guides that are accredited by the Swiss Alpine Club are available at many other resorts as well, and usually remain in close contact with the staffs at the local tourist offices.

SKIING   Skiing in Switzerland, a tradition that goes back 2 centuries, is big business—an estimated 40% of the tourist dollar is spent on it. There are more than 1,700 mountain railways and ski lifts, and ski schools, ski instructors, and the best ski equipment in the world are available throughout the country.

Switzerland, which faces heavy competition from Austria (for a complete guide to resorts, see *Frommer's Austria*), has been called Europe's winter playground. What were once simple alpine farming villages have been transformed into bustling ski resorts, and there are more than 200 throughout the country. Nearly all of them have ski-rental shops.

All the cantons have skiing centers, most of which are in the Bernese Oberland, the Grisons, and the Valais. The ideal ski season is from January to late March. At the very highest resorts, the season begins around mid-December. Even at some of the resorts at lower elevations, there is a ski season that begins before Christmas if there are adequate weather conditions and snow is adequate. February is the peak month, in which reservations are most difficult to come by. Skiing in some areas of the country continues until late April or, in other areas such as Zermatt, throughout the summer around the Klein Matterhorn.

Most slopes are nothing short of spectacular in Switzerland, as are the facilities, which cater to every type of skier from the beginner to the Olympic champion.

Europeans have always sought out family-oriented villages for inexpensive ski vacations, whereas Americans have traditionally preferred the more famous meccas such as St. Moritz and Gstaad. Happily, that is changing now, and many Americans (and Canadians) are choosing ski packages in the smaller alpine villages.

At the tourist offices of most resorts, ask for an area map depicting the various slopes. These maps also grade the ski trails for difficulty. Be sure to familiarize yourself with the resort's signs before hitting the slopes. Obviously, avalanche zones are particularly important to learn.

At more than 50 resorts in Switzerland, the Swiss Rent-a-Ski program prevails. This service allows you to rent skis (either downhill or cross-country), poles, and boots on a weekly basis.

Founded in 1863, the **Swiss Alpine Club** promotes ski tours and mountaineering at lofty alpine altitudes. For more details about membership, see "Mountaineering," above.

Swiss Ski School is the most famous such institution in Europe. Federally run, it provides on-site instruction for beginners as well as advanced skiers. The majority of instructors speak English. Most of these ski schools—found at all major resorts—reduce their charges for five half-day classes. However, all-day classes are usually recommended.

Warning: Always carry plenty of sunscreen, even in winter. The reflection of sunlight off the snow is intense.

Summer skiing, or glacier skiing, takes place on glaciers that retain their snow throughout July and August, and ski schools and lifts are open all summer. Locals say that glacier skiing is best before lunch, especially during the early-morning hours. The best glacier ski resorts are Zermatt, St. Moritz, Engelberg, Saas-Fee, Gstaad, and Pontresina.

Experienced skiers may wish to take a popular spring ski tour, the Haute Route, which crosses the French Alps into Switzerland; it's a weeklong tour that is usually offered between March and May. Led by a professional guide, skiers stop overnight and for noon rests at cabins maintained by the Swiss Alpine Club (see "Mountaineering," above, for more information on this club).

Cross-country skiing, or *langlauf,* is the fastest-growing sport in Europe, especially at St. Moritz, Pontresina, and Montana. You go at your own speed and are not at the whim of slope conditions. There are no age limits or charges for use of the well-marked cross-country trails.

From December 18 to March 31, you can get information on conditions in major Swiss ski areas by linking up with Switzerland Tourism Office's **snow report** at **www.switzerlandtourism.com**.

The best resort for families is **Arosa** (see chapter 13). It is very family-oriented and offers runs suitable for every level of skier, especially beginners. Most of the runs, however, are intermediate.

Expert skiers head for the resort of **Zermatt** (see chapter 9). In just minutes skiers can be more than 3,600m (11,808 ft.) up on the Klein Matterhorn. Zermatt claims that it can guarantee a skier a vertical drop of some 2,700m (8,856 ft.) regardless of the snowfall.

Beginning skiers, often those with families, find the resort of **Grindelwald** (see chapter 8) ideal, the best base for skiing the Jungfrau area. It offers cable cars, lifts, funicular railways, and more than 160km (100 miles) of downhill runs.

A great center for intermediates is the resort of **Davos** (see chapter 13) along with its twin resort of **Klosters.** The ski terrain at Davos extends for some 35km (22 miles) in a relatively sheltered valley floor. Of course, these resorts have peaks for the more daring expert skier but offer miles of easy terrain for the intermediate as well.

The chic resort of **St. Moritz** in the Engadine (see chapter 14) has more nightlife possibilities than any resort in Switzerland. All the major ski resorts have an active après-ski life, but St. Moritz offers more diversity, from pubbing to high casino action.

In a virtual ski valley, **Verbier** (see chapter 9) is ideal for early- or late-season skiing. Its upper ski area, which culminates at Mont-Fort at 3,255m (10,676 ft.), is filled with a widely varied set of *pistes.* The snow falls early and lingers late into the spring.

FOR THE NONSKIER   The number of nonskiers at ski resorts is growing. It's estimated that at such fashionable resorts as Gstaad, Pontresina, Arosa, and Davos, one out of two guests is a nonskier. Most resorts offer a host of other activities, such as sunbathing on mountain terraces, day hikes in the forest, sleigh rides, sightseeing excursions, and of course, partying in the local bars and clubs. So if some of your family members ski and others don't, everyone will still be happy and entertained.

SNOWBOARDING   All the resorts mentioned under skiing offer snowboarding. The best centers are Celerina, Grindelwald, Gstaad, Kandersteg, St. Moritz, Wengen, and Zermatt. However, the top snowboard resort of Europe is Davos, which offers ideal slope conditions, snowboard schools, and a snowboard hotel. The resort also hosts national and international snowboarding events. Snowboarders will find a wide range of equipment to hire in all the resorts mentioned, with the largest concentration of sports shops in Davos.

Spa Vacations

Switzerland has 22 resorts with natural curative springs. Most of these spas, which have been approved by the Association of Swiss Health Spas and the Swiss Society of Balneology and Bioclimatology, include a medical examination, along with thermal baths and excursions, in their package plans for visitors. Many of them are open all year. All the spas offer various treatments, along with Turkish baths, mud baths, whirlpools, exercise/weight-loss programs, antistress programs, massages, and diets. You can request information from **Switzerland Tourism,** Tours Dept., 608 Fifth Ave., New York, NY 10020 (© **877/794-8037**). For very specific data about individual spas, phone **Great Spas of the World** (© **800/SPA-TIME** or 212/889-8170; www.greatspas.com).

For a spa vacation in Switzerland, one resort towers over all the rest—chic **St. Moritz** in the Engadine. Its thermal springs were known 3,000 years ago. St. Moritz-Bad was the original spa resort lying at the base of the lake, although modern housing has spoiled much of its former character. For more details, refer to "Spas" under St. Moritz, in chapter 14.

OUTFITTERS

Be it rafting, canoeing, sea kayaking, sailing, biking, hiking, paragliding, or horse-and-wagon trips, **Eurotrek,** Militarstrasse 52, CH-8021 Zurich (© **044/295-59-59;** www.eurotrek.ch), has a tour for you. All ages, tastes, and levels of fitness participate in these tours, from absolute beginners to experienced athletes. The outfit uses skilled travel guides, instructors, skippers, and coach drivers. Rafting adventures, for example, are arranged in the Bernese Oberland or on the Lütschine, the wild river at the foot of the Eiger and Jungfrau. Sailing trips are arranged on both Lake Thun and Lake Maggiore, and horse-and-wagon treks explore both the Emmental and the Jura in covered wagons. You can bungee jump in the alpine regions around Davos, or book a 3-day bike tour through the Ticino.

15 Getting Around

BY TRAIN

The Swiss Federal Railway is noted for its comfort and cleanliness. Most of the electrically operated trains have first- and second-class compartments. International trains link Swiss cities with other European centers. Intercity trains coming from Holland, Scandinavia, and Germany require a change at Basel's station, where a connection is usually available on the same platform. Most intercity trains offer the fastest connections, and since trains leave the Basel station hourly, there's never too long a wait.

It's advisable to purchase European train tickets before leaving home, especially when your itinerary is specific and complicated. All tickets are available through your travel agent.

SWISS PASS/SWISS FLEXIPASS The most practical and convenient ticket for your trip to Switzerland is the **Swiss Pass,** which entitles you to unlimited travel on the entire network of the Swiss Federal Railways, as well as on lake steamers and most postal motor coaches linking Swiss cities and resorts. The Swiss Pass is good for a predetermined number of consecutive days.

A 4-day pass goes for $270 for first class and $180 for second class, an 8-day pass is $380 for first class and $255 for second class, a 15-day pass is $465 for first class and $310 for second class, a 22-day pass is $540 for first class and $360 for second class, and a 1-month pass costs $600 for first class and $400 for second class. The Swiss Pass is issued at half price to children ages 6 to 15 and is free for children 5 and under. The pass can be purchased in Switzerland.

A variation of the Swiss Pass is the **Swiss Flexipass,** good for a predetermined number of days to be used anytime during a 30-day period of time. A 3-day pass goes for $258 for first class and $172 for second class, a 4-day pass is $308 in first class and $206 in second class, a 5-day pass is $358 in first class and $240 in second class, a 6-day pass is $408 for first class and $274 for second class, and an 8-day pass is $480 in first class and $322 in second class. The **Swiss Family Card** is just for families traveling together. This card allows children under 16 to travel free when accompanied by a parent. It's valid when traveling on a Swiss Pass or a Swiss Flexipass. Probably the best part of all about the Swiss Family Card is that it is free. Just request it when you purchase your Swiss Pass from Rail Europe.

An economical alternative is the **Swiss Saverpass,** which offers five consecutive-day durations to choose from including 4, 8, 15, or 22 days unlimited travel or 1 month unlimited travel. This pass requires a minimum of two people traveling together at all times and offers the choice of first- or second-class train travel. An individual traveling in first class for 4 days costs $230, 8 days $323, 15 days $395, 22 days $459, or 1 month $510 with a $17 fee for the optional Rail Protection Plan. Individual prices for one adult traveling in second class are for 4 days $153, 8 days $217, 15 days $264, 22 days $306, or 1 month $340 with a $17 fee for the optional Rail Protection Plan.

Those under the age of 26 might consider the **Swiss Youth Pass,** which is a discounted version of the Swiss Pass. This pass also offers five consecutive-day durations to choose from including 4, 8, 15, or 22 days unlimited travel or 1 month unlimited travel. A 4-day pass goes for $203 for first class and $135 for second class, 8-day pass is $285 for first class and $192 for second class, 15-day is $349 for first class and $233 for second class, 22-day is $405 for first class and $270 for second class, and a 1-month pass costs $450 for first class and $300 for second class with a $10 optional fee for Rail Protection Plan.

SWISS REGIONAL RAIL PASSES
One of the country's most unusual transportation bargains is offered in the form of regional passes that divide Switzerland into about half a dozen districts. Passes, most of which are good for 5 days of unrestricted rail travel, are offered for the Lake Geneva region, the Graubunden (Grisons), the Ticino, central Switzerland, and the Bernese Oberland. If you plan to devote a block of days to exploring one of these specific regions, you might find one of these passes a great savings.

One of the most popular of these passes is the **Bernese Oberland Regional Pass (Regional Pass für das Berner Oberland),** which comes in variations of 3 travel days out of 7 calendar days, and 5 travel days out of 15 calendar days. They're available from any railway station in the Bernese Oberland. The 3-day option sells for 220F ($180) in second class and 263F ($216) in first class. The 5-day option costs 265F ($217) in second class and 316F ($259) in first class. Either variation allows free transport during the appropriate time frames on all but a handful of the cog railways, buses, cable cars, ferryboats, and SBB trains within the region. Note to holders of either the Swiss Pass or the Swiss Card: If you present either of those documents at the time of purchase, you'll get a 20% discount off the above-mentioned prices.

SWISS CARD   This pass is valid for 1 month, entitling the holder to a free transfer from any Swiss airport or border point to any destination within Switzerland and a second free transfer from any destination in Switzerland to any Swiss airport or border point. Each transfer has to be completed within 1 day. Additionally, the Swiss Card gives the holder unlimited half-fare trips on the entire Swiss travel system, including trains, postal coaches, lake steamers, and most (not all) excursions to mountaintops. The pass costs $175 for first class and $130 for second class. Children are charged half price.

For more information on Swiss railway passes, call **Switzerland Tourism** at ℂ **212/757-5944.**

EURAILPASSES   The Eurailpass is one of Europe's greatest bargains, permitting unlimited first-class rail travel through 17 countries in Europe, including Switzerland. Passes are for periods as short as 15 days or as long as 3 months and are strictly nontransferable.

Your best bet is to buy a **Eurailpass** outside Europe (it's available in Europe but will cost more). It costs $588 for 15 days, $762 for 21 days, $946 for 1 month, $1,338 for 2 months, and $1,654 for 3 months. Children 3 and under travel free provided they don't occupy a seat (otherwise they're charged half fare); children 4 to 11 are charged half fare. If you're under 26, you can purchase a **Eurail Youthpass,** entitling you to unlimited second-class travel for $382 for 15 days, $495 for 21 days, $615 for 1 month, $870 for 2 months, and $1,075 for 3 months.

If you'll be traveling for 2 weeks or a month, think carefully before you buy a pass. To get full advantage of a pass for 15 days or a month, you'll have to spend a great deal of time on the train.

The **Eurail Flexipass** allows you to travel through Europe with more flexibility. It's valid in first class and offers the same privileges as the Eurailpass. However, it provides a number of individual travel days that you can use over a much longer period of consecutive days. That makes it possible to stay in one city and yet not lose a single day of travel. There are two passes: 10 days of travel in 2 months for $694, and 15 days of travel in 2 months for $914. The **Eurail Youth Flexipass** is identical except that it's sold only to travelers under 26 and costs less: $451 for 10 days of travel within 2 months, and $594 for 15 days of travel within 2 months.

The **EurailDrive Pass** offers 4 days of train travel and 2 days of Avis or Hertz car rental. You have 2 months to complete your travel. The cost of a package is $858 for two adults with first-class train travel and a compact-car rental.

WHERE TO BUY RAIL PASSES Travel agents in all towns and railway agents in major North American cities sell all these tickets, but the biggest supplier is **Rail Europe** (ℂ 877/257-2887; www.rail europe.com), which can also give you informational brochures.

Many different rail passes are available in the United Kingdom for travel in Britain and continental Europe. Stop in at the **International Rail Centre,** Victoria Station, London SW1V 1JY (ℂ **0870/ 5848-848** in the U.K.). Some of the most popular passes, including InterRail and Euro Youth, are offered only to travelers under 26 years of age; these allow unlimited second-class travel through most European countries.

INTERRAIL   European travelers can travel throughout Europe for up to 1 month by train with the InterRail ticket. In your home country you get a 50% reduction on the normal price. Only supplements, reservations, and special trains like the Eurostar cost extra. The ticket is sold at all European travel agents. All you need is a passport and the fee, of course.

BY CAR

Switzerland has excellent roads and superhighways, all marked by clear road signs. Alpine passes are not difficult to cross, except in snowstorms, when they may shut down suddenly. Special rail facilities are provided for drivers wishing to transport their cars through the alpine tunnels of the Albula, Furka, Lotschberg, and Simplon. A timetable highlighting the various rates is available from the Swiss National Tourist Office.

CAR RENTALS   Several American companies operate in Switzerland. One of the most reliable firms is **Budget** (© **800/472-3325**; www.budget.com); its prices are competitive with those offered by **Avis** (© **800/331-1212**; www.avis.com) and **Hertz** (© **800/654-3131**; www.hertz.com). Under certain circumstances, the companies offer a discount if you prepay your rental 21 days or more in advance. Budget offers one-way rentals between any two of its more than 20 Swiss offices with no extra drop-off charge. **Kemwel Holiday Autos** (© **800/678-0678**; www.kemwel.com) offers a sometimes viable alternative to more traditional car rental companies, such as Budget, Hertz, and Avis, that actually own their automobiles outright. Kemwel leases blocks of cars a year in advance at locations throughout Switzerland, then rents them to qualified customers who prepay the entire rental. Kemwel, along with its competitor, Auto Europe (see below), offers the advantage of issuing vouchers in advance of your departure, the price of which includes taxes, airport surcharges, unlimited mileage and—if you ask for it—insurance premiums. The company's address is 106 Calvert St., Harrison, NY 10528.

Auto Europe (© **800/223-5555**; www.autoeurope.com) is an equivalent company that leases cars, on an as-needed basis, from larger car-rental companies throughout Europe. They represent at least 100 car-rental locations throughout Switzerland, including all the major cities and airports, at rates that are sometimes less than what's being offered at Hertz and Avis. In a system that's equivalent to the one used by Kemwel (see above), vouchers are issued in advance for car rentals, with most or all incidentals included. Advance payment of between 20% and 60%, depending on the value of the car, is required. Their address is 39 Commercial St., Portland, ME 04101.

Note that there is a 6.5% government tax on car rentals in Switzerland, in addition to a tax of 12% of the total rental usually imposed for rentals at many of the country's airports, including Zurich. With this in mind, you might choose to skip getting a car at the airport and pick up a vehicle at one of the hundreds of downtown rental agencies run by Budget, Hertz, and Avis.

AUTOMOBILE PERMIT   Apart from the auto and train tunnel trips mentioned above and a toll on the road through the Great St. Bernard Tunnel, there are no toll roads in the country. Instead of tolls, Switzerland levies a single annual fee of 40F ($33) per car, or 80F ($66) for trailers, motor homes, and RVs, for use of the nation's superhighways; when the fee has been paid, a permit sticker is affixed to the car. Drivers of cars without the permit sticker face a fine of more than twice the permit's cost. Most rental cars come equipped with this certificate. Otherwise, the appropriate permits may be purchased at any post office in Switzerland, at the Customs office at any Swiss border, or from one of the automobile associations.

If you didn't rent your car in Switzerland, you'll probably have to purchase the permit. Permits are available at border crossings and are valid for multiple reentries into Switzerland within the licensed period. To avoid long lines at border crossings, you can buy the permit sticker in advance at the Swiss National Tourist Office in Italy, Austria, or Germany (it is not sold in France). *Note:* If you drive into Switzerland on a secondary road, you don't need a permit sticker, but if you drive on a Swiss superhighway without one, you risk facing that heavy fine.

GAS The cost varies across the country. Gas stations are usually open daily from 8am to 10pm. U.S. gasoline credit cards generally are not accepted for payment. At stations along Swiss autobahns, gas prices are higher than along secondary roads. Autobahn stations usually give 24-hour service, and electronic machines accept 10- and 20-franc Swiss notes.

DRIVER'S LICENSE U.S. and Canadian driver's licenses are valid in Switzerland, but if you're at least 18 and touring Europe by car, you may want to invest in an international driver's license. Although you may not actually need one, many travelers like the added security blanket of having one, as they are recognized worldwide whereas your local driver's license isn't. In case of an accident, an international driver's license is easier to read among parties who may not understand your local license. In the United States you can apply for one at any local branch of the **American Automobile Association (AAA)** (© **800/AAA-HELP** or 407/444-4300; www.aaa.com). Include two 2×2-inch photographs, a $10 fee, and a photocopy of your state driver's license. Canadians can get the address of the nearest branch of the **Canadian Automobile Club** by phoning its national office (© **613/247-0117;** www.caa.ca).

Note that your international driver's license is valid only if accompanied by your home state or provincial driver's license.

In Switzerland, as elsewhere in Europe, to drive a car legally, you must have in your possession an international insurance certificate, known as a **Green Card (Carte Verte).** Your car-rental agency will provide one as part of your rental contract.

DRIVING RULES The legal minimum age for driving in Switzerland is 18. Note, however, that car-rental companies often set their own minimum age, usually 20 or 21.

Drive on the right side of the road and observe the speed limit for passenger vehicles; it's 120kmph (about 75 mph) on superhighways, 80kmph (about 50 mph) on other highways, and 50kmph (about 30 mph) in cities, towns, and villages, unless otherwise posted. Non-Swiss drivers who exceed the speed limit by 50kmph (about 30 mph) or more are fined 1,200F ($984) on the spot. Swiss citizens similarly caught have their driver's licenses revoked.

When driving through tunnels, be sure to turn on and dim your headlights, as required by law. Never pass another car from the right, even on superhighways. Always wear your seat belt. Don't permit children under 12 to ride in the front seat. And, needless to say, don't drink and drive; driving while under the influence of alcohol is a serious offense in Switzerland.

BREAKDOWNS/ASSISTANCE The Automobile Club of Switzerland and its branch offices will assist motorists at all times. For help, contact **Automobil Club der Schweiz,** Wassergasse 39, CH-3000 Bern 13 (© **031/328-31-11;** www.acs.ch), or **Touring Club Suisse,** 9, rue Pierre-Fatio, CH-1211 Geneva 3 (© **022/417-27-27;** www.tcs.ch). The Automobile Club der Schweiz offers 24-hour **breakdown service.** Motorists in need of help can call © **031/328-31-11.** Most mountain roads have emergency call boxes.

MAPS The best maps, available at major bookstores, are *Michelin 427 Switzerland* and the various Michelin regional road guides. An excellent map for those who plan extensive touring is published by

Hallwag. Local tourist offices provide city maps.

BY PLANE

Switzerland does not have an abundance of airports, partly because of the alpine terrain and partly due to the Swiss peoples' own resistance to having planes disturb their peace and quiet. To compensate, Switzerland has one of Europe's best railway systems, linking every major city in the country. This is particularly advantageous for cities such as Bern, the capital; it relies almost exclusively on rail transport to Zurich, Geneva, and Basel for air connections to the rest of the world.

If you want to fly within Switzerland, or from Switzerland to one of about 30 regional cities in Austria, Italy, Germany, or France, **Swiss** (*C* **0848/85-2000;** www.swiss.com), a domestic airline, schedules flights from and to Basel and Amsterdam, Geneva and London, and Lugano and Geneva.

BY BUS

The extremely dense network covered by the Swiss postal buses is useful for trips into the mountains. Hopping on one of the popular yellow buses is a much safer and more comfortable way of seeing the Alps than trying to do your own driving in those regions.

BY BOAT

In the summer, passenger boats sail on Switzerland's major lakes and rivers. More than 100 boats, with accommodations for 60,000 passengers, operate on the lakes and along stretches of the Rhine and the Aare; most of them have dining. Evening trips, with music and dancing, are also quite popular. The old paddle-steamers on the lakes of Brienz, Geneva, Lucerne, and Zurich, dating from before World War I, are particularly attractive and romantic.

Remember that your Swiss Pass or Swiss Card (half-fare travel card) entitles you to unlimited travel on lake steamers.

16 Tips on Accommodations

HOTELS

Most hotels in Switzerland are clean, comfortable, and efficiently run. Many in the luxury category are among the finest in the world (two in Zurich, in fact, are regarded as the best in Europe). After all, César Ritz came from Switzerland.

There are several categories of hotels. An *alkoholfrei* hotel is one that doesn't serve liquor. A hotel *garni* is one that serves breakfast and beverages but no other meals. You can judge a hotel and its prices by its stars (as judged by Swiss travel authorities): Five stars signify deluxe; four stars, first class; three stars, superior; and two stars, standard. One star indicates "minimum." A minimum hotel, with the most limited of facilities, can nevertheless be clean and reasonably comfortable, and standard hotels are among the country's best travel values.

Reservations can be made directly with the hotel, through any recognized travel agency, or through various reservations systems that have toll-free numbers. The hotel is entitled to request a deposit when you make your reservation; the amount will vary from hotel to hotel.

If you want a total deluxe-hotel-chain trip, you'll find the Hilton with more choices, each ideally located. These include the Basel Hilton and Le Palace Hilton Geneva, which is one of the finest chain hotels in Switzerland. The latter hotel occupies an entire city block.

The chains do not dominate the hotel scene in Switzerland as they do in some countries. The Inter-Continental weighs in with such heavy-duty choices as the Royal Plaza Inter-Continental Montreux, but we find this one often filled with convention

Impressions

The Swiss managed to build a lovely country around their hotels.
—George Mikes, *Down with Everybody*, 1951

people as the convention center is just next door.

If you're looking for a chain bargain, and your tastes aren't too demanding, you can book into any Novotel (there's one at the Zurich airport, for example).

Among the leading German chains, with minor but choice representation in Switzerland, is the German-owned Steigenberger. Hotels in this chain include the Steigenberger Belvedere at Davos Platz and the chic Steigenberger Gstaad-Saanen outside Gstaad.

All accommodations listed in this guide have private bathrooms unless otherwise noted.

To cut costs, you may consider a package tour (or book land arrangements with your air ticket). You'll often pay 30% less than individual rack rates (off-the-street, independent bookings). Also, be sure to ask about winter discounts. Some hotels won't grant them, but many will, especially if bookings that week are light. The price you'll pay in inexpensive hotels depends on the plumbing. Rooms with only showers are much cheaper than those with private bathrooms. Even cheaper is a room with only a sink and a *cabinette de toilet* (toilet and bidet).

When you check in, remember to ask if there's a surcharge on local or long-distance telephone calls (these can often be lethal, up to 40%).

ALTERNATIVES TO HOTELS

BED & BREAKFASTS   The Swiss concept of a bed-and-breakfast is different from that in the United States and Canada. In Switzerland many bed-and-breakfast places are more like small, cozy hotels than like private homes. Called "E + G Hotels"—a voluntary chain of 220

guesthouses—they can be found throughout the country. A folder listing addresses and phone numbers of E&Gs is available from the Swiss National Tourist Office.

PRIVATE HOMES   In Swiss mountain and rural areas, a list of private accommodations can be obtained from most local tourist offices. Look for the following signs advertising such an accommodation (generally, a single room): ZIMMER FREI in German, CHAMBRE A LOUER in French, and AFFITASI CAMERA in Italian.

CHALET, HOUSE & APARTMENT RENTALS   For a list of U.S. agencies handling such rentals, contact the Swiss National Tourist Office. Local tourist offices in Switzerland also provide listings of apartments and chalets to rent. The Swiss prefer to do business in writing rather than on the phone, so it's strongly recommended that you write to the home owners directly; allow about 20 days for a reply.

The best agency for arranging vacation homes in Switzerland is a Swiss-based company called **INTERHOME,** which represents some 20,000 properties throughout Europe—some 4,000 of these in Switzerland. Travelers have easy access to chalets and condos in all the major resort areas, from modest studio apartments at budget prices to luxurious chalets with all the modern amenities. The U.S. branch of INTERHOME, Inc., is at 1990 NE 163 St., Suite 110, North Miami Beach, FL 33162 (© **800/882-6864;** fax 305/940-2911; www.interhome.us). Contact them for a catalog of vacation homes outlining some 4,000 listings in almost 200 locations.

In addition, **Hometours International, Inc.,** 1108 Scottie Lane, Knoxville, TN

Cheese, Cheese & More Cheese

Cheese making is an integral part of the Swiss heritage. Cattle breeding and dairy farming, concentrated in the alpine areas of the country, have been associated with the region for 2,000 years, since the Romans ate *caseus Helveticus* (Helvetian cheese). Today more than 100 different varieties of cheese are produced in Switzerland. The cheeses, however, are not mass produced—they're made in hundreds of small, strictly controlled dairies, each under the direction of a master cheese maker with a federal degree.

The cheese with the holes, known as Switzerland Swiss or Emmenthal, has been widely copied, since nobody ever thought to protect the name for use only on cheeses produced in the Emme Valley until it was too late. Other cheeses of Switzerland, many of which have also had their names plagiarized, are Gruyère, Appenzeller, raclette, royalp, and sapsago. The names of several mountain cheeses have also been copied, including *sbrinz* and *spalen,* closely related to the *caseus Helveticus* of Roman times.

Fondue   Cheese fondue, which consists of cheese (Emmenthal and natural Gruyère used separately, together, or with special local cheeses) melted in white wine flavored with a soupçon of garlic and lemon juice, is the national dish of Switzerland. Freshly ground pepper, nutmeg, paprika, and Swiss kirsch are among the traditional seasonings. Guests surround a bubbling *caquelon* (an earthenware pipkin or small pot) and use long forks to dunk cubes of bread into the hot mixture. Other dunkables are apples, pears, grapes, cocktail wieners, cubes of boiled ham, shrimp, pitted olives, and tiny boiled potatoes. Other fondues include fondue bourguignon made with chunks of beef and red wine, usually from Burgundy, and fondue *chinois,* with a base of vegetable, herb, and meat-flavored bouillon, into which is dipped chunks of meat on long forks.

Raclette   This cheese specialty is almost as famous as fondue. Popular for many centuries, its origin is lost in antiquity, but the word *raclette* comes from the French word *racler,* meaning "to scrape off." Although raclette originally was the name of the dish made from the special mountain cheese of the Valais, today it describes not only the dish itself but also the cheese varieties suitable for melting at an open fire or in an oven.

A piece of cheese—traditionally half to a quarter of a wheel of raclette—is held in front of an open fire. As it starts to soften, it is scraped off onto one's plate with a special knife. The unique flavor of the cheese is most delicious when the cheese is hottest. The classic accompaniment is fresh, crusty, homemade dark bread, but the cheese may also be eaten with potatoes boiled in their skins, pickled onions, cucumbers, or small corncobs. You usually eat raclette with a fork, but sometimes you may need a knife as well.

37919 (© **865/690-8484;** hometours @aol.com), offers chalet apartments and apartment hotels in Zermatt overlooking the Matterhorn. Hometours also rents chalet apartments in the center of the resort in Interlaken.

FARM VACATIONS   A unique way to get to know Switzerland, this program lets you experience firsthand the working world and home life of a Swiss farming family. A brochure called *Swiss Farm Holidays* tells exactly how it can be done; it's available from the Swiss National Tourist Office.

YOUTH HOSTELS   About 75 youth hostels exist in Switzerland, open to single people, families, or both. Fees range from $18 to $30 per person including bed linen and breakfast, depending on the hostel. There is no upper age limit, but in peak season travelers 25 and younger have priority. For more information, contact **Hostelling International USA,** 8401 Colesville Rd., Silver Springs, MD 20910 (© **202/783-6161;** fax 202/783-6171; www.hiusa.org.

17 Recommended Reading

Read a few of the books below to get a feel for Switzerland—its people, atmosphere, and history—before you visit.

- *Why Switzerland?* (Cambridge University Press, by Jonathan Steinberg), provides the best look at Swiss society, culture, and history.
- *A Tramp Abroad* (Oxford Press, by Mark Twain) is the eternal tongue-in-cheek travelogue for "Innocents Abroad" touring the Swiss Alps.
- *Scrambles Amongst the Alps* (Dover Publishers, by Edward Whymper) is the latest reprint of this classic mountaineer's account of his conquest of the Matterhorn.
- For some light reading, *Ticking Along with the Swiss* (Bergli Books, by Dianne Dicks), is an amusing collection of personal tales from travelers to Switzerland.
- For the reader who wants to explore Switzerland in depth and on foot, *Walking Switzerland—The Swiss Way* (Mountaineers Books, by Marcia and Philip Lieberman) is a useful guide for those who want to walk through the tiny country, as hundreds do.

FAST FACTS: Switzerland

Business Hours **Banks** are usually open Monday through Friday from 8:30am to 4:30pm (closed on legal holidays). Foreign currency may be exchanged at major railroad stations and airports daily from 8am to 10pm. Most **business offices** are open Monday through Friday from 8am to noon and 2 to 6pm. **Shops** are usually open Monday through Friday from 8am to 12:15pm and 1:30 to 6:30pm, and on Saturday from 9am to 4pm. In most major cities, shops and supermarkets in the main train station are open on Sundays—generally between 11am and 4pm. In large cities most shops don't close during the lunch hour, although many do so on Monday morning.

Climate See "When to Go," earlier in this chapter.

Currency/Currency Exchange See "Money," earlier in this chapter.

Driving Rules See "Getting Around," earlier in this chapter.

Drug Laws A word of warning: Penalties for illegal drug possession are more severe in Switzerland than they are in the United States and Canada. You could go to jail or be deported immediately.

Drugstores Switzerland has excellent pharmacies. Yet outside the main cities it can be difficult to get a prescription filled after business hours.

Electricity Switzerland's electricity is 220 volts, 50 cycles, AC. Some international hotels are specially wired to allow North Americans to plug in their appliances, but you'll usually need a transformer for your electric razor, hair dryer, or soft-contact-lens sterilizer. You'll also need an adapter plug to channel the electricity from the Swiss system to the flat-pronged American system. Don't plug anything into the house current in Switzerland without being certain the systems are compatible.

Embassies & Consulates Most embassies are located in the national capital, Bern; some nations maintain consulates in other cities such as Geneva. There's an **Australian consulate** in Geneva at Chemins des Fins 2 (© 022/799-91-00). The **Canadian embassy** is at 88 Kirchenfeldstrasse, Bern (© 031/357-32-00). In Geneva the consulate is at 1, chemin du Pré-de-la-Bichette (© 022/919-92-00). **New Zealand** has no embassy in Switzerland, but there's a consulate in Geneva at chemin des Fins (© 022/929-03-50). The embassy of the **United Kingdom** is at Thunstrasse 50, Bern (© 031/359-77-00), and there is a British consulate in Geneva at 37-39, rue de Vermont (© 022/918-24-00). The embassy of the **United States** is located at Jubilaumstrasse 93, Bern (© 031/357-70-11), with consulates in Zurich at Dufourstrasse 101 (© 043/499-29-60) and in Geneva at Versonnex 7 (© 022/840-51-60).

Emergencies Dial © **117** for the police (emergencies only) and © **118** to report a fire.

Gasoline See "Getting Around," earlier in this chapter.

Hospitals A prime location for medical aid is the **Geneva University Hospital** (rue Micheli-du-Crest 24, CH-1211 Genève; © 022/372-60-19; www.hug-ge.ch). Most physicians speak English and German.

Language The three major languages are German, French, and Italian, although most people in the tourist industry speak English.

Legal Aid This may be hard to come by in Switzerland. The government advises foreigners to consult their embassy or consulate (see "Embassies & Consulates," above) in case of a dire emergency, such as an arrest. Even if your embassy or consulate declines to offer financial or legal help, it will generally offer advice on how to obtain help locally.

Liquor Laws The official drinking age is 16. As in many European countries, the application of laws governing drinking is flexible and enforced only if a problem develops or if decorum is broken. Driving while intoxicated, particularly if it results in damage to property or persons, brings swift and severe punishment involving sizable fines and possible imprisonment.

Mail Post offices in large cities are open Monday through Friday from 7:30am to noon and 2 to 6:30pm, and on Saturday from 7:30 to 11am. If you have letters forwarded to a post office to be collected after you arrive, you'll need a passport for identification. The words "Poste Restante" must be clearly written on the envelope. Letters not collected within 30 days are returned to the sender. Letters are either first class, meaning air mail, or surface mail, rated second class. To send letters and postcards to America, weighing up to 20 grams, the cost is 1.80F ($1.50) for first class or 1.40F ($1.15) for surface. To Great Britain, the charge is 1.30F ($1.05) in first class or 1.20F ($1) for surface.

Newspapers & Magazines Swiss papers are published in German, French, or Italian (depending on the region). Most news kiosks in major cities stock the British dailies, plus the latest editions of the *International Herald Tribune,* which, although edited in Paris, is printed in Zurich. *USA Today,* the latest copies of *Time* and *Newsweek,* and other U.S. and British magazines are also widely available.

Passports **For residents of the United States:** Whether you're applying in person or by mail, you can download passport applications from the U.S. State Department website at **http://travel.state.gov.** For general information, call the **National Passport Agency** (*©* **877/487-6868**). To find your regional passport office, either check the U.S. State Department website or call.

   For residents of Canada: Passport applications are available at travel agencies throughout Canada and from the central **Passport Office,** Department of Foreign Affairs and International Trade, Ottawa, ON K1A 0G3 (*©* **800/567-6868;** www.ppt.gc.ca).

   For residents of the United Kingdom: To pick up an application for a standard 10-year passport (5-year passport for children under 16), visit your nearest passport office, major post office, or travel agency, or contact the **United Kingdom Passport Service** (*©* **0870/521-0410;** www.ukpa.gov.uk).

   For residents of Ireland: You can apply for a 10-year passport at the **Passport Office,** Setanta Centre, Molesworth Street, Dublin 2 (*©* **01/671-1633;** www.irlgov.ie/iveagh). Those under age 18 and over 65 must apply for a 12€ 3-year passport. You can also apply at 1A South Mall, Cork (*©* **021/272-525**) and at most main post offices.

   For residents of Australia: You can pick up an application from your local post office or any branch of Passports Australia, but you must schedule an interview at the passport office to present your application materials. Contact the **Australian Passport Information Service** (*©* **131-232;** www.passports.gov.au).

   For residents of New Zealand: You can pick up a passport application at any New Zealand Passports Office or download it from the website. Contact the **Passports Office** (*©* **0800/225-050** in New Zealand or 04/474-8100; www.passports.govt.nz).

Pets Dogs and cats brought into Switzerland require veterinary certificates stating that the animals have been vaccinated against rabies not less than 30 days and not more than 1 year prior to entry into the country. This regulation also applies to dogs and cats returning after a temporary absence from Switzerland, but not to animals transported through the country by rail or air traffic.

Police Dial *©* **117** for emergencies.

Radio & TV Television programming transmits in German, French, or Italian (again, depending on the region), but films in English are often shown, with the local language appearing in subtitles. Most hotels have radios on which you can hear British broadcasts. The BBC can often be picked up on transistor sets, as can the American Forces Network. First-class hotels often subscribe to CNN.

Restrooms Most public restrooms are clean and modernized. However, in this multilingual country you have to know what you are looking for. Depending on the part of Switzerland, public restrooms may be WC (water closet), *Toiletten, toilettes,* or *gabinetti.* Women's rooms may be identified as *"Damen"* or *"Frauen," "Signore"* or *"Donne," "Femmes"* or *"Dames;"* and men's rooms may be labeled *"Herren"* or *"Männer," "Signori"* or *"Uomini," "Hommes"* or *"Messieurs."* Public restrooms can be found at bus stations, railway terminals, and cable-car platforms. If these aren't handy, use the restrooms in cafes. Most public lavatories are not free.

Safety Crimes of violence, such as muggings, are rare in Switzerland. It is generally safe to walk the streets of cities day and night. The most common crime reported by visitors is a picked pocket.

Taxes A value-added tax (VAT) of 7.6% is added to bills. In addition, drivers entering Switzerland are required by law to purchase a windshield sticker for 40F ($33), valid for travel on Swiss roads for 1 year. Stickers are sold at all Customs posts upon entering Switzerland.

Telephone/Telex/Fax The telephone system is entirely automatic and connects the entire country. **Helpful numbers** to know are: ✆ **111** for directory assistance, ✆ **120** for tourist information and snow reports, ✆ **140** for help on the road, ✆ **162** for weather forecasts, and ✆ **163** for up-to-the-minute information on road conditions. Hotels add substantial service charges for calls made from your room; it's considerably less expensive to make calls from a public phone booth.

To use a **coin-operated telephone,** lift the receiver and insert 40 centimes to get a dial tone. Be sure to have enough coins on hand, as you must insert more for each message unit over your initial deposit. If you insert more coins than necessary, the excess amounts will be returned. A pay phone will accept up to 5F ($4.10).

To make a local call, dial directly after you hear the dial tone (no area code needed); for other places in Switzerland, dial the area code and then the number. To call a foreign country, dial the code of the country first, then the area code, and then the number.

The country code for Switzerland is **41.** When calling from the United States dial **011,** the country code, the city code (dropping the zero), then the number. For example, the city code for Zurich is **1;** use this code if calling from outside Switzerland. If you're within Switzerland but not in Zurich, use **01.** When calling within Zurich, leave off the code and dial the regular phone number.

Time Switzerland's clocks are usually 6 hours ahead of Eastern Standard Time in the United States, and 1 hour ahead of Greenwich Mean Time. However, because Switzerland and the United States switch their clocks every spring and fall during different weeks, the time difference is sometimes only 5 hours.

Tipping A 15% service charge is included in all hotel and restaurant bills, although some people leave an additional tip for exceptional service. For taxis, a tip is usually included in the charges (a notice will be posted in the cab).

Tourist Offices See "Visitor Information," earlier in this chapter.

Water Tap water is safe to drink in all Swiss towns and cities. But don't drink from rivers or mountain streams, regardless of how clean the water may appear.

Weather American Express Travel Related Service Company provides hourly reports on current weather conditions and 3-day forecasts for more than 900 cities in Europe. For Switzerland, dial ℂ **900/WEATHER** (there's a 95¢-per-minute charge for the call) and press the first three letters of the desired city: BAS (Basel), BER (Bern), GEN (Geneva), LUC (Lucerne), STM (St. Moritz), or VAD (Vaduz, Liechtenstein).

3

Suggested Switzerland Itineraries

If you have unlimited time, one of Europe's greatest pleasures is getting lost in the Swiss Alps, wandering about at random, making new discoveries off the beaten path, and finding untrampled villages deep in the mountains.

But few of us have such a generous amount of time in the speeded-up 21st century. Vacations are getting shorter, and a "lean-and-mean" schedule is called for if you want to experience the best of any country in a short amount of time.

If you're pressed for time, the first two itineraries in this chapter ("Switzerland in 1 Week" or "Switzerland in 2 Weeks") may be most helpful for skimming the highlights. If you've been to Switzerland before, exploring such well-trodden tourist meccas as Zurich, Bern, Geneva, and Lucerne, you may want to discover a different area of the country this time. Consider our itinerary for "The Grisons, the Engadine & Ticino." We also suggest an itinerary for families.

If you stick to the main highways, Switzerland offers some of the best maintained roads in Europe. But when you wander off the beaten trail—in particular heading up to the mountains—you'll find your driving skills tested. Switzerland is one alpine-high country, although it has miles upon miles of rolling meadowland, often filled with grazing cows, as well.

Switzerland is blessed with one of the world's most efficient rail systems, which will get you to the high spots, with Zurich and Geneva being main transportation hubs in different parts of the country. The itineraries here take you to major attractions such as Bern and Lausanne, but also direct you to more secluded beauty spots and lesser known resorts such as Silvaplana and Morcote.

The pace may be a bit breathless for some visitors, so skip a town or sight occasionally to have some chill-out time—after all, you're on a holiday.

1 Switzerland in 1 Week

The very title of this tour is a misnomer. No one can see all of Switzerland in 1 week—it's time enough merely for a few of its highlights. But you can have a memorable vacation in Switzerland in 1 week if you budget your time carefully. Because of its great highways and rail connections, you can virtually cross the country from one end to another in 1 day. Of course, that wouldn't leave much time for sightseeing.

One week, however, provides just enough time, although barely, to introduce yourself to the most visited cities in the country, which include Zurich, Lucerne (our favorite), Bern (next on our list), Lausanne, and Geneva. On an even more rushed schedule, if you have to choose between Geneva and Zurich, make it Geneva as it is far more scenic and grand.

Days ❶ & ❷ Zurich: Gateway to Switzerland ☆☆☆

Because of its superior transportation connections, chances are you'll arrive in Zurich, especially if you're winding your way across the Alps. If you can, hit the town as early as possible in the morning to get in a full round of the city's attractions. After checking into a hotel, take our **walking tour of Bahnhofstrasse** (p. 110), which is lined with some of the world's most elegant shops. Even if you can't afford to purchase anything, it's fun to just look at the luxury merchandise, especially the Swiss watches and jewelry. Follow this with a **boat trip along Lake Zurich**, departing from the lake end of Bahnhofstrasse. Depending on your time, tours last from 1½ to 4 hours. In the afternoon take the city's best walk by promenading along the quays of Zurich, such as the finest and most famous, **Limmatquai** (p. 103). As the afternoon fades, check out the stained-glass windows at the church, **Fraumünster** (p. 103). That night, dine at Zurich's most famous beer hall, **Bierhalle Kropf** (p. 94) or at the **Zeughauskeller** (p. 95), a formal arsenal dating from 1487.

Begin **Day 2** with a **walking tour of Zurich's Altstadt (Old Town)** (p. 112). Check out the Romanesque and Gothic cathedral of **Grossmünster** (p. 103) as you continue the walk. Before lunch, head for **Landesmuseum (Swiss National Museum;** p. 107), which is a virtual case history of the culture of the Swiss people. After lunch, head in the afternoon to the **Kunsthaus Zürich** (fine art museum; p. 107), with one of the greatest art collections in Europe. With time remaining in the afternoon, take another tour, this one by boat and aerial cableway to **Felsenegg** at 795m (2,608 ft.) (p. 125). One of the greatest panoramas in this part of

Switzerland can be viewed from here, a fit ending for your sightseeing before setting out in the morning on another adventure.

Days ❸ & ❹ Lucerne: Mountain Magic ☆☆☆

Either by rented car or train, head 50km (31 miles) south of Zurich to the city most favored by American visitors, lying on the western edge of Lake Lucerne. Check in to a hotel for 2 nights. In the late morning take our **walking tour of Lucerne** (p. 357), which will not only be a beautiful experience but will give you an orientation of the area. After lunch visit the major attraction, the **Verkehrshaus der Schweiz (Swiss Transport Museum),** one of the finest such museums in the world (p. 362). With time remaining, you can take in one or two of the minor sites that interest you—notably the **Picasso Museum** (p. 360), the **Glacier Garden** (p. 361), or the **Neues Kunstmuseum (Modern Art Museum;** p. 361). For atmosphere and good food, dine that night at the **Old Swiss House** (p. 370).

While based in Lucerne, **Day 4** can be devoted to two mountain excursions, each among the most important attractions in all of Switzerland. First, head to **Mount Pilatus** (p. 376), 15km (9 miles) south of Lucerne. The best way to go is to take a steamer from Lucerne to Alpnachstad, where you transfer to a cog railway. With discreet planning, you can also visit **Rigi** (p. 377), 24km (15 miles) east of Lucerne. Rigi (1,680m/5,510 ft.) is the most famous mountain-view in Switzerland. Even Mark Twain climbed it. Return to Lucerne for a final night.

Day ❺ Bern: The Great Medieval Capital ☆☆☆

On **Day 5** leave Lucerne early, traveling by train or car 111km (69 miles) west to

Days 1 & 2
1 Zurich

Days 3 & 4
2 Lucerne

Day 5
3 Bern

Day 6
4 Lausanne

Day 7
5 Geneva

Bern, the capital of Switzerland. Trains leave every 30 minutes during the day, the trip taking 1½ hours. Check in to a hotel for the night and set out to discover a city declared a World Treasure by UNESCO in 1983 because of its medieval architecture. To see the highlights, take our **2-hour walking tour** of the historic **Altstadt (Old Town),** finishing at the Swiss Parliament (Bundeshaus; p. 194). Sample a typical lunch like bratwurst and rösti (see p. 188 for dining options), head for **Mount Gurten** (p. 194) at 844m (2,768 ft.), for the grandest panoramic vista in the area. By the afternoon, visit the **Kunstmuseum (Fine Arts Museum;** p. 193) to see the world's largest collection of paintings by Paul Klee. No visit to Bern is complete without a stop at the famous **Bärengraben (Bear Pits;** p. 193). Spend the better part of the evening enjoying the regional food and plenty of wine at **Klötzlikeller** (p. 200), the oldest wine tavern in Bern.

Day ❻ Lausanne: Gateway to Lake Geneva ✶✶✶

From Bern, travel 101km (63 miles) southwest to the lakeside city of Lausanne, where you can enjoy not only boat trips but wander the medieval labyrinth of its **Vieille Ville (Old Town).** Enjoying a great heyday under the Romans, the town has long been a favorite of expats and a choice watering hole for the literati, everybody from Dickens to Thackeray. T. S. Eliot even wrote *The Wasteland* here.

After checking in to a hotel for the night, wander for 2 hours or so around **Haute Ville** (p. 274), the Upper Town, visiting the **Cathedral of Lausanne** (p. 278), and other sights before lunch. Spend the afternoon exploring **Ouchy** (p. 276), the port and resort area of Lausanne, opening onto Lake Geneva. You can enjoy 2 or 3 leisurely hours exploring the quayside flower gardens, which stretch for half a mile. The lakeside promenades of **quai de Belgique** and **quai d'Ouchy** are of particular interest. You can also rent *pédolas* (pedal boats) for fun in the lake itself.

Day ❼ Geneva: A Summer Garden ✸✸✸

In just 60km (37 miles), you can arrive by car or train (just 50 min.) in a city very different from Lausanne. Straddling the Rhone River as it opens onto Lac Léman (Lake Geneva), the city itself will easily fill up one very busy day of sightseeing, so arrive as early in the morning as you can. The morning can be spent exploring **Vieille Ville (Old Town).** The highlight is the **Cathédrale de St.-Pierre** (p. 337). For a fast preview, take our 2-hour walking tour of Geneva's quays and Old Town (p. 339), viewing the famous fountain, **Jet d'Eau,** and the **Flower Clock** in the Jardin Anglais. At some point before the afternoon fades, consider one of the "Boat Tours" (p. 343) of Lac Léman itself. Stay overnight in Geneva, which is one of the major transportation hubs of Switzerland. In Geneva you can usually link up by train or plane to where you're going next in Europe. It can also be a link in your journey homeward.

2 Switzerland in 2 Weeks

With 2 weeks to explore Switzerland, you have a bit more breathing time, and you can take in some of the more esoteric destinations, such as Gruyères (of cheese fame) and Appenzell (capital of folkloric religion). The second week will also allow you to visit not only the cities previewed above, but less touristy centers such as Basel.

Days ❶ & ❷ Geneva: Your Entry into Switzerland ✸✸✸

On this trip we enter Switzerland from its French-speaking western frontier, the international city of Geneva. If you arrive early enough, take our morning **walking tour** (p. 339), which will allow you to see the highlights of the quays and the Old Town, including such attractions as the famous fountain, Jet d'Eau, trademark of the city. You can also explore such Old Town landmarks as Place di Bourge-de-Four. In the afternoon visit **Musée Ariana** (p. 334), one of Europe's top pottery and glass museums (allow less than an hour), and the **Musée d'Arte et d'Histoire (Museum of Art and History;** p. 334), with a fabulous collection of relics, everything from Swiss timepieces to Picasso. Allow another hour for a visit

here. Only if time allows, duck into the **Palais des Nations** (p. 336), former seat of the League of Nations. Overnight in Geneva.

On **Day 2,** while still based in Geneva, take a **full-day tour of Lac Léman (Lake Geneva;** see p. 343 for full details). Departures are at 9am daily, with a return at 8:45pm. You'll be back in Geneva in time for a late dinner.

Day ❸ Montreux: Chief Resort of the Swiss Riviera ✸✸

It's best to rent a car when you leave Geneva for an exploration of Switzerland. After a distance of 100km (62 miles) east from Geneva, you arrive at this chic resort on Lac Léman. Expect a balmy climate as you explore **Château of Chillon** (p. 297), which Lord Byron wrote about in his *The*

Switzerland in 2 Weeks

Days 1 & 2
1 Geneva

Day 3
2 Montreux

Days 4 & 5
3 Vevey
4 Lausanne

Day 6
5 Gruyères
6 Fribourg

Days 7 & 8
7 Murten
8 Bern

Day 9
9 Solothurn
10 Basel

Days 10 & 11
11 Lucerne
12 Mount Pilatus
13 Rigi

Day 12
14 Appenzell

Days 13 & 14
15 Zurich

Prisoner of Chillon. The château will be the man-made highlight of your visit. After lunch head for **Rochers-de-Naye** (p. 297), at 2,042m (6,698 ft.), reached by cogwheel train from Montreux. One of the greatest vistas in all of western Switzerland unfolds at the top. That night, if you're a gambler, you can descend on **Casino de Montreux** (p. 302).

Days ④ & ⑤ Vevey ✈ & Lausanne ✈✈

In the morning drive 6km (4 miles) northwest of Montreux, arriving in Vevey, the home of Nestlé chocolate. Many famous artists have lived here, and Charlie Chaplin in exile chose it as his final residence. Start your exploration at **Grand-Place** (p. 292), the large market

square and town nerve center. All of the museums are minor, but if you have time for one, make it **Musée du Vieux-Vevey** (p. 293), viewing, if rushed, its section on winemaker relics. Have lunch at **Café de La Clef** (p. 292), where Jean Jacques Rousseau stayed in 1730, before continuing in Lausanne, which lies 18km (11 miles) to the west. Check in to a hotel in Lausanne for 2 nights.

In the afternoon explore **Ouchy** (p. 276), the port area along the lakefront, especially the promenades, **Quai de Belgique** and **Quai d'Ouchy.** Filled with tropical plants, these gardens stretch for half a mile.

On the morning of **Day 5,** explore Lausanne's **Haute Ville** or Upper Town (p. 274). Allow 45 minutes for a visit.

You will still have time for a visit to the **Château de Beaulieu et Musée de l'Art Brut** (p. 278), a château from 1756 with a museum of paintings by the criminally insane. For a change-of-pace venture, take one of the lake steamers leaving every hour in summer, heading for **Evian-les-Bains** (p. 277), one of the leading resorts of Lake Geneva but lying across the French border. Along the way you can take in the beauty of the lake (Lac Léman is French). Once at Evian, you can walk its fashionable lakeside promenade before returning to your hotel in Lausanne for the night.

Day ❻ Gruyères ⚜ & Fribourg ⚜⚜

Leave Lausanne in the morning heading to the small town of Gruyères, seat of the counts of Gruyères and known for its château and its famous cheese sold all over the world. Gruyères lies 56km (35 miles) northeast of Lausanne. The highlight of a visit here is the **Château Gruyères** (p. 171), which is filled with art and antiques. Allow 1 hour for a visit. You can also visit in an hour the **Fromagerie de Démonstration** (p. 170), a model dairy where the famed cheese is made. If you find yourself in Gruyères for lunch, order raclette, if you're into cheese. This traditional Swiss specialty is served all over town.

After lunch continue on to **Fribourg** for the night, a distance of 35km (22 miles) north of Gruyères. You can stroll around this university city, set between lakes and mountains, with a visit to its major attraction, **St. Nicholas's Cathedral** (p. 167). Allow 30 minutes for visit. If time remains, duck into its **Eglise des Cordeliers** (p. 167), a historic Franciscan church. Overnight in Fribourg.

Days ❼ & ❽ Murten ⚜⚜ & Bern ⚜⚜⚜

Leave Fribourg in the morning, driving north to Murten, a distance of 18km (11 miles). Allow an hour for a walk along its

medieval ramparts (p. 173), plus another 40 minutes to stroll its main street, **Hauptgasse** (p. 173). You can also pay a 45-minute visit to the **Musée Historique** (p. 173), installed in an 8th-century mill.

You can remain in Murten for lunch before setting out for Bern, the capital of Switzerland. Check in to a hotel for 2 nights. With time remaining in the afternoon, you can visit the famous **Bärengraben** (Bear Pits; p. 193), and the **Cathedral of St. Vincent,** with its celebrated tympanum (p. 193) over the main portal.

On the morning of **Day 8,** spend at least 1½ hours in the **Kunstmuseum (Fine Arts Museum),** with the world's largest collection of the works of painter Paul Klee. Before the morning ends, take our 2-hour **walking tour of Altstadt** (p. 195). After lunch spend about an hour visiting the **Bernisches Historisches Museum (Bern Historic Museum;** p. 194), followed by a tour of the **Bundeshaus** (p. 194), a Renaissance palace housing the Swiss Parliament. To cap your visit, take the cable train to **Mount Gurten** at 844m (2,768 ft.) for one of the grandest panoramas in the area. Spend your final night in Bern by going to a famous old wine tavern, the **Klötzlikeller** (p. 200).

Day ❾ Solothurn ⚜ & Basel ⚜⚜⚜

Leave Bern in the morning and drive north to Solothurn, a distance of 43km (27 miles). At the foot of the Jura mountains, Solothurn offers a rewarding 3 hours of exploration, as you visit its **Old Town** (p. 165) on the left bank of the Aare River, taking in its **Cathedral of St. Ursus** (p. 165). With 45 minutes remaining, call at the **Kunstmuseum Solothurn (Municipal Fine Arts Museum),** taking in such paintings as the *Madonna of Solothurn* by Holbein the Younger (p. 165).

After lunch continue to drive north into Basel, a distance of 69km (43 miles). Try to visit Basel's two main attractions, the **Zoologischer Garten Basler** (p. 154), one of the greatest zoos in the world, and **Fondation Beyeler** (p. 152), one of Switzerland's finest museums of modern art. Overnight in Basel.

Days ⑩ & ⑪ Lucerne: Lake Tours & Mountain Vistas ✿✿✿

From Basel, drive southeast to the city of Lucerne, a distance of 96km (60 miles). After checking in to a hotel for 2 nights, set out to conquer this lakeside town by spending 2½ hours taking our walking tour (p. 357), which covers the scenic highlights. In the afternoon call on the major attraction, the **Swiss Transport Museum** (p. 362), one of the finest such museums of its kind in the world. If time remains, visit **Neues Kunstmuseum** (**Modern Art Museum;** p. 361), with both a permanent collection and temporary exhibitions.

Spend all **Day 11** by taking two of Switzerland's most popular—and justifiably so—mountain excursions: one to **Mount Pilatus** in the morning (p. 376), the other to **Rigi** in the afternoon (p. 377). These are described under **Day 4,** above, under "Switzerland in 1 Week."

Day ⑫ Appenzell: Strong on Folklore ✿

From Lucerne, drive 129km (80 miles) to Appenzell, the most folkloric town of northeastern Switzerland. You can arrive in time to explore the town in about 2 hours, doing some shopping along its Hauptgasse for regional handcrafts. Have lunch at **Hof** (p. 136), before heading out in the afternoon to visit **Ebenalp** (p. 136) a distance of 6km (4 miles). This jagged promontory at 1,620 m (5,314 ft.) offers one of the most stunning panoramas of the Appenzell district. For an even grander look, visit **Mount Säntis** (p. 136), the highest peak at 2,463m (8,079 ft.), for the single most spectacular view of

eastern Switzerland. The location is 14km (9 miles) west of Appenzell. Return to Appenzell for the night.

Days ⑬ & ⑭ Zurich ✿✿✿

For your final look at Switzerland, head west from Appenzell for 99km (62 miles) to Zurich, the country's largest city. This is the site of the world's largest gold exchange and the fourth-largest stock exchange. But there is reason to go here even if you don't dress in an Armani suit and carry a briefcase. For general orientation, talk our **two walking tours** (p. 110 and p. 112), which will take you into the **Altstadt** and along the historic quays by the Limmat River.

In the afternoon pay a visit to one of the city's greatest attractions, the **Landesmuseum** (**Swiss National Museum;** p. 107). This is your best introduction to the history and culture of the Swiss people.

On **Day 14**, your final day in Switzerland, see the stained-glass windows of the **Fraumünster** (p. 103), the Romanesque and Gothic cathedral of **Grossmünster** (p. 103), and call at the **Kunsthaus Zurich** (**Fine Arts Museum;** p. 107) to see its treasure trove of art.

After lunch take in the **Botanischer Garten** (p. 108) and the **Foundation E. G. Bührle Collection** (p. 108), filled with works of the Impressionists. If time remains, take the mountain railway to **Uetliberg** (p. 126), for one of the great panoramic views of the area. Return to the city center for the night, perhaps spending it at **Bierhalle Kropf** (p. 94), the city's most famous beer hall, serving a hearty regional cuisine.

The next morning you'll find that Zurich has the best rail and air connections of any city in Switzerland if you're returning home or going somewhere else in Europe.

3 Switzerland for Families

Many of Switzerland's pleasures and pastimes, such as alpine skiing and mountain trekking, are strictly adult-oriented. Nonetheless, it is one of the great outdoor countries in Europe, and all its major cities, such as Geneva and Zurich, offer activities that the entire family can enjoy. Perhaps your main concern with having children along is pacing yourself with enough museum time.

If you're on a rushed weeklong schedule, our suggestion is to spend only 1 night in the two main cities, Geneva and Zurich, but 2 nights each in the more kid-friendly cities of Interlaken and Lucerne, because of all the thrilling mountain excursions possible from these two resorts.

Day ❶ Zurich: Your Arrival Point ✦✦✦

On **Day 1** arrive as early as you can to crowd in as much sightseeing as possible, since you have only a day. The best and quickest way to see the city is to walk about the famous **quays of Zurich** (p. 103), which are riverside promenades along the Limmat. Many of these quays open onto beautiful gardens where the entire family can rest their feet. The town's major attraction is the **Landesmuseum** (**Swiss National Museum;** p. 107), which has something for all ages, even antique dollhouses built over various periods for the very young. Older boys will be fascinated by the display of weapons and armor, and there are always special exhibitions. After lunch families can head for the **Botanischer Garten** (p. 108), with some 15,000 living specimens. At the tourist office you can pick up a map listing 80 different playgrounds. No kid turns down an invitation to visit **Franz Carl Weber** (p. 109), the largest toy shop in Europe. Only if you've gotten through the day with time to spare, you can visit either the **Zuricher Spielzeugmuseum** (**Zurich Toy Museum;** p. 110), or one of the best zoos in Europe, **Zoologischer Garten** (p. 109).

Days ❷ & ❸ Lucerne: Mountains & Lakes ✦✦✦

On **Day 2** leave Zurich heading 50km (31 miles) south to Lake Lucerne and its "queen," the city of Lucerne itself. Check in to a hotel for 2 nights, and take the whole family on our walking tour (p. 357), which will take you by the big attractions. The major sight of Lucerne is something the whole family can enjoy, the **Verkehrshaus der Schweiz** (**Swiss Transport Museum;** p. 362). There's everything here from spaceships to an adventure ride called the Gotthard Tunnel Show. There's even the Longies planetarium where space travel is simulated. In the afternoon take the kids to **The Bourbaki Panorama** (a replica of the famous 19th-century battle; p. 360), followed by an excursion on one of the flotilla of lake steamers plying across Lake Lucerne. Some **summer boat excursions** last 4 hours, and there is a cafeteria onboard. (Ships are operated by Lake Lucerne Navigation Co.; p. 363).

On **Day 3,** while still based in Lucerne, take your family on two of the most famous mountain excursions in Switzerland. Because of public transportation, such as a cog railway, getting there is part of the fun. The excursions to **Mount Pilatus** and **Rigi** are previewed under **Day 4,** earlier, under "Switzerland in 1 Week."

Day ❹ Bern: Capital of Switzerland ✦✦✦

On **Day 4** leave Lucerne heading for the capital city of Bern, 111km (69 miles) to the west. Swiss politics will hold little interest for children but the **Bärengraben** (**Bear Pits;** p. 193) is a surefire winner.

Day 1
1 Zurich

Days 2 & 3
2 Lucerne

Day 4
3 Bern

Days 5 & 6
4 Interlaken

Day 7
5 Geneva

These pampered bears are the best fed in Europe, a carrot being their favorite food. Families also visit the **Zytgloggeturm** (**Clock Tower;** p. 193), which, 4 minutes before the hour, stages the oldest and biggest horological puppet show, with mechanical bears and the like. Other attractions to fill a day include a visit to **Dählhölzli Tierpark** (p. 194), one of the best zoos in Switzerland, with everything from exotic reptiles to mush oxen. Later an excursion to **Mount Gurten** at 844m (2,768 ft.) is in order. You get not only a panoramic view, but there's also a children's fairyland on-site. After a final stroll along **Marktgasse,** the main street of Old Town, you can call it a day.

Days ⑤ & ⑥ Interlaken: The Bernese Oberland ✹✹✹

On **Day 5** drive 54km (34 miles) southeast of Bern to reach the tourist capital of the Bernese Oberland, which can be your launch pad for exploring the mighty **Jungfraujoch** at 3,400m (11,152 ft.), reached by traveling to the highest railway station in Europe.

Arriving in the morning in Interlaken, check in to a hotel for 2 nights and spend the rest of the morning exploring parklike **Höheweg** (p. 205), covering 14 hectares (35 acres) in the center of town. All ages admire the view of Jungfrau mountain and the famous flower clock. In the afternoon take an excursion to the Wilderswil/Schynige Platte at 1,936m (6,350 ft.)

Once here, you'll find an alpine garden. If time remains, try to fit in an excursion to **Giessbach Falls** (p. 215), accessible by funicular, allowing about 2 hours for the excursion. Return to Interlaken for the night.

On the morning of **Day 6,** set out by Jungfrau Railways (p. 212) for a day's excursion to the afore-mentioned **Jungfraujoch** (p. 212). Families can purchase a Family Card for the whole brood. Attractions at the top include the famous **Eispalast (Ice Palace),** and there are lofty alpine restaurants as well. Later you can take the family on a sleigh ride pulled by huskies. Departures from Interlaken are daily at 8am, with a return at 4pm. Overnight once again in Interlaken.

Day ❼ Geneva 𝕬𝕬𝕬
On your final day in Switzerland, Day 7, leave Interlaken in the morning and drive across some of the most beautiful scenery in the country, both lake and mountain, until you come to Geneva, a distance of 218km (135 miles) to the southwest. After checking in to a hotel, set out to discover one of Europe's most regal cities. Kids delight in seeing the famous fountain, Jet d'Eau (p. 339), and the Flower Clock (p. 340) in the Jardin Anglais. A walk through the Old Town or Vieille Ville (p. 305) can be a highlight of the trip. Wind down in the Parc Mon-Repos (p. 338), perhaps securing the makings of a picnic. Later you can visit the Jardin Botanique (Botanical Garden; p. 338), with its alpine garden and little zoo. Older children are often interested in the adventure movie and exhibitions at the Musée International de la Croix-Rouge at du Croissant-Rouge, devoted to the Red Cross (p. 335). Overnight in Geneva.

4 The Grisons, the Engadine & Ticino

Graubünden (the Swiss name for the Grisons) is crowned by St. Moritz but also shelters such fabled resorts as Klosters and Davos. The province covers more than one-sixth of Switzerland and many—certainly the local residents—consider it the most beautiful part of the entire country. Its geographic landscape has staggering statistics: 615 lakes, 150 valleys, and 937 mountain peaks.

Bordering it is the dramatically different Ticino, centering around Locarno and Lugano. This is Switzerland with an Italian accent, and the look of the resorts with their date palms and manicured gardens is Mediterranean. In its heart, the Ticino belongs to sunny Italy, but German-speaking Switzerland dominates the district politically. However, their culture and language are strictly Italian.

Day ❶ Klosters: Prince Charles & Movie People 𝕬𝕬
Begin your trip to the Grisons in the Prättigau Valley resort of Klosters, a favorite retreat for Prince Charles and his sons today, or such literary figures in the past as Robert Louis Stevenson, who wrote *Treasure Island* here. If you're driving here from Zurich, your gateway city can be Chur, which is 122km (76 miles) southeast of Zurich. Once at Chur, you still have a 29km (18-mile) drive east to arrive at Klosters. If you visit in winter, you've come to ski. But most visitors making these driving tours do so in the summer. In that case, you can spend the rest of the afternoon taking in the mountain beauty of the resort. Both the **Madrisa** (p. 405) and the **Gotschna-Parsenn** (p. 405) cable cars will take you to the most scenic points in the mountains where you can hike through woods and alpine meadows along well-marked trails. Allow at least 4 hours for these treks. Overnight in Klosters.

Day 1
1 Klosters

Days 2 & 3
2 St. Moritz

Day 4 & 5
3 Bellinzona
4 Locarno

Days 6 & 7
4 Lugano
6 Morcote

Days ❷ & ❸ St. Moritz: The Ne Plus Ultra ✶✶✶

On the morning of **Day 2,** leave early to get some sightseeing time in Davos, 11km (7 miles) south of Klosters, its rival resort. Many expat writers and artists have preferred Davos to Klosters. Take the cableway to **Weissflühgipfel** (p. 411) at a height of 2,778m (9,112 ft.) for the best panorama in this part of eastern Switzerland. Transit time is only half an hour.

After a return to your car, continue the drive 80km (50 miles) south of Davos to St. Moritz, where you can check in to a hotel for 2 nights. Although St. Moritz is at its ritzy best in winter, it also attracts summer visitors to the mountain beauty of the Engadine (you've left the Grisons at

this point). After lunch in St. Moritz, you can visit the **Engadine Museum** (p. 427) to view artifacts of the history of the region. Part of the fun of a summer visit is to select from an array of **summer sports** (p. 428) that include windsurfing on the lakes, golfing, tennis, hiking, and even fishing. Plan an activity that fits your interest or else just spend the day walking around the streets of this posh resort window-shopping (or if your budget allows, actually doing some purchasing).

If you're into panoramas, you can go to **Piz Nair** (p. 427), the highest skiable mountain at 3,251m (10,663 ft.). The trip up takes 30 minutes by funicular to Corviglia. You go the rest of the way by cable car and on foot. Your reward from the terrace of the upper cable-car station is to look down on the Upper Engadine and its lakes, a vast panorama embracing the Bernina Alps.

On the morning of **Day 3,** while still based in St. Moritz, set out to explore some of the mountain scenery and the satellite towns of Engadine. One of the great drives in the area is to head southwest from St. Moritz, going through the resorts of Silvaplana and Sils-Maria until you reach to **Maloja Pass** (p. 418) at 1,786m (5,858 ft.). Hikers come to Maloja to begin one of the great walks in the Engadine—all of Switzerland, for that matter—going for 14km (8½ miles) to the resort of Silvaplana, taking about 3 to 3½ hours for this alpine trek. If you'd like something far less strenuous, take the 2-hour drive to the **Bernina Pass** (p. 418), going 55km (34 miles) between St. Moritz and Tirano in Italy. This is one of the great drives in Europe, possible from June to September. Return to St. Moritz for a final night.

Days ❹ & ❺ Bellinzona & Locarno 𝕬𝕬

Leave St. Moritz on the morning of **Day 4,** going via the Julierpass as you cut across a broad stretch of some great mountain scenery of southeastern Switzerland. Follow the signs to the **Passo del S. Bernardino,** which you can take south into the Ticino, that Italian-speaking part of southern Switzerland. Your first stop can be in the town of **Bellinzona,** 152km (94 miles) southwest of St. Moritz. The town has three medieval fortifications. The best views are possible from **Schwyz Castle** (p. 446).

After a lunch stopover, press on to the southwest, a distance of 22km (14 miles) from Bellinzona. Plan to stay 2 nights in Locarno, a vacation resort opening onto Lake Maggiore. You probably will arrive too late in the day for much sightseeing, but you can at least explore the main

square, **piazza Grande** (p. 450), and take a lakeside promenade.

On the morning of **Day 5,** visit the **Santuario della Madonna del Sasso** (p. 450), lying on a wooden crag above the resort in Orselina, where you will be rewarded with a panoramic view. For a dramatic drive, explore the **Gambarogno Riviera** (p. 450), with its evocative Ticinese villages spread across a distance of 11km (6½ miles) stretching to the Italian border. While still based in Locarno, and as part of the same day's activities, drive southwest to the resort of **Ascona,** a distance of only 4km (2½ miles). You can spend at least 2 hours visiting its Old Town and wandering its narrow streets, checking out the botanical garden on the **Isole di Brissago** (p. 456). If time remains, head for the little village of **Ronco** (p. 456), lying along the corniche, a distance of 18km (11 miles). A Mediterranean-style village, it's one of the most evocative in the Ticino. Return to Locarno for the night.

Days ❻ & ❼ Lugano 𝕬𝕬𝕬 & Morcote 𝕬𝕬

On the morning of **Day 6,** drive 39km (24 miles) southeast of Locarno to the even larger and more famous waterfront resort of Lugano, which tops even Locarno for natural beauty and architecture. Check in to a hotel for 2 nights. Before lunch, walk around the city park, **Parco Civico** (p. 462), opening onto Lake Lugano. There may even be time to duck into **Chiesa di Santa Maria degli Angeli** (p. 462) to see its famous frescoes by Bernardino Luini.

In the afternoon we suggest renting a bike (perhaps from your hotel) and getting a map from the tourist office. Set out to explore the nature reserve of **Origlio Lake** (p. 463) and the villages of **Tesserete** and **Colla** (p. 463). In all, the 4-hour trips goes for 37km (23 miles) and will give you some real atmosphere of the Ticino landscape. Return to Locarno.

On the morning of **Day 7,** drive to the town of **Morcote,** 11km (7 miles) south of Lugano. We consider this the most idyllic in the Ticino. You can also reach it by a summer boat. Spend at least 2 hours exploring this village and plan on an early lunch at one of its fine restaurants. In the afternoon head back to Lugano where you can go shopping for Ticino crafts or else participate in one of a dozen or so summer activities—not only golf or tennis, but boating, sailing, swimming at the Lido, or waterskiing and windsurfing. See **"The Active Vacation Planner"** (p. 463) for suggestions. From Lugano you can make connections the following morning for a long trip back home or else another destination in Switzerland or Europe.

4

Zurich

Switzerland's largest city is surely among the most beautiful in all of Europe, and even today, Zurich retains much of its 19th-century charm. Situated on the northern shore of Lake Zurich in the heart of the country, the city is both large enough to offer all amenities to its visitors and small enough for you to discover on your own.

Zurich is the capital of a canton of the same name that joined the Swiss Confederation in 1351. Most of the more than 380,000 residents speak a form of German called Schwyzerdütsch (Schweizerdeutsch, in standard German). A former seat of the Reformation, Zurich is a staunchly Protestant—some say Puritan—city.

Although Zurich is highly industrialized, its skies remain relatively unpolluted because the factories run on electricity. Zurich is also a major center of international finance; the headquarters of five major banks are on Bahnhofstrasse, in the heart of the city. The bankers are sometimes referred to as gnomes because many of the banks store mountains of gold in underground vaults.

Zurich produces one-fifth of the nation's income, but it's far from being a dreary city of commerce. It's long been a great center of liberal thought, attracting such scholars as Lenin, Jung, Joyce, and Mann. The Dadaist school was founded here in 1916. And the increase of visitors in the last 2 decades has spurred the development of a livelier nightlife and entertainment scene.

Built between the wooded slopes of the Uetliberg and the Zürichberg, Zurich is split by the Limmat River. There is no finer pleasure to be had in Zurich than walking along its quays, which line the banks of the Limmat and Lake Zurich. Sailboats and motorboats take visitors across Lake Zurich. Zurich's Altstadt (Old Town) is one of the most intriguing in Switzerland, with two giant cathedrals and dozens of streets ideal for exploring at leisure. It is also a city of parks and gardens, with a particularly outstanding botanical garden.

While based in Zurich you can also take easy side trips to some of the most panoramic views of Switzerland, including to the Uetliberg, the king of picnic spots and known as the "top of Zurich."

1 Orientation

ARRIVING

BY PLANE   Kloten Airport (*©* **044/816-22-11;** www.zurich-airport.com), the international airport of Zurich, is the biggest airport in Switzerland and the most popular gateway to the country; in fact, it's among the 10 busiest airports in Europe. Located approximately 11km (7 miles) north of the city center, the trip by taxi costs between 55F and 60F ($45 and $49). A far better and cheaper option is to take the Swiss Federal Railways train service; for 5.80F ($4.70)—press the solid red button on the automated ticket machine—you'll arrive in less than 15 minutes at the **Zurich**

Hauptbahnhof, the main railway station in the center of town. Zurich is a fairly compact town—from the train station, you can walk or hop on a tram or bus to most Zurich hotels in less than 30 minutes. (The train ticket you purchase at the airport is valid for 1 hour and includes connecting travel on the trams and buses within central Zurich. Alternatively, you can purchase a 24-hour version of the same ticket for 12F/$9.80—press the solid red button followed by the silver button with arrows). The train runs every 15 to 20 minutes between 5:36am and 12:20am. You can also take bus no. 768 (Zurich Airport–Seebach), but you'll have to change to tram no. 14 to get to the center of town.

BY TRAIN   Several trains bound for Switzerland leave from the Gare de l'Est in Paris. Without a stop, a train departs **Paris** at 10:43pm daily, arriving in Zurich at 6:45am. Other connections are via Basel. One train leaves Paris daily at 2:43pm, arriving 9:22pm in Zurich; yet another leaves Paris at 5:19pm, also going via Basel, arriving in Zurich at 12:06pm. From **Munich,** the Gottfried Keller Express departs daily at 6:15pm with a 10:23pm arrival in Zurich. The Bavaria leaves Munich daily at 8:15am, arriving in Zurich at 12:26pm. All trains arrive at the **Zurich Hauptbahnhof** (© **0900/300-300**).

BY BUS   Zurich's bus routes function only as feeder lines from outlying suburbs, which lie off the train lines, into the vicinity of the town's railroad station.

BY CAR   From Basel, take N3 east, and from Geneva, take N1 northeast, going via Bern, where you'll connect with E4 and E17 heading east into Zurich.

BY BOAT   The **Zurichsee-Schifffahrtsgesellschaft,** Mythenquai 333 (© **044/482-10-33;** www.zsg.ch), offers regularly scheduled service on modern passenger ships as well as old steamers plying both sides of Lake Zurich. The service is operated from Easter to October, going from Zurich as far as Rapperswil.

VISITOR INFORMATION

The **Zurich Tourist Office,** Bahnhofplatz 15 (© **044/215-40-00;** www.zuerich.com), is in the main railway station. It's open November to April, Monday to Saturday from 8:30am to 7pm and Sunday 9am to 6:30pm; May to October, Monday to Saturday 8am to 8:30pm and Sunday 8:30am to 6:30pm.

CITY LAYOUT

Zurich lies situated on both shores of the Limmat River, which flows from the northern end of Lake Zurich. The Sihl River, a tributary of the Limmat, also flows through the city, and quays line the riverbanks and the lake. The city spreads across a ravine in the eastern hills between the wooded slopes of the Zürichberg and Kääferberg hills into the Glatt River Valley.

The hamlet that became Zurich began at the **Lindenhof,** which is where you, too, may begin your orientation to the city. This square is the architectural center of historic Zurich. From here, you can survey the city as it rises on both banks of the Limmat from Bahnhofbrücke (*brücke* means bridge) to Quailbrücke. Between these two bridges are four other spans over the river: Muhle-Steg, Rudolf Brun-Brücke, Rathausbrücke, and Münsterbrücke.

Below this square runs **Bahnhofstrasse,** one of the most elegant and expensive shopping streets in the world. It begins in the north, at the Hauptbahnhof (the railway station), opening onto Bahnhofplatz, and runs south to the lake. It crosses **Paradeplatz,** a converging point for trams and the modern center of the city. From

Paradeplatz you can continue east, passing Fraumünster church and crossing Münsterbrücke to reach the right bank of the river. Here, the narrow streets of the **Limmatquai** are the second-best place in the city to shop. Running parallel to Limmatquai is **Niederdorfstrasse,** in the so-called red-light district of Zurich.

Old Town, or **Altstadt,** was developed during the early medieval period and is focused on Lindenhof, Fraumünster, Grossmünster, and St. Peter's. It expanded to **Weinplatz,** the oldest market square, and **Strehlgasse.** By the 11th century, the city developed on the right bank with such centers as **Kirchgasse** and **Neumarkt.**

FINDING AN ADDRESS   In a system that developed during the Middle Ages, all Swiss cities, including Zurich, begin their street-numbering system with the lowest numbers closest to the center of town. In Zurich the center is the **Hauptbahnhof.** All even numbers lie on one side of the street, and all odd numbers are on the other.

MAPS   The best map, published by Falk, is a pocket-size Stadtplan (city plan) with an index. Copies are available at various newsstands and bookstores. Try the **Travel Book Shop,** Rindermarkt 20 (© **044/252-38-83;** www.travelbookshop.ch). Hours are Monday 1 to 6:30pm, Tuesday through Friday from 9am to 6:30pm, and Saturday 9am to 4pm.

NEIGHBORHOODS IN BRIEF

Zurich is divided by the Limmat River into the following two general areas:

West or Left Bank This district is dominated by Bahnhofplatz, center of rail connections, and Bahnhofstrasse, which is the main commercial and banking thoroughfare. This is the Zurich world of high finance and elegant shops. The venerable Fraumünster church, on Fraumünsterstrasse, dominates the west bank.

East or Right Bank Opposite Fraumünster, on the other side of the river,

rises Grossmünster church, on Grossmünsterplatz; its two Gothic towers are an east-bank landmark. The historic guildhalls of Zurich, such as the Zunfthaus zur Saffran, rise on the east bank of the river. So, too, does the Rathaus, the city's town hall, completed in 1698. On the east bank you can explore the eastern part of Altstadt, strolling along Neumarkt, one of the best preserved of the old streets. The area beyond is Niederdorf, the center of the town's hot spots.

2 Getting Around

Zurich is an easy city to navigate, and the trams (streetcars) and buses are reliable.

BY PUBLIC TRANSPORTATION

The public transport system of Zurich is operated by VBZ Züri-Linie, or **Zurich Public Transport** (© **044/212-37-37;** www.vbz.ch). The modern and extensive network of trams and buses (there is no subway) runs daily from 5:30 to 12:30am. You should have to wait no longer than 6 minutes during rush hours. Most trams and buses connect at the Zurich Hauptbahnhof, in the heart of the city.

You can buy tickets from automatic vending machines located at every stop. You must have a ticket before you get on a vehicle; if you're caught without one, you'll pay a fine of 50F ($41). The fare is 3.30F ($2.70) for a trip of up to four stops, and 4.10F ($3.35) for longer journeys. Visitors can get the most for their money by ordering a

Tageskarte (1-day ticket), which costs 7.50F ($6.15) and allows you to travel on all city buses and trams for 24 hours.

BY TAXI

Taxis are very expensive. The budget-conscious will only want to use them as a last resort. Your hotel will usually be glad to call a taxi for you, but if you're making the call yourself, call **Taxi-Zentrale Zurich** (© **044/272-44-44**). The basic charge before you even get into the vehicle is 6F ($4.90), plus 3.50F ($2.85) for each kilometer you travel.

BY CAR

We don't recommend attempting to see Zurich by car—the city is way too congested, and parking is too scarce and too expensive. Save the car for exploring the environs.

RENTAL CARS   All the major car-rental firms are represented in Zurich, with offices at both Kloten Airport and downtown. Representative firms include **Avis,** with offices at Gartenhofstrasse 17 (© **044/296-87-87**) or at the airport (© **044/800-77-33**); **Budget,** with an office at Steinstrasse 21 (© **044/450-75-35**); and **Hertz,** with a base at Morgartenstrasse 5 (© **044/298-84-84**).

PARKING   You should get a street plan (see "Maps" under "Orientation," above), which indicates parking garages with a "P" sign; a similar leaflet is available from the Zurich police. Some hotels have their own parking garages, for which there is an extra charge; others, especially those in congested Old Town, do not. You'll have to inquire at your hotel for the location of the nearest public garage. Parking costs range from 6F to 10F ($4.90–$8.20) per hour in most of the city's public garages.

BY BIKE

Biking is a good way to get around Zurich, especially in the outlying areas. Bicycles can be rented at the baggage counter of the railway station, the **Hauptbahnhof** (© **051/222-29-04**), for 27F ($22) per day for a city bike or 21F ($17) for a half day. Hours are daily from 7am to 7:30pm.

ON FOOT

Zurich and its quays are ideal for walking, and many of the places of interest, such as the sights of Altstadt on both sides of the Limmat, are conveniently grouped together.

FAST FACTS: Zurich

Babysitters If enough advance notification is given (at least a day in advance), virtually any hotel in Zurich can arrange for a babysitter. Another option is the child-care facilities at one of Zurich's largest department stores, **Jelmoli,** Seidengasse 1 (© **044/220-44-11**).

Banks Banks are generally open Monday to Wednesday and on Friday from 8:15am to 4:30pm and on Thursday from 8:15am to 6pm. Two well-known banks are **Union Bank of Switzerland,** at ShopVille (© **044/234-11-11**), and **Swiss Bank Corporation,** Bahnhofstrasse 70 (© **044/224-21-42**). Both banks have locations throughout Zurich, and both are open Monday to Friday 8am to 7pm.

Climate Summers in Zurich are not as warm as on the French Riviera, but the lake is usually warm enough to swim in during July and August. Many days are chilly, and spring and fall can be quite cold. In winter the temperature rarely goes below zero. The average temperature in January is 30°F (–1°C); in July the average is only 61°F (16°C). On cloudy days the view of the Alps is obscured.

Consulates If you lose your passport or have another emergency, go to the **U.S. Consulate,** Dufourstrasse 101 (*℃* **043/499-29-60**). The **Consulate of the United Kingdom** is at Minervastrasse 117 (*℃* **044/383-65-60**). Canadians and Australians should contact their respective embassies in Bern, and New Zealanders should apply to their consulate-general in Geneva (see "Fast Facts: Switzerland" in chapter 2).

Currency Exchange Most banks and travel agencies will exchange money for you. There's also an exchange office of **Credit Suisse** at the Zurich Hauptbahnhof, the main railway station, open daily from 6:30am to 11:30pm at Minervastrasse 117. Incidentally, there are ATMs all over the city.

Dentists Emergency dental problems can be solved by calling *℃* **044/269-69-69**. An appointment with an English-speaking dentist can be arranged for you.

Doctors Contact the **Zurich Universitätsspital (University Hospital),** Rämistrasse 100 (*℃* **044/255-11-1**).

Drugstores For 24-hour service, **Bellevue Apotheke,** at Theaterstrasse 14 (*℃* **044/266-62-22**; www.bellevue-apotheke.com), lies off Bellevueplatz.

Emergencies Call the **police** at *℃* **117**. For **first aid,** phone *℃* **47-47-00**; for the **City Ambulance Service,** dial *℃* **144**. There's an accident center at the **University Hospital,** Rämistrasse 100 (*℃* **044/255-11-11**). For a fire, dial *℃* **118**.

Hairdressers & Barbers Women do not need a reservation at **Gidor,** Theaterstrasse 8 (*℃* **044/251-90-18**). Men can get their hair cut at the Hauptbahnhof (rail station).

Hospitals See "Doctors" or "Emergencies," above.

Information See "Visitor Information," earlier in this chapter.

Internet Access Head for an Internet cafe such as **Telefon-Corner,** Kanzleistrasse 57 (*℃* **044/297-20-80**), open Monday to Thursday 9am to midnight, Friday and Saturday 9am to 2am, and Sunday 10am to 11pm.

Laundry/Dry Cleaning One of the best and most centrally located of Zurich's self-service laundries is **Waschbär,** Mühlegasse 11 (*℃* **044/252-37-95**). A dry-cleaning service is also on-site.

Libraries The main branch of the **Pestalozzi Bibliothek (Pestalozzi Library),** the largest in Zurich, is at Zähringerstrasse 17 (*℃* **044/261-78-11**). You must maintain a permanent address in Switzerland to be able to borrow books, but even if you don't, you're welcome to browse the stacks and read anything you want on-site. It's open Monday to Friday 10am to 7pm and Saturday 10am to 2pm (till 4pm Sept–May).

Lost Property There is a lost-property office at Werdmühlestrasse 10 (*℃* **044/216-51-11**), open Monday to Friday 7:30am to 5:30pm.

Luggage Storage/Lockers These are available at several locations throughout the vast Hauptbahnhof (*℃* **044/211-25-51**).

Newspapers/Magazines The major newspaper of Zurich is the German-language **Neue Zürcher Zeitung.** The **International Herald Tribune** is printed in Zurich. Several German-language magazines are published in Switzerland, and the latest copies of **Newsweek** and **Time** (European editions) are available at most newsstands and in big-hotel lobbies.

Police See "Emergencies," above.

Post Office The main post office is the **Sihlpost,** Kasernenstrasse 95-97 (**©** **044/ 296-21-11**), across the Sihl River from Löwenstrasse; an emergency-service window is open from 6:30am to 10pm daily. Most post offices—listed under "Post" in the phone directory—are open Monday to Friday 7:30am to 6:30pm and on Saturday from 6:30 to 11am.

Restrooms Public toilets are located at all central points, including the Hauptbahnhof and such locations as Bellevueplatz, Paradeplatz, and Heimplatz. They are open daily, generally from 5am to midnight.

Safety Zurich is one of the safest cities in Europe, both during the day and at night. The most potentially dangerous place is Niederdorf, the red-light district in Altstadt.

Taxes A 7.5% VAT (value-added tax) is added to hotel and restaurant bills. There are no other special taxes.

Taxis See "Getting Around," earlier in this chapter.

Telephone/Telex/Fax A telephone, telex, and fax office is open at the **Zurich Hauptbahnhof,** the main railway station, Monday to Friday from 7am to 10:30pm and on Saturday and Sunday from 9am to 9pm.

Transit Information For bus and tram information, call **©** **044/288-48-48.**

Weather See "Climate," above.

3 Where to Stay

Zurich is an ideal place to get acquainted with Swiss hospitality. More than 120 hotels offer accommodations ranging from the most sumptuous suites in Europe to simple, clean pensions (boardinghouses). Finding a room can be a problem, however. The top hotels are usually filled with business travelers, and the city is a frequent host to conventions and fairs. So, if possible, make a reservation in advance.

For top-rate comfort in Zurich, you'll have to pay. Inexpensive hotels are often spartan and definitely have no frills. Furthermore, many of the budget hostelries are in dire need of renovation. Don't believe the myth that you can't find a bad hotel in Switzerland: It's not true and probably never was.

The division between the left bank and the right bank of Zurich isn't as sharply divided as it is in Paris, for example. You stay on the left bank for greater convenience, as it is the site of the rail terminus, all the major banks, and some of the grandest shops and restaurants. However, the right bank is the site of the Altstadt (Old Town), and for many visitors this section of Zurich has far greater atmosphere. It is also the site of some of the historic guildhalls of Zurich (some of which are now restaurants). A stay here is for those who seek ambience and an old-style atmosphere when lodging in a European capital.

Where to Stay in Zurich

Alden Hotel Splügenschloss **22**
Bar Hotel Seehof **19**
Baur au Lac **21**
Hotel Ambassador **18**
Hotel Bristol **3**
Hotel Dolder Waldhaus **12**
Hotel du Theatre **7**
Hotel Goldenes Schwert **13**

Hotel Helmhaus **16**
Hotel Kindli **9**
Hotel Limmatblick **6**
Hotel Opéra **17**
Hotel Romantic Florhof **10**
Hotel Schweizerhof **4**
Hotel St. Gotthard **5**
Hotel Walhalla **2**

Hotel Zum Storchen **14**
Hotel Zurichberg **11**
Lady's First **20**
Savoy Baur en Ville **15**
Widder Hotel **8**
X-tra Hotel Limmat **1**

Note: Rooms in all our recommended hotels have private bathrooms with tub and shower unless otherwise indicated.

ON THE LEFT BANK
VERY EXPENSIVE
Alden Hotel Splügenschloss 🎔🎔 *Finds*   A little city-*palais,* and a Relais & Châteaux, this is a gem of a hotel, each room a suite. At the turn of the 20th century, it was a luxury apartment house, home to rich merchants, but its historic decor has been successfully adapted into the midsize charmer that you see today. Bedrooms are spacious and tastefully furnished, including such extras as a sitting area and a luxury bathroom with tub or shower. Many of the accommodations contain antique wardrobes and are decked out in soothing shades of pastels. One, for example, has been paneled in Graubünden pine from eastern Switzerland. The location is just a 6-minute walk from the Bahnhofstrasse and a 3-minute walk from the Enge rail depot. The restaurant is a virtual art gallery and serves a refined cuisine of international dishes.

Splügenstrasse 2, CH-8002. Zurich. ℂ **044/289-99-99.** Fax 044/289-99-98. www.alden.ch. 22 units. 700F–1,100F ($574–$902) junior suite; 900F–1,500F ($738–$1,230) suite. AE, DC, MC, V. Tram: 5, 6, 7, or 13. **Amenities:** 2 restaurants; bar; limited room service; laundry service. *In room:* A/C (on request), TV, dataport, minibar, hair dryer, safe.

Baur au Lac 🎔🎔🎔   One of the world's great hotels, owned by the same family since it opened in 1844, Baur au Lac is ideally located at the end of Bahnhofstrasse, right next to the Schanzengraben Canal. The constantly renovated three-story stone building is surrounded by a private park that's filled with red geraniums in summer. In style, grandeur, service, and amenities, it is superior to its nearest competitor, the Widder. The dining facilities are among the finest in Zurich.

In rooms where Richard Wagner and Franz Liszt once entertained at the piano, guests today are treated to Jugendstil glass, tapestries, antiques, marble floors, and Oriental carpets. All bedrooms and suites are luxuriously and uniquely furnished. Suites have the best antiques, but regular rooms may have an Empire piece, a style from one of the Louis periods, or modern furnishings. Try for a room with a lake view.

Talstrasse 1, CH-8022, Zurich. ℂ **044/220-50-20.** Fax 044/220-50-44. www.bauraulac.ch. 125 units. 660F ($541) double; from 1,600F ($1,312) suite. AE, DC, MC, V. Parking 27F ($22). Tram: 4. **Amenities:** 3 restaurants; bar; disco; fitness club; limited room service; massage; laundry/dry cleaning. *In room:* A/C, TV, dataport, minibar, coffeemaker, hair dryer, iron, safe (in some).

Hotel St. Gotthard 🎔   A longtime favorite of the Swiss, Hotel St. Gotthard is located on the main shopping street, only a block from the railroad station. For more than a century, it has been convenient for shops, transportation, business centers, bus terminals, and restaurants. Rooms and suites, including a collection of business-class units, are generously furnished in various styles and come in a range of sizes. Amenities include voice mail and videos, along with deluxe toiletries in the bathrooms. Suites and business-class rooms have fax machines. The welcome here is warmer and more personal than it is at the giants recommended elsewhere in this section.

Bahnhofstrasse 87, CH-8023 Zurich. ℂ **800/457-4000** in the U.S. or 044/227-77-00. Fax 044/227-77-50. www.hotel stgotthard.ch. 150 units. 425F–480F ($349–$394) double; 600F–700F ($492–$574) suite. AE, DC, MC, V. Parking 35F ($29). Tram: 6, 7, 11, or 13. **Amenities:** 2 restaurants; 3 bars; health club; sauna; solarium; 24-hr. room service; massage room; babysitting; laundry service/dry cleaning; nonsmoking rooms. *In room:* A/C (in some), TV, dataport, minibar, coffeemaker, hair dryer, iron (in some), safe.

Hotel Schweizerhof 🎔🎔   Located in one of the city's busiest areas, the landmark Schweizerhof is accessible from anywhere in town by tram. This is a grand old station hotel in turn-of-the-20th-century tradition, although major renovations have kept it in step with the times. When stacked up against the Baur au Lac, Widder, and Savoy, it would definitely be number four, although the Schweizerhof is far superior to the average station hotel in a European capital. The stone building has gables, turrets, and columns and is decorated with flags. Inside, the public rooms are pleasant and unpretentious. The ideal rooms are the semicircular corner units. In spite of its central location, rooms are generally quiet because of the triple-glazing on the windows. Most units are roomy and filled with many thoughtful extras, including spongy carpeting, alarm clocks, fruit baskets, and deluxe toiletries. They even provide umbrellas.

Bahnhofplatz 7, CH-8023 Zurich. © **044/218-88-88.** Fax 044/218-81-81. www.hotelschweizerhof.com. 115 units. 530F–620F ($435–$508) double; 690F ($566) junior suite; 1,080F ($886) suite. Rates include buffet breakfast. AE, DC, MC, V. Parking 25F ($21). Tram: 3 or 4. **Amenities:** 2 restaurants; bar; business center; 24-hr. room service; babysitting; laundry service/dry cleaning; nonsmoking rooms. *In room:* A/C, TV, dataport, minibar, coffeemaker, hair dryer, iron, trouser press.

Hotel zum Storchen ⓕⓕ

This hotel claims to be the oldest in Europe, with origins going back to 1357. However, it was completely rebuilt in 1939, just at the outbreak of World War II. A traditional government-rated four-star hotel, it is an unusual choice for Zurich. Although Zurich's deluxe hotels are far better known, this is the only one directly on the Limmat River and seems more overrun with tourists than the more prestigious Baur au Lac, which also lures discerning clients seeking an old-world ambience. Supposedly named for the storks that nested on the roof, the Storchen is undeniably romantic. A favorite feature is the cafe terrace, which provides a sweeping panorama of Old Town. The midsize rooms are warmly and invitingly decorated and maintained in state-of-the-art condition. The most desirable units have French windows opening onto the water, across to the floodlit Rathaus. Be sure to reserve ahead of time, especially in summer.

Am Weinplatz 2, CH-8001 Zurich. © **800/457-4000** in the U.S., or 044/227-27-27. Fax 044/227-27-00. www.storchen.ch. 73 units. 555F–680F ($455–$558) double; 750F–1,050F ($615–$861) suite. Rates include buffet breakfast. AE, DC, MC, V. Parking 30F ($25). Tram: 4 or 15. **Amenities:** 2 restaurants; bar; 24-hr. room service; babysitting; laundry service/dry cleaning. *In room:* A/C, TV, dataport, minibar, coffeemaker, hair dryer.

Savoy Baur en Ville ⓕⓕⓕ

Savoy Baur en Ville is a Zurich landmark and has been since 1838. It's a grand and elegant choice, although coming nowhere near the grandeur of Baur au Lac. A conservative and refined hotel, it's one of the premier spots of Zurich. Its six stories are conspicuously located amid stores on Paradeplatz, a 5-minute walk from the lake. The public rooms contain high ceilings and are decorated with occasional touches of gilt and expensive accessories. The bedrooms are quietly dignified and decorated in a wide range of styles. Rooms on the sixth floor have balconies, with space for sunbathing or breakfast.

Am Paradeplatz, CH-8022 Zurich. © **044/215-25-25.** Fax 044/215-25-00. www.savoy-baurenville.ch. 112 units. 720F ($590) double; 1,400F ($1,148) suite. Rates include continental breakfast. AE, DC, MC, V. Parking 27F ($22). Tram: 4, 6, 11, or 13. **Amenities:** 2 restaurants; bar; salon; 24-hr. room service; babysitting; laundry service/dry cleaning. *In room:* A/C, TV, dataport, minibar, coffeemaker, hair dryer, safe (in some).

Widder Hotel ⓕⓕⓕ

Today this is Zurich's most up-to-date deluxe hotel, rivaled in the neighborhood only by the superior Baur au Lac, but well ahead of the Savoy in overall tranquillity and comfort. In the early 1990s the Union Bank of Switzerland managed to acquire 10 interconnected buildings—some associated with the city's medieval butchers' guild—clustered around a central courtyard in the capital's historic core. The well-respected architect they hired, Ms. Tilla Theus, successfully emphasized, rather than diminished, the buildings' individual differences when they were combined into this sophisticated international hotel, creating an architectural ensemble that is praised by architects and cultural authorities.

During the renovations, great care was used to retain the original stone walls, murals, frescos, and ceilings. The result is a unique hotel where every room is different—sometimes radically so—from its neighbors, and where the color scheme (pastel beige, pink, blue, or yellow) reflects the color of the exterior of whichever of the 10 buildings you happen to be in. Interior furnishings range from the metallic, minimalist, and very modern to the traditional. Views from the bedrooms extend out over either the Rennweg, the Augustinergasse, or the buildings' inner courtyard, and some enjoy vistas of the stately Augustinerkirche nearby.

Rennweg 7, CH-8001 Zurich. ✆ 044/224-25-26. Fax 044/224-24-24. www.widderhotel.ch. 49 units. 665F–790F ($545–$648) double; 920F–1,510F ($754–$1,238) suite. Rates include breakfast. AE, DC, MC, V. Parking 30F ($25). Tram: 6, 7, or 11. **Amenities:** Restaurant; bar; health club; 24-hr. room service; babysitting; laundry service/dry cleaning. *In room:* TV, fax, dataport, minibar, coffeemaker, hair dryer, safe (in some).

MODERATE
Hotel du Theatre ★ *(Finds*   This bed-and-breakfast hotel is aptly named, as it harbored a German-speaking Broadway-style stage in the 1950s before its conversion to a top-notch urban hotel. The tall, thin architecture of the building itself, along with a glass facade, sets the stage for the drama going on inside. The tranquil, comfortably furnished rooms are more traditional than theatrical. However, they possess character and are equipped with a cornucopia of audio books, plays, music, drama, crime stories, philosophy tomes, and even erotica. When this library of goodies has tired you, you're prepared for a rest before breakfast the following morning in a beautiful room. The city center, only a short walk away, can be seen from the dining room, and the location is a 5-minute walk from the Bahnhof.

Seilergraben 69, CH-8001 Zurich. ✆ 044/267-267-0. Fax 044/267-267-1. www.hotel-du-theatre.ch. 50 units. 195F–260F ($160–$213) double; 235F–290F ($193–$238) junior suite. AE, DC, MC, V. Tram: 4 or 10. **Amenities:** Nonsmoking rooms; rooms for guests w/limited mobility. *In room:* TV, dataport, minibar, safe.

Hotel Kindli ★   Set at the end of a steep street (Rennweg) in Old Town, in a pedestrian zone, this 16th-century building is one of Zurich's most well-recommended middle-bracket hotels. It's been completely renovated, with a different color scheme designed for each of the nice-size bedrooms, and a flowery overlay of Laura Ashley fabrics throughout. Each room contains an eclectic blend of old and new furniture and an efficient bathroom.

Pfalzgasse 1, CH-8001 Zurich. ✆ 043/888-76-76. Fax 043/888-76-77. www.kindli.ch. 20 units. 340F–370F ($279–$303) double. Rates include continental breakfast. AE, DC, MC, V. Parking 32F ($26). Tram: 7, 11, or 13. **Amenities:** Restaurant. *In room:* A/C, TV, minibar.

Hotel Zürichberg ★ *(Kids*   This hotel stands on a hillside 2.2km (1¼ miles) east of Zurich's center. In 1994 a team of architects and entrepreneurs radically renovated a century-old, brick-sided hotel, and added a futuristic-looking annex, interconnecting them with an underground tunnel stretching beneath a lavish garden. Views from the spacious bedrooms encompass either the forest or the lakes and mountains. Because of the convenient and frequent tram service, you do not need a car to stay here. Since its inauguration, several prestigious architectural awards have been lavished upon the property for its successful merging of late-Victorian and avant-garde styles. The curved sides of the annex have been compared to the exterior of the Guggenheim

museum in New York. Separating the buildings are two children's playgrounds, the above-mentioned garden, and a warm-weather terrace where tables from the hotel's cafe, Colibri, and its more substantial restaurant, the Kiebitz, are placed during clement weather. Bedrooms are minimalist, accented with as much full-grained wood as possible and occasional touches of bamboo.

Orellistrasse 21, CH-8044 Zurich. ✆ 044/268-35-35. Fax 044/268-35-45. www.zuerichberg.ch. 67 units. 270F–420F ($221–$344) double. Rates include breakfast. AE, DC, MC, V. Parking 10F ($8.20). Tram: 6. **Amenities:** 2 restaurants; cafe; 24-hr. room service; laundry service/dry cleaning. *In room:* TV, dataport, minibar, hair dryer, safe.

INEXPENSIVE

Hotel Bristol ✻ *Value*   This small hotel stands on a hill near the main train station, behind the major road to the airport. For many years, Hotel Bristol has been one of Zurich's best-known and most successful small hotels despite its lack of amenities. The bedrooms are well maintained, frequently renovated, and furnished to a high standard of comfort. The helpful staff makes you feel right at home in the center of Zurich. No alcoholic beverages are sold, and only breakfast is served.

Stampfenbachstrasse 34, CH-8035 Zurich. ✆ **044/258-44-44.** Fax 044/258-44-00. www.hotelbristol.ch. 53 units. 150F–210F ($123–$172) double; 190F–240F ($156–$197) triple; 220F–290F ($180–$238) quad. Rates include continental breakfast. AE, DC, MC, V. Tram: 11 or 14. **Amenities:** Limited room service; laundry service/dry cleaning; rooms for guests w/limited mobility. *In room:* TV, hair dryer, iron, safe.

Hotel Walhalla *Value*   Set close to the railway station, this hotel is one of the relatively cheap bargains in central Zurich. It occupies two five-story buildings, one with more up-to-date bedrooms. The other is older and a bit dowdier, with high-ceilinged bedrooms and very little architectural flair. All rooms and bathrooms, however, are comfortable and well maintained. The dining room serves breakfast only.

Limmatstrasse 5, 8005 Zurich. ✆ **044/446-54-00.** Fax 044/446-54-54. www.walhalla-hotel.ch. 48 units. 140F–200F ($115–$164) double; 250F ($205) triple. AE, DC, MC, V. Tram: 3 or 14. **Amenities:** Restaurant; lounge; breakfast room; nonsmoking rooms; rooms for guests w/limited mobility. *In room:* TV.

X-Tra Hotel Limmat ✻ *Finds*   The Limmat is one of the most durable of the cost-conscious hotels of downtown Zurich. The hotel occupies part of a four-story building erected in 1935 in the Bauhaus style as a convention center, and whose boxy-looking facade is today protected as a historic monument. You can expect more here than just a place to stay: Its management, in place since 1997, is one of the largest organizers of rock-'n'-roll concerts in Switzerland, often staging their acts in the cavernous restaurant and nightclub that occupies the ground floor. Consequently, members of the bands that play here are often in residence within the hotel, a policy that adds to the cachet of the place for counterculture rock-'n'-roll enthusiasts across Switzerland. (Hotel guests receive a 15F/$12 discount off their admission to the nightclub.) Accommodations are streamlined, partially paneled, and outfitted in a style you may identify as Danish modern. Eight single units do not contain private bathrooms, but toilets and showers lie just off the corridors.

In the Limmathaus, Limmatstrasse 118, CH-8005 Zurich. ✆ **044/448-15-95.** Fax 044/448-15-96. www.x-tra.ch. 43 units (35 with bathroom). 130F–150F ($107–$123) double without bathroom; 154F–205F ($126–$168) double with bathroom; 188F–235F ($154–$193) triple with bathroom; 225F–265F ($185–$217) quad with bathroom. Rates include breakfast. Parking 15F ($12) per night. AE, DC, MC, V. Tram: 4 or 13 to Limmatplatz. **Amenities:** Restaurant; bar; cafe with outdoor terrace; nightclub; discounted admission at a nearby health club; self-service laundry. *In room:* TV, minibar.

ON THE RIGHT BANK
EXPENSIVE

Hotel Ambassador ✿   The grand and ornate facade of this government-rated four-star hotel is in sharp contrast to a stripped-down interior, which is more efficiently decorated, and more streamlined, than you may have thought. Built late in the 19th century, in beige stone with lots of Beaux Arts–style carvings, it rises from a point near the tramway junction at the Bellevueplatz, near the Opera House. Bedrooms are high-ceilinged and generally spacious. A well-trained staff attends to your comfort, providing the services that a traveling business representative may need. In this category, the Ambassador lacks the frills and flourish of its competitors, Florhof and Dolder Waldhaus, but its devotees prefer the simplified no-nonsense atmosphere.

Falkenstrasse 6, CH-8008 Zurich. ✆ 044/258-98-98. Fax 044/258-98-00. www.ambassadorhotel.ch. 44 units. 390F–460F ($320–$377) double; 580F ($476) suite. Rates include buffet breakfast. AE, DC, MC, V. Parking 25F ($21). Tram: 4. **Amenities:** Restaurant; bar; 24-hr. room service; laundry service/dry cleaning. *In room:* A/C (in some), TV, dataport, minibar, coffeemaker, hair dryer.

Hotel Dolder Waldhaus ✿ *Finds*   Surrounded by forest in the Dolder residential section of Zurich, this hotel offers an experience in country living yet is only 15 minutes from the center of town and easily accessible by public transportation. It is preferred by many because of its resortlike facilities, almost completely lacking, of course, in hotels in the city center. The hotel consists of two towers, one housing 75 rooms and a suite, the other 25 apartments. All doubles have a kitchenette and a balcony. Apartments, on the other hand, offer a kitchenette and terrace and are mainly for long-term clients (they can be rented nightly if available). Accommodations above the tree line offer panoramic views of the lake. A 9-hole golf course, tennis courts, and an outdoor pool are a 10-minute walk away, but their use is included in hotel rates.

Kurhausstrasse 20, CH-8030 Zurich. ✆ 044/269-10-00. Fax 044/269-10-01. www.dolderwaldhaus.ch. 100 units. 360F–460F ($295–$377) double; 550F ($451) 1-bedroom apt; 850F ($697) 2-bedroom apt. AE, DC, MC, V. Free parking. Tram: 3, 8, or 15. **Amenities:** Restaurant; indoor pool; minigolf course; sauna; 24-hr. room service; massage; babysitting; laundry service/dry cleaning. *In room:* A/C (in some), TV, minibar, kitchenette, coffeemaker, hair dryer.

Hotel Romantik Florhof ✿ *Value*   This is the most charming and tranquil of the little boutique hotels of Zurich, located on the eastern edge of the Old Town. Originally built in the 15th century as a merchant's home, these premises became a hotel during the 1920s. The Florhof represents top value in Zurich and is known as a gracious and well-managed hotel with a loyal clientele. Although the public rooms retain much of their antique glamour (including a noteworthy blue-and-white Kachelofen often used long ago for heating), many of the bedrooms are modern and functional in their inspiration. The single units are a bit small, but most doubles are of decent size and are nicely outfitted with plasterwork on the ceilings, exceedingly comfortable beds, stone-topped nightstands, and generous bathrooms.

Florhofgasse 4, CH-8001 Zurich. ✆ 044/250-26-26. Fax 044/250-26-27. www.florhof.ch. 35 units. 330F–380F ($271–$312) double; 480F–580F ($394–$476) junior suite. Rates include continental breakfast. AE, DC, MC, V. Parking 17F ($14). Tram: 3. **Amenities:** Restaurant; limited room service; laundry/dry cleaning. *In room:* TV, minibar.

MODERATE

Bar Hotel Seehof   Set close to the opera house and the promenade that parallels the lake, this small-scale, postmodern hotel was opened in 1999 after a radical renovation and modernization of the original 1930s-era private house. Whereas the hotel retains the original russet-colored exterior, the interior decor is angular and efficient, with stark white walls and the kind of black furniture that you'd expect in a trendy art gallery. Fortunately, the angularity is softened, in both the public areas and the bedrooms, with varnished and beautifully crafted oaken floors and a revolving series of artworks, usually photographs, by Swiss artists. Many of the rooms are reserved by opera singers performing at the nearby Opera House.

Seehofstrasse 11, CH-8008 Zurich. © 044/254-57-57. Fax 044/254-57-58. www.hotelseehof.ch. 19 units. 250F–280F ($205–$230) double; 320F–340F ($262–$279) triple; 350F–380F ($287–$312) suite. Rates include buffet breakfast. AE, DC, MC, V. Tram: 4. **Amenities:** Restaurant (open Mon–Fri for lunch only); bar (closed weekends July–Aug); limited room service; laundry service/dry cleaning. *In room:* TV, minibar, hair dryer, safe (in some).

Hotel Helmhaus ⚘   In the center of Zurich, Helmhaus is 5 minutes from Paradeplatz/Bahnhofstrasse, the opera house, major museums, and the lake. Set on a boat-landing square, it stands a block from the river at the corner of Limmatquai. The hotel is one of the best in its price range with a pleasantly personal atmosphere. The bedrooms are newly furnished, often in bright florals, and the bathrooms are of medium size.

Schifflände 30, CH-8001 Zurich. © 044/266-95-95. Fax 044/266-95-66. www.helmhaus.ch. 24 units. 240F–342F ($197–$280) double. Rates include buffet breakfast. AE, DC, MC, V. Parking 27F ($22). Tram: 4 from the Hauptbahnhof, or shuttle-bus service between the hotel and the airport. **Amenities:** Business center; laundry service/dry cleaning. *In room:* A/C, dataport, minibar, hair dryer, iron.

Hotel Opera   This cozy choice, next to the Opera House, may be short on facilities, but it's a favorite among many business travelers seeking a central location. Try for one of the corner rooms or an accommodation on the fourth or fifth floor. The Opera boasts a large, carpeted lobby, with an assortment of armchairs, where you can purchase beer and soft drinks.

Dufourstrasse 5, CH-8008 Zurich. © 044/258-99-99. Fax 044/258-99-00. www.operahotel.ch. 62 units. 330F–420F ($271–$344) double. Rates include buffet breakfast. AE, DC, MC, V. Parking 28F ($23) nearby. Tram: 4. **Amenities:** Restaurant; bar; limited room service; laundry service/dry cleaning. *In room:* A/C, TV, dataport, minibar, hair dryer, safe.

Lady's First ⚘ *Finds*   The first hotel of its type in Switzerland, this is a boutique hotel with its top two floors catering just to women. It is installed in an elegant town house from the 1880s, which was renovated by Pia Schmid, a well-known architect. The house lies close to the core of town and Lake Zurich. The top floors also embrace a first-class spa area where sauna, massage, and cosmetic treatments are offered to women as well as a rooftop terrace and recreation area. Bedrooms come in various shapes and sizes, and each is furnished in a sleekly modern and tasteful way with well-maintained bathrooms with tub or shower. The best accommodations open onto a small balcony with a view of the lake. Along with its chic furnishings, rooms have parquet floors and high ceilings. Grace notes include a fireplace in the lounge and a summer rose garden.

Mainaustrasse 24, CH-8008 Zurich. © 044/380-80-10. Fax 044/380-80-20. www.ladysfirst.ch. 28 units. 245F–280F ($201–$230) double; 365F ($299) suite. Rates include breakfast. AE, DC, MC, V. Tram: 2 or 4. **Amenities:** Spa; sauna; steam room; massage. *In room:* TV, dataport.

INEXPENSIVE

Hotel Goldenes Schwert   The "Golden Sword" caters to a clientele that's almost exclusively out, proud, and eager to patronize some of the many nightlife options that ring it within this bustling neighborhood of Zurich's historic Altstadt. Set behind a simple white stucco facade within a century-old building, it maintains a pair of gay nightclubs (separately recommended—see "Zurich After Dark," later in this chapter) on its lower floors, and comfortable bedrooms on floors 4, 5, and 6, each accessible by elevator from the street level. Each of the rooms is individually decorated and outfitted in styles that range from the artfully minimalist to several that are a bit more cluttered, in a cozy way, with wooden furniture and original paintings.

Marktgasse 14, CH-8001 Zurich. ✆ **044/250-70-80.** Fax 044/250-70-89. www.gayhotel.ch. 22 units. 155F–235F ($127–$193) double; 250F–378F ($205–$310) suite. AE, DC, MC, V. Tram: 4 or 15. **Amenities:** Limited room service; laundry/dry cleaning. *In room:* A/C, TV, dataport.

Hotel Limmatblick   This hotel, owned by the Leonhard family, is located in the Old Town, a 2-minute walk from the main railroad station. The hotel is well maintained, but the rooms are small. They contain twin beds and are equipped with rather cramped bathrooms with shower. In contrast to the bedrooms, the hotel's inviting restaurant, Arvenstube, is cozy and traditional, like something you'd find in the Tyrol. In summer there's a terrace overlooking the water. In addition, a coffee shop, Wyss-Müllirädli, serves such Zurich specialties as bratwurst with onions and rösti (Swiss hash browns).

Limmatquai 136, CH-8001 Zurich. ✆ **044/254-60-00.** Fax 044/254-60-10. www.limmatblick.ch. 16 units. 200F–230F ($164–$189) double. Rates include continental breakfast. AE, DC, MC, V. Closed Dec 15–Jan 6. Tram: 4 or 15. **Amenities:** Restaurant; coffee shop; bar; room service; laundry. *In room:* TV, dataport, minibar, hair dryer, safe.

4 Where to Dine

Zurich restaurants feature a selection of both international and Swiss specialties. The local favorite is *rösti* (potatoes grated and fried). You should also try *Züri-Gschnätzlets* (shredded veal cooked with mushrooms in a cream sauce laced with white wine) and *Kutteln nach Zürcherart* (tripe with mushrooms, white wine, and caraway seed). Another classic dish is *Leberspiesschen* (liver cubes skewered with bacon and sage and served with potatoes and beans).

Among local wines, the white Riesling Sylvaner is outstanding and great with fish. The light Clevner wines, always chilled, are made from blue Burgundy grapes that grow around the lake. You should be able to order wine by the glass, even in first-class restaurants.

ON THE LEFT BANK
VERY EXPENSIVE
Sukhothai ✦✦ THAI   With a deliberately simple interior graced with photographs of the royal family of Thailand and a discreet scattering of Thai objets d'art, this restaurant is the premier Thai restaurant in Switzerland. Food is presented in varying degrees of spiciness, and may include lemon-grass soup studded with chicken, a papaya-based Thai salad, brochettes of chicken or shrimp, a selection of rice-based dishes, and a varied array of exotic fish flown in from the waters of East Asia and prepared according to traditional Thai recipes. The chef does an admirable job with all of these dishes, and the flavors are bracing and aromatic, a marvelous change of pace from the typical Swiss cuisine. In the words of one habitué, this restaurant has awakened the sleepy taste buds of Zurichers.

Erlachstrasse 46. ✆ **044/462-66-22.** www.sukhothai.ch. Reservations recommended. Main courses 62F–95F ($51–$78); menu surprise 160F ($131). AE, MC, V. Tues–Fri 11am–2:30pm; Tues–Sat 5:30–11pm. Closed July 12–Aug 10. Tram: 9 or 14.

EXPENSIVE
Cantinetta Antinori ✦ ITALIAN   The Antinori marchesi launched the vineyards that became a wine empire some 26 generations ago. Their first wine bar (still going)

was installed in a 15th-century *palazzo* in Florence. Today this Zurich branch brings their high-quality ingredients, often from Antinori farms, as well as their aromatic wines to the city on the Limmat. The waiters speak all known languages (well, almost) and are most helpful in guiding you through the delectable menu. Over the bar a sign reads TARTUFFO, ANCORA, TARTUFF, SOLO TARTUFFO, meaning "Truffles, more truffles, and only truffles." This seems to be a mantra that the chefs live by, as evoked by their superb filets of veal with a generous portion of white truffles. Some of the specialties seemed to have arrived intact from their Florentine branch, including sausages with white haricot beans and thick oven-roasted Chiana beef. Top off your meal with an espresso macchiato, accompanied by a small dish of Cantuccini (biscuits with almonds).

Augustinergasse 25. (℗ **044/211-72-10.** Reservations recommended. Main courses 40F–65F ($33–$53). AE, DC, MC, V. Daily 11am–11pm. Tram: 6, 7, or 11.

Piccoli Accademia *⟨R⟩⟨R⟩* ITALIAN   The finest and most elegant Italian restaurant in Zurich, Piccoli Accademia is much appreciated at lunchtime by bankers and businesspeople, who use it to entertain their clients. In an Art Deco setting scattered with a collection of oil paintings, a uniformed staff politely serves Italian regional dishes, ranging from Venetian to Neapolitan. Specialties include several succulent versions of pasta, risotto with mushrooms, and veal liver *alla Veneziana.* Daily specialties, when in season, may include various game dishes, including pheasant, venison, wild boar, and partridge. You are almost never disappointed with the offerings here. It may not be imaginative cuisine, but it's certainly good.

Rotwandstrasse 48. (℗ **044/241-42-02.** Reservations recommended, especially in summer. Main courses 43F–66F ($35–$54). AE, DC, MC, V. Mon–Fri noon–2pm; Mon–Sat 6pm–midnight. Tram: 2, 3, 9, 10, or 14.

Veltliner Keller *⟨R⟩* SWISS/ITALIAN/FRENCH   If endurance and longevity are hallmarks of a good restaurant, this dining room would emerge near the top. Veltliner Keller has been a restaurant since 1551; before that it was a wine cellar. Located next to St. Peter's Church in Old Town, it has an ancient interior of carved mountain pine wood called arve (grown only in Switzerland). The chef prepares familiar Swiss specialties, and does so exceedingly well, including the classic chopped-veal dish of Zurich. Several Italian dishes are also featured, including veal piccata and *osso buco.* A lot of the seafood is grilled or poached, including salmon. Ingredients change with the season, but you can always count on the house's signature dish, a Veltliner pot—baked macaroni with meat and beef liver cooked in a casserole.

Schlüsselgasse 8. (℗ **044/225-40-40.** Reservations recommended. Main courses 42F–50F ($34–$41). AE, DC, MC, V. Mon–Fri 11:30am–2pm and 6:30–9:30pm. Closed July 18–Aug 15. Tram: 2, 9, 11, or 13.

Widder Restaurant & Türmstübli *⟨R⟩* INTERNATIONAL   When this restaurant opened in the mid-1990s, many of its clients came as an excuse to view the iconoclastic architecture of the hotel that contained it (see "Where to Stay," earlier in this chapter). But since then, these twin dining rooms have taken on a life of their own, and are now sought out as independent eateries in their own right. Although the Widder Restaurant is outfitted in a rustic, folksy style, and the Türmstübli is angular, minimalist, and devoid of most alpine reminders, the same menu is served in both. Look for a clientele from Zurich's financial community, along with a scattering of wealthy bohemians. Menu items include well-prepared versions of chicken mousse served in crepe-style pastry with applesauce; a sumptuous breast of Barbary duckling in an orange-flavored crust served with a pumpkin-and-lettuce-based piccata sauce and

Where to Dine in Zurich

galettes of sweet corn; a delectable scampi with morel-stuffed ravioli in a pepper-flavored butter sauce; and a particularly delicious gratin of salmon-trout with cucumber sauce, dill weed, and new potatoes.

In the Widder Hotel, Rennweg 7. ⓒ 044/224-25-26. www.widderhotel.ch. Reservations recommended. Main courses 30F–55F ($25–$45). AE, DC, MC, V. Daily 11:30am–2pm and 6:30–11pm. Tram: 6, 7, 11, or 13.

MODERATE

Brasserie Lipp FRENCH/SWISS   Everything about this place emulates the decor and seating configuration of Lipp, one of Paris's most famous Art Nouveau brasseries. So authentic is the duplication, in fact, that the Zurich version paid a royalty to the original in Paris for the right to use the name and a re-creation of its decor. The venue is loud, fast paced, and, during the noon rush, frenzied as waiters squeeze between narrowly spaced tables bearing trays of *choucroute* (sauerkraut); platters of fresh fish such as sole meunière, smoked salmon, and filets of herring in cream sauce; terrines; many kinds of cold salad; and such daily specials as Moroccan couscous. Don't expect to linger for hours at a table. Nonetheless, the French-inspired ambience is a refreshing change from the Teutonic overtones of many of this restaurant's competitors. The bar, the Jules Verne, is recommended under "Zurich After Dark," later in this chapter.

Uraniastrasse 9. ⓒ 044/888-66-66. Reservations recommended, especially Fri–Sat. Main courses 30F–50F ($25–$41). AE, DC, MC, V. Mon–Sat 11:30am–11pm (till 1am Fri–Sat). Tram: 6, 7, 11, or 13.

INEXPENSIVE

Bierhalle Kropf ⑥ (Kids) SWISS/BAVARIAN/AUSTRIAN   Everyone in Zurich goes to "Der Kropf" for its old-fashioned ambience and generous portions at reasonable prices. The restaurant is in one of the oldest burgher houses in town, a few steps from Paradeplatz. Its dining room has stained-glass windows, polished paneling, chandeliers, and plaster columns. On the walls hang stag horns and painted hunting scenes. You get authentic and well-prepared dishes here. Almost no one, including visiting personalities, local political figures, or finicky children, leaves disappointed. Bring along a healthy appetite. Specialties include chopped veal with rösti, stewed meats, pork shank, and *pot-au-feu* Zurich-style. For dessert, we recommend *Palatschinken* (a chocolate crepe) or *Apfelstrudel* (apple strudel).

In Gassen 16. ⓒ 044/221-18-05. Reservations recommended. Main courses 15F–46F ($12–$38). AE, MC, V. Mon–Sat 11:30am–11:30pm. Closed Easter, Dec 25, and Aug 1. Tram: 2, 8, 9, or 11.

Hiltl VEGETARIAN/INDIAN   Founded in 1898 but completely redecorated in 1993, this bright, inviting place is Zurich's leading vegetarian restaurant. Its main attraction is a large salad bar, containing more than 40 different types of freshly prepared vegetables. House creations include vegetable paella, mushrooms Stroganoff, and curry colonial. There's a vast choice of fruit juices, teas, draft beer, and wines priced by the glass. The restaurant is also known for its vegetarian Indian specialties, and after 6pm it features an Indian buffet.

Sihlstrasse 28. ⓒ 044/227-70-00. Reservations recommended. Main courses 19F–36F ($16–$30); Indian buffet 40F–65F ($33–$53). AE, MC, V. Mon–Sat 7am–11pm; Sun 11am–11pm. Tram: 6, 7, 11, or 13.

Restaurant Kaufleuten (Finds) INTERNATIONAL   Despite its location in the heart of one of Europe's most gilt-edged neighborhoods, a few steps from the Bahnhofstrasse, there's something artfully disheveled and happy-go-lucky about this restaurant. You'll find a deliberately mismatched collection of tables and chairs. The menu is just as eclectic, with offerings derived from virtually everywhere. These include favorites from Thailand (including *tom kha kai,* made of chicken, coconut, and fiery spices); Japan (sushi and miso soup); and Austria (Wiener schnitzel). Also available are tender steaks and several kinds of saltwater and freshwater fish, including salmon, sole, and sea bass. The setting is pleasant, and the place is a fine cost-conscious alternative to more-formal spots nearby. The site contains a worn, heavily trafficked bar area that's open daily from 9am till whenever the restaurant closes, and a nightclub that's separately recommended in "Zurich After Dark," later in this chapter.

Pelikanstrasse 18. (€ 044/225-33-33. Reservations recommended. Main courses 22F–47F ($18–$39). AE, DC, MC, V. Mon–Fri 11:30am–2pm; daily 7pm–2am (till 3am Fri–Sat). Tram: 6, 7, 11, or 13.

Restaurant Reithalle INTERNATIONAL   One of Zurich's most genuinely unpretentious restaurants occupies the battered premises of what was originally built as a stable and horseback-riding rink. Cost-conscious locals frequent the Reithalle, which is set on a small island in downtown Zurich, bordered by the Schanzengraben Creek and the Seil Canal. It's at its most fun in midsummer when picnic tables are set up on the quiet, cobblestone inner courtyard, which is mobbed every day at lunch and dinner. The rest of the year, tables are moved into the severe-looking, heavily timbered interior that once sheltered horses and riding equipment from the city and weather outside. Menu items are hearty and generous and include beef curry; peppered paillard of veal; Iranian-style lamb stew; grilled squid with lemon sauce; and several kinds of pastas and salads. Saturday nights from 11pm till around 3am, the interior of this place becomes a disco, charging an entrance price of 12F ($9.85) per person. (Patrons of the restaurant enter free.)

In the Theaterhaus Gessnerallee, Gessnerallee 8. (€ 044/212-07-66. Reservations not necessary. Main courses 11F–32F ($9–$26) lunch, 20F–36F ($16–$30) dinner. AE, DC, MC, V. Mon–Fri 11am–midnight; Sat–Sun 6pm–midnight. Tram: 3.

Zeughauskeller *☞* SWISS   This mammoth restaurant, dating from 1487, was once an arsenal; its vast dining room now seats 200. Large wooden chandeliers hang from cast-iron chains, and the walls are decorated with medieval halberds and illustrations of ancient Zurich noblemen. Generous portions of traditional and tasty Swiss dishes are served with steins of local beer. Owners Kurt Andreae and Willy Hammer say that patrons consume some 30 tons of potato salad a year. Hurlimann draft beer is poured from 1,000-liter barrels. Specialties, and excellent ones at that, include calves' liver, Wiener schnitzel, and regional sausages, such as *saucisson* of Neuchâtel. For 77F ($63), you can order a meter-long sausage—enough to feed four hungry people. Service is quick and efficient.

Bahnhofstrasse 28a (near Paradeplatz). (€ 044/211-26-90. www.zeughauskeller.ch. Reservations recommended. Main courses 13F–44F ($11–$36). AE, MC, V. Daily 11:30am–11pm. Tram: 2, 6, 7, 8, 9, 11, or 13.

ON THE RIGHT BANK
VERY EXPENSIVE
Haus Zum Rüden *☞☞* SWISS/FRENCH   The Gothic room in this historic guild house dating from 1295 contains one of the best restaurants in the city. It's especially popular with foreign visitors, even though they often get a somewhat stuffy greeting from the staff. The spacious yet intimate dining room has a hardwood ceiling and stone walls decorated with medieval halberds and stag horns. The chef specializes in *cuisine du marché* (market-fresh cuisine). Foie gras sautéed with a salad makes a stunning opening, followed by salmon prepared in the style of Carcassonne or aromatic roast Scottish lamb delectably flavored with mustard grains.

Limmatquai 42. ✆ **044/261-95-66.** Reservations required. Main courses 53F–68F ($43–$56); fixed-price lunch 55F ($45). AE, DC, MC, V. Mon–Fri noon–2pm and 6:30–9:30pm. Tram: 4 or 15.

Jacky's Stapferstube ☆☆ SWISS   In a manor house that dates back some 200 years, this restaurant near the university is famous throughout the city for its beef and veal dishes. Manager Jacky Donatz is well known among a crowd of fashionable regular clients. In a typically Swiss dining room with white walls, oil paintings, and darkened beams, you can enjoy perfectly prepared veal cutlets, veal shanks, boiled beef, and a wide array of tender steaks. Meat is priced according to its weight, but the staff can advise you on sizes and cuts. Many diners begin with a miniplatter of stuffed mushrooms. Other dishes include pasta and lobster salad, and there's a well-chosen wine list.

Culmannstrasse 45. ✆ **044/361-37-48.** Reservations required. Main courses 37F–100F ($30–$82). AE, DC, MC, V. Tues–Sat 11:30am–3pm and 6–10pm. Closed mid-July to mid-Aug. Tram: 9 or 10.

EXPENSIVE

Blue Monkey THAI   It may seem incongruous to find a Thai restaurant, replete with Thai paintings and sculptures, and a staff that seems to have been trained in Bangkok, within this medieval-looking building in the center of historic Zurich. But once you get there, you may appreciate its cultural ironies, and even be grateful for a break from too constant a diet of Teutonic food. The street-level venue, known as the Bistro, has tables that are a bit more crowded together, and prices that are a bit lower, than the setting upstairs (the restaurant), where there's a bit more privacy (theoretically at least), better service, and greater attention to detail. Menu items on either level include four different kinds of curry (red, brown, green, and yellow) to accompany, among others, pork, chicken, tofu, or fish; as well as such Thai staples as lemon-grass soup; fish (red snapper, tuna, sea bass, and sole) with coconut sauce or lemon sauce; green papaya salad; and spring rolls. Fried chicken with chili sauce is very pleasant, and vegetarians appreciate the wide array of dishes without meat or fish.

Stüssihofstatt 3. ✆ **044/261-76-18.** Reservations recommended. Main courses in street-level bistro 26F–27F ($21–$22); main courses upstairs in restaurant 31F–47F ($25–$39). AE, DC, MC, V. Mon–Fri 11am–2pm; daily 6–11:30pm. Tram: 4 or 15.

Kronenhalle ☆ SWISS/FRENCH   This is one of Zurich's most famous restaurants, and it also serves some of the best cuisine. This celebrity favorite has attracted such greats as Thomas Mann, James Joyce, Joan Miró, Georges Braque, Pablo Picasso, Richard Strauss, and Igor Stravinsky. More recent guests have included Plácido Domingo, Catherine Deneuve, and Yves Saint-Laurent.

The restaurant is in a five-story, gray Biedermeier building with gold crowns above the six windows on the first floor. Traditional Swiss cuisine and international dishes are served in the two dining rooms. The decor includes original paintings by Klee, Chagall, Matisse, Miró, Kandinsky, Braque, Bonnard, and Picasso. Regional specialties are served on a trolley and include smoked pork with lentils and *bollito misto* (boiled beef, chicken, sausage, and tongue). For a main dish, try shredded calves' liver with rösti or filet of sole baked with olives and tomatoes. You may also enjoy *bündnerfleisch*—thinly sliced, smoked, dried beef. This is one of the most outstanding and consistently reliable restaurants in Zurich. In the Kronenhalle Bar the specialty is the Ladykiller.

Rämistrasse 4. ✆ **044/251-66-69.** Reservations required. Main courses 34F–55F ($28–$45). AE, DC, MC, V. Daily noon–midnight. Closed Dec 24. Tram: 2, 4, 5, 9, 11, or 15.

Lasalle 𝕬 INTERNATIONAL   One of the most hip and sought-after restaurants in Zurich today is set within a severe-looking factory built during the 19th century to manufacture boats and lake cruisers. Today it's the centerpiece of an urban renewal known as Zuri-West, wherein affluent hipsters congregate in ways you might have expected in New York's SoHo or TriBeCa. A team of architects labored to maintain the original battered shell of the redbrick factory. Their avant-garde solution involved enclosing the restaurant within an enormous but delicate-looking high-tech box of steel beams and plexiglass, all of it suspended from the building's ceiling and redbrick walls. Centered within the area's core is a massive blown-glass (Murano) chandelier whose delicacy is in ironic contrast to the industrial muscle that otherwise surrounds you on all sides. Menu items seem deceptively simple when listed on the stark white menu, and except for an occasional gaffe, are incredibly flavor-filled and artful upon delivery. Examples include Indian-style entrecôte of lamb with raita; grilled filet of salmon with artichokes, tomatoes, and herbs; and a vegetarian version of tortilla with guacamole and sour cream. Either of these might be accompanied with an all-vegetarian gratin of celeriac and potatoes.

Schiffbaustrasse 4. ℂ **044/258-70-71.** Reservations necessary. Main courses 31F–48F ($25–$39). AE, DC, MC, V. Mon–Fri 11:30am–10:45pm; Sat–Sun 5:30–10:45pm. Tram: 4 or 13.

Restaurant Conti 𝕬 ITALIAN   Many people eat dinner here, see a show, and then return for dessert and coffee. The menu is based on seasonal specialties. Try a dish of homemade pasta, followed by either scaloppine *al limone* or entrecôte Robespierre. The menu includes freshwater and ocean fish, as well as game dishes such as pheasant. You can always count on a warm welcome and good food at this crowded, cheerful spot. The cuisine is fine-tuned and served in abundant portions.

Helmstrasse 41. ℂ **044/745-86-86.** www.conti.ch. Reservations required. Main courses 33F–55F ($27–$45); fixed-price lunch 36F ($30). AE, DC, MC, V. Mon–Fri 11:30am–2:30pm; Mon–Sat 6pm–midnight. Closed 1 month during July–Aug (dates vary). Tram: 2 or 4.

Rosaly's 𝕬 SWISS/INTERNATIONAL   Set about a block from the Bellevueplatz and the clamor of its tram junctions, this restaurant occupies what looks like a mountain chalet that's incongruously perched on a narrow alleyway amid the midtown urban sprawl. There's a bar on the premises—a half-moon-shaped affair whose clients spill out into the dining room as the evening gets late—but the real appeal here is the reasonably priced, well-prepared food. Part of its allure lies in the hints of California you may detect in the cuisine and the relaxed charm of the staff. (The owner named the restaurant after one he once visited in San Francisco.) The chef here is particularly proud of his butter-braised calves' liver, braised strips of veal prepared "Zurich-style" in cream sauce, and a wide range of salad, vegetarian, and fish dishes. A particularly well-received side dish is "Rosaly's rice," prepared with herbs and cheese. During clement weather, consider dining at one of the geranium-flanked tables lined up along the alleyway outside.

Freieckgasse 7. ℂ **044/261-44-30.** Reservations recommended. Main courses 18F–40F ($15–$33). AE, MC, V. Daily noon–2pm and 6–10pm (till 11pm Thurs–Sat). Bar stays open to between midnight and 2am, depending on business. Tram: 2, 4, 7, 9, 11, or 13.

Zunfthaus zur Zimmerleuten 𝕬 SWISS   With foundations dating from 1336, when it was originally the carpenters' guildhall, the building you see today is from 1708, with few changes made since then. An architectural showpiece of Zurich, it now functions as one of the city's most enduring restaurants. A flight of baroque stairs leads from the street level to the elegant dining room, which is decorated with rows of leaded-glass windows and an impressive collection of hunting trophies. Menu items include "Lake Zurich fish soup," served with a garlic rouille; morel toasts; freshwater bouillabaisse with local catch; filet of pike-perch poached in Savoy cabbage; and a local specialty, *ratsherrentopf*, composed of three different filets with rösti and butter sauce. The reward for the kitchen's vigilance is a loyal clientele of discerning palates, who enjoy the full-bodied dishes.

Limmatquai 40. © **044/252-08-34.** Reservations recommended. Main courses 27F–53F ($22–$43). AE, DC, MC, V. Mon–Sat 11:30am–2pm and 6–11pm. Closed mid-July to mid-Aug. Tram: 4 or 15.

MODERATE
Fischstube Zürichhorn *Kids* SWISS   Ideal on a summer evening, this seafood restaurant with outdoor tables is built on pilings over the lake. The scenery, service, and cuisine make it a worthy choice if the weather is balmy. We recommend the lake trout, filet of Dover sole Champs-Elysées, grilled lobster with curry butter, and lake fish sautéed in butter and served with market-fresh vegetables. The cuisine here has a sprightly, original taste, flavored with a dash of this or a dab of that. The chefs rely on the sound principles of simplicity and accurate timing in all their dishes, and the servings are generous. Kids delight at sitting outside overlooking the lake and even like the vegetables cooked here since they're so fresh and delectably cooked.

Bellerivestrasse 160. © **044/422-25-20.** Reservations required. Main courses 28F–45F ($23–$37); fixed-price lunch 39F ($32). AE, MC, V. Daily 9:30am–11pm. Closed Sept 26–Easter. Tram: 2 or 4.

Mère Catherine PROVENÇAL/FRENCH   This small courtyard restaurant nestled among the back streets of Old Town offers quiet cafe tables, ivy, and, at times, a lot of sun. Anybody who knows backstreet Paris or a small town in France will feel at home here. Unpretentious French food, especially Provençal bistro fare, is served here. Fresh sea fish is a feature, but the specials change every day. You can always find various meatless platters on the menu. *Salade paysanne* with a Roquefort sauce is the most popular appetizer, and you can usually order snails *en brioche* or, for something more exotic, terrine of quail. The dishes are painstakingly prepared and usually get diners salivating in no time flat. You may want to arrive before your reservations to have an aperitif at the Bar Philosophe, the cozy marble bar next to the restaurant.

Nägelihof 3. © **044/250-59-40.** Reservations required. Main courses 24F–38F ($20–$31); menu surprise 17F–24F ($14–$20) lunch Mon–Fri only. AE, DC, MC, V. Daily 11:30am–2:30pm and 6–11:30pm. Tram: 4 or 15.

INEXPENSIVE
Blockhus *Value* SWISS/FRENCH   On the richly paneled street level of a wooden house more than 2 centuries old, this restaurant emulates the glamour and flair of a French bistro. You'll get a warm welcome and be offered well-prepared dishes such as steak au poivre, rack of lamb with rosemary and a touch of garlic, mussels in white wine and herb sauce, and what might be the widest assortment of French cheeses in Zurich. The food is rustic yet urbane, and flavors are well matched. No dish is ever smothered in sauces but is prepared so that its true flavor asserts itself.

Schifflande 4. © **044/252-14-53.** Reservations recommended. Main courses 20F–37F ($16–$30); fixed-price lunch 28F ($23). AE, MC, V. Mon–Sat 11:30am–2pm and 6pm–midnight. Tram: 2, 4, 8, or 11.

Crazy Cow *Finds* SWISS   This is a hipster's version of an old-fashioned Swiss inn, with a strong sense of satire and a menu that makes virtually everyone laugh. It's one of the most visible places in Zurich where you can see the Swiss poking fun at their own sense of folksy isolationism, as portrayed in the decor with replicas of drug-trip-ping cows and crazed versions of Heidi looking for a goatherd. Even if your knowl-edge of German is rudimentary, spend some time deciphering the Swiss dialect in which the menu is printed, since even the Swiss find it irreverently amusing. (Grilled duck breast with olive-lemon sauce is listed as Äntäpüppi; gratin of shredded potatoes with vegetables and cream sauce is listed as Röschti mit G'mües.) The alpine version of macaroni comes with onions and apple wedges, and drinks of choice include all-Swiss versions of hard cider, beer, or wine.

Bahhofstrasse 4. © 044/728-95-95. Reservations recommended. Main courses 15F–39F ($12–$32). AE, DC, MC, V. Daily 11am–11:30pm. Tram: 6, 7, 10, or 15.

Le Dézaley *Finds* VAUDOIS   Named after a remote corner of the Vaud region of French-speaking Switzerland, this restaurant celebrates the food and traditions of the countryside north of Lake Geneva. Many of the regular clients speak French as they dine on an array of fondues (cheese, chinoise, and bourguignonne) or other dishes such as minced liver, veal kidneys with rösti, pork sausages flavored with leeks, and shredded veal Zurich-style. The chefs are more obsessed with flavor than novelty, and they certainly succeed. Many wines from the Dézaley region, some rather rare, are offered. The large, wood-paneled dining room is set in a pair of interconnected houses originally built during the late 13th century. In summer you can dine in a little gar-den out back. The restaurant is located close to the Grossmünster church.

Römergasse 7-9. © 044/251-61-29. Reservations recommended. Main courses 22F–27F ($18–$22); fondues 30F–46F ($25–$38). AE, DC, MC, V. Mon–Sat 11:30am–2pm and 6pm–midnight. Tram: 4 or 15.

Restaurant Movie AMERICAN/INTERNATIONAL   This is one of the most con-sistently popular theme restaurants in Zurich. Hip, artful, and fun, and positioned adja-cent to one of the city's biggest movie theater complexes, it boasts a campy faux-Hollywood decor that includes a gilded version of the Statue of Liberty, industrial-style ventilation tubes, and the kind of lighting fixtures you'd expect on the original sound stage of *Gone With the Wind.* Even the place mats are emblazoned with publicity stills from about-to-be-screened American movies, with menus printed on round alu-minum canisters that traditionally hold a reel of celluloid. Many of the dishes are named after movies and actors. All of this would be hopelessly corny if the food weren't gen-uinely well prepared and the place packed, especially during the dinner and after-dinner bar hour. Menus include pastas, sandwiches, salads, quesadillas, fajitas, and grills. Don't overlook the bar area at this place as a California-inspired (and very popular) nightlife option. Outfitted with a black-and-gold ancient Egyptian theme, it has tables spilling out onto the Beattenplatz and dance music that actually encourages you to rock 'n' roll.

Bahnhofquai 7, at Beattenplatz. © 044/211-66-77. Reservations not necessary. Main courses 14F–28F ($11–$23). AE, MC, V. Daily 11:30am–midnight. Tram: 6 or 10.

SOUTH OF THE CENTER

Peter's Kunststuben *Finds* CONTINENTAL   The Zagat European edition pro-claims this the best restaurant in Europe. We might not go that far but we'd cite it as the best restaurant in Switzerland. Since it opened in the early 1980s, this restaurant has attracted most of the well-heeled gastronomes in Zurich, as well as such notables as the emperor of Japan and the Swiss president. Relentlessly elegant, but with a staff that's more hip and alert than you may expect, it lies 10km (6 miles) south of Zurich in the hamlet of Küsnacht, near Rapperswil, within a house whose date of construc-tion (1873) is marked above a wood-burning stove in the dining room.

Most of the year, the restaurant accommodates only 55 diners, but in summer an outdoor terrace ringed with flowering shrubs and flowers adds another 20 places. Amid a collection of upscale accoutrements and well-rehearsed service rituals, you can enjoy such inventive dishes as a tartare of beef and caviar with a potato galette, roasted duck with honey-lemon sauce, lobster with a purée of celery, lobster-studded potato salad with a leek-based cream sauce, stuffed squid with a confit of fennel, and young hen stuffed with shrimp. Dessert may include a gratin of wild strawberries with can-nelloni stuffed with almond paste. You'll find almost anything you order irresistible.

Seestrasse 160, Küsnacht. ⓒ 044/910-07-15. Reservations required. Main courses 58F–85F ($48–$70); fixed-price 6-course menu 195F ($160). AE, DC, MC, V. Tues–Sat noon–2pm and 7pm–midnight. Closed 2 weeks in Feb and 2 weeks Aug–Sept. Take a taxi or the train from Zurich's Hauptbahnhof to Küsnacht, then walk for 5 min.

EAST OF THE CENTER

Blu INTERNATIONAL   This is an offbeat choice. The site of this restaurant and shopping complex originated in the late 1800s, when a Swiss entrepreneur assembled a flotilla of barges to take in laundry, using the waters of Lake Zurich to flush the dirt out of clothes and bedding. Later, the boats were permanently moored to the lakeside, and an enormous clothes-washing complex was built beside the lake, centered around a redbrick smokestack that still remains in place today, a 15-minute drive from the center of town. In the 1990s a team of trend-conscious architects transformed the site into a complex of boutiques, offices, and condominiums, one of the highlights of which is this artfully minimalist restaurant that's favored by the young, the arts-con-scious, and the upwardly mobile. It's at its most relaxing in summer, when tables are lined up beside a marina that's loaded with tall-masted sailboats. People travel here from far away in any season to experience the unusual design of the starkly minimal-ist duplex-style dining room. Menu items are deeply entrenched in the seasons and include, among others, gnocchi with grilled shrimp and cherry tomatoes; cutlet of beef (Milan-style); a symphony of fish—sea wolf, shrimp, and mussels—served with a lemon-flavored wine sauce; slow-braised rack of lamb with herbs; several prepara-tions of fresh fish; meal-size salads; and a deliberately undercooked version of bitter-sweet chocolate cake.

Seestrasse 4-7. ⓒ 044/488-65-65. Reservations recommended for dinner. Main courses 25F–47F ($21–$39). AE, DC, MC, V. Sun–Fri 11:30am–2pm; daily 4:30–11pm. Bus: 160 or 165.

WEST OF THE CENTER

Caduff's Wine Loft ⭐ *Finds* CONTINENTAL   Set within a hilly and verdant res-idential neighborhood 3km (2 miles) west of Zurich's center, this hip and stylish restaurant occupies what was originally, from around 1900, an industrial warehouse. Today, much renovated and much fussed over by a team of designers and decorators, it's a minimalist-chic bastion of Pan-European charm, with sleek furniture, sophisti-cated lighting, a strategically placed potted cactus or two, and one of the most appeal-ing wine cellars in Zurich. Don't expect much of a view, since the windows look out on the surrounding neighborhood. Instead, you'll be beguiled and seduced by a sea-sonally changing menu that reflects very fresh ingredients. The best examples include platters of shrimp and scallops drizzled with saffron sauce and served with fresh asparagus; a mixed grill that includes portions of calves' liver, veal, beef, and chicken; house-made ravioli stuffed with a mixture of tomatoes and basil; medallions of veal served with saffron-flavored risotto and rosemary; turbot in champagne sauce; and filets of venison with port wine sauce and ricotta-flavored gnocchi. The cellar—where the caches of wine are stored—contain two especially atmospheric dining tables, which are sometimes sought after by groups of friends or families planning reunions.

Kanzleistrasse 126, Unit 4. © **044/240-22-55**. Reservations recommended. Main courses 20F–52F ($16–$43); fixed-price 3-course lunch 52F ($43); fixed-price dinner 95F ($78) for 4 courses and 110F ($90) for 5 courses. AE, DC, MC, V. Mon–Fri 11:30am–2pm and 5pm–midnight; Sat 4pm–midnight. Bus: 32. Tram: 2, 3, or 8.

Iroquois INTERNATIONAL   The Swiss have never really gone ga-ga over American-style bars and grills, but of the several that exist within Zurich, this is the busiest and most popular. Always crowded and sometimes mobbed, it's a neighborhood tavern whose rough edges and spilled beer add to its image as a rough-and-ready burger-and-fajitas joint that just happens to have a distinctive Swiss accent. Come here for sports TV and the possibility of striking up a neighborhood friendship. The house cocktail is an Iroquois, made with vodka, Galliano, maracuja (star fruit), and orange juice. If you come with a group that tends to get the munchies, consider a Surfer's Platter prepared for multiple diners at a time, that mixes chicken wings, tortilla chips, quesadillas, and guacamole. Other food choices include ostrich-meat fajitas, burritos, chicken chili burgers, and turkey tacos. Don't expect grandeur, as virtually everything and everyone here is aggressively unpretentious.

Seefeldstrasse 120. © **044/383-70-77**. Reservations not necessary. Main courses 16F–32F ($13–$26). AE, MC, V. Daily 11am–2pm and 6–10pm. Bar open daily 5pm–midnight. Tram: 2 or 4.

NORTH OF THE CENTER

Giesserei Oerlikon *Finds* INTERNATIONAL   It's fun and funky. Until 2000, the battered-looking building containing this place had lain empty, a former foundry whose grimy walls had once reverberated with the sound of hammers and heavy machinery. Today, despite a setting that might remind you of a prison camp in Siberia, it's a sought-after address for Zurich's trendsetters, who seek it out as a change from a usual diet of manicured efficiency and predictable Swiss comforts. Don't be dismayed by the concrete and cinder-block severity of the setting. (Some local wits—who invariably have a good time here—compare it to dining in the Gulag.) A tongue-in-cheek team of decorators enhanced the Sputnik-era angularity with a stainless-steel bar, artful lighting, and occasional touches of whimsy. The menu, which will be recited in English or German by the waitstaff, changes daily, and will usually include a choice of only three starters and three main courses. On the evening of our visit, well-prepared menu choices included grilled eggplant with air-dried beef and tabbouleh; fresh cantaloupe with Serrano ham; a "summer salad" with shrimp; a terrine of chanterelle mushrooms; and a ragout of swordfish.

Birchstrasse 108, in Oerlikon. © **044/311-70-44**. Reservations recommended. Main courses 37F–43F ($30–$35). AE, MC, V. No credit cards. Mon–Fri noon–2pm; Mon–Sat 6–11pm. Tram: 11.

CAFES

Café/Bar Odéon   This legendary 1912 bohemian landmark is a popular singles and gay hangout in the evening. Lenin came here during World War I to make such pronouncements as "The neutrality of Switzerland is a bourgeois fraud and means submission to the imperialist war." Thornton Wilder also sloshed down a few here, as did Mussolini and Mata Hari. The intimate, Art Nouveau cafe has banquettes and cubbyholes. It also sports a curved bar and many sidewalk tables.

Limmatquai 2. © **044/251-16-50**. Light meals 8.50F–26F ($6.95–$21); coffee 4F–6F ($3.30–$4.90). No credit cards. Mon–Thurs 6:30am–2:30am; Fri–Sat 7am–4:30am; Sun 9am–2:30am.

Café Schober   One of the most select cafes in Zurich is located in Zum grossen Erker (The Great Alcove), a building dating from 1314 that was turned into a confectionery and coffee shop by Theodor Schober after 1875. When the last Schober retired, the well-known meeting place was bought and renovated by Teuscher, the epicurean name brand in chocolates. The old-fashioned cafe, with its beautiful lighting fixtures and molded ceilings, is known for its hot chocolate. It also offers an array of homemade pastries, cakes, and ice cream.

Napfgasse 4. ℂ 044/251-80-60. Hot chocolate 9F ($7.40). Mon–Fri 8am–6:30pm; Sat 8am–5:30pm; Sun 10am–5:30pm.

A PASTRY SHOP

Confiserie Sprüngli   This old-fashioned pastry shop on Bahnhofstrasse, founded in 1836, is comparable to the legendary Demel in Vienna. Many Zurichers remember this place fondly from their childhood. A variety of pastries and chocolates are sold on the ground floor. The famous Lindt chocolates and the house specialties are about the best you'll ever find. You'll also find fixed-price lunches, tea, and coffee. Many old-time Zurichers journey across town for a cup of hot chocolate here.

Am Paradeplatz. ℂ 044/224-47-31. www.confiserie-spruengli.ch. Fixed-price lunch 22F–29F ($18–$24); tea or coffee from 4F ($3.30). AE, DC, MC, V. Mon–Fri 7am–6:30pm; Sat 7:30am–5:30pm.

5 Attractions

Zurich has a rich history and many reminders of its past. There are 20 museums, nearly 100 galleries, and 24 archives, including one devoted to Thomas Mann. The historic buildings, religious monuments, and quays are worth discovering, as are the well-preserved homes of rich burghers, lovely parks, and gardens. Even if you don't have time to visit all those museums and galleries, a walk along the quays of Zurich shouldn't be missed.

You can also visit Uetliberg, southwest of Zurich, the northernmost peak in the Albis ridge (see "Side Trips from Zurich," later in this chapter).

SUGGESTED ZURICH ITINERARIES

If You Have 1 Day

Take **"Walking Tour 1: Zurich's Bahnhofstrasse"** to Lake Zurich, where you can board a steamer for a 1½-hour ride on the lake. Return to shore and visit either the **Kunsthaus Museum** or the **Landesmuseum.** In late afternoon take **"Walking Tour 2: Zurich's Altstadt,"** along the famous quays of Zurich and through Old Town, where you might have a raclette dinner in an old tavern. (Both walking tours are detailed later in this section.)

If You Have 2 Days

Spend the first day as suggested above. In the morning visit **Fraumünster** or **Grossmünster,** the two most famous churches of Zurich. Enjoy lunch in a typical Zurich cafe. In the afternoon leave Zurich for **Uetliberg** for a panoramic view of the Alps and the city. Have a beer and listen to the oompah band at the **Bierhalle Wolf** in the evening.

If You Have 3 Days

Spend the first 2 days as outlined above. On the third day, see all the attractions you've missed before, including two museums: the **Rietberg,** with its great non-European art collection, and the **Bührle,** with its collection of modern art. Visit the **Botanischer Garten (Botanic Garden)** and the **zoo** in the afternoon, if time remains.

If You Have 4 Days

Spend the first 3 days as outlined above. On the morning of the fourth day, go to **Winterthur,** only a 25-minute ride from Zurich, to see its many attractions, including the Museum Oskar Reinhart, the Kunstmuseum, and the Schloss Kyburg.

THE TOP ATTRACTIONS

The **quays of Zurich** 𝕮𝕮, with their promenades, are among the city's most popular attractions. They're made for walking. The most famous is **Limmatquai,** in the center of Zurich. It begins at the Bahnhof Bridge and extends east to the Rathaus (town hall) and beyond. Many of the quays have lovely gardens. **Uto Quai** is the major promenade along Zurichsee (Lake Zurich), running from Badeanstalt Uto Quai (a swimming pool) to Bellevueplatz and Quai Brücke. The pool is open daily from 8am to 7pm. If you stroll as far as **Mythenquai,** you'll be following the lake along its western shore and out into the countryside.

Fraumünster   This church, with its slender, blue spire, is on the left bank overlooking the former pig market, Münsterhof. Münsterhof is one of the historic old squares of Zurich and is well worth a visit. A Benedictine abbey was founded at the site in 853 by Emperor Ludwig (Louis the German), the grandson of Charlemagne. His daughter became the first abbess. The present church dates from the 13th and 14th centuries, but the crypt of the old abbey church is preserved in the undercroft.

The chief attractions of Fraumünster are five **stained-glass windows** 𝕮—each with its own color theme—designed by Marc Chagall in 1970. They are best seen in bright morning light. The Münster is also celebrated for its elaborate organ. The basilica has three aisles; the nave is in the Gothic style.

From Fraumünster you can cross the Münsterbrücke, an 1838 bridge that leads to Grossmünster. On the bridge is a statue of Burgomaster Waldmann, who was beheaded in 1489 when his political enemies seized power. During his rule the city gained influence over much of the surrounding lands.

Fraumünsterstrasse. No phone; inquire at tourist office. Free admission. May–Sept Mon–Sat 9am–noon, daily 2–6pm; Oct, Mar–Apr Mon–Sat 10am–noon, daily 2–5pm; Nov–Feb Mon–Sat 10am–noon, daily 2–4pm. Tram: 4 to City Hall.

Grossmünster   This Romanesque and Gothic cathedral was, according to legend, founded by Charlemagne, whose horse bowed down on the spot marking the graves of three early Christian martyrs. The cathedral has two three-story towers and is situated on a terrace above Limmatquai, on the right bank. Despite the legend, construction actually began in 1090 and additions were made until the early 14th century. The choir contains stained-glass windows completed in 1932 by Augusto Giacometti. (Augusto is not to be confused with his more celebrated uncle, Alberto Giacometti, the famous Swiss abstract.) In the crypt is a weather-beaten, 15th-century statue of Charlemagne, a copy of which crowns the south tower.

Finds **An Open Sesame & Bargain Pass**

Inaugurated in 2003, the ZurichCARD offers 50% reduction on public transportation, free visits to 43 museums, reduced prices at the zoo, and a welcome drink at more than two dozen restaurants. The pass is widely available, sold at such outlets as the Zurich Main Rail Station, the airport, and at certain hotels. It costs 15F ($12) for 24 hours or 30F ($25) for 72 hours.

Zurich Attractions

Dolderbahn

Forsterstrasse
Llabuhlstrasse
Kraftstrasse
Bergstrasse
Kleinjoggigasse
Riestelbergstrasse
Toblerstrasse
Hadlaubstrasse
Gladbachstrasse
Hochstrasse
Bolleystrasse
Schmelzbergstrasse
Voltastrasse
Gloriastrasse
Zürichbergstrasse
Attenhoferstrasse
Electorastrasse
Hofstrasse
Dolderstrasse
Ilgenstrasse
Asylstrasse
Gemeindestrasse
Pestalozzistrasse
Plattenstrasse
Freiestrasse
Hottingerstrasse
Zeltweg
Spöndlistrasse
Haldenbachstrasse
Universitätstrasse
Culmannstrasse
Federal Institute of Technology (ETHZ)
Rämistrasse
Gloriastrasse
Künstlergasse
Heimstrasse
Rämistrasse
Bahnhof Stadelhofen
Vogelsangstrasse
Stapferstrasse
Sonneggstrasse
Clausiusstrasse
Leonhardstrasse
Hirschengraben
Seilergraben
Mühlegasse
Brunngasse
Spiegelgasse
NIEDERDORF
Oberdorfstrasse
Turnerstrasse
Weinbergstrasse
Sumatrastrasse
Stampfenbachstrasse
Central
polybahn
Niederdorfstrasse
Limmatquai
Münsterg.
Grossmünster-platz
Limmatquai
Beckenhofstr.
Nordstrasse
Neumühlequai
Limmat River
Walcher Br.
Bahnhof-Br.
Bahnhofquai
Mühlsteg (Ped bridge)
Rud. Brun-Br.
Fortunagasse
Oetenbachg.
Rathaus Br.
Storchengasse
Münster Br.
Limmat River
Stadthausquai
Fraumünsterstr.
PLATZSPITZ
Zoll-Br.
Hauptbahnhof (Main Train Station)
Bahnhof-platz
Post-Br.
Beaten-platz
Bahnhofstrasse
Uraniastrasse
Rennweg
Bahnhofstrasse
St. Peterstr.
Bahnhofstrasse
Bastei-platz
Bärengasse
Paradeplatz
Talstrasse
Bleicherweg
Sihlquai
Ausstellungsstrasse
Limmatstrasse
Heinrichstrasse
Josefstrasse
Neugasse
Langstrasse
Hafnerstrasse
Zollstrasse
Löwenstrasse
Gessner Allee
Kasernenstrasse
Sihl River
Talackerstrasse
Pelikanstrasse
Selnaustrasse
Stauffbr.
Brandschenkestrasse
Gartenstr.
Freigutstr.
Teilstrasse
Kanonengasse
Lagerstrasse
Militärstrasse
Zeughausstrasse
Müllerstrasse
Bäckerstrasse
Sihlbr.
Stauffacher-platz
Werdstrasse
Morgartenstrasse
Stauffacherstrasse
Sihlhölzlistrasse
Stauffacherstrasse
LEFT BANK
Dienerstrasse
Hohlstrasse
Kernstrasse
Langstrasse
Badenerstrasse
Zweierstrasse
Ankerstrasse
Birmensdorferstrasse
Schimmelstr.

RIGHT BANK

SWITZERLAND

Basel • Zurich
Bern ✶
Geneva •

Train Station

Zürichsee/
Lake Zürich

St. Peter Kirche (St. Peter's Church) **5**
Thomas Mann Archives **17**
Tonhalle Gesellschaft **9**
Urania Observatory **2**
Wasserkirche **11**
Zoologischer Garten **18**
Zunfthaus zur Meisen **7**
Zürcher Spielzeugmuseum **4**

Landesmuseum
(Swiss National Museum) **1**
Lindenhof **3**
Münsterhof **6**
Museum Rietberg **22**
Opernhaus **10**
Rathaus **13**
Schauspielhaus **16**

Botanischer Garten
(Botanic Garden) **20**
Foundation E.G. Bührle Collection **21**
Fraumünster **8**
Friedhof Fluntern (Cemetery) **19**
Grossmünster **14**
Helmhaus **12**
Kunsthaus Zurich (Fine Arts Museum) **15**

Zurich Street Parade

You'll either flock to or flee from this bash, depending on your personality and music preferences. The Zurich Street Parade is one massive rave/techno dance party, filling the city streets for 1 day and night each August in an outdoor, over-the-top party. The event, meant to symbolize love, peace, freedom, generosity, and tolerance, started in 1992 with 2000 partiers and has mushroomed to attract over half a million international visitors in 2005. Modeled after Berlin's Loveparade (which, at press time, has been cancelled 2 years running), the Zurich Street Parade kicks off on a Saturday in early August with a parade of floats (lovemobiles) blaring their way along city streets, each with its own dance and music theme. On my visit, my two favorite lovemobiles contained orange jumpsuit–clad revelers jamming to a hard-core techno beat and another featuring green angels swaying to trance. When I tired of dancing, I lounged at an outdoor table with a beer and enjoyed hours of prime people-watching. In three words: exuberant, energetic, and fun. And just as the party starts winding down (around 3am), special cleaning vans sweep and clean the streets, leaving the town spotless and perfect by the next day—only in Switzerland. If this is your thing, book early, or plan to stay in an nearby city such as Basel or Lucerne (both 1 hour away by train). If this sounds like your biggest nightmare, stay away. For dates and details, visit the Street Parade's official website, www.streetparade.ch.

—*Caroline Sieg*

The cathedral is dedicated to the patron saints of Zurich: Felix, Regula, and Exuperantius. In the 3rd century the three martyrs attempted to convert the citizens of Turicum (the original name for Zurich) to Christianity. The governor, according to legend, had them plunged into boiling oil and forced to drink molten lead. The trio refused to renounce their faith and were beheaded. Miraculously, they still had enough energy to pick up their heads and climb to the top of a hill (the present site of the cathedral), where they dug their own graves and then interred themselves. The seal of Zurich honors these saints, depicting them carrying their heads under their arms. The remains of the saints are said to rest in one of the chapels of the Münster (cathedral).

The cathedral was once the parish church of Huldrych Zwingli, one of the great leaders of the Reformation. He urged priests to take wives (he himself had married) and attacked the "worship of images" and the Roman sacrament of mass. In 1531 Zwingli was killed in a religious war at Kappel. The hangman quartered his body and soldiers burnt the pieces with dung. The site of his execution is marked with an inscription: "They may kill the body but not the soul." In accordance with Zwingli's beliefs, Zurich's Grossmünster is austere, stripped of the heavy ornamentation you'll find in the cathedrals of Italy. The view from the towers is impressive.

Grossmünsterplatz. © **044/252-59-49.** Free admission to cathedral; towers 2F ($1.65). Cathedral Mar 15–Oct daily 9am–6pm; Nov–Mar 14 daily 10am–4pm. Towers Mar–Oct daily 9am–6pm (weather permitting); off season Sat–Sun 10am–4pm (weather permitting). Tram: 4.

Kunsthaus Zürich (Fine Arts Museum) 𝄞𝄞 One of the most important art museums in Europe, the Kunsthaus Zürich is devoted mainly to the 19th and 20th centuries, although the range of paintings and sculpture reaches back to antiquity. The museum was founded in Victorian times and was overhauled in 1976. Today it's one of the most modern and sophisticated museums in the world, both in its lighting and its display of art.

Our favorite exhibits include Rodin's *Gate of Hell*, near the entrance, and the Giacometti wing, showing the development of this Swiss-born artist. The collection of modern art includes works by all the greats—Bonnard, Braque, Chagall, Lipschitz, Marini, Mondrian, Picasso, and Rouault. The gallery owns the largest collection outside Oslo of works by the Norwegian artist Edvard Munch. Two old masters, Rubens and Rembrandt, are also represented. To brighten a rainy day, come see the pictures by Cézanne, Degas, Monet, Toulouse-Lautrec, and Utrillo.

Heimplatz 1. ⓒ **044/253-84-97**. www.kunsthaus.ch. Admission 13F ($11) adults, 11F ($9) seniors and students, free for children 16 and under; special exhibitions 14F ($11) adults, 7F ($5.75) children. Tues–Thurs 10am–9pm; Fri–Sun 10am–5pm. Tram: 3 (marked KLUSPLATZ).

Landesmuseum (Swiss National Museum) 𝄞𝄞𝄞 This museum offers an epic survey of the culture and history of the Swiss people. Its collection, housed in a feudal-looking, 19th-century building behind the Zurich Hauptbahnhof, contains works of religious art, including 16th-century stained glass from the Tanikon Convent and frescoes from the church of Mustair. Some of the Carolingian art dates from the 9th century. The altarpieces are carved, painted, and gilded.

The prehistoric section is also exceptional. Some of the artifacts are from the 4th millennium B.C. There's a large display of Roman clothing, medieval silverware, 14th-century drinking bowls, and 17th-century china, as well as painted furniture, costumes, and dollhouses of various periods. A display of weapons and armor shows the methods of Swiss warfare from 800 to 1800. There's also an exhibit tracing Swiss clockmaking from the 16th to the 18th centuries.

Special exhibitions are presented twice annually, lasting between 3 and 6 months. Themes are always different; a recent one was devoted to Swiss fashion design.

Museumstrasse 2. ⓒ **044/218-65-11**. www.musee-suisse.com. Admission 5F ($4.10), 3F ($2.45) students and seniors; special exhibitions 8F–12F ($6.55–$9.85). Tues–Sun 10am–5pm. Tram: 3, 4, 5, 11, 13, or 14.

Museum Rietberg 𝄞 *Finds* A real discovery, the neoclassical Villa Wesendonck was once occupied by Richard Wagner, who wrote his *Wesendonck Songs* to the lady of the manor. Today that mansion and an adjoining one, Park-Villa Rieter, have been converted into an exquisite museum that showcases Asian, African, and other non-European art. The setting is the lush Rieter-Park overlooking Zurich. The collection grew from an initial trove collected by Baron von der Heyt. The collection is rich in highly acclaimed exhibits of Japanese, Chinese, and Indian drawings and paintings, including Bodhisattvas from India, China, Tibet, and Nepal. Here you can enjoy viewing everything from Tibetan bronzes to jade Chinese funereal art, even the bizarre Japanese Noh masks. The location of the museum is along Seestrasse, 1.75km (1 mile) south of the center.

Gablerstrasse 15, Kreis 2. ⓒ **044/206-31-31**. www.rietberg.ch. Admission 6F ($5.20) adults, 3F ($2.45) students and children. Tues–Sun 10am–5pm; Wed 10am–8pm. Tram: 7.

MORE ATTRACTIONS

Botanischer Garten (Botanic Garden) ✦   The gardens contain 15,000 living species, including some rare specimens from New Caledonia and Southwest Africa. The herbarium contains three million plants. The gardens, owned by the University of Zurich, were laid out on the site of a former private villa.

Universität Zurich, Zollikerstrasse 107. Ⓒ 044/634-84-61. Free admission. Park Mar–Sept Mon–Fri 7am–7pm, Sat–Sun 8am–6pm; Oct–Feb Mon–Fri 8am–6pm, Sat–Sun 8am–5pm. Greenhouses daily 9:30–11:30am and 1–4pm. Tram: 11 to Hegibachplatz, or 2 or 4 to Höschgasse. Bus: 33 to Botanischer Garten.

Foundation E. G. Bührle Collection ✦✦   This jewel of a collection is most popular for its French Impressionist works, including those by Monet, van Gogh, Cézanne, Gauguin, Degas, Renoir, and Manet. See Picasso's *The Italian Girl.* The private collection also includes paintings by Rubens, Rembrandt, and Guardi. There's a limited but very special section of 24 sculptures from the Middle Ages.

Zollikerstrasse 172. Ⓒ 044/422-00-86. Admission 9F ($7.40) adults, 7F ($5.75) students and seniors. Tues, Wed, Fri, and Sun 2–5pm. Tram: 2 or 4.

Friedhof Fluntern (Fluntern Cemetery)   James Joyce, the author of *Ulysses,* lived in Zurich from 1915 to 1919, at Universitätsstrasse 38. In 1941 he returned to Zurich from Paris, only a month before his death. Near his tomb is a statue depicting the great Irish writer sitting cross-legged with a book in his hand. Elias Canetti, winner of the Nobel Prize for literature in 1981, died in August 1994; his grave lies to the left of Joyce's. The grave of Johanna Spiri (1827–1901), who wrote the famous story *Heidi,* is in the Central Cemetery.

Zürichberg district. Free admission. May–Aug daily 7am–8pm; Mar–Apr and Sept–Oct daily 7am–7pm; Nov–Feb daily 8am–5pm. Tram: 6 to zoo.

St. Peter Kirche (St. Peter's Church)   Built in the 13th century, St. Peter's—on the left bank south of Lindenhof—is the oldest church in Zurich. It has the largest clock face in Europe: 9m (30 ft.) in diameter; the minute hand alone is almost 4m (13 ft.) long. Inside, the choir is Romanesque, but the three-aisle nave is baroque.

St. Peterhofstatt 1. Ⓒ 044/211-25-88. Free admission. Mon–Fri 8am–6pm; Sat 9am–4pm.

Thomas Mann Archives   Thomas Mann, the German writer who won the Nobel Prize for literature in 1929 for such works as *Death in Venice* and *The Magic Mountain,* died in Kilchberg, near Zurich, in 1955. An opponent of the Nazi regime, he had lived outside Germany after 1933—in the United States and Switzerland during most of the period. The archives, located next to the university, contain manuscripts and mementos.

Swiss Federal Institute of Technology, Schönberggasse 15. Ⓒ 044/632-40-45. Free admission. Wed and Sat 2–4pm. Tram: 5, 6, or 9.

Urania Observatory   The observatory is halfway between Bahnhofstrasse and the Limmat River on Uraniastrasse. On clear days you can look through the telescope, while on bad days the observatory doesn't open. Call in advance to find out. The observatory has been at this site since 1907. Because of its central location, you have a panoramic view not only of Zurich but also of the lake and the distant Alps. You can see the stars, planets, and galaxy through a big Zeiss telescope that weighs 20 tons.

Uraniastrasse 9. Ⓒ 044/211-65-23. Admission 10F ($8.20) adults, 5F ($4.10) children. Apr–Sept Tues–Sat noon–4pm and 7–11pm; Oct–Mar Tues–Sat noon–4pm and 6–9pm. Tram: 7, 11, or 13.

Zunfthaus zur Meisen Across the bridge from the Wasserkirche is one of the city's famous old guildhalls. It has a wrought-iron gatehouse that opens onto Münsterhof. Dating from 1752, it's a branch museum of the overstuffed Swiss National Museum. It's devoted mainly to 18th-century Swiss ceramics, the porcelain of Zurich, and several antiques. The beauty of the stuccoed rooms competes with the exhibits.

Münsterhof 20. ℭ **044/221-28-07.** Admission 3F ($2.45) adults, free for children under 16. Tues–Sun 10:30am–5pm. Closed holidays. Tram: 3.

ESPECIALLY FOR KIDS

There are 80 playgrounds in Zurich. For the one nearest your hotel, inquire either at your hotel or at the local tourist office (see "Visitor Information," earlier in this chapter). Most boat trips (see "Organized Tours," below) leave from the end of Bahnhofstrasse on the right. You may also combine a train ride with a trip to an attraction outside Zurich.

Select theaters also offer changing programs for children. Ask at the tourist office or get a copy of *Zurich Weekly Official,* available at most newsstands.

Several stores may be fun spots to visit with your kids. The largest toy shop in Europe is **Franz Carl Weber,** Bahnhofstrasse 62 (ℭ **044/211-29-61**), named for the famous toy collector. There's also a specialist toy shop, **Pastorini,** Weinplatz 3 (ℭ **044/228-70-70**). Pastorini specializes in wooden toys and is one of the biggest toy stores in Zurich, spread over five floors.

The best-stocked children's bookstore in Switzerland is **Kinderbuchladen Zurich,** Oberdorfstrasse 32 (ℭ **044/261-53-50**), which carries many English-language books.

In addition, the following two attractions may be of special interest to children:

Zoologischer Garten (Zoological Garden) ⊛ One of the best-known zoos in Europe, Zurich's Zoological Garden contains some 2,200 animals of about 260

Frommer's Favorite Zurich Experiences

Shopping along Bahnhofstrasse It has been called the most beautiful shopping street in the world, and perhaps it is. Built a century ago on the site of the ancient moat, it's a stroller's paradise. In stores on both sides of the street is some of the world's greatest merchandise.

Taking a Boat Trip on Lake Zurich On a sunny day, this is the best way to spend time in Zurich. Cruises on one of Europe's most beautiful lakes last 1½ to 4 hours. Boats depart from Bürkliplatz, the lake end of Bahnhofstrasse.

Visiting Uetliberg If the day is sunny, you can take an electric train to this parklike, 840m (2,755-ft.) hill. Once here, you can wander about, enjoying the natural surroundings and scenic vistas at every turn. It's best to take a picnic.

Biking & Swimming on the Lake In July and August, one of the most peaceful experiences is to bike from Seebach station through the forest to Katzenruti, where you'll find several places ideal for a picnic. After lunch you can cycle to the Katzensee with its sandy beach, returning later via Affoltern. The tourist office in Zurich will help you plot this course, which takes about 1½ hours to go the full 13km (8 miles).

species. It also has an aquarium and an open-air aviary. You can visit the Africa house, the ape house, and the terrariums, along with the elephant house and the giant-tortoise house. There are special enclosures for red pandas, otters, and snow leopards, and a house for clouded leopards, tigers, Amur leopards, and Indian lions.

Zürichbergstrasse 221. © 044/254-25-00. Admission 22F ($18) adults, 11F ($9) children, free for children 5 and under. Mar–Oct daily 8am–6pm; Nov–Feb daily 8am–5pm. Tram: 6 from the Hauptbahnhof; the zoo is in the eastern sector of the city, called Zürichberg, on a wooded hill.

Zürcher Spielzeugmuseum (Zurich Toy Museum)   This museum, in one of the oldest parts of the city, contains more than 1,200 antique toys from all over Europe. The collection is displayed on the fifth floor of a house and is accessible by elevator.

Fortunagasse 15. © 044/211-93-05. Free admission. Mon–Fri 2–5pm; Sat 1–4pm. Tram: 6, 7, 11, or 13.

WALKING TOUR 1	ZURICH'S BAHNHOFSTRASSE

Start:	Bahnhofplatz.
Finish:	Bellevueplatz.
Time:	1 hour.
Best Times:	Monday through Friday from 9am to 5pm or on Saturday from 9am to 1am (when most stores are open).
Worst Times:	Rush hours, Monday through Friday from 8 to 9am and 5 to 6pm.

If you do nothing else in Zurich, walk along world-famous Bahnhofstrasse. One of the most beautiful shopping streets on earth was built on the site of a "frogs' moat." The street is free from all traffic except trams.

Begin the tour at:

❶ Bahnhofplatz

The site of the Hauptbahnhof, the central railroad station, this is the beginning of Bahnhofstrasse. The square itself is rather drab, but the scenery improves as you go along (the street extends almost a mile to the lake). The Hauptbahnhof was built in 1871.

Escalators take you from Bahnhofplatz past an underground shopping mall called ShopVille to:

❷ Bahnhofstrasse

With your back to the railway terminus, you can head up Bahnhofstrasse, which is lined with linden trees as well as some of the world's most prosperous banks and expensive shops, selling such luxury merchandise as Swiss watches and jewelry.

Continue up the street to:

❸ Pestalozzi Park

The park appears on your right, 2 blocks from Bahnhofplatz, between Schweizergasse and Usteristrasse. You can stop here and rest on one of the park benches by a statue of Johann Heinrich Pestalozzi (1746–1827), an educational reformer who had import on school standards in the United States.

Farther along, near Augustinergasse and Pelikanstrasse, you'll see a small pedestrian walkway where you can stop to admire the sculpture in the area. After you pass St. Peter Strasse and Bärengasse, you'll reach:

❹ Paradeplatz

This is the hub of Zurich and the central tram interchange. In the 18th century, it was a cattle market. The square is dominated by the 1876 mansion of Crédit Suisse. East of the plaza is the Savoy Baur en Ville hotel.

Walking Tour 1: Zurich's Bahnhofstrasse

1 Bahnhofplatz
2 Bahnhofstrasse
3 Pestalozzi Park
4 Paradeplatz
   Confiserie Sprüngli
5 Bürkliplatz
6 Bellevueplatz

TAKE A BREAK
At Bahnhofstrasse 21 (Am Paradeplatz) is the **Confiserie Sprüngli** (☎ 044/224-47-31; www.confiserie-spruengli.ch), the most elegant and fashionable place on this chic shopping street to meet for tea and pastries, which are the best in the city. You can also enjoy daily lunch specials.

Continue along Bahnhofstrasse until you reach:

❺ Bürkliplatz

On the shore of Lake Zurich, this is the point where the Limmat River empties into the lake. This square overlooks Quaibrücke, a bridge across the Limmat that connects the left bank with the right bank. After stopping to admire the lake, you may also consider a boat excursion if it's summer.

If you cross Quaibrücke, you'll arrive on the right bank at:

❻ Bellevueplatz

Here you can enjoy the view of the lake and river as you rest on a park bench and watch all of Zurich pass by.

WALKING TOUR 2   ZURICH'S ALTSTADT

Start:	Münsterhof.
Finish:	Helmhaus.
Time:	1½ hours.
Best Times:	Any sunny day between 10am and 4pm (when there's less traffic).
Worst Times:	Rush hours, Monday through Friday from 8 to 9am and 5 to 6pm.

Situated on both sides of the Limmat River, Altstadt (Old Town) is known for its squares, narrow cobblestone streets, and winding alleys. There are fountains, medieval houses, art galleries, boutiques, quaint restaurants, hotels (many moderately priced), and antiques shops. To walk its old streets is to follow in the footsteps of such famous figures as Charlemagne, Goethe, Einstein, and Lenin. The oldest houses date from the 1100s.

A former swine market, a good place to begin your exploration of Altstadt is:

❶ Münsterhof

This square, on the left bank, is near such landmarks as Fraumünster and the Rathaus. You can reach it by walking along Schlüsselgasse. At Münsterhof 8 is the guildhall Zunfthaus zur Waag, erected in 1637, with late Gothic windows and a gabled facade.

Across the square is:

❷ Fraumünster

The entrance is on Fraumünsterstrasse. A church has stood on this site since 853, when it was a convent for noblewomen. It contains artwork by Chagall and Giacometti, among others.

After the church, your next target can be:

❸ Lindenhof

To get here, you must climb narrow medieval alleyways from Fraumünster. Continue north along Schlüsselgasse, heading in the direction of the railroad station. Shaded by trees, the belvedere square of Lindenhof is one of the most scenic spots in Zurich, especially romantic at twilight. Once the site of a Celtic and later a Roman fort, Lindenhof is a good place from which to view the Limmat River; the lookout point has a fountain. There's also a good view of the medieval old quarter, which rises in layers on the right bank.

Walking Tour 2: Zurich's Altstadt

1 Münsterhof
2 Fraumünster
3 Lindenhof
4 Weinplatz
5 Rathausbrücke
6 Rathaus
7 Wasserkirche
8 Helmhaus
Café Odéon

SWITZERLAND

Basel
Zurich
Bern
Geneva

Train Station

0   200 yds
0   100 m

From Lindenhof, head down Pfalzgasse, forking left onto Strehlgasse to Waggengasse and Rathausbrücke, the city hall bridge spanning the Limmat. You have arrived at the landmark square:

❹ Weinplatz

The site of the Corn Exchange until 1620, this is presumably the oldest market square in Zurich. It's named for its 1909 Weinbauer fountain, which depicts a Swiss winegrower with a basket of grapes in hand. Most visitors pause to photograph the Flemish-roofed burghers' houses on the opposite bank.

Here you can also look at the:

❺ Rathausbrücke

The present City Hall Bridge spanning the Limmat was built in 1878, at the site of the first span in Zurich.

Cross the bridge to visit the:

❻ Rathaus

Here you'll find the late Renaissance town hall of Zurich, which opens onto Limmatquai. Built in the late 17th century, it has darkly paneled rooms and antique porcelain stoves. Canton councils still meet here in a setting of rich sculptural adornment. The town hall is open on Tuesday, Thursday, and Friday from 10 to 11:30am. Admission is free, but you should tip your guide.

Walk south along Limmatquai until you reach Münsterbrücke, a bridge across the Limmat, and the site of:

❼ Wasserkirche

Also called Water Church, this church got its unusual name because it was surrounded by water when it was built in 1479. There's a statue of Zwingli, the famous Swiss reformer, here.

Directly north of the church at Limmatquai 31 is the:

❽ Helmhaus

Built in 1794, the Helmhaus has a fountain hall and a gallery on the second and third floors, where the city shows changing exhibitions of Swiss art. The gallery is open Tuesday through Sunday from 10am to 6pm and also on Thursday from 8 to 10pm.

At the end of your walking tour, you can continue over to Zurich's most famous cafe:

❾ Café Odéon

This Belle Epoque cafe, Limmatquai 2 (✆ **044/251-16-50**), is the place where Lenin sat out most of World War I, plotting the Russian Revolution. It was also popular with the iconoclastic Dada artists of the same era. Stop for a cup of coffee in this historic setting.

ORGANIZED TOURS

TRAM TOURS   The quickest and most convenient way to get acquainted with Zurich is with a 2-hour trolley tour, which rolls through various neighborhoods of interest. There's no live spokesperson pointing out the sights, but you'll be given a headset, which delivers a running commentary in seven languages. Between May and October, for a fee of 32F ($26) per person, there are tours daily at 9:45am, noon, and 2pm. The tour takes in the commercial and shopping center and Old Town, and goes along the lakefront for a visit to Fraumünster or one of the historic guildhalls beside the Limmatquai.

CABLEWAY TOUR   Another tour of Zurich is by boat and aerial cableway ascending to the Felsenegg at 795m (2,608 ft.). From here, there's a panoramic view over the lake and the Alps beyond. It departs daily at 9:30am between May and September. Make your arrangements in advance with the tourist office in the main hall of Zurich's railway station, although your actual departure will be from a bus parked beside the Sihlquai, at a point that will be communicated to you in advance.

BOAT TOURS   At some point during your stay in Switzerland's largest city, you'll want to take a lake steamer for a tour around Lake Zurich. Walk to Bahnhofstrasse's lower end and buy a ticket at the pier for any of the dozen or so boats that ply the waters from late May to late September. The boats are more or less the same so it doesn't matter which one you take. Most of the steamers contain simple restaurant facilities, and all have two or three levels of decks and lots of windows for wide-angle views of the Swiss mountains and shoreline. During peak season, boats depart at approximately 30-minute intervals. The most distant itinerary from Zurich is to Rapperswil, a historic town near the lake's southeastern end. A full-length, round-trip tour of the lake from Zurich to Rapperswil will require 2 hours each way, plus whatever time you opt to explore towns en route. This trip is the highlight of the boat tours offered, and if you can spare the time, you'll find it a rewarding way to see the area in and around Zurich. Many visitors opt for shorter boat rides encompassing only the northern third of the lake; the total trip takes about 90 minutes.

The full-length tour of the lake costs 20F ($16) in second class and 33F ($27) in first class. The shorter boat ride on the northern third of the lake costs 5.40F ($4.45).

You may also want to take a 55-minute boat trip along the Limmat River for a closer view of Zurich's historic bridges and riverfront buildings. Boats depart daily at 30-minute intervals in the summer months, costing 4.60F ($3.75) per person. Boats depart from a pier in front of the Landesmuseum, near Zurich's main railway station, and travel downriver to the lake as far as the Zurichhorn or the Wollishofen railway station before retracing their paths upriver back to the pier.

For more information on all the boats mentioned above, contact the **Zürichsee Schifffahrtsgesellschaft** by calling ✆ **044/487-13-33,** or go online at www.zsg.ch.

WALKING TOURS   One of the most appealing walking tours in Zurich is a 2-hour guided stroll through the Old Town. If you're interested in participating, meet in the main hall of Zurich's railway station, at the Tourist Service office (✆ **044/215-40-00**). The cost of the tour is 20F ($16) for adults, 10F ($8.20) for children 6 to 16, and free for children under 6. From April through October, tours are operated Monday through Friday at 3pm (in German and English), and on Saturday and Sunday at 11am (in German and English) and at 3pm (in Spanish and English). From November to March, they are offered only at 11am on Wednesday and Saturday, and only in German and English.

ACTIVE PURSUITS

Zurichers are not big on spectator sports—they like to get out and participate.

Many of the larger hotels have added swimming pools and tennis courts or handball and racquetball facilities to their attractions. Some also have fitness centers. The best one for the sports-minded is **Dolder Waldhaus.**

GOLF   The premier golf club in Switzerland, **Golf & Country Club Zurich,** Wied 9, Aiderstrasse, in the suburb of Zumikon (✆ **044/918-00-50**), 12km (7½ miles) southeast of the center, was laid out in 1931 and has the most prestigious reputation in the country. An 18-hole, par-72 course, it welcomes nonmembers who phone in advance, but only if they have a handicap of 30 or less, and only if they present a membership at a golf club in another part of the world. Greens fees are 200F ($164) per person, and clubs can be rented for 30F ($25) per set. To get there from downtown Zurich, take the Forchbahn tram from the Stadelhofen Bahnhof, near the Zurich opera house, then ride for 20 minutes to the tram station in the suburb of Zumikon. From there, it's a 6-minute walk to the golf course.

HIKING   Zurich has seven "Vita-Parcours," or keep-fit trails. Someone at the Zurich Tourist Office, Bahnhofplatz 15 (© **044/215-40-00**), will map these trails for you.

JOGGING   The nearest woodland jogging route is on the **Allmend Fluntern,** which is a wide-open public park, crisscrossed with jogging paths, on the northeastern outskirts of Zurich, near the zoo. To get here from the center, take tram no. 6. Joggers are also seen frequently along the quays and elsewhere in the city.

SWIMMING   You can go swimming in Lake Zurich, which has an average summer temperature of 68°F (20°C). The finest beach is the **Tiefenbrunnen.** To get to Tiefenbrunnen (which is also popular with the gay crowd), take tram no. 4 from central Zurich (Bahnhofplatz) to Tiefenbrunnen Bahnhof, a ride of about 15 minutes. The city and many hotels offer indoor and outdoor swimming pools. The **public pool** at Sihlstrasse 71 also has a sauna with its indoor swimming facilities.

6 Shopping

In the heart of Zurich is a square kilometer (about ⅓ sq. mile) of shopping, including the exclusive stores along **Bahnhofstrasse,** previewed in the "Attractions," earlier. Your shopping adventure might begin more modestly at the top of the street, at Bahnhofplatz. Below this vast transportation hub is a complex of shops known as **ShopVille.**

ShopVille is opened from 8am to 8pm every day except Christmas. Most shops are open Monday to Friday from 8am to 6:30pm and on Saturday from 8am to 4pm. Some of the larger stores stay open until 9pm on Thursday, and other shops are closed on Monday morning.

ART
Art-Repro *(Value)*   If you've always wanted a Degas or a Renoir but have not been able to afford one, this trove of high-quality reproductions of the world's famous masterpieces may provide a reasonably priced alternative. An impressive array of artists' works is available, including copies of paintings by Picasso, Miró, Chagall, and van Gogh, as well as such old masters as Rembrandt. Scheideggstrasse 95. © **044/482-60-45.**

Wühre 9-Art Deco *(Finds)*   This shop is noted as one of Europe's richest repositories of objects crafted in the increasingly valuable Art Deco and Art Nouveau styles. The inventory includes everything from furniture to decorative accessories. There are no copies, and the establishment's buyers comb the art markets of France, Italy, England, and North America to replenish the stock. Wühre 9. © **044/221-67-57.**

BOOKS
Orell Füssli   Zurich's premier book department store stocks a large inventory of German- and English-language books. In addition to books on Switzerland, you'll find everything from the latest novels to your favorite classics, as well as many contemporary nonfiction titles on every subject. Füsslistrasse at Bahnhofstrasse. © **044/455-56-17.**

The Travel Book Shop   This shop has a complete selection of travel books, as well as one of Europe's best map collections. Many of the books are in German, but about half the stock is in English. Maps for trekking and mountaineering from all over the world are also sold. Rindermarkt 20. © **044/252-38-83.**

CHOCOLATES
Sprüngli   In a country famous for its chocolates, Sprüngli is the most famous chocolatier, although we still consider it second best to Teuscher (see below). The

inventory of virtually everything dark and "meltable in your mouth" is featured at this temple to chocolate. Adjacent to the store, you'll find a coffee shop, a small restaurant with a limited menu, and a room designated exclusively for mailing your next high-caloric gifts to friends and family abroad. Additional outlets of Sprüngli are located at Bahnhofstrasse 67, Löwenplatz, Stadelhoferplatz, and, to tempt last-minute buyers, the Zurich International Airport. Paradeplatz. ✆ 044/224-47-11.

Teuscher   Located on a narrow cobblestone street in Old Town, this small store is the original epicurean chocolate shop. You can tell you're in the area by the smell of chocolate truffles, which come in such flavors as champagne, orange, and cocoa. Storchengasse 9. ✆ 044/211-51-53.

CRAFTS

Schweizer Heimatwerk *Finds*   In 1930, in an effort to help economically distressed areas, a nonprofit society, Schweizer Heimatwerk, was created to keep traditional crafts alive. Today Heimatwerk shops sell only items designed and made in Switzerland, most of them handcrafted. Items include copperware, ceramics, woodcarvings, ironwork, jewelry, toys, nave paintings, crystal, tinware, baskets, music boxes, and paper-cutout pictures. Puzzles, games, puppets, even a Noah's ark with its carved wooden animals, are sold here as well. The headquarters shop and four other outlets of Schweizer Heimatwerk are in Zurich. The prices range from reasonable to expensive. Other branches are at Bahnhofstrasse 2, at Rennweg 14, at the Hauptbahnhof, and at the Zurich airport in Transit Halls A and B. Rudolf Brun-Brücke. ✆ 044/217-83-17.

Teddy's Souvenir Shop   Swiss-made handicrafts here evoke a nostalgia for old-fashioned Switzerland with the type of gifts a Teutonic Santa Claus might stuff into his bag of Christmas gifts. Items for sale include cuckoo clocks, T-shirts with an assortment of Swiss-inspired sayings, an impressive array of music boxes and beer steins, Swiss Army knives, and woodcarvings. Anything you buy can be shipped abroad. Limmatquai 34. ✆ 044/261-22-89.

DEPARTMENT STORES

Grieder les Boutiques   This is one of the best department stores in Switzerland, offering both ready-to-wear and couture by such designers as Valentino, Dior, Escada, and Montana. The store fills two floors of a stone building on Zurich's most fashionable commercial street, where the salespeople tend to be bilingual and formidably well dressed. The accessories, including purses, scarves, and leather goods, are well selected. There's a wide choice of shoes—many Swiss-made—for both men and women, plus a good men's department. Bahnhofstrasse 30. ✆ 044/224-36-36.

Jelmoli Department Store   This Zurich institution has everything a large department store should have, from cookware to clothing. Founded more than 150 years ago by the Ticino-born entrepreneur Johann Peter Jelmoli, the store is a legend in the Zurich business community. Seidengasse 1. ✆ 044/220-44-11.

FASHIONS

Le Mouton a Cinq Pattes   This is the Zurich branch of a well-known Paris-based discount outlet for high-end fashion for men and women. It maintains direct pipelines to upscale manufacturers including Moschino, Issey Miyake, Thierry Mügler, Cerrutti 1881, Armani, Versace, Gucci, Cavalli, and—for the very youthful-looking—Exte. Unless you're a very tall, very muscular, or very bulky man, the store will probably have something to fit you. Ask the multilingual staff for help. They're genuinely charming and willing to help. Usteristrasse 23. ℰ **044/212-00-68**.

Modeshaus Feldpausch   Spread across four floors, this outlet is devoted mainly to women's wear. With some of the deepest discounts available in the basement, inventories include designs from fashion moguls Mark Kane, Hugo Boss, Orvell, and Akris. On the street level they sell casual wear along with a selection of clothing for young women. On the next level is the house's selection of designer clothing, with cocktail dresses and ensembles on the floor above. Check for sales in late summer and late winter. Bahnhofstrasse 88. ℰ **044/225-11-11**.

Sormustin   This is one of the most sophisticated clothing stores of Zurich, lying in the gentrified Aussersihl district. A genius in textiles, Anne Koskiluoma, has teamed with Barbara Egg, a leading fashion designer, to create this clothing store for women. Among some of their more intriguing selections are pants and coats with patterns and colors inspired by the kimono designs of Tokyo. Ankerstrasse 41. ℰ **044/240-26-06**.

GIFTS

Meister Silber   This elite shop, on prestigious Paradeplatz in the center of Zurich, has one of the widest selections of gift items in Switzerland. The prices are high but reasonable, considering that every article is either exquisitely handcrafted or comes from producers internationally known for quality and fine design. Bahnhofstrasse 28A. ℰ **044/221-27-30**.

JEWELRY

Les Ambassadeurs   Benefiting from a stylish location on the city's most prestigious shopping street, this well-known jeweler sells gemstones and such watches as Breitling, Cartier, Longines, Omega, and Constantin. Also featured are the baubles of Italian jeweler Mandredi and the Cleopatra line. Bahnhofstrasse 64. ℰ **044/227-17-17**.

Tiffany & Co.   The Swiss branch of America's most famous jeweler, this well-upholstered boutique sells the full line of products originally made famous in New York, including those by artists such as Paloma Picasso. No crystal or china is offered, but small gift items are sold, as well as a choice of the famous gold and silver chains. Bahnhofstrasse 14. ℰ **044/211-19-45**.

Türler   On the ground level of the Savoy Hotel, this outlet has a goldsmith and a watchmaker on staff and is known throughout Zurich for its custom-made watches and jewelry. If you have a special design, they'll make it for you. They also carry a wide variety of watches from other designers—some 30 different brands in all—and they sell both these and a selection of jewelry in a wide range of prices. Bahnhofstrasse 28. ℰ **044/221-06-08**. www.tuerler.ch.

LEATHER GOODS

Leder-Locher   Established 150 years ago, this venerable leather store has maintained high standards despite the changing tides of fashion throughout the years. Its inventory includes handbags, purses, wallets, suitcases, garment bags, and an unusual collection of small but charming gift items and accessories. The store maintains another branch at Bahnhofstrasse 91. Münsterhof 18-19. ℰ **044/211-18-64**.

Mädler   Stephanie Mädler and her family have owned this leather-goods shop since 1951. The store, which specializes in leather bags, wallets, and suitcases, has a massively stocked second floor. Bahnhofstrasse 26. ℰ **044/211-75-70**.

LINENS & COTTONS

Albrecht Schläper   For about a century, well-heeled Swiss have come here for access to upscale table and bed linens, some of it richly embroidered in places including Sankt Gallen and Appenzell. The venue is plush and the merchandise includes the kind of densely woven high-end consumer goods that evoke the haute bourgeoisie of central Europe even after the goods have been unwrapped, used repeatedly, and laundered. Kappellergasse 1. © **044/211-57-47.**

Spitzenhaus   An air of old-fashioned charm permeates this store specializing in carefully crafted linens, cottons, and silks for the dining table. Most of the linen comes from Bern and Zurich (both specialists in linen), while most of the lace is handmade in either St. Gallen or Appenzell. The place also sells embroidered blouses and table scarves. Börsenstrasse 14. © **044/211-55-76.**

Sturzenegger   This century-old, wood-paneled store is a good place to buy all kinds of delicate hand-embroidered items, including Swiss-made lace. Several rooms contain a variety of intricately patterned tablecloths, place mats, doilies, and napkins. Also sold are blouses, handkerchiefs, shawls, scarves, and children's frocks. Upstairs is a large assortment of nightgowns, pajamas, and women's lingerie. Bahnhofstrasse 48. © **044/211-28-20.**

MUSIC

Musik Hug   This is the largest branch of the best music chain in Switzerland. Conveniently located in the center of Zurich, it stocks thousands of tapes from around the world and has a helpful staff. Its selection of Swiss folkloric music, classical recordings, and modern jazz is especially rich and varied. Limmatquai 28-30. © **044/251-68-50.**

PERFUMES

Parfumerie Schindler   This store on the Paradeplatz is devoted exclusively to one of the city's most comprehensive selections of perfumes and fragrances. If you can name it, this store will probably have it. Bahnhofstrasse 26. © **044/221-18-55.**

PORCELAIN

Ursula Riedi   Whatever you do, don't make any sudden moves in this shop. It's loaded from floor to ceiling with some of the most exquisite and valuable antique Meissen porcelain in Zurich. Everything is breathtakingly fragile, and breathtakingly valuable, a safe haven for aficionados of Europe's most ephemeral art form—antique porcelain. Leave the kids at home. Torgasse 5. © **044/252-35-10.**

SHOES

Andy Jllien, C. Q.   This is the quintessential boutique, with a carefully chosen but limited inventory of shoes that might appeal to fashion-conscious women. Torgasse 5-6. © **044/252-19-11.**

Bally Capitol   This is the place to buy Bally shoes. The prominently situated store is the world's largest official outlet of this famous Swiss chain. The store carries the complete line, along with accessories and clothing for men, women, and children. Bahnhofstrasse 66. © **044/224-39-39.**

Graziella   Graziella's inventory of shoes comes from throughout Europe. There's everything from sensible oxfords to the kind of flimsy but oh-so-attractive footwear a woman might wear to a Hollywood premier or a glamorous casino. Löwenstrasse 30. © **044/221-11-93.**

WATCHES

Beyer   If you have your heart set on buying a timepiece in Zurich, try this well-established store midway between the train station and the lake. Besides carrying just about every famous brand of watch made in Switzerland—Rolex, Corum, Cartier, and Patke Philippe—it also has a museum in the basement, containing timepieces from as early as 1400 B.C. Exhibitions include all kinds of water clocks, sundials, and hourglasses. Bahnhofstrasse 31. © 044/344-63-63.

Bucherer   A longtime name in the Swiss watch industry, this store also carries an impressive collection of jewelry. Some of the most famous names in watchmaking are represented in their latest offerings, including Chopard, Rado, and Rolex. Bahnhofstrasse 6. © 044/967-53-53.

7 Zurich After Dark

The city's nightlife is becoming less conservative, but don't expect it to be too wild. Most of the nightspots in Zurich close down early, so you should begin early. Concerts, theater, opera, and ballet all flourish here.

To learn what's on during your visit, pick up a copy of *Zurich News,* available free at the tourist office and distributed at the front desks of most hotels.

THE PERFORMING ARTS

No special discount tickets are granted, but for regular tickets to operas, theaters, and concerts, go to **Billettzentrale** (BiZZ for short), Bahnhofstrasse 9 (© 044/221-22-83), open Monday to Friday from 10am to 6:30pm and on Saturday from 10am to 2pm.

The **Zurich Opera** is the most outstanding local company, performing at the Opernhaus. The **Zurich Tonhalle Orchestra,** performing at Tonhalle, also enjoys an international reputation.

Opernhaus   Zurich Opera House, near Bellevueplatz in the center of the city, was founded in 1891. The history of the opera house forms part of the cultural history of Europe; the house was the venue of several world premiers, including performances of *Lulu* by Alban Berg and *Mathis der Maler* by Hindemith. The opera house is also a repertory theater, hosting ballets, concerts, and recitals. The hall is dark in July and August. Box office open daily from 10am to 6:30pm. Falkenstrasse 1. © 044/268-66-66. www.opernhaus.ch. Tickets 16F–230F ($13–$189).

Schauspielhaus   This is one of the most important theaters in Switzerland, generally performing plays in German that range from classic to modern. It's a repertoire theater that performs different works nearly every evening, not long-running shows. Box office open daily from 10am to 7pm. Closed mid-June to September. Rämistrasse 34, at Heimplatz. © 044/268-66-66. www.schauspielhaus.ch. Tickets 23F–97F ($19–$80).

Tonhalle Gesellschaft   This concert hall facing Bürkliplatz is the biggest and most famous concert hall in Zurich, with 1,500 seats in the big hall and 700 seats in the small hall. Brahms opened Tonhalle Gesellschaft in 1895 with a presentation of "Song of Triumph." It's home to the Zurich Tonhalle Orchestra and the venue for appearances by many internationally known soloists. Recitals and chamber music presentations are also staged here. Try to purchase your tickets as early as possible because many seats are sold by subscription. Reservations can be made 2 weeks prior to any concert. Box office open daily from 10am to 6pm, except concert days when it closes at performance time. Claridenstrasse 5. © 044/206-34-34. www.tonhalle.ch. Tickets 20F–141F ($16–$116).

My, what an inefficient way to fish.

Ring toss, good. Horseshoes, bad.

Faster! Faster! Faster!

We take care of the fiddly bits, from providing over 43,000 customer reviews of hotels, to helping you find our best fares, to giving you 24/7 customer service. So you can focus on the only thing that matters. Goofing off.

travelocity
You'll never roam alone.™

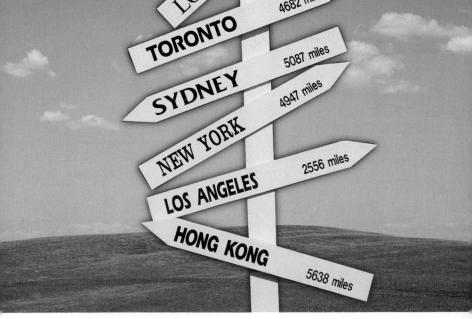

THE CLUB & MUSIC SCENE

Adagio   In a city building frequently used for public meetings (the Kongresshaus), this nightclub sets strict standards of respectability for its relatively conservative clientele, generally attracting an over-35 crowd. Adagio is a dance club—mainly ballroom stuff in a big hall decorated like a church. The staff wears ancient costumes, and fresh flowers and burning candles abound. The club is extremely crowded on weekends. Open year-round Sunday to Thursday 5pm to 2am, Friday and Saturday 5pm to 4am. In the Kongresshaus, Gothardstrasse 5. © **044/206-36-66.** No cover.

Bierhalle Wolf   With 160 seats, this is the best-known beer hall in Zurich, drawing people of all ages and all walks of life. It features "evergreen music" in a sometimes rowdy but safe environment. Folk music is played by an oompah band in regional garb whose instruments include a tuba, accordion, saxophone, clarinet, and bass. The large beer hall is decorated with pennants and flags of different cantons. Beer is available in tankards costing 6.50F ($5.35) and up. Live music is presented every day from 4 to 6:30pm and from 8:30pm to midnight, and every Sunday morning from 10am to noon. During the breaks, slides of alpine scenery are shown. You can also dine here on hearty robust fare, with main courses starting at 13F ($11). Open daily from 11am to 2am. Limmatquai 132. © **044/251-01-30.** Cover 4F–5F ($3.30–$4.10).

Gastro Annoncen AG Casa-Bar   When Zurichers want to hear New Orleans–style, Dixieland jazz, they head here. Some rhythm and blues from the '50s and '60s is regularly featured as well. The dark-paneled decor is inspired by the forests of Switzerland. On a busy night, at least 60 patrons of varying ages can crowd in here. A beer costs 10F ($8.20) and up. Or you can order hard liquor beginning at 16F ($13). Wine by the glass costs from 16F ($13). Open daily from 5pm to 2am. Münstergasse 30. © **044/261-20-02.** No cover.

Kaufleuten   This club attracts a wide cross section of Zurich society, partly because of the central location and partly because of the comfortably battered, old-fashioned interior whose mismatched tables and chairs imply a certain unstructured comfort. Inside are four different bar areas with mostly house and garage music playing. The Restaurant Kaufleuten is separately recommended in "Where to Dine," earlier in the chapter. Open daily 11pm to 2am (till 4am Fri–Sat). Pelikanstrasse 18. © **044/225-33-22.** Cover 15F–25F ($12–$21), depending on the night of the week.

Palais X-tra   This is the largest nightclub in Zurich, a cavernous, high-ceilinged, affair partially painted in strident colors of red and black, with a long, long bar, an outdoor terrace, and restaurant facilities that seem to be less popular than the bar and rock-'n'-roll club that fill the same place. Between bouts of recorded music, a changing ensemble of live acts will appear, drawing counterculture and youthful fans from throughout Switzerland. This is a trendy and creative address, beloved by persons in their 20s, and respected by parents throughout the city as a spot where their children are likely, at least once, to have spent some time meeting and mingling. Open Monday, Wednesday, and Saturday 8pm to 2am. In the Limmathaus, Limmatsrasse 118. © **044/ 448-15-00.** www.x-tra.ch. Cover 30F–45F ($25–$37) depending on the performers.

THE BAR SCENE

Blaue Ente   Although Blaue Ente is best known as a restaurant, many locals, especially young professionals, come here for its bar. In a high-tech setting, you can enjoy beer beginning at 5F ($4.10), or whiskey at 14F ($11). Although the restaurant is open daily, the bar is closed on Sunday. Open Monday through Saturday from 11:30am to 12:30am. Both the bar and its restaurant are closed from July 25 to August 17. Seefeldstrasse 223 at Mühle Tiefenbrunnen. ℂ **044/388-68-40.**

James Joyce Pub   The furnishings and paneling of this pub were acquired in the early 1970s by the Union Bank of Switzerland, when Jury's, an 18th-century hotel in Dublin, was demolished. The Union Bank reassembled the bar (with slightly more comfortable banquettes) near Bahnhofstrasse to entertain business clients and named it after famous Dubliner James Joyce, who had described its decor in certain passages of *Ulysses.* The blackboard menu lists the daily specials *(Plattes).* In December, Irish stew is traditionally served. Other fare includes fish and chips, hamburgers, and fried chicken legs. Open Monday to Friday 11am to midnight and on Saturday from 11am to 6pm. Pelikanstrasse 8. ℂ **044/221-18-28.**

Jules Verne   To reach the bar, you'll have to ride an elevator to the 11th floor, after passing through the street-level restaurant (Brasserie Lipp—see "Where to Dine," earlier in this chapter) with which it's associated. Views from the windows encompass the center of Zurich and some of the surrounding scenery, and the decor includes nostalgic references to what the bar's namesake envisioned as the technology of the future. The place can get crowded with talkers and drinkers in their 30s and 40s as music plays in the background. You can expect conviviality but not necessarily intimacy here. It's a great happy-hour spot. Open daily from 11:30am to midnight (till 1am Fri–Sat). Uraniastrasse 9. ℂ **044/211-11-55.**

Rosaly's   The structure looks a lot like a geranium-studded alpine chalet that's oddly positioned on a narrow alleyway near the most congested part of the Bellevueplatz, a busy downtown tram junction. During the dinner hour, patrons huddle around a half-moon-shaped bar area, leaving most of the tables to diners. Later in the evening, however, more and more of the tables—both indoor and outdoor—become devoted to the bar. There's a sense of hipness and whimsy to this place, and an occasional subtle reference to big-city life in faraway California. The list of cocktails include kamikazes, Rob Roys, side cars, and margaritas. Open daily from 4pm to midnight or 1am, depending on business. Freieckgasse 7. ℂ **044/261-44-30.**

Schmuklerski   There isn't that much to the decor of this place, other than a sheathing of mirrors, a kind of glossy minimalism, and tables that spill out into a garden in back during clement weather. But it rates as one of the bars of the minute in trend-conscious Zurich, thanks to its ownership by a local soccer star, Thomas Bickel, whose cachet and contacts draw in a bevy of sports stars and fans, models and mannequins, graphic designers and media people. Look for such cocktails as caipirinhas and mojitos, many kinds of beer, and a contagious sense of hip. The bar is open Monday from 4pm to midnight, Tuesday and Wednesday 9am to midnight, Thursday and Friday 9am to 2am, Saturday noon to 2am, and Sunday noon to midnight. 101 Badenerstrasse. ℂ **044/241-15-41.**

2 Akt   By daylight, this place resembles a simple bistro, with varnished pine paneling, high ceilings, and accessories that hint at its beer-hall-style origins around the turn of the 20th century. A simple menu of Wiener schnitzels and roasted chicken accompanies mugs of beer and glasses of wine. By nightfall, however, the place is filled with the young and the restless, and on nights when a DJ spins state-of-the-art dance music, the place is mobbed. It isn't a disco per se, but rather a bar and restaurant that just happens to play dance music, and which just happens to attract a crowd of TV announcers, journalists, and artists in modern-day Zurich. As such, you'll probably be tapping your feet to the music but not actually dancing, unless a group of rowdies breaks loose from their drinking and spontaneously begins to gyrate. The weekly schedule of which spin-meister will be on duty is clearly marked on a blackboard several days in advance, adding an element of star quality to the artist who's actually selecting the music. Food is served Monday to Saturday from 9am to 10pm, and Sunday from 5 to 10pm. A DJ plays Thursday to Saturday from 9pm to 4am. Open Monday to Saturday from 9am to 2 or 4am, Sunday from 5pm to 2am. Seinaustrasse 2. ✆ **044/201-65-64.**

THE GAY SCENE

Barfüsser   This is the premier jeans-and-leather bar for gay men in Zurich, although in recent years an increasing number of gay women have shown up as well. It proudly lays claim to being the oldest continuously operated gay bar in Europe, with a well-worn dark and woodsy decor and a loyal clientele who have patronized the place since its establishment in 1956. Most show up after 8pm, and it's especially popular on week-ends. On-site is a sushi bar, which serves continuously throughout the day until 11pm. It's open Monday to Wednesday from 11am to 1am, Thursday 11am to 2am, Friday and Saturday 11am to 3am, and Sunday 3pm to 1am. Spitalgasse 14. ✆ **044/251-40-64.**

Club Aaah!   Set within the same all-gay hotel recommended previously (see Hotel Goldenes Schwert on p. 89), this is a techno-rock dance club with a bar, a minimal-ist, vaguely industrial-looking decor, and an animated, rather sweaty dark room in back. It isn't for everybody, although if you're absolutely intent on exploring as many gay dives as possible during one of your counterculture explorations of a town whose gay life has considerably expanded recently, it's worth a brief hello. There's a cover charge of 25F ($21) per person that's imposed only on Friday and Saturday nights. Otherwise, entrance is free, and beers cost around 7F ($5.75) each. Open daily 9:30pm to 2am. In the Hotel Goldenes Schwert, Marktgasse 14. ✆ **044/266-18-90.**

Cranberry's   Of the many gay bars that compete with the convivial and deeply entrenched Barfüsser, this one is the most successful. It's definitely not a disco (no one comes here to dance), but for an ambience that's like that of a classy and minimalist-looking American-style cocktail bar, and where virtually everyone is gay or gay-friendly, it's a solid and reliable bet. Scattered over two floors of a building in Zurich's historic Altstadt, cocktails cost from 10F to 17F ($8.20–$14) each. It's open Monday to Wednesday from 5pm to 1am, Thursday 5pm to 2am, Friday and Saturday 5pm to 3am, and Sunday 5pm to 12:30am. Metzgergasse 3. ✆ **044/261-27-72.**

Labor Bar   Most of the week, this place operates like a well-oiled, mostly heterosex-ual club where teeny-boppers release pent-up energy, and where recent divorcés min-gle and flirt and sometimes get lucky. Upcoming musical venues are scheduled online (www.laborbar.ch) several months in advance, and if you happen to be caught in the flashbulbs of the resident paparazzi, it's likely that it will be posted on the Internet within a day or two. But every Sunday night, beginning around 7pm, the place goes gay, and if, when it does, a recently divorced (presumably heterosexual) single happens to wander in, he or she usually tends to have a marvelous time. Entrance is usually free for these "Trash Sundays," and beers cost around 7F ($5.75) each. Open Friday and Saturday from 10pm to 3am, Sunday 9pm to 2am. Schiffbaustrasse 3. ✆ **044/272-44-02.**

The Labyrinth   Depending on the night of the week, this place might switch-hit between its straight and gay identities. But at press time the prevalent wisdom assigned Wednesday, Friday, and Saturday (from around 9:30pm till between 1 and 3am, depending on business) to a mostly gay—and youthfully so—clientele. There's a bar or two on the premises, but most of the crowd comes here just to dance, dance, dance, and perhaps to explore the shadowy premises this place maintains in its nether areas. Entrance costs 25F ($21) per person, a price that includes the first drink. Open Friday and Saturday from 11:30pm till late. Pfingstweidstrasse 70. No phone.

Predigerhof   This is a warm, friendly, and sometimes very busy men's pub that makes every effort to welcome the widest possible cross section of the local gay community. Despite its attempts at even-handedness, it tends to attract the kind of machos you might have expected in a high-altitude hut in the Swiss Alps. Sandwiches, salads, and soups are served, each item priced from 5F to 10F ($4.10–$8.20). Beers cost 4.90F ($4). Open Sunday to Thursday 11am to 2am, Friday and Saturday 11am to 4am. Mühlegasse 15. ℂ 044/251-29-85.

T&M Club   It's deliberately tacky, even "artfully cheesy," according to its fans, and if you're shocked or offended by German-accented males of all possible body types trying to look as drag-bitch glamorous as possible, this is definitely not the place for you. It's located one floor above street level within a room loaded with Teutonic kitsch. Feeling nostalgic for Berlin between the wars? This place might evoke some aspects of that time and era for you. Drag shows are presented nightly at 10pm, sometimes with later shows presented sporadically, if at all, around 1am. Entrance costs 25F ($21) per person. Within the same hotel, two floors above street level, you'll also find Club A, described in greater detail above. Open Tuesday to Saturday from 9:30pm. In the Hotel Goldenes Schwert, Marktgasse 14. ℂ 044/266-18-90.

8 Side Trips from Zurich

Zurich is surrounded by some of the most interesting sightseeing areas in Switzerland. The following are a few of exceptional interest. All these attractions can easily be reached on a short trip from your hotel in Zurich, either by train or by lake steamer.

GREAT RIDES THROUGH THE ENVIRONS

A few fun, quick tours you can take on your own make use of funiculars and trains. If you have time for only one of these trips, make it the Uetliberg (see below).

THE DOLDERBAHN ⌖   Take the Dolderbahn for a short aerial cable ride to the **Dolder Recreational Area,** 596m (1,955 ft.) above the city. Trains leave every 10 minutes from Römerhofplatz, which you can reach by taking tram no. 3, 8, or 15. The recreational area is open year-round and has restaurants, nature trails, old rustic taverns, a path to the zoo, a miniature golf course, and, from October to March, a huge ice-skating rink. There's a place to swim, the **Dolder Schwimmbad** (ℂ 044/267-70-80), which is carved into a hillside with a view of Zurich. The swimming area is a 5-minute walk along a forest trail from the end of the cable-car line; follow the signs to Dolder Wellenbad. Admission to the pool with its artificial waves is 8F ($6.55), 5F ($4.10) for children under 6. The Dolderbahn funicular ride costs 2.50F ($2.05); buy your tickets from the machine.

THE FORCHBAHN   For a close-up view of some of the most desirable residential real estate in Zurich, consider a ride on the Forchbahn, a short-haul railway line originating in downtown Zurich at the Stadelhofen Bahnhof, which lies at the junction of the Bellevueplatz and the Limmatquai, adjacent to the Quaibrücke (ℂ 044/434-41-11 for more information). The Forchbahn travels through the capital's staid and endlessly respectable suburbs (local wits refer to it as "The Gold Coast") to end points at

Esslingen and Forch, both of which lie within 30-minute rides south of the city center. The area is noted for its sunlight, and as such, gardening seems to be a passionate pastime for local residents. You can get off the train at any of the stops, and pick any of the signposted trails that meander to nearby points of scenic interest. (The tourist office in Zurich is a good source of information. Otherwise, just ask a local or set out on a brief excursion on your own.) The shores of both the Greifensee and the Zurichsee are good bets for a walk, with paths that meander down from many points en route. Trains on the Forchbahn run without conductors, so you must buy your tickets from a machine at whatever point you happen to get on.

A round-trip ticket from Stadelhofen Bahnhof to Forch costs 15F ($12); a round-trip ticket from Stadelhofen Bahnhof to Esslingen costs 18F ($15). Trains depart from downtown Zurich (Bellevueplatz) at 30-minute intervals throughout the day and evening.

FELSENEGG 🎿   An excursion to the alpine aerie at Felsenegg isn't as vertiginous as other mountain stations in higher-altitude regions of Switzerland, but its proximity to Zurich makes it one of the most consistently popular. To reach it, take one of the frequent (every 25 min.) trains from Zurich's Hauptbahnhof for the 14-minute ride to the residential suburb of Adliswil, 10km (6 miles) south, for a cost of 7.50F ($6.15) each way. Get off in Adliswil, then embark on a brisk, 10-minute uphill climb to an aerial cable car, the Luftseilbahn Adliswil-Felsenegg (LAF; ℂ **044/710-73-30**), for a 6-minute uphill ride to the top of Felsenegg, at 795m (2,608 ft.) above sea level. Expect to pay 7.20F ($5.90) round-trip. From here, it's a 10-minute hike to the **Restaurant Felsenegg** (ℂ **044/710-77-55;** www.felsenegg.com), serving typical alpine food on a panoramic outdoor terrace or indoors. Main courses range in price from 9.50F to 28F ($7.80–$23). From May to September, the restaurant is open daily from 8am to 10pm; from October to April, 9am to 8pm. Every Saturday night year-round, it stays open till 11pm. It's closed 2 weeks in early November.

ALPAMARE   We also recommend a visit to **Alpamare** (ℂ **055/415-15-87;** www.alpamare.ch), Europe's largest water park as certified in the *Guinness Book of World Records.* It lies at Churstrasse 111, in the village of Pfäffikon on Lake Zurich, offering year-round fun in and around the water on four body flumes and both indoor and outdoor tube slides. There's also an indoor swimming pool with breakers, a bubbling hot spring, and an open-air pool with underwater music and massage jets, as well as 90m (295 ft.) of lazy river. An outdoor thermal pool contains iodine. The attraction is open daily from 10am to 10pm. Weekdays adults pay 36F ($29) for a visit of up to 4 hours or 46F ($38) for a daylong visit. Children under 16 are charged 29F ($24) for a visit of up to 4 hours or 38F ($31) for a daylong visit. Weekends adults pay 39F ($32) and 46F ($38), respectively, and children 31F ($25) and 38F ($31). Children 2 and under are not allowed in the water.

KILCHBERG   If you're an admirer of Thomas Mann, we recommend a visit to Kilchberg, 6km (4 miles) from Zurich along the southwestern shore of the lake. Mann spent the last years of his life here and was buried on the south side of the small church in the village in 1955. His wife died here in 1980. Fans of the author still flock here to see the grave site, but Kilchberg is more famously associated with the 19th-century Swiss author Conrad Ferdinand Meyer. Train S8 departs from the Zurich Hauptbahnhof every half-hour for an 11-minute ride to the village. If traveling by car, proceed along the southwestern shore route of Lake Zurich following the signposts to Kilchberg.

UETLIBERG   Southwest of Zurich, Uetliberg, the northernmost peak in the Albis ridge, is one of the most popular excursions from the city, reached in only 15 minutes. Take the mountain railway Uetlibergbahn from the Selnau station in Zurich. A round-trip costs 14F ($11) and takes half an hour. You arrive near the Sihl River, at an elevation of 840m (2,755 ft.).

From the station, you can hike 10 minutes to the summit, where there's a cafe and restaurant. The tower is a climb of about 170 steps; from the lookout, on a clear day, you can see as far away as the Black Forest. For more information about the train, call ℂ **044/206-45-11.**

WINTERTHUR

This industrial town in the Toss Valley, 20km (12 miles) northeast of Zurich, is also a music and cultural center, with an art collection that makes the 15-minute train trip from Zurich worthwhile. Winterthur was once a Roman settlement and became the seat of the counts of Kyburg. It later was a stronghold of the Hapsburgs, until it was sold to Zurich. In the United States the name Winterthur conjures up the du Pont mansion in Delaware with its museum of Americana, or a reference to the financial giant, Winterthur Insurance. Both of these take their name from this Swiss industrial city.

Winterthur is best explored on foot. City officials have signposted an itinerary that takes in the history, architecture, and culture of the town.

A **tourist office** is at Im Hauptbahnhof (ℂ **052/267-67-00**), open Tuesday to Friday 8:30am to 6:30pm, and on Saturday from 8:30am to 4pm.

From Zurich's Hauptbahnhof, trains depart about every 20 minutes throughout the day (trip time: 20–26 min.).

SEEING THE SIGHTS

The skyline of Winterthur is dominated by the twin towers of its parish church, the Stadtkirche, built from 1264 to 1515 (the towers were added later).

Kunstmuseum ⟡   Located a 10-minute walk north of the Stadthaus on Stadthausstrasse and Lindstrasse, this fine-arts museum contains an impressive collection of European and American art and sculpture from the late 19th century to the present. Giacometti and such French artists as Bonnard and Vuillard are well represented. Highlights are works by van Gogh, Miró, Magritte, Mondrian, Kokoschka, Calder, and Klee. There are sculptures by Rodin, as well as works by Medardo Rosso and Maillol. The permanent collection is on display from June to August; temporary exhibits are presented the rest of the year.

Museumstrasse 52. ℂ 052/267-51-62. Admission 10F ($8.20) adults, 7F ($5.75) seniors and students 16–18, children under 16 with adult enter free. Tues 10am–8pm; Wed–Sun 10am–5pm. Bus: 1, 3, or 6 to Stadthaus.

Museum Oskar Reinhart am Stadtgarten ⟡⟡   Oskar Reinhart, a famous art collector who died in 1965, willed many of his treasures to the city. Displayed in this gallery are works of Austrian, German, and Swiss artists, with a fine representation of the Romantic painters, including Blechen, Friedrich, Kersting, and Runge. Many canvases are by Hodler. There are some 600 works in all, from the 18th to the 20th centuries.

Stadthausstrasse 6. ℂ 052/267-51-72. www.museumoskarreinhart.ch. Admission 8F ($6.55) adults, 6F ($4.90) children under 8. Wed–Sun 10am–5pm; Tues 10am–8pm. Bus: 1, 3, or 6.

Schloss Kyburg   Six kilometers (4 miles) from Winterthur, Schloss Kyburg is the largest castle in eastern Switzerland, dating from the Middle Ages. The stronghold was the ancestral home of the counts of Kyburg until 1264, when the Hapsburgs took over. These counts were local rulers and of little interest to visitors today, as their history has long been overshadowed by the more powerful and more famous Hapsburg dynasty. It was ceded to Zurich in the 15th century and is now a museum of antiques and armor. There's a good view from the keep. You may also visit the residence hall of the knights, parapet, and chapel.

Kyburg 8314. (C) **052/232-46-64**. www.schlosskyburg.ch. Admission 8F ($6.55) adults, 6F ($4.90) students and seniors, 3F ($2.45) children 6–16, free for children 5 and under. Feb–Nov Tues–Sun 10:30am–4:30pm (May–Oct till 5:30pm). Closed Dec–Jan. From Zurich, take the Winterthur rail line, get off at the Fretekon stop, and transfer to a bus for the 10-min. ride to the castle; buses depart every hour throughout the day. The castle is not on a street (or road) map.

Swiss Technorama   Technorama is the Swiss National Center for Science and Technology. Its permanent exhibition is divided into eight areas, with many interactive experiments and phenomena: Physics, Energy, Water/Nature/Chaos, Mechanical Music, Mathe-Magic, Materials, Textiles, and Automation. Technorama also boasts the world's greatest tin-plate train collection. In the hands-on Youth Laboratory, children can learn from some 100 experiments about science, mathematics, and biology. A self-service restaurant is at the site, and a big park features a steam train and muscle-powered flying machines.

Technoramastrasse 1. (C) **052/243-05-05**. www.technorama.ch. Admission 17F ($14) adults, 11F ($9) students and seniors, 9F ($7.40) children 6–19, free for children 5 and under. Tues–Sun 10am–5pm. Closed Dec 25. Take motorway N1, exit at Oberwinterthur, and drive a mile toward Winterthur. Or take a train to the Winterthur main station and switch to bus no. 5, marked TECHNORAMA.

WHERE TO DINE

Schloss Wulflingen SWISS   This long-enduring favorite lies 4km (2½ miles) west of the center. The rustic stone, stucco, and slate building was built in 1644 and still has many of its original ceramic stoves in the dining rooms. In the summer the owners adorn the intricate shutters of the step-gabled house with garlands, and cafe tables are set out in front. Specialties include beef in red- and green-pepper sauce with gratin potatoes, sole, catfish, salmon, giant shrimp, and other seafood. A simpler menu is offered at lunch, including veal stuffed with country ham, a mousse of foie gras served with tiny homemade noodles, and fresh-fish dishes.

Wulflingerstrasse 240, Winterthur-Wulflingen. (C) **052/222-18-67**. Reservations recommended. Main courses 38F–69F ($31–$57). AE, DC, MC, V. Wed–Sun 10am–midnight. Bus: 2 from Winterthur.

5

Northeastern Switzerland

The northeastern region of Switzerland—one of the country's most unspoiled areas—contains the cantons of Appenzell, Glarus, St. Gallen, Schaffhausen, and Thurgau, and such wondrous natural sights as St. Gallen's Rhine Valley and the Rhine Falls. St. Gallen is the region's bustling cultural and economic center, and some of the most abundant orchards in the country dot the shores of Lake Constance.

For the athletic, there's plenty of sports and adventure to be found. Skiing, snowboarding, tobogganing, and hiking are easily accessible in the mountain areas. Sailing schools abound in the lakeside communities of Rorschach and Kreuzlingen, and the flat countryside along the lake is perfect for biking.

The northeastern region is also a sensible destination economically, as food and lodging prices are among the lowest in the country.

For an overnight stopover in the area, our money is on Stein-am-Rhein, one of the most perfectly preserved medieval villages in Europe and also one of the most charming of all Swiss towns. It lies at the point where the Rhein leaves Lake Constance. It also has the most charming old-world hotels.

However, that doesn't mean that other towns in northeastern Switzerland are without their allure. If you like your cities historic, make it St. Gallen, the largest city in eastern Switzerland. However, if you've come to the area for its folkish charm, head for Appenzell, the country's most traditional town (some Swiss speak of locals here as virtual hillbillies).

If boating and views of Lake Constance are your passion, take a promenade along the seafront, then settle into one of the resorts along Lake Constance—Rorschach has the widest choice of hotels and restaurants.

1 St. Gallen ★ ★

85km (53 miles) E of Zurich; 156km (97 miles) E of Basel; 15km (9 miles) SW of Rorschach

At 660m (2,165 ft.) above sea level, this valley is one of the primary stops in northeastern Switzerland. St. Gallen, which is the highest city of its size in Europe, is a good base for exploring Lake Constance (a 15-min. drive away), Mount Säntis, and the Appenzell countryside. This ancient town in the foothills of the Alps was founded by Gallus, an Irish monk who built a hermitage here in 612. By the 13th century his humble cell had developed into an important cultural outpost. St. Gallen became a free imperial city in 1212, and in 1454 it joined the Swiss Confederation. With a population of approximately 75,000, St. Gallen is the capital of a canton of the same name.

St. Gallen is the embroidery and lace capital of Europe; here, three dozen seamstresses worked for a year and a half to make a lace gown for Empress Eugénie, the wife of Napoleon III. Today most of the embroidery is done by computer-driven machines. However, you can still purchase handmade items (see "Shopping," below).

Freudenberg, 3km (2 miles) south of St. Gallen, at an altitude of 900m (2,952 ft.), offers a panoramic view of Mount Säntis, St. Gallen, and Lake Constance (known in this part of the country as Bodensee).

ESSENTIALS

GETTING THERE St. Gallen is on the main train lines connecting Zurich with Munich. At least a dozen trains per day arrive from both directions. Trip time from Zurich is about 75 minutes. St. Gallen is the railway linchpin for at least four local lines. Call ℭ **0900-300-300** (no area code) for more information.

As in most other Swiss cities, bus connections in St. Gallen are meant to supplement railroad service. Buses connect St. Gallen mainly with such outlying villages as

Rorschach and Appenzell, with many stops at local villages along the way. Call the tourist office (see below) for more information.

By car from Zurich, head east on N1 (also called E17).

VISITOR INFORMATION   The **St. Gallen Tourist Office** is located at Bahnhofplatz 1A (© **071/227-37-37;** www.st.gallen-bodensee.ch). It's open Monday to Friday from 9am to noon and 1 to 6pm, Saturday 9am to noon.

EXPLORING THE TOWN

The **Old City** 🎔 is the thing to see here, with its restored, half-timbered houses and their turrets and oriels. Wander the lanes and alleys laid out during the Middle Ages; some of them are closed to traffic.

The Protestant Reformation was victorious in St. Gallen, but the **Benedictine monastery at Klosterhof** remained virtually unaffected. The monastery contains the Catholic bishop's residence, the abbey library, and the canton's government offices. This area is also the site of the Domkirche (see below). The buildings that remain of the abbey date from the 17th and 18th centuries. Its walls were razed, and the best view is from the abbey yard, called the Klosterhof. To reach the abbey from Marktplatz in the center of town, take Marktgasse south, past St. Lawrence's Church, to the large Klosterhof.

St. Gallen offers many sports facilities, including tennis courts and three outdoor swimming pools. The region's best golf course lies 4km (2½ miles) from St. Gallen at the **Waldkirch Golf Park,** Golfpark Waldkirch, St. Gallen (© **071/434-67-67**). To get here, follow the road signs to Gosau. An 18-hole round of golf costs from 70F to 90F ($57–$74) per person. Because much of the area is relatively flat, consider renting a bicycle (available at the federal rail station). The tourist office (see "Essentials," above) is helpful in outlining bike routes that aren't too strenuous.

Serious climbers tend to dismiss the region around St. Gallen as being too flat, and they will consequently direct you to loftier altitudes near Appenzell. But if you don't mind a softly undulating landscape that's forested with deciduous trees, and accessible even to those not in the best shape, consider an 8km (5-mile) trip that incorporates the best and most panoramic of the local low-lying hills. From the center of St. Gallen, take bus no. 5 to the satellite hamlet of Reithüsli. From there, you'll climb a low hill, **Bernegg,** whose views sweep out over the Bodensee. There's a cozy wood-sheathed restaurant near its summit (the **Falkenburg Restaurant;** © **071/222-55-81**), where air-dried beef and hearty stews and steaks are the norm every day at lunch and dinner. Walk about a mile to **Drei Weiher,** a trio of small, clear lakes, where you can swim. Afterwards you can walk back to St. Gallen directly, or retrace your steps to the hamlet of Reithüsli. The complete excursion can last between 4 and 6 hours, depending on how much you dawdle en route. For more information on this and other treks near St. Gallen or Appenzell, contact the local tourist office.

Domkirche (Cathedral)   The twin-towered Domkirche at Klosterhof is Switzerland's best example of baroque architecture. It was erected in 1756 on the site of the celebrated 14th-century Gothic abbey. Be sure to check out the cathedral chancel, one of its more interesting architectural features.

Klosterhof. © **071/227-34-88.** Free admission. Daily 9am–7pm.

Stiftsbibliothek (Abbey Library) 🎔🎔🎔   This world-famous library contains some 130,000 volumes, including manuscripts dating back to the 8th through the

15th centuries (several of the Renaissance manuscripts have well-preserved illustrations). The library hall is built in a rococo style, with stucco art and ceiling paintings. A plan of the St. Gallen Abbey in the year 830 is displayed, preserved under glass.

Klosterhof 6. ✆ **071/227-34-16.** Admission 7F ($4.55) adults, 5F ($3.25) students and seniors, free for children 15 and under. Apr–Nov Mon–Fri 10am–5pm; Dec–Mar Mon–Fri 10am–noon and 1:30–4pm.

SHOPPING

Many shoppers come to St. Gallen seeking embroideries. The best place to look is **Sturzenegger Broderie,** Spisergasse 2 (✆ **071/222-45-76**), established in 1883. Here you'll find a large variety of tablecloths, place mats, doilies, and napkins, both hand- and machine-made. Sturzenegger also sells blouses, handkerchiefs, shawls, scarves, and children's frocks, as well as a large assortment of nightgowns, pajamas, and women's lingerie.

You can find real bargains when the local textile factories have clearance sales, usually in January and July. The tourist office (see "Essentials," above) will advise.

Another good source for textiles and embroidery is **Saphir,** Bleichestrasse 9 (✆ **071/223-62-63**), which sells high-quality goods, including the finest table linens and hand-embroidered handkerchiefs. They also sell bolts of St. Gallen lace and tasteful fabrics by the yard.

To see how the embroideries—both hand- and machine-made—of St. Gallen are produced, call **Försterhoner Embroiderie,** Flurhofstrasse 150 (✆ **071/243-15-15**), which is 10 minutes by car from the center of town in the direction of Bodensee. You need an appointment, but they'll show you the factory and explain the process to you.

Finally, **Graphica Antiqua,** Marktgasse 26 (✆ **071/223-50-16**), is a real shopping find, selling an array of antique prints of Swiss landscapes, including the Alps and "Heidi meadows." Prints are available from all parts of Switzerland, and each region is clearly identified in the shop.

WHERE TO STAY
EXPENSIVE
Einstein Hotel ★★   The most desirable hotel in town, the Einstein is near the center of the historic district. Built some 150 years ago, originally as a Swiss embroidery factory, it was converted in 1983 into a stylish provincial hotel. It has a gray-and-white neoclassical facade and a marble lobby, and you're likely to hear live piano music playing in the pub/cocktail bar. The midsize guest rooms are conservatively furnished and well maintained, each fitted with neatly kept bathrooms.

Berneggstrasse 2, CH-9001 St. Gallen. ✆ **071/227-55-55.** Fax 071/227-55-77. www.einstein.ch. 113 units. 250F–380F ($205–$312) double; 425F–510F ($349–$418) suite. AE, DC, MC, V. Parking 20F ($13) in the garage, free outside. Bus: 1, 3, or 11. **Amenities:** Restaurant; bar; limited room service; laundry service/dry cleaning. *In room:* TV, minibar, hair dryer.

MODERATE
Hotel Ekkehard   Located in the center of town, this typical government-rated three-star Swiss hotel is neat and well maintained, with small but pleasant rooms. All are equipped with tidily kept bathrooms. The hotel offers a wood-trimmed restaurant with modern decor serving Austrian food at reasonable prices (closed July 13–Aug 9), as well as a more upscale option.

Rorschacher Strasse 50, CH-9000 St. Gallen. ✆ **071/222-04-44.** Fax 071/222-04-74. www.ekkehard.ch. 29 units. 158F–240F ($130–$197) double. Rates include buffet breakfast. AE, DC, MC, V. Bus: 1 or 7. **Amenities:** 2 restaurants; limited room service; laundry service. *In room:* TV, dataport, minibar, hair dryer.

Hotel Gallo   This hotel—a former apartment house—lies along a busy traffic artery, about a 10-minute walk from the town center. Windows are double-glazed to shut out the noise. Some of the details of its Art Nouveau facade are still visible. The recently renovated rooms have tall windows and contain big tiled bathrooms. Our favorites are two cozy attic rooms under beamed ceilings with dormer windows.

St. Jacobstrasse 62, CH-9000 St. Gallen. ☎ **071/242-71-71.** Fax 071/242-71-61. www.hotelgallo.ch. 24 units. 220F–240F ($180–$197) double; 270F ($221) triple. Rates include buffet breakfast. AE, DC, MC, V. Dogs welcome for 15F ($12) fee. Parking 20F ($16). Bus: 3. **Amenities:** Lounge; breakfast room; laundry service/dry cleaning. *In room:* A/C, TV, dataport, minibar, hair dryer, trouser press.

Hotel Walhalla *✎*   This modernized Best Western is a first-class hotel in the shopping district. It faces the main railroad station and parking garage and is about a 3-minute walk from the Old Town. Many visitors use the Walhalla as a base for excursions to Appenzellerland and the Lake Constance area. The rooms are nicely furnished and include well-scrubbed bathrooms. The hotel has a Mediterranean-style restaurant, which also serves typical Swiss cuisine.

Bahnhofplatz, CH-9001 St. Gallen. ☎ **800/528-1234** in the U.S. or 071/228-28-00. Fax 071/228-28-90. www.hotel walhalla.ch. 57 units. 180F–220F ($148–$180) double; 280F ($230) suite for 2. Rates include buffet breakfast. AE, DC, MC, V. Parking 30F ($25) in garage (only 2 spaces), 20F ($16) outside. Bus: 1. **Amenities:** 2 restaurants; bar; 24-hr. room service; laundry service/dry cleaning; nonsmoking floors. *In room:* TV, dataport, minibar, hair dryer.

Im Portner & Pförtnerhof *✎Value*   Simple and unpretentious, this solid and reliable middle-bracket hotel offers lodgings within two separate buildings that lie on opposite sides of a street (Bankgasse 7 and Bankgasse 12) in St. Gallen's historic core. The newer of the buildings (#12) was built about 30 years ago and houses the reception area and the smaller, slightly cheaper, and slightly less evocative rooms, and as such, tends to be favored by business travelers from other parts of Switzerland. The older section, at Bankgasse 7, has bedrooms with greater numbers of antiques, greater amounts of regional nostalgia, and a greater sense of decorative history. (Interestingly, whereas the main, and newer, building is owned by an individual investor, the hotel's older section, which dates from the 1500s, is owned by a local church.) The five-story newer section contains the hotel's restaurant, which is open for lunch and dinner every day except Monday. If you opt for a room in the two-story older section, you'll be given a key to its front door, since there's no on-duty receptionist inside.

Bankgasse 12, CH-9000 St. Gallen. ☎ **071/222-97-44.** 24 units. 200F–280F ($164–$230) double. Rates include breakfast. AE, DC, MC, V. Bus: 1. **Amenities:** Restaurant; cafe-bar; laundry service/dry cleaning. *In room:* TV, minibar (in older annex only), safe.

INEXPENSIVE

Hotel Dom   This simple but adequate hotel is one floor above street level, near the cathedral in the center of town. Originally built in 1966, it has been renovated slowly and gradually many times since. The hotel offers small, basic units with comfortable furniture, some with private bathrooms. No meals other than breakfast are served, but many restaurants and taverns can be found nearby.

Webergasse 22, CH-9000 St. Gallen. ☎ **071/227-71-71.** Fax 071/227-71-72. www.hoteldom.ch. 40 units (32 with bathroom). 110F ($90) double without bathroom, 190F ($156) double with bathroom. Rates include continental breakfast. AE, DC, MC, V. Parking 10F ($8.20). Bus: 1. **Amenities:** Breakfast room; lounge; limited room service; nonsmoking rooms; rooms for guests w/limited mobility. *In room:* TV.

WHERE TO DINE

In the restaurants recommended below, as well as in the area's tearooms and inns, make an effort to try the famous local sausage—bratwurst—and to sample St. Gallen's rich regional pastries.

Am Gallusplatz ☆☆ FRENCH/SWISS   Am Gallusplatz is the most famous restaurant in the Old Town and has a dining room that dates from 1606. Finding it is part of the pleasure of dining here. It's opposite the cathedral, behind a low wall and a pink facade. The five- or seven-course "menu surprise" dinner includes wine and champagne, and the regular menu changes frequently and is always based on fresh ingredients. If available, we recommend bouillabaisse "chef," *pot-au-feu* of fish, garnished goose liver with fresh herbs, grilled sole and salmon Florentine style, and lamb medallions Provençal. The savory dishes are prepared with flair, with perfectly balanced flavors and textures. The wine list, one of the most extensive in Switzerland, includes 450 choices, the oldest dating from 1893. The restaurant also offers a nice selection of Armagnacs and brandies.

Gallusstrasse 24. ℂ **071/223-33-30.** Reservations recommended. Main courses 26F–64F ($21–$52); fixed-price lunch 56F ($46); 5-course menu surprise 150F ($123); 7-course menu surprise 260F ($213). AE, DC, MC, V. Tues–Fri and Sun 11:30am–2:30pm; Tues–Sun 6pm–midnight. Closed last week of July through the 1st 2 weeks of Aug. Bus: 1.

Einstein Hotel Restaurant FRENCH/SWISS   One of the finest restaurants in the city is located on the fifth floor of the Hotel Einstein, with the best panoramic view in town. The decor blends rustic timber with marble trim. Specialties include calves' liver with garden herbs, grilled veal schnitzels, cream of spinach soup with salmon strips, and filet of sole with artichokes and sherry-flavored butter. The food is rather hearty but often prepared with a sense of delicacy too.

Berneggstrasse 2. ℂ **071/227-55-55.** Reservations recommended. Main courses 24F–62F ($20–$51); fixed-price lunch 42F ($34); fixed-price dinner 90F ($74). AE, DC, MC, V. Daily noon–2pm and 6–10pm. Bus: 1, 3, or 11.

Restaurant Neubad ☆☆☆ SWISS/FRENCH/ITALIAN   Set in a 300-year-old house in the historic center of St. Gallen, this restaurant contains a street-level bistro and a more formal (and expensive) restaurant upstairs, which is one of the finest in northeastern Switzerland. The setting's antique charm is most visible in the two dining rooms upstairs. Here, a *cuisine du marché,* featuring menu items that change with the seasons, may include roast haunch of venison with fresh spätzle, several preparations of fresh fish, filet of veal with alpine herbs and vegetable risotto, and roast lamb with rosemary sauce and garlic. Wild-game dishes are featured in autumn, and the salads are usually very, very fresh. The dishes prepared here seem more engaging year after year, and you can always count on first-rate cuisine.

Bankgasse 6. ℂ **071/222-86-83.** Reservations recommended for the restaurant, not required for the bistro. Restaurant main courses 31F–59F ($25–$48); fixed-price 3-course lunch 58F ($48); fixed-price 4-course tasting menu 88F ($72); fixed-price 5-course surprise menu 98F ($80). Bistro main courses 15F–39F ($12–$32). AE, DC, MC, V. Mon–Fri 10am–2pm and 6–10:30pm. Closed 2 weeks in July. Bus: 1.

ST. GALLEN AFTER DARK

Many locals head for the town's main hotel, **Einstein Hotel** (see "Where to Stay," above), which has the best pub/cocktail bar in town. If you're lucky, you'll catch a set of live piano music in this dark, leathery enclave.

Another good spot on the after-dark circuit, for those who like a bustling, noisy Teutonic atmosphere, is the **Weinstube zum Bäumli,** Schmiedgasse 18 (ℂ **071/222-11-74**), convenient to the Old Town, which has been in business for 5 centuries. It has the town's best wine collection, and you can order inexpensive food here, mainly regional fare such as bratwurst. It's closed Sunday and Monday.

You can also check the program at the local tourist office to find out what's scheduled at the **Stadttheater,** Museumstrasse 24 (© **071/242-05-05**), which presents at least 200 concerts and dramatic performances during its annual season from September to June. Ticket prices depend on the presentation.

Local bands often appear at the **Trischli,** Brühlgasse 18 (© **071/226-09-00**), which also sponsors the occasional karaoke or theme night. The club is open in July and August daily from 10pm to 5:30am, and from September to June daily from 9pm (closing hours vary). There's a cover charge of 10F ($8.20) on Friday and Saturday. A DJ spins different kinds of music every night at the **Ozon,** Goliathgasse 28 (© **071/224-81-24**), with its flashing lights and steep beer prices. The club is open Wednesday and Thursday from 10:30pm to 2am and Friday and Saturday from 10:30pm to 3am. Cover is from 13F to 25F ($11–$21).

2 Appenzell ✦

18km (11 miles) S of St. Gallen; 20km (12 miles) SW of Altstätten

In the rolling, verdant foothills of the Alpstein, south of Lake Constance, the Appenzell district retains some of Switzerland's strongest folklore. However, in recent years, in an attempt to attract the tourist purse, it has become somewhat self-conscious and commercial about its traditions. Its hamlets contain intricately painted houses whose colorful decorations are distinctive to the region. The inhabitants, proud of their cultural distinctions, sometimes wear folk costumes, which include an elaborate coif with large wings made of a fabric called tulle. Local men are known for their rakish earrings and their habit of going barefoot in the summer.

Appenzell is famous for three reasons: for its baked goods such as pear bread and chocolates, for the artists who adhere to a certain school of naive art (which some observers compare to paintings by the late American primitivist Grandma Moses), and for its status as the yodeling headquarters of Switzerland. For centuries the district was relatively isolated from the rest of Switzerland, but modern roads and trusty cable cars now ferry sightseers across the otherwise inaccessible terrain.

Appenzell's main square, **Landsgemeindeplatz,** and its main street, **Hauptgasse,** are lined with traditional painted houses. Here, shops sometimes sell the famous embroidery of the area—but examine items carefully before you buy, as some embroideries are made in China or Portugal. Appenzell is an excellent base for exploring two nearby peaks, the **Ebenalp** and **Mount Säntis.**

ESSENTIALS

GETTING THERE   From Zurich, you can take a slow local train without transferring; you'll reach Appenzell in about 2 hours. A faster way is to take an express train from Zurich to Gossau, a satellite village of St. Gallen, and transfer to the local train. Trip time from St. Gallen or Gossau to Appenzell on one of the 30 or so daily locals is about 45 minutes. Call © **0900-300-300** for information.

The town's only bus line goes between Appenzell and St. Gallen via a meandering path through local villages not serviced by rail. From St. Gallen, you'll have to transfer buses in a village called Teufen. For more information, call © **071/227-37-37.**

By car from St. Gallen, drive south from the city toward Teufen, where the road is signposted south to Appenzell.

VISITOR INFORMATION   The **Appenzell Tourist Office** is at Hauptgasse 4 (© **071/788-96-41;** www.appenzell.ch), and is open Monday to Friday from 9am to noon and 2 to 6pm, Saturday and Sunday 10am to noon and 2 to 5pm.

SHOPPING

The main street is filled with shops hawking souvenirs and gifts, some of dubious origin. However, for the best and most authentic handicrafts, head for **Trachtenstube,** Hauptgasse 23 (© **071/787-16-06**). On the second floor of this outlet you'll find a wide array of traditional Appenzeller clothing, along with farmers' floral work shirts and hand-embroidered handkerchiefs. A wide selection of lace, embroidery, and crafts are sold here as well. Even the locals come here to shop for costumes during festivals.

Another outlet on the main street, **Margreiter,** Hauptgasse 29 (© **071/787-33-13**), offers machine-made work produced in neighboring factories that's often quite stunning. Embroideries decorated with edelweiss or other alpine flora seem to be the fastest-moving items.

WHERE TO STAY

Hotel Appenzell 🎘 *(Finds)*   Located on the town's main square, this cozy retreat, built in 1983, is painted with whimsical folk colors on its gabled facade with shuttered windows. The comfortable rooms include conservative, modern walnut furniture, and the bathrooms are lined with marble. It's rather luxurious for the prices charged.

The hotel's street-level cafe, with an outdoor terrace, is a comfortable stop for daily meals, which are really well prepared based on fresh ingredients. Through the cafe is an elaborately paneled dining room, which is suitable for a more intimate experience.

Landsgemeindeplatz, CH-9050 Appenzell. © 071/788-15-15. Fax 071/788-15-51. www.hotel-appenzell.ch. 16 units. 186F–281F ($153–$230) double. Rates include buffet breakfast. AE, DC, MC, V. Free parking. Closed 3 weeks in Nov. **Amenities:** 2 restaurants; bar; lounge; limited room service; babysitting; laundry service/dry cleaning; nonsmoking rooms; rooms for guests w/limited mobility. *In room:* TV, dataport, minibar, hair dryer.

Hotel Hecht   This 300-year-old hotel, in the center of town opposite the Catholic church, is the biggest alpine inn in Appenzell. The Knechtle family has owned the place for more than 50 years, keeping it clean, attractive, and conservative. The overall effect is cheerful and comfortable. Bedrooms are small but tastefully furnished with private bathrooms, most of which contain tub/shower combinations.

Hauptgasse 9, CH-9050 Appenzell. © **071/788-22-22.** Fax 071/788-22-88. www.hecht-appenzell.ch. 42 units. 170F–270F ($139–$221) double. Rates include buffet breakfast. AE, DC, MC, V. **Amenities:** Breakfast room; laundry service/dry cleaning. *In room:* TV, hair dryer, minibar.

Romantik Hotel Säntis 🎘🎘   Appenzell's best hotel in the town center is decorated with dozens of stenciled, symmetrical designs. Its traditional rooms are cozy, and many are filled with regional antiques. Try for a room in the old wing, dating from 1835, if you like painted beams and provincial wooden furnishings. Some accommodations have four-poster or canopy beds. There's a small Appenzell-style dining room with a wood ceiling and colorful tablecloths (see "Where to Dine," below). The Heeb family offers a cordial welcome.

Landsgemeindeplatz 3, CH-9050 Appenzell. © **071/788-11-11.** Fax 071/788-11-10. www.saentis-appenzell.ch. 37 units. 180F–300F ($148–$246) double; 320F ($262) suite. Rates include buffet breakfast. Parking 5F ($4.10). AE, DC, MC, V. **Amenities:** Restaurant; limited room service; laundry/dry cleaning; nonsmoking rooms; rooms for guests w/limited mobility. *In room:* TV, hair dryer.

WHERE TO DINE

Hof ⊛ SWISS   One of Appenzell's most consistently crowded and popular restaurants occupies a prominent location in the town center, within a relatively modern-looking decor that's accented with many yards of varnished pinewood planking. Inside, you'll find a collection of local sports trophies and memorabilia, rustic artifacts straight from an alpine farm, wooden tables and chairs, and a fireplace that burns brightly throughout the winter. Menu items include all manner of grilled steaks and meats, fondues, spätzle with cheese, and a house potato-based specialty loaded with ham, cheese, onions, and spices known as Rösti Hof.

Upstairs are 20 cozy but compact bedrooms, each with private bathroom (tub/shower combination) and TV. None have air-conditioning, but in view of the relatively cheap price (140F/$115 double with breakfast), they tend to be popular.

Engelgasse 4. ℂ 071/787-22-10. Fax 071/787-58-83. Reservations not necessary. Main courses 14F–29F ($11–$24); fixed-price 3-course menu 25F ($21). AE, DC, MC, V. Daily noon–10pm.

Restaurant Säntis ⊛⊛ SWISS   This restaurant on the first floor of the popular Romantik Hotel Säntis offers a view over the elaborately detailed houses of the main square. The menu changes frequently. Typical appetizers include a nourishing bouillon or alpine dried beef garnished with pickles and onions. Main courses may include loin of lamb Provençal or roast filet of pork. Some of the meat and fish dishes are accompanied by homemade noodles, served with al dente carrots and spinach.

In the Romantik Hotel Säntis, Landsgemeindeplatz 3. ℂ 071/788-11-11. Reservations recommended. Main courses 29F–53F ($24–$43); fixed-price lunch 19F–25F ($16–$21); fixed-price dinner 57F ($47); menu degustation 88F–110F ($72–$90). AE, DC, MC, V. Daily 11am–2pm and 6:30–11pm. Closed Jan 15–Feb.

EASY EXCURSIONS

Either of the following excursions would be ideal for a picnic, with some of the most dramatic mountains in eastern Switzerland as your backdrop. Before heading here, pick up supplies in Appenzell and the day is yours. We hope it's a sunny one.

EBENALP ⊛⊛   Visit Ebenalp, 6km (4 miles) away, for a spectacular view of the hills and pastures of the Appenzell district. The jagged promontory is at an elevation of 1,620m (5,314 ft.). Wear sturdy walking shoes so that you can walk down to **Wild-kirchli**—a chapel in a grotto, inhabited by hermits from the mid–17th to the mid–19th centuries. Paleolithic artifacts discovered here at the turn of the 20th century indicate that it is the oldest prehistoric settlement found in Switzerland so far.

To get here, drive to the end of the Weissbad-Wasserauen road, then take a cable car for an 11-minute ride to the summit. The cable car leaves every 45 minutes in season; a round-trip costs 25F ($21) for adults, 10F ($8.20) for people 25 and under. For information, call ℂ 071/799-12-12; www.ebenalp.ch.

MOUNT SÄNTIS ⊛⊛⊛   The major attraction in the area is Mount Säntis, the highest peak (2,463m/8,079 ft.) in the Alpstein massif. It offers a panoramic view of

---

Tips A Must-Have Picnic Item

If you're planning a picnic in the mountains, stock up on some of the local Appenzeller cheese at **Chäs Sutter**, Marktgasse 8 (ℂ 071/787-13-33). This cheese tastes like nothing else found in Europe.

eastern Switzerland, including the Grisons, the Bernese Alps, the Vorarlberg mountains, Lake Constance, and even Lake Zurich. On a clear day you can see as far as Swabia in southern Germany.

To reach the departure point for the cable car (whose German name is Säntis Schwebebahn), drive 14km (9 miles) west of Appenzell, following the signs pointing to Urnäsch and Schwägalp. The cable car departs at 30-minute intervals year-round; round-trip passage costs 36F ($30). For more information, call © **071/365-65-65;** www.saentisbahn.ch.

Instead of driving, you can take one of the most dramatic walks in the area from the village of Wasserrauen to the village of Schwägalp, at which point you can take a cable car to the belvedere overlooking Säntis. Hourly trains from Appenzell will take you to Wasserrauen. The walk between Wasserrauen and Schwägalp is 8km (5½ miles), taking anywhere from 4½ to 5½ hours, depending on your stamina. As you hike along, you'll see some of the most scenic panoramas in this part of Switzerland.

3 Lake Constance ★★★

Lake Constance is divided into three parts, although the name is frequently applied to Bodensee, the largest part. At the western end of Bodensee, the lake splits into two branches: a long fjord called Überlingersee and an irregular marshland known as Untersee. Untersee is connected to the rest of the lake by a narrow channel of water, which is actually the young Rhine River. The blue felchen, a pike-like fish found only in Lake Constance, furnishes the district with a tasty and renowned specialty.

The 261km (162-mile) shoreline of the lake is shared by three countries—Switzerland, Germany, and Austria. The surrounding hills are covered with vineyards and orchards and are dotted with many farming villages. Vacationers are drawn here by the sunny, mild climate and nice beaches.

The Swiss gateway to Lake Constance is **Rorschach,** 11km (7 miles) northeast of St. Gallen. You can get here by train from Zurich in 1½ hours (the train departs every hour) or from St. Gallen in 20 minutes. From Rorschach, you can continue on—by frequent local trains or buses along the lake—to the three major centers: **Arbon, Horn,** and **Romanshorn.** A well-organized network of modern passenger ferries links all these towns along the shore and connects Switzerland with Germany and Austria.

The **Rorschach Tourist Office,** Hauptstrasse 63 (© **071/841-70-34**), provides an up-to-date timetable for all forms of transportation. They are open Monday to Friday from 9:30am to 5:30pm. You can also contact one of the most popular boat lines, **Schiffahrtsbetrieb Rorschach** (© **071/846-60-60**), the best and most economical way to cruise from one town along the lake to another, thereby transforming a commuter trip into a cruise. This is easiest to do from May to September.

Your choice of towns along Lake Constance will depend almost entirely on your selection of a hotel. The towns and attractions are so similar that it is hard to tell where one town ends and another begins. All of them offer lakeside promenades and flower gardens overlooking the lake, and all of them can become centers for pleasure boating and trips on the lake. The towns are also so close together that even if you're in Romanshorn in the west, you can arrive at Rorschach in the east in minutes. Because it has a greater choice of hotels, we'd give the nod to Rorschach.

Once at Lake Constance, you'll find dozens of bike trails, each marked with a red sign, and each running around the southern tier (the Swiss side) of the lake.

RORSCHACH

This medieval harbor town at the foot of the Rorschacher Berg is at the southern tip of the lake. It has lakeside gardens, an extensive promenade, a good choice of hotels, and facilities for sailing, rowing, swimming, fishing, and windsurfing. Passenger ships pass through Rorschach en route to Germany, Austria, and Liechtenstein.

Rorschach's illustrious past is reflected in its buildings, which include the **Kornhaus,** a granary built in 1746; the former **Mariaberg cloister;** and **18th-century painted houses** with oriel windows along Hauptgasse. If you'd like to bike along the lake, you can go to the railway station and rent a bike for the day for about 30F ($25).

WHERE TO STAY & DINE

Hotel Mozart   Opened in 1986, this comfortable hotel with its own garage is situated between the main street of town and the lake. The polished-granite building has well-maintained, midsize rooms, eight overlooking the lake.

The old-world ambience of the hotel's Café Mozart complements its variety of famous pastries. Another specialty is tea—19 varieties, including essence of kiwi, linden blossom, and tea leaves grown on the foothills of Mount Everest. The cafe also offers simple meals.

Hafenzentrum, CH-9400 Rorschach. © 071/844-47-47. Fax 071/844-47-48. www.mozart-rorschach.ch. 33 units. 150F–185F ($123–$152) double; 220F–350F ($180–$287) suite. Rates include buffet breakfast. AE, DC, MC, V. Free parking. **Amenities:** Restaurant; lounge. *In room:* TV, minibar.

Parkhotel Waldau 🐟🐟   This country manor was built after World War II as a private school for boys, then transformed into a government-rated five-star hotel, the best in town. The hotel sits on a hill overlooking the lake 6km (4 miles) southwest of the center. As a first-class hotel, Parkhotel Waldau, as opposed to its more modest and smaller competitor, the Mozart, has far larger and better-furnished rooms and more spacious and well-equipped bathrooms. In addition, it has all the amenities of a deluxe hotel (including a swimming pool as well as tennis courts and a health club), with which no other hotel in town can compete. And if that wasn't enough, Parkhotel Waldau also has the finest and most varied cuisine in town.

Seebleichestrasse 42, CH-9400 Rorschach. © 071/858-70-70. Fax 071/858-70-71. www.parkhotel-waldau.ch. 42 units. 192F–205F ($157–$168) double; 260F ($213) junior suite. Rates include buffet breakfast. AE, DC, MC, V. Free parking. **Amenities:** Restaurant; indoor pool; tennis court; health club; sauna; limited room service; babysitting; laundry service/dry cleaning. *In room:* TV, dataport, minibar, hair dryer, safe.

HORN

This old fishing hamlet is a 5-minute drive east of Arbon. Set in the canton of Thurgau, it provides another base for exploring the shores of Lake Constance. Frankly, the main reason to visit is to stay or dine at the Hotel Bad Horn; otherwise, you'll find more facilities at Rorschach, only a 10-minute car or bus ride to the east.

WHERE TO STAY & DINE

Hotel Bad Horn 🐟 *Finds*   This large blue-and-white hotel is located in the town center at the end of a small peninsula on the lakefront. Built in 1827, it is fully restored with big windows, gables, a tile roof, rooftop terraces, and an expanse of lawn extending almost to the lake. The midsize bedrooms are well furnished and comfortably appointed, each with a neatly kept bathroom.

At the Captain's Grill, with its nautical decor, specialties include aiguillettes of pink duck, quenelles of local fish, scampi with calvados, and filet of beef with Armagnac.

Seestrasse 36, CH-9326 Horn. (**071/841-55-11**. Fax 071/841-60-89. www.badhorn.ch. 54 units. 190F–250F ($156–$205) double; 310F ($254) suite. Rates include buffet breakfast. AE, DC, MC, V. Free parking. **Amenities:** 2 restaurants; limited room service; laundry service/dry cleaning. *In room:* TV, dataport, minibar, hair dryer, safe.

ARBON ⚑

One of the best spots along the lake is Arbon, the lakefront promenade that offers a view of Constance, the German shore, and the Alps. It has far more facilities than Horn (see above), although the views and ambience are pretty similar. If lakeside walks appeal to you, this might be the place, as most of the town lies on a promontory jutting out into Lake Constance. In summer you're surrounded by orchards and lake meadows, so strolling is what to do here. Facilities include a large boat harbor, swimming pools, and a school for sailing and surfing. The town was built on the site of an ancient Celtic community and was called Arbor Felix by the Romans.

After leaving Rorschach, continue northwest along Route 13 for 15 minutes until you reach Arbon. The town is also a major stopover for all the trains and buses running along the southern tier of Lake Constance.

The town's most visible monument is its 13th- or 14th-century castle, **Schloss Arbon,** Hauptstrasse ((**071/446-10-58**), which broods over the town from its hilltop. Most of its interior is devoted to a technical school for adults, but you can visit the small-scale museum during its limited open hours. Exhibits include ancient Roman artifacts unearthed in the region, and displays relating to the once-potent, now-defunct industries that used to call Arbon home. Premier among these is the Saurer Truck Company, which employed up to 3,000 local workers between its 1906 founding and its merger with Mercedes-Benz in 1982. Frankly, unless you're terribly interested in the history of the local region, you can skip this museum entirely. Between May and September, the museum is open daily from 2 to 5pm; March, April, October, and November, it's open Sunday only, from 2 to 5pm. It's closed December to February. Admission costs 4F ($3.30) for adults and 2F ($1.65) for children 14 and under.

For tourist information, go to **Infocenter Arbon,** Schmiedgasse 6 ((**071/440-13-80**), open Monday to Friday 9 to 11:30am and 2 to 6pm. From mid-June to August it is also open on Saturday from 9 to 11:30am.

WHERE TO STAY & DINE

Gasthof Bräuerei Frohsinn ⚑   Originally built in 1822, and located near the edge of the Bodensee, within a 5-minute walk west of the town center, this historic hotel, restaurant, and brewery was renovated in 1986. Today the four-story premises contain 13 simple and nostalgically decorated bedrooms, a brewery that chugs out many gallons of both light and dark beer (the brand name is Frohsinn), a popular bowling alley, and a trio of restaurants. The most formal and gourmet-conscious of the three is the Fisch Restaurant. Focusing on upscale, gourmet-inspired Continental food, prices begin at 75F ($62) for a fixed-price menu.

Less lofty, and less ambitious in their cuisine, are Le Bistro and, in the cellar, the Bräukeller. Both restaurants charge from 19F to 47F ($16–$39) for rib-sticking main courses that include grilled steaks; calves' liver with bacon; roulades of beef, chicken, or veal layered with herbs and cheese; noodles studded with ham and a cream-flavored cheese sauce; and as much beer from the local brewery as you can handle.

Romanshornerstrasse 15, CH-9320 Arbon. Tel. **071/447-84-84**. Fax 0714/464-142. www.frohsinn-arbon.ch. 13 units. 160F–175F ($131–$144) double; 250F ($205) suite. Rates include breakfast. AE, DC, MC, V. **Amenities:** 3 restaurants; laundry service; bowling alley. *In room:* TV.

Hotel Metropol ✿   This hotel, across from the train station, is part of a lakeside complex that exemplifies creative urban planning. It's Arbon's best choice for overnighting. The complex includes a department store, a grocery store, and a busy cafeteria. The hotel lobby is Nordic modern, and the rooms are comfortable but plain, each with a loggia facing the lake and well-maintained bathrooms. The best place to dine is the second-floor restaurant, serving Swiss cuisine and specializing in fish caught in the lake.

Bahnhofstrasse 49, CH-9320 Arbon. ℂ **071/447-82-82.** Fax 071/447-82-80. www.metropol-arbon.ch. 42 units. 190F–220F ($156–$180) double; 190F–290F ($156–$238) suite for 1–3. Rates include buffet breakfast. AE, DC, MC, V. Free parking. **Amenities:** 2 restaurants; bar; outdoor pool; sauna; limited room service; laundry service/dry cleaning. *In room:* TV, minibar, hair dryer, safe.

Hotel Rotes Kreuz   This is a stucco house with a lake terrace built in 1760. The handful of rooms it contains are simple, small, and well scrubbed. All contain a private bathroom. You can dine in a glass-enclosed solarium or a cozy pine-paneled room. Specialties include a variety of lake fish.

Hafenstrasse 3, CH-9320 Arbon. ℂ **071/446-19-18.** Fax 071/446-24-85. www.hotelroteskreuz.ch. 20 units. 150F ($123) double. Rates include continental breakfast. MC, V. Free parking. **Amenities:** Restaurant; lounge. *In room:* TV.

ROMANSHORN

This industrial town is the largest port on the lake and the base for Swiss steamers. In spite of the industrial overlay, Romanshorn is also a successful summer lakeside resort. Popular with Swiss, German, and Austrian tourists, it's set against a backdrop of panoramic views of the Austrian and Swiss mountains nearby. The resort offers a swimming pool, a sailing school, a water-skiing school, and tennis courts. There's also a park as well as a zoo.

A year-round ferry service links Romanshorn with Friedrichshafen, Germany. Boats operated by the **Schweizerische Bodensee Schiffahrtsgesellschaft** (ℂ **071/446-78-88;** www.sbsag.ch) make hourly transits to Friedrichshafen, beginning at 8:30am daily between May and October, and ending between 6:30 and 7:30pm, depending on the day of the week. One-way transit, which requires about an hour, costs 13F ($11). The attractions on the German side of the lake are actually far more interesting than anything on the Swiss border, and there's no hassle or fees to cross, so we recommend you take the chance to visit **Friedrichshafen.** Here you can stroll its lakefront promenade, with a sweeping view of the Swiss Alps. Biking along the broad Seestrasse is also a delight. A kiosk within the Stadtbahnhof (local rail station) rents bikes. You can also visit the **Zeppelin Museum** in the Hafenbahnhof on Seestrasse 22, with its fascinating re-creation of the historic *Hindenburg,* which exploded in a fire in New Jersey in 1937, possibly because of sabotage.

In summer, boat trips are organized to Mainau, a German island about 6km (4 miles) north of Constance that was once the home of the grand duke of Baden. Boats operated by the **Schweizerische Bodensee Schiffahrtsgesellschaft** (ℂ **071/466-78-88;** www.sbsag.ch) make two daily transits from May to October, from Romanshorn to Mainau. Transit takes 90 minutes each way and costs 27F ($22) round-trip. You'll have to pay an entrance fee of 6F ($4.90) to gain access to the island. **Mainau Island** is well worth your time. Because of the mild climate, the island is almost tropical, filled with palms and orange trees, along with fragrant flowers in bloom year-round—even though the island lies practically in the shadow of the snow-covered Alps. In the center of the island is a botanical garden, set on the site of an ancient castle, once a residence of the Knights of the Teutonic order.

In Romanshorn two other worthy options involve hopping aboard any boat operated by Schweizerische Bodensee Schiffahrtsgesellschaft (see above). If you go on the one bound for Rorschach (three departures per day), you'll pay about 13F ($11) one-way. Then you can explore the town of Rorschach before returning to Romanshorn by any of the many trains (a 20-min. ride).

A second option involves sailing from Romanshorn to **Kreuzlingen** or the German town of **Konstanz,** a 1-hour ride (between two and three departures per day), and taking the train back (a 20-min. ride). One-way boat transit to either Kreuzlingen or Konstanz costs 12F ($9.85).

For tourist information in Romanshorn, contact **Verkehrsbüro,** Bahnhofplatz (✆ **071/463-32-32**), open Monday to Friday from 8am to noon and 2 to 6pm, Saturday 9am to noon. If you'd like to bike along the lake, you can go to the railway station, where a kiosk rents bikes from 28F to 33F ($23–$27) per day.

WHERE TO STAY & DINE

Park-Hotel Inseli ☞   This model hotel, the best in town, is secluded in a grove of trees a 10-minute walk from the center, directly on the lake. Its comfortable and spacious bedrooms offer views of the park or the lake; the public rooms are decorated with chrome and plush carpeting. Manager Anton Stager and his family keep up the hotel's informal ambience. There's a sunny, indoor-outdoor cafe and a more formal rotisserie where French cuisine is served daily. There's a pretense to grandeur, and those in the know order the local fish caught from Lake Constance. The cafe offers a panoramic view all the way to Austria.

Inselistrasse 6, CH-8590 Romanshorn. ✆ 071/466-88-88. Fax 071/466-88-77. www.inseli.ch. 39 units. 190F–260F ($156–$213) double. Rates include buffet breakfast. AE, DC, MC, V. Free parking. **Amenities:** 2 restaurants; bar; lounge; gym; sauna; limited room service; laundry service/dry cleaning. *In room:* TV, minibar, hair dryer, safe.

4 Stein-am-Rhein ☞☞

20km (12 miles) east of Schaffhausen; 27km (17 miles) N of Winterthur

Dating from 1094, Stein-am-Rhein is pure old-town, one of the most authentic and best-preserved medieval towns in Switzerland. It's on the right bank of the Rhine, west of Untersee, an arm of Lake Constance. The town is blessed with the finest half-timbered houses in northeastern Switzerland, and the foundations of some of them dip into the river itself. Flower-decked fountains and oriel-windowed houses are grace notes. The facades, which are often fully painted, beckon the photographer in all of us. Nearby was the first Roman bridge ever built over the Rhine.

ESSENTIALS

GETTING THERE   Stein-am-Rhein lies midway along the railway link connecting Schaffhausen with Kreuzlingen, on the edge of Lake Constance. From Zurich, passengers take an express train to Schaffhausen, then change for a less frequent local train to Stein-am-Rhein; trip time from Zurich is just under 2 hours. There are also good train connections to Stuttgart, Germany. For rail schedules or more information, call ✆ **0900/300-300.**

The only bus connection to Stein-am-Rhein crosses the border into a German village named Singen, from which there are rail connections to Stuttgart, Germany. Call ✆ **0900-300-300** for information.

By car the trip from Zurich takes less than an hour. Head north on N1 until a point near Winterthur, where you connect with E41 going north to Schaffhausen. This route becomes N4, connecting with Route 13, heading east toward Stein-am-Rhein.

VISITOR INFORMATION   The Stein-am-Rhein **Tourist Office,** at Oberstadt 10 (© 052/741-28-35), maintains up-to-date bus and rail schedules. It's open Monday to Friday from 9 to 11am and 2 to 5pm.

SEEING THE SIGHTS

A number of quaint houses line **Rathausplatz (Town Hall Square)** and **Hauptstrasse (Main Street).** Many have oriel windows, rich frescoes, timberwork, and fountains.

The **Historische Sammlung (Historical Museum)** is in one of the rooms of the town hall, on Rathausplatz (© 052/741-21-42). The collection includes weapons, banners, and stained glass. Admission is 3F ($2.45). The exhibit keeps no set hours; you have to call and arrange for an appointment to view it.

A Benedictine abbey was built near Rathausplatz during the 11th century; it was abandoned during the Protestant Reformation in 1524. Today it's the **Kloster-museum St. Georgen (St. George's Abbey Museum)** (© 052/741-21-42), devoted to local history and art. The rooms, because of their rich ceilings, paneling, and 16th-century murals by Thomas Schmid and Ambrosius Holbein, are often more interesting than the exhibits. Admission to the museum is 3F ($2.45) for adults, 1.50F ($1.25) for children. The museum is open March to October, Tuesday to Sunday 10am to noon and 1 to 5pm. The restored Convent Church of St. George, a Romanesque basilica built by the Catholics and later transformed into a Protestant church, has sections dating from the 12th century.

Wohnmuseum Lindwurm, Understadt 18 (© 052/741-25-12), lies in an old, 19th-century *bürgerhaus* (community center). With exhibits and artifacts, it re-creates life here in that century. You learn how the townspeople and their servants lived, and something about their farming methods. It's open March to October, Wednesday to Monday from 10am to 5pm, charging 5F ($4.10) for adults and 3F ($2.45) for children.

If riding a bike appeals to you, consider renting one from the kiosk (© 052/741-21-34) within the railway station, and then heading off for a 20km/13-mile (each way) westbound excursion to Schaffhausen, or a 29km/18-mile (each way) eastbound excursion to Kreuzlingen. The cost is about 32F ($26) per day. The edges of both the Rhine and the Bodensee are flanked with "velo-routes" (bicycle paths) that are clearly marked with red-and-white signs that display a bicycle.

Ecologically and panoramically, the area where the Rhine widens into a lake is particularly interesting for sightseeing and cruising. If you're in Stein-am-Rhein, you'll find yourself midway along the route of a series of cruises that depart from Schaffhausen, to the west, and meander their way into the Untersee, the lake just to the west of the Bodensee. The terminus of the cruise is in the Swiss town of Kreuzlingen, just across the water from the German city of Konstanz. If you opt for a full round-trip excursion from Schaffhausen to Kreuzlingen, a travel time of 4 hours each way, you'll spend a full day in some of the most appealing waterways of central Europe. The cost is 30F ($25) round-trip. There are between three and four departures per day from both Schaffhausen and Kreuzlingen, but only between April and early October. For reservations and more information, contact **Schiffahrtsgesellschaft Untersee und Rhein,** Freierplatz 7, 8202 Schaffhausen (© 052/634-08-88;** www.urh.ch).

SHOPPING

Most of the town's shopping options line either side of the **Understadt,** a thorough-fare that some old-time residents still refer to as Hauptstrasse. Set near the town's rail-way station and Rathaus, its most appealing shop is **Heimatwerk,** Understadt 28 (© **052/741-33-92**). Devoted to the merchandising of artifacts made exclusively in Switzerland, it inventories glass, ceramics, woodcarvings, textiles, Swiss Army knives and watches, and lots of small and usually inexpensive art objects guaranteed to col-lect dust after you display them in your home for a while.

WHERE TO STAY

Hotel Chlosterhof ✿✿✿   The finest hotel in town, situated on the Rhine east of Rathausplatz, was created from an abandoned shoe factory and now has a brick facade with angled glass. Its interior includes an open fireplace and a lobby with a cruciform vault. The rooms, which come in various shapes and sizes, are stylized; 10 have four-poster beds and most of the suites open onto the Rhine. All units contain neatly kept bathrooms. The restaurant, Le Bâteau, offers fine dining amid a nautical decor, and Le Jardin is a little in-house bistro.

Oehningerstrasse 2, CH-8260 Stein-am-Rhein. © **052/742-42-42**. Fax 052/741-13-37. www.chlosterhof.ch. 69 units. 270F–310F ($221–$254) double; 370F–600F ($303–$492) suite. Rates include buffet breakfast. AE, DC, MC, V. Parking 15F ($12). **Amenities:** 2 restaurants; bar; pool; sauna; limited room service; laundry service/dry cleaning. *In room:* TV, dataport, minibar, hair dryer, safe.

Hotel-Restaurant Adler ✿ *(Finds)*   This tasteful, comfortable hotel has one of the most flamboyant facades in the old city: It's painted with characters from Rhenish leg-ends, depicting such medieval scenes as a tree of life, martyrs at the stake, and charac-ters groveling before Asian potentates. The hotel has two sections: One dates from 1461, and the other, less interesting guesthouse annex was built in 1957. The rooms, streamlined with a Nordic design and equipped with firm beds, often attract traveling families.

Rathausplatz, CH-8260 Stein-am-Rhein. © **052/742-61-61**. Fax 052/741-44-40. www.adlersteinamrhein.ch. 25 units. 170F–190F ($139–$156) main house double; 120F–150F ($98–$123) annex double. Rates include continental breakfast. AE, DC, MC, V. **Amenities:** Restaurant; lounge; laundry (self-service, coin-operated); rooms for guests w/limited mobility. *In room:* TV, hair dryer.

Hotel Rheinfels ✿   This is a large and commodious building built in 1448 near the entrance to Stein-am-Rhein beside the Rhine. It's well known for its pleasantly deco-rated bedrooms and for its popular restaurant with family-style tables. Bedrooms range from small to midsize, and each is traditionally furnished with comfortable beds. Upstairs from the restaurant is an antique room with wide, creaking floorboards, massive chandeliers, old portraits, and a collection of medieval armor.

Rhygasse 8, CH-8260 Stein-am-Rhein. © **052/741-21-44**. Fax 052/741-25-22. www.rheinfels.ch. 16 units. 180F–250F ($148–$205) double. Rates include continental breakfast. AE, MC, V. **Amenities:** Restaurant; lounge; room service; laundry service. *In room:* TV, minibar; hair dryer.

WHERE TO DINE

Hotel Rheinfels Restaurant SWISS   This regional restaurant offers a view of the head of the Rhine, where it exits from Lake Constance. Typical dishes include filet of fera (a lake fish) with lemon and capers, fricassee of Rhenish fish with baby vegetables, hot Bauernschinken (farmer's ham), and grilled veal steak. A potpourri of desserts is offered. The cuisine is based on very fresh and quality ingredients that are deftly han-dled by the kitchen staff.

Rathausplatz. ℂ **052/741-21-44.** Reservations recommended. Main courses 35F–52F ($29–$43). AE, MC, V. Thurs–Tues 11am–2pm and 6–9:30pm.

Restaurant Sonne ✦✦✦ SWISS/FRENCH   Located near the well-preserved marketplace, the Sonne, set in a 15th-century building, is the most famous—and best—restaurant in town. Chef/owner Philippe Combe prepares cuisine moderne for guests in the intimate dining room decorated with damask and Biedermeier. Typical dishes include delectable fresh river crabs in a vinaigrette sauce, a savory wild game in a Beaujolais sauce served with wild mushrooms sautéed in butter, and a tender roast hare with mustard sauce. The menu may also include ravioli stuffed with lobster or a superb sea bass with fresh asparagus. Good wines complement the fine food, and smooth desserts, such as chocolate mousse, provide the perfect finish.

Rathausplatz 127. ℂ **052/741-21-28.** Reservations required. Main courses 39F–50F ($32–$41); fixed-price menu 53F–100F ($43–$82). AE, MC, V. Thurs–Mon 11:30am–2pm and 6–9:30pm.

STEIN-AM-RHEIN AFTER DARK

Most city residents head home after work in a city that's not noted for its raucous nightlife. But the bar that attracts more business than any other, **Le Papillon** is in the Hotel Chlosterhof (see above), Oehningerstrasse 2 (ℂ **052/742-42-42**). It opens every night at 6pm and offers lots of varnished paneling, a woodsy kind of coziness, and views of the river. They will happily stay open until the last customer leaves.

5 Schaffhausen ✦ & the Rheinfall ✦✦

51km (32 miles) N of Zurich, 27km (17 miles) N of Winterthur

Once a major depot for river barges, Schaffhausen is built on terraces along the steeply inclined right bank of the Rhine. Although many sections of the city are modern and heavily industrialized, Schaffhausen retains its medieval spirit, exemplified by its romantic fountains and old, brown-roofed houses, dotted with oriel windows and decorated with statues in niches. It's a center for visiting the Rhine Falls (Rheinfall), one of the most popular sights in northeastern Switzerland.

Once ruled by the Hapsburgs, Schaffhausen became an imperial free city and later the capital of a Swiss canton of the same name. Germany borders the canton on three sides, heavily influencing the Teutonic flavor of much of the city's architecture.

ESSENTIALS

GETTING THERE   Schaffhausen is on all major north-south train lines between Stuttgart and Milan. There are at least 14 express trains from Zurich every day (trip time is 40 min.). Call ℂ **0900-300-300** for more information.

If driving from Zurich, head north on Route 4 all the way, which takes about 1 hour.

VISITOR INFORMATION   The Schaffhausen **Tourist Information Office** is at Fronwagturm (ℂ **052/625-51-41**) and is open in summer Monday to Friday from 10am to 6pm, Saturday 10am to 4pm, and Sunday 10am to 1pm; winter, Monday to Friday 10am to 5pm and Saturday 10am to 2pm.

SEEING THE SIGHTS

Spend a morning touring the **Old Town** ✦ on foot. There's a good view of the town from the battlements of the **Munot,** which dates from 1564. The round fortress has a tower, platform, and parapet walks. It can be reached by stairs and has a covered footbridge across the moat. The Munot is the only fortress to be based on a book by

Albrecht Dürer, published in Nürnberg in 1527. It's open May to September daily from 9am to 8pm; October to April daily from 10am to 5pm. Admission is free.

The crowning glory of the Old Town is the **Münster (All Saints' Church),** on Münsterplatz. Now Protestant, it was formerly a Benedictine monastery, consecrated in 1052. Its Romanesque architecture is stern and plain. In a nearby courtyard is the 15th-century bell that inspired Schiller's poem "Song of the Bell" and the opening of Longfellow's "Golden Legend."

The most characteristic street is **Vordergasse** ⊛, where visitors usually stop to photograph the frescoed Haus zum Ritter, dating from 1485. On Fronwegplatz you'll find two outstanding fountains from the 1520s.

Museum zu Allerheiligen (All Saints' Museum) ⊛, Baumgartenstrasse (⊘ 052/633-07-77), is one of the most important national museums in Switzerland. The exhibits range from prehistoric times to the present, including traditional garb of the province, old weapons, and period furnishings. Visit the "Treasury" in the former abbots' salon. The museum is open year-round, Tuesday to Sunday from 10am to noon and 2 to 5pm (10am–5pm Sat and Sun Mar–Oct). Admission is free.

A SPECTACULAR WATERFALL

The Rheinfall (or Rhine Falls) is the most celebrated waterfall in central Europe. It's also the most powerful—700 cubic meters of water per second rush over a width of 137m (449 ft.). The water falls 21m (69 ft.), a sight that inspired Goethe to liken it to the "source of the ocean." This natural wonder is most spectacular in early summer when it's fed by mountain snows.

From the bus station at Schaffhausen, take bus no. 1. There are frequent departures for the 10-minute ride. A train runs every 30 minutes during the day from the station at Schaffhausen to Rheinfall.

To get to the Rheinfall from Zurich, take a train from the Hauptbahnhof to Neuhausen and get off at the Rheinfall stop. The trip takes less than an hour. It's a 15-minute walk from the train depot at Neuhausen to the waterfall. To further enhance the experience, you can take a 7F ($5.75) boat trip to the rock in the center of the Rheinfall from April to October.

In addition, the falls can be viewed from the belvedere of **Laufen Castle** on the left bank. The castle has been converted into a restaurant with a staircase that leads to the view. Bring a raincoat.

You can also take a ferry across the river to Neuhausen and the little castle of **Schlöseli-Wörth** (⊘ 052/672-24-21), built in the 12th century as a Customs post. Today it's a restaurant, open daily from March through November.

SHOPPING

Consistent with its role as a hardworking, industry-conscious border town, Schaffhausen doesn't place too much emphasis on folklore, so the handful of kitschy souvenirs you're likely to find will probably be sold from small shops around the railway station, or from nondescript outlets beside either of the town's main shopping streets, **Vordergasse** and **Fronwegplatz.** More appealing are two shops that specialize in equipment designed for climbing, skiing, and virtually every other sport you can think of: **Benz,** Fronwegplatz (⊘ 052/624-56-93), and **Elite Sport,** Vorstadt 3 (⊘ 052/625-18-43). In addition to everything from tennis racquets to snowshoes, each of these sells clothing suitable for any weather Switzerland can dish out.

WHERE TO STAY

Hotel Park Villa ℛ   This chiseled gray hotel is located near the train station in a municipal park with massive trees. Originally built as an opulent private home around 1900, it was converted into a hotel in the 1960s. It's designed very much like a castle, with towers and steep roofs. The interior is as graceful as the exterior is rough, containing crystal chandeliers and several public rooms with fresh flowers, comfortable chairs, and oil paintings. A few bedrooms are decorated regally with antiques; others are in an uninspired modern style. All units are well maintained.

Parkstrasse 18, CH-8200 Schaffhausen. ℂ **052/635-60-60.** Fax 052/635-70-70. www.parkvilla.ch. 20 units. 179F–229F ($147–$188) double; 250F–308F ($205–$253) suite. Rates include breakfast. AE, DC, MC, V. Free parking. **Amenities:** Restaurant; lounge; tennis court; limited room service; laundry service/dry cleaning. *In room:* TV, dataport, minibar, hair dryer.

Rheinhotel Fischerzunft ℛℛℛ   Located on Freier Platz next to a promenade along the Rhine, this is an inviting inn that was formerly occupied by the fishermen's guild. The Jaeger family converted it to a hotel in 1898. The main public room has Chinese decor. Since there are so few bedrooms, and this place is so well known, reservations are especially important in summer. The château-style, contemporary bedrooms at first appear out of place in such a medieval city, but they're soothingly comfortable. The six with views of the Rhine carry higher price tags.

The excellent restaurant mixes classic European and Asian influences, featuring curried chicken consommé with Chinese ravioli, filet of venison with five Chinese spices and sautéed mustard cabbage, ravioli of crayfish, and an assortment of dim sum. The dishes are rich in taste, texture, and presentation. The desserts include a medley of passion fruit and papaya.

Rheinquai 8, CH-8202 Schaffhausen. ℂ **052/632-05-05.** Fax 052/632-05-13. www.fischerzunft.ch. 10 units. 280F–330F ($230–$271) double; 440F ($361) junior suite. Rates include buffet breakfast. AE, DC, MC, V. **Amenities:** Restaurant; lounge; limited room service; laundry service/dry cleaning. *In room:* TV, dataport, minibar, hair dryer, safe.

WHERE TO DINE

Consider an elegant dinner at the Rheinhotel Fischerzunft (see above), which is one of the top three restaurants in Switzerland.

Restaurant Gerberstube ITALIAN   The Guidi family runs the finest Italian restaurant in Schaffhausen. The dining room is in a 17th-century guildhall, which contains a changing exhibit of modern paintings. You may begin with stracciatella, the famous egg-and-consommé soup of Rome, and follow it with spaghetti, cannelloni, or a veal schnitzel pizzaiola. They also serve many classic dishes, including chateaubriand with béarnaise sauce and various preparations of veal and pasta. The cooking, although not exactly innovative or exciting, is always reliable and satisfying and is prepared with quality ingredients.

Bachstrasse 8. ℂ **052/625-21-55.** Reservations required. Main courses 40F–45F ($33–$37); fixed-price 3-course lunch 60F ($49); fixed-price 5-course dinner 95F ($78). AE, DC, MC, V. Tues–Sat 11am–3pm and 6–10:30pm.

Wirschaft zum Frieden ℛ SWISS   One of Schaffhausen's most folkloric and "romantic"-looking restaurants occupies five richly paneled dining rooms within the thick and solid walls of a building that dates from 1445. In summer expect masses of flowers on the building's balconies, and even more pleasingly, one of the city's finest gardens in back, where tables are set up beneath wisteria vines and venerable trees as a means of appreciating the seasonal warmth. Menu items include carpaccio of beef;

fresh-made soups that include cream of broccoli and cream of tomato with basil; Zurich-style minced veal in an herb-flavored cream sauce; an excellent version of calves' liver with rösti potatoes; and a mixed grill that combines portions of veal, beef, calves' liver, and chicken. Dessert may include a satisfying dish of poached seasonal fruit (including plums, peaches, and/or apricots), sometimes garnished with ice cream.

Herrenacker 11. ℂ 052/625-4715. Reservations recommended only for dinner on weekends. Main courses 28F–52F ($23–$43); fixed-price 4-course menu 39F ($32). AE, DC, MC, V. Mon–Sat 11am–2:30pm and 6pm–midnight. Bus: 1, 2, 6, or 10.

SCHAFFHAUSEN AFTER DARK

Many night owls gravitate toward Schaffhausen's **Saffrangasse,** a narrow historic street with the most crowded and popular bars in town. Two of them stand out: The **Bar Orient,** Saffrangasse 13 (ℂ **052/633-02-02**), a loud, sometimes raucous hangout for folks under 35, offers high-energy, foaming mugs of beer and occasional bouts of live music. Its most visible competitor is the smaller, somewhat calmer **Cuba Club,** Saffrangasse 2 (ℂ **052/625-34-98**), which is also favored by clients under 40. Catering to an older and somewhat more sedate crowd is the **Piano Bar Eckhaus,** Stadthausgasse 1 (ℂ **052/624-55-55**), where stiff drinks, a cozy setting, and live piano music help keep the conversation rolling. Most spots are open 7 days a week.

6

Basel & the Jura

Northwestern Switzerland, with its valleys, waterfalls, and old-world villages, is one of the most beautiful regions in the country. Most of the region has a medieval feel, reflected mainly in the ancient architecture.

The area lies at the juncture of Germany and France and encompasses the Jura mountain range, Basel, and the surrounding towns. During this part of your journey, you'll zigzag between two cultures, and the names of the towns—for example, Morat in French and Murten in German—will often confuse you. Most citizens of Basel, for instance, speak German, although many, living so close to France, also speak French and often English. To confuse the cultural brew, every weekday some 30,000 commuters from both France and Germany cross into Basel to work, returning to their homes in the evening.

Some of the towns may sound familiar to you: Gruyères is well known for its cheese. Other places, such as the walled university town of Fribourg and historic Neuchâtel, are also well worth a visit. You'll probably be based in Basel (or *Basle*), which straddles the Rhine, between Alsace in France and the Jura in Switzerland.

The canton of Jura was established in 1979 as the 23rd member of the Swiss Confederation. A total of 82 communes make up the canton, with Delemont as its capital. Nearly 88% of the population is Roman Catholic, and French is the predominant language.

Situated between the Rhine and the Rhône, the geological folds and faults of the Jura mountain range form the border between Switzerland and France and extend from Geneva, in the southwest, to Schaffhausen, along the northern border. Vastly different in height and character from the Alps, few peaks in the Jura exceed 1,650m (5,412 ft.).

The center of the Swiss watchmaking industry is here. Winter-sports resorts also thrive throughout the region, although most of them draw a local rather than an international clientele.

1 Basel ★★★

85km (53 miles) NW of Zurich; 98km (61 miles) N of Bern

The third-largest city in Switzerland, Basel stands on the Rhine at the point where the French, German, and Swiss borders meet. At the entrance to the Swiss Rhineland, Basel is the capital of the half-canton of Basel-Stadt. On its borders are the French Vosges, the German Black Forest, and the Swiss Jura Mountains. Grossbasel (Greater Basel) lies on the steep left bank, and Kleinbasel (Lesser Basel) is on the right bank. The old imperial city stood at Grossbasel. The two parts of the city are linked by half a dozen bridges, plus four ferries powered by river currents. The first bridge, erected in 1225, was for centuries the only one spanning the Rhine; it has since been replaced by the Mittlere Rheinbrücke (Middle Rhine Bridge).

The town was a Roman fort in A.D. 374, named Basilia, and was later ruled by prince-bishops for about 1,000 years. The Great Council met in Basel between 1431 and 1448, during which time a pope was crowned here. After Basel joined the Swiss Confederation in 1501, it became a Protestant region. During the onset of the Reformation in 1529, it served as a refuge for victims of religious persecution. They flooded in from Holland, Italy, and France, bringing renewed vitality to Basel and laying the foundation for the city's great golden age in the 18th century.

As one of Switzerland's most important cultural centers, Basel saw the development of the printing press and the book trade. In 1516 Erasmus, the great Dutch humanist and writer, published here the first edition of the New Testament in the original Greek. He is buried in the cathedral. Other notable Basel residents were the painter Holbein the Younger, who made portraits of Erasmus; the German philosopher Friedrich Nietzsche, who taught at the University of Basel; Theodor Herzl, who addressed the first Zionist World Congress here in 1897; and Jacob Burckhardt, a native, who achieved fame with his history of the Italian Renaissance.

Today the cultural traditions of Basel live on in its many museums (27 in all), art galleries, and schools. The city has become known as an international marketplace for art and antiquities. In 1967 its citizens voted by referendum to purchase two well-known works by Picasso, *The Seated Harlequin* and *The Two Brothers*. Picasso was so moved that he donated four other paintings to Basel.

Basel, which is also a banking and industrial center, is headquarters of the Bank for International Settlement. In addition, Basel's chemical and pharmaceutical industry is one of the most important in the world.

Except at Carnival, the citizens of Basel are self-restrained and industrious. The German dramatist Rolf Hochhuth has observed: "English understatement looks like megalomania when compared to the people of Basel."

ESSENTIALS

GETTING THERE   **EuroAirport** (© **061/325-25-11**) lies across the border in France and is shared by Basel, Mulhouse (France), and Freiburg (Germany). The location is 9km (5½ miles) northwest of Basel. Many major European cities have direct flights into EuroAirport, but the nearest intercontinental airport is 80km (50 miles) southeast of Basel at Zurich.

Located on the major rail lines between Paris and Zurich, Basel is the most important railroad junction in the Juras. Trip time from Paris is between 4½ and 5 hours, depending on the train; from Zurich, an express train can take as little as an hour. Call © **0900/300-300** (no area code) for **rail information.**

Basel is a junction point for highways from all over Europe. From Bern, head north on N1, continuing north on N2 at the junction. From Zurich, drive west on the same N1, turning north onto N2 at the junction.

Tips The Mobility Ticket

Any tourist staying in Basel at paid accommodations is entitled to a **mobility ticket,** which allows free use of Basel's public transport for the duration of your stay. The reception desk at your hotel should provide you with your ticket upon check-in.

(Tips An Open Sesame to Discounts in Basel

While at the **tourist office** (see above), you can purchase a **Basel Card** for 25F ($21), good for 24 hours and entitling you to a guided walking tour, discounts at some restaurants, and admission to all city museums. It's a worthy investment.

ARRIVING   If you're flying to Basel, your plane will land at the **EuroAirport Basel-Mulhouse-Freiburg** (see above). A road links the Swiss sector of the airport with Switzerland. A city bus runs between the airport and Basel's main railway station, departing every 30 minutes daily between 5:10am and 11:30pm; the 15-minute trip costs 3.75F ($3.10) one-way. A taxi costs from 40F ($33) and takes from 15 to 30 minutes depending on traffic.

Basel has three railroad stations—Swiss, French, and German—making it one of the largest rail junctions in Europe. The SNCF station is on Centralbahnplatz, as is the SBB station. The DB station is across the Rhine and down Richenstrasse.

VISITOR INFORMATION   The **Basel Tourist Office,** Schifflände 5 (© 061/268-68-68;** www.baseltourismus.ch), is open year-round Monday to Friday from 8:30am to 6pm and Saturday from 10am to 4pm.

GETTING AROUND   Basel has a good, relatively cheap public transportation system. Bus or tram tickets must be purchased at a station in advance. Clear maps will help you find your way. For 3.60F ($2.95) you can buy a ticket allowing you unlimited travel in two geographical zones for a 24-hour period. A single, once-only tram ride costs 2.80F ($2.30) within one zone.

Basel is best covered on foot, as most of its attractions radiate from the historic heart of this ancient city on the Rhine. When you need to go farther afield, you can take public transportation such as a tram. Taxis tend to be expensive.

Another way of getting around is to rent a bike at the kiosk next to the information booth at the rail station in the center of town. The cost is 34F ($28) per day, and an ID deposit is required. Bikes are rented daily from 7am to midnight.

SPECIAL EVENTS   Dating from the Middle Ages, **Fasnacht** is the most exciting time to be in Basel. All the city seems caught up in the revelry beginning the Monday after Ash Wednesday (usually in late Feb or early Mar). Motorized and horse-drawn parades highlight the activities, along with music from dozens of bands—fifes, trumpets, trombones, and drums.

The **Basel Art Fair** in mid-June (© **061/686-20-20** for more information) grows larger every year, with 260 dealers displaying the work of some 1,000 artists. The fair also generally hosts more than two dozen solo shows. Basel's most traditional festival is **Vogel Gryff Volksfest,** when a griffin, a lion, and a "wild man of the woods" float down the Rhine on a raft. This event occurs either on January 13, 20, or 27 (it changes every year). The event is followed by street dancing. The Wilder Mann, the lion, and the griffin are traditional symbols for the three main neighborhoods of Basel.

SEEING THE SIGHTS

As a city, Basel is visited primarily for its urban attractions such as museums and shopping. However, if you'd like to escape the congestion and get out and see some countryside, you're at the right place. On the outskirts of the city are 1,198km (744 miles)

Basel Attractions

Information ⓘ
Train Station 🚇

Basel Tourist Office
  (Offizielles
  Verkehrsbüro Basel) **2**
Dreiländereck **1**
Historisches Museum
  Barfüsserplatz **11**
Kunsthalle **10**
Kunstmuseum
  (Fine Arts Museum) **12**

Münster (Cathedral) **6**
Museum für Gegenwartskunst
  (Museum for Contemporary Art) **8**
Museum Jean Tinguely **7**
Rathaus **5**
Spalentor **3**
Stadtcasino **9**
University of Basel **4**
Zoologischer Garten Basel **13**

of **Wanderweg,** which are marked trails crisscrossing the scenic highlights of the area. To get you going on your journey, catch bus no. 70 to Reigoldswil. Here you can board the Gondelbahn cable to take you to the mountain peak of Wasserfallen at 922m (3,024 ft.). Once here, you can set off on hikes in many directions. Call ⓒ 061/601-15-35 for information about the best hikes in the Reigoldswil and Wasserfallen region.

THE TOP ATTRACTIONS

Fondation Beyeler ✦✦✦   Some half a century ago, Ernest and Hildy Beyeler set out to acquire some modern paintings to decorate their home. By the turn of the millennium, they had collected one of the greatest private art collections of Switzerland, which they now share with the public in the suburb of Riehen, 15 minutes by tram from the center near the Swiss borders with France and Germany. Talk about name dropping: Andy Warhol, Georges Seurat, Jackson Pollock, Mark Rothko, Joan Miró, Léger, Max Ernst, van Gogh, Kandinsky, Edgar Degas, Cézanne, Alexander Calder, and Georges Braque among others. These artists' works are stunningly displayed in Renzo Piano's avant-garde building, which is evocative of a ship lying at anchor. One of our favorite arrangements is a Monet water lily triptych that seemingly spills from the canvas into a reflecting pool outdoors.

Seek out, in particular, Picasso's 1944 *Woman in Green,* believed to be his final portrait of Dora Maar, his longtime mistress and muse. A Picasso oddity is his sculpture of the head of Marie-Thérèse Walter. The protuberances and hollows of her face evoke male and female genitalia. The Picasso is remarkable, although Matisse is more thinly represented except for some dazzling cutouts.

A series of eight Giacometti bronze figures are complemented by some of his magnificent portraits in oil. Francis Bacon's canvas, *Lying Figure,* from 1969 depicts a naked man writhing on a striped mattress. Paul Klee painted *MOMOM Sinks, Drunk, Into the Chair* in black paste on mounted paper 3 months before his death in 1940.

Baselstrasse 101, Riehen. ⓒ **061/645-9700.** www.beyeler.com. Admission 21F ($17) adults, 18F ($15) seniors, 12F ($9.85) students, 6F ($4.90) children 11–19, free for children 10 and under. Daily 9am–8pm. Tram: 6.

Historisches Museum Barfüsserplatz ✦   This former 14th-century Franciscan church on "Barefoot Square" (named for the unshod friars) contains many relics of medieval Basel, including rare 15th-century tapestries and specimens of ecclesiastical art. One of the best-known sculptures is in the late Gothic style, depicting a babbling king. Its greatest exhibit is a reliquary bust of St. Ursula, in silver and gold, commissioned by the people of Basel to contain the saint's relics.

Barfüsserplatz. ⓒ **061/211-05-05.** Admission 5F ($4.10) adults, 3F ($2.45) students, free for children 15 and under. Wed–Mon 10am–5pm. Tram: 1 or 7.

Kunsthalle   A 5-minute walk from the Kunstmuseum (see below), this gallery offers experimental works by contemporary artists. Banners displayed throughout the town announce current exhibitions. Since 1872 its changing program of exhibitions has featured many of the leading artists of classical modern and abstract expressionism before they became household names. Since the early 1980s it has been among the leading spaces in Switzerland to exhibit the most recent trends in modern art.

Steinenberg 7. ⓒ **061/206-99-00.** www.kunsthallebasel.ch. Admission 10F ($8.20) adults, 6F ($4.90) seniors and children. Sat–Sun 11am–5pm; Tues, Wed, and Fri 11am–6pm; Thurs 11am–8:30pm. Tram: 1, 2, 6, 8, or 14. Go left from the Kunstmuseum on St. Alban–Graben, cross Bankenplatz, and follow Theaterstrasse.

Kunstmuseum (Fine Arts Museum) ✦✦✦   This is the oldest museum in Switzerland, offering one of Europe's most remarkable collections—everything from the old masters to 20th-century paintings. You approach the massive building through a courtyard graced with sculptures by Rodin, Calder, and others. The collections represent the development of art of the Upper Rhine Valley from the 14th to the 17th centuries, as well as works by outstanding modern artists.

In addition to paintings by Holbein the Younger (who lived in Basel from 1515 to 1538) and Konrad Witz, the Kunstmuseum has a collection of Impressionist and modern art, including works by van Gogh, Picasso, Gauguin, Klee, Chagall, and Giacometti.

St. Alban–Graben 16. ✆ 061/206-62-62. www.kunstmuseumbasel.ch. Admission 12F ($9.85) adults, 10F ($8.20) seniors and children. Tues–Sun 10am–5pm. Tram: 2 or 15.

Münster (Cathedral)   This red sandstone building towering over the Old Town was consecrated way back in 1019. Destroyed by an earthquake in 1356, it was rebuilt along Romanesque and Gothic lines with a green-and-yellow tile roof. The cathedral has functioned as an Evangelical Reformed church since 1529.

The facade is richly decorated, depicting everything from prophets to virgins. The pulpit, which dates from 1486, was carved from a single block of stone. One of its many treasures, at the end of the south aisle, is an 11th-century bas-relief. There's a monumental slab on one of the pillars honoring Erasmus of Rotterdam, who died in Basel in 1536. The church also contains the tomb of Anna von Hohenberg, wife of Rudolf of Hapsburg. The double cloister can be entered from Rittergasse; it was erected in the 15th century on the foundations of a much earlier Roman structure. Visitors will find an excellent view from the twin Gothic towers of the cathedral. There are also two famous views of the cathedral—from the right bank of the Rhine and from the back of the Pfalz (palace). This 20m (65-ft.) terrace also provides a splendid panorama of the Rhine and Germany's Black Forest.

Münsterplatz. ✆ 061/271-21-82. Free admission to cathedral; towers 3F ($2.45). Easter to Oct 15 Mon–Fri 10am–5pm, Sat 10am–4pm, Sun 1–5pm; Oct 16 to Easter Mon–Sat 11am–4pm, Sun 2–4pm. Tram: 1, 6, 8, or H.

Museum für Gegenwartskunst (Museum for Contemporary Art) ✦   This is one of Europe's leading museums, highlighting artists from the 1960s to the present, with works by Bruce Nauman, Richard Long, Jonathan Borofsky, Joseph Beuys, Frank Stella, and Donald Judd.

Alban-Rheinweg 60. ✆ 061/272-81-83. Admission 10F ($8.20) adults, 8F ($6.55) students and seniors, free for children 15 and under. Tues–Sun 11am–5pm. Tram: 2.

Museum Jean Tinguely ✦ *Finds*   The museum is dedicated to the work of Jean Tinguely, one of Switzerland's greatest sculptors, who died in 1991. The 70 mechanical sculptures in the collection span 4 decades of artistic evolution beginning with reliefs and printing machines from the 1950s and progressing to later pieces like the Mengele-Totentanz cycle and huge, clanking metaharmonies. Further insight into the artist's life and times can be found in the many drawings and writings that document his projects around Europe and the United States.

The museum is a delight. All four levels are alive with ponderous movement, musical with the clean notes of working machinery. "Works of art usually make their statements silently," said Mario Botta, the Swiss architect who designed the museum specifically to house the collection. "These works are the exception, for they communicate through sound engendered by their movements." Many of the exhibits in the museum were donated by Tinguely's wife and fellow artist, Niki de Saint Phalle.

Botta's dramatic architectural vision has made the museum building an attraction in its own right, a modern landmark in Solitude Park on the right bank of the River Rhine. The red sandstone building is topped by the "barca," a bold steel construction.

Paul Sacher–Anlage 1. ℂ **061/681-93-20.** www.tinguely.ch. Admission 10F ($8.20) adults, 7F ($5.75) seniors and students, free for children 16 and under. Tues–Sun 11am–7pm. Tram: 2 or 15.

Zoologischer Garten Basel 🐾🐾🐾 Established in 1874, the Zoologischer Garten is one of the greatest zoos in the world, famous for breeding endangered species in captivity. Covering 11 hectares (26 acres) in an urban setting within a 7-minute walk of the railway station, it has some 4,500 animals of 600 different species. Trained elephants and sea lions perform tricks. The Vivarium is filled with everything from penguins to reptiles.

Binningerstrasse 40. ℂ **061/295-35-35.** www.zoobasel.ch. Admission 16F ($13) adults, 6F ($4.90) children, 35F ($29) family ticket. May–Aug daily 8am–6:30pm; Mar–Apr and Sept–Oct daily 8am–6pm; Nov–Feb daily 8am–5:30pm. Tram: 1, 2, 6, 8, 10, or 17.

MORE ATTRACTIONS

The **Rathaus (town hall)** on Marktplatz dominates the market square of Basel. It was built in 1504 in the late Burgundian style, but additions have been made since. The sandstone building is decorated with shields of the ancient city guildhall and adorned with frescoes.

You may also want to visit the **University of Basel,** on the south side of Petersplatz. Founded in 1460, it's one of the oldest academic institutions in Switzerland (the school's charter was signed by Pope Pius II). Its library contains a collection of rare manuscripts, as well as works by Martin Luther, Erasmus, and Zwingli.

Spalentor (Spalen Gate), west of the university, marks the end of the medieval sector. It's one of the most beautiful gates in the country. Built in the 1400s, it was heavily restored in the 19th century, and has a pointed roof and two towers with battlements.

Finally, **Dreiländereck (Three Countries' Corner),** which juts out into the Rhine, is one of Basel's more unusual sites. If you walk around a pylon marking the spot, in just a few steps you can cross from Switzerland into Germany and then into France—and you don't even need a passport.

ORGANIZED TOURS

Basel is a popular embarkation point for cruises on the Rhine. In summer (between May and Oct), **Basler Personenschiffahrt,** Blumenrain 2 (ℂ **061/639-95-00**), conducts cruises to Rheinfelden. Ships leave May to mid-October, Monday to Saturday at 1:45pm and on Sunday at 9:15am. A one-way ticket costs 26F ($21), or 49F ($40) round-trip; children travel for half price. Evening cruises are often conducted, costing 50F to 75F ($41–$62), depending on the cruise. The theme of the night cruise changes daily—a fondue cruise, a captain's dinner, a Gypsy evening. Check with the tourist office or with Basler Personenschiffahrt for last-minute changes in these schedules.

SHOPPING

Cosmopolitan, sophisticated, and prosperous, Basel shelters a medley of shops whose merchandise rivals that found in much larger cities. The finest antiques shop in the region is **Antiquités M. & G. Ségal,** Aeschengraben 14 (ℂ **061/272-39-08**). Founded in 1862, it's run by the articulate and knowledgeable fourth-generation owner, Georges Ségal, and his North Carolina–born wife, Margaret. Their specialties include 18th-century Continental paintings, silver, furniture, ceramics (including antique Meissen porcelain), and art objects, all of which are displayed over four floors of a building bulging with treasures. You'll also find two impressive art galleries in town. The immensely prestigious **Ernest Beyeler Gallery,** Baunleingasse 9 (*℡* **061/ 206-97-00**), is a cultural focal point that's famous throughout Europe for its roster of Impressionist, modern, and contemporary paintings. Also, a more avant-garde gallery with more emphasis on minimalist, hypercontemporary art, is the well-respected **Galerie Gisele Linder,** Elisabethenstrasse 54 (*℡* **061/272-83-77**).

Upscale housewares, with an emphasis on grandeur and social correctness, are displayed at a store beloved by brides-to-be, **Füglistaller,** Freie Strasse 23 (*℡* **061/261- 78-78**). Here, in a setting that includes a monumental staircase worthy of Scarlett O'Hara, look for quality porcelain, crystal, silverware, and gift items.

Seeking a suitcase to pack the loot you've already acquired in Basel? Head for **Droeser,** Eisengasse 11 (*℡* **061/261-42-53**), where wallets, valises, purses, handbags, shaving kits, even gym bags, offer leather making at its best. Shoes and clothing for both men and women can be found at **Bally Schuhfabriken,** Freie Strasse 38 (*℡* **061/261-18-97**), a three-level emporium that works hard at supplying what upscale consumers really want. Men's goods are showcased one floor above street level; women's shoes and clothing lie on street level and in the cellar. And if you have a yen for fine tobaccos, check out **Davidoff,** Aeschenvorstadt 4 (*℡* **061/272-47-70**), where brierwood and meerschaum pipes, along with cigarettes and cigars from around the world (including Cuba), are sold along with their appropriate accessories. And finally, dozens of emporiums in Basel are ready, willing, and able to sell you a wristwatch. One of the city's most upscale shops is **Gübelin,** Freie Strasse 27 (*℡* **061/261-40-33**). More closely geared to the mass market and less expensive is **Juwelier Kurz,** Freie Strasse 39 (*℡* **061/261-26-20**).

The premier chocolatier in town is **Confiserie Schiesser,** 19 Marktplatz (*℡* **061/ 261-60-77**), which sells expensive but delectable confections in its downstairs shop. Upstairs is a Viennese tearoom founded in 1870, where you can order delicate pastries and tasty little sandwiches while enjoying views of the bustling market square and the Gothic City Hall.

The best place to shop for handicrafts and gifts is **Heimatwerk,** Schneidergasse 2 (*℡* **061/261-91-78**), which carries an array of tasteful merchandise from all parts of the country. You'll find everything here from ceramics to wooden toys.

If you're just seeking general merchandise, head for the leading department store in Basel, **Globus,** Marktplatz 2 (*℡* **061/268-45-45**).

WHERE TO STAY

Keep in mind that it's almost impossible to get hotel reservations during the Swiss Industries Fair, which attracts about a million visitors every spring. Rooms are also impossible to find at Carnival time, when hotels often raise their prices by as much as 40%. Check with the Basel tourist office for exact dates. Even when hotels aren't raising their prices in Basel, the prices strike many visitors as being extremely high, even

---

Impressions

Once people have been to Basel, they keep coming back. The only difficulty we have is in getting them to come for the first time.

—Urs Hitz, 1992

when they shouldn't be for what they offer. That's because Basel can most often fill up its rooms with business clients and doesn't have to rely primarily on tourist patronage.

VERY EXPENSIVE

Hotel Drei Könige (Hôtel des Trois Rois) ☆☆☆   Established in 1026, this is the oldest government-rated five-star hotel in Europe, although most of the building you see today was constructed in the 18th century. Originally named Zur Blume ("At the Flower"), the white building, situated on the Rhine, houses a guest book, now a museum piece, containing the names of Voltaire, Napoleon, Princess (later Queen) Victoria, and Kaiser Wilhelm II. History records that soon after the establishment of the inn, three kings (Conrad II, emperor of the Holy Roman Empire; his son, Henry III; and Rudolf III, the last king of Burgundy) drew up a treaty here that divided western Switzerland and southern France.

A tapestry resembling a Gobelin tapestry hangs in the wood-paneled lobby; the bar area is accented with pin lights and brass detail. Some of the traditional guest rooms have their original ornamentation on the ceilings. Even the stables and old servants' quarters have been converted into comfortable rooms. Most units are spacious, and all are up-to-date with soft robes and well-kept bathrooms. Try, if possible, for a room opening onto the river.

Blumenrain 8, CH-4001 Basel. ℂ 061/260-50-50. Fax 061/260-50-60. www.drei-koenige-basel.ch. 88 units. 475F–600F ($390–$492) double; from 1,400F ($1,148) suite. AE, DC, MC, V. Parking 30F ($25). Tram: 1, 6, 8, 14, or 15. **Amenities:** 2 restaurants; bar; 24-hr. room service; babysitting; laundry service/dry cleaning. *In room:* A/C, TV, dataport, minibar, hair dryer, safe.

Hotel Euler und Central ☆   This hotel offers everything you'd expect from a grand hotel in Basel. Built in 1865 near the railroad station, it's elegantly detailed in white, with gray-stone half columns. The bedrooms are luxuriously paneled and impeccable, having housed everyone from Greta Garbo to Elizabeth Taylor over the years. Rooms have traditional styling with original paintings, some period furnishings, and such extras as spacious closets. All the bathrooms are maintained in excellent condition with heated towel racks. The chandeliered dining room, Le Bonheure, serves first-class dinners. The cuisine is mainly French with a lot of fish and a changing menu that takes advantage of the best of seasonal produce. The famous bar is richly ornamented with leather, wood, and red velvet, and is a favorite of visiting businesspeople and local bankers.

Centralbahnplatz 14, CH-4002 Basel. ℂ 061/275-80-00. Fax 061/275-80-50. www.hoteleuler.ch. 64 units. 330F–640F ($271–$525) double; 660F–1,000F ($541–$820) suite. AE, DC, MC, V. Tram: 6, 10, 16, or 17. **Amenities:** 2 restaurants; bar; limited room service; babysitting; laundry service/dry cleaning; nonsmoking rooms. *In room:* TV, dataport, minibar, hair dryer, safe.

EXPENSIVE

Hilton Basel ☆☆   Visitors can expect the customary Hilton service in this black steel-and-glass hotel built in 1975. In the center of town, it's connected via an underground shopping arcade to the main railway station. Bedrooms are generally roomy and comfortable, with built-in furnishings, blackout draperies, abstract paintings, and easy chairs, plus plenty of work space. Bathrooms are large and well equipped. There are even some rooms for tall people. The Wettstein Restaurant is one of the city's best restaurants.

Aeschengraben 31, CH-4002 Basel. ℂ 061/275-66-00. Fax 061/275-66-50. www.basel.hilton.com. 214 units. 280F–530F ($230–$435) double; from 750F ($615) suite. AE, DC, MC, V. Parking 24F ($20). Tram: 1, 2, or 8. **Amenities:** 2 restaurants; bar; indoor pool; health club; sauna; car-rental desk; 24-hr. room service; massage; babysitting; laundry service/dry cleaning; nonsmoking rooms; rooms for guests w/limited mobility. *In room:* A/C, TV, dataport, minibar, hair dryer, iron, safe.

Hotel Drachen *(Finds)* With a history going back some half a century, this hotel has been completely renewed and is now better than ever. The hotel lies in the heart of the city, convenient for business or shopping, and within only 2 blocks of the Kunstmuseum and other cultural monuments, such as 20 more museums or several art galleries. The hotel is stylishly decorated, in a traditional motif enhanced by the work of 14 Spanish artists who used the walls and ceilings to create scenes or landmarks of cityscapes such as the Blue Mosque in Istanbul or the Rialto Bridge in Venice. Each comes with a lovely little bathroom with both tub and shower. Even if you're not staying here, consider a visit to sample its international and Italian dishes or else a savory pizza.

Aeschenvorstadt 24, CH-4010 Basel. © **061/270-23-23**. Fax 061/270-23-24. www.drachen.ch. 43 units. 238F–280F ($195–$230) double; 360F–450F ($295–$369) suite. Rates include breakfast. AE, DC, MC, V. Tram: 2, 8, 10, 11, or 14. Parking 25F ($16). **Amenities:** 3 restaurants; 2 bars; limited room service; laundry service/dry cleaning. *In room:* A/C, TV, dataport, minibar, hair dryer, safe.

Hotel Europe *(* Centrally located next to the Swiss Industries Fair and within easy access of the Swiss and German railway stations, this renovated hotel offers modern comforts and contemporary style. Most of its bedrooms overlook a quiet roof garden, and all units contain neatly kept bathrooms. Some readers have praised these bathrooms—"storage enough for a platoon"—and enjoyed the two 1.5m-wide (5-ft.) mirrors. Le Quatre Saisons, the hotel's luxury restaurant, is among the top three in Basel, although some find it overrated and overpriced. An international market-fresh cuisine is served.

Clarastrasse 43, CH-4005 Basel. © **800/223-5652** in the U.S. and Canada or 061/690-80-80. Fax 061/690-88-80. www.balehotels.ch. 158 units. 260F–420F ($213–$344) double; 290F–520F ($238–$426) suite. Children 12 and under stay free in parent's room. Rates include buffet breakfast. AE, DC, MC, V. Parking 15F ($12); 30F ($25) for fairs and congresses. Tram: 2, 6, or 8. **Amenities:** 2 restaurants; bar; cafe; 24-hr. room service; babysitting; laundry service/dry cleaning; nonsmoking rooms. *In room:* TV, dataport, minibar, hair dryer, safe.

Hotel Krafft *(Finds)* Located across the river from the Old Town's Rathaus and Münster, this elegant little mansion is a real discovery, its terrace cafe and its bedrooms opening directly on the waterfront of Basel's right bank. The public rooms are decorated with 19th-century antiques, oversize gilt mirrors, and Oriental rugs. The comfortable, modernized rooms often have good views, and contain Oriental carpets and artwork. All units offer showers with some containing tub/shower combinations. The Waldmeyer-Schneiter family also manages the well-known restaurant Zem Schnoogge-loch (Mosquito's Den) and the Restaurant Petit Bâle, serving French and Swiss cuisine.

Rheingasse 12, CH-4058 Basel. © **061/690-91-30**. Fax 061/690-91-31. www.hotelkrafft.ch. 52 units. 230F–290F ($189–$238) double. Children 12 and under stay free in parent's room. Rates include continental breakfast. AE, DC, MC, V. Parking 25F ($21). Tram: 8. **Amenities:** 2 restaurants; lounge; laundry service/dry cleaning. *In room:* TV.

Hotel Mérian am Rhein *(* This 1972 hotel lies just off the quay where a 13th-century bishop commissioned the construction of the only bridge across the Rhine between Lake Constance and the sea. Located in the oldest part of the city, the Mérian has updated conveniences, including very comfortable beds. Rooms with river-view balconies of the Rhine are more expensive. Ranging from midsize to spacious, units are well equipped with modern furnishings, glass-topped cocktail tables, well-lit desk space, and tiled bathrooms.

With its black lacquer and beech furnishings, the Café and Restaurant Spitz on the ground floor of the hotel is famous locally, especially because of its terrace by the Mittlerebrücke and the Rhine.

Rheingasse (at Greifengasse 2), CH-4058 Basel. ✆ **061/681-00-00.** Fax 061/685-11-01. www.bestwestern.ch. 65 units. 260F–290F ($213–$238) double. Rates include continental breakfast. AE, DC, MC, V. Parking 14F ($11). Tram: 6, 8, or 14. **Amenities:** 2 restaurants; bar; lounge; 24-hr. room service; laundry service/dry cleaning; nonsmoking rooms; rooms for guests w/limited mobility. *In room:* TV, dataport, minibar, hair dryer.

Hotel St. Gotthard

Opposite the train station, this building is graced with arched canopies stretching above the two doors and three picture windows. The hotel, run by the third generation of the Geyer-Arel family, offers comfortable, well-maintained, and individually decorated bedrooms. All contain neatly kept bathrooms with shower stalls. The staff is friendly and helpful.

Centralbahnstrasse 13, CH-4002 Basel. ✆ **800/780-7234** in the U.S. or 061/225-13-13. Fax 061/225-13-14. www. bestwestern.ch. 104 units. 240F–360F ($197–$295) double. Rates include buffet breakfast. AE, DC, MC, V. Parking 25F ($21). Tram: 1, 2, or 8. **Amenities:** Lounge; bar; laundry service/dry cleaning. *In room:* A/C, TV, dataport, minibar, hair dryer, iron, safe, trouser press.

Kultur Gasthaus der Teufelhof ⟨⟨⟨ *Finds*

This is one of the most unusual hotels in Switzerland, if not all of Europe. Set in what was originally a 19th-century private home in the Spalen district, near the Academy of Music, it contains two restaurants, a charming bar, and handsomely decorated bedrooms featuring decor that's been written up in newspapers across the city. Each room was entrusted to the artistic inspiration of a different Swiss, Italian, or German "environmental artist." Each artist was given carte blanche to create whatever he or she decided. The result gives you the impression of living inside a work of art that happens to be exceedingly comfortable, with cozy chairs and modern plumbing. ***Heads up:*** There is no air-conditioning, no room TV. Even if you don't stay here, consider the hotel's dining possibilities.

Leonhardsgraben 47, CH-4051 Basel. ✆ **061/261-10-10.** Fax 061/261-10-04. www.teufelhof.com. 33 units. 255F–370F ($209–$303) double; 295F–450F ($242–$369) suite. Rates include breakfast. AE, MC, V. Parking 27F ($22). Tram: 3. **Amenities:** 2 restaurants; bar; limited room service; laundry service/dry cleaning. *In room:* Hair dryer.

Royal Hotel ⟨ *Finds*

This boutique hotel in a former office building is a bit of an oddity but one with charm for some clients, especially young travelers. Its bedrooms are aligned according to proper feng shui, and individually designed with your comfort in mind, complete with multilingual fax machines and high-speed Internet access. The size—called "spatial environment" here—is generous with a certain elegant functionalism. The belief here is that "less is more." Each comes with a bathroom with tub and shower. Opt for a meal in the 70-seat Royal Restaurant, where you can enjoy light, imaginative cuisine in its bright, airy rooms. Or you can choose a table in the garden.

Schwarzwaldallee 179, CH-4058 Basel. ✆ **061/686-55-55.** Fax 061/686-55-99. www.royal-hotel.ch. 15 units. 220F–270F ($180–$221) double. AE, DC, MC, V. Tram: 2 or 6. **Amenities:** Restaurant; bar; lounge; 24-hr. room service; laundry service/dry cleaning. *In room:* TV, dataport, minibar, hair dryer, safe.

MODERATE

Hotel Münchnerhof

In front of the Basel Fair and Conference Center and close to the railroad station, Hotel Münchnerhof is housed in a brownish-ocher building with white trim and small balconies. Bedrooms are small to midsize, each well maintained and comfortable. Furnishings are a combination of modern and traditional. In addition to the hotel, the Früh family also operates a restaurant, known for its French, Swiss, and Italian cuisine.

Riehenring 75, CH-4058 Basel. ✆ **061/691-77-80.** Fax 061/691-14-90. www.muenchnerhof.ch. 32 units. 140F–350F ($115–$287) double. Rates include buffet breakfast. AE, DC, MC, V. Parking 25F ($21). Tram: 1, 2, 6, or 14. **Amenities:** Restaurant; Bavarian cellar; bar; limited room service; laundry service/dry cleaning. *In room:* TV, dataport, iron, safe.

Hotel Schweizerhof ⭐ Located near the train station across from a landscaped park, this ornate hotel is six stories high, with a terrace and wrought-iron balconies. It has been in the Goetzinger family for three generations. Built in 1864, it was once the most luxurious hotel in Basel, entertaining such greats as Casals, Menuhin, and Toscanini. Today it remains the traditional favorite of town, but is likely to attract more business travelers than its former clientele of the wealthy chic. The salons are decorated with Oriental rugs and some 19th-century antiques, while the bedrooms are both modern and traditional, sometimes blending Biedermeier with pine and beech. Half the accommodations are air-conditioned.

Centralbahnplatz 1, CH-4002 Basel. ✆ 061/271-28-33. Fax 061/271-29-19. www.schweizerhof-basel.ch. 75 units. 198F–300F ($162–$246) double. Rates include continental breakfast. AE, DC, MC, V. Free parking. Tram: 6, 10, 16, or 17. **Amenities:** Restaurant; bar; laundry service/dry cleaning. *In room:* A/C, TV, dataport, minibar, hair dryer, safe.

INEXPENSIVE

Au-Violon ⭐⭐ *(Finds)* One tries to avoid overnighting in a prison, but not in this case. This historic site, once a 12th-century cloister for priests and from 1835 to 1995 a famous prison, is now an offbeat hotel of comfort and grace. If you want that jail-house feeling, ask for one of the bedrooms fronting the courtyard. These units still adhere to their cellblock plan, and space is tight. Accommodations whose windows open onto the Altstadt are larger and more comfortable. All units come with well-maintained but rather small private bathrooms with shower stalls. Some of the doors leading to the bedrooms are 1.5m (5 ft.) tall, so be duly warned. Even if you don't stay here, consider a visit to its charming old-world brasserie with its classic French cuisine. Tables are placed outside on a terraced garden in fair weather.

Im Lohnhof, CH-4051 Basel. ✆ **061/269-87-11.** Fax 061/269-87-12. www.au-violon.com. 20 units. 140F–190F ($115–$156) double. Tram: 3. **Amenities:** Restaurant; laundry service/dry cleaning. *In room:* TV, hair dryer.

BildungsZentrum 21 *(Value)* More than a hotel, this building is also the headquarters of the Evangelische Missionswerk (Protestant Mission) of Basel and every profit made goes to their work. However, this isn't just a good place to stay for the religious. The hotel's central location, beautiful garden, and comfortable rooms make it a good value choice for any traveler. Most of the rooms are inexpensive, priced at the lower end of the scale. Zum Rosengarten, the on-site restaurant, is fine, but guests go here more for the convenience than for the food. The extensive library is a grace note.

Missionsstrasse 21, Postfach CH-4003 Basel. ✆ **061/260-21-21.** Fax 061/260-21-22. www.bildungszentrum-21.ch. 69 units. 135F–350F ($111–$287) double. Rates include breakfast. AE, DC, MC, V. Free parking. Tram: 1. **Amenities:** Restaurant; business services; nonsmoking rooms; rooms for guests w/limited mobility. *In room:* TV, dataport.

WHERE TO DINE

Five centuries ago the humanist Enea Silvio de' Piccolomini (who later became Pope Pius II) said about Baslers: "Most of them are devotees of good living. They live at home in style and spend most of their time at the table." Not much has changed.

VERY EXPENSIVE

La Rôtisserie des Rois ⭐ SWISS This elegant restaurant is famous for its riverside terrace, where in midsummer tables are set close to the waters of the Rhine. The restaurant offers a *cuisine du marché*—that is, a cuisine based on the best of market-fresh ingredients. Original seasonings as well as a sound classic technique characterize this refined cuisine, which is exceptionally flavorful. No wonder the locals flock here. Specialties change with the seasons; you may try homemade terrine of goose liver, guinea fowl with chanterelles, chicken breast with leek-flavored cream sauce, potato pancakes with caviar, or chateaubriand in a confit of shallots.

In the Hotel Drei Könige, Blumenrain 8. © 061/261-52-52. Reservations recommended. Main courses 29F–130F ($24–$107); 6-course gourmet menu 160F ($131). AE, DC, MC, V. Daily 11:15am–2:45pm and 7–10pm. Tram: 1, 6, 8, 14, or 15.

Restaurant Stucki Bruderholz 🏵🏵🏵 FRENCH   Located a short distance south of the city limits, Hans and Susi Stucki's gourmet restaurant is renowned throughout Switzerland, an elegant shrine of haute cuisine. Customers may dine inside or on the backyard terrace by the garden. The former private residence is decorated with antiques and oil paintings. Our favorite room is the Salon Vert, with its green napery, Empire chairs, and light-patterned Oriental rug.

The chef produces a refined yet lively cuisine known for its intense flavor and use of top-quality ingredients. Specialties may include a filet of saltwater red mullet with coriander, a terrine of foie gras, sliced veal kidneys in a tarragon vinaigrette sauce, or a lobster ragout with truffles and baby leeks. The *selle d'agneau* (lamb) is cooked with a gratin of green beans, and the sweetbreads are masterful. For dessert, we'd suggest a compote of pears or a soufflé made with the fresh fruits of the season.

Bruderholzallee 42. © 061/361-82-22. www.stucki-bruderholz.ch. Reservations required. Main courses 68F–170F ($56–$139); fixed-price lunch 90F ($74); 6-course menu surprise 200F ($164). AE, DC, MC, V. Tues–Sat 11:30am–am. Bus: 15.

EXPENSIVE

Chez Donati 🏵🏵 ITALIAN   This is Basel's best Italian restaurant, the creation of Romano Villa and Peter Wyss, whose viands are just as fine as those south in Italy itself. This has long been a favorite of artists visiting Basel and was a former haunt of Andy Warhol and Jean Tinguely. Ancient statuary is placed against periwinkle blue walls, and chandeliers overhead light the dark woodwork. This is a mere backdrop for the first-class cuisine, which some critics have hailed as the finest Italian dining in the entire country. The chefs are justifiably celebrated for the best antipasti table in this part of the world. One of their best dishes is *osso buco* (braised veal knuckles). The meat is incredibly tender, and this Lombard specialty would hold up against any competition in Milan. Braised beef and fresh fish are other specialties, and all of this fare is enjoyed on a white-covered table with a view of the fast-flowing Rhine.

48 St. Johanns-Vorstadt, Grossbasel. © 061/322-09-19. Reservations required. Main courses 58F–75F ($48–$62). No credit cards. Tues–Sat 11:30am–2pm and 6pm–midnight. Closed July 11–Aug 11. Tram: 11. Bus: 3.

Kunsthalle Restaurant 🏵 FRENCH/ITALIAN   This elegant restaurant houses pictures from the Kunsthalle (art gallery) on its walls to complement the chandeliers, handsome rugs, stone arches leading into the bar, and murals on the walls. In the main dining room, cold specialties are served buffet style, and white-jacketed waiters will take your orders for hot courses. You can order a salad of arugula with mushrooms and cheese, followed by a double entrecôte with risotto or grilled sea bass served with potatoes. You can also eat supper in the bar from the same a la carte menu offered in the main restaurant. Though hardly the best cuisine in Basel, the food is consistently reliable, and diners usually leave satisfied.

Steinenberg 7. © 061/272-42-33. Reservations recommended. Main courses 43F–63F ($35–$52). No credit cards. Daily 11am–2pm and 6pm–midnight. Tram: 6, 10, or 16.

St. Alban-Eck 🏵 *(Finds* SWISS/FRENCH   Set in the antiques district and filled with architectural charm, this small and intimate restaurant is a 5-minute walk from the

Museum of Fine Arts. The historic 750-year-old building has retained its beautiful original stone and oak door. The kitchen is known for its high-quality French and Swiss specialties. You might try the homemade ravioli stuffed with salmon in a creamy truffle sauce, grilled turbot with potatoes and vegetables, or suprême of duckling with honey sauce or coriander. The chef also prepares grilled U.S. beef with arugula and rack of veal with potatoes and chanterelles. We are exceedingly fond of this place, and after sampling the meticulously prepared cuisine, we think you will be too.

Malzgasse–St. Alban–Vorstadt 60. © 061/271-03-20. Reservations recommended. Main courses 40F–56F ($33–$46); fixed-price 5-course menu 85F ($70). AE, DC, MC, V. Mon–Sat 11:30am–2:30pm and 7–11:30pm. Closed July 16–Aug 16. Tram: 2 or 14.

Schloss Binningen ๙๙ FRENCH   This 16th-century château and its grounds are owned by the township but managed by independent entrepreneurs. The entrance hall is appropriately baronial, and the grand dining rooms contain an antique loggia (presumably used long ago by chamber orchestras). The wine cellar is among the best in the region, with at least 50 vintages not listed on the menu (the wine steward will make appropriate suggestions). The menu changes at least three times a year but is likely to include a *timbale de langoustines* (crawfish served in a pie crust) with caviar, a *selle de chevreuil rösti* (saddle of roast roebuck), or fresh lobster, followed by a cold soufflé. This restaurant is tranquil and charming. Dishes are carefully prepared, and lighter versions of classic dishes appear frequently.

Schlossgasse 5, Binningen. © 061/421-20-55. Reservations required. Main courses 32F–66F ($26–$54); fixed-price lunch 55F ($45); fixed-price dinner 110F ($90). AE, DC, MC, V. Tues–Sat noon–2pm and 7–9:30pm. Closed 2 weeks in Feb. Tram: 2, 10, or 17.

MODERATE

Safran-Zunft ๛ SWISS   Upon entering this medieval stone building, you'll notice the wrought-iron depiction of the restaurant's logo, a gluttonous monk inhaling the aroma from a goblet of wine. That sets the tone for this time-tested favorite attracting faithful devotees, primarily those drawn by its bargain lunches. Inside, the restaurant is set up tavern style, with red-checked tablecloths, wood paneling, and oversize Gothic windows.

The kitchen serves elaborate specialties and good-tasting appetizers such as caviar and smoked salmon. And while you'll regularly find veal steak and chateaubriand on the menu, most guests order the delectable fondue Bacchus, with veal and all the condiments. The soups are especially good.

Gerbergasse 11. © 061/269-94-94. Reservations recommended. Main courses 23F–40F ($19–$33); fixed-price lunch 27F ($22). AE, DC, MC, V. Sept–June Mon–Sat 11:30am–11pm; July–Aug Mon–Fri 10am–2pm and 5pm–midnight. Tram: 1, 6, 8, 11, or 14.

Schlüsselzunft ๙๙ FRENCH   This is one of the oldest guildhalls in Basel, begun in the 12th century by cloth merchants. The restaurant has a menu offering seasonal specialties, including various types of fish and, in the autumn, venison. The cooking is careful, and the talented kitchen delivers on solid flavors, using quality ingredients. Regular specialties include veal curry, tenderloin steak with goose liver and morels, shredded calves' kidney in a Madeira sauce, and shredded veal and kidney in a cream sauce with Spätzle. It also serves well-prepared traditional soups and a fine selection of pasta, including cannelloni au gratin.

Freie Strasse 25. © 061/261-20-46. Reservations recommended. Main courses 34F–57F ($28–$47); fixed-price lunch 50F ($41), fixed-price dinner 70F ($57). AE, MC, V. Mon–Sat 11:30am–3pm and 6pm–midnight. Tram: 6 or 14.

Zum Goldenen Sternen CONTINENTAL   Set near the edge of the Rhine and established in 1421, this is one of the oldest restaurants in Switzerland. Renovated in a conservative mixed style of old and modern architectural elements in the early 1990s, it's known to many different generations of Baslers. The well-prepared dishes are traditional, influenced by neighboring France. Dishes include smoked eel, smoked trout, terrine maison, turbot in a potato crust, lobster soup, roast rack of lamb, filet of veal with lemon, and roast guinea fowl with a mushroom ragout.

St. Albanrheinweg 70. ✆ 061/272-16-66. Reservations recommended. Main courses 32F–40F ($26–$33); fixed-price menu 62F–80F ($51–$66). AE, DC, MC, V. Daily noon–2pm and 6–10pm. Tram: 6 or 12.

INEXPENSIVE

Brauerei Fischerstube BREWERY   No one comes to this restaurant expecting a mind-boggling culinary experience. People visit because they want to drink one of the fresh-brewed local lagers and ales. Order the house ale, named Ueli Bier after a Fasnacht clown, and you'll be expected to drink every drop of the mammoth 5-liter serving you're given. If you'd rather drink at a slower pace in the comfort of your own hotel room, the brewers also sell 15-liter kegs. The food here isn't anything special. Expect such hearty fare—good with beer—as regional sausages and a big serving of rump steak. This is one of the most fun spots in Basel for devotees of the brew.

Rheingasse 45. ✆ 061/692-66-35. Reservations not required. Main courses 15F–36F ($12–$30). MC, V. Mon–Thurs 10am–midnight; Fri–Sat 10am–1:30am; Sun 5pm–midnight. Tram: 6, 8, or 14.

Da Roberto Value ITALIAN   Located on a narrow side street 1 block from the central train station, this restaurant attracts younger Baslers, many of whom appreciate its nonsmoking area. Depending on what you order, you can dine here rather inexpensively, enjoying good food, a lively atmosphere, and polite but informal service. There are three separate seating areas, decorated with checkered tablecloths and paneled walls. At night the young crowd often drops in for the tasty pizzas. The soups are a good value, as are the 15 different spaghetti dishes.

Kuchengasse 3. ✆ 061/205-85-50. Main courses 18F–32F ($15–$26); pizzas and salads 15F–30F ($12–$25); fixed-price lunch 20F–30F ($16–$25). AE, DC, MC, V. Sun–Fri 11:45am–2pm; daily 5:30–11pm. Tram: 1, 2, 8, 10 or 11.

BASEL AFTER DARK

Regardless of which language you speak, you'll find lots of options for nightlife, whether you're looking for a sophisticated cocktail lounge or a funky alternative club. A worthwhile cluster of them are in the **Stadtcasino,** Barfüssenplatz (✆ 061/225-93-93), a venue that contains a stage (Musik Halle) for live musical acts, plus at least three other bars and restaurants. On Steinenberg 14, look for the American-inspired **Papa Joe's** (✆ 061/225-93-94), a restaurant containing vague references to Hemingway and a commodious bar area. A few steps away, at Steinenberg 7, directly opposite the whimsical fountain designed by mega-artist Jean Tinguely, is the **Campari Bar** (✆ 061/272-83-83), a youthful site for drinking, gossiping, or whatever.

An appealing and discreetly prosperous bar, **The Old City Bar,** is in the previously recommended Basel Hilton International, Aeschengraben 31 (✆ 061/271-66-22). Its decor evokes a prestigious men's club in London. Here, you'll get the distinct feeling that everything from billion-dollar bank transfers to romantic assignations have been discreetly and stylishly conducted. Several notches upscale, with older and more prestigious antecedents, is the **Euler Bar,** in the Hotel Euler, Centralbahnplatz 14 (✆ 061/275-80-00). Popular with the international business community, it contains a lavishly coffered ceiling, a live pianist, lots of leather upholstery, a noise level that rarely rises above a murmur, and stiff drinks. More raucous and earthy is the popular bar in the oldest hotel in Europe, the **Drei Könige,** Blumenrain 8 (© **061/260-50-50**), which is smaller and more bohemian than the previously recommended bars.

Next door to the Hotel Drei Könige is **Queens,** Blumenrain 10 (© **061/271-00-50**), a safe and well-recommended disco with an appealing cross section of youthful and middle-age partygoers, both gay and straight. Admission is free. The music is a mix of '60s, '70s, and '80s. Music lovers head for the city's most deeply entrenched bastion of electronic music, avant-garde jazz, and rock 'n' roll, the **Café Atlantis,** Klosterberg 13 (© **061/228-96-96**). Favored by rock-star hopefuls and college students, it contains a labyrinth of bars and balconies, and views of the medieval cathedral from the second-floor windows. On Friday and Saturday nights, it becomes a disco. During the week it has occasional live music. Admission is free. The quintessential smoke-filled cafe is **Zum Roten Engel,** 15 Andreasplatz (© **061/261-2008**), filled mainly with students and other young people.

Young Basel, enjoying their position at the "crossroads" of Europe, are constantly discovering and patronizing new bars and nightspots that keep them on the cutting edge, making Bern look absolutely provincial. Follow the sound of soul and funk echo to **NT/Areal,** 21-23 Erlenstrasse (© **061/683-83-22**), a music spot that grows hotter as the night grows long.

You're always likely to strike up an interesting conversation when you drop in at any of Basel's gay bars, which tend to get going relatively late at night, around 11pm. Try **Elle et Lui,** Rebgasse 39 (© **061/692-54-79**).

On a more cultural note, the **Basel Stadttheater,** Theaterstrasse 7 (© **061/295-11-33**), presents an array of opera, operetta, dance concerts, and plays in German. The box office is open Monday to Saturday from 10am to 1pm and 3:30 to 5:30pm, and 1 hour before any performance. It is closed in July and August.

2 Solothurn ⭐

43km (27 miles) N of Bern; 25km (16 miles) NE of Biel

The capital of a canton by the same name, Solothurn, according to a 16th-century rhyme, is "the oldest place in Celtis save Trier." Located on the banks of the Aare at the foot of the Jura Mountains, it has been fortified many times. Roman inscriptions calling it Salodurum have been found, as have the remains of a Roman castrum. But today the town is celebrated for its baroque architecture—reason enough for a visit.

Many guidebooks ignore the town completely, and many visitors relegate it to a day trip from Bern, but there are rewards to be found here.

ESSENTIALS

GETTING THERE   Solothurn has frequent train connections to the major cities of Switzerland, including Zurich (65 min.), Geneva (2 hr.), and Biel (1 hr.). Call © **0900-300-300** (no area code) for **rail information.**

If driving, head north from Bern on the N1, veering west at the turnoff to Solothurn.

VISITOR INFORMATION   The Solothurn tourist office, the **Verkehrsbüro,** Hauptgasse 69, am Kronenplatz (© **032/626-46-46**), will provide you with a map and pinpoint some of the best hiking in the area. Open Monday to Friday from 8:30am to noon and 1:30 to 6pm, Saturday 9am to noon.

SEEING THE SIGHTS

Solothurn is Switzerland's finest baroque town. It was at its peak from the 16th to the 18th centuries, when it was the residence of the French ambassadors to the Swiss Confederation. Solothurn became part of the Confederation as early as 1481.

Exploring Solothurn on foot is the typical way to see the town's attractions, although you may opt for a **rental bike** instead. At the Solothurn rail station on Hauptbahnhofstrasse (© **0512/26-98-15**), you can rent a bike for 30F ($25) daily from 8am to 7pm.

Solothurn's **Old Town** ☞ is on the left bank of the river, partially enclosed by 17th-century walls. Inside those walls you'll find many Renaissance and baroque buildings. The Old Town is entered through the **Biel Gate,** or the Basel Gate. The heart of the old sector is **Marktplatz,** with its clock tower and a produce market on Wednesday and Saturday mornings from 9am to noon. The 15th-century **Rathaus (town hall)** has a notable Renaissance doorway. The two most colorful streets are **Hauptgasse** and **Schaalgasse,** where you'll find many wrought-iron signs and brightly painted shutters.

The baroque **Cathedral of St. Ursus** ☞—said to stand on the spot where its namesake was martyred—dates from the 18th century and has been the seat of the bishop of Basel since 1828. The cathedral, just inside Basel Gate, was constructed by builders from Ticino, which explains its Italian artistry. Try to visit the gardens on the east side.

The **Jesuitenkirche (Jesuits' Church),** on Hauptgasse between the cathedral and the marketplace, dates from 1680 and contains a frescoed, **three-bay nave** ☞.

After you've absorbed the town's beauty, you might want to see some of the **Juras,** which tower in the background. There are many marked trails in the area for biking or hiking. The most scenic trail leads from the center of Solothurn to the Weissenstein Alpine Center, which will take about 2 hours by foot. Start out at the corner of Wengisteinstrasse and Verenawegstrasse in Solothurn and follow signs leading to Weissenstein. Once there you can board a chairlift that takes you down from Weissenstein to a station in Oberdorf where you can return to Solothurn by rail.

In summer consider a **boat tour** leaving from the quays at Solothurn to the towns of Biel, Murten, or Neuchâtel. A round-trip fare costs 47F ($31), and the tourist office (see above) keeps a list of departure times, which vary depending on the weather.

Kunstmuseum Solothurn (Municipal Fine Arts Museum) ☞   Visit this museum

if only to see the *Madonna of Solothurn,* by Holbein the Younger. Also outstanding is a 15th-century painting on wood from the Rhenish school, the *Virgin with Strawberries.* The museum emphasizes Swiss art from the mid–19th century to the present. A collection of excellent works represent Frölicher, Hodler, Vallotton, Trachsel, Amiet, Berger, Gubler, and others.

Werkhofstrasse 30. © **032/622-23-07.** Free admission. Tues–Fri 10am–noon and 2–5pm; Sat–Sun 10am–5pm.

Museum Altes Zeughaus (Old Arsenal)   Slightly to the northwest of the cathe-

dral stands this museum, which houses one of the largest collections of weapons in Europe. There are fascinating exhibits of medieval weaponry, flags, and Swiss military uniforms.

Zeughausplatz 1. © **032/623-35-28.** Admission 6F ($4.90) adults, 4F ($3.30) children and seniors, 10F ($8.20) family ticket, free for children 7 and under. June–Oct Tues–Sun 10am–noon and 2–5pm; Nov–May Tues–Sun 2–5pm, Sat–Sun 10am–noon.

WHERE TO STAY

Hotel Krone ⟨ This hotel is clearly the front-runner in town. Hotel Krone, near the Clock Tower, is one of the oldest inns in the country and basks in its reputation as the hotel where Napoleon's wife, Josephine, stayed for several days in 1811. Run by the Küng family, the inn still attracts history buffs. The gilt lettering on the pink facade spells out the name in French—Hôtel de la Couronne. The bedrooms are old-fashioned but exceedingly comfortable and well maintained. Most of the units are quite spacious, and all contain neatly kept bathrooms.

Hauptgasse 64, CH-4500 Solothurn. ⟨ **032/626-44-44.** Fax 032/626-44-45. www.hotelkrone-solothurn.ch. 42 units. 220F–260F ($180–$213) double. Rates include buffet breakfast. AE, DC, MC, V. Parking 12F ($9.85). **Amenities:** Restaurant; bar; limited room service; laundry service/dry cleaning. *In room:* TV, minibar, hair dryer, safe.

Roter Turm Parts of this hotel date from the 1100s; others were added throughout the centuries to create the inner labyrinth of rooms and corridors that make the architecture of this place the most complicated and intriguing in town. An inn has been on-site since the 1840s, and the current Swiss family owners provide modern, comfortable bedrooms; the largest overlook the front square. Accommodations come in a range of sizes and shapes, and most furnishings are traditional. All units are equipped with well-maintained bathrooms. The staff keeps the place in tip-top shape.

Hauptgasse 42, CH-4500 Solothurn. ⟨ **032/622-96-21.** Fax 032/622-98-65. www.roterturm.ch. 36 units. 195F–230F ($160–$189) double. Rates include breakfast. AE, DC, MC, V. **Amenities:** 2 restaurants; laundry/dry cleaning. *In room:* TV, dataport, minibar, hair dryer.

WHERE TO DINE

Zum Alten Stephan ⟨⟨⟨ SWISS This restaurant is the finest in this region of Switzerland. Parts of the structure that contain this place were built 1,000 years ago as housing for the staff of a nearby chapel, St. Stephan's Kappelle. Later it functioned as the point of demarcation from which most of the streets of Solothurn were laid out. Today it's the oldest restaurant in the canton and the most charming and amusing place in town, with two distinctly separate venues, menus, and price scales.

We usually prefer the simpler, street-level dining room, where varnished pine, marble floors, bare-wood tables, and oil paintings in gilded frames provide an uncluttered dignity. Upstairs is a smaller, more intimate and hushed ambience where the cuisine is more thoughtful and cerebral (and more fussed over) than in the brasserie. Menu items in the brasserie include several kinds of rösti, which many locals consider a meal in itself. According to your wishes, it will include any combination of ham, onions, cheese, bacon, and fried eggs. There's also pasta, salads, soups, meat, and fish. Upstairs, look for such dishes as Scottish salmon in puff pastry with broad beans and soy sauce, duck breast with white asparagus, Parmesan ravioli in a spinach pasta wrapper, filet of U.S. beef served with vegetables and wild mushrooms, and such desserts as four-fruit sorbet with fresh berries.

Friedhofplatz 10. ⟨ **032/622-11-09.** Reservations recommended, especially for the upstairs restaurant. Upstairs restaurant fixed-price lunch 64F ($52), fixed-price dinner 160F ($131). Street-level brasserie main courses 18F–55F ($15–$45); fixed-price menu 25F ($21). AE, DC, MC, V. Restaurant Tues–Sat 11am–2pm and 5pm–midnight. Brasserie daily 11am–midnight.

3 Fribourg ⟨⟨

35km (22 miles) SW of Bern; 53km (33 miles) NE of Vevey

Once a sovereign republic, set between lakes and mountains, Fribourg was founded in 1157 and today has a population of some 40,000 and a university. It was a stronghold of Catholicism for centuries and was known for its dyers, weavers, and tanners. In 1481 it joined the Swiss Confederation, and today it's the capital of a canton of the same name. Visitors arrive today to see Switzerland's most rural canton, famous for its Holstein cows. It's a charming place with narrow medieval town houses. To wander its ancient precincts is well worth a day or at least an afternoon of your time.

ESSENTIALS

GETTING THERE   Fribourg is on the main train lines that connect Zurich and Bern with Lausanne and Geneva. Travel time from Lausanne is about 45 minutes; from Bern, about 25 minutes. Call © **0900-300-300** for **train schedules** and information.

If you're driving, head southwest from Bern on N12; from Vevey, on Lake Geneva, go northeast on N12.

VISITOR INFORMATION   The **Office du Tourisme** is at 1, place de la Gare (© **026/821-31-75**), and is open Monday to Friday from 9am to 12:30pm and 1:30 to 6pm, Saturday 9am to noon and 1:30 to 4pm (closed Sat afternoon Oct–Apr).

SEEING THE SIGHTS

Fribourg's major attraction is **St. Nicholas's Cathedral** *&*, on place Notre-Dame (© **026/347-10-40**), with its lofty 15th-century Gothic bell tower that dominates the medieval quarter. The most remarkable feature is the main porch **tymphanum** *&&*, surmounted by a rose window. Depicted are such subjects as the Last Judgment and "heaven and the inferno." The nave dates from the 13th and 14th centuries, although the choir was reconstructed in the 17th century. La Chapelle Saint-Sépulcre, from the 15th century, has some remarkable stained glass and a celebrated organ.

In the vicinity of the cathedral, you'll find **old patrician houses.** On foot, you can explore this architecturally interesting part of Fribourg—its Gothic houses, small steep streets, and squares adorned with fountains.

Whether it's called the Rathaus (in German) or the Hôtel de Ville (in French), the **town hall** of Fribourg is a notable 16th-century building. Located on route des Alpes, its best feature is its octagonal clock tower where mechanical figures strike the hours. Outside the town hall, the seat of the parliament of Fribourg, traditionally dressed farmers' wives sell produce on Wednesday and Saturday—the most colorful days to visit the city.

Another important religious site is the Franciscan church **Eglise des Cordeliers** (© **026/347-11-60**), located north of place Notre-Dame, where St. Nicholas stands. The choir at the Franciscan church is from the 13th century, the nave is from the 18th century, and the church has an outstanding wood triptych carved in 1513. Its chief attraction is an altarpiece that rises from the main altar, the work of the "Masters of the Carnation," 15th-century artists who signed their works with a white or a red carnation.

The city also has an outstanding art and history museum, the **Musée d'Art et d'Histoire** or Museum für Kunst und Geschichte, 12, rue de Morat (© **026/305-51-40**). Housed in the 16th-century Hôtel Ratze and a former slaughterhouse, it has archaeological collections of prehistoric, Roman, and medieval objects, as well as a remarkable series of Burgundian belt buckles. The epic sweep of Fribourg's history comes alive in the sculptures and paintings from the 11th to the 20th centuries. There are also displays on the political, military, and economic life of the canton. Other exhibits include numerous 15th- to 18th-century stained-glass windows and the largest collection in Switzerland of wood sculpture from the first half of the 16th century. The museum is open Tuesday to Sunday from 11am to 6pm (till 8pm Thurs). Admission is 8F ($6.55) for adults, 5F ($4.10) for students and seniors.

To reach the upper town of Fribourg, you can take a funicular. At some point you'll want to see the **Ponte de Berne,** a covered wooden bridge built in 1580.

The best way to sample Fribourg life is from **small cafes** along rue de Romont or rue de Lausanne. Here you can see the city folk pass by—30% calling themselves Freiburger in German, the remaining viewing themselves as Fribourgeois in French.

From a hill rising above the river, Fribourg offers a panoramic view of the **Bernese Alps.** If you're feeling energetic, rent a bike from the train station on place de la Gare for 30F ($25) and go exploring. The best attraction in the environs is Schwarzee (Black Lake), a distance of 27km (17 miles) from the center. It is reached from Fribourg along N74. This can be either a summer or winter excursion, and the scenic setting is one of the most memorable in the area.

SHOPPING

The folkloric souvenirs you'll see in Fribourg revolve around the canton's dairy and cheese-making traditions, with lots of emphasis on objects with heraldic shields and coats-of-arms. If you want to buy some, stroll along the town's main shopping streets, **rue de Romont** and **rue de Lausanne,** or head directly to any of the three addresses listed below. A good inventory of handicrafts is stocked in the city's **Office de Tourisme,** 1, place de la Gare (© **026/321-31-75**), and in a shop that's wholeheartedly devoted to French-speaking Switzerland's folklore, **La Clef du Pays,** 1, rue du Tilleul (© **026/322-51-20**). Barring that, consider rummaging through the town's largest department store, **La Placette,** 30, rue de Romont (© **026/350-66-11**), where you'll find everything you want and more, including gift items, clothing, and any necessities you may have overlooked while packing for your trip.

WHERE TO STAY

Hôtel Alpha *Value*   Located a 15-minute walk from the train station, this modern hotel is one of the best bargains in town. Each of the modern furnished rooms is simple but adequate, and generally tranquil. Beds are firm, and maintenance is high in all units and bathrooms. A restaurant and bar on the first landing are independent of the hotel. Call © **026/322-69-33** for information about the restaurant.

13, rue du Simplon, CH-1700 Fribourg. © **026/322-72-72.** Fax 026/323-10-00. www.alpha-hotel.ch. 27 units. 140F–180F ($115–$148) double; 200F–280F ($164–$230) junior suite. Rates include continental breakfast. AE, DC, MC, V. Parking 12F ($9.85). Bus: 1 or 2. **Amenities:** Restaurant; bar; limited room service; movie cinema. *In room:* TV, dataport, minibar, hair dryer.

Hôtel de la Rose   Occupying a grand sandstone building near the cathedral, this is a historic property, which has been renovated in a rather pristine way. The flowered ceiling in the lobby—the hotel's most dramatic feature—contains elements of the original construction from the 1600s. The midsize bedrooms are modern and comfortably furnished, each with a firm bed and a neat bathroom.

Place Notre-Dame, 1, rue de Morat, CH-1700 Fribourg. © **026/351-01-01.** Fax 026/351-01-00. www.hoteldela rose.ch. 36 units. 140F–230F ($115–$189) double; 230F ($189) suite. Rates include buffet breakfast. AE, DC, MC, V. Parking 6F ($3.90). Bus: 1 or 2. **Amenities:** 2 restaurants; bar; room service; laundry service/dry cleaning. *In room:* TV, minibar, hair dryer, safe, trouser press.

Hôtel Duc Berthold   Yes, there was a Duke Berthold, who once lived in this building, although it's unlikely that he'd recognize it after its conversion to a hotel in 1969.

It's in a fairly noisy part of town, on a busy street alongside the cathedral and the Zähringen Bridge, which is why the hotel's windows are triple-glazed. Some bedrooms are more modernized than others; many retain an antique aura with reproductions of traditional furniture and soft, cream-colored bed linens. The size and shape of the rooms vary but all are comfortably furnished, with good maintenance.

5, rue des Bouchers, CH-1700 Fribourg. © 026/350-81-00. Fax 026/350-81-81. 36 units. 180F–240F ($148–$197) double. Rates include breakfast. AE, DC, MC, V. Bus: 1 or 2. **Amenities:** 2 restaurants; bar; limited room service; babysitting; laundry service/dry cleaning. *In room:* TV, dataport, minibar, hair dryer, safe, trouser press.

WHERE TO DINE

Auberge de Zähringen 𝒢 SWISS   This 17th-century, former private residence attracts seasoned diners. On the ground floor the owners have established both a brasserie and a more intimate French restaurant. The restaurant offers such seasonal specialties as rack of rabbit and pikeperch, plus a ragout of fresh mushrooms in a Gruyère cream sauce and game cock sautéed with fresh mushrooms. The brasserie has drinks, light meals, and platters of food available during the afternoon.

13, rue de Zähringen. © 026/322-42-36. Reservations required in the restaurant. Restaurant main courses 20F–50F ($16–$41); fixed-price menu 60F–105F ($49–$86). Brasserie fixed-price menu 35F–58F ($29–$48). AE, DC, MC, V. Mon 7:30–10:30pm; Tues–Sun noon–1:30pm and 6:30–9:30pm. Closed Sun July–Aug. Bus: 1 or 2.

La Fleur-de-Lys 𝒢𝒢𝒢 FRENCH   This is the most outstanding restaurant in Fribourg, dwarfing the competition. Elegant and charming, the restaurant is a showcase for the culinary skills of Pierre-Andre Ayer, who offers a magic combination: great food at affordable prices. The service is formal without being stiff, and Ayer shops for only the finest ingredients in any season, which he shapes into an array of specialties that show both inventiveness and a solid technique. Typical seasonal specialties include in May and June a delectable lake perch served with an asparagus-stuffed ravioli and crunchy vegetables. In spring you can also enjoy fresh cherries poached in red wine. From November to March a ravioli stuffed with black sausage appears on the menu, a dish made even more delightful by its accompaniment of wild berries and a cider-flavored butter.

18, rue des Forgerons. © 026/322-79-61. Reservations required. Lunch main courses 14F–52F ($11–$43); dinner main courses 60F–100F ($49–$82). AE, DC, MC, V. Tues–Sat noon–2pm and 7–10pm. Closed Feb 25–Mar 6 and Aug.

FRIBOURG AFTER DARK

You'll find more cafes and hole-in-the-wall bars around Fribourg's railway station than anywhere else in town, especially along either side of boulevard de Pérolles, rue de Romont, and rue de l'Hôpital. A particularly cozy bar is **La Cave de la Rose,** in the cellar of the Hôtel de la Rose, 1, rue de Morat (© 026/351-01-01). **Le Macumba,** 17, route de Tavel (© 026/481-33-88), is a high-energy, high-volume disco favored by folks under 30. A bit more mellow and sedate is the disco in the cellar of the **Restaurant l'Escale,** 3, route de Belfaux, in the suburb of Givisiez (© 026/466-27-67), about 1km (half a mile) west of Fribourg's commercial core.

The latest hot spot is **Planet Edelweiss,** Mariahilf, Düdingen (© 026/492-05-05), an 18th-century inn converted into a bustling restaurant and dance club. It draws a young crowd to its location a 5-minute ride northeast of the center. The club keeps the latest hours in the area: until 2am Sunday to Tuesday, 3am Wednesday and Thursday, and 4am Friday and Saturday.

4 Gruyères ✶✶

6km (4 miles) S of Bulle; 64km (40 miles) SW of Bern; 43km (27 miles) E of Palézieux

This small town, which once belonged to the counts of Gruyères, is known for its castle and its cheese. It's a highlight for anyone taking the "cheese route" through Switzerland. It's also a good base for exploring the district of Gruyère (the region is spelled without an "s").

In the canton of Fribourg, the little town of Gruyères seems to slumber somewhere back in the Middle Ages. Enclosed by 12th-century ramparts, it's dominated by a castle, where the counts lived from the 12th to the 16th centuries. Their crest, which bears a crane, is still used in Gruyères.

Cars are forbidden to enter between Easter and the first of November (and on Sun year-round). Therefore you must park your car outside the gates and walk into town. Everything can be explored on foot.

ESSENTIALS

GETTING THERE   From either Lausanne or Zurich, most Gruyères-bound passengers transfer at the busy railway junction of Palézieux. From here, a secondary railway spur leads to Gruyères, stopping at about 20 other hamlets along the way. Trip time from Zurich to Gruyères is about 4½ hours; from Palézieux to Gruyères, about 1 hour. For **train information,** call ✆ 0900-300-300.

About seven buses a day connect Gruyères with the rail and bus junction of Bulle, a 10-minute drive northwest of Gruyères. From Bulle, you can make bus connections to Fribourg and rail connections to the rest of Switzerland. For **bus schedules** and information, call ✆ 026/913-05-21.

If you're driving from Bern, head southwest along N12 and take the southeast turnoff to Bulle; Gruyères is signposted from there.

VISITOR INFORMATION   The **Office du Tourisme** (✆ 026/921-10-30) is in the village center, open Monday to Friday 9am to noon and 1:30 to 5pm, Saturday and Sunday 10am to 4pm. Street names aren't used—the village is very small.

SEEING THE SIGHTS

If you're here when the tour buses aren't, you'll discover one of the most charming villages on the Continent.

At the entrance to town, at the foot of a hill near the railway station, the Swiss Cheese Union operates a model dairy, **Fromagerie de Démonstration,** près de la Gare, at Pringy (✆ 026/921-84-00), for demonstration purposes. Here you can see workers produce the famed Gruyère cheese (a single wheel weighs 75 lb.), which is a more piquant version of the equally famous Emmenthaler. An audiovisual show reveals how the cheese is made. The dairy is open daily from 9am to noon and 1:30 to 7pm, but it's best to go between 10 and 11am or 2 and 3pm, when the cheese is actually being made. In July and August, daily hours are 7am to 7pm. For more information, contact the tourism office (see above).

The traditional lunch in all the restaurants here is **raclette.** A machine is usually placed on your table, so you can melt and scrape the cheese at your own speed. You can eat right down to the rind, which is crunchy and considered by many to be the best part of the raclette. In the right season, you can finish with a large bowl of fresh raspberries in thick cream.

(Moments Fantasy-Porn, Gynecological Obsessions & More

There's nothing quite like the **H. R. Giger Museum**, Château St-Germain (© **026/921-22-00**), in all of Switzerland. The Swiss-born graphic artist H. R. Giger won an Oscar for the special effects he created for the film *Alien*. He brought his obsessions of sexualized surrealist visions to the quaint town of Gruyères, where he opened this museum. Many of his key works are on display here, including grotesque paintings and sculpture, bizarre furniture, and film designs, many from the early 1960s. On the top floor is a permanent display of Giger's own private collection. Wait until you see the glowing red room with "erotic aliens" in compromising positions—it's something to write home about. Admission is 12F ($9.85) for adults and 8F ($6.55) for students. April to October hours are daily 10am to 6pm. In winter hours are Tuesday to Friday 11am to 5pm, Saturday and Sunday 10am to 6pm.

You can walk the cobblestone road to the **Château Gruyères** ✦ (© **026/921-21-02**), passing the house of the famed court jester Chalamala. Dating mostly from the 15th century, the castle, or château, is owned today by the canton of Fribourg. In 1848 the Bovy family of Geneva acquired it and ordered many of its embellishments. Several famous artists, including Corot, have lived here. The château is filled with objets d'art, the most outstanding of which are three mourning copes from the Order of the Golden Fleece—part of the bounty grabbed up in the Burgundian wars. The castle is open to the public June to September daily from 9am to 6pm; March to May and October daily from 9am to noon and 1 to 6pm; and November to February daily from 9:30am to noon and 1:30 to 4pm (till 5pm on weekends). Admission is 6F ($4.90).

WHERE TO STAY

Hostellerie de St-Georges ✦✦✦   This peaceful hideaway is the best place to stay in the region. The building, which dates from the 1500s, offers well-furnished bedrooms, all with new beds and bathrooms.

There's a cozy cafe suitable for drinks, snacks, and light lunches. But many guests prefer the old-world charm of the formal dining room in back, where specialties include filet of beef served on a slate platter, breast of duckling with green peppercorns, and a quiche made with—of course—Gruyère cheese.

CH-1663 Gruyères. (© **026/921-83-00**. Fax 026/921-83-39. www.st-georges-gruyeres.ch. 14 units. 160F–280F ($131–$230) double. Rates include continental breakfast. AE, DC, MC, V. Closed Nov and last 2 weeks of Jan. **Amenities:** 2 restaurants; lounge; laundry service. *In room:* TV, minibar, hair dryer, safe.

Hostellerie des Chevaliers ✦✦   This atmospheric hotel is set at the end of a private driveway near the main town square and thus avoids the bus hordes who descend upon Gruyères. The restaurant section is in a 1950s private villa. The comfortable, conservative, midsize bedrooms are situated a few steps away in a more recent addition, and the best rooms offer sweeping views of the valley. All units are well maintained and contain neatly kept bathrooms.

Both guests and nonguests are welcome to visit the three elegant dining rooms. The one with the best view is covered from floor to ceiling with garden lattices. The others have a scattering of antiques, Delft tiles, and paneling.

CH-1663 Gruyères. © **026/921-19-33.** Fax 026/921-25-52. www.gruyeres-hotels.ch. 30 units. 160F–260F ($131–$213) double. Rates include breakfast. AE, DC, MC, V. Free parking. Closed Jan. **Amenities:** Restaurant; lounge; limited room service; laundry service/dry cleaning. *In room:* TV, minibar.

Hôtel de Ville *Value*   In a historic building in the center of the Old Town, Michel Murith's hotel offers comfortable, pleasantly furnished rooms, all of which contain tidy bathrooms. There is a terrace cafe in front. The restaurant, one of the best bargains in town, serves such specialties as ham and trout.

CH-1663 Gruyères. © **026/921-24-24.** Fax 026/921-36-28. www.hoteldeville.ch. 8 units. 180F–220F ($148–$180) double; 280F–300F ($230–$246) junior suite. Rates include continental breakfast. AE, DC, MC, V. **Amenities:** Restaurant; lounge; laundry service/dry cleaning. *In room:* TV, safe.

WHERE TO DINE

Restaurant le Chalet de Gruyères *Finds* SWISS   One of the most popular and evocative restaurants in town specializes in any dish that can be made with the region's most famous product—cheese. Built in the 1700s a few paces from the château, and functioning as a traditional restaurant since the early 20th century, it counts former U.S. president Jimmy Carter as one of its patrons. Amid aged timbers, honey-colored planks, and polished farm tools, you can order *assiettes gruyèriennes* (Gruyères plates) piled high with ham, cheese, sausages, and air-dried beef; Gruyère salads; *croûtes aux Gruyère* garnished with salad and ham; several kinds of fondues with bread and potatoes; and raclettes. For anyone not interested in cheese, there's a savory mixed grill of meats and sausages.

Rue Principale. © **026/921-21-54.** Reservations recommended. Main courses 16F–50F ($13–$41). AE, DC, MC, V. Daily 11am–10:30pm.

5 Murten

18km (11 miles) N of Fribourg; 30km (19 miles) W of Bern

Of the many ancient towns in Switzerland, we find Murten to be one of the most idyllic and beautifully preserved. The town sits on what is called the "language demarcation line," and its residents speak either French or German, and quite often both. Lying on the southern side of the lake Murtensee, known in French as Lac de Morat, Murten forms a gateway into French-speaking Switzerland. Outside Murten, on June 22, 1476, a fierce battle was fought between the Confederates and Charles the Bold of Burgundy.

ESSENTIALS

GETTING THERE   Murten is connected by direct rail line to Fribourg, a 30-minute ride away. About 20 trains a day make the run, stopping off at about six hamlets along the way. Murten also has good connections to the nearby town of Ins, which lies directly on most of the train routes between Zurich and Paris. For **train information,** call © **0900-300-300.** If you'd like to rent a bike, stop in at the station; a kiosk rents bikes for 29F ($24) a day.

A **boat ride** is quite a restful way to reach Murten over the lakes that lie to the north and west. Ferries cross between Neuchâtel and Murten about five times daily between late May and late September. It takes about 1¾ hours to cross the two lakes (Lac de Neuchâtel and Murtensee) and the canal (La Broye) that connects them; the one-way boat fare is 18F ($15). Call © **026/670-26-03** for more information.

In midsummer another way to reach Murten is from Biel (Bienne). Between late May and late September, a ferry departs Tuesday to Sunday from the central piers in

Biel at 11:20am, arriving in Murten at 3:30pm. One-way transit costs 35F ($29) and will take you through three lakes (Bielersee, Lac de Neuchâtel, and Murtensee) and across the canals connecting them.

If you're driving, head west from Bern on Route 10 and turn south to Murten at the junction with Route 22.

VISITOR INFORMATION   The **Murten Tourist Information Office** is at Französische Kirschgasse 6 (© **026/670-51-12**). It's open Monday to Friday from 9am to noon and 2 to 6pm, Saturday 10am to 2pm.

EXPLORING THE AREA

Many houses date from the 15th to the 18th centuries, and the town itself is surrounded by **medieval ramparts** 🐾 with a wall walk. Today you can stroll along the wall, taking in the view over Altstadt (Old Town) with the castle, lake, and Jura Mountains as a backdrop.

Duke Peter of Savoy built the town's **castle** in the 13th century. It's bleak and foreboding, but impressive nevertheless, and from its inner courtyard (which you can enter for free), there's a vista of the lake and the Jura foothills.

The main street, **Hauptgasse** 🐾, is the major attraction of Murten, running through the center of the old quarter. It leads to the baroque **Bernegate,** which contains one of the oldest clock towers in the country, dating from 1712.

Musée Historique, adjacent to the castle (© **026/670-31-00**), contains everything from archaeological excavations revealing the city's earliest history to a diorama of the 15th-century Battle of Morat. It's housed in an 8-century-old mill a few steps from the walls of the castle. The museum shows a film featuring the Battle of Murten, one of the defining moments in the history of the Swiss cantons. It's open April 3 to October 30, Tuesday to Saturday from 2 to 5pm, Sunday 10am to 5pm. Admission is 6F ($4.90) for adults, 5F ($4.10) for seniors, 2F ($1.65) for students and children 6 to 16, and free for children 5 and under.

Nearby, **Murtensee** 🐾, or Lac de Morat, spread over nearly 26 sq. km (10 sq. miles), has a maximum depth of 45m (148 ft.). Between late May and September, you can take boat trips and circular tours on the three lakes from Murten to Neuchâtel to Biel (Bienne), with trips through the canals in the Great Marshes. Check with the tourist office for information on these excursions.

One of the most enchanting **bike rides** in this part of Switzerland is around Lake Murten. The tourist office (see above) will provide maps, and you can set out on your own. You can rent a bike at the rail station and visit such lakeside villages as Faoug, Salavaux, Bellerive, and Vully. Allow about 4 hours for this 40km (25-mile) jaunt.

WHERE TO STAY & DINE

Hotel Krone (Hôtel de la Couronne) *Value*   This is a heavily gabled building in the center of town that was originally a 15th-century inn. It offers well-maintained, orderly accommodations at reasonable prices. All units contain neatly kept bathrooms. Some rooms are small; those opening onto the lake are the most sought after. The owners, Werner and Christine Nyffeler, oversee service at the hotel's five eating areas. You can opt for the street-level pizzeria, which also serves fondue, or the adjacent Café-Brasserie. A large sunny restaurant and open-air terrace can be found one floor above the lobby, offering a salad bar with as many as two dozen varieties of vegetables.

Rathausgasse 5, CH-3280 Murten. ℭ **026/670-52-52**. Fax 026/670-36-10. www.krone-murten.ch. 33 units. 160F–200F ($131–$164) double. Rates include continental breakfast. AE, DC, MC, V. Free parking. Closed Nov 10–Dec 10. **Amenities:** 3 restaurants; bar; laundry service. *In room:* TV, minibar.

Hotel Schiff   Lying at the edge of the lake near the harbor, this hotel is surrounded
by parks and operates a lakeside cafe. The building, with 19th-century gables and
porches, has a modern extension containing well-decorated public rooms, with Persian rugs, antiques, and lots of gilt. All units are comfortable and well maintained.

The hotel's restaurant, Lord Nelson, has large windows offering a view of lawns and
chestnut trees down to the lake. The French menu is changed every 2 months; in September, during the hunting season, it features game selections. The hotel's dance club
is yet another option for evening activity. Indoor and outdoor swimming pools are a
short walk away.

Ryf 53, CH-3280 Murten. ℭ **026/670-27-01**. Fax 026/670-35-31. www.hotel-schiff.ch. 15 units. 170F–280F ($139–$230) double. Rates include continental breakfast. AE, DC, MC, V. Parking 10F ($8.20). **Amenities:** 2 restaurants; bar; nightclub; limited room service; laundry service/dry cleaning. *In room:* TV, dataport, minibar, hair dryer.

Hotel Weisses Kreuz (Hôtel de la Croix Blanche) 🕸🕸   This is a superb, recently
renovated, attractive hotel, with a gracious staff. It's situated on the lake about a 10-
minute walk from the train station. The historic buildings—one of which was originally a stable—are set behind a screen of roses on a cobblestone street in the center of
the Old Town. The hotel has a scattering of antiques; the midsize bedrooms have
either a modern or an antique decor. Some of the bedrooms are across the street on a
block without views of the lake. However, don't reject these too quickly, as the accommodations here are among the best in Murten, furnished in a combination of styles
ranging from Biedermeier to Louis XVI, and from Empire to Art Nouveau.

Rathausgasse 31, CH-3280 Murten. ℭ **026/670-26-41**. Fax 026/670-28-66. www.weisses-kreuz.ch. 27 units. 160F–280F ($131–$230) double. Rates include continental breakfast. AE, DC, MC, V. Closed Dec–Feb. **Amenities:** Restaurant; lounge; limited room service; laundry service/dry cleaning. *In room:* TV, hair dryer, safe.

Le Vieux Manoir au Lac 🕸🕸🕸 *(Finds)*   Located 2.4km (1½ miles) west of the town
center (a 5-min. taxi ride from the train station), this is a gabled, stucco building in an
idyllic setting. With a sun deck and balconies overlooking Lake Morat, this is the finest
place to stay in the entire area. In the Belle Epoque era, a French military officer—
homesick for his native Normandy—constructed this manor with the turrets and half-
timbers of his homeland. Inside, the decor blends many periods and styles, with objects
such as Persian rugs collected from all over the world. The nice-size bedrooms are comfortable, furnished with individual style and decor. Country prints abound, making for
a cozy atmosphere, and the bedrooms open onto either a landscaped park or the lake.

The restaurant, which has a collection of antiques from around the region, serves
excellent French cuisine.

Rte. de Lausanne, CH-3280 Murten-Meyriez. ℭ **026/678-61-61**. Fax 026/678-61-62. www.vieuxmanoir.ch. 33 units. 390F–510F ($320–$418) double; 510F–630F ($418–$517) suite. Rates include continental breakfast. AE, DC, MC, V. Free parking. Closed mid-Nov to mid-Apr. **Amenities:** Restaurant; lounge; limited room service; babysitting; laundry service/dry cleaning. *In room:* TV, dataport, minibar, hair dryer, safe, robes.

6 Neuchâtel 🕸🕸

46km (29 miles) W of Bern; 30km (19 miles) SW of Biel

Neuchâtel lies at the border of a lake of the same name and at the foot of the green
slopes of Chaumont (1,161m/3,808 ft.). It's the capital of the canton of Neuchâtel,

created in 1815 out of a Prussian principality that had joined the Swiss Confederation. The majority of Neuchâtel's population are Protestant and French-speaking (indeed, they're said to speak the finest French in Switzerland). They acquired their fame for watchmaking as early as the 18th century.

Situated at the foot of the Jura Mountains, in the midst of vineyards, Neuchâtel enjoys an idyllic setting. Many of its limestone houses have a distinctive yellow or ocher color, which inspired Alexandre Dumas to describe the town as having been carved out of a "block of butter."

Neuchâtel is also a notable seat of culture and learning, with a university that was founded in 1838.

The French influence is evident in its architecture. Many houses in the old town date back to the 16th century; some were built with defensive towers. The spirit of old Neuchâtel is best seen at the **Maison des Halles,** the market square, where you may want to buy some well-known local cheese—de Jura—for a picnic around the lake after you've walked the long promenade.

No cars are allowed in the center of the old sector.

ESSENTIALS

GETTING THERE   Neuchâtel lies at the junction of major rail lines linking Geneva with Basel and Zurich with Paris. Travel time to Neuchâtel from Geneva is about 90 minutes; from Zurich, about 2½ hours. For **train information,** call ✆ **0900-300-300.**

Ferries arrive in Neuchâtel about five times a day, in both winter and summer, from Murten (Morat). The trip takes about 1¾ hours. The one-way boat fare is 20F ($16). For **ferry information,** call ✆ **032/729-96-00.** For a longer boat itinerary, available only in the summer, see "Essentials" under section 5, earlier in this chapter.

If you're driving from Bern, take Route 10 west, then Route 5 south to Neuchâtel.

VISITOR INFORMATION   For more information, contact the **tourist office** at Hotel des Postes (✆ **032/889-68-90**), open Monday to Friday 9am to 12:30pm and 1:30 to 5:30pm, Saturday 9am to noon.

SEEING THE SIGHTS

The medieval core of Neuchâtel is dominated by three architectural attractions: a castle (château), a *collégial* (University Church), and the Prison Tower (Tour des Prisons), standing on the highest peak of the city. Of the three, the building that has been altered most over the centuries is the **castle** ✵ (✆ **032/889-68-00**). Its oldest section, the west wing, dates from the 12th century, but most of what you'll see today was added during the 15th, 16th, and 17th centuries. The structure is stern and forbidding; from some of its ramparts you get a panoramic view of the old town. To visit the castle's interior, apply to the building's concierge (you'll find him near the gate to the castle, under an archway). Accompanied visits, for a minimum of two or three people, are conducted Monday to Saturday at 10 and 11am, and 2, 3, and 4pm; and Sunday at 2, 3, and 4pm. The castle is open daily from 10am to 6pm. Admission is free.

Next door, the **Eglise Collégial** was built during the 12th and 13th centuries, though sections of it, most notably the western towers, were a 19th-century embellishment, constructed when the church underwent (some say suffered) a major overhaul. The building's highlight, found in the Romanesque choir, is a monument to the counts of Neuchâtel, created during the 14th century. Adorned with 15 painted effigies of almost-forgotten noblemen, this is the most spectacular Gothic memorial in the country. The collégial is open daily from 8am to 8pm (to 6pm in the winter); admission is free.

Tour des Prisons, rue Hochberg, offers a panoramic view. It was a jail until 1850. It's open 8am to 6pm every day from Easter to September. Admission, via a Metro-style turnstile, is .50F (40¢).

The **Griffin Fountain,** from 1664, stands nearby on rue du Château. It's one of the most famous fountains in the country, thanks to Henri II of Orléans, who in 1657 had it filled with 1,300 gallons of red wine to honor his entry into Neuchâtel.

Stroll into the garden of the **Hôtel du Peyrou,** faubourg de l'Hôpital, dating from 1764. This excellent patrician house was constructed for Monsieur du Peyrou, who was a friend of Jean-Jacques Rousseau and published some of his works. *The Bather,* a statue in the pool, is by Ramseyer.

For a view of the Lake of Neuchâtel and the distant Alps, take a funicular to the **Crête du Plan,** a height of 589m (1,932 ft.). Approach from rue de l'Ecluse, on the border of the medieval sector.

Neuchâtel doesn't lack for shopping options, many of which lie near the railway station in the heart of town. Three of your best bets for crafts and souvenirs are the **Magazin Cachet,** 2, rue de Saint-Honoré (© **032/721-20-22**); a somewhat less elegant competitor, the **Magazin Naville,** place Pury (© **032/724-47-50**); and a relatively upscale alternative, **Unip,** 3, rue des Epancheurs (© **032/724-79-00**).

In and around Neuchâtel are 403km (250 miles) of signposted **mountain bike trails.** Free trail maps are distributed by the tourist office (see above). Mountain bikes are rented at **Alizé,** place du 12-Septembre (© **032/724-40-90**).

WHERE TO STAY

Beau-Rivage ⭐⭐⭐ This is the grandest place to stay in town. A hotel since the 1800s, this graceful lakeside property has been splendidly rejuvenated and should last long into the 21st century. When you pull back the draperies of your bedroom window, you're rewarded with a panoramic alpine view. In the heart of Neuchâtel, this tranquil oasis reopened in 1993 after a long slumber. It's in the grand hotel tradition with luxurious bedrooms, spacious and airy and comfortably furnished. Only one-third of the bedrooms lack lakeside views. Elegant fabrics and cherrywood furnishings and paneling add to the allure of the hotel. The cuisine at the restaurant here is imaginative, with an array of seasonal produce and fine wines.

1, esplanade de Mont-Blanc, CH-2001 Neuchâtel. © **032/723-15-15.** Fax 032/723-16-16. www.beau-rivage-hotel.ch. 390F–470F ($320–$385) double; 600F–1,500F ($492–$1,230) suite. Children up to 16 stay free in parent's room. AE, DC, MC, V. **Amenities:** Restaurant; bar; 24-hr. room service; babysitting; laundry service/dry cleaning. *In room:* TV, dataport, minibar, hair dryer, safe, robes.

Hôtel Beaulac ⭐ Set near the intersection of quai Léopold-Robert and quai du Port, this hotel's angular modernity strikes a glaring note when compared to the 18th-century sandstone buildings surrounding it. Nevertheless, it's one of the city's leading hotels. Across from the Museum of Art and History, its lakefront location offers panoramic vistas facing the Alps. The bedrooms are well maintained and comfortable, but not stylish, often containing Formica, 1960s tiles, and vinyls. Guests can watch the activity of the nearby marina from cafe tables on the hotel's waterside terrace.

2, esplanade Léopold-Robert, CH-2000 Neuchâtel. © **032/723-11-11.** Fax 032/725-60-35. www.beaulac.ch. 81 units. 250F–320F ($205–$262) double; 370F–630F ($303–$517) suite. Rates include continental breakfast. AE, DC, MC, V. Parking 12F ($9.85). Bus: 1. **Amenities:** 2 restaurants; lounge; sauna; solarium; limited room service; laundry service/dry cleaning; rooms for guests w/limited mobility. *In room:* TV, dataport, minibar, hair dryer, safe.

Hôtel du Marché   Stay here to avoid the high prices of many surrounding hotels. The location is in the center of town, opening onto Place des Halles. You can walk to most places of interest. Don't expect too much in the way of the rooms. They are small and furnished with minimum pieces, yet they are well maintained and offer reasonable comfort. Double-glazing cuts down the noise. There are no private bathrooms and only one communal bathroom per floor. At rush hours, lines can form, so be duly warned. An on-site restaurant serves regional fare as well as international dishes. If you're on the run, you can stop in for a drink and a quick plate at the combined cafe/bar.

4, place des Halles, CH-2000 Neuchâtel. © 032/723-23-30. Fax 032/723-23-30. www.hoteldumarche.com. 10 units. 140F ($115) double; 150F ($123) triple. Rates include breakfast. AE, DC, MC, V. **Amenities:** Restaurant; cafe; laundry service. *In room:* TV.

La Maison du Prussien ⚘ *Finds*   The setting for this historic inn lies, ironically, within an industrial zone of Neuchâtel, 5km (3 miles) west of the center, but thanks to a protective barrier of trees, you'd imagine yourself in a sylvan corner of the Swiss forest. The site was the setting for a series of mills—at least three of them—that first appeared in 1614, and a brewery that was founded in 1798. In 1991 it was transformed into a hotel and then a restaurant. Today it's a stylish enclave of good food and comfort, with its original ocher-colored stone walls (local geologists refer to it as "stone from Hautrive"), half-timbering, and a sprawling terrace that encompasses a view of the waterfall that used to turn the grinding wheels of the mills. Each of the bedrooms has at least one wall of the exposed original stone, as well as comfortable furnishings. Although the rooms are attractive, most guests come here for the food, which is centered around the local produce, fish, and game, and local wines.

Au Gor du Vauseyon, CH-2006 Neuchâtel. © 032/730-54-54. Fax 032/730-21-43. www.hotel-prussien.ch. 10 units. 165F–310F ($135–$254) double. AE, DC, MC, V. From the center, follow the signs to La Chaux-de-Fonds, then turn off toward Pontarlier-Vauseyon. Signs point to the hotel. **Amenities:** Restaurant; lounge. *In room:* TV, minibar, hair dryer.

WHERE TO DINE

La Maison des Halles ⚘ CONTINENTAL   One of the most appealing and deeply entrenched restaurants in town lies in the pedestrian zone of the commercial center. One floor above street level is the relatively exclusive restaurant gastronomique. Here, amid white walls and pink napery, and with service rituals patterned after the grand bourgeois restaurants of Paris or Lyon, you'll dine on food that's fussier and more delicate (and more expensive) than in the earthier, more raucous, brasserie downstairs. Stellar examples include filet of duckling with orange sauce, or sweetbreads with a mustard sauce. In the street-level brasserie, look for lots of varnished wood, turn-of-the-20th-century-style mirrors, leather banquettes, and such rib-sticking food as freshwater fera from the nearby lake that's served with a sauce Neuchâtelois made from white wine, cream, baby onions, and capers; or filet of lake perch with butter-flavored parsley sauce.

4, rue du Trésor. © 032/724-31-41. Reservations recommended. Restaurant main courses 29F–46F ($24–$38); fixed-price menus 80F–115F ($66–$94). Brasserie main courses 12F–32F ($9.85–$26); fixed-price menu 80F–115F ($66–$94). MC, V. Restaurant Tues–Sat noon–2pm and 7pm–midnight. Brasserie Tues–Sat 11am–midnight.

NEUCHÂTEL AFTER DARK

As a university town, Neuchâtel is lively when the sun goes down. The hot spot is the **Casino de la Rotonde,** Faubourg du lac 14 (© 032/724-48-48), with a trio of dance clubs. The town has popularized the *bar musicaux* in this part of Switzerland, and many places now stay open until dawn, offering food and music. The best of these is **Garbo,** a bar and disco at 5-7, rue de Chavannes (© **032/724-31-81**), where you can eat, drink, and dance the night away from 9pm to 6am Tuesday to Sunday. Its chief rival, keeping the same hours, is **Dakota,** 3, av. de la Gare (© **032/710-07-05**). A young crowd mostly composed of students flocks nightly to the town's hottest pub, **Le Shakespeare,** 7, rue des Terreaux (© **032/725-85-88**). On weekends this pub often imposes a 20F ($16) cover charge.

7

Bern

As the Swiss capital, Bern is an important city of diplomats and the site of many international organizations and meetings. It's one of the oldest and loveliest cities in Europe, with origins going back to the 12th century. Since much of its medieval architecture remains today, Bern evokes the feeling of a large provincial town rather than a city. In 1983 the United Nations declared it a World Cultural Landmark.

Over the years the city landscape has been praised by many famous visitors, including Horace Walpole, who called it "the most Faire city." Dorothy, sister of William Wordsworth, gushed, "There is a beautiful order, a solidity, a gravity in this city, which strikes one at first sight and then never loses its effect."

The modern mingles harmoniously with the old in this charming city, and in recent years residents have discreetly added contemporary-style homes and structures to the historic environment. Such coexistence between the old and new is also evident in Bern's university, known equally for traditional studies and pioneering scientific research.

Bern joined the Swiss Confederation in 1353. In 1848, it replaced Zurich as the seat of the federal government. The city stands on a thumb of land that's bordered on three sides by the Aare River, hence the several bridges connecting various sections of the city.

Market days in Bern are Tuesday and Saturday. People from the outlying areas come to town to sell their produce and wares. The fourth Monday of November features the centuries-old **Zwiebelmarkt** (Zibelemärit, in the local dialect), or Onion Market. This is the city's last big event before winter, and residents traditionally stock up on onions in anticipation of the first snows. In Bern's historic core, vendors arrive before dawn to set up stalls featuring plaited strings of onions. It is customary to sell some 100 tons of onions in 1 day during the festival. It's not all salesmanship either—buffoons disguised as onions run about, barrels of confetti are thrown, and a good time is had by all. Naturally, local restaurants feature all their special dishes made with onions at the time.

Bern is also a popular starting point for many excursions, especially to the lakes and peaks of the Bernese Oberland (see chapter 8), a vast recreational area only minutes from the capital.

1 Orientation

ESSENTIALS

GETTING THERE

BY PLANE   The **Bern-Belp Airport** (✆ **031/960-21-11**) is 9.6km (6 miles) south of the city in the town of Belpmoos. International flights arrive from London, Paris, and Nice, but transatlantic jets are not able to land here. Fortunately, it's a short hop to Bern from the international airports in Zurich and Geneva.

A taxi from the airport to the city center costs about 35F to 50F ($29–$41), so it's better to take the shuttle bus that runs between the airport and the Bahnhof (train station)—it costs 14F ($11) one-way.

BY TRAIN   Bern has direct connections to the Continental rail network that includes France, Italy, Germany, the Benelux countries, and even Scandinavia and Spain. The TGV high-speed train connects Paris with Bern in just 4½ hours. Bern also lies on major Swiss rail links, particularly those connecting Geneva (90 min.) and Zurich (75 min.). For **rail information** and schedules, call ✆ **0900/300-300.**

The **Bahnhof** rail station, on Bahnhofplatz, is right in the center of town near all the major hotels. If your luggage is light, you can walk to your hotel; otherwise, take one of the taxis waiting outside the station.

BY CAR   Bern lies at a major expressway junction, with E17 coming in east from Zurich, N2 heading south from Basel, and N12 running north from Lake Geneva.

VISITOR INFORMATION

Bern Tourist Office, in the Bern Bahnhof, on Bahnhofplatz (✆ **031/328-12-12;** www.bernetourism.ch), is open June to September daily 9am to 8:30pm; October to May Monday to Saturday 9am to 6:30pm and on Sunday from 10am to 5pm. If you need help finding a hotel room, the tourist office can make a reservation for you in the price range you select.

CITY LAYOUT

MAIN ARTERIES & STREETS   The geography of the city is neatly pressed into a relatively small area, so getting about is quite easy. You can walk to most of the major sights. **Altstadt,** or Old Town, lies on a high rocky plateau that juts out into a "loop" of the Aare River. Most of the major hotels and attractions lie within this loop.

Most arrivals are at the Bahnhof on Bahnhofplatz, in the center of town. From here you can walk along the major arteries of Bern: **Spitalgasse, Marktgasse, Kramgasse,** and **Gerechtigkeitsgasse.** The town's major squares include **Theaterplatz,** with its famed Zytgloggeturm (Clock Tower), **Kornhausplatz** and its much-photographed Ogre Fountain, and **Rathausplatz,** on which stands the old Rathaus (town hall), seat of the cantonal government.

The three major bridges crossing the Aare into this historic loop are **Kirchenfeld-brücke, Kornhausbrücke,** and **Lorrainebrücke.**

FINDING AN ADDRESS   In a system developed during the Middle Ages, street numbers in the city begin in the center of Altstadt, and the numbers increase as they fan out. Even numbers lie on one side of the street, odd numbers on the other.

MAPS   Good local maps are available at the Bern Tourist Office (see above).

NEIGHBORHOODS IN BRIEF

Only two of Bern's many neighborhoods are of particular interest to tourists:

   Altstadt   This is the heart of Bern, lying inside a bend of the Aare River. Filled with flower-decked fountains, it encompasses some 6km (3½ miles) of arcades and medieval streets, many reserved for pedestrians only. Its main street is Marktgasse, filled with luxury shops and 17th- and 18th-century houses.

   South of the Aare   You can reach this sprawling district by crossing the

Kirchenfeldbrücke. The neighborhood has three major museums: Swiss Alpine Museum, Bern Historical Museum, and Natural History Museum.

2 Getting Around

ON FOOT   This is the only practical means of exploring Altstadt and its many attractions. You can see what there is to see here in about 2½ hours.

Don't overlook the possibility of walks in Greater Bern, including Bern's own mountain, **Gurten,** a popular day-trip destination reached in 25 minutes by tram no. 9 and rack railway. Once here, you'll find walks in many directions and can enjoy a panorama over the Alps. There's also a children's playground.

Walks in and around Bern include 250km (155 miles) of **marked rambling paths.** One of the most scenic runs along the banks of the Aare through the English gardens, the Dählhölzli Zoological Gardens, Elfenau Park, and the Bremgarten woods.

For **jogging and running,** the best spots are the Aare River Run (Dalmaziquai), stretching 4km (2¼ miles), or the Aare River Run—Bear Pits, which is 5km (3 miles) long.

BY BUS & TRAM   The public transportation system, the **Stadtische Verkehrsbetriebe (SVB),** is a reliable, 77km (48-mile) network of buses and trams. Before you board, purchase a ticket from one of the automatic machines (you'll find one at each stop) because conductors don't sell tickets. If you're caught traveling without one, you'll be fined 60F ($49) in addition to the fare for the ride. A short-range ride (within six stations) costs 1.70F ($1.40); a normal ticket, valid for 45 minutes one-way, goes for 2.60F ($2.15).

To save time and money, you might purchase a Bern Card for 17F ($14), which entitles you to unlimited travel on the SVB network. Just get the ticket stamped at the automatic machine before beginning your first trip. Tickets are available at the Rail City Tourist Center, and in some hotels and museums.

BY TAXI   You can catch a taxi at the public cab ranks, or call a dispatcher. **Nova Taxi** is at ✆ **031/331-33-13, Bären Taxi** at ✆ **031/371-11-11.** The basic rate is 6.80F ($5.60), plus 3.10F ($2.55) per kilometer.

BY CAR   Seeing Bern by car is very impractical due to traffic congestion in Old Town, its confusing layout of one-way streets, and a lack of on-street parking. If you have a car, it's best to park in a public garage and explore the city on foot; its miles of arcades were designed to protect pedestrians from rain, snow, and traffic.

If you want to rent a car to explore the environs, arrangements can be made at **Hertz,** Kasinoplatz at Kochergasse 1 (✆ **031/318-21-60**); or **Avis,** Wabernstrasse 41 (✆ **031/378-15-15**).

BY BICYCLE   Altstadt is compressed into such a small area that it's better to cover the historic district on foot rather than on a bike (bicycles aren't allowed on many pedestrian-only streets, anyway). However, in greater Bern and its environs, there are 399km (248 miles) of cycling paths. These are marked on a special cycling map available at the tourist office (see above). The narrow yellow lanes throughout the road network are reserved for bikers. The point of departure for most official routes is Bundesplatz in Parliament Square. Special red signs will guide you through a wide variety of landscapes. Bikes can be checked out free at the **Bahnhofplatz** (✆ **079/277-28-57**). For a 20F ($16) deposit, plus your passport, you can ride the bikes for the day. If you keep the bikes longer, it's 20F ($16) a day.

FAST FACTS: Bern

The following is a quick-reference guide to Bern. For more information, see "Fast Facts: Switzerland," in chapter 2.

Babysitters Babysitting can be arranged through most hotels. Try to make arrangements as far in advance as possible.

Bookstores The best for English-language books is **Buchanlung Stauffacher,** Neuengassan 25-37 (© **031/313-63-63**).

Business Hours Banks are open Monday to Friday from 8am to 4:30pm (on Thurs until 6pm). Most offices are open Monday to Friday from 9am to 5pm, and on Saturday from 9am to noon.

Car Rentals See "Getting Around," above.

Currency Exchange This is available on the lower level of the Bahnhof, on Bahnhofplatz, open daily from 6am to 10pm.

Dentists Call © **0900/57-67-47** for a referral to an English-speaking dentist.

Doctors Call © **0900/57-67-47** for a referral to an English-speaking doctor.

Drugstores Try **Central-Apotheke Volz & Co.,** Zeitglockenlaub 2 (© **031/311-10-94**). It's near the Clock Tower in Old Town. The staff speaks English and can suggest over-the-counter substitutes for foreign drugs that can't be found in Europe. It's open on Monday from 9am to 6:30pm, Tuesday to Friday 7:45am to 6:30pm, and on Saturday from 7:45am to 4pm. **Aperto,** at the Bahnhofplatz (© **031/311-41-15**), is open daily from 6am to 10pm.

Embassies & Consulates The **U.S. Embassy** is at Jubiläumsstrasse 93 (© **031/357-70-11**). Other embassy addresses are: **Canada,** Kirchenfeldstrasse 88 (© **031/357-32-00**); and **United Kingdom,** Thunstrasse 50 (© **031/359-77-00**). **New Zealand** citizens should call their consulate-general in Geneva (© **022/929-03-50**).

Emergencies Call © **117** for the police, © **144** for an ambulance, © **118** to report a fire, or © **140** for the road patrol, but only for an emergency.

Eyeglasses **Augenwerk,** Marktgasse 52 (© **031/311-02-02**), can replace both eyeglasses and contact lenses.

Hairdressers/Barbers One of the city's best-known hairdressers is **Erminio,** Marktgasse 50 (© **031/312-22-33**). There are separate sections for men and women. Hours are Monday to Friday 9am to 6:30pm and Saturday 8am to 1pm.

Hospital The city's largest is **Insel Hospital,** Freiburgstrasse (© **031/632-21-11**), the clinic affiliated with the University of Bern.

Information See "Visitor Information," above.

Internet Access Internet access is available at **BEKB Meeting Center,** Bundesplatz 8 (© **031/666-60-03**).

Laundry/Dry Cleaning **Jet Wash** is a coin-operated, conveniently located laundry at Dammweg 43 (© **031/330-26-38**). For dry cleaning, try **Textilpflege** (© **031/312-00-77**), which is located in the main railway station.

Lost Property The lost-property office at Predigergasse 5 (© **031/321-50-50**) is open Monday to Friday from 10am to 4pm (till 6pm Thurs).

Luggage Storage/Lockers Storage facilities are available on the lower level of the Bahnhof, on Bahnhofplatz.

Photographic Needs Go to **Coop Ryfflihof,** Aarbergergasse 53 (© 031/329-71-11), which has a big film and photography department.

Police The police station is at Waisenhausplatz 32 (© 031/321-21-21).

Post Office The main post office (Schanzenpost), at Schanzenstrasse 4 (© 031/386-61-11), is open Monday to Friday from 7:30am to 9pm, on Saturday from 8am to 4pm, and Sunday 4 to 9pm.

Restrooms You'll find public facilities in the Bahnhof and in some squares in Old Town.

Safety Bern is Europe's safest capital. Nevertheless, you should take the usual precautions; protect your valuables. It's generally safe to walk the streets at night, and crimes against women are rare.

Taxes A 7.6% value-added tax (VAT) is included in the price of all goods and services rendered, including hotel and restaurant bills. There are no other special taxes.

Taxis See "Getting Around," above.

Telegrams/Telex/Fax Most hotels will arrange the expedition of faxes and telegrams. If not, head for the main post office (see above).

Transit Information Call © **0900/300-300** for **rail information** or © **031/370-88-88** for **postal-bus information.**

3 Where to Stay

There are accommodations for most budgets in Bern. As the federal capital, Bern hosts many conventions and international meetings, so the hotels are frequently fully booked. Make a reservation. You can reserve a hotel room in advance either by phone (© **031/328-12-12**) or by Internet (www.bernetourism.ch). The service is free.

Altstadt is built on a peninsula so compact that everything is literally "around the corner," including nearly all hotels, more than 150 restaurants, the major sights, 6km (3½ miles) of arcades for shopping—even the weekly farmers market and the Houses of Parliament.

VERY EXPENSIVE

Bellevue Palace 🏛🏛🏛   Built in 1913, the grand old dame of Bern reopened in 2003 after massive renovations and improvements next to the Bundeshaus, the seat of the Swiss government. It is the most lavish and opulent choice in town, in direct contrast to the Schweizerhof, which is the bastion of stiff formality on a definite nonpalatial and more intimate scale. The Bellevue Palace has carved Corinthian columns and ornate details, one of its grand salons covered with a stained-glass ceiling. The setting is definitely old-world, and the service is impeccable. The spacious and beautifully furnished bedrooms open onto views of the Jungfrau and the Bernese Alps. The trappings of the Belle Epoque era have been combined with a state-of-the-art infrastructure that still pays homage to its architectural heritage. The market-fresh cuisine is some of the most sophisticated in town, a parade of gourmet delicacies. Dining on the renowned Bellevue Terrace is one of the reasons to come to Bern.

Kochergasse 3-5, 3001 Bern. © **031/320-45-45.** Fax 031/311-47-43. www.bellevue-palace.ch. 130 units. 350F–540F ($287–$443) double; 550F–950F ($451–$779) suite. AE, DC, MC, V. Parking 28F ($23). Tram: 3, 9, or 12. **Amenities:** 2 restaurants; bar; 24-hr. room service; babysitting; laundry service/dry cleaning; nonsmoking rooms. *In room:* A/C, TV, dataport, minibar, hair dryer, safe, robe and slippers.

Hotel Schweizerhof Bern ✹✹✹   This centrally located hotel managed by the
Gauer family is popular with diplomats. Built in 1859, it has undergone many renovations since then, and remains one of the grandest hotels in the Swiss capital. It contains many antiques and some of the best decorative art in Bern—18th-century drawing-room pieces, wall-size tapestries, and crystal chandeliers. Each room is uniquely decorated, but all offer comfortably upholstered chairs and sofas, with a fairly good chest, desk, or table, as well as neatly maintained bathrooms. There are several formal restaurants, including Yamato, the first Japanese restaurant to open in Bern.

Bahnhofplatz 11, CH-3001 Bern. © **031/326-80-80.** Fax 031/326-80-90. www.schweizerhof-bern.ch. 84 units. 415F–455F ($340–$373) double; from 625F ($513) suite. AE, DC, MC, V. Parking 30F ($25). Tram: 3, 9, or 12. **Amenities:** 2 restaurants; bar; 24-hr. room service; babysitting; laundry service/dry cleaning; nonsmoking rooms. *In room:* A/C, TV, dataport, minibar, hair dryer.

EXPENSIVE

Allegro Bern ✹✹   We stay here just for the panoramic view of the medieval town center of Bern and the Swiss Alps. That's reason enough to check in—that and the fact that this is one of the top three hotels in town in comfort and grace. The hotel runs as efficiently as a Swiss clock. There is grand comfort everywhere, especially in the midsize to spacious bedrooms, which are well furnished, immaculately kept, and each equipped with a combination tub/shower in the immaculate and well-accessorized bathrooms. The best accommodations are in the Panorama Club at the front of the hotel. These are especially sought out for their view of the Bernese Alps. All units have large beds, modern equipment, and excellent service from a well-trained staff.

Kornhausstrasse 3, CH-3000 Bern. © **031/339-55-00.** Fax 031/339-55-10. www.allegro-hotel.ch. 171 units. 330F–380F ($271–$312) double. AE, DC, MC, V. Parking 24F ($20). **Amenities:** 3 restaurants; 2 bars; exercise room; free bike rental; 24-hr. room service; babysitting; laundry service/dry cleaning; rooms for guests w/limited mobility. *In room:* A/C, TV, dataport, minibar, coffeemaker, iron, safe.

Belle Epoque ✹✹✹ *(Finds)*   This is the hippest, most savvy, and most sophisticated small-scale hotel in town, with a countercultural slant, a charming and hardworking staff, and a flair for elegance and charm. In 1989 an interconnected pair of historic Bern medieval houses were gutted, renovated, and turned into this hotel, devoted to the promotion of Teutonic Art Nouveau (Jugendstil). Each of the bedrooms is outfitted with jewel-toned colors, big windows, turn-of-the-20th-century furniture and lighting fixtures, and unusual antique paintings and engravings. Minibars and closets are artfully concealed within *trompe l'oeil* replicas of steamer trunks, in a style that's in pleasing contrast to bathrooms that are immaculately tiled (some have Jacuzzis) and very modern, with free condoms on offer. Public rooms are somewhat cramped but beautifully decorated and convivial. They include a cozy bar whose cafe tables extend out under the 17th-century arcades in front.

Gerechtigkeitsgasse 18, CH-3011 Bern. © **031/311-43-36.** Fax 031/311-39-36. www.belle-epoque.ch. 17 units. 280F–340F ($230–$279) double; 245F–480F ($201–$394) suite. Rates include breakfast. AE, DC, MC, V. Bus: 12. **Amenities:** Restaurant; bar; room service; babysitting; laundry service/dry cleaning; nonsmoking rooms. *In room:* TV, dataport, minibar, hair dryer.

Where to Stay in Bern

Allegro Bern **3**

Belle Epoque **12**

Bellevue Palace **10**

Hotel Ambassador **5**

Hotel Bern **11**

Hotel Continental **8**

Hotel Goldener
Schlüssel **9**

Hotel-Pension
Marthahaus **2**

Hotel Schweizerhof
Bern **6**

Innere Enge **1**

Jardin **4**

Savoy Hotel **7**

Zum Goldener Adler **13**

Hotel Bern ⓐ   This six-story hotel, a frequent host to diplomats and business travelers, sits behind one of Bern's most striking Art Deco facades ornamented with arches, columns, and a series of iconoclastic sculptures. The midsize guest rooms are comfortable and well furnished, with breakfast areas and firm beds, plus tidy bathrooms. The best rooms look out onto a garden courtyard. The hotel has nine dining rooms, but most of these are reserved for groups and banquets. The Grill Room is more formal, serving French cuisine.

Zeughausgasse 9, CH-3011. ⓒ 031/329-22-22. Fax 031/329-22-99. www.hotelbern.ch. 100 units. 280F–350F ($230–$287) double; 370F ($303) suite. Rates include buffet breakfast. AE, DC, MC, V. Tram: 9. **Amenities:** 2 restaurants; bar; limited room service; laundry service/dry cleaning. *In room:* TV, dataport, minibar, hair dryer, safe.

Innere Enge ⓐⓐⓐ *(Finds)*   When you tire of Bern's impersonal bandbox hotels, head for this converted inn in a building from the 1700s. This small but choice hotel, a 20-minute walk from the center of town, has windows that open onto views of the Bernese Oberland, and the grass and trees around the building make for quite a tranquil setting. The atmosphere in the public rooms is that of Jugendstil or a Teutonic Art Nouveau. The well-kept and individually designed bedrooms are often spacious and filled with sunshine. Furnishings are traditional, and maintenance meets the high standards set by the manager. The most romantic units are on the top floor, resting under the eaves with sloped ceilings. The Louis Armstrong Bar, also called Marians Jazzroom, is linked to the hotel, offering drinks, food, and traditional jazz performances February to June and September to December.

Engestrasse 54, CH-3012 Bern. ⓒ 031/309-61-11. Fax 301/309-61-12. www.zghotels.ch. 26 units. 260F–320F ($213–$262) double; 550F ($451) suite. Rates include continental breakfast. AE, DC, MC, V. Free parking. Bus: 21. **Amenities:** Restaurant; bar; limited room service; babysitting; laundry service/dry cleaning; rooms for guests w/limited mobility. *In room:* TV, dataport, minibar, coffeemaker, hair dryer.

MODERATE

Hotel Ambassador ⓐ   This nine-story hotel is the tallest building in a neighborhood of old houses with red-tile roofs. The guest rooms come with refrigerators, and many have a view of the federal palace, the Bundeshaus. They tend to be smallish and furnished rather impersonally, but they are well maintained with firm beds and neat bathrooms. Since the hotel caters to business travelers, its rooms offer fax and computer hookups. It's located about a mile from the train station and easily reached by tram. Dining choices include the Japanese Teppan Restaurant, surrounded by a Japanese garden.

Seftigenstrasse 99, CH-3007 Bern. ⓒ 031/370-99-99. Fax 031/371-41-17. www.fhotels.ch. 99 units. 205F–230F ($168–$189) double. AE, DC, MC, V. Free parking. Tram: 9. **Amenities:** 2 restaurants; lounge; pool; sauna; room service; babysitting; laundry service/dry cleaning. *In room:* A/C, TV, dataport, minibar, hair dryer, safe.

Hotel Continental   Another of those fairly anonymous hotels clustered around the Bern rail station, this government-rated three-star choice achieves a grace note with flower boxes blooming in spring at its bedroom windows. Filled with shops at ground level, the building lures mainly business travelers during the week, although weekends are more devoted to visitors, often the Swiss themselves. The smallest bedrooms are a bit lackluster, but still well maintained and furnished with both traditional and modern pieces. Breakfast is served in fair weather under a canopied terrace upstairs.

Zeughausgasse 27, CH-3011 Bern. ⓒ 031/329-21-21. Fax 031/329-21-99. www.hotel-continental.ch. 43 units. 130F–180F ($107–$148) double. Rates include buffet breakfast. AE, DC, MC, V. Tram: 3 or 9. **Amenities:** Lounge; nonsmoking rooms; babysitting; laundry service. *In room:* TV.

Savoy Hotel *Value*   Close to the main rail depot and the commercial center, this is a traditional Bern hotel of some charm and grace, achieving a four-star rating from the government. The fabled arcaded shopping streets of Bern lie just outside the door. The owners, the Gauer family, have long tired of hearing that this is the "budget version" of the Schweizerhof, a more deluxe choice. This place is more welcoming than many straitlaced Bern hotels; you're even given a free welcome drink. The five-story building shares its entrance with a bank. Rooms are fairly standardized and plain but have recently been renovated and are quite comfortable, with mostly combination tub/shower bathrooms (15 with shower only). Soundproof windows keep the noise outside, and there is also individually adjustable ventilation.

Neuengasse 26, CH-3011 Bern. ℂ 031/311-44-05. Fax 031/312-19-78. www.zghotels.ch. 56 units. 230F–250F ($189–$205) double; 295F ($242) junior suite. AE, DC, MC, V. **Amenities:** Cafe-bar; limited room service; laundry service/dry cleaning; rooms for guests w/limited mobility. *In room:* TV, dataport, minibar, hair dryer.

Zum Goldener Adler   Once this was a patrician town house of a wealthy city merchant, but in 1489 it started housing wayfarers arriving in Bern by coach. That building is long gone, but the current hotel dates from 1764 and has been run by the same family for more than a century. Its dramatic old-fashioned exterior makes you anticipate a real period piece inside. However, Vreni and Peter Balz, the innkeepers, have done the relatively modest rooms in a functional modern. There is comfort here but not a lot of style. The linoleum-floored bathrooms have shower stalls, and there is a reliance on Formica furnishings. Nonetheless, this is a heavily patronized and long-favored local inn.

Gerechtigkeitsgasse 7, CH-3011. ℂ 031/311-17-25. Fax 031/311-37-61. www.goldener-adler-bern.ch. 40 units. 150F–180F ($123–$148) double. Rates include breakfast. AE, DC, MC, V. Bus: 12. **Amenities:** Restaurant; laundry service/dry cleaning. *In room:* A/C, TV.

INEXPENSIVE

Hotel Goldener Schlüssel ⟨⟩   In the heart of Altstadt, opening onto Rathausgasse, the building housing this cozy little inn dates from the 13th century, when it was used as a stable. Any hint of its origins has long been removed, and the house today is beautifully maintained. Some of the carpeted bedrooms have wood-paneled walls. It's fairly busy on the street outside, so ask for one of the rooms in the rear if you prefer it quieter. Immaculate linens on the beds and fresh tiles in the shower-only bathrooms reflect the good housekeeping. If you're a bargain hunter, ask for a room without a shower; the hallway plumbing is adequate. The hotel's sidewalk cafe does a thriving business throughout the summer, and the restaurant (see "Where to Dine," below) offers reasonably priced meals.

Rathausgasse 72, CH-3011 Bern. ℂ 031/311-02-16. Fax 031/311-56-88. www.goldener-schluessel.ch. 29 units (21 with bathroom). 115F ($94) double without bathroom, 155F ($127) double with bathroom; 155F ($127) triple without bathroom, 205F ($168) triple with bathroom. Rates include buffet breakfast. AE, MC, V. Free parking. Tram: 9. Bus: 12. **Amenities:** Restaurant; cafe; limited room service. *In room:* TV, hair dryer.

Hotel-Pension Marthahaus *Value*   Set within a verdant suburb about a 12-minute walk to the city center, this is a five-story hotel that was originally built around 1900 and has comfortably battered, semiantique bedrooms that may remind some visitors of a slightly dowdy college dormitory. There's a tiny elevator to carry guests upstairs, and a simple but respectable and clean format that symbolizes good value in an otherwise expensive town. Present management—an organization that directs a pension and retirement fund for women—has been in place here since the 1970s. The better rooms contain small private bathrooms, most of which contain tub/shower combinations.

Wyttenbachstrasse 22A, CH-3013 Bern. (C) **031/332-41-35.** Fax 031/333-33-86. www.marthahaus.ch. 40 units (6 with bathroom). 95F ($78) double without bathroom; 125F ($103) double with bathroom. MC, V. Parking 10F ($8.20). Bus: 20. **Amenities:** Lounge; bikes; nonsmoking rooms; communal kitchen; TV room. *In room:* TV, dataport.

Jardin *Value*   Set about .8km (½ mile) north of Bern's center, Jardin lies within a leafy residential suburb with lots of parking. This establishment functioned only as a restaurant and apartment building between the year it was built (ca. 1900) and 1985. Then its apartments were transformed into modern, warmly appealing hotel rooms that are larger than virtually anything else within their price category. All rooms are equipped with private bathrooms. Your hosts are identical twins Andy and Daniel Balz. Joggers and nature enthusiasts appreciate the large verdant spaces (part of a military academy) across the street from this russet-brown, four-story hotel.

Militärstrasse 38, CH-3014 Bern. (C) **031/333-01-17.** Fax 031/333-09-43. www.hotel-jardin.ch. 18 units. 100F–150F ($82–$123) double; 140F–205F ($115–$168) triple. Rates include breakfast. AE, DC, MC, V. Free parking. Tram: 9 to Breitenrainplatz. **Amenities:** Restaurant; lounge; laundry service/dry cleaning. *In room:* TV, hair dryer.

4 Where to Dine

Bern is a city of international cuisine. There are dozens of specialty restaurants offering everything from paella to porterhouse, in addition to the famous Swiss potato dish, rösti. We recommend sampling one of the charming country inns on the outskirts.

VERY EXPENSIVE

Restaurant la Terrasse *G* INTERNATIONAL   For a unique gastronomic experience with the Alps as a backdrop, try the refined cuisine in this dining room high above the Aare River. The kitchen is resolutely contemporary, although drawing inspiration from the classic repertoire. All the ingredients are carefully selected and inventively paired. This is the quintessential choice for haute-cuisine dining in Bern. The menu may begin with smoked salmon or a mushroom salad, followed by langoustine with olive rice and fresh basil, or else sole in cream sauce with shiitake mushrooms. In fair weather, grilled fish is often served on a summer salad. A pianist adds to the soothing atmosphere.

In the Bellevue Palace, Kochergasse 3. (C) **031/320-45-45.** Reservations recommended. Main courses 40F–80F ($33–$66). AE, DC, MC, V. Daily noon–2pm and 6–11pm. Closed for dinner in winter. Tram: 3, 9, or 12.

Wein & Sein *GGG* INTERNATIONAL   In terms of underground, word-of-mouth chic, this is the most fashionable and hip restaurant in Bern today. Set within the cellar of a historic building in the city's medieval core, it's accessible via a steep staircase that leads you past an open kitchen where a view of the staff comprises part of the allure. Chef and owner Beat Blum, a celebrity whose fame derives from his former administration of a more expensive restaurant near Lucerne, is the impresario who directs the show here. Within a severely spartan-looking dining room, you'll have only one choice: a fixed-price menu that's written on a blackboard, and which doesn't allow a lot of room for either variety or indecision. On the night of our latest visit, it consisted of such heavenly concoctions as braised tuna and free-range chicken served with braised pepperoni in a sweet-and-sour sauce; terrine of melon; beef filet with a vegetable purée; and a quark (white cheese) mousse served with pineapple and homemade ice cream. You'll select your wine from racks at one end of the dining room, a system that affords lots of interplay with the staff over whatever it is that you propose drinking with your meal.

Münstergasse 50. (C) **031/311-98-44.** Reservations required. Fixed-price menu 90F ($74). MC, V. Tues–Sat 6pm–midnight. Closed 2 weeks in July–Aug. Tram: 3, 5, or 9. Bus: 10 or 12.

EXPENSIVE

Della Casa ☝ CONTINENTAL   Entering the hotel, you'll find yourself immersed in what has been called Switzerland's "unofficial Parliament headquarters." The inner room, often filled with chattering diners, contains the day's newspapers. You'll find a quieter, more formal dining room upstairs. The menu features Continental and Italian dishes, such as *bollito misto* (a medley of mixed boiled meats) and rack of lamb. Two local favorites are the *ravioli maison* and the fried zucchini; a popular meat specialty is a filet mignon a la bordelaise with Creole rice. For the more adventurous, try the boiled veal head served with onions, tomatoes, and potatoes with an herbed vinaigrette. The cuisine is very authentic, very savory, and very satisfying.

Schauplatzgasse 16. ☏ 031/311-21-42. Reservations recommended. Main courses 25F–40F ($21–$33); fixed-price menu 28F ($23). AE, DC, MC, V (downstairs only). Mon–Fri 11am–2pm and 6–9:30pm; Sat 9:30am–3pm. Upstairs level closed July. Tram: 3, 5, or 9.

Frohsinn *Finds* FRENCH/SWISS   This restaurant, with only a dozen tables, stands in the shadow of the Zytgloggeturm (Clock Tower). It attracts businesspeople, journalists, and politicians as much for its traditional cuisine as for its cozy atmosphere. The menu may include filet of beef with whiskey sauce, goose-liver mousse, liver with rösti, or filet of rabbit with watercress. Other dishes reflect a southern Italian influence, especially the homemade ravioli. Sabayon with strawberries is a seasonal specialty. You'll relish most of the dishes, as they are prepared with first-rate ingredients.

Münstergasse 54. ☏ 031/311-37-68. Reservations required. Main courses 24F–43F ($20–$35). AE, DC, MC, V. Tues–Sat 8am–2pm and 6–10pm. Closed July 15–Aug 15. Tram: 54.

Gourmanderie Café Moléson ☝ *Finds* INTERNATIONAL   It looks like your basic cafe but the food at this joint is rather uncafe-like. Market-fresh ingredients and a skilled preparation go into the good-tasting dishes, attracting politicians from the Swiss Parliament and even artists, a not-always-compatible combination except at this cafe. The friendly staff speaks English and will guide you through their specials of the day. Slices of cold organic veal roast are served with a tuna fish cream sauce, and you can also feast on fresh-roasted lamb from the neighboring meadows as well as grilled organic salmon steak in a creamy foam sauce with spinach, cherry tomatoes, and lemon-flavored rice.

Aarbergerasse 24, 3011 Bern. ☏ 031/311-44-63. www.moleson-bern.ch. Reservations not required. Main courses 26F–45F ($21–$37); fixed-price dinner 66F ($54) 3 courses, 77F ($63) 4 courses. AE, DC, MC, V. Mon–Fri 11:30am–2:30pm; Mon–Sat 6–11:30pm.

Jack's Brasserie (Stadt Restaurant) ☝☝ FRENCH/CONTINENTAL   Although this restaurant is one of the less formal choices within the Hotel Schweizerhof, it's a nice spot for an important meal or even a celebratory dinner. Decorated along the lines of a Lyonnais bistro, replete with paneling, banquettes, and etched glass, it bustles in a way that's chic, friendly, and matter-of-fact, all at the same time. Menu items include fish soup; the kind of Wiener schnitzels that hang over the sides of the plate; succulent versions of sole meunière and sea bass; veal head vinaigrette for real regional flavor; and smaller platters piled high with salads, risottos, and succulent pastas. You will smack your lips over these luscious and full-flavored dishes inspired by the chef's mood and what's at the market.

In the Hotel Schweizerhof, Bahnhofplatz 11. ☏ 031/311-45-01. Reservations recommended. Main courses 26F–60F ($21–$49); fixed-price menu 85F ($70). AE, DC, MC, V. Daily 11:45am–10:45pm. Limited menu daily 1:45–6:15pm. Tram: 3, 9, or 12.

Räblus FRENCH/SWISS REGIONAL   The building containing this restaurant is more than 200 years old, making it the oldest on the street. Centrally located near the Clock Tower, it offers dinner guests a chance to stop for an aperitif in the ground-floor bar before proceeding upstairs to the richly paneled and sculpture-filled dining room. The chef prepares French cuisine with a definite Swiss/German influence. Dishes include potpourri of seafood with Pernod, saffron-flavored sole, citrus-flavored veal, and those old reliables, tournedos Rossini and veal kidney flambé, that have appeared on French menus forever. If not terribly imaginative, the cuisine is satisfying, especially on a cold day. The kitchen is talented, and local produce is deftly handled.

Zeughausgasse 3. ⓒ 031/311-59-08. Reservations required. Main courses 24F–39F ($20–$32); fixed-price 3-course menu 35F–60F ($29–$49). AE, DC, MC, V. Mon–Wed 6pm–1:30am; Thurs 6pm–2:30am; Fri–Sat 6pm–3:30am. Tram: 3 or 9.

Ratskeller *(Kids)* SWISS   This historic establishment offers old masonry, modern paneling, and a battalion of busy waitresses serving ample portions of good, rib-sticking food. This dining room has long been the family favorite of locals. Swiss parents who take their children here once were taken here by their parents. Specialties include rack of lamb *a la diable* for two, an omelet soufflé aux fruits, veal kidneys Robert, and *côte de veau* (veal steak) in butter sauce. Your best bet is the tiny filet of perch (*egli* in German) with white sauce on a bed of spinach. Prized by gourmets, this tiny fish is native to the lakes around Bern.

Gerechtigkeitsgasse 81. ⓒ 031/311-17-25. Reservations recommended. Main courses 24F–42F ($20–$34). AE, DC, MC, V. Daily 11:30am–2pm and 6–11pm. Tram: 9.

Restaurant Harmonie SWISS/BERNESE   Located at the corner of Münstergasse, a few blocks from the Houses of Parliament, this Art Nouveau local favorite evokes 1890s Paris with its grimy overlay. It has been in the hands of the Gyger family since 1915. Service is efficient, and tables are spaced far enough apart to allow a feeling of privacy. There are two separate dining rooms and a handful of sidewalk tables set behind banks of potted geraniums. You get the same regional specialties that Grandmother Gyger might have served between the wars: pork sausage with rösti, tripe with tomatoes, and cheese fondues. If you're not ravenously hungry, go for the simple platter of cooked ham with pickles, pickled onions, and sliced bread.

Hotelgasse 3. ⓒ 031/313-38-40. Reservations recommended. Main courses 24F–50F ($20–$41). MC, V. Mon–Fri 8am–11:30pm. Closed mid-July to mid-Aug. Tram: 9.

Restaurant Zimmermania *(Value)* FRENCH   This is a small and charming French bistro that's set on a quiet street of Bern's historic core. Inside, you'll find two dining rooms outfitted like something you might have expected in a small French town in the 1920s, a marble-topped service bar, and a menu that emphasizes many classic brasserie-style dishes from France. In addition to a short but well-chosen wine list, you can expect such well-prepared French classics as foie gras of duckling, carpaccio of beef, marinated herring with apple slices and sour cream, fresh oysters, veal kidneys in mustard sauce, rack of lamb with green beans, steak tartare, and guinea fowl roasted with rosemary.

Brunngasse 19. ⓒ 031/311-15-42. Reservations recommended. Main courses 29F–60F ($24–$49); fixed-price lunch 25F–41F ($21–$34). AE, MC, V. Tues–Sat 12:30–2pm and 6–10pm. Closed July. Tram: 12.

Verdi Ristorante, Bar & Enoteca ITALIAN   This is a charmingly decorated Italian hideaway that's more elegant and more sophisticated than its reasonable prices would imply. Set near the eastern terminus of one of the most important medieval streets of the Old Town, it includes at least three different dining areas, simultaneously evoking both a brick-lined trattoria and a grand gourmet restaurant. Accessories include a zinc-topped bar, a vast array of wine that's artfully arranged in a replica of an antique wine cellar, an antipasti buffet, and a fireplace that blazes merrily throughout the winter. Food items are good, classic, and Italian. The best examples include braised artichokes in herb-flavored olive oil, with Parma ham; medallions of anglerfish with white-wine-and-saffron sauce; diced filets of rabbit with mushrooms, olives, and rosemary, served with risotto; and grilled filets of beef with arugula-basil sauce and risotto.

Gerechtigkeitsgasse 5. (C) 031/312-63-68. Reservations recommended. Pastas 20F–32F ($16–$26); main courses 33F–40F ($27–$33). AE, DC, MC, V. Daily 11am–2pm and 6–11pm. Bus: 12.

Zum Zähringer (R) *Finds* CONTINENTAL   No restaurant in Bern projects such a high mountain atmosphere. It occupies a weathered chalet that sits across a quiet street from the surging waters of the Aare, at the bottom of the steep cliff whose top contains the cathedral and the rest of medieval Bern. Many aspects, particularly its riverfront terrace, evoke a country inn that's far removed from the politics of the Swiss capital, but with a menu that's much more modern than you might have expected. Menu items are creative and filled with flair. They include asparagus mousse served with a tartare of salmon; veal shank in wine sauce; house-made terrine with green peppercorn and chutney; braised chicken livers with arugula; pikeperch with chive-flavored cream sauce; an artfully composed "hamburger" of goose meat with Asian vegetables and basmati rice; and scallops with spring vegetables served with olive-studded mashed potatoes.

Badgasse 1 (corner of Aaregasse). (C) 031/311-32-70. Reservations recommended. Main courses 25F–60F ($21–$49); fixed-price menu 50F–75F ($41–$62). MC, V. Tues–Fri 11am–2:30pm; Mon–Sat 6–11:30pm.

MODERATE

Gaumentranz (R) *Finds* SWISS/PACIFIC RIM   This is a good example of the new and hip restaurants sweeping through the Swiss capital. Small and artsy, it has a decor that leans toward industrial and high-tech design, and a kitchen that's open for viewing. Chef Max Zwahlen prepares a Continental menu that's fused with international and Asian overtones, and which changes every 6 weeks. Stellar examples include shrimp with lemon grass, strips of asparagus, and raspberry vinaigrette; pink chicken breast served with salsa verde, galettes of black rice, and spring vegetables; and exotic peppered filets of kangaroo steak with caramelized onions and asparagus in a mustard-flavored cream sauce. Dessert, depending on the inspiration of the chef that night, may include a sumptuous crème brûlée infused with white chocolate.

Gerechtigkeitsgasse 56. (C) 031/311-64-84. Reservations recommended. Main courses 26F–33F ($21–$27); fixed-price lunch 16F–17F ($13–$14). AE, MC, V. Tues–Sat 11am–2pm and 6–10pm.

Goldener Schlüssel (R) SWISS   As you dine at this very Swiss restaurant, you can relish both the cuisine and the atmosphere. Overhead is the old planking and stonework of a 13th-century building, and you're surrounded by the endless bustle of a workaday restaurant. Serving wholesome and good-tasting food in ample portions, the restaurant is on the street level of a budget-priced hotel of the same name (see "Where to Stay," above). Specialties include a well-flavored *mignon d'agneau au poivre vert* (tenderloin of lamb with green-pepper sauce and corn croquettes), *Schweinbratwurst mit Zwiebelsauce* (butter-fried sausage with onion sauce), and rösti.

Rathausgasse 72. ℂ **031/311-02-16**. Reservations recommended. Main courses 25F–34F ($21–$28); fixed-price lunch 22F–26F ($18–$21). AE, MC, V. Sun–Thurs 7am–11:30pm; Fri–Sat 7am–12:30am. Tram: 9. Bus 12.

Mille Sens *&* EUROPEAN FUSION   This old factory building converted into a restaurant by Urs Messerli is an intimate choice and one of the leading restaurants of Bern. The open kitchen and accessible wine cellar add to the warm ambience of this sophisticated eatery. Light menu items include a chicken club sandwich with curried mayonnaise, tomatoes, and pickles, and a vegetable-stuffed crepe with a sweet-and-sour sauce topping. If you want a more substantial meal, we recommend you start with the seasonal green salad with melon and summer herbs, or cured Parma ham slices in a roulade with walnut oil vinaigrette. For your main course, enticing dishes include sautéed breast of corn-fed chicken with strips of cured ham and saffron-flavored risotto, and filet of Angus beef in a red-wine sauce along with strips of Mediterranean polenta.

Markethalle, Bubenbergplatz 9. ℂ **031/329-29-29**. www.millesens.ch. Reservations recommended. Main courses 28F–37F ($23–$30). AE, DC, MC, V. Mon–Thurs 11am–11:30pm (till 1:30am on Fri); Sat 4pm–1:30am.

INEXPENSIVE

Altes Tramdepot Brauerel & Restaurant *(kids* INTERNATIONAL   One of the most visible and popular restaurants on Bern's tourist circuit lies immediately adjacent to the Bear Pits, within what was built around 1900 as a tramway depot. In 1999 the space beneath its soaring, heavily trussed ceiling was transformed into a brewery and brasserie. You'll have to descend into the cellar to see the complicated vats and pipes of the brewery, where any of three kinds of beer—blonde, dark, and white (wheat) beer—are likely to be percolating and fermenting. Many clients gravitate toward the sprawling terrace looking out over the city. Menu items focus on a hearty, wholesome cuisine that goes beautifully with beer. Good-tasting examples include pork sausages with onion sauce and rösti; sliced veal Zurich-style with mushroom sauce and rösti; Wiener schnitzels; beef filet Stroganoff with noodles or rice; grilled spareribs, steak, or shrimp; salads and sandwiches; and at least four different wok-prepared dishes inspired by the cuisine of Thailand. There's even a special menu, each dish of which is named after a species of bear, for children.

Am Bärengraben, Gr. Muristalden 6. ℂ **031/368-14-15**. Reservations necessary. Main courses 16F–34F ($13–$28); children's platters 6F–16F ($4.90–$13). AE, DC, MC, V. Daily 11am–11:30pm. Tram: 12.

Arlequin SWISS/ITALIAN   Bern's society and intelligentsia are attracted to this informal restaurant in the city center rustically decorated with art and bronze pieces. Typical and well-prepared Swiss dishes include chicken pâté with morel mushrooms in puff pastry, farmhouse ham-and-potato salad, and goulash soup. From Wednesday to Friday, the chef is known for turning out Bern's best Wiener schnitzel. There are also the usual offerings of pasta dishes and fresh salads. During the summer, tables are set up on the pergola-shaded outdoor terrace.

Gerechtigkeitsgasse 51. ℂ **031/311-39-46**. Reservations recommended. Main courses 15F–30F ($12–$25); fixed-price menu 20F ($16). MC, V. Daily 11am–1pm and 5–10pm. Tram: 9.

5 Attractions

Before you rush off to sample the sightseeing attractions of the capital of Switzerland, stop in at the **Brasserie zum Bärengraben,** Muristalden 1 (ℂ **031/331-42-18**), immediately across the street from the Bear Pits, the town's major attraction (see below). At a table here you can enjoy a slice of local life better than anywhere else. Many habitués settle down to read the morning news, ordering their favorite coffee, a beer, or a glass of wine.

THE TOP ATTRACTIONS

Bärengraben (Bear Pits) ⚘ is a deep, moon-shaped den where the bears, Bern's mascots, have been kept since 1480. According to legend, when the duke of Zähringen established the town in 1191, he sent his hunters out into the surrounding woods, which were full of wild game. The duke promised to name the city after the first animal slain, which was the *Bär* (bear). Since then, the town has been known as Bärn (Bern). Today the bears are beloved, pampered, and fed by both residents and visitors (carrots are most appreciated). The Bear Pits lie on the opposite side of the **Nydegg Bridge (Nydeggbrücke)** from the rest of Old Town. The bridge was built over one of the gorges of the Aare River; its central stone arch has a span of 54m (177 ft.) and affords a sweeping view of the city. Below the Bear Pits, you can visit the **Rosengarten (Rose Gardens),** with its much-photographed view of the medieval sector of the city.

Zytgloggeturm (Clock Tower) ⚘ (*Zeitglocketurm* in standard German), on Kramgasse, was built in the 12th century and restored in the 16th century. Four minutes before every hour, crowds gather for the world's oldest and biggest horological puppet show. Mechanical bears, jesters, and emperors put on an animated performance. Staged since 1530, it's one of the longest-running acts in show business.

Cathedral of St. Vincent ⚘⚘
The Münster is one of the "newer" Gothic churches in Switzerland, dating from 1421. The belfry, however, was completed in 1893. The most exceptional feature of this three-aisle, pillared basilica is the tympanum over the main portal, which depicts the Last Judgment and contains more than 200 figures. You'll see mammoth 15th-century stained-glass windows in the chancel, but the most remarkable window, the *Dance of Death,* can be found in the Matter Chapel. The cathedral's 90m (295-ft.) belfry dominates Bern and offers a panoramic sweep of the Bernese Alps; to reach the viewing platform, you must climb 270 steps. The vista also includes the old town, its bridges, and the Aare River. Outside the basilica on Münsterplatz is the Moses Fountain, built in 1545.

Münsterplatz. ☏ **031/312-04-62.** Free admission to cathedral; viewing platform 3F ($1.95) adults, 1F (65¢) children. Cathedral Easter to Oct Tues–Sat 10am–5pm, Sun 11am–5pm; rest of year Tues–Fri 10am–noon and 2–4pm, Sat 10am–noon and 2–5pm, Sun 11am–2pm. Viewing platform closes half an hour before cathedral. Bus: 12.

Kunstmuseum (Fine Arts Museum) ⚘⚘
The world's largest collection of works by Paul Klee ⚘⚘⚘ is the star attraction here. The painter was born in Switzerland in 1879, the same year that this building was constructed. The collection includes 40 oils, 2,000 drawings, and many gouaches and watercolors.

The museum also contains works by other artists, with an emphasis on the 19th and 20th centuries. There's a collection of Italian 14th-century primitives, including Fra Angelico's *Virgin and Child.* Swiss primitives include some from the "Masters of the Carnation." Hodler, the romantic artist, is represented by allegorical paintings depicting day and night. Impressionists include Monet, Manet, Sisley, and Cézanne, along with Delacroix and Bonnard. Surrealistic painters represented here include Dalí, Seligman, Oppenheim, and Tschumi. You'll also see works by Kandinsky, Modigliani, Matisse, Kirchner, Soutine, and Picasso, as well as contemporary Swiss artists.

Hodlerstrasse 12. ☏ **031/328-09-44.** Permanent collection 7F ($5.75) adults, 5F ($4.10) seniors; special exhibitions 14F–18F ($11–$15) extra. Tues 10am–9pm; Wed–Sun 10am–5pm. Bus: 20.

MORE ATTRACTIONS

IN TOWN

The town's old but dignified **Rathaus (town hall),** on Rathausplatz, is still a center of political life. Built in 1406 in the Burgundian Gothic style and restored during World War II, the town hall has a double staircase and a covered porch.

Bernisches Historisches Museum (Bern Historical Museum) ⭐⭐   This neo-Gothic castle is built in the Swiss fortress style of the 16th century. The museum contains historical relics, along with archaeological, ethnographic, and numismatic collections. The main attraction is a series of seven 15th-century tapestries. A tapestry called *The Thousand Flowers,* plus four others telling the story of Julius Caesar, once belonged to the dukes of Burgundy. A number of rural and urban rooms, filled with period furnishings and artifacts, are also open to the public.

Helvetiaplatz 5. ℭ **031/350-77-11.** Admission 5F ($4.10) adults, 3F ($2.45) students and seniors, free for children 16 and under. Tues–Sun 10am–5pm. Tram: 3 or 5.

Botanischer Garten (Botanical Garden)   Medicinal and fiber plants, examples of tropical and subtropical alpine plants, woodland and water plants, and a collection of plants from the cold steppes of central Asia are just some of the attractions in this vast garden arranged in descending terraces to the banks of the Aare River. Vegetation from various ecological zones is grown both in greenhouses and outdoors.

Altenbergrain 21. ℭ **031/631-49-44.** Free admission. Garden Mon–Fri 7am–6pm; Sat–Sun 8am–5pm. Greenhouses daily 8am–5pm. Bus: 20.

Bundeshaus   This Renaissance building, the Federal Palace, contains the two chambers of Switzerland's Parliament. Inaugurated in 1902, the Parliament building has a glass dome that displays the coats of arms of all 22 Swiss cantons. Of interest are the stained-glass windows, which symbolize education, public works, defense, and justice. In the ground-floor rotunda a relief depicts the legend of the origin of Switzerland as dramatized in Schiller's saga of *Wilhelm Tell.* You can also visit the Chamber of the National Council, dominated by a large fresco by Gyron, and the Chamber of the Council of States, decorated with a mural painting by Albert Welti.

Bundesplatz. ℭ **031/322-85-22.** Free admission. Tours given on the hour Mon–Sat 9–11am and 2–4pm; Sun 10am, 11am, 2pm, and 3pm, except when Parliament is in session. Closed public holidays. Tram: 9.

NEARBY

The most panoramic attraction in the immediate vicinity of Bern is the belvedere atop **Mount Gurten** ⭐⭐ at 844m (2,768 ft.). There's a children's fairyland and a walking area as well as the lookout point. The belvedere is connected to Bern by the Gurten-bahn, a cable-train that's one of the fastest in Europe. The train departs from a station beside the Monbijoustrasse, about a half mile from Bern's center. To reach the departure platform, take tram no. 9, costing 2.80F ($2.30) each way, to the Gurtenbahn station. The trip takes 4 minutes each way. If driving, follow the road signs to Thun. A parking lot in the hamlet of Wabern is a short walk from the cable-train station.

Round-trip passage on the cable-train to the belvedere costs 9F ($7.40). The train operates year-round daily from 7:30am to sunset (depending on the season). For information, contact **Gurtenbahn Bern,** Eigerplatz (ℭ **031/961-23-23**).

ESPECIALLY FOR KIDS

Dählhölzli Tierpark, Tierparkweg (ℭ **031/357-15-15**), is one of the most interesting zoos in Europe. It offers a complete range of European creatures, from the tiny harvest mouse to the mighty musk oxen. You can admire more than 2,000 animals, including exotic birds, reptiles, and fish in the vivarium. Admission is 7F ($5.75) for adults, .50F (40¢) for children 6 to 16, free for children under 6. The zoo is open April through September daily from 8am to 6:30pm; off season daily 9am to 5pm. Take bus no. 18.

Kids also enjoy the **Zytgloggeturm (Clock Tower)** and the **Bärengraben (Bear Pits).** The **Naturhistorisches Museum,** Bernastrasse 15 (© **031/350-71-11;** www-nmbe.unibe.ch), with its fascinating reptile collection and gallery of stuffed African beasts, is best for a rainy day, and a picnic at **Mount Gurten** is a good way to cap any child's visit to Bern.

WALKING TOUR	BERN'S ALTSTADT

Start:	Bahnhofplatz.
Finish:	Swiss Parliament.
Time:	2 hours.
Best Times:	Any sunny day.
Worst Times:	Rush hours, Monday through Friday from 8 to 9am and 5 to 6pm.

Start at Bahnhofplatz, site of the Bern railroad station, the Bahnhof, facing the:

❶ Hotel Schweizerhof Bern

Many ambassadors and presidents have stayed at this famous landmark hotel.

Opening onto Bahnhofplatz is the:

❷ Church of the Holy Ghost

Also called the Heiliggeistkirche, this church dates from 1729 and is somehow out of place in such a traffic-congested area.

From the church, head east up Spittalgasse, coming first to:

❸ Bagpiper Fountain

The Pfeiferbrunnen, which depicts a bagpiper atop a column and capital, was erected in about 1545, presumably by Hans Gieng.

Directly east of the fountain, at Bärenplatz, is the:

❹ Prison Gate

Called the Käfigturm, this gate dates from the 1200s. It now shelters a tiny museum devoted to the cultural and business life of the city.

Continue east along:

❺ Marktgasse

This is the main street of Old Town, filled with fashionable shops and florists. Many of its buildings date from the 17th century.

The street leads into one of the principal squares of Altstadt:

❻ Kornhausplatz

This square is the site of the Ogre Fountain, which is a representation of a carnival figure, with a pillar and capital erected about 1544. The Kornhaus, an old granary from the 1700s, also stands on the square; today it's a restaurant and wine cellar.

TAKE A BREAK
The "nerve center" of Bern, **Café des Pyrénées,** Kornhausplatz (© **031/311-30-63**), is frequented by international journalists and visitors drawn to its sidewalk terrace. This bistro cafe also attracts many expatriates in Bern. Stop in for a drink—half a dozen types of Spanish brandy, for example—or any of the sandwiches and pasta dishes. Open Monday to Friday 9am to 12:30am and Saturday 8am to 5pm.

Also opening onto this square is the celebrated:

❼ Clock Tower

Also called the Zytgloggeturm, the Clock Tower was the town's west gate from 1191 to 1250. Its chimes start pealing at 4 minutes before every hour. A picture postcard of this scene is the most popular souvenir of Bern.

Leaving Kornhausplatz, continue east along:

❽ Kramgasse

A continuation of Marktgasse, this street contains many old houses with corner turrets and oriel windows.

Another major fountain standing on this street is the:

❾ Zähringer Fountain

This fountain was a monument to the city founder, Berchtold von Zähringen. Here you can see the Bern bear, mascot of the city, along with the Zähringer coat of arms. The pillar, capital, and figure were erected in 1535 by Hans Hiltprand.

Continuing, at Kramgasse 49 you come to:

❿ Albert Einstein's Home

In 1905 the famous physicist wrote his *Special Theory of Relativity* here.

The next fountain encountered on this same street is the:

⓫ Samson Fountain

This notable fountain is an allegory of strength, with a pillar and capital from 1527 and the figure from 1544.

Continue east along the street, which now changes its name to Gerechtigkeitsgasse. In the center of the street stands yet another famous fountain, the:

⓬ Justice Fountain

This fountain is an allegory of Justice, with worshipping subjects, including the pope, at her feet. The statue was erected in 1543.

Walk to the end of the street and continue across the river, crossing the Nydeggbrücke, until you reach Bern's most visited sight:

⓭ The Bear Pits

The Bärengraben is immediately on your right. The city of Bern is named after the bear (now its official mascot), and bears have resided in these pits since 1480.

Cross back over the bridge, and this time take the street to the left, heading west along Junkerngasse until you reach the:

⓮ Cathedral of St. Vincent

In Münsterplatz, the cathedral's first stone was laid in 1421, but building went on until 1573. From the tower you'll get a panoramic view of Bern.

After leaving the cathedral, continue west along Münstergasse until you reach Theaterplatz, one of Altstadt's major squares. Continue west, following the same street, which has now changed its name to Amthausgasse. You'll then approach Bundesplatz, site of the:

⓯ Federal Palace

Also called the Bundeshaus (Swiss Parliament) and capped with a massive dome, it was inspired by the Italian Renaissance Cathedral in Florence. This is the seat of Swiss democracy and one of the nation's treasured symbols.

ORGANIZED TOURS

We highly recommend the 2-hour **bus tour** that leaves from the tourist office at the railway station at Bahnhofplatz. You'll have an English-speaking guide as you travel through the city's residential quarters, past museums, and down to the Aare River, which flows below the houses of Parliament. You'll see the Rose Gardens and the late-Gothic cathedral and stroll under the arcades to the Clock Tower. After visiting the Bear Pits, you'll be led through medieval streets back to the railroad station. Tours are offered June to September daily at 2pm; April, May, and October Monday to Saturday at 2pm; and November to March only on Saturday at 2pm. The cost is 30F ($25) for adults, 18F ($15) for children 6 to 16, free for children 5 and under.

The tourist office also conducts **walking tours** of Bern from May through October. The daily meeting point is either at the tourist office at 11am or at Zytgloggeturm

Walking Tour: Bern's Altstadt

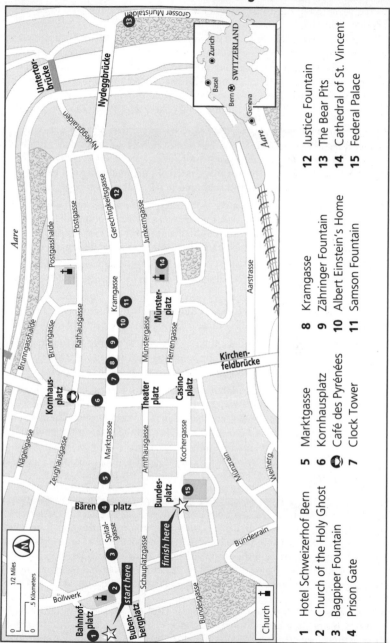

Legend / Points of interest:

1. Hotel Schweizerhof Bern
2. Church of the Holy Ghost
3. Bagpiper Fountain
4. Prison Gate
5. Marktgasse
6. Kornhausplatz
7. Clock Tower
8. Kramgasse
9. Zähringer Fountain
10. Albert Einstein's Home
11. Samson Fountain
12. Justice Fountain
13. The Bear Pits
14. Cathedral of St. Vincent
15. Federal Palace

at 11am. The cost is 12F ($9.85) for adults, 5F ($4.10) for children 6 to 16, free for children 5 and under.

We also recommend an organized **railway tour** (© 0900-300-300). The tour is an alpine adventure, traveling first through Interlaken, Lauterbrunnen, Wengen, and Kleine Scheidegg, then over the Jungfraujoch via Grindelwald and Interlaken, and back to Bern. Jungfraujoch, at 3,400m (11,152 ft.), has the highest railway station in Europe and offers panoramic views over glaciers and the Alps, including the so-called Ice Palace. The cost is 174F ($143) in second class and 210F ($172) in first class.

6 Outdoor Pursuits

The people of Bern are not particularly addicted to spectator sports, but they're very fond of recreational sports. The vast playground of Europe, the Bernese Oberland (see chapter 8), is at their doorstep, and they tend to take full advantage of it.

BIKING   There are approximately 2,993km (1,860 miles) of roadway in the Bernese Oberland around Bern. Pick up a bicycle map that outlines the routes at the tourist office, then rent a bike at the Bahnhof and set off on your adventure. See "By Bicycle" in "Getting Around," earlier in this chapter, for more information.

FITNESS, SAUNA, SOLARIUM   Go to the **STB Training Center,** Seilerstrasse 21 (© 031/381-26-06), where full facilities are available to keep you in shape.

GOLF   If you're a member of a golf club back home and have your membership card, you can patronize the **Golf and Country Club** in Blumisberg (© 026/496-34-38), 18km (11 miles) west of Bern near Flamatt (on the road to Fribourg).

HIKING   There are an estimated 250km (155 miles) of marked walking trails in the area surrounding Bern. You can pick up a rambling map at the tourist office. See "On Foot" in "Getting Around," earlier in this chapter, for more information.

SWIMMING   The city's best indoor pool, along with a Turkish bath and sauna, is the **Hirschengraben Indoor Pool,** Maulbeerstrasse 14 (© 031/381-36-56). The pool is open Monday, Wednesday, and Saturday from 8am to 6pm; Tuesday, Thursday, and Friday from 8am to 9pm. Admission is 6.50F ($5.35) to the pool and 17F ($14) to the sauna. The pool is closed July and August.

TENNIS   Courts are available at **Thalmatt,** Mettlenwaldweg 19, Herren-schwanden (© 031/307-33-33).

7 Shopping

With a few exceptions, stores in the city center are open on Monday from 2 to 6:30pm; on Tuesday, Wednesday, and Friday from 8:15am to 6:30pm; on Thursday from 8:15am to 9pm; and on Saturday from 8:15am to 4pm. They're closed on Sunday.

With 6km (4 miles) of arcades, stores of all types are sheltered in Bern. The main shopping streets are **Spitalgasse, Kramgasse, Postgasse, Marktgasse,** and **Gerechtigkeitsgasse.**

You can begin your shopping excursion at **Globus,** Spitalgasse 17 (© 031/313-40-40), a major department store comparable to Bloomingdale's, with departments for everything. Many people from the Bernese Oberland come into Bern just to shop at Globus. Also in the center of town, **Loeb ag Bern,** Spitalgasse 47 (© 031/320-71-11), has a little bit of everything but is known chiefly for its high-quality fashions.

The best handcrafts, souvenirs, and gifts are found at **Oberlander Heimat,** Kramgasse 61 (© **031/311-30-00**), located on a historic street near the Clock Tower. This outlet sells handcrafts from all over Switzerland, including textiles, woodcarvings, music boxes, and jewelry.

A collection of Art Nouveau pewter pieces is found at **Galerie Trag-art,** Gerechtigkeitsgasse 9 (© **031/311-64-49**). You'll find toys from all over the world at **Kunsthandwerk Anderegg,** Kramgasse 48 (© **031/311-02-01**).

For antiques, dolls, and toys, the best outlet is **Puppenklinik,** Gerechtigkeitsgasse 36 (© **031/312-07-71**).

The coin and stamp collector should head for Bern's most famous dealer, **Zumstein,** Zeughausgasse 24 (© **031/312-00-55**).

A good outlet for leather footwear is **Bally,** Spitalgasse 9 (© **031/311-54-81**), a branch of the famous Swiss shoe manufacturer that carries the complete line. Spitalgasse lies right off Bahnhofplatz. On the same street, **Gygax Mode,** Spitalgasse 4 (© **031/311-25-61**), is a leading name in leather goods. It sells locally produced items as well as some of the best from neighboring countries such as Italy.

For fashion, women gravitate to **Ciolina Modehaus,** Marktgasse 51 (© **031/328-64-64**), where clothes have fine styles and high prices. A leading men's store is **Zwald,** Neuengasse 23 (© **031/311-71-29**). Fashions here reflect a Continental flair.

Swiss chocolates (not always made in Switzerland these days) are sold at **Beeler,** Spitalgasse 29 (© **031/311-28-08**), one of the city's leading chocolatiers, and **Abegglen,** Spitalgasse 36 (© **031/311-21-11**).

Hats and handbags are the specialties at **KB Accessories,** Münstergasse 12 (© **031/312-01-15**), as designed by funky fashion iconoclasts Brigitte Keller and Stephan Billeter. Look for the kind of unusual and hip millinery that, if you're brave enough to wear proudly and with good posture, will evoke memories and comparisons to Marlene Dietrich.

Many of the art objects at **Galerie Granero/Erg du Ténéré,** Nydeggasse 15 (© **031/311-71-41**), derive from Africa's dusty sub-Sahara region, especially the arid and folklore-rich countries of Chad and Mali. The Swiss-born owners scour that region for silver jewelry crafted by members of the Tuareg tribes, some of which come adorned with mystical symbols that are believed to ward off evil and empower the wearer.

Chalk **Llhasa,** Münstergasse 51 (© **031/311-61-06**), up to offbeat shopping. Switzerland's status as a neutral nation has encouraged the emigration to Bern of some of Tibet's spiritual leaders. This shop acts as a focal point for some of them. You'll find meditative aids, exotic jewelry, carpets and weavings, clothing, incense, and books describing various aspects of Tibet's unique points of view about politics, philosophy, and religion. A second branch is at Bubenbergplatz 5 (© **031/311-01-88**).

Here's a random sampling of funky shops in funky Bern. **Irmak und Wirz,** GmbH, Kramgasse 10 (© **031/312-06-04**), specializes in tribal rugs from Iran, many of them woven high in the Iranian mountains according to age-old geometric designs of the Quashquai tribes. **Trouvaillen am Münster,** Münstergasse 16 (© **031/312-79-82**), is dusty and overcrowded, containing an intriguing, sometimes bizarre collection of African and Swiss hunting trophies, antique lighting fixtures, bric-a-brac, and oddities that include an elephant embryo from the 1950s and a barely used motorcycle from the 1930s. This is counterculture Bern at its most genuinely eccentric. Visit **Marcopolo,** Münstergasse 47 (© **031/311-88-44**), for artifacts from the developing world, all arranged in glittering arrays of jewelry and weavings from Africa, India,

Uzbekistan, and Afghanistan. Everything here seems exotic and ironically positioned a bit like a cleaned-up version of a Middle Eastern bazaar.

8 Bern After Dark

Most Bern residents get up early on weekday mornings, so they usually limit their evening entertainment to a drink or two at a historic cellar such as the Kornhauskeller or the Klötzlikeller. Nevertheless, the city offers several late-night clubs, with dancing and cabaret, for the nocturnally active international crowd. *This Week in Bern,* distributed free by the tourist office, keeps a current list of cultural events.

THE PERFORMING ARTS

The **Bern Symphony Orchestra,** one of the finest orchestras in Switzerland, is conducted by the acclaimed Russian-born Dmitrij Kitajenko, whose services are supplemented by frequent guest conductors from around the world. Concerts by the orchestra are usually performed at the concert facilities in the **Bern Casino,** Herrengasse 25 (© **031/311-42-42**). Except for a summer vacation usually lasting from July until mid-August, the box office is open Monday through Friday from 12:30 to 3pm. Tickets range from 20F to 55F ($16–$45).

Concerts with fewer musicians, especially chamber music, are often performed in any of four or five churches; in the auditorium at the **Konservatorium für Musik,** Kramgasse 36 (© **031/311-62-21**); or in the concert and recording facilities of **Radio Studio Bern,** Schwarztorstrasse 21 (© **031/388-91-11**).

Major opera and ballet performances are usually staged in what is generally acknowledged as Bern's most beautiful theater, the century-old **Stadttheater,** Kornhausplatz 20 (© **031/329-51-11**). Performances are usually in German, and to a lesser degree in French, but even if you don't understand those languages, you might want to attend a performance. Other plays and dance programs, including ballet and cabaret, are presented in the **Theater am Käfigturm,** Spitalgasse 4 (© **031/311-61-00**). Contemporary German-language dramas, comedies, tragedies, and satires are featured in the **Kleintheater,** Kramgasse 6 (© **031/320-26-26**).

THE CLUB & BAR SCENE

Bar aux Petits Fours   This is the newest of several contenders for the title of best gay bar in Bern, attracting a multilingual, attractive, and international group of gay people, mostly men. There's no dance floor and no restaurant on the premises, but what you get is a low-key bar, filled with regular clients, where a newcomer with a bit of effort can usually break the glacial freeze of Swiss reserve. Open daily from 6:30pm to 12:30am. Kramgasse 67. © **031/312-73-74.**

Come Back Bar   This isn't a gay bar in the strictest sense of the word, but a tavern that's cosmopolitan and tolerant, and likely to attract lots of genuinely cool artists and hipsters in Bern. It occupies the cellar vaults below the medieval buildings of the Rathausgasse. Inside, blinking lights frame a discreet dance floor and a long bar functions as a local hangout for many of the gay and gay-friendly residents of the Old Town. It's especially crowded on weekends, with a calmer, more low-key approach to things during weeknights. Open daily from 6pm to 12:30am (until 3:30am Fri–Sat). Rathausgasse 42. © **031/311-77-13.**

Klötzlikeller   The oldest wine tavern in Bern is near the Gerechtigkeitsbrunnen (Fountain of Justice), the first fountain you see on your walk from the Bärengraben

(Bear Pits) to the Zytgloggeturm (Clock Tower). Watch for the lantern outside an angled cellar door. The well-known tavern dates from 1635 and is leased by the city to an independent operator. Some 20 different wines are sold by the glass, with prices starting at 8.50F ($6.95). The menu is changed every 6 weeks. The appetizing snacks are always traditional, including sliced cheese, with prices ranging from 14F to 28F ($11–$23). The traditional Bernese kitchen produces various dinner plates, reflecting regional specialties and costing 24F to 48F ($20–$39). Open Tuesday to Saturday 4pm to 12:30am. 62 Gerechtigkeitsgasse. ℂ **031/311-74-56.**

Marians Jazzroom   The Louis Armstrong Bar, site of this jazz venue, has its own separate entrance from the Innere Enge Hotel. Unique in Bern, it serves up not only food and drink, but the finest traditional jazz performed live by top artists from around the world. From Tuesday to Thursday, hours are 7:30pm to midnight, Friday 7:30pm to 1am, and Saturday 7:30pm to 2am. On Saturday there is a Concert Apéro from 4 to 6:30pm, and on some Sundays there is a Jazz Brunch from 10am to 1:30pm. Closed June 6 through Sept 7. In the Innere Enge Hotel, Engerstrasse 54. ℂ **031/309-61-11.** Cover 15F–47F ($9.75–$31), depending on the act.

Samurai Bar Disco   This gay bar draws people who work in the local embassies, Bern locals, and young men from the Bernese Oberland in for a night on the town. Women are also welcome. Guys gyrating to the sounds of hot music fill the dance floor. Open Monday to Thursday from 8pm to 2:30am, Friday and Saturday from 8pm to 3:30am. Aarbergergasse 35. ℂ **031/311-88-03.**

GAMBLING

Grand Casino Koursaal Bern, Kornhausstrasse 3 (ℂ **031/339-55-55**), is the only place in town to gamble. Indeed, it's a great spot for novices to learn because serious money rarely changes hands here. It's open daily from noon to 3:30am, and admission is free. Drinks cost 10F to 15F ($8.20–$12). There are three restaurants and two bars, plus a dance hall that charges a 10F ($8.20) cover. It's open Friday and Saturday from 9pm to 3:30am, and on Sunday from 3 to 10pm.

8

The Bernese Oberland

The Bernese Oberland is one of the greatest tourist attractions in the world, mainly because it's one of the best areas for winter sports. The region sprawls between the Reuss River and Lake Geneva, with the Rhône forming its southern border. The area contains two lakes, the Thun and the Brienz, and takes in a portion of the Alps (culminating in the Finsteraarhorn at 4,207m/13,799 ft.). The canton of Bern, which encompasses most of the area, is the second largest in Switzerland and contains about 160 sq. km (100 sq. miles) of glaciers.

The best center for exploring the Bernese Oberland is Interlaken, most popular as a summer resort. Other cities in the region, such as Gstaad, Grindelwald, Kandersteg, and Mürren, are both summer and winter playgrounds. You can ski the mountains during winter and swim, sail, and water-ski on Lake Thun in the summer.

1 Exploring the Bernese Oberland

To compensate for the region's almost impossible geography, Swiss engineers have crisscrossed the Oberland with cogwheel railways (some of them still driven by steam), aerial cableways, and sinuous mountain roads. Though often a confusing experience, getting to a particular resort can be part of the fun. The region's busiest railroad junction, and the point where most travelers change trains for local railways, is **Interlaken.**

You can buy a **transportation pass** for the Bernese Oberland from the Swiss Rail System. The train ticket is valid for 7 days and costs 195F ($160) in second class and 233F ($191) in first class. Another pass, valid for 15 days, costs 240F ($197) in second class and 287F ($235) in first class. With the 7-day pass, you'll travel free for 3 days and pay a reduced fare for the final 4 days. With a 15-day pass, you'll travel free for 5 days and pay reduced fares for the rest of the time. Children travel at half price. The pass is valid on most railroads; all mountain trains, cable cars, chairlifts, and steamers on Lakes Thun and Brienz; and most postal-bus lines in the area. The ticket also qualifies you for a 25% reduction on the Kleine Scheidegg-Eigergletscher-Jungfraujoch railway, the Mürren-Schilthorn aerial cable line, and the bus to Grosse Scheidegg and Bussalp. You must purchase the pass at least 1 week before you arrive. For information about the pass, call © **800/794-7795.**

Since Interlaken is the focal point of one of the most complicated networks of ski lifts in the world, most visitors opt to buy a comprehensive pass that allows unlimited access to the cog railways, buses, cable cars, chairlifts, and gondolas (incorporating every mechanical lift in and around Interlaken, Wengen, Grindelwald, and Mürren). Sold at the Interlaken tourist office (see "Interlaken," below) and tourist offices at the other leading resorts, it's called the **Jungfrau Top Ski Region Pass.** You can buy the 2-day pass for 118F ($97), the 5-day pass for 248F ($203), or the 7-day pass for 312F ($256). Discounts of 10% are offered to seniors 62 and older, discounts of 20% to youths ages 16 to 20, and discounts of 50% to children 6 to 15. Kids 5 and under travel for only 10% of the above rates. This pass incorporates access to 45 ski lifts, 204km (127 miles) of well-groomed downhill runs, 99km (60 miles) of prepared walking and cross-country ski paths, and 50km (31 miles) of tobogganing runs. It covers the region around Grindelwald, Wengen, and Mürren.

Other passes include the following:

- **First Region Ski Pass** is a small-scale cluster of ski lifts, favored by beginners and intermediates, that includes six lifts and a gondola. It's available only for the region immediately around Grindelwald and does not include Wengen. A 1-day pass costs 62F ($51), a 2-day pass 112F ($92).
- **Kleine Männlichen and Scheidegg Pass** offer the same scale of difficulty as the First Region Ski Pass, as well as the same price (1- and 2-day passes are the only

offerings). Unlike the First Region Pass, it's available to residents of either Wengen or Grindelwald, but residents of Mürren are not invited to this particular cluster of runs.

BY MOUNTAIN BIKE   Hundreds of miles of cycling paths riddle the Bernese Oberland, and most of them begin in Interlaken. Separate from the network of hiking paths, the bike routes are signposted and marked on rental maps distributed at bike-rental agencies. Of course, it's the law to use only specially signposted routes and not destroy plant and animal life or ride across private fields. Hikers, incidentally, are given the right of way over bikers.

There are 13 railroad stations in the Bernese Oberland offering bike-rental services. Rates are reasonable. Families can rent four bikes (two for adults, two for children 15 and under) for an all-inclusive price of 60F ($49) per day or 420F ($344) per week. Individual rentals cost 30F ($25) per day or 210F ($172) per week. Reservations must be made the evening before the tour. You can make reservations in Interlaken at either of its rail stations, **Interlaken East** (© **033/828-73-19**) or **Interlaken West** (© **033/826-47-50**).

ON FOOT   The Bernese Oberland is ideal for walkers and hikers. The natural terrain here will satisfy everyone from the most ambitious mountain hiker to the casual stroller.

Trails designed for walkers branch out from almost every junction. Most are paved and signposted, showing distances and estimated walking times. Most tourist offices will suggest itineraries for walkers.

For the more athletic, itineraries include long hikes far afield in the mountains, with suggestions for overnight accommodations en route.

Even if you don't feel up to scaling alpine peaks, you can still go on walks. Take one of the Swiss postal-bus rides uphill to a village, then stroll back down to Interlaken, for example. Be warned, however, that walking downhill in Switzerland can still strain your calf muscles.

2 Interlaken ⟨★⟨★⟨★

54km (34 miles) SE of Bern; 130km (81 miles) SW of Zurich

Interlaken is the tourist capital of the Bernese Oberland. Cableways and cog railways designed for steeply inclined mountains connect it with most of the region's villages and dazzling sights, including the snowy heights of the Jungfrau, which rises a short distance to the south. Excursion possibilities from Interlaken are both numerous and dazzling.

This "town between the lakes" (Thun and Brienz) has been a vacation resort for over 300 years. Although it began as a summer resort, it developed into a year-round playground, altering its allure as the seasons change. During the winter skiers take advantage of the town's low prices. Interlaken charges low-season prices in January and February, when smaller resorts at higher altitudes are charging their highest rates of the year. The most expensive time to visit Interlaken is during midsummer, when high-altitude and snowless ski resorts often charge their lowest rates.

An Augustinian monastery was founded in Interlaken in 1130 but was later closed during the Reformation; the ruins can still be seen in a park in the center of town. Tourism to the area is said to have begun in 1690, when Margrave Frederic Albert of Brandenburg journeyed into the snow-covered rocks of the Jungfrau massif. However, tourism as we know it today dawned at the beginning of the 19th century, when artists and writers—many of them British—were drawn to the town by its scenery. As the country's railroad and steamer services improved, a steady stream of visitors followed, including such notables as Mark Twain, Goethe (who seems to have lived everywhere), Wagner, Mendelssohn, and representatives of European royal families.

ESSENTIALS

GETTING THERE   There are several trains daily between Zurich and Interlaken (2 hr.) and between Bern and Interlaken (40 min.). Frequent train service also connects Geneva with Interlaken (2½ hr.). For additional **rail information,** call © **0900/300-300.**

Note: Although the town has two different railway stations, Interlaken East and Interlaken West, West is most convenient to the city's center.

If you're driving from Bern, head south on N6 to Spiez, then continue east on N8 to Interlaken.

VISITOR INFORMATION   The **Tourism Organization Interlaken** is in the Hotel Metropole at Höheweg 37 (© **033/826-53-00**). It's open in July and August, Monday to Friday 8am to noon and 1:30 to 6:30pm, Saturday 8am to 5pm, and Sunday 5 to 7pm; the rest of the year, Monday to Friday 8am to noon and 2 to 6pm and Saturday 8am to noon.

A **Visitor's Card** is granted to persons registered at local hotels and confers certain discounts to some of the local attractions.

GETTING AROUND   Train arrivals are at either Interlaken East or Interlaken West. If you're loaded with luggage, you'll want to grab a taxi. However, after you've been deposited at one of the local hotels (nearly all of which are in the city center), you'll rarely need a taxi—the town is closely knit and best explored on foot. Buses are convenient for connections to the satellite towns and villages or heading to the outskirts. The **bus station** is at Areckstrasse 6 (© **033/828-88-28**).

EXPLORING THE AREA

It's very simple—the best way to see everything in Interlaken is to walk. You can either randomly stroll around, enjoying the panoramic views in all directions, or follow a more structured walking tour. If you'd like some guidance, go to the tourist office (see above) and ask for a copy of *What to Do in Interlaken.* It maps out walks for both young and more mature visitors.

The **Höheweg** 🔍🔍 covers 14 hectares (35 acres) in the middle of town between the two train stations. Once the property of Augustinian monks, it was acquired in the mid–19th century by the hotel keepers of Interlaken, who turned it into a park. As you stroll along Höhenpromenade, admire the famous view of the Jungfrau mountain. Another beautiful sight is the flower clock at the Kursaal (casino). You're also sure to see some *fiacres* (horse-drawn cabs). The promenade is lined with hotels, cafes, and gardens.

Cross over the Aare River to **Unterseen,** built in 1280 by Berthold von Eschenbach. Here you can visit the parish church, with its late-Gothic tower dating from 1471. This is one of the most photographed sights in the Bernese Oberland. The Mönch appears to the left of the tower, the Jungfrau on the right.

Back in Interlaken, visit the **Touristik-Museum der Jungfrau-Region,** am Stadthausplatz, Obere Gasse 26 (© **033/822-98-39**), the first regional tourism museum in the country. Exhibitions show the growth of tourism in the region throughout the past 2 centuries. The museum is open from May to mid-October,

Tuesday to Sunday from 2 to 5pm. Admission is 4F ($3.30), or 3F ($2.45) with a Visitor's Card. Children are charged 2F ($1.65).

To see the sights of Interlaken, Matten, and Unterseen by *fiacre,* line up at the Interlaken West train station. The half-hour round-trip tour costs 39F ($32) for one or two, plus 11F ($9) for each additional person; children 7 to 16 are charged half fare, and those 6 and under ride free.

Other attractions in the area include animal parks, afternoon concerts, and steamers across Lakes Brienz and Thun. During the summer visitors can sit in covered grandstands and watch Schiller's version of the William Tell story and the formation of the Swiss Confederation. We also recommend the delectable pastries sold in the local cafes.

OUTDOOR ACTIVITIES

If you're feeling energetic, or just looking to work off an excess of fondue dipping, Interlaken offers many opportunities for sports—sailing, windsurfing, rowing, fishing, golf, tennis, mountain trekking, and glider flying. There's also a swimming pool in town. More information is available at the tourist office.

GOLF   You can play at the **Interlaken-Unterseen course** (© 033/823-60-16) from April to October. The cost is 90F ($74) Monday to Friday and 105F ($86) Saturday and Sunday. With a Visitor's Card, the cost is reduced to 80F ($66).

HORSEBACK RIDING   There are several bridle paths between Lake Thun and Lake Brienz. The **Voegeli Riding School,** Scheidgasse 66, in Unterseen (© 033/822-74-16), offers guided rides costing 40F ($33) for 1 hour and 75F ($62) for 2 hours.

SWIMMING   There's a public **indoor pool** and a public open-air pool, **Bödeli** (© 033/827-90-90), behind the Kursaal. The indoor pool has a sauna and a solarium as well as a fitness room. This pool is open year-round Monday from 9am to 9pm, Tuesday through Friday from 9am to 9:45pm, and Saturday and Sunday from 9am to 6pm. Entrance is 8F ($6.55) for adults, 4.80F ($3.95) for children 6 to 16, and free for children 5 and under. The outdoor pool, with its changing cabins and 9.9m (32-ft.) diving board, is open mid-May through September daily from 9am to 7pm. Keep in mind, though, that even July and August might be too chilly for you. Entrance is 5F ($4.10) for adults and 3F ($2.45) for children.

TENNIS   Use of a court at the **Höhematte** costs 24F ($20) per hour for visitors. If you're alone and willing to be matched up with another person, it will cost you half the court fee. For reservations, phone © **033/822-14-72.** The courts are open from mid-April to mid-October daily from 8am to 8 or 9pm.

SHOPPING

True to its role as the nerve center of the entire Oberland region, Interlaken stocks an ample supply of souvenirs and sports equipment. You'll find all the handicrafts and art objects you could possibly need beside the resort's main street, Höheweg, and around the Interlaken West railway station. One of the best of these is **Heimatwerk Interlaken,** Höheweg 115 (© **033/823-16-53**). It's been a fixture for tourists since the turn of the 20th century. It stocks only goods manufactured in Switzerland, including a wholesome and comprehensive roster of wood-carved children's toys, tablecloths and linens, cutting boards and cheese boards, ceramics, and glass. Since Interlaken has higher-altitude ski and hill-climbing resorts stretching upward on virtually all sides, you won't lack for purveyors of sporting-goods equipment. Two of the best are **Intersport,** Postgasse 16 (© **033/822-06-61**), and **Harry Sport,** Bahnhofstrasse 8 (© **033/822-73-22**).

WHERE TO STAY
VERY EXPENSIVE
Lindner Grand Hotel Beau-Rivage 🦌🦌🦌   This government-rated five-star and reconstructed Belle Epoque-style hotel between Höheweg and the Aare River is one of Interlaken's grand hotels. Only Victoria-Jungfrau is better. The Beau-Rivage sells luxury on a smaller, more intimate scale than its competitors, and is located in a very tranquil spot. It's only a short distance from the Interlaken East rail station, which makes it a good center for excursions in all directions. The central tower has an ascending series of covered loggias decorated with carvings and flowers, a triangular pediment, and a mansard roof. There are two wings with gables and wrought-iron balconies. The renovated rooms are conservatively modern with excellent beds and nicely kept bathrooms. The front rooms open onto the Jungfrau, and the rooms in the rear are not only quieter but front the river.

Höheweg 211, CH-3800 Interlaken. ✆ **033/826-70-07.** Fax 033/823-28-47. www.lindner.de. 101 units. 290F–410F ($238–$336) double; 700F–1,500F ($574–$1,230) suite. Rates include buffet breakfast. AE, DC, MC, V. Free parking outdoors. **Amenities:** Restaurant; bar; pool; health club; sauna; limited room service; babysitting; laundry service/dry cleaning. *In room:* TV, minibar, dataport, hair dryer.

Victoria-Jungfrau Grand Hotel & Spa 🦌🦌🦌 *(Kids)*   Since 1865, this grand hotel has reigned as one of the most important resort properties in Switzerland. The owner of the Victoria Hotel, Edouard Ruchti, united it with the Jungfrau Hotel in 1895, and the landmark property has stood ever since. Through its corridors has passed everyone from the emperor of Brazil to the king of Siam to Mark Twain. During World War II the hotel served as headquarters of the Swiss commander in chief, General Henri Guisan. Designed in a richly ornate Victorian style, it sits right in the town center at the foot of rigidly symmetrical gardens. The hotel boasts valuable antiques and one of the best-trained staffs in Interlaken. The most expensive rooms open onto views of the Jungfrau. The midsize to spacious accommodations are luxurious.

Höheweg 41, CH-3800 Interlaken. ✆ **800/223-6800** in the U.S. or 033/828-28-28. Fax 033/828-28-80. www.victoria-jungfrau.ch. 212 units. Summer 560F–760F ($459–$623) double; winter 450F–610F ($369–$500) double, 810F–900F ($664–$738) junior suite, 1,580F–4,500F ($1,296–$3,690) suite. Half board 110F ($90) per person extra. AE, DC, MC, V. Free parking outside, 25F ($21) in garage. **Amenities:** 3 restaurants; 2 bars; pool; tennis courts; spa; Jacuzzi; sauna; kids' club; limited room service; massage; babysitting; laundry service/dry cleaning. *In room:* TV, dataport, minibar, hair dryer, safe.

EXPENSIVE
Hotel Interlaken 🦌   This is the resort's oldest hotel, receiving overnight guests since 1323, first as a hospital, later as a cloister and, beginning in the early 1400s, as a tavern and inn. Guests have included Byron and Felix Mendelssohn. The hotel, directly east of the casino, has been gutted and rebuilt since, with a salmon-colored facade sporting baroque touches. The most expensive rooms have a few 19th-century antiques; the rest have conservative, modern furnishings with excellent beds and well-maintained bathrooms.

Höheweg 74, CH-3800 Interlaken. ✆ **033/826-68-68.** Fax 033/826-68-69. www.interlakenhotel.ch. 60 units. 210F–345F ($172–$283) double. Rates include buffet breakfast. Half board 45F ($37) per person extra. AE, DC, MC, V. Free parking. **Amenities:** Restaurant; bar; sauna; limited room service; laundry service/dry cleaning; nonsmoking rooms. *In room:* TV, dataport, minibar, hair dryer, safe.

Hotel Metropole 🦌🦌   Americans often prefer this sleek, modern hotel in the city center, the only skyscraper in the Bernese Oberland, to the aging palaces of Interlaken. The 18-story building was built in 1976 and has since been stylishly renovated. It's the most

up-to-date and best-managed hotel in town. The small, standardized rooms have plush carpeting, modern furniture, and balconies. All units have neatly kept bathrooms. Those facing south have a panoramic view of Interlaken and the towering mountains. Try to steer clear of the 18 units in the annex, as they are a bit lackluster and have no views.

Höheweg 37, CH-3800 Interlaken. © 800/223-5652 in the U.S. or 033/828-66-66. Fax 033/828-66-33. www. metropole-interlaken.ch. 95 units. May–Oct 295F–360F ($242–$295) double, 590F ($484) suite; Nov–Apr 250F–270F ($205–$221) double, 480F ($394) suite. Half board 55F ($45) per person extra. AE, DC, MC, V. Parking 8F ($6.55) outside, 14F ($11) in garage. **Amenities:** 2 restaurants; bar; indoor pool; sauna; limited room service; babysitting; laundry service/dry cleaning. *In room:* TV, dataport (in some), minibar, hair dryer.

MODERATE
Hotel Weisses Kreuz   This safe and tranquil hotel is located on the famous Höheweg, right in the center of Interlaken. The interior is pleasantly decorated yet simple, and the bedrooms are newly renovated. Each has a well-maintained bathroom. Owned and managed by the Bieri family since 1911, the hotel offers a brasserie-style restaurant with Italian/Swiss cuisine. In summer guests gravitate to its boulevard terrace for people-watching, drinks, and pastries.

Höheweg (at Jungfraustrasse), CH-3800 Interlaken. © 033/822-59-51. Fax 033/823-35-55. www.weisseskreuz.ch. 56 units. 170F–220F ($139–$180) double. Rates include buffet breakfast. AE, DC, MC, V. Free parking. **Amenities:** Restaurant; lounge. *In room:* TV.

Park-Hotel Mattenhof ⟨ᚷ   This large, old-fashioned, government-rated four-star hotel is in a secluded area at the edge of a forest 2km (1¼ miles) south of the center; you can reach it by heading away from the center toward Wilderswil. The exterior looks like a private castle, with its high, pointed roof, tower, loggias, and balconies. It was originally built as a simple and sedate pension in 1897, but adopted most of its mock-medieval form after a massive enlargement in 1906. During World War II it functioned as a hospital for injured soldiers, but for the past 30 years it has been managed by Peter Bühler and his family. They offer a calm retreat with terraces, manicured lawns, and panoramic views of the Alps. The salons are warmly decorated and sunny, and some of the well-furnished but small bedrooms have a view of the Jungfrau and the Niederhorn. All have well-kept bathrooms, and several also are equipped with a balcony.

Hauptstrasse, Matten, CH-3800 Interlaken. © 033/821-61-21. Fax 033/822-28-88. www.park-mattenhof.ch. 76 units. June–Sept and Dec 26–Jan 1 200F–260F ($164–$213) double; off season 140F–170F ($115–$139) double. Rates include buffet breakfast. AE, DC, MC, V. Free parking. **Amenities:** 2 restaurants; 2 bars; indoor pool; tennis court; health club; laundry service/dry cleaning. *In room:* TV, dataport, minibar, hair dryer.

Royal St. Georges ⟨ᚷ   Built in 1907, this oft-restored hotel is a historical landmark structure. In spite of several renovations, it has retained its traditional character. In contrast to the old-style architecture, the bedrooms are as up-to-date as tomorrow, ranging in size from small to exceedingly spacious. Some of the suites are in the Victorian style. Bathrooms are generous in size and often stylized, such as a special Art Nouveau bathroom. The hotel is divided into two parts, the Royal Wing and the St. Georges Wing, both linked to each other through a gangway. Unlike most peas-in-a-pod hotel rooms, this government-rated four-star choice offers individualized bedrooms—you can hardly find two rooms that are identical. Each unit contains a private bathroom with either shower or combination tub/shower.

Höheweg 139, CH-3800 Interlaken. © 033/822-75-75. Fax 033/823-30-75. www.royal-stgeorges.ch. 95 units. 125F–300F ($103–$246) double; 260F–390F ($213–$320) suite. Rates include breakfast. AE, DC, MC, V. **Amenities:** Restaurant; bar; Jacuzzi; steam room; sauna; 24-hr. room service; laundry service/dry cleaning. *In room:* TV, dataport, minibar, hair dryer, safe.

INEXPENSIVE

Hotel Alphorn ❧ This bed-and-breakfast oozes charm the old-fashioned way. From the flower boxes that adorn the ground-floor windows to the vibrant colors of the breakfast room, this place has an inviting ambience. The rooms are small but have a private bathroom with shower and toilet, as well as cable TV—which the host is proud to tell you includes CNN. There is a bar where patrons go after a long day, but don't expect a rowdy crowd because this is a family-oriented and family-operated type of place.

Rugenaustrasse 8, CH-3800 Interlaken. ℂ **033/822-30-51.** Fax 033/823-30-69. www.hotel-alphorn.ch. 10 units. 110F–140F ($90–$115) double. Rates include buffet breakfast. AE, MC, V. **Amenities:** Breakfast room; bar. *In room:* TV.

Hotel Lötschberg ❧ *Finds* A hotel that's sure to transmit an old-fashioned sense of Swiss charm is this sprawling villa-style building that rises from the city's commercial core, a 3-minute walk from the railway station. Originally built in 1906 as a cost-conscious pension, and painted a striking shade of blue, it has been frequently improved, repaired, and renovated between 1994 and 1998. All but three of the units have a TV set, and the three that don't are located within a simple, century-old guesthouse a short walk away. Rooms come in a wide variety of sizes, ranging from small units to medium-size ones (two to three guests), and even very spacious rooms, each comfortable enough for four persons. By far the best part about this place is the personalized attention offered by Susi and Fritz Hutmacher, who pride themselves on providing advice that usually leads guests to less frequently visited sites in and around Interlaken. Breakfast is the only meal served within this hotel, but on the premises, under separate management, is an Asian restaurant that serves lunch and dinner. You can rent mountain bikes from the Hutmachers or even check your e-mail for a small fee.

Général Guisanstrasse 31, CH-3800 Interlaken. ℂ **033/822-25-45.** Fax 033/822-25-79. www.lotschberg.ch. 19 units. 98F–190F ($80–$156) double; 85F–110F ($70–$90) apt. Rates include breakfast. AE, DC, MC, V. Free parking. Closed Jan. **Amenities:** Lounge; laundry (self-service, coin-operated); dry cleaning. *In room:* TV, dataport.

The Swiss Inn *Value* This small Edwardian inn with balconies and gables offers good value. Mrs. Vreny Müller Lohner rents tasteful, simply decorated one- to three-room apartments equipped with good beds and well-kept bathrooms with tub/shower combinations in one half, only showers in the others. They accommodate two to six guests, and children's beds or cots are available. The inn has a lounge, a sitting area with a fireplace, and a grill for barbecues in the garden.

Général Guisanstrasse 23, CH-3800 Interlaken. ℂ **033/822-36-26.** Fax 033/823-23-03. www.swiss-inn.com. 9 units. 130F–210F ($107–$172) double; 100F–170F ($82–$139) apt for 2; 230F–250F ($189–$205) apt for 4. AE, MC, V. Free parking. **Amenities:** Lounge; laundry (self-service; coin-operated); dry cleaning. *In room:* TV, kitchenette (in some).

WHERE TO DINE

Most guests dine at their hotels, which partially explains why such a world-famous resort as Interlaken has so few independent restaurants worth noting.

EXPENSIVE

Gasthof Hirschen *Value* SWISS This hotel restaurant offers some of the best and most reasonably priced meals in town. The menu is varied; the potato soup with mountain cheese is the finest we've ever tasted. Another tasty appetizer is the ravioli filled with salmon. For a main dish, we recommend sautéed calves' liver, filet of beef bordelaise, beef goulash, broiled trout, or chateaubriand. The Hirschen also operates its own farm, which supplies Bio-Angus beef, veal, cheese, fresh vegetables, and herbs. Fresh berries and honey are also brought in from the farm during summer.

Hauptstrasse 11, Matten. ⓒ 033/822-15-43. Reservations recommended. Main courses 21F–52F ($17–$43). AE, DC, MC, V. Thurs–Mon 11:30am–2pm; Wed–Mon 6:30–9:30pm.

Il Bellini ⓡⓡ INTERNATIONAL   This is one of the finest restaurants in the Bernese Oberland. Established in 1994, it sits one floor above the lobby in the tallest hotel in Interlaken, the Metropole, and is outfitted in a graceful 19th-century rendition of pale pinks and greens. The fresh, good-tasting food is served with a discreet panache you might have expected in Italy, and includes an assortment of antipasti. You can order individual selections of hors d'oeuvres, including prosciutto with melon or smoked salmon and carpaccio. The soups, especially the homemade minestrone, are tasty, and the main courses include such delectable specialties as tender beefsteak Florentine, saltimbocca, and chicken breast grilled with tomatoes and mozzarella. The fish selections are limited but well chosen.

In the Hotel Metropole, Höheweg 37. ⓒ 033/828-66-66. www.metropole-interlaken.ch. Reservations recommended Fri–Sun. Main courses 19F–59F ($16–$48); pastas 14F–26F ($11–$21). AE, DC, MC, V. Tues–Sat 11:30am–2pm and 6:30pm–midnight.

Im Gade ⓡ SWISS/INTERNATIONAL   Set on the eastern perimeter of town, near the monumental-looking Hotel Victoria Jungfrau, this elegantly folkloric restaurant was established about a century ago, during the early days of modern tourism in Switzerland. A staff of dirndl-clad waitresses service a pair of interconnected dining rooms, one of which (the Stübli) is more deliberately old-fashioned-looking than its neighbor. Menu items are well prepared and usually accompanied with fresh and seasonal vegetables. The best examples include at least three kinds of soup, including carrot, gratin of onion, and fish soup; a "variation" of shrimp, duckling breast with orange sauce, and almond dumplings; beefsteaks—including a meaty version of chateaubriand—with Choron sauce; curried chicken with rice; and poached filet of sole with Pernod sauce. Expect an elegant venue, with attentive service and lots of well-established charm.

In the Hotel du Nord, Höheweg 70. ⓒ 033/827-50-50. Reservations recommended. Lunch main courses 17F–30F ($14–$25); dinner main courses 30F–50F ($25–$41). Set-price lunches 26F–50F ($21–$41); set-price dinners 30F–50F ($25–$41). AE, DC, MC, V. Daily noon–9:45pm, with a limited menu available 2–6pm. Closed Nov.

MODERATE

Schuh SWISS/CONTINENTAL   This attractive restaurant and tearoom in the center of town has been known for its pastries since 1885. They are still the town's finest. The alpine building has a thick roof arched over the fourth-floor windows and, in back, a sunny terrace with a view of the Jungfrau and a well-kept lawn. The dining room has large windows and a Viennese ambience. A pianist provides music.

Höheweg 56. ⓒ 033/822-94-41. www.schuh-interlaken.ch. Main courses 15F–46F ($12–$38); fixed-price meal 35F–40F ($29–$33). AE, DC, MC, V. Tues–Sun 8am–11pm. Closed Oct 25–Dec 9.

Spice India ⓡ INDIAN   The Mathur family waited a long time for a restaurant of their own and when they got it, they didn't disappoint. Ideally located in between the Hotel Metropole and the Chalet Hotel Oberland, this is a place where anyone who likes Indian food can enjoy a good meal served by people who are passionate about their restaurant. Among the top menu options are the Barrah kabobs—oven-grilled lamb marinated in yogurt with garlic and ginger paste—fish curry, filets of chicken, and basmati rice. There is also a vegetarian section from the menu and from that we recommend the *baingan ka bharta* (chargrilled eggplant with yogurt and cheese) and the *aloo ghobi,* a potato-and-cauliflower dish. The decor is a little bland for an exotic restaurant, but the food makes up for it.

Postgasse 6. ℂ **033/821-00-91.** www.spice-india.net. Reservations required for large groups only. Main courses 16F–38F ($13–$31). AE, DC, MC, V. Tues–Sun noon–2:30pm; daily 6–10:30pm.

Zum Bären SWISS   Set within a richly folkloric setting whose origins go back to 1674, this is a worthwhile excursion for clients who want to perhaps escape the restrictions of their in-house dining plan for a view of old-fashioned alpine folklore. Expect lots of weathered and congenially battered paneling, dented wooden tables, chairs that have borne the weight of thousands of previous diners, and a standardized, mostly Swiss menu that's redolent with rösti, schnitzels of both pork and veal, grilled filet of beef with peppercorn or béarnaise sauce, and minced veal in cream sauce, Zurich style. It all goes well with beer that's served here in foaming mugfuls. Prerecorded "evergreen music" usually accompanies your meal.

Seestrasse 2, Unterseen. ℂ **033/822-75-26.** Reservations recommended. Main courses 25F–42F ($21–$34); set–price menu 56F ($46). AE, MC, V. Oct–Apr Tues–Sun 8:30pm–midnight; May–Sept daily 8:30pm–midnight.

INTERLAKEN AFTER DARK
Merchants in Interlaken have always known how to inject their town with enough razzle-dazzle to keep visitors coming back. As such, Interlaken boasts one of the highest per-capita rates of nightclubs of any town its size in Switzerland. The town's business is so transient—composed mostly of short-term visitors on their way to somewhere else—the clientele of any particular bar or club is likely to change virtually every week. Given that, here's a roster of those that at this writing were the most animated and/or fun.

You'll usually find a drinking buddy in the folksy, amiably kitschy **Victoria Bar** in the town's stateliest hotel, the Victoria-Jungfrau, Höheweg 41 (ℂ **033/828-28-28**). The **Sternen Bar,** set amid a cluster of shops on the all-pedestrian precinct of Jungfraustrasse (ℂ **033/822-34-25**), is the closest thing to a big-city wine bar in Interlaken, complete with the requisite platters of food and an alpine version of daytime soap-opera intrigue. **Buddy's Pub,** in the Hotel Splendid, Höheweg 33 (ℂ **033/ 822-76-12**), provides a cozy, richly paneled setting that evokes an upscale version of a smoke-stained pub in Ireland.

If you want to combine drinking with dancing, head to **Johnny Carlton's Club,** in the Hotel Carlton, Höheweg 92 (ℂ **033/822-38-21**). Although the dance floor is comically small, the music is danceable. Because there are never enough banquettes and chairs for the crowd, everyone seems to mingle extra freely. Its leading competitors include **Hollywood,** in the Hotel Central, Bahnhofstrasse (ℂ **033/823-10-33**), where live bands sometimes play. Call ahead here first though to see if anything is going on because sometimes it can get slow. The disco **High-Life,** Rugenparkstrasse 2 (ℂ **033/822-15-50**), has been a staple for local residents for many years, especially for off-duty restaurateurs from throughout the surrounding valleys. It plays enough disco tunes from the 1970s and 1980s to unthaw the Big Chill. Somewhat more restrained is the **Black and White,** in the Hotel Metropole, Höheweg 37 (ℂ **033/ 828-66-66**), where a somewhat better-dressed crowd in their 30s and 40s mingles happily together.

Access to virtually every disco in Interlaken costs 7F ($5.75) on Friday and Saturday nights, and is free every other night. Things begin happening a bit earlier than you might expect—many are rocking by 11pm.

Despite its allegiance to the music coming out of London and Los Angeles, Interlaken also places a lot of emphasis on folklore and alpine schmaltz. **The Casino Kursaal,** Höheweg at Strandbadstrasse (© **033/827-61-00;** www.casino-kursaal.ch), is the venue for the dinner-and-entertainment **Swiss Folklore Show,** a somewhat self-conscious duplication of the quirks and yodels that made alpine Switzerland so unique. The show is in a cavernous convention hall, Monday to Saturday beginning at 7:30pm during July and August, with a less dependable schedule during May and June and again in September and October. Access to the show, which at its most fun can be sudsy and the teeniest bit raucous, costs 24F ($20); access to the show that includes a fixed-price menu ranges from 42F to 70F ($34–$57), depending on the meal you order.

Interlaken's most intense doses of folk schmaltz take the form of the **Tellfreilichtspiele,** a secular version of a Teutonic morality play that's presented in an open-air amphitheater in Interlaken's suburb of Matten, a village en route to Grindelwald, reached after a brisk 15-minute walk from Interlaken's center. A sweeping cast of as many as 250 presents Schiller's pageant play *William Tell,* complete with galloping horses, flaming torches, flower-draped cows, apple-shooting scenes, and an all-German text delivered in the lilting diphthongs of the Schwyzerdeutsch accent. Tickets for the 2½-hour show cost 25F to 40F ($21–$33), and are available from **Tellbüro,** Bahnhofstrasse 5 (© **033/822-37-22**). The play is presented at 8pm every Thursday and Saturday between mid-June and early September. Bring a jacket or sweater, or rent one of the blankets from an on-site kiosk, as the alpine chill seems to enhance this epic tale of the struggle for Swiss independence from the tyranny of neighboring Austria.

EASY EXCURSIONS FROM INTERLAKEN

By making the mountains of the Bernese Oberland accessible by train and cable car, Swiss engineers paved the way for visitors to this popular region to explore some of the most scenic and enjoyable spots in the country. There are many organized excursions, as adventurous as they are varied, and Interlaken is the most sensible starting point.

JUNGFRAUJOCH ✻✻✻

A train trip to Jungfraujoch, at 3,400m (11,152 ft.), is often considered the trip highlight by visitors. For more than a century, it's been the highest railway station in Europe. It's also one of the most expensive: A round-trip tour costs 179F ($147) in first class, 167F ($137) in second class. However, families can fill out a Family Card form, available at the railway station, which allows children 16 and under to ride free. Departures are usually daily at 8am from the east station in Interlaken; expect to return around 4pm. To check times, contact the sales office of **Jungfrau Railways,** Höheweg 37 (© **033/828-71-11** or 033/828-72-33; www.jungfraubahn.ch).

With luck, you'll get good weather for your day trip; you should always consult the tourist office in Interlaken before boarding the train. The trip is comfortable, safe, and packed with adventure. First you'll take the Wengernalp railway (WAB), a rack railway that opened in 1893. It will take you to Lauterbrunnen, at 784m (2,572 ft.), where you'll change to a train heading for the Kleine Scheidegg station, at 2,029m (6,655 ft.)—welcome to avalanche country. The view includes the Mönch, the Eiger Wall, and the Jungfrau, which was named for the white-clad Augustinian nuns of medieval Interlaken (Jungfrau means "virgin").

At Kleine Scheidegg you'll change to the highest rack railway in Europe, the Jungfraubahn. You have 9.6km (6 miles) to go; 6.4km (4 miles) of that will be spent in a tunnel carved into the mountain. You'll stop briefly twice, at Eigerwand and Eismeer, where you can view the sea of ice from windows in the rock (the Eigerwand is at 2,830m/9,282 ft. and Eismeer is at 3,110m/10,201 ft.). When the train emerges from the tunnel, the daylight is momentarily blinding, so bring a pair of sunglasses to help your eyes adjust. Notorious among mountain climbers, the Eigernordwand (or "north wall") is incredibly steep.

Once at the Jungfraujoch terminus, you may feel a little giddy until you get used to the air. There's much to do in this eerie world high up Jungfrau, but take it slow— your body's metabolism will be affected and you may tire quickly.

Behind the post office is an elevator that will take you to a corridor leading to the famed **Eispalast (Ice Palace)** *. Here you'll be walking inside "eternal ice" in caverns hewn out of the slowest-moving section of the glacier. Cut 19m (62 ft.) below the glacier's surface, these caverns were begun in 1934 by a Swiss guide and subsequently enlarged and embellished with additional sculptures by others. Everything in here is made of ice, including full-size replicas of vintage automobiles and local chaplains.

After returning to the station, you can take the Sphinx Tunnel to another elevator. This one takes you up 107m (351 ft.) to an observation deck called the **Sphinx Terraces,** overlooking the saddle between the Mönch and Jungfrau peaks. You can also see the Aletsch Glacier, a 23km (14-mile) river of ice—the longest in Europe. The snow melts into Lake Geneva and eventually flows into the Mediterranean.

Astronomical and meteorological research is conducted at a scientific station here. There's a research exhibition that explains weather conditions, and a video presentation.

There are five different **restaurants** from which to choose. The traditional choice is Jungfraujoch Glacier Restaurant. Top of Europe, opened in 1987, offers several different dining possibilities, and there's also a self-service cafeteria. As a final adventure, you can take a **sleigh ride,** pulled by stout huskies.

On your way back down the mountain, you'll return to Kleine Scheidegg station, but you can vary your route by going through Grindelwald, which offers panoramic views of the treacherous north wall.

HARDER KULM **

For a somewhat less ambitious excursion, set out from Interlaken East for this belvedere at 1,301m (4,267 ft.). The funicular ride takes 15 minutes and costs 22F ($18) round-trip for adults and 11F ($9) for children. From the lookout, you can see Interlaken, the Bernese Alps, and the two lakes, Thun and Brienz, that give Interlaken its name. Departures are every half-hour daily from May until the end of October. The first funicular departs at 9:10am, the last one back leaving at 6pm (6:30pm July–Aug). There's a mountain restaurant at Harder Kulm, with observation terraces. For details, call *C* **033/828-72-16** or 033/822-34-44.

HEIMWEHFLUH *

You can also take the funicular trip up to Heimwehfluh, at 669m (2,194 ft.), where you'll be rewarded with panoramic views of both lakes and the classic trio of Jungfrau, Mönch, and Eiger. In addition to the lookout tower, there's a cafe and restaurant. The funicular station is about a 6-minute walk from the Interlaken West rail station at the southern end of Rugenparkstrasse. The ride takes about 5 minutes and costs 12F ($9.85) round-trip for adults, 7F ($5.75) for children. Departures are April to October daily from 9:30am to 5:30pm.

ST. BEATUS-HÖHLEN

According to legend, these caves in the cliffs above Lake Thun were once a dragon's lair until Beatus, a 6th-century Irish missionary, slew the beast and set up residence here. The caves came to be known as Grottes de St-Béat in French and St. Beatus-Höhlen in German. They can be reached by boat, bus, car, or even by foot.

The caves can be explored to a depth of 990m (3,247 ft.), along a path lit by electricity. There's a reproduction of a prehistoric cave settlement. The museum section also includes the cell of St. Beatus. Tours are available through the huge caverns and grottoes featuring the striking stalactites and stalagmites. The caves are open from April to October daily from 10:30am to 5pm. Tours depart every 20 to 30 minutes and cost 16F ($13) for adults and 6F ($4.90) for children. For details, call © 033/ 841-16-43.

Just inside the cave entrance is a well-managed restaurant. You can have a meal or a snack inside the cozy dining area or outside on the cave terrace.

The caves can be reached in a number of ways: The bus from Interlaken is the shortest route. From Interlaken bus station, take STI bus no. 21 for a 15-minute ride to the entrance of the caves. Round-trip tickets cost 5F ($4.10) and buses depart every hour at 15 minutes to the hour. You can drive from Interlaken taking N8 toward Thun. Follow signs leading to the caves. It's a half-hour boat ride to the caves from Interlaken West. The arrival spot is an approximately 20-minute walk from the caves' entrance. Tickets cost 5F ($4.10) round-trip. Walkers and hikers can make it a 2½-hour trip: Start at Interlaken West station and follow signs for the caves.

WILDERSWIL/SCHYNIGE PLATTE ✯✯✯

Less than 3km (2 miles) south of Interlaken, Wilderswil stands on a plain between Lakes Brienz and Thun, at the foot of the Jungfrau Mountains. It's both a summer resort and a winter resort, as well as the starting point for many excursions. The resort has 16 levels of accommodations, ranging from hotels to guesthouses, but most tourists stay in Interlaken and visit Wilderswil to take the excursion to **Schynige Platte** (© 033/822-34-31; www.schynigeplatte.ch). To get to Wilderswil, take the 6-minute train ride from the Interlaken East station. Switch to a cogwheel train for the harrowing, steep ascent to the Schynige Platte, at 1,936m (6,350 ft.). The rack railway, which opened in 1893, climbs the 7km (4½-mile) slope in less than an hour, with gradients of up to 25%. There are more than a dozen trips a day in season, June to October, costing 47F ($39) round-trip.

There's an alpine garden in Schynige Platte, containing some 500 species of plants; admission is 3F ($2.45). From a nearby belvedere, visitors command a splendid view of the Eiger, Mönch, and Jungfrau. The resort's restaurant offers good food and drink.

LAKE THUN ✯✯

Occupying an ancient terminal basin of a glacier, Lake Thun (Thunersee) was once connected to Lake Brienz (Brienzersee). The lake is 27km (17 miles) south of Bern and there is frequent rail service, which continues east to Interlaken. The Lutschine River deposited so much sediment at Interlaken that the one body of water eventually became two. Lake Thun, once beloved by Brahms, is 21km (13 miles) long and 3km (2 miles) wide.

Because of its mild climate, Lake Thun is known as the Riviera of the Bernese Oberland. Popular lake sports include water-skiing, yachting, and windsurfing. Onshore there are excellent swimming pools (indoor and outdoor), windsurfing schools, golf courses, tennis courts, horse stables, and caves.

The lake's major resort is **Thun,** a small city that was founded on an island where the Aare River flows out of Lake Thun. The city has since expanded onto the banks of the river to become the political and administrative center of the Bernese Oberland and the gateway to the Bernese mountains.

The most interesting part of the city is on the Aare's right bank. The busy main street, **Hauptgasse,** has walkways built above the arcaded shops. There's a 17th-century town hall on Rathausplatz, where you can climb a covered staircase up to the formidable **Schloss Thun (Castle Kyburg)** ✿. The castle is now a historical museum (✆ 033/223-20-01). It was built by the dukes of Zähringen at the end of the 12th century. Later it was the home of the counts of Kyburg, as well as the Bernese bailiffs. The massive residential tower has a large Knights' Hall, which contains a Gobelin tapestry from the time of Charles the Bold and a fine collection of halberds and other weapons. Other rooms have important archaeological finds, an exhibit of military uniforms, period furniture, and toys. From the turrets, there's a panoramic view of the surrounding area. The museum is open daily April to October from 9am to 6pm and November to March from 10am to 4pm. Admission is 6F ($4.90) for adults, 2F ($1.65) for children.

LAKE BRIENZ ✿

Lake Brienz, directly east of Interlaken, is the smaller of the two Oberland lakes. It's about 14km (9 miles) long and up to 3km (2 miles) wide. Most North American visitors bypass the many vacation areas and resorts along its shores in favor of the more traditional resorts on Lake Thun. Europeans, on the other hand, tend to prefer Lake Brienz.

The resort of **Brienz** is at the northern end of the lake, facing Giessbach Falls. The town is famous for its woodcarvers, whose work can be found in souvenir shops throughout Switzerland. It's also known for its violin makers.

Brienz has good rail links with Interlaken. Trains run in both directions every hour. For **train schedules** and information, call ✆ **0900-300-300.**

The town's most popular excursion is a cogwheel railway trip to **Brienzer Rothorn,** where you'll get a panoramic vista of the Bernese Alps and Lake Brienz. The tour requires about 2 hours and takes you to an elevation of 2,310m (7,577 ft.). Nine trips run each day from June to October. A round-trip costs 72F ($59) per person.

Giessbach Falls ✿✿, some of the most dramatic falls in the Bernese Oberland, are accessible by funicular, which leaves from a platform across the lake. You can get there by car or boat. The funicular costs 6F ($4.90) for adults, 3F ($2.45) for children 6 to 16, and is free for children 5 and under. The boat to the funicular departs from the lakeshore wharf in the center of Brienz. Allow about 2 hours for the entire excursion. For more information about excursions in the area, call the **Brienz Tourist Office** at ✆ **033/952-80-80.**

For a glimpse of Switzerland's rural history, you can visit the **Swiss Open-Air Museum of Rural Dwellings and Lifestyle** ✿ at Ballenberg, near Brienz (✆ **033/951-11-23**). This is a living, breathing museum—not a dusty, boring complex. Thirteen scenic areas, comprising more than 809 hectares (2,000 acres), lie within the jurisdiction of this museum; they include clusters of typical old farm buildings, tiny settlements, and gardens and fields that Swiss farmers cultivate using time-tested regional methods. The various sections of the museum, which include both a nature park and the still alpine waters of Lake Wyssen, are connected by good roads. The museum's acreage lies between the villages of Hofstetten and Brienzwiler, and various sections document architecture specific to different cantons and regions of Switzerland.

Lake Tours

A fleet of ships with a total capacity of 6,720 passengers operates on **Lake Thun** daily from April to October. A 4-hour voyage from Interlaken West to Beaten-bucht, Spiez, Overhofen, Thun, and back costs 60F ($49) in first class, 40F ($33) in second class.

Boat trips on **Lake Brienz** are also available daily from June to September. There are five motor ships and one steamship, with a total capacity of 3,160 passengers. A 3-hour voyage from Interlaken East to Iseltwald, Giessbach, Brienz, and back costs 48F ($39) in first class and 32F ($26) in second class. For details, call **B.L.S.** (© **033/334-52-11**).

A tour of the museum takes about 3 hours. It's open April 15 through October daily from 10am to 5pm. Admission is 16F ($13) for adults and 8F ($6.55) for children. Guided tours are available by request, but reservations are necessary; plus there's a minimum charge of 100F ($82).

For those driving to the museum, there's parking at the Hofstetten and Brienzwiler entrances. You can also take a train along the Interlaken-Meiringen-Lucerne line to the Brienz railroad station and transfer there for a bus to the museum.

MEIRINGEN ✦

This resort lies about 13km (8 miles) from Brienz and can be easily visited on a day trip from Interlaken. Several trains headed to Meiringen stop at Interlaken's two rail-way stations every day. Travel time each way is about 50 minutes.

Strategically centered between three alpine passes (the Grimsel, the Brunig, and the Susten), this old town is a suitable base from which you can explore the eastern sections of the Bernese Oberland and the wild upper reaches of the Aare River. Classified as the major town in the Haslital district and set above the waters of Lake Brienz, Meiringen is famous throughout Europe for its meringue, a dessert that was suppos-edly invented here.

Rich in scenery and wildlife, the district attracts mountaineers, rock climbers, and hikers. Surrounding the town, you'll find more than 298km (185 miles) of marked hiking trails through unspoiled natural settings, with a complicated network of lifts to reach panoramic vantage points. Destinations for excursions include the Aare Gorge, the Rosenlaui Glacier, and the Reichenbach Falls. The district also has a folklore museum, a crystal grotto, an antique water mill, and a pathway across a glacier. Almost everyone visits the parish church in the upper part of the village. Its crypt was built during the 11th century.

From Meiringen, you can set out for Grindelwald, a distance of some 27km (17 miles) and one of the great walks in the Jungfrau region. Along the way you can absorb the stunning panoramas of the massif, the Eiger, with its massive gray rock walls. Soaring summits and white glaciers form your backdrop as you walk along. If you get tired along the way, there are bus stops where you can board public transporta-tion to take you into Grindelwald. This is also an option should the weather turn bad. Otherwise, depending on your stamina, the walk takes from 6½ to 9 hours.

If you're in the mood for meringue, you can buy one or two at a local bakery. According to legend, the dessert was created when Napoleon visited the town and the local chef in charge of the welcoming banquet had a lot of leftover egg whites.

Inspired, he created the puffy mounds and served them in a saucer brimming with sweet mountain cream, much to the general's delight.

Aare Gorge ⟨✶✶⟩ is full of recesses, grottoes, precipices, and arches—all fashioned by the Aare's waters over centuries. The cleft is 1,371m (4,497 ft.) long and 195m (640 ft.) deep, carved in the Kirchet, a craggy barrier left over from the ice age. In some places the towering rock walls of the gorge are so close together that only a few rays of sunshine can penetrate, just before noon. A unique natural wonder of the Swiss Alps, the gorge can only be reached by car, via the Grimsel-Susten road along the Kirchet. Admission is 6F ($4.90) for adults and 3.50F ($2.85) for children. The gorge is open May to October daily from 10am to 5pm; in July and August its extended hours are from 8am to 6pm.

If you're a fan of Sherlock Holmes, you'll enjoy an excursion to **Reichenbach Falls** ⟨✶⟩, where the rivers of the Rosenlaui Valley meet. The impressive beauty of the falls has lured many visitors, beginning with the British in the 19th century. One visitor, Sir Arthur Conan Doyle, creator of Holmes, was so impressed with the place that he used it as the setting for the scene in *The Final Problem,* in which the villain, Professor Moriarty, struggles with the detective and tosses Holmes into the falls. You can see a Sherlock Holmes commemorative plaque near the upper station of the funicular. The falls can be visited from mid-May to mid-September. The funicular takes you to a point at 834m (2,734 ft.) near terraces overlooking the water. Handrails provide safety. Departures are every 10 minutes daily from 8:15 to 11:45am and 1 to 6pm. The cost of admission is 7F ($5.75) for adults and 3.50F ($2.85) for children. The price includes the cost of the funicular. It's a 10-minute walk from Meiringen to the base of the funicular. If you're driving from Meiringen, take the road to Grimsel and turn right toward Reichenbach Falls and Mervenklinik. For more information, call ✆ **033/971-40-48.**

The Murder of Sherlock Holmes

In 1891 the English writer Sir Arthur Conan Doyle, creator of the most famous detective in all fiction, Sherlock Holmes, acted too hastily in killing off his fictional hero. In a story entitled *The Final Problem,* after a battle with Professor Moriarty (called "the Napoleon of Crime"), Holmes and the fiendish villain were sent plunging to their deaths into Reichenbach Falls at Meiringen.

Although the Sherlock Holmes stories had proven successful, Conan Doyle apparently decided that he'd had enough of Sherlock's sleuthing. His rather outraged public disagreed, so Conan Doyle was forced to virtually call back Sherlock Holmes from the dead, and the detective went on to solve at least 60 more crimes.

The wonder of the falls is reason enough to visit the site, but Holmes devotees wanted more, so in May 1991 the town leaders opened a **Sherlock Holmes Museum,** Bahnhofstrasse 26 (✆ **033/971-42-21**), in an old Anglican church at Meiringen. There, you can visit a re-creation of Sherlock Holmes's sitting room at 221B Baker St. in London, with exhibits donated by fans from around the world. The museum is open May through September Tuesday to Sunday from 1:30 to 6pm, and October to April Wednesday to Sunday 4:30 to 6pm. Admission costs 4F ($3.30) for adults and 3F ($2.45) for children.

After admiring the cascade, you can hike through the river valley. The footpath through the **Rosenlaui Valley** is marked. After 90 minutes you'll arrive at the entrance to Rosenlaui Gorge. The surfaces of the sheer rock faces echo the sounds of the many small waterfalls within. The **glacier gorges** ✦, which have been hollowed out by the waters from the melting ice of the Rosenlaui Glacier, are a spectacular sight. You can walk from one end of this gorge to the other in about 30 minutes. A small hotel and seasonal restaurant are near the entrance. Most visitors turn around at the uppermost reaches of the gorge and make the 2-hour trek back to Reichenbach Falls to pick up the funicular back to Meiringen. The gorge can be visited May through October daily from 9am to 5pm. The cost is 6F ($4.90) for adults and 3.50F ($2.85) for children.

3 Mürren ✦✦

11km (7 miles) S of Lauterbrunnen; 30km (19 miles) S of Interlaken

This village has a stunning location, high above the Lauterbrunnen Valley. At 1,624m (5,327 ft.), Mürren is the highest year-round inhabited village in the Bernese Oberland. It's an exciting excursion from Interlaken in the summer and a major ski resort in the winter. Downhill and slalom skiing were developed here in the 1920s. Mürren is also the birthplace of modern alpine racing.

ESSENTIALS

GETTING THERE   Take the mountain railway from the Interlaken East rail station to Lauterbrunnen (trip time: 1 hr.). Once at Lauterbrunnen, you can take a cogwheel train the rest of the way to Mürren. Departures from Lauterbrunnen are every half-hour from 6:30am to 8:30pm daily, costing 9.80F ($8.05) one-way.

A regular postal-bus service goes once an hour from Lauterbrunnen to Stechelberg; the rest of the way you must travel by cable car, costing 31F ($25) round-trip. Departures are every half-hour, and the trip takes about 10 minutes.

Mürren is not accessible to traffic. You can drive as far as Stechelberg, the last town on the Lauterbrunnen Valley road, and switch to the cable car discussed above.

VISITOR INFORMATION   The **Mürren Tourist Information Bureau** is at the Sportzentrum (© **033/856-86-86**). There is no street plan—follow the clearly indicated signs to the various hotels and commercial establishments. The office is open Monday to Friday 9am to noon and 2 to 7pm, Saturday and Sunday 2 to 6:30pm.

OUTDOOR FUN
IN TOWN

There are miles of downhill runs in the area. Mürren, one of the finest ski resorts of Switzerland, provides access to the Schilthorn at 2,923m (9,587 ft.), the start of a 15km (9-mile) run that drops all the way to Lauterbrunnen. It also has one funicular railway, seven lifts, and two cable cars. A 1-day ski pass that includes the area around Schilthorn costs 55F ($45), a 7-day pass goes for 260F ($213). For cross-country skiers, there's a 12km (7½-mile) track in the Lauterbrunnen Valley, 10 minutes by railway from Mürren.

The alpine **Sportzentrum (Sports Center),** in the middle of Mürren (© **033/856-86-86**), is one of the finest in the Bernese Oberland. The modern building has an indoor pool, a lounge, a snack bar, an outdoor skating rink, a tourist information office, and a children's playroom and library. There are facilities for squash, tennis, and curling. Hotel owners subsidize the operation, tacking the charges onto your hotel

On the Trail of James Bond

The **Schilthorn,** with its aerial cableway and steep snow slopes, was the setting for the most exciting scenes in the film *On Her Majesty's Secret Service,* one of the classic Bond thrillers. The incomparable location, the dramatic view of ice-covered peaks, and the fact that the imposing summit house is accessible only by aerial cableway convinced United Artists to select the Schilthorn as the film site.

Between October 1968 and April 1969, an army of volunteers transformed the Schilthorn into the film's "Piz Gloria." A landing pad for helicopters was constructed that was also used as a curling rink in the film and now serves as a sun terrace. The film was the breakthrough that made Schilthorn the world-famous attraction it has become. Today the imitation-blood trails have long been washed away, the fake bodies carted off, and the revolving restaurant never really exploded. A James Bond video in the Touristorama reminds visitors of this spectacular scenic film adventure.

bill. Supplemental charges include 20F to 30F ($16–$25) per hour for tennis, 16F ($13) per 45-minute session for squash, 16F ($13) per 2 hours use of the sauna. The facility is usually open Monday to Friday from 9am to noon and 1 to 6:45pm, and from Christmas to April and July to mid-September also on Saturday from 1 to 6:30pm and Sunday from 1 to 5:30pm; but check locally as these times can vary.

NEARBY

The famous **Mürren-Allmendhubel Cableway** leaves from the northwestern edge of Mürren. From the destination, there's a panoramic view of the Lauterbrunnen Valley as far as Wengen and Kleine Scheidegg. Between mid-June and late August, the alpine meadows are covered with wildflowers. A walk in this hilly region might be a highlight of your trip to Switzerland. The cable car operates daily throughout the year from 8am to 5pm. However, there are annual closings for maintenance in May and November. It costs 12F ($9.85) per person round-trip. For information, call ☎ 033/826-00-07.

The most popular excursion from Mürren is a cable-car ride to the **Schilthorn** ✹✹✹, famous for its 360-degree view. The panorama extends from the Jura to the Black Forest, including the Eiger, Mönch, and Jungfrau. The Schilthorn is also called "Piz Gloria" after the James Bond film *On Her Majesty's Secret Service* (the most dramatic scenes in the movie were filmed here). Today Piz Gloria is the name of the revolving restaurant on-site. The summit is the start of the world's longest downhill ski race. The cable car to Schilthorn leaves every 30 minutes, and the round-trip costs 94F ($77). The journey to the top takes 20 minutes. For details, call ☎ **033/826-00-07.**

SHOPPING

Commercial real estate in Mürren is expensive, particularly since the terrain is so inhospitable and supplies have to be hauled up by cable car or helicopter. Consequently, many of the resort's store owners make it a point to cram as much as possible into their shops, hoping to catch impulse buyers during shopping sprees. Therefore, the rule is, don't make any assumptions that shops here won't have what you want, as they're deceptively all-encompassing. Two of the resort's most interesting shops combine displays loaded with both sporting equipment and handcrafts. These are **Sporthaus Abegglen** (© 033/855-12-45) and **Sporthaus Stäger** (© 033/855-23-55).

WHERE TO STAY
EXPENSIVE

Anfi Palace Hotel ⍟   Built early in the 20th century, this hotel lies under a black mansard roof and indented loggias with wrought-iron balconies. There's a modern extension jutting off to one side. A change of management in the early 1990s arranged the gradual renovation and improvement of this property, which underwent several name changes throughout the 1970s and 1980s. The bedrooms are the most spacious, best furnished, and also the most comfortable in Mürren. The beds are excellent, and the bathrooms are nicely maintained.

CH-3825 Mürren. © 033/856-99-99. Fax 033/856-99-98. www.muerren.ch/palace. 44 units. Summer 270F–330F ($221–$271) double, 350F ($287) suite, 400F–610F ($328–$500) apt; winter 300F–360F ($246–$295) double, 380F ($312) suite, 520F–660F ($426–$541) apt. Rates include buffet breakfast and dinner. Half board 35F–45F ($29–$37) per person extra. AE, DC, MC, V. **Amenities:** 3 restaurants; 2 bars (1 a club); indoor pool; Jacuzzi; sauna; limited room service; babysitting; coin-operated and laundry service/dry cleaning. *In room:* TV, dataport, minibar, hair dryer.

Hotel Eiger ⍟   Founded in the 1920s and last renovated in 1994, this chalet is the longest-established hotel in Mürren. The public rooms are warmly decorated, and many of the windows have panoramic views. The bedrooms are small, cozy, and comfortable and decorated in a typical alpine style. All units have tidy bathrooms. The hotel, managed by Annelis Stähli-von Allmen and family, lies across the street from the terminus of the cable car from Lauterbrunnen.

CH-3825 Mürren. © 033/856-54-54. Fax 033/856-54-56. www.hoteleiger.com. 44 units. 280F–320F ($230–$262) double; 370F–410F ($303–$336) triple; 460F ($377) quad. Rates include breakfast. AE, DC, MC, V. Closed Easter to early June and mid-Sept to Dec 19. **Amenities:** Restaurant; bar; indoor pool; sauna; limited room service; babysitting; laundry service/dry cleaning. *In room:* TV, dataport, hair dryer.

MODERATE

Hotel Alpenruh   Set in the most congested yet charming section of the village, the Alpenruh possesses an interior that's plusher than its chalet-style facade implies. The old building was upgraded in 1986 to government-rated three-star status without sacrificing any of its small-scale charm. The small rooms have pine paneling and a mix of antique and contemporary furniture, and most of them open onto a view of the Jungfrau. The hotel is owned by the company that operates the aerial cable cars to the Schilthorn's Piz Gloria, and you can get a voucher to have breakfast there.

CH-3825 Mürren. © 033/856-88-00. Fax 033/856-88-88. www.muerren.ch/alpenruh. 26 units. 180F–270F ($148–$221) double. 50% reduction for children 12 and under sharing parent's room. Rates include buffet breakfast. Half board 35F ($29) per person extra. AE, DC, MC, V. **Amenities:** Restaurant; bar; lounge. *In room:* TV, minibar, hair dryer.

Hotel Jungfrau/Haus Mönch   This government-rated, three-star, 19th-century building, located a 3-minute walk from the Mürrenbahn, lies under gables behind green shutters, stucco, and brick walls. A comfortable annex was constructed in 1965; both buildings have an inviting, modern decor with open fireplaces, clusters of armchairs, and a shared dining room. The small bedrooms are bright and appealing. Twenty of the rooms are in the Hotel Jungfrau and 29 are across the street in the lodge. Units are equal in comfort. All contain neatly kept bathrooms.

CH-3825 Mürren. © **033/855-45-45.** Fax 033/855-45-49. www.hoteljungfrau.ch. 49 units. 190F–210F ($156–$172) double; 240F–270F ($197–$221) triple; 320F ($262) quad. Rates include buffet breakfast. AE, DC, MC, V. Closed mid-Apr to late May and mid-Oct to mid-Dec. **Amenities:** Restaurant; bar; limited room service; laundry service. *In room:* TV, dataport.

WHERE TO DINE

Eiger Stübli ⚘ SWISS   The best food in Mürren is served here in a festive ambience. The Eiger Stübli's cuisine includes fondue and an international range of hearty and well-prepared specialties well suited to the alpine heights and chill. Main dishes include a delectable roast lamb shoulder with lentils, a whole sole from the grill, beef Stroganoff, a savory cheese fondue, a perfectly prepared roast breast of duck with orange sauce, or poached filet of trout. All main dishes may be ordered with rösti (Swiss hash browns). Dessert specialties include vodka sherbet and iced soufflé Grand Marnier.

In the Hotel Eiger. © **033/856-54-54.** Reservations recommended. Main courses 21F–50F ($17–$41). AE, DC, MC, V. Daily 11:30am–2pm and 6–9pm. Closed Easter to mid-June and mid-Sept to mid-Dec.

Hotel Alpenruh ⚘ FRENCH   This small hotel contains one of the finest restaurants in Mürren, offering a large and varied menu. The place is always a reliable bet for lunch or dinner, even during the rainy months of April and May and again in November when many of the other restaurants and hotels in Mürren are closed. Both its dining rooms have attractive alpine themes and wide terraces with a panoramic view of the surrounding mountains. Appetizers include dried tomato strips with sage butter and tortellini with ricotta. You can dive enthusiastically into such dishes as veal steak with a Dijon mustard sauce and lamb cutlet with a garlic-herb sauce. The steaks are delectable. The fish courses may include sole Colbert and anglerfish medallions with jumbo shrimp. For dessert, try the fresh pineapple with caramel mousse or a gratiné of kiwi and oranges.

In the Hotel Alpenruh. © **033/856-88-00.** Reservations recommended in winter. Main courses 16F–39F ($13–$32); fixed-price menu 40F ($33). AE, DC, MC, V. Daily 7am–11pm.

Restaurant im Gruebi SWISS   This popular restaurant offers a sunny outdoor terrace on the lobby level of the Hotel Jungfrau. The large hexagonal dining room has views of the mountains and ski slopes. You get authentic Swiss flavor here and first-rate ingredients. Some specialties are prepared for two, including chateaubriand, New York steak, rack of lamb flavored with herbs, and veal filets with fruits in a cognac sauce. It also offers the classic fondue bourguignon. Ten different types of rösti are served, including the classic Jungfrau version—ham, tomatoes, and raclette cheese. The chef also features what he calls "week-hits," a different specialty every night. One night may feature a salad and an all-you-can-eat array of meat fondues. Another night may be pasta night, grill night, and so on. There's even a cheese night, featuring raclette, fondues, and various types of Swiss cheese preparations.

In the Hotel Jungfrau. © **033/855-45-45.** Reservations recommended in midwinter. Main courses 24F–36F ($20–$30); fixed-price menu 34F ($28). AE, DC, MC, V. Daily 7:30am–9:15pm. Closed mid-Apr to mid-June and mid-Oct to mid-Dec.

Restaurant Piz Gloria ⚘ *Finds* SWISS   Piz Gloria is the most dramatically located restaurant in Europe, with a setting so inhospitable and an architecture so futuristic that it was used as the setting for the James Bond film *On Her Majesty's Secret Service.* Designed like a big-windowed flying saucer and anchored solidly to the alpine bedrock, it was built at staggering expense in one of Switzerland's highest locations, the Schilthorn. Closed during blizzards, the restaurant has a terrace where newcomers should beware of becoming seriously sunburned by the rays of the high-altitude, unfiltered sunlight. You'll dine inside at long wooden tables, each with a wraparound view. The menu includes hearty dishes suited to the climate. There are both weekly and daily specials, ranging from chicken *cordon bleu* to filet of codfish with rice and vegetables. One spaghetti dish is named for James Bond; it's made with peppers, mushrooms, bacon, and Italian veal sausages. Another dish often served is puff pastry filled with veal and served with a white sauce. The 007 for dessert is a bowl of five different scoops of ice cream topped with fruits.

Schilthorn. © 033/856-21-40. Main courses 12F–43F ($9.85–$35); daily special 22F ($18). AE, DC, MC, V. Daily from the 1st cable car's arrival until the last cable car's afternoon departure. The first departure from Stechelberg is at 7:25am in summer and at 7:55am in winter. The cable car's last departure from Schilthorn's summit is at 6pm in summer and 5pm in winter. Closed Nov 15–Dec 4 and 1 week after Easter. The only access is via the Schilthorn cable car, which departs from the relatively low-lying town of Stechelberg and stops at 3 way stations, the most prominent of which is Mürren. Round-trip fare from Stechelberg 89F ($73); round-trip fare from Mürren 60F ($49).

MÜRREN AFTER DARK

Every hotel in Mürren contains a bar offering maximum amounts of alpine coziness. Two that deserve special mention, however, are the **Bliemlichäller,** a sudsy, popular, and sometimes raucous disco in the Hotel Blumental (© **033/855-18-26**); and an equivalent disco, the **Inferno-Bar,** in the Hotel Palace (© **033/856-99-99**). Both open in the late afternoon, then crank up in midwinter and midsummer around 10:30pm into roaringly high-energy discos. More correctly perceived as a pub for après-skiing or après-hill climbing is the winter-only **Tächibar** in the Hotel Eiger (© **033/855-13-31**).

4 Wengen (★ (★ (★

26km (16 miles) S of Interlaken; 5km (3 miles) NE of Mürren

The Mönch, Jungfrau, and Eiger loom above this sunny resort town built on a sheltered terrace high above the Lauterbrunnen Valley, at about 1,248m (4,093 ft.). Wengen (pronounced *Ven*-ghen) is one of the more chic and better-equipped ski and mountain resorts in the Bernese Oberland. It has 30 hotels in all price categories, as well as 500 apartments and chalets for rent.

In the 1830s, the International Lauberhorn Ski Race was established here. At that time Wengen was a farm community. The British were the first to popularize the resort, after World War I. Today parts of the area retain their rural charm. The main street, however, is filled with cafes, shops, and restaurants welcoming tourists. Robert Redford is a frequent visitor. No cars are allowed in Wengen, but the streets are still bustling with service vehicles and electric luggage carts.

ESSENTIALS

GETTING THERE   Take the train from Interlaken West to Wengen. Departures are every 45 minutes from 6:30am to 11:30pm, costing 14F ($11) one-way. After a stopover at Wengen, the train goes on to Kleine Scheidegg and Jungfraujoch. For **rail information,** call © **0900/300-300.**

If you're driving, head south from Interlaken toward Wilderswil, following the minor signposted road to Lauterbrunnen, where you'll find garages and open-air spaces for parking. You cannot drive to Wengen but must take the train (see above). You can park in one of the garages at Lauterbrunnen for 12F ($9.85) a day. Trains from Lauterbrunnen to Wengen leave at the rate of one every 15 minutes from 6am to midnight, costing 6.20F ($5.10) one-way.

VISITOR INFORMATION   There are no street names; hotels, restaurants, and other major establishments are signposted with directional signs, which make them relatively easy to find. The **Wengen Tourist Information Office** (© 033/855-14-14) is in the center of the resort. It's open mid-June to mid-September and mid-December to Easter only, Monday to Saturday 9am to noon and 2 to 5pm.

EXPLORING THE AREA

The **ski area** around Wengen is highly developed, with ski trails carved into the sides of Männlichen, Kleine Scheidegg, Lauberhorn, and Eigergletscher. A triumph of alpine engineering, the town and its region contain three mountain railways, two aerial cableways, one gondola, 31 lifts, and 250km (155 miles) of downhill runs. You'll also find a branch of the Swiss Ski School, more than 11km (7 miles) of trails for cross-country skiing, an indoor and outdoor skating rink, a curling hall, an indoor swimming pool, and a day nursery.

During the summer the district attracts hill climbers from all over Europe. The **hiking trails** are well maintained and carefully marked, with dozens of unusual detours to hidden lakes and panoramas. Wengen also has five public tennis courts available through the tourist office (see above), a natural skating rink (Natureisbahn), and a partially sheltered indoor rink (Kunsteisbahn). The hours these rinks keep are subject to change, so check with the tourist office for details.

NEARBY ATTRACTIONS   From Wengen and Grindelwald, there are a number of excursions up and down the Lauterbrunnen Valley. You can visit **Trümmelbach Falls** ᏬᏬᏬ , which plunges in five powerful cascades through a gorge. You can take an elevator built through the rock to a series of galleries (bring a raincoat). The last stop is at a wall where the upper fall descends. The falls can be visited from the end of May through June and in September and October daily from 9am to 5pm; in July and August daily from 9am to 5:30pm. They're closed during other months. Admission is 10F ($8.20) for adults, 4F ($3.30) for children 6 to 16, and free for children 5 and under. It takes about 45 minutes to reach the falls on foot. For information, call © 033/855-32-32. A postal bus from Lauterbrunnen (only 15 min. from Wengen by train) stops at Trümmelbach Falls. It costs only 3F ($2.45) for adults, 2F ($1.65) for children, and departs once an hour from Lauterbrunnen. For information, call © **033/828-70-38.**

You might also want to visit the base of the **Staubbach Waterfall** ᏬᏬ , which plunges nearly 300m (984 ft.) in a sheer drop over a rock wall in the valley above Lauterbrunnen. Lord Byron compared this waterfall to the "tail of the pale horse ridden by Death in the Apocalypse." Staubbach can be reached from the resort village of Lauterbrunnen, which lies only 15 minutes from Wengen by train (see "Essentials," above). From the center of Lauterbrunnen, follow the signposts along a walkway running along a creek and then be prepared for some steep stairs to reach the viewing point for the falls.

SHOPPING

Despite its proximity to the wide open spaces of the big-sky Alps, don't be disappointed by the distinctly nonalpine-looking shops here. The well-recommended **Boutique zur Vase,** Dorfstrasse (© 033/855-26-27), offers fragile and exquisite cutlery, porcelain, and flatware. Two of the town's most successful shops for ski and other sports equipment are **Alpia Sport,** Dorfstrasse (© 033/855-26-26), and **Central Sport,** Dorfstrasse (© 033/855-23-23). If you're interested in capturing the scenery that unfolds on all sides, head for **Foto-Haus,** Dorfstrasse (© 033/855-11-54). In addition to film and cameras, it also sells one of the town's widest rosters of hand-crafted souvenirs to commemorate your stay in the Oberland.

WHERE TO STAY

All the hotels in Wengen are mobbed most of the winter, so make reservations if you plan to arrive during ski season.

Hotel Alpenrose ✶✶ A longtime favorite of ours, this hotel is invitingly traditional with a family atmosphere. Most of the cozy, well-furnished bedrooms have views over the Lauterbrunnen Valley, lots of light, and plenty of pine paneling. Accommodations facing south are slightly higher in price and more desirable because they get more sunlight. The hotel is efficiently run and filled with cozy public rooms and a large formal dining area where, if you've been gathering wildflowers that day, you'll probably find them in a vase at your supper. In ski season, fans of this hotel, all sports lovers, fill up the rooms. Staying on-site for your meals is hardly a hardship, as the food is well prepared with fresh ingredients whenever possible. Old favorites pepper the menu, including fondue bourguignon, trout with almonds, and terrine maison. Other than skiing, winter sports include curling, tobogganing, and hiking.

CH-3823 Wengen. ☎ 033/855-32-16. Fax 033/855-15-18. www.alpenrose.ch. 50 units. Summer 214F–338F ($175–$277) double; winter 244F–394F ($200–$323) double. AE, DC, MC, V. **Amenities:** Dining room; bar; limited room service; nonsmoking rooms; rooms for guests w/limited mobility. In room: TV, safe.

Hotel Eiger ✶ Rustic timbers cover the walls and ceilings of this attractive hotel behind the railway station. Karl Fuchs and his family offer spacious, attractive rooms with balconies. The suites, which are rented on a weekly basis only, are often sold out a year in advance. All rooms come equipped with well-maintained bathrooms. There's a modern dining room with views of the Jungfrau massif and the Lauterbrunnen Valley. In the hotel lobby you'll find an inviting sitting area with a fireplace.

CH-3823 Wengen. ☎ 033/856-05-05. Fax 033/856-05-06. www.eigerhotel-wengen.ch. 33 units. Summer 235F ($193) double; winter 310F ($254) double. Rates include buffet breakfast. Half board 25F ($21) per person extra. AE, DC, MC, V. Closed mid-Apr to June 1 and Nov. **Amenities:** Restaurant; bar; laundry service. In room: TV, dataport.

Hotel Regina ✶✶ Wengen's most time-honored hotel lies in an embellished Victorian elephant of a building with balconies and lots of charm. Guido Meyer has been known to arrange unusual concerts for his guests (once, during our stay, a group of Oklahoma high school students gave a concert on the front lawn). One of the public rooms has a baronial carved-stone fireplace. The midsize to spacious bedrooms are comfortable and cozy, each well furnished and immaculately maintained. All units contain tidily kept bathrooms. Maintenance is high, as is the level of service.

CH-3823 Wengen. ☎ 033/856-58-58. Fax 033/855-15-74. www.wengen.com/hotel/regina. 90 units. Summer 320F ($262) double; winter 450F ($369) double. For a suite add 20F ($16) per person. Rates include half board. AE, DC, MC, V. Closed Oct 15–Dec 15. **Amenities:** 2 restaurants; bar; health club; sauna; room service; babysitting; laundry service. In room: TV, dataport, minibar, hair dryer.

Hotel Silberhorn ✶ Famous for the cluster of restaurants and nightclubs located on its first two floors, this first-class family-owned hotel also offers comfortable modern rooms filled with pine and chintz, many with wooden balconies, and a few with kitchenettes. The simple Victorian building has been modernly equipped. The most spacious, most comfortable, and most attractive rooms are in the older wing. The restaurants located here shine in midwinter.

CH-3823 Wengen. ℂ 033/856-51-31. Fax 033/855-22-44. www.silberhorn.ch. 71 units. Summer 206F–262F ($169–$215) double, 264F–345F ($216–$283) apt for 2, 326F–376F ($267–$308) apt for 4; winter 250F–388F ($205–$318) double, 402F–543F ($330–$445) apt for 3, 464F–604F ($380–$495) apt for 4. Children 5 and under stay free in parent's room. Rates include buffet breakfast. Half board 25F ($21) extra. AE, DC, MC, V. **Amenities:** 3 restaurants; nightclub (in winter only); bar (in winter only); Jacuzzi; sauna; salon; limited room service; babysitting; laundry service (and coin-operated); disco; hairdresser. *In room:* TV, dataport, minibar, hair dryer.

Sunstar Hotel   Originally constructed in 1910 as the Metropole Hotel, this present hostelry is from the mid-1970s. Today it's a government-rated four-star hotel in the heart of the village, with wraparound balconies and a modern design inspired by traditional alpine architecture. The Kirche family are the helpful hosts. The nice-size rooms are well furnished and comfortable, many opening onto balconies with panoramic views of the Alps. All units are equipped with well-kept bathrooms. Guests can relax in the spacious lounge with a fireplace or retreat to the hotel's cozy bar.

CH-3823 Wengen. ℂ 033/856-52-00. Fax 033/856-53-00. www.sunstar.ch. 76 units. Summer 228F–256F ($187–$210) double, from 284F ($233) junior suite; winter 252F–328F ($207–$269) double, from 328F ($269) junior suite. Rates include buffet. AE, DC, MC, V. Closed Easter to end of May and mid-Oct to mid-Dec. **Amenities:** Restaurant; bar; indoor pool; sauna; limited room service; babysitting; laundry service. *In room:* TV, dataport, minibar, hair dryer, safe.

Zum Bären *(Value)*   Looking for comfortable lodging and good views near the city center of Wengen? This cozy chalet inn, popular with families and backpackers alike, fits the bill. There are no fancy amenities here, but the accommodations are clean and most look out over the Swiss mountains. A buffet-style breakfast is served before guests depart to ski or take in the sights. If you're really on a budget, you can stay in one of two dorms that contain 10 communal beds. It will run you about 35F ($29) including breakfast.

CH-3823 Wengen. ℂ 033/855-14-19. Fax 033/855-15-25. www.baeren-wengen.ch. 14 units. Summer 130F–160F ($107–$131) double; winter 180F–200F ($148–$164) double. Rates include breakfast. AE, DC, MC, V. Closed mid-Oct to mid-Dec. **Amenities:** Restaurant; cafe. *In room:* No phone.

WHERE TO DINE

Arvenstube SWISS   This is a local favorite, with pinewood panels and a polite crew ready to serve you. The well-prepared menu may include smoked trout with horseradish, air-dried alpine beef, smoked breast of goose, Bernese-style beef with mushrooms, filet of fera (a lake fish), and veal steak Alfredo and morels. Three kinds of fondue are also offered. The fondue bourguignon is particularly stunning with 40 garnitures—you must order it a day in advance. The Valais-style braserade of beef cooks over a small flame at your table.

In the Hotel Eiger. ℂ 033/856-05-05. Reservations recommended. Main courses 15F–56F ($12–$46); fixed-price lunch 18F ($15), fixed-price dinner 56F ($46). AE, DC, MC, V. Daily 11am–2pm and 6–9:30pm (open all day in winter). Closed May.

Hotel Bernerhof Restaurant SWISS/ITALIAN   The Schweizers run this old family favorite with wine-red shutters. There's an alpine-themed bar, which fills up in the early evening with beer drinkers returning from the slopes. Hearty alpine food, including raclette and fondue, is served in the dining room. Several savory Italian dishes are also featured. Justifiably favorite dishes include grilled trout with horseradish sauce, Burgundy-style snails, and a delectable fondue bourguignon.

CH-3823 Wengen. ℂ 033/855-27-21. Reservations recommended (and sometimes required). Main courses 17F–44F ($14–$36). AE, MC, V. Daily 8am–11:30pm.

Hotel Hirschen Restaurant *(Finds)* SWISS   This quiet retreat at the foot of the slopes has true alpine flavor. The rear dining room is decorated with hunting trophies, pewter, and wine racks. Johannes Abplanalp and his family offer a dinner special called Galgenspiess—filet of beef, veal, and pork flambéed at your table. Other dishes include filet of breaded pork, rump steak Café de Paris, and fondue Bacchus (in white-wine sauce), *bourguignon* (hot oil), or *chinoise* (hot bouillon). A hearty lunch is *Winz-errösti*, consisting of country ham, cheese, and a fried egg with homemade rösti.

CH-3823 Wengen. © 033/855-15-44. Reservations recommended. Main courses 12F–47F ($9.85–$39); fixed-price menu 42F–77F ($34–$63). MC, V. Sat–Sun 11:30am–2:30pm; Wed–Mon 5–11pm (closed Mon in summer and Tues for nonguests all year). Closed mid-Apr to May and late Sept to Dec 15.

WENGEN AFTER DARK

Except for the **Disco Carrousel** in the Hotel Regina (© **033/855-15-12**), which is open only 1 week during ski championships and then 1 week over Christmas and New Year's, Wengen has only one disco, the popular **Disco Tiffany.** Set in the cellar of the Hotel Silberhorn (© **033/856-51-31**), near the arrival point for the cog-railway cars from Lauterbrunnen, it's small, crowded, and painted in tones of navy blue and black. Look for nightly openings between mid-December and early April, and openings on Friday and Saturday nights the rest of the year. No cover; show up after 10:30pm.

More reliable and prevalent than discos in Wengen are the resort's hard-drinking bars and sudsy pubs. The two wildest are the **Tanne Bar,** Dorfstrasse (no phone), across the street from the Sunstar Hotel; and **Sina's Pub,** Dorfstrasse (© **033/855-31-72**), where karaoke mics and monitors are pulled out from storage whenever things begin to look dull. An enduring favorite is the **Pickel Bar,** in the Hotel Eiger (© **033/856-05-05**). Set in a trapezoidal room lined with thick unfinished planks and stout timbers, it's illuminated with candlelight and can take all the punishment a rowdy core of skiers can dish out. At the **Hot Chili Peppers Bar,** Dorfstrasse (© **033/855-50-20**), there's drinking, flirting, and gossiping every night. One spot with touches of village-life kitsch is the **Kegelbahn Bar,** Dorfstrasse (© **033/856-68-68**). It contains three billiard tables, a bowling alley, and some dart boards. It's located in the cellar of Wengen's only movie theater.

5 Grindelwald ⋆⋆⋆

22km (14 miles) S of Interlaken; 192km (120 miles) SW of Zurich

The "glacier village" of Grindelwald, at 1,033m (3,388 ft.), is set against a backdrop of the Wetterhorn and the towering north face of the Eiger. It's both a winter and a summer resort.

Unlike Wengen and Mürren, it's the only major resort in the Jungfrau region that can be reached by car. Because of its accessibility, Grindelwald is often crowded with visitors, many of whom come just for the day.

Grindelwald is surrounded by folkloric hamlets, swift streams, and as much alpine beauty as you're likely to find anywhere in Switzerland. Although at first the hiking options and cable-car networks might seem baffling, the tourist office will provide maps of the local peaks and valleys and help clear up any confusion.

ESSENTIALS

GETTING THERE   The **Bernese Oberland Railway (BOB)** leaves from the Interlaken East station. The trip takes 35 minutes. Call © **0900-300-300** for information.

If you're driving, take the Wilderswil road south from Interlaken and follow the signs all the way to Grindelwald.

VISITOR INFORMATION   The resort doesn't use street names or numbers; instead of street names, hotel direction signs are used to locate places. If you're booked into a hotel or tourist home in Grindelwald, request a pass at your hotel that will entitle you to many discounts, especially on mountain rides.

The tourist office is at the **Sportszentrum,** on Hauptstrasse (✆ **033/854-12-12**). It's open July and August, Monday to Friday from 8am to 7pm, Saturday 8am to 5pm, and Sunday 9 to 11am and 3 to 5pm; September to June, Monday to Friday 8am to noon and 2 to 6pm, Saturday 8am to noon and 2 to 5pm.

THE GREAT OUTDOORS

For details about the tours below, including seasonal changes, consult the tourist office (see above).

GLACIER TOURS   The town maintains a sheltered observation gallery, adjacent to the base of the **Lower Grindelwald Glacier (Untere Gletscher),** that offers a close look at the glacier's ravine. The half-mile gallery stretches past the deeply striated rocks, which include formations of colored marble worn smooth by the glacier's powers of erosion. The gallery is easy to reach on foot or by car. Round-trip bus service is available from Grindelwald for 12F ($9.85), and there's a parking lot and restaurant nearby.

HIKING & MOUNTAIN CLIMBING   If you've come to Switzerland to see the Alps, Grindelwald and its surroundings offer dozens of challenging paths and mountain trails that are well marked and carefully maintained. Outdoor adventures range from an exhilarating ramble across the gentle incline of an alpine valley to a dangerous trek with ropes and pitons along the north face of Mount Eiger. The choice depends on your inclination and your skills. A map showing the region's paths and trails is available at the town's tourist office.

If you're adventurous enough to be tempted by peaks 3,900m (12,792 ft.) high or higher, or if you'd like to learn the proper way to climb rocks and ice, contact the **Bergsteigerzentrum** (✆ **033/853-52-00**), which lies adjacent to the Sunstar Hotel in Grindelwald. Far more modest in its scope is a 1-day hiking tour that's recommended to everybody capable of hiking in boots for 2 or 3 hours. After a scenic mountain train ride from Grindelwald to Eigergletscher, you'll be led by a local mountain guide to the Bergsteigerzentrum Grindelwald, a husky-breeding center. Then you'll hike along the foot of the north face of Mount Eiger. Along the way, your guide will narrate the history of this famous wall, providing interesting stories. Back down in Alpiglen, you can rest and enjoy a lunch of toasted cheese sandwiches. The train will transport you back to Grindelwald. Try to make reservations 2 to 3 days in advance.

Faulhorn, at 2,639m (8,796 ft.), is a historic vantage point from which you can view a panorama of untouched alpine beauty. Near the summit is the mountain hotel **Faulhorn Hotel** (✆ **033/853-27-13**), which has been here for over 150 years and can be reached in a 7-hour hike from Grindelwald. Less committed hikers usually opt for cable-car or bus transfers to Bussalp, to First, or to Schynige Platte, and then continue their hike on to Faulhorn from any of those three points. Hikes to Faulhorn from Bussalp take 2¾ hours; from First, 2½ hours; and from Schynige Platte, 4 hours.

A 30-minute ride on a six-passenger gondola ("bubble car") will take you to **First Mountain** ☆☆, at 2,134m (7,000 ft.). You can stop at the intermediate stations of Bort and Grindd as you cross the alpine meadows to the First Mountain terminal and sun terrace. You'll have many hiking possibilities into the neighboring Bussalp or Grosse Scheidegg area, and you can return by bus. An hour's brisk hike will take you to idyllic Lake Bachalp. Besides the 2½-hour trek to Faulhorn, you can trek on foot to the Schynige Platte in 6 hours. A round-trip gondola ride between Grindelwald and First costs 48F ($39). There's a large restaurant at First, **Bergrestaurant First** (© 033/ 853-12-84), where you can order lunch.

Grosse Scheidegg ☞, at 1,930m (6,330 ft.), is a famous pass between the Grindelwald and Rosenlaui valleys. You can hike here in 3 hours from Grindelwald, or take the bus for 40 minutes. Our preference is usually to take a bus to Grosse Scheidegg and then begin our hill walking away from the village traffic and crowds. Round-trip bus passage from Grindelwald to Grosse Scheidegg is 34F ($28) per person.

If you want to climb in the upper regions of the Oberland, you might consider this **itinerary:** Take a bus from Grindelwald to Grosse Scheidegg. Walk for 2½ hours from Grosse Scheidegg to **Schwartzwaldalp.** The peaks of the First and Wetterhorn will loom on either side of you. After a panoramic respite in Schwartzwaldalp, you can take a bus, which will retrace your steps, first to Grosse Scheidegg, then to Grindelwald. This excursion is only possible in the summer; the total bus fare is 40F ($33) per person. Also only in the summer, a short aerial cable-car ride will take you to **Pfingstegg,** at 1,369m (4,490 ft.), from which you can hike to the Lower and Upper Grindelwald glaciers. The round-trip cost is 16F ($13). A hike to **Baregg-Stieregg** (1 hr.) is highly recommended as a 1-day journey, as is the trek to **Banisegg** (2 hr.). You'll get a view of the Eismeer and the Fiescherwand, and they're both worth the hike.

An especially popular half-day hike from Grindelwald goes to **Milchbach,** where melting glacial ice forms a milk-colored stream laden with gravel sediment. After about an hour's climb from Grindelwald, you'll find yourself at the base of the Upper Grindelwald Glacier (Obere Gletscher). The Blue Ice Grotto, which is about 45 minutes' walking distance above the Milchbach, can be visited as part of the same half-day excursion. After your visit, you can return by either hiking back to Grindelwald or by climbing aboard any of the postal buses that connect the Blue Ice Grotto to Grindelwald at hourly intervals.

From Grindelwald, it's also easy to visit **Kleine Scheidegg** ☞☞, which is the departure point for the final ascent to Jungfraujoch by train. The rack-and-pinion railway from Grindelwald to Kleine Scheidegg costs 46F ($38) round-trip or 28F ($23) each way. For information on this and all trains departing from Grindelwald, call the **Grindelwald railway station** (© 033/828-75-40).

SKIING   In winter Grindelwald is one of the major ski resorts of Europe, perfect as a base for skiing in the Jungfrau ski region. It has 22 lifts, eight funiculars, a trio of cable cars, and more than 160km (100 miles) of downhill runs. Snowboarders and novice skiers are also welcome. It's a ski circus for all ages and various skills.

In the winter skiers take the cableway to **Männlichen,** at 2,200m (7,216 ft.), which opens onto a panoramic vista of the treacherous Eiger. From here there is no direct run back to Wengen; however, skiers can enjoy an uninterrupted ski trail stretching 7.2km (4½ miles) to Grindelwald. The cost of the Männlichen cable car (Grindelwald-Grund to Männlichen) is 33F ($27) each way, or 48F ($39) round-trip. For information, call the departure point for the **Männlichen Bahn** in Grindelwald (© 033/854-80-80).

SHOPPING

There are a lot more shops in Grindelwald than the seasonal local economy can sometimes support. Most of them line the crowded edges of the resort's main thoroughfare, a sometimes traffic-clogged highway. A half dozen of these shops specialize in sporting goods and ski equipment, many stockpiling inventory from prestigious, high-tech manufacturers from around Europe and North America. The best of them include **Buri-Sport,** Hauptstrasse (© **033/853-14-27**), and **Bernet Sport,** Hauptstrasse (© **033/853-13-09**). If you're in the market for a timepiece, **Casa Grande,** Hauptstrasse (© **033/853-50-15**), has a wide inventory of all kinds of Swiss watches and— to a much lesser extent—simple jewelry.

WHERE TO STAY
EXPENSIVE

Belvedere This is a vastly renovated government-rated four-star hotel dating from 1904. It once declined the offer of a higher rating from the Swiss government so that it could keep its prices within reason. It has the most spectacular view in Grindelwald, and its luxurious public rooms include a fireplace and comfortable armchairs. There's also another lounge for nonsmokers decorated in the antique Louis Philippe style with well-preserved old pieces and Bohemian crystal chandeliers. The attractive and spacious bedrooms all have balconies and private bathrooms. Twenty-two of the double rooms are classified as "luxury twins" or "junior suites." The hotel is a 5-minute walk from the center of the resort and easily accessible by the mountain railway systems.

CH-3818 Grindelwald. © 033/854-54-54. Fax 033/853-53-23. www.belvedere-grindelwald.ch. 57 units. 410F–430F ($336–$353) double; 460F–570F ($377–$467) junior suite for 2. Rates include half board. AE, DC, MC, V. Free parking. **Amenities:** 2 restaurants; bar; lounge; indoor pool; health club; Jacuzzi; sauna; limited room service; massage; babysitting; laundry service. *In room:* TV, dataport, minibar, hair dryer, safe, beverage maker.

Grand Hotel Regina Across from the Grindelwald train station, this hotel is part rustic and part urban slick and dates from the turn of the 20th century. It became a hotel in 1953 and still evokes the glamour of that era. The facade of the oldest part has an imposing set of turrets with red-tile roofs. One of the salons has Victorian chairs clustered around bridge tables, with sculpture in wall niches. The collection of art includes etchings, gouaches, and oil paintings. The large bedrooms, done in various styles, are comfortable and contain well-maintained bathrooms. These elegantly furnished rooms are your finest choice for a vacation here in either summer or winter. Most bedrooms enjoy panoramic views.

CH-3818 Grindelwald. © 800/223-6800 in the U.S. or 033/854-86-00. Fax 033/854-86-88. www.grandregina.ch. 90 units. 450F–560F ($369–$459) double; 660F–2,160F ($541–$1,771) suite. AE, DC, MC, V. Free parking outside, 17F ($14) in garage. Closed mid-Oct to Dec 18. **Amenities:** 2 restaurants; 2 bars; 2 pools (1 indoor); 2 tennis courts; health club; sauna; salon; limited room service; massage; babysitting; laundry service. *In room:* TV, dataport, minibar.

Romantik Hotel Schweizerhof Originally built in 1912 on the site of what had until then been an ironmonger's and blacksmith's shop, this spacious and gracious hotel sits on the main street of Grindelwald, close to the railway station, behind a facade of very dark wood that resembles an oft-expanded chalet. The public areas are comfortably outfitted with deep-upholstered wing chairs and sofas, and bedrooms have tile-sheathed bathrooms, carved-pine panels, comfortable furniture, and lots of folkloric charm. Staff is helpful and friendly.

CH-3818 Grindelwald. © 033/853-22-02. Fax 033/853-20-04. www.hotelschweizerhof.com. 52 units. 480F–690F ($394–$566) double; 719F–1,140F ($590–$935) suite. Rates include buffet breakfast. AE, DC, V. Closed Oct 5–Dec 20 and Apr 6 to late May. **Amenities:** 2 restaurants; bar; indoor heated swimming pool; health club; sauna; salon; limited room service; babysitting; laundry service/dry cleaning; nonsmoking rooms; bowling alley. *In room:* A/C, TV, dataport, minibar, hair dryer, safe, beverage maker, trouser press.

MODERATE

Best Western Hotel Derby   This is a large and modernized mountain chalet, rated three stars by the government. Peter and Christiane Märkle carry on the century-old family tradition. The present building, with a twin-peaked roof and several irregularly shaped balconies, dates from 1973. The pine-paneled bedrooms are brightly furnished and comfortable if a bit small. All contain well-kept bathrooms, which for the most part contain tub/shower combinations. The Derby offers some of the best restaurant and bar options in town.

CH-3818 Grindelwald. ✆ 033/854-54-61. Fax 033/853-24-26. www.bestwestern.ch. 70 units. 214F–264F ($175–$216) double; 310F–413F ($254–$339) triple; 248F–298F ($203–$244) junior suite. Rates include buffet breakfast. Half board 32F ($26) per person extra. AE, DC, MC, V. Free parking. **Amenities:** 3 restaurants; bar; sauna; limited room service; laundry service. *In room:* TV, dataport, minibar, hair dryer.

Hotel Eiger   This hotel looks like a collection of interconnected balconies from the outside, each on a different plane and built of contrasting shades of white stucco and natural wood. The interior is attractive, simple, and unpretentious, with lots of warmly tinted wood, hanging lamps, and contrasting lights. The small to midsize bedrooms are comfortable, well furnished, and alpine cozy. All are equipped with tidily kept bathrooms. Maintenance is high, and the hotel staff is extremely inviting and hospitable.

CH-3818 Grindelwald. ✆ 033/844-31-31. Fax 033/654-31-30. www.eiger-grindelwald.ch. 50 units. Summer 220F–340F ($180–$279) double, 280F–500F ($230–$410) suite; winter 300F–360F ($246–$295) double, 350F–510F ($287–$418) suite. Rates include buffet breakfast. Half board 35F ($29) per person extra. AE, DC, MC, V. Free parking outdoors, 6F–12F ($4.90–$9.85) in garage. **Amenities:** 2 restaurants; 2 bars; massage studio; sauna; salon; babysitting; laundry service. *In room:* TV, dataport, minibar.

Hotel Kreuz & Post ✿   This angular, modern hotel is ideally located on the main square of town, across from the Sports Center. The Konzett family takes advantage of the location by setting up an outdoor cafe on the sidewalk in front. The interior is decorated in part with 18th-century antiques and engravings. Many of the rooms have balconies. Ranging from small to midsize, the tidy units are traditionally furnished and equipped with neatly kept bathrooms. The welcome here is warm in any season. There's a sun terrace on the roof with a panoramic view of the mountains.

CH-3818 Grindelwald. ✆ 033/854-54-92. Fax 033/854-54-99. www.kreuz-post.ch. 42 units. Summer 260F–290F ($213–$238) double, 300F–440F ($246–$361) suite; winter 290F–400F ($238–$328) double, 330F–600F ($271–$492) suite. Rates include buffet breakfast. Half board 45F ($37) per person extra. AE, DC, MC, V. Free parking. **Amenities:** 2 restaurants; bar; lounge; fitness center; Jacuzzi; sauna; babysitting; laundry service. *In room:* TV, dataport, minibar, hair dryer.

Hotel Restaurant Steinbock *Value*   Mentioned as a tavern for the first time in chronicles in 1798, the rebuilt Steinbock basks in its tradition. It is a cozy, chalet-style, government-rated three-star hotel, just opposite the Sunstar Hotel and lying near the bottom of the First gondola leading to the First skiing area in winter or a hiking Valhalla in summer. The ski bus stop for Klein Scheidegg/Männlichen areas is located just next to the Steinbock. Completely rebuilt in 1992, the hotel is run by the Ponzio family, who also operate the on-site Pizzeria da Salvi, where the best pies in town emerge piping hot from a wooden stove. Bedrooms are small but handsomely and comfortably furnished in a modern alpine style. The hotel's Grappa Bar offers 100 different kinds of grappas.

CH-3818 Grindelwald. ✆ 033/853-89-89. Fax 033/853-89-98. www.steinbock-grindewald.ch. 22 units. 260F–280F ($213–$230) double. Rates include breakfast. MC, V. **Amenities:** Restaurant; bar. *In room:* TV, hair dryer.

Parkhotel Schoenegg   This hotel, established by the Stettler family in 1890, is today a modern expansive property. The bedrooms are cozy and comfortable, some with private balconies. Each is furnished in an alpine decor, and beds are excellent, as is the housekeeping. All units are also equipped with neatly kept bathrooms. The hotel's dining room serves French cuisine. Local ski runs terminate at the hotel; a lift to the ski school is close to the front door.

CH-3818 Grindelwald. © 033/854-18-18. Fax 033/854-18-19. www.parkhotelschoenegg.ch. 50 units. Summer 300F–330F ($246–$271) double; winter 320F–350F ($262–$287) double. Rates include buffet breakfast. AE, MC, V. Parking 8F–14F ($6.55–$11). Closed May and Nov. **Amenities:** Restaurant; bar; lounge; indoor pool; health club; sauna; limited room service; massage; babysitting; laundry service/dry cleaning. *In room:* Hair dryer, safe.

INEXPENSIVE

Central Hotel Wolter   It's more modern and boxy than the other hotels in town, but its central location just a few steps from several more expensive hotels makes it a solid and reliable choice. On the ground floor there's a popular outdoor cafe and a substantial restaurant. Upstairs is the reception area and a salon that resembles a room in a private home. It has armchairs, a few antiques, and a compact bar. The small bedrooms are simply decorated, all with comfortable beds and well-kept bathrooms.

CH-3818 Grindelwald. © 033/854-33-33. Fax 033/854-33-39. www.central-wolter.ch. 35 units. 170F–230F ($139–$189) double. Rates include buffet breakfast. Half board 40F ($33) per person extra. AE, DC, MC, V. Parking 5F ($4.10). Closed Nov 7–Dec 17. **Amenities:** 2 restaurants; bar; limited room service; free entrance to sports center. *In room:* TV, minibar, hair dryer.

Hotel Gletschergarten ☆ *Finds*   One of the oldest and most evocative hotels in town is this family-run (by the Breitensteins) hotel that originally opened in 1899 as a cafe and restaurant, and which by 1906 had become a full-fledged, full-service hotel. Ongoing renovations since then, especially the major refurbishment that took place in the summer of 1982, have kept the place looking spiffy. It sits at the eastern edge of the main street of Grindelwald, nearly adjacent to the town's church, behind a time-blackened wooden facade with lots of folkloric detailing. Bedrooms are tasteful and cozy, with views over the mountains and their permanent snowfields. Those on the corners of the building tend to be a bit larger than the others. Each has access to a balcony, which in midsummer is likely to be festooned with flowering plants. Expect goodly doses of cozy comfort at this place, as well as a gracious welcome. The food is very good and reasonably priced.

CH-3818 Grindelwald. © 033/853-17-21. Fax 033/853-29-57. www.hotel-gletschergarten.ch. 26 units. Winter and midsummer (July 5–Aug 22) 220F–230F ($180–$189) double; off season 190F–230F ($156–$189) double. AE, DC, MC, V. Closed late Mar to late May and early Oct to Dec 20. **Amenities:** Restaurant and bar (open to hotel residents only); sauna; steam room; solarium; coin-operated laundry facilities. *In room:* TV, hair dryer, safe.

Hotel Hirschen *Value*   In the government-rated three-star Hirschen, the Bleuer family offers one of the best values in town. The hotel, which has an attractive modern facade, is both comfortable and affordable with rooms in a variety of styles. Each is well furnished with good beds and equipped with neatly kept bathrooms.

CH-3818 Grindelwald. © 033/854-84-84. Fax 033/854-84-80. www.hirschen-grindelwald.ch. 28 units. 150F–220F ($123–$180) double. Rates include continental breakfast. Half board 30F ($25) extra. AE, DC, MC, V. Free parking outside, 8F ($6.55) in garage. Closed Nov–Dec 19. **Amenities:** Restaurant; bar; limited room service; laundry service; bowling alley. *In room:* TV, dataport.

Hotel Jungfrau Swiss Mountain Lodge   This establishment consists of two hotels, the Jungfrau (with 18 rooms, built in 1903) and the Crystal (with 29 rooms, built in 1972), located across the street from one another at the edge of the village, a 3-minute walk from the railway station. Both the reception area and the dining room, called "Mr. Chicken," are in the Jungfrau, but both offer clean, comfortable rooms at favorable prices with equal extras. The lounge has a view of the fierce north face of the Eiger, and it expands during warm weather onto an outdoor terrace. The bedrooms were recently renovated in a Canadian mountain lodge style. All come equipped with neatly kept private bathrooms, which mostly contain tub/shower combinations.

CH-3818 Grindelwald. ℂ **033/854-41-41**. Fax 033/854-41-42. www.jungfraulodge.ch. 47 units. Summer 110F–140F ($90–$115) double; winter 130F–170F ($107–$139) double. Rates include buffet breakfast. AE, DC, MC, V. Free parking. Closed Nov. **Amenities:** Restaurant; bar; lounge; limited room service; laundry service. *In room:* TV.

WHERE TO DINE
EXPENSIVE
La Pendule d'Or/Jägerstube ⚜ SWISS/FRENCH   Some of the best cuisine in Grindelwald is served in these two dining rooms. In La Pendule d'Or men must wear jackets and ties, but not in Jägerstube, an elegant version of a hunter's retreat, and our preferred choice. Typical dishes include poached eel with crayfish tails, French snails, Russian caviar, steak tartare, scampi flambéed with Chivas Regal, and aiguillettes of veal in a saffron sauce. The cooking, if not always sublime, is exceedingly professional. Flavors are balanced and ingredients are first rate. Both restaurants serve the same menu, but fondue is offered only in the Jägerstube. Service is formal and correct.

In the Grand Hotel Regina. ℂ **033/854-86-00**. Reservations recommended. Main courses 39F–110F ($32–$90); fixed-price menu 80F–110F ($66–$90). AE, DC, MC, V. La Pendule d'Or daily noon–2pm and 7–10pm. Jägerstube daily 7–10pm. Closed mid-Oct to Dec 18.

Restaurant Français ⚜⚜ INTERNATIONAL   This is the best restaurant in Grindelwald. The owner, Urs Hauser, is always in the dining room during meal hours to aid and advise diners. Special buffets are a feature of the restaurant. As you listen to the soothing sounds of a live pianist, you can study the menu (which will have changed by the time of your visit). Just to give you an idea, you may be served an appetizer of game terrine, Grindelwald air-dried meat, or thinly sliced lamb carpaccio. Fish dishes may include poached filet of turbot served on zucchini and potato rounds with a yellow-red pepper sauce or fried filet of salmon with a truffle butter sauce. Main dishes are likely to include lamb entrecôte in a coating of peppercorns or breast of guinea fowl with red wine and prunes. The cuisine intelligently blends flavors with imagination and zest. The cooks in the kitchen really know their stuff, and their wine list is among the finest in the area.

In the Hotel Belvedere. ℂ **033/854-54-54**. Reservations recommended. Main courses 28F–50F ($23–$41); fixed-price menu 56F–72F ($46–$59). AE, DC, MC, V. Daily noon–1pm and 6:45–9pm.

MODERATE
Il Mercato ITALIAN/SWISS   The decor is elegant and alpine, with Italian touches you might expect in the Ticino. The dining room's visual centerpiece is a large window with a sweeping view over the mountains. During warm weather, tables are set out on a terrace dotted with flowers. Menu items include virtually everything from the Italian repertoire, with an emphasis on cold-weather dishes from the Val d'Aosta (northern Italy's milk and cheese district). There is a tempting array of salads, pizzas, pastas, risottos, and grilled veal, beef, and chicken dishes, always with fresh ingredients.

In the Hotel Spinne. ℂ **033/854-88-88**. www.spinne.ch. Reservations recommended. Main courses 15F–47F ($12–$39). AE, DC, MC, V. Daily 11am–2pm and 6:30–11pm. Closed Oct to mid-Dec.

Restaurant Alte Post ☆ *(finds* SWISS   Often fully booked at least a day in advance, this Swiss, pine-paneled charmer serves traditional specialties, often to local residents of Grindelwald, with efficient service. Typical dishes include a terrine of morels, smoked filet of trout, asparagus with air-dried ham, filet steak with green peppers, scallop of veal cordon-bleu, and beef Stroganoff. Because of the first-rate cooking and the quality ingredients, this is one of the most satisfying choices in town.

CH-3818 Grindelwald. ☎ 033/853-42-42. Reservations required. Main courses 14F–47F ($11–$39). AE, MC, V. Thurs–Tues 11:30am–2pm and 6:30–9pm. Closed end of Oct to mid-Dec.

Restaurant Fiescherblick ☆ INTERNATIONAL   One of the best restaurants in town occupies a green-and-brown-toned dining room whose windows open onto a sweeping view over the mountains. Within an environment sheathed in wood paneling, with attentive and well-trained service rituals, you'll enjoy a menu that changes with the seasons, and which might include, depending on the day of your arrival, marinated duck liver with a compote of figs; roasted king prawns with salsa; and tournedos of local beef grilled beneath a layer of peppers served with truffle juice. Dessert may include selections from a cheese tray or a gratin of seasonal berries served with kirsch and mint-flavored ice cream.

In the Hotel Fiescherblick. ☎ 033/854-53-53. www.fiescherblick.ch. Reservations recommended. Main courses 14F–49F ($11–$40); fixed-price menu 35F–70F ($29–$57). AE, DC, MC, V. Daily 7–9:30pm. Closed mid-Oct to mid-Dec.

Restaurant Kreuz & Post SWISS/INTERNATIONAL   Explore this alpine restaurant before choosing a table. Tucked away in the corner is an attractive room, the Challi-Stube; the ceiling and paneling are especially well crafted. Everything in here is made of wood from a farmhouse that was torn down in 1748. The menu here is in English. Hearty alpine flavor and first-class ingredients characterize the cuisine. Typical appetizers are smoked salmon and oxtail soup. For a main course, steak, pork, and fish are offered, including blue trout sautéed in butter. For a traditional Swiss dish, try sliced veal Zurich style with rösti, or veal steak with a morel-cream sauce. The chef specializes in the two classic fondues, *chinoise* and *bourguignon,* served for two.

In the Hotel Kreuz & Post. ☎ 033/854-54-92. Reservations recommended. Main courses 15F–56F ($12–$46); 3-course fixed-price lunch 29F ($24); 5-course fixed-price dinner 48F ($39). AE, DC, MC, V. Tues–Sun 11:30am–1:30pm and 6:30–10:30pm. Closed Apr 14–May 21.

Restaurant Sportzentrum SWISS   This rustic, timbered dining room in the modern Sports Center is in the middle of the resort. Windows look down over an indoor swimming pool on one side and an enormous ice-hockey rink on the other. It opens early in the morning and serves snacks and drinks until late. The menu offers many Swiss specialties, including cheese fondue, beef bourguignon, and Wiener schnitzel. Come here for typically soul-satisfying Swiss food, each dish well prepared and reasonable in price too.

CH-3818 Grindelwald. ☎ 033/853-32-77. Reservations not accepted. Main courses 16F–40F ($13–$33). MC, V. Daily 7:30am–11:30pm.

INEXPENSIVE

Onkel Tom's Hütte PIZZAS & SALADS   Set within a rustic-looking A-frame house whose indestructible furniture and plank floors have seen thousands of snow-and-mud-covered boots tramping across its surface, this is Grindelwald's most visible and popular pizza place. There's a wide selection of beer and wine available, and a multilingual staff member will bring any of the three sizes of pizza to your amiably scarred and battered table. Varieties of pizza include the Onkel Tom (tomatoes, cheese, pepperoni, and assorted vegetables), the Rustica (tomatoes, cheese, broccoli, and garlic), and an Al Capone (tomatoes, cheese, braised leeks, bacon, and onion).

At the top of Hauptstrasse, near the Firstbahn cable-car station. ℂ **033/853-52-39**. Reservations not accepted. Pizzas 10F–29F ($8.20–$24); salads 7F–12F ($5.75–$9.85). MC, V. Daily noon–2:30pm and 3:30–10:30pm. Closed Nov and June.

GRINDELWALD AFTER DARK

After sundown Grindelwald transforms itself into one of the liveliest towns in the Bernese Oberland. In addition to the following choices, many of the hotels sponsor get-together parties at least once a week for residents, and each contains at least one bar. Bars that are noteworthy in their attempts at aggressively searching out the patronage of non-residents include the **Cava Bar,** in the Derby Hotel (ℂ 033/854-54-61). From their site near the railway station, they throw in the occasional live band. The **Challi Bar,** in the Hotel Kreuz & Post (ℂ **033/854-54-92**), does a roaring business—mostly from drinkers, less so from dancers—inside what looks like the re-creation of an alpine barnyard lined with roughly textured planks. Both bars are only open in the winter.

Don't be fooled by the name of the **Espresso Bar,** in the Hotel Spinne (ℂ 033/854-88-88), a cramped, hot, and crowded venue with the inner walls of a log cabin and a penchant for suds and schnapps. Only a handful of its clients actually opt for coffee. The same hotel is the site of everybody's favorite ethnic hideaway, the **Disco Mescalero.** Here, tacos, tortillas, and refried beans are served until around 10pm, after which lots of very danceable music is unleashed. Over the summer, the Mexican restaurant is closed; the disco, however, still opens 3 days a week. Offhandedly elegant is **Regina Bar,** the entertainment focal point of the Grand Hotel Regina (ℂ 033/854-86-00), and **Le Plaza-Club,** a prosperous-looking disco favored by prosperous-looking people in the Hotel Sunstar (ℂ 033/854-77-77). A replica of a smoke-stained English pub on the street level of the Bellevue Hotel, Hauptstrasse, is **Ye Olde Spotted Cat** (ℂ 033/853-12-34). Finally, the **Gepsi-Bar,** in the Hotel Eiger (ℂ 033/854-31-31), is appealingly conducive to dialogue and flirtation. There's no dancing here, but musicians sometimes arrive to perk things up a bit.

6 Kandersteg ⊛

26km (16 miles) S of Spiez; 43km (27 miles) SW of Interlaken

Lying between Grindelwald and Gstaad, Kandersteg is a popular resort at one of the southern points of the Bernese Oberland. It's a tranquil, lovely mountain village with rust- and orange-colored rooftops and green Swiss meadows. The summer and winter resort is spread over 4km (2½ miles), so nothing is ever too crowded. The village itself lies at the foot of the Blumlisalp chain (3,600m/11,808 ft.) and provides access to six remote alpine hamlets.

Kandersteg developed as a resting point on the road to the Gemmi Pass, which long ago linked the Valais with the Bernese Oberland. The village still has many old farmhouses and a tiny church from the 16th century. It's very proud of its traditions.

ESSENTIALS

GETTING THERE   Kandersteg is at the northern terminus of the 15km (9-mile) **Lotschberg Tunnel,** which, ever since the beginning of World War I, has linked Bern with the Rhône Valley. The railroad that runs through the tunnel can transport cars.

Trains leave every 30 minutes; no reservations are necessary. The resort is also served by the Berne-Lotschberg-Simplon railway. Call © **0900/300-300** for **rail information.**

If you're driving from Interlaken, take N8 west to Spiez, where the Kandersteg road then heads south into the mountains. The journey from Spiez to Kandersteg takes only 20 minutes along the well-built road.

VISITOR INFORMATION   In lieu of street names, directional signs are used. All guests who have a room in Kandersteg are given a **Visitor's Card,** entitling them to certain price reductions, including a discount on the town's network of cable cars.

Kandersteg Tourist Office, Hauptstrasse, CH-3718 Kandersteg (© **033/675-80-80**), dispenses information Monday to Friday from 8am to noon and 2 to 6pm.

EXPLORING THE AREA
IN TOWN

In summer qualified riders in proper clothes can rent horses at the local riding school at the **Royal Park Hotel** (see below). For walkers, there's an extensive network of level footpaths and strategically located benches around Kandersteg. These paths are open year-round.

In winter the resort attracts cross-country skiers and downhill novices (top-speed skiers go elsewhere). It has a cable car, two chairlifts, and four ski tows; the National Nordic Ski Center offers a ski-jumping station. The 2km (1½-mile) cross-country ski trail is floodlit in the evening. Other facilities include an indoor and outdoor ice rink.

If you select Kandersteg for your winter vacation, don't expect the breadth and diversity of ski slopes that are available in the much larger, more varied Jungfrau region accessible from Wengen, Mürren, Interlaken, and Grindelwald. Kandersteg's ski trails lie on the slopes of a bowl-shaped depression whose sides slope down into the waters of Oeschinensee, and incorporate 13km (8 miles) of downhill runs, 76km (47 miles) of cross-country trails, and eight ski lifts, three of which are short "baby lifts" for beginners. Adults pay 66F ($54) for a 2-day pass, 144F ($118) for a 5-day pass, and 191F ($157) for a 7-day pass. Skiers looking for more far-flung pastures can add access to the Lauchernalp slopes, a neighboring, narrowly defined, and somewhat limited network of ski slopes, for a supplement of around 20%.

Discounts of around 10% are offered to seniors over age 62, and discounts of between 20% and 50% are available to children, depending on their ages and whether they buy their passes in conjunction with passes sold to their parents or guardians.

NEARBY

The most popular excursion from Kandersteg is to **Oeschinensee (Lake Oeschinen)** ⟨✹✹✹⟩, high above the village. The lake is surrounded by the snow-covered peaks of the Blumlisalp, towering 1,800m (5,904 ft.) above the extremely clear water. You can walk to it from the Victoria Hotel or take a chairlift, costing 17F ($14) round-trip or 12F ($9.85) one-way, to the Oeschinen station and walk down from that point. If you opt to walk, allow about 1½ hours, or 2 hours if you'd like to stroll. Many visitors who take the chairlift decide to hike back to Kandersteg. Be warned, however, of the steep downhill grade.

Another popular excursion is to the **Klus Gorge** ⟨✹✹⟩. Park your car at the cable station's lower platform at Stock and walk 3km (2 miles) to the gorge, which was formed by the abrasive action of the Kander River. The rushing water creates a romantic, even primeval, setting. However, watch your step—the path gets very slippery in places.

The spray coats the stones and pebbles and has fostered a layer of moss. There's a tunnel over the gorge. During the winter the access route is icy and dangerous.

SHOPPING

Kandersteg's small size doesn't allow for too many shops, but of the limited number available, the best include **Käthy Sport,** Hauptstrasse (© **033/675-16-09**), which is in two connected buildings. The smaller is a century-old house dispensing folkloric Oberland souvenirs (woodcarvings, glass, ceramics, textiles, and the like); the larger sells sporting equipment, with emphasis on hill climbing and skiing. Its most appealing competitor is **Grossen-Sport,** Hauptstrasse (© **033/675-00-16**), where special emphasis during warm-weather months is on tennis equipment and mountain bikes, and, in winter, on ski and ice hockey equipment.

WHERE TO STAY & DINE
EXPENSIVE

Royal Park Hotel 🐾🐾🐾   The brown-and-white facade of this four-story hotel doesn't adequately convey the luxury you'll find inside. One of the finest hotels in Switzerland, it has been owned by the Rikli family for three generations. The interior has flagstone floors covered with dozens of Oriental rugs, Louis XIII–style armchairs, a collection of antiques, and rococo lighting fixtures. Around the fireplaces are clusters of carved armchairs covered with gray brocades. The spacious bedrooms are sumptuous, each individually furnished in a classical style with soft colors; large windows open onto views. All the bathrooms have been recently redone with deluxe appliances.

The lovely grounds include gardens, evergreens, and lawns. From the back garden, there's a mountain vista. In summer, hiking excursions are arranged, and guests can ride one of the many horses or bicycles. If you love horses, bring your riding clothes and boots. The hotel operates at least three impressive boats—both motorized and sailing craft—which are moored nearby and are available for the use of hotel guests. Lake Thun is 10 minutes away. In winter alpine and cross-country skiing are available.

CH-3718 Kandersteg. © **800/874-4002** in the U.S. or 033/675-88-88. Fax 033/675-88-80. www.royalkandersteg.com. 31 units. 360F–700F ($295–$574) double; 600F–820F ($492–$672) junior suite; 700F–1,160F ($574–$951) suite. AE, DC, MC, V. Free parking outside, 20F ($16) in garage. Closed Mar 26–May and Oct–Dec 17. **Amenities:** 3 restaurants; bar; 2 pools (1 indoor); tennis courts; health club; Jacuzzi, sauna; bike rental; salon; 24-hr. room service; massage; babysitting; laundry service; horseback riding. *In room:* TV, dataport, minibar, hair dryer, safe.

MODERATE

Chalet-Hotel Adler 🐾   An open fire crackling in the foyer sets the tone of this warm, cozy inn. A wood-sided chalet originally built in 1906 and rebuilt in 2002, it's set on the main street near the center of town. The fourth-generation owner, Andreas Fetzer, and his Finnish-born wife, Eija, offer comfortable midsize bedrooms paneled in pinewood, each with a tidily kept bathroom. Most accommodations open onto a private balcony; six rooms have Jacuzzis, and two offer a private fireplace. The Adler-Bar, which fills most of the ground floor, is one of the most popular après-ski hangouts in town.

CH-3718 Kandersteg. © **033/675-80-10.** Fax 033/675-80-11. www.chalethotels.ch. 24 units. Feb–Mar and July–Sept 180F–210F ($148–$172) double; off season 170F ($139) double. Rates include buffet breakfast. Half board 30F ($25) per person extra. AE, DC, MC, V. Free parking. Closed Nov 22–Dec 27. **Amenities:** 2 restaurants; bar; exercise room; sauna; room service; laundry service. *In room:* TV, dataport, minibar, hair dryer.

Hotel Victoria Ritter 🐾*Kids*   This is a longtime favorite. The original part of this hotel was built as a coaching inn in 1789 and named the Ritter (knight), after a local nobleman. In 1912 the Victoria, a larger and more opulent hotel, was added. Today the two hotels form a single architectural unit, and although much of the interior has been modernized, they still retain their original exterior detailing. The midsize bedrooms are contemporary, with neatly kept bathrooms. The premises boast a kindergarten for small children as well.

CH-3718 Kandersteg. ℂ 033/675-80-00. Fax 033/675-81-00. www.hotel-victoria.ch. 75 units. 170F–270F ($139–$221) double; 230F–290F ($189–$238) family apt; 250F–290F ($205–$238) junior suite. Rates include buffet breakfast. Half board (minimum 2 days) 35F ($29) per person extra. AE, DC, MC, V. Free parking. Closed mid-Oct to mid-Dec. **Amenities:** Restaurant; bar; pool; 2 tennis courts; limited room service; massage; babysitting; laundry service/dry cleaning; kindergarten. *In room:* TV, dataport, hair dryer.

INEXPENSIVE

Hotel Alpenblick   Built in 1902, this small chalet in the center of town is a 5-minute walk from the train station. Though small, bedrooms are traditionally furnished with alpine comfort, each with tidy bathroom. Register for your room near the bar of the locally popular hotel brasserie, the Oberlanderstube. The owner plays the clarinet, and his band performs on Friday nights during the busy season.

CH-3716 Kandersteg. ℂ 033/675-11-29. Fax 033/675-21-29. 12 units. 90F–110F ($74–$90) double. Rates include continental breakfast. AE, DC, MC, V. Free parking. **Amenities:** Brasserie; bar; lounge. *In room:* No phone.

KANDERSTEG AFTER DARK

Every hotel in the region offers at least one comfortable, often panoramic showcase, usually with a blazing fireplace, perfect for a drink or two on starry evenings. Two of the most convivial and animated deserve mention. The **High Moon Pub,** in the Hotel Alfa-Soleil (ℂ **033/675-84-84**), is a faithful replica of an English pub, replete with battered paneling, billiards, darts, and hints of the Edwardian age. At least twice a month, and sometimes more often, when business justifies the effort, the site is transformed into a disco. The **Adler-Bar,** in the Hotel Adler (ℂ **033/675-80-10**), has textured timbers, pine paneling, a pianist who adds ambience in winter beginning around sundown, and lots of clients mellowing out after a day in the great outdoors.

7 Gstaad ★★

61km (38 miles) SW of Thun; 42km (26 miles) SE of Bulle

Against a backdrop of glaciers and mountain lakes, Gstaad is a haven for the rich and famous. Frequent visitors include King Juan Carlos II of Spain, Elizabeth Taylor, and Julie Andrews.

Built at the junction of four quiet valleys near the southern tip of the Bernese Oberland, Gstaad was once only a place to change horses during the grueling voyage through the Oberland. But as the railroad lines developed, it grew into a resort. After the opening of the deluxe Alpina Grand Hotel, wealthy Russian and Hungarian families started coming, bringing their entourages of valets, nannies, and translators. In 1912, 2 years before the outbreak of World War I, a hotel that was to become one of the most legendary in Switzerland, the Palace, opened, promising the ultimate in luxury. In 1916 Le Rosey school (listed in the Guinness Book of World Records as "the most expensive prep school in the world") opened its doors in the satellite town of Tolle. The school contributed to the fame of Gstaad, as prestigious visitors, including King Leopold of Belgium, came to see their children.

The town, by far the most chic in the Bernese Oberland, retains much of its turn-of-the-20th-century charm. Some first-time visitors, however, say that the resort is a bore if you can't afford to stay at the Gstaad Palace or mingle with the stars in their private chalets. Yet the town has many moderately priced hotels, taverns, and guest-houses with an allure of their own. Many of the bistros and cafes close from late April to mid-June and from October to mid-December.

ESSENTIALS

GETTING THERE   Gstaad is on the local train line connecting Interlaken with Montreux and several smaller towns in central-southwest Switzerland. About a dozen trains come into Gstaad every day from both of those cities, each of which is a railway junction with good connections to the rest of Switzerland. Travel time from Montreux can be as little as an hour and 20 minutes; from Interlaken, about 30 minutes, some-times with a change of train at the hamlet of Zweisimmen. Call ℂ **0900/300-300** for **rail schedules** and information.

If you're driving from Spiez, head southwest on Route 11; from Bulle, head south and then east on Route 11.

VISITOR INFORMATION   Some streets have names; others are placed outside street plans, but there are directional signs to lead you to hotels and restaurants. The **Gstaad-Saanenland Tourist Association,** CH-3780 Gstaad (ℂ **033/748-81-81**), is a useful source of information, open July and August, Monday to Friday from 8:30am to 6:30pm, Saturday 9am to 6pm, and Sunday 10am to 5pm; September to June, Monday to Friday 8:30am to noon and 2 to 6pm, Saturday 9am to noon.

FUN IN THE OUTDOORS

Gstaad is a resort rich in entertainment and sports facilities. Many skiers stay in Gstaad by night and venture to one of the nearby ski resorts during the day. Cable cars take passengers to altitudes of 1,500m and 3,000m (4,920 and 9,840 ft.)—at the higher altitudes there's skiing even in the summer. Other facilities include tennis courts, heated indoor and outdoor swimming pools, and about 320km (200 miles) of hiking trails. Many of these scenic trails are possible to walk or hike year-round (the tourist office will advise). The **Gstaad International Tennis Tournament,** beginning the first Saturday in July, is the most important tennis event in Switzerland.

Skiers setting off from Gstaad have access to 70 lifts, mountain railroads, and gon-dolas. The altitude of Gstaad's highest skiable mountain is 1,965m (6,445 ft.), with a vertical drop of 1,066m (3,496 ft.). Most beginner and intermediate runs are east of the village in Eggli, a ski area reached by cable car. Eggli has a sunny, southern expo-sure. Wispellan-Sanetch is favored for afternoon skiing, with lots of runs down to the village. At its summit is the Glacier des Diablerets, at a height of 2,970m (9,741 ft.). Wasserngrat, reached from the south side of the resort, is yet another skiing area. Advanced skiers prize Wasserngrat for its powder skiing on steep slopes.

Swiss Ski School at Gstaad (ℂ **033/744-18-65**) has first-class teachers and qualified mountain and touring guides. Special classes for children are offered. Some 100 private instructors are available. It receives stiff competition from the **Schweizer Schi Schule (Swiss Ski School)** (ℂ **033/744-36-65**) in the nearby satellite resort of Schönried.

Gstaad has several satellite resorts, which many visitors prefer. Saanen and Schön-ried are both summer and winter resorts, with excellent accommodations. **Saanen,** at 1,051m (3,447 ft.), is east of Gstaad; some of its wooden chalets date from the 1500s. The **Menuhin Festival** draws an international music-loving crowd from late July to mid-September. The resort can be reached easily by car or by the Montreux-Oberland railway; there's also a small airfield at Saanen for visitors who fly in. **Schönried,** some

4km (2½ miles) northeast of Gstaad, is appreciated for its arguably better snowfall and accommodations, notably the Alpenrose Hotel.

Whichever resort you choose—Gstaad, Saanen, or Schönried—you'll be surrounded by dramatic glaciers and bucolic alpine pastures. This part of the country, called **Saanenland,** is undoubtedly one of the most beautiful parts of Switzerland.

The funiculars and chairlifts around Gstaad are configured into a system that services the slopes of at least six other resorts scattered over four valleys of the Bernese Oberland. In addition to Gstaad, the region's star, the resorts include Saanen, Saanen-Möser, Schönreid, and Sankt Stephan. An all-inclusive ski pass—known locally as a **"Ski Gstaad Pass"**—is sold at the departure point of any of the region's funicular stations, and allows automatic access to 250km (155 miles) of downhill slopes and 70 chairlifts and gondolas.

All-inclusive passes ("Ski Gstaad Passes") may vary depending on what point in the season you buy them, but generally cost 99F ($81) for 2 days, 222F ($182) for 5 days, and 290F ($238) for 7 days, with a complicated set of discounts for children depending on their age and to what degree they're traveling as part of a family unit.

If you're in Gstaad for only 1 day, it's probably smarter to buy a limited pass for access to just a few slopes and chairlifts. The less comprehensive pass (known as a pass for Eggli-La Vide Manette) is sold only in 1-day increments for a price of 49F ($40). Frankly, for anyone planning on 2 or more days of skiing, it's a lot more appealing, and not that much more expensive, to go for the more comprehensive pass.

SHOPPING

Stores along Gstaad's main shopping street, **Hauptstrasse,** seem more upscale, more lavish, and more aggressively tuned to the big-city affluence of Paris, London, and Munich than in virtually any other ski resort in Switzerland. Most of the shops that sell sporting goods in Gstaad inventory other sorts of casual and formal clothing as well, allowing buyers one-stop shopping for the layered look that keeps you warmer on the slopes. Two worthy outlets are **Brand,** Palace Strasse (℡ **033/744-17-75;** www.brandsport.ch); and **HermenJat,** Hauptstrasse (℡ **033/744-15-47;** www.hermenjat-gstaad.com). If you want to check out the kinds of jewelry bought by the resort's most glamorous clients, consider a visit to **Villiger,** Promenade (℡ **033/744-11-22**). Barring that, you can always visit any of the aggressively upscale, relentlessly chic luxury boutiques in the Palace Hotel.

Von Siebenthal, Promenade (℡ **033/744-12-81**), is a three-story housewares emporium filled with high-performance Swiss-made gadgets, ranging from wooden molds for making anise cookies to fondue sets.

Pernet, Promenade (℡ **033/748-70-68**), is to Gstaad what Fauchon is to Paris. Even the designer Valentino, when not in Rome, might be seen shopping here among truffle pâté, smoked salmon, grappa, and more than two dozen different cooking oils. The best bookstore for reading on a cold alpine night is **Buchhandlung,** Hauptstrasse (℡ **033/744-39-90**).

WHERE TO STAY

Gstaad is not known for its inexpensive hotels. Prices soar in the winter. When business is slow, many of the hotels close; the dates of these closings can vary from year to year.

VERY EXPENSIVE

Grand Hotel Park ✦✦✦ This landmark hotel lives again. In 1990 one of the Oberland's most venerable hotels was demolished and rebuilt in a style that reflects the

1910 original. Associated with and partially owned by investors in the Palace Hotel, it sits astride a hill overlooking the center of the town and across from the Palace. Its design, including the bedrooms, evokes a mixture of the Edwardian age with a posh ski resort you might find in Vail, Colorado. Standard rooms measure a generous 35 sq. m (377 sq. ft.), and the more expensive rooms facing south open onto views of the Wispile, Eggli, and Glacier des Diablerets. Each accommodation comes with an immaculately kept bathroom. Although some of the original turn-of-the-20th-century furniture was incorporated into the new design, much of the interior is new, sleekly modern, and richly accessorized with decorative and structural bands of chiseled granite, polished marble, and burnished pine. It is also home to the first Louis Vuitton boutique in a hotel in Europe.

CH-3780 Gstaad. © **033/748-98-00.** Fax 033/748-98-08. www.grandhotelpark.ch. 93 units. Summer 450F–800F ($369–$656) double, from 1,200F ($984) suite; winter 670F–1,540F ($549–$1,263) double, from 2,860F ($2,345) suite. Rates include half board. AE, DC, MC, V. Parking 20F ($16) in winter, free in summer. Closed Mar 23–June 10 and Sept 26–Dec 17. **Amenities:** 5 restaurants; 3 bars; 2 pools (1 indoor saltwater); tennis courts; health club; sauna; Louis Vuitton boutique; salon; 24-hr. room service; babysitting; laundry service/dry cleaning; hairdresser. *In room:* TV, dataport, minibar, hair dryer, safe.

Palace Hotel Gstaad ✯✯✯   This other landmark hotel on a wooded hill overlooks the center of Gstaad. Opened in 1912, the Palace has mock-fortified corner towers and a neomedieval facade. The designer, Valentino, called the architecture a "brutal Sleeping Beauty castle." It's one of the most sought-after luxury hideaways in the world, attracting corporation heads, movie stars, and fashionable aristocrats, many of whom return every winter and stay a long time, earning the Palace the reputation as "Switzerland's largest family boardinghouse." Owner and manager Ernst Scherz's motto is: "Every king is a client, and every client is a king." It's true—if you can afford it.

The nerve center of this chic citadel is an elegantly paneled main salon, with an "eternal flame" burning in the baronial stone fireplace. This flame isn't so eternal—it burns only in winter. Radiating hallways lead to superb restaurants, bars, discos, and sports facilities. The plush, spacious rooms are tastefully furnished and very distinguished; all come equipped with beautifully maintained bathrooms. However, be duly warned: Those facing north open onto a parking lot. Nonetheless, accommodations here are among the most sumptuous in Europe.

CH-3780 Gstaad. © **800/223-6800** in the U.S. or 033/748-50-00. Fax 033/748-50-01. www.palace.ch. 104 units. Summer 590F–960F ($484–$787) double, 980F–1,180F ($804–$968) junior suite, 1,227F–2,554F ($1,006–$2,094) suite; winter 610F–1,660F ($500–$1,361) double, 1,090F–2,220F ($894–$1,820) junior suite, 1,727F–5,310F ($1,416–$4,354) suite. AE, DC, MC, V. Free parking outside, 20F ($16) in garage. Closed end of Mar to mid-June and late Sept to shortly before Christmas (dates vary). **Amenities:** 5 restaurants; 2 bars; nightclub; 2 pools (1 indoor); tennis courts; health club; sauna; salon; 24-hr. room service; massage; babysitting; laundry service/dry cleaning. *In room:* TV, dataport, minibar, hair dryer, safe.

EXPENSIVE
Grand Hotel Bellevue ✯   A venerable favorite still holding its own, this hotel is from 1912. Gstaad's leading government-rated four-star hotel, it stands in a serene park with tall, old trees in the midst of the town. The rooms are spacious and well lit, in a calming color palette. The furnishings are traditional and exceedingly comfortable, as reflected by the deluxe beds and the well-maintained bathrooms.

Hauptstrasse, CH-3780 Gstaad. © **033/748-00-00.** Fax 033/748-00-01. www.bellevue-gstaad.ch. 52 units. 380F–720F ($312–$590) double; 720F–920F ($590–$754) junior suite; 1,020F–1,900F ($836–$1,558) suite. AE, DC, MC, V. Free parking outside. Closed Oct 22–Dec 22. **Amenities:** Restaurant; bar; indoor pool; 2 tennis courts; 24-hr. room service; laundry service/dry cleaning; curling hall. *In room:* TV, fax, dataport, minibar, hair dryer, safe.

Hostellerie Alpenrose ★★★ *(Finds)*   For those who seek the charm of a small inn, this is the preferred choice in the area, the only Relais & Châteaux listing within 48km (30 miles). The pine-paneled rooms are exquisitely decorated with rustic furnishings, and the small bedrooms are comfortable and tastefully appointed. All are equipped with well-maintained bathrooms. Its kindly host, Michel von Siebenthal, is a memorable fellow, setting the fashionable tone of the chalet, which is famous for its restaurant (see "Where to Dine," below).

Saanenmoserstrasse, CH-3778 Schönried-Gstaad. ✆ 033/744-67-67. Fax 033/744-67-12. www.relaischateaux.com/alpenrose. 19 units. 220F–490F ($180–$402) double; 450F–750F ($369–$615) suite. Rates include buffet breakfast. Half board 50F ($41) per person extra. AE, DC, MC, V. Free parking. Closed Nov. **Amenities:** 2 restaurants; 2 bars; lounge; sauna; whirlpool; limited room service. *In room:* TV, minibar.

Hotel Bernerhof ★ *(Kids)*   This hotel lies in the center of the resort town about half a block from the rail station. Built on the site of a hotel dating from 1904, it offers modern comforts and attracts a loyal clientele that keeps in touch via a hotel newsletter. Wooden balconies extend across the front. Thomas and Claudia Frei offer well-furnished rooms with neatly kept bathrooms. Children are catered to at the hotel, and many activities are planned for them. The restaurant is recommended in "Where to Dine," below. The Stöckli Bar is a popular place for drinks.

CH-3780 Gstaad. ✆ 033/748-88-44. Fax 033/748-88-40. www.bernerhof-gstaad.ch. 47 units. 270F ($221) double; 330F–380F ($271–$312) suite. Rates include breakfast. Half board 25F ($21) per person extra. AE, DC, MC, V. Free parking outside, 12F ($9.85) in garage. Closed Nov 20–Dec 1. **Amenities:** 3 restaurants; bar; indoor pool; health club; Jacuzzi; sauna; children's activities; limited room service; babysitting; laundry service/dry cleaning. *In room:* TV, minibar, hair dryer.

Hotel Le Grand Chalet   Tucked away near the mountains in Gstaad is this cozy and distinctly Swiss family-run hotel. The rooms use light wood furniture and moldings, white walls and linens, and strategically places lights to make the accommodations elegant and seemingly spacious. Every room has a desk and a plethora of closet space. The double rooms here are much nicer than the suites, which tend to be on the gaudy and dim side. However, the views from their balconies are panoramic, so it's a trade-off. During your stay, treat yourself to a specialty prepared by head chef Stève Willié at the hotel's restaurant La Bagatelle.

Le Grand Chalet, CH-3780 Gstaad. ✆ 033/48-76-76. Fax 033/748-76-77. www.grandchalet.ch. 25 units. 260F–520F ($213–$426) double; 420F–750F ($344–$615) suite. Rates include breakfast. AE, DC, MC, V. **Amenities:** 2 restaurants; heated outdoor pool (summer only); sauna; steam bath; limited room service; laundry service. *In room:* TV, kitchenette (in some), minibar, hair dryer, safe.

Hotel Olden ★★   This is one of the most low-key and gracefully unpretentious hotels in Gstaad, a sort of Victorian country inn set amid a sometimes chillingly glamorous landscape—or at least a chillingly expensive landscape. The Olden has a facade painted with regional floral designs and pithy bits of folk wisdom. Embellishments are carved or painted into the stone lintels around many of the doors. The small to mid-size rooms are generally furnished in a typical alpine style, although the bathrooms have been modernized. Some guests are housed in the adjacent chalet wing, where the comfort level and amenities are the same.

Hauptstrasse, CH-3780 Gstaad. ✆ 033/748-49-50. Fax 033/744-61-64. www.hotelolden.ch. 16 units. Summer 280F–500F ($230–$410) double, 450F–670F ($369–$549) junior suite, 670F–1,500F ($549–$1,230) suite; winter 280F–500F ($230–$410) double, 450F–670F ($369–$549) junior suite, 550F–1,400F ($451–$1,148) suite. Rates include continental breakfast. AE, DC, MC, V. Parking 20F ($16). Closed late Apr to late May. **Amenities:** Restaurant; bar; limited room service; laundry service/dry cleaning. *In room:* TV, minibar.

Wellness & Spa Hotel Ermitage-Golf ⭐⭐   This is a government-rated five-star hotel designed and built in 1958. Its developers had intended that a golf course surround it on all sides. Although the building permit for the golf course was eventually refused by the city, the name remained in place. There's a 9-hole golf course, however, about 3km (2 miles) away. Today this is a large and comfortable hotel, with a helpful staff and lots of alpine warmth. In the winter it's a toasty, cozy retreat; in the summer it's a pleasure chalet, as red geraniums bloom on its balconies and chaise longues are set up on its lawns. Heiner Lutz and Laurenz Schmid offer paneled bedrooms, each individually furnished. Some have Oriental rugs and offer grand comfort.

Hauptstrasse, CH-3778 Schönried-Gstaad. ✆ **033/748-60-60.** Fax 033/748-60-67. www.ermitagegolf.ch. 69 units. 300F–910F ($246–$746) double. Rates include half board. AE, DC, MC, V. Parking 10F–18F ($8.20–$15). Closed Oct 25–Dec 18. **Amenities:** 3 restaurants; 2 bars; 2 pools (1 indoor); tennis court; health club; Jacuzzi; sauna; Turkish bath; 24-hr. room service; massage; babysitting; laundry service/dry cleaning. *In room:* TV, minibar, hair dryer, safe.

MODERATE

Hotel Alphorn *Finds*   Located at the base of the Wispile cable car, this intimate chalet is a small, relatively unpublicized hotel owned by the Bruriswill family. The hotel, built in 1970 and enlarged and upgraded in 1992, has a ski shop on the premises. The small rooms are comfortable and snug, each fitted with a well-kept private bathroom.

Steigstrasse, CH-3780 Gstaad. ✆ **033/748-45-45.** Fax 033/748-45-46. www.gstaad-alphorn.ch. 30 units. 172F–288F ($141–$236) double. Rates include buffet breakfast. Half board 30F ($25) per person extra. AE, DC, MC, V. Free parking. **Amenities:** Restaurant; lounge; sauna; babysitting; laundry service/dry cleaning. *In room:* TV, minibar, hair dryer.

Posthotel Rössli *Value*   The Rössli is an authentic and traditional chalet in the center of Gstaad. Often attracting a young crowd, it's well heated and furnished with modern conveniences in its small but cozy and comfortable bedrooms. All are equipped with neatly kept bathrooms. Every week Ruedi Widmer, mountain guide, ski teacher, and owner of the hotel, organizes walks and grill parties in summer or skiing days in winter. Guests are invited to participate at no extra charge. Locals mix with guests in the *bierstube* (beer tavern), the Stübli.

Hauptstrasse, CH-3780 Gstaad. ✆ **033/748-42-42.** Fax 033/748-42-43. www.posthotelrossli.ch. 36 units. 185F–250F ($152–$205) double. Half board 33F ($27) per person. Rates include breakfast. AE, DC, MC, V. Free parking. **Amenities:** Restaurant; lounge. *In room:* TV, minibar, hair dryer.

WHERE TO DINE

Most visitors dine at their hotel, so there are few independent restaurants in Gstaad. The following choices include some worth venturing out for, as well as others in previously recommended hotels.

VERY EXPENSIVE

The Restaurant ⭐⭐⭐ FRENCH/INTERNATIONAL   The hotel opens up to three different dining rooms, each elegantly paneled and boasting impeccable service and the finest haute cuisine. Some of the finest chefs in the Bernese Oberland create dishes here for an extremely demanding clientele. Formal attire is essential—men without ties or jackets will be asked to dine in the Sans-Cravatte.

For an appetizer, caviar and foie gras abound, but there are also superb hors d'oeuvres, including beefsteak tartare, and delicate soups and consommés. Some especially delectable dishes include crisp rack of Scottish lamb with eggplant lasagna, grilled sole flavored with oregano, crispy duck for two, and chicken Taj Mahal with curry and many side condiments. This wide repertoire includes imaginative interpretations of old favorites. Most desserts are elaborate, but if you wish, you can order a simple sorbet.

In the Palace Hotel. ℂ **033/748-50-00**. Reservations required. Main courses 60F–160F ($49–$131); 3-course fixed-price lunch 80F ($66), 5-course fixed-price dinner 115F ($94). AE, DC, MC, V. Daily 12:30–2:30pm and 7:30–10:30pm. Closed end of Mar to mid-June and mid-Sept to shortly before Christmas.

Restaurant Chesery *€€€* FRENCH/SWISS   At an elevation of 1,097m (3,598 ft.), this is one of the 10 best restaurants in Switzerland. The floors are pink marble and the walls are polished pine. The menu changes daily, based on the freshest ingredients available. The chef is a perfectionist and shops far and wide for only the finest of produce with which to dazzle his clients—grouse from Scotland, Charolais beef from France, truffles from Umbria. You may sample his salt-crusted sea bass with wild rice or his chicken Houban (a very special breed from France). Try also his Scottish lamb with a crust of fresh herbs or rack of venison with whortleberries. In the basement bar, Casino, a piano player entertains nightly, and the bar is open from 6pm to 3am, when the last ski bunny departs.

Lauenenstrasse. ℂ **033/744-24-51**. Reservations required. Main courses 37F–68F ($30–$56); fixed-price lunch 52F–65F ($43–$53), fixed-price dinner 110F–152F ($90–$125). AE, DC, MC, V. Tues–Sun 11:30am–2:30pm and 7pm–midnight. Closed mid-Oct to mid-Dec, Easter–June 10, and in winter (Tues–Fri) for lunch.

EXPENSIVE
Hostellerie Alpenrose *€€* SWISS/FRENCH   During the summer the paneled dining rooms are full of local residents and guests from the surrounding chalets. Michel von Siebenthal is your chef; his father built the first ski lift in the region in 1935. He has elevated a modest pension into a culinary citadel known throughout Switzerland for its cuisine. The varied menu changes every 3 weeks. Lobster is almost always on the menu, but look for marinated salmon, which remains a delectable house specialty. Begin, perhaps, with the duck-liver terrine or a velvety-smooth imaginative soup made of nettles. One savory dish is a cassoulet of mushrooms. The grilled turbot is prepared with several different sauces, including an unusual carrot sauce, and you can also order a superb wild duck in a juniper-berry sauce. Consider having an after-dinner drink in the nightclub, Sammy's.

Hauptstrasse, Schönried-Gstaad. ℂ **033/744-67-67**. Reservations recommended. Main courses 29F–67F ($24–$55); 4-course fixed-price menu 75F ($62). AE, DC, MC, V. Daily 6:30–10pm; Wed–Thurs noon–2pm; Fri–Sun noon–2:30pm. Closed mid-Oct to mid-Dec.

MODERATE
Olden Restaurant *€€* MEDITERRANEAN/ITALIAN   This is the most formal restaurant of the several dining choices in this previously recommended hotel. On the street level, it attracts the latest visiting celebrity with its country charm. Meals are formally served in the pine-paneled dining room. The always-tempting menu might include smoked salmon, fresh goose-liver terrine, shrimp bisque with green peppercorns, house-style tagliatelle, raclette, veal cutlet Milanese, Scottish lamb, and sea bass with olives, potatoes, tomatoes, and onions. Although there are grander restaurants in Gstaad, as well as dining rooms serving a more haute cuisine, the Olden remains our most satisfying choice year after year.

In the Hotel Olden, Hauptstrasse. ℂ **033/744-34-44**. Reservations recommended. Main courses 25F–70F ($21–$57). AE, DC, MC, V. Tues–Sun noon–2:30pm and 6:30–10:30pm. Closed mid-Apr to mid-May and 2 weeks in Nov.

Posthotel Rössli SWISS   Set within a 150-year-old chalet in the heart of town, nearly adjacent to the Stadtkirche, this restaurant welcomes many generations of diners, most of whom have appreciated the paneled interior, small windows, and agrarian artifacts scattered throughout. Menu items—most of which are on the lower end of the price scale—are hearty, alpine-inspired, and served in generous portions. Examples include pork and veal schnitzels, tender beefsteaks in a mushroom-flavored cream sauce, velvety fondues, chicken roulades layered with ham and cheese, and several variations on Italian pastas. Salads are fresh, and the beer is cold.

Hauptstrasse 1. ℂ 033/748-42-42. Reservations not accepted. Main courses 13F–43F ($11–$35); fixed-price menu 32F ($26). AE, MC, V. Daily 11:30am–2:30pm and 4:30–10pm.

Restaurant Stafel (Kids) INTERNATIONAL   This tavern-style restaurant at the previously recommended hotel attracts plenty of discerning devotees. A longtime family favorite, it serves a menu so wide-ranging there's almost always something to please everybody. Along with the standard international dishes, it also offers a selection of excellent Swiss regional specialties, including a fondue with veal liver. Asian culinary delicacies are featured in the blun-chi section, and every day a large variety of succulent fresh pasta dishes are prepared. The hotel also houses the popular après-ski Stöckli Bar.

In the Hotel Bernerhof. ℂ 033/748-88-44. Reservations recommended. Main courses 16F–44F ($13–$36). AE, DC, MC, V. Daily 11:30am–2:30pm and 6:30–10:30pm. Closed Nov 20–Dec 1.

Ristorante Rialto ITALIAN   One of the finest Italian restaurants in the Bernese Oberland, the Rialto lies in the heart of Gstaad. The proprietors, Peter and Tanja Burri, use only the freshest ingredients, and the menu changes with the season. You may begin with a selection of always-tempting antipasti, followed by the luscious salmon carpaccio with a truffle-cream sauce or one of the pasta dishes, including pappardelle. The flavor-filled risotto with fresh asparagus and the chef's sea bass Mediterranean style are both excellent.

Promenade. ℂ 033/744-34-74. Reservations recommended. Main courses 22F–47F ($18–$39). AE, DC, MC, V. Open daily 24 hr. Main meals served Mon–Sat noon–2pm and 8:30–11:30pm; Sun noon–2pm (light dishes, drinks, and salads through the day). Closed Mon May–June and Nov.

GSTAAD AFTER DARK

Much more than its competitors, Gstaad has been accused of attracting glamorous folk who care more about the resort's social scene than they do about skiing. As such, the resort supports a healthy roster of nightspots that range from boozy to glamorous. In midwinter your options include alpine coziness in at least two mountain huts accessible only by cable car, the **Berghaus Eggli,** on the Eggli ski slopes (ℂ 033/748-96-12), and the **Berghaus Wispile,** on the Wispile ski slopes (ℂ 033/748-96-32). Access to either requires an 8-minute ascent on the Eggli (south of the center) and Wispile (north of the center) cable cars *(Gondelbahns).* Both are infused with the odors of simmering raclette and fondues, both are open only during the height of the winter season, and both encourage guests to ski home after a night of alpine *Gemütlichkeit* (a Swiss term for cozy, good times shared with sympathetic souls). Don't even think of riding the cable car uphill for a meal or drink at either of these places after dark without a reservation, as their scheduling and priorities are as haphazard as anything at the resort.

More conventional evening diversions include the **Palace Hotel** (ℂ 033/748-50-00), which contains a supremely upscale bar adjacent to the pine-sheathed lobby where the comings and goings could fill any Robin Leach production. The hotel also contains the most exclusive—and sometimes somewhat stuffy—disco in Gstaad, the **Green Go Disco,** where pinpricks of light illuminate a mysterious semipsychedelic decor of orange, green, and black. Call ahead, as it operates only during midwinter and selected weekends in the peak of midsummer.

In the heart of Gstaad, there's a bar, the **Hostellerie Chesery,** Lauenenstrasse (© 033/744-24-51), that hosts both piano music and dance music (later in the evening). Its main focus, its restaurant, is separately recommended above. An appealingly battered hangout reminiscent of England is **Richie's Pub,** Hauptstrasse (© 033/744-57-87). Nobody dances here, but the place is a town favorite. A few steps away is a worthy and much more elegant competitor, the **Rialto Bar,** in the Ristorante Rialto, Hauptstrasse (© 033/744-34-74). There is a large terrace in the summer, and in the winter there's sometimes live music in the restaurant.

9

The Valais

The Valais is a region in southern Switzerland that borders on Italy and consists mostly of the valley around the upper Rhône River. The valley was called Vallis Poenina by the Romans, and the Germans refer to it as Wallis. The main attractions here include the Matterhorn, the Great St. Bernard Pass, and Zermatt. The area offers excellent skiing and other winter sports (Zermatt has one of the longest ski seasons in Switzerland).

The Valais is surrounded by the Alps, with more than 50 major mountain peaks, but the Matterhorn, at 4,410m (14,465 ft.), is by far the most majestic. The Valais contains the largest glacier in Switzerland as well as several others that send tributaries to feed the Rhône, which flows northwest to Lake Geneva, then on through France to the Mediterranean. The Valais also contains about 8 sq. km (5 sq. miles) of lakes.

Often called the hiking capital of Switzerland, the Valais is riddled with well-maintained and well-marked mountain paths. Some of this former network of alpine mule paths are called Roman roads, because in ancient times the Simplon and Great Saint Bernard passes were the gateways to the Valais from Italy. Walks along irrigation channels—called bisses—are among the most intriguing for nature lovers.

For centuries the Rhône Valley has been a major route through the Alps. The Celts used the Great St. Bernard Pass and Simplon Pass, and then the Gauls held the territory for 500 years. Hannibal and Napoleon both passed through on their

way to conquest. Today wide highways and tunnels provide a direct route to Italy.

Protected by mountains, the Valais enjoys a sunny, stable climate, with weather comparable to that of northwestern Spain and France's Provence. The vineyards are second only to those of the Vaud, and the local wine is known for its fruity bouquet and delicate flavor. Dairy farming is widespread. Raclette, the classic Swiss dish, is usually made of the rich, unskimmed milk from the Bagnes Valley, near the Great St. Bernard Pass. Just outside most of the regional towns, you'll see *mazots* or *raccards,* small, elevated grain-storage barns.

Most residents in the western part of the Valais, from Lake Geneva to Sierre, speak French, while those living to the east speak a German dialect. Many people speak both languages as well as some English. Most residents of the Valais are Roman Catholic, evident in the number of churches, abbeys, and monasteries.

The Valais is an increasingly popular year-round travel destination, but not to worry: The growth of resorts and recreation facilities has not disturbed the natural splendor and tranquillity of the alpine countryside.

Chances are if you're visiting the Valais by train you'll land at the major rail terminus of Martigny, which attracts visitors heading across the Great St. Bernard Pass. Visitors going to the ski resort of Verbier also pass through here. Frequent trains arrive in Martigny from Lausanne every hour, taking 30 minutes; from Montreux, every 30 minutes, taking 30 minutes; and from Sion, every 15 minutes, taking 30 minutes.

If you'd like to take one of the most scenic bike trips in the Valais, rent a bike at the kiosk at the **train station** (© **0900/ 300-300**), costing 25F ($21) per day. The **tourist office** at Martigny, 9, place Centrale (© **027/721-22-20**), will provide you with maps of the area. The office is open September to June, Monday to Friday from 9am to noon and 1:30 to 6pm and on Saturday from 9am to 2pm; in July and August hours are daily 9am to 6pm.

From Martigny you can cycle through a beautiful region of the lower Valais, heading across the Rhône River to the villages of Fully, Chataigner, Mazembroz, and Saillon.

1 Verbier ⋆

128km (80 miles) E of Geneva; 40km (25 miles) N of Great St. Bernard Tunnel; 29km (18 miles) E of Martigny; 58km (36 miles) SW of Sion

Verbier sits on a vast, sunny plateau in the Bagnes Valley in Switzerland's southernmost Alps. It looks toward the Combin and Mont Blanc mountains, which are covered with snow year-round, even when the town is bursting with leafy trees and flowers. At 1,500m (4,920 ft.), Verbier was a pastureland before developing into an outstanding sports center. The area is protected from harsh winds by the surrounding mountains. The predominant language of the resort is French.

Verbier doesn't have the architectural distinction of Zermatt. Everything from souvenir shops to the fast-food joints to the chalets is modern. But you don't concentrate on the man-made architecture—the draw is the panoramic site of the resort itself, as its buildings are scattered over a slope of the Bagnes Valley surrounded by snow-covered mountains.

ESSENTIALS

GETTING THERE   From the railway junction of Martigny, take the train along a secondary spur route to Le Châble. Call © **0900-300-300** for **train schedules.** At Le Châble you can transfer to a postal bus. Le Châble is also the departure point for an aerial cableway leading directly to Verbier. The cost of one-way transport on the cable car is 7F ($5.75) per person.

During the peak of the ski season, a consortium of hotels operates a shuttle bus that travels directly from Martigny to Verbier that's timed to coincide with the arrival of important trains into Martigny. The one-way cost is 15F ($9.75). Regrettably, it operates only during winter, and only on Friday afternoon (one bus) and on Saturday (three buses). For **shuttle bus information** and reservations, call © **0900-300-300.**

If you're driving, take N9 as far as Martigny on the Great St. Bernard route. Turn left for Verbier at Sembrancher.

VISITOR INFORMATION   Some areas have no street names, so many establishments are signposted. The **Verbier Tourist Office,** place Centrale (© **027/775-38-88;** www.verbier.ch), dispenses information. It's open Monday to Friday 8am to 12:30pm and 2 to 6:30pm, Saturday and Sunday 9am to noon and 2 to 4:30pm.

SKIING & OTHER SPORTS

Skiing tops the list of attractions. The area offers 306km (190 miles) of ski runs, serviced by 47 lifts. Téléverbier, a company founded in 1950, oversees one of the biggest conveyance systems in all of Switzerland. A recent addition, a heavy-duty cable car

("Le Jumbo"), whose cables are strung between the region of La Chaux and the Col des Gentianes, is the largest lift in the country.

In cooperation with neighboring regions, visitors can use their Téléverbier passes on more than 98 additional lifts in the area known as Les 4 Vallées (valleys) and L'Entremont. From Verbier, a single lift ticket can take skiers as high as 3,300m (10,824 ft.). The permit also authorizes cross-country skiing, and several circuits are possible. One goes from Verbier to Mont-Gelé, Mont-Fort, and La Chaux and then back to Verbier. Another circuit goes from Verbier to Tortin, Mont-Fort, and La Chaux. For information on skiing in the Téléverbier network, contact **Téléverbier S.A.,** CP 419, CH-1936 Verbier (© **027/775-25-11;** www.televerbier.ch).

Throughout the winter, comprehensive passes that entitle skiers to access on all the ski lifts and slopes in the 4 Vallées region cost 115F ($94) for 2 days, 263F ($216) for 5 days, and 306F ($251) for a full week. Children ages 6 to 16 and seniors 63 or older pay only 60% of these rates.

The **Swiss Ski School (Ecole Suisse de Ski)** (© **027/775-33-63**) has 170 instructors and in winter offers group lessons daily from 9:15 to 11:45am and more individualized lessons every day in winter from 2:10 to 4:30pm. Private lessons can be arranged as well.

The inauguration of **Le Centre Sportif (Verbier Polysports Center)** (© **027/771-66-01**) has greatly expanded sports offerings in all seasons. Facilities include a covered swimming pool, 10 indoor curling lanes, an indoor ice rink, nine tennis courts, squash courts, saunas, whirlpools, a solarium, and a games area. The center, open daily from 10am to 9pm, also contains a simple restaurant.

Besides sports, Verbier abounds in alpine beauty. The **Haut Val de Bagnes Nature Reserve (Haut Val de Bagnes Réserve Naturelle)** ✿✿, whose terrain can be safely visited only between mid-May and early October, has a rich variety of flora and fauna, including some rare species of plants. You might see alpine aquilegia, white gentian, yellow pond lily, edelweiss, and several kinds of orchids. Botanical walks are organized in the summer; inquire at the tourist office. There's a sweeping view of the Bagnes Valley from the Combe des Violettes. In the distance you can see Mont-Pleureur, with Italy in the blue mist on the horizon.

There are about 21km (13 miles) of footpaths in and around Verbier that are open for **hiking** in summer and hiking or cross-country skiing in winter. These are carefully maintained and signposted by the municipality. A bit farther afield from Verbier, you'll find almost 402km (250 miles) of hiking trails of varying degrees of difficulty. Maps are available (see the tourist office, under "Essentials," above). There are usually signs posted to indicate the estimated time it takes the average hiker to reach each destination.

If you'd prefer to participate in activities more strenuous than mere walking and hiking, you can try one of several alpine adventures. Trained mountain guides lead jaunts in rock climbing, mountaineering, and cliff climbing, often on excursions of 3 days or more. Call the **Bureau des Guides de Verbier,** a branch of the above-recommended ski school (© **027/775-33-64;** www.guide-verbier.ch), or one of its competitors, **La Fantastique** (© **027/771-41-41;** www.lafantastique.com), for more information about hiring a mountain guide.

Golf Club de Verbier (© **027/771-53-14**) is an 18-hole course open from June to October. It is one of the finest in the Valais, set against a scenic alpine backdrop, at an altitude of 1,574m (5,163 ft.). Greens fees Monday to Friday are 75F ($62), going up to 83F ($68) on weekends. Every hole provides stunning views of such mountain ranges as Combin, Rogneux, and even Mont-Blanc.

SHOPPING

Much of the merchandising that keeps Verbier's economy pumping involves alpine sports, summer or winter, and as such, you'll find half a dozen sporting-goods stores in town. Three of the best are **Philippe Roux Sport,** place Centrale (© 027/771-47-12); its nearby competitor, **Médran-Sport,** route de Verbier (© 027/771-60-48); and located close to the departure point for most of the cable cars and ski lifts, **La boit'askis,** rue de Médran (© 027/771-34-87; www.boitaskis.com). If you're more interested in handcrafts than state-of-the-art ski and mountaineering equipment, head for Verbier's largest dealer of the ceramic and carved wooden artifacts that the Valais produces in such abundance, **Bagn'Art,** rue de la Poste (© 027/771-5060).

WHERE TO STAY

In the peak of the winter season, hotels often require Saturday-to-Saturday bookings.

EXPENSIVE

Hôtel Les 4 Vallées 🏨🏨   The hotel stands near the main square and the Médran lift station, and was built in the early 1980s in a contemporary chalet style. Each of its often sunny rooms has pine paneling, plush carpeting, and a balcony, many of which look southward toward the mountains. A copious breakfast buffet is served in a room with large windows and paneling.

Rue de Médran, CH-1936 Verbier. ℂ 027/775-33-44. Fax 027/775-33-45. www.les4vallees.com. 20 units. Summer 250F–310F ($205–$254) double; winter 270F–350F ($221–$287) double. Rates include continental breakfast. AE, DC, MC, V. Free parking. Closed May–June and Sept–Nov. **Amenities:** Bar; free use of nearby indoor swimming pool; sauna; laundry service. *In room:* TV, dataport, minibar, hair dryer, safe.

Hôtel Rosalp 🏨🏨🏨   This Relais & Châteaux establishment is the plushest resort here. Roger and Anita Pierroz built the Rosalp in 1945, and Anita's cooking brought early fame to the place. But their son, Roland, put it on Europe's gastronomic map. Today first-class rooms and refined cuisine are available, the suites are excellent, and the small public salon is a tranquil retreat. The bedrooms are decorated with flair and filled with modern comforts. Many have dark paneling and some contain a sun deck. Suites for four contain two rooms, two bathrooms, and a private salon. The hotel has the area's premier restaurant, Le Restaurant Pierroz (see "Where to Dine," below).

Route de Médran, CH-1936 Verbier. ℂ 027/771-63-23. Fax 027/771-10-59. www.rosalp.ch. 18 units. Summer 355F–400F ($291–$328) double; 910F ($746) suite for 4; winter 415F–520F ($340–$426) double, 1,150F ($943) suite for 4. Rates include continental breakfast. Half board 75F ($62) per person extra. AE, DC, MC, V. Parking free outside, 15F ($9.75) in garage. Closed May–June and Oct–Nov. **Amenities:** 2 restaurants; bar; fitness center; Jacuzzi; sauna; limited room service; laundry service/dry cleaning. *In room:* TV, dataport, minibar, safe, hair dryer.

Hôtel Vanessa 🏨   One of the biggest hotels in Verbier is also one of the resort's finest. This government-rated four-star, six-floor hotel dating from 1980 has comfortable and modern midsize rooms; most resemble suites and offer bright upholstery and balconies. The beds are exceedingly comfortable, and the maintenance is among the finest in town. Each unit is fitted with a well-maintained bathroom.

Place Centrale, CH-1936 Verbier. ℂ 027/775-28-00. Fax 027/775-28-88. www.hotelvanessa.ch. 56 units. Summer 179F–260F ($147–$213) double; 203F–330F ($166–$271) duplex, 290F–520F ($238–$426) suite; winter 240F–350F ($197–$287) double, 255F–600F ($209–$492) duplex, 310F–840F ($254–$689) suite. Rates include breakfast. Half board 50F ($33) per person extra. AE, DC, MC, V. Parking 15F ($12). Closed Apr–June and mid-Oct to Dec 1. **Amenities:** Restaurant; piano bar; exercise room; Jacuzzi; sauna; limited room service; babysitting; laundry service. *In room:* TV, dataport, minibar, hair dryer.

MODERATE

Golf Hôtel 🏨   The rooms in this government-rated three-star chalet are equivalent to four-star accommodations in other towns. Opened in 1953, the hotel sits in isolated grandeur a short walk below the main square. The public areas, including the lobby, contain architectural details that emulate antique models. Contrary to the hotel's name, it's not affiliated with a nearby golf course—most of its business comes from midwinter skiers. The midsize rooms contain Oriental carpets, pine paneling, and conservative furniture. Most have private balconies.

Rue de Verbier, CH-1936 Verbier. ℂ 027/771-65-15. Fax 027/771-14-88. www.golfhotelverbier.ch. 25 units. Summer 140F–170F ($115–$139) double; winter 190F–230F ($156–$189) double. Rates include half board. AE, DC, MC, V. Free parking. Closed Apr–June and Oct–Dec 10. **Amenities:** Restaurant; piano bar; fitness room; sauna/steam bath; limited room service; laundry service. *In room:* TV, safe.

Hôtel de la Poste *(Kids)*   This red-shuttered chalet on the main street near the central square has long been a family favorite. Despite its lack of special facilities or programming for children, this family-owned and -run resort stands out against the other more upscale, adult-oriented hotels in the market as being a family spot. Constructed in 1955, it was rebuilt in 1962 and then drastically altered in 1980, which accounts for its present look. The small rooms are snug and comfortable with a modern alpine decor, and each comes with an adequate tiled bathroom. The hotel restaurant, La Tana, serves typical Swiss alpine cuisine.

Rue de Médran, CH-1936 Verbier. © **027/771-66-81.** Fax 027/771-34-01. www.hotelposteverbier.ch. 30 units. Summer 225F–255F ($185–$209) double; winter 310F–350F ($254–$287) double. Rates include half board. AE, DC, MC, V. Free parking. Closed mid-Apr to mid-June and Sept 15–Dec 10. **Amenities:** Restaurant; bar; indoor pool. *In room:* TV, minibar.

WHERE TO DINE

Verbier has several excellent restaurants, many serving traditional Swiss dishes and Continental cuisine. Most of the best restaurants are connected with hotels.

EXPENSIVE

Le Restaurant Pierroz *(★★★)* FRENCH   The finest food in the Valais is served at this Relais & Châteaux selection. Roland Pierroz is one of the great chefs of Switzerland; gourmets drive across national borders to sample his light cuisine moderne and regional specialties. The menu changes frequently but could include roulades of carpaccio of sea bream with tomatoes en confit; a theatrical but delicious version of fried foie gras in a beet-and-onion "cage"; red mullet soup studded with shellfish; a divine poached chicken with truffles and baby vegetables (for two); and tournedos of lamb with a mousseline of local potatoes (rattes), garlic, and crispy sauerkraut. The cheese trolley emerges with at least 35 selections, followed by desserts such as a crisp and tasty apple tart with ice cream that was celestial. The finest meal we've ever had in Switzerland was had here.

In the Hôtel Rosalp, rue de Médran. © **027/771-63-23.** Reservations required at least a day ahead. Main courses 59F–74F ($48–$61); fixed-price menus 140F ($115), 160F ($131), and 190F ($156). AE, DC, MC, V. Daily noon–2pm and 7–9:30pm. Closed May–June and Oct–Nov.

MODERATE

Au Vieux Verbier SWISS   One of the few restaurants in Verbier not affiliated with any hotel, the Old Verbier is on a hillside a few paces from the town's ski slopes. It's set in a building that functions as the nerve center for the surrounding hillside cable cars. Its decor features brightly polished brassware, ceiling beams, and stone. The kitchen defines its cuisine as *bonne cuisine bourgeoise,* which is rich, traditional, and filling, exemplified by such featured dishes as La Potence—a grilled steak flambéed at your table with a red-wine sauce. Grilled fish and roasted rack of lamb are among the more delectable items to order. The specialty of the house—and it's a delight for connoisseurs—is pigs' feet in Madeira with rösti, but it's only served in autumn.

Gare de Médran. © **027/771-16-68.** Reservations required for dinner. Main courses 19F–45F ($16–$37); fixed-price menus (summer only) 30F–40F ($25–$33). AE, DC, MC, V. Daily noon–3pm and 6:30pm–midnight. Closed early May to mid-July and Mon in summer and fall.

La Pinte *★ (Finds)* SWISS   This is master chef Roland Pierroz's second, more reasonably priced restaurant, on the ground floor of the Hôtel Rosalp. The 19th-century paneling is decorated with painted flowers; in the back a snug room displays hunting trophies. The cuisine features simmered and grilled specialties. A typical meal includes a to-die-for tart made with leeks or Gruyère cheese. Meats, ranging from a brochette of lamb to tournedos, are grilled over an open fire. He offers several regional dishes, including a savory sausage with lentils. Specials change daily.

In the Hôtel Rosalp, rue de Médran. © 027/771-63-23. Reservations required. Main courses 26F–48F ($17–$31). AE, DC, MC, V. Daily noon–2pm and 7–9:30pm. Closed May to mid-Dec.

Le Caveau SWISS   Set in a cozy cellar, the entrance to the restaurant overlooks the town's main square. "The Cave" has a warmly rustic decor, a convivial bar near the entrance, and a menu offering the most famous dishes of the French-speaking alpine world. Specialties include five different kinds of fondues, raclettes, pepper steak, peppered filet of lamb, a fondue of chanterelles, and grilled steaks served with *gratin dauphinois* or rösti. The fondues are the resort's finest. No one will mind if you just drop in for a drink. Few other restaurants in town are as willing to close down whenever the weather is clear and sunny. Presumably when that happens, the staff rushes to the slopes because it's almost certain that the restaurant will be empty.

Place Centrale. © 027/771-22-26. Reservations recommended. Main courses 13F–47F ($11–$39); all-you-can-eat raclette 38F ($31). AE, DC, MC, V. Daily 11:30am–1am. Closed May–June.

Le Sonalon ⭐ *Finds* SWISS/CONTINENTAL   Some 4km (2½ miles) northwest of Verbier's center, this discovery lies near the edge of one of Verbier's less frequently used ski slopes (la piste de Savolère). This wood-sided chalet was built in the mid-1980s and has been known as a warm, comfortable dining spot ever since. You can reach it by car, following the directions listed below, or take the cable car to the Savolère station, then trek downhill on a steeply inclined 10-minute walk. In a dining room sheathed in light-colored wood paneling, or on an outdoor terrace with panoramic views encompassing the entire village of Verbier, you'll enjoy well-prepared meals whose gusto seems enhanced by the high altitudes. Menu items include raclette (available at dinner but not at lunch), several kinds of fondue, grilled lamb chops with aromatic herbs, filets of beef prepared with pepper sauce or mushrooms, and such palate-pleasing fish as pikeperch, filet of sole, and salmon. Calorie-conscious dishes such as grilled chicken in a sweet-and-sour sauce are classified as "fitness platters," although their weight-reducing benefits are usually offset by such desserts as crème brûlée, tiramisu, or a particularly succulent version of pears marinated in red wine and spices, served with cinnamon-flavored ice cream.

Piste de Savolère. © 027/771-72-71. Reservations recommended. Main courses 12F–55F ($9.85–$45). AE, DC, MC, V. Daily 11:30am–2pm and 7–10pm. Closed mid-Apr to May and Nov, and Mon–Tues in June and Sept–Oct. From place Centrale in Verbier, follow the signs to Savolère and Carrefour, then branch off on a dirt road signposted LE SONALON.

INEXPENSIVE

Pizzeria Fer à Cheval *Value* PIZZA/GRILLS   Although it defines itself as a pizzeria, this is among the best cost-conscious restaurants of Verbier, offering more than the dozen types of pizza for which it's best known. Crowded and friendly, with additional seating on another floor, it lies a short walk uphill from the resort's main square. It has an outdoor terrace that's used throughout the summer and on nice days the rest of the year, and an interior with large windows and pinewood paneling. The menu includes pizzas, such pastas as lasagna and spaghetti, all sorts of salads, and grills such as tenderloin of pork and filet steaks. A great between-meals snack is a *croûte au fromage*— a slice of bread covered with melted Gruyère and white-wine sauce, garnished with sliced ham or a fried egg.

Rue de Médran. ℂ **027/771-26-69.** Reservations recommended. Salads 7F–19F ($5.75–$16); pizzas and pastas 12F–25F ($9.85–$21); platters 25F–40F ($21–$33). AE, DC, MC, V. Daily 8am–midnight. Closed May–June and Sept to early Nov.

Restaurant au Robinson SWISS   This stucco-sided brasserie, hidden away on the side of Verbier's main square, is popular with local residents and the maintenance crews who keep the town's ski slopes and tourist facilities running. No one will mind if you order just a drink, but if you want a full-fledged meal, the staff is happy to accommodate you. Among the most popular and tasty items are beefsteaks, fondue *chinoise* or bourguignon, and a regional dish known as La Pirade—morsels of beef, duck, or chicken cooked on a hot platter directly at your table. Accompanying sauces include curry, calypso, or tartar sauce. Also available are *assiette valaisanne* (air-dried alpine beef with pickles and onions), filet of beef Stroganoff, and pastas.

Place Centrale. ℂ **027/771-32-13.** Reservations recommended. Main courses 13F–46F ($11–$38). MC, V. Tues–Sat noon–2pm and 7–10pm. Closed Aug–Sept 1.

VERBIER AFTER DARK

Partly because of its cosmopolitan mixture of English, French, and Swiss clients, many of whose youthful high spirits rise to alpine levels during ski and hill-climbing vacations, Verbier has more discos (at least four, all open only in the winter) and bars than you'd expect. The disco most popular with English-speaking tourists is the **Farm Club,** route de Verbier (ℂ **027/771-42-77**). Here, amid weathered beams, sturdy and amiably battered furniture, and a modern decor that includes several fireplaces, you can drink and dance to your heart's content. It's open every night between December and April, and things really get going after 10:30pm. Its most visible competitor is the **Tara Club,** route des Creux (ℂ **027/771-45-35**), with loud and danceable music, plank-covered walls, and alpine detailing. It's open only during midwinter, with hours that depend on how many dance-crazed clients are in Verbier at the time.

Even if you arrive during the off season when the discos are closed, you can always drink in any of the dozen or so bars and pubs. The most English of the lot is the neo-Victorian **Nelson Pub,** in the Hotel Vanessa, place Centrale (ℂ **027/771-31-51**). Look for cheeseburgers, croque-monsieur, and platters of air-dried alpine beef, along with at least 40 brands of beer from virtually everywhere. A less theme-ish, less aggressively Olde English venue is **Le Crok,** route des Creux (ℂ **027/771-69-34**), with tiny tables, leather-upholstered banquettes, and a modern decor. The place offers stiff drinks and frequent live music. The **Bar New Club,** rue de la Poste (ℂ **027/771-22-67**), re-creates the glossy, comfortable living room of an affluent bachelor, with couches perfect for conversation and comfortable drinking. Two noteworthy hotel bars are **Jacky's Bar,** in the Hôtel du Golf, rue de Verbier (ℂ **027/771-65-15**), and the **Bar L'Auin,** in the Hotel Rosalp, rue de Médran (ℂ **027/771-63-23**), which wins as the most conservative, discreet, elegant, and comfortable bar in town. The fireplace there gives a warm glow.

GREAT ST. BERNARD PASS ✵✵✵: AN EASY EXCURSION FROM VERBIER

Because of the danger of avalanches and road blockage, most winter drivers headed between the Valais and northern Italy travel through the 6km (4-mile) Great St. Bernard Tunnel instead of negotiating overland roads that are treacherous or impassable. In the summer, however, many visitors make the pilgrimage over the St. Bernard Pass instead, often to conclude that the drive is one of the highlights of their trip. The overland road is usually open only from mid-June to early October; its highest point lies about an hour's drive from Martigny, 40km (25 miles) away. If you're staying in Verbier and you'd like to visit the pass, you can drive east from Verbier along a winding road until you come to the village of Sembranchen. From here, E21 leads directly south to this historic pass. Follow the signs pointing uphill to Hospice St-Bernard. Travel time by car from Verbier is about 1¼ hours.

St. Bernard dogs are beloved in Switzerland, even though they no longer roam the snowy passes on missions of mercy with brandy in their casks. The dogs are still bred by Augustinian monks in one of the oldest monasteries in Europe, the **Great St. Bernard Hospice,** Le Grand-St-Bernard, 1946 Bourg-St-Pierre (© **027/787-12-36**). Set on the Swiss side of the vertiginous Swiss-Italian border, it was founded in 1050 and was mostly rebuilt of somber-looking gray stone in the 1600s. Year-round, the hospice houses only four or five Franciscan monks, many native to the Valais, as well as monks from other parts of Europe who stay for short-term bouts of meditation and prayer. Visitors can arrive by car only between June 15 and early October; the rest of the year, all roads are snowbound and transit is possible only via special skis. (See below for details.)

The monastery shelters a treasury of religious artifacts, a museum showcasing the often-tragic history of the pass, and historic kennels that are devoted to the perpetuation of the bloodlines of the St. Bernard breed of dog. During the winter visitors are forced to make a strenuous 6km (4-mile) uphill trek, on specially accessorized skis, from a parking lot near the Swiss entrance to the St. Bernard Tunnel. Don't even think of trying this without warning the monastery of your plans in advance, as the brothers will discourage you in the event of impending storms or avalanches. Proper equipment is required, including sealskin sheathing for your skis for traction during the uphill trek. In the event of an emergency, midwinter guests can be evacuated by snowmobile or helicopter.

In summer, between June 15 and early October, the kennels and the museum can be visited every day from 8:30am to 7pm. Admission to the public areas of the monastery and its chapel is free; admission to the museum and the kennels costs 5F ($4.10) per person. The rest of the year, visits can be made only by special arrangement.

During limited warm-weather periods, you can stay in the wood-sheathed interior of the **Hôtel de l'Hospice du Grand-St-Bernard,** Le Grand-St-Bernard, 1946 Bourg-St-Pierre (© **027/787-11-53;** fax 027/787-11-92). The four-story, gray-stone building was built in 1899. It's owned by the monastery, leased to a private entrepreneur, and contains 33 rooms. None have a TV or phone, and furnishings are simple and vaguely monastic. But views sweep out over both the Swiss and Italian Alps, and the food in the in-house restaurant is plentiful and reasonably priced. The hotel is open only between early June and mid-October, when it welcomes hill climbers, nature lovers, and members of religious organizations. The rest of the year it's locked tight, and the intrepid visitors who make the uphill trek on skis are housed, space and circumstances permitting, in the monastery itself. Per-person rates are 55F ($45), single or double occupancy, with breakfast and dinner included. MasterCard and Visa are accepted.

WHERE TO STAY & DINE

Auberge du Vieux-Moulin *(Finds*   This is a remote oasis. Part of a rocky hill was blasted away to make room for this small roadside inn in the hamlet of Bourg-St-Pierre, which lies on the way to the monastery (see above). Built in 1964 and recently renovated, the small rooms are streamlined and comfortable, with good beds. Guests in a room without private bathroom will find clean corridor facilities. Private bathrooms are small but neat with shower stalls.

CH-1946 Bourg-St-Pierre. (𝒞 **027/787-11-69**. Fax 027/787-11-92. 19 units, 9 with bathroom. 50F–84F ($41–$69) double with or without bathroom. Rates include continental breakfast. AE, DC, MC, V. **Amenities:** Restaurant; gas station; currency exchange. *In room:* No phone.

2 Sion ★/★

27km (17 miles) E of Martigny; 53km (33 miles) W of Visp

The capital of the Valais, the ancient city of Sion is known for its glorious springs and autumns and for its ancient status as a trading post on the trails between France and Italy. Dating from Roman times, the town is dominated by the silhouettes of the castles of Valère and Tourbillon. Most of its population speaks French.

Most of the towns of the Valais are sports oriented, but Sion is one of the exceptions. Come here if you want to see a beautifully preserved old Swiss town with a lot of history and plenty of impressive walks in all directions. It's not as tourist oriented as such cities as Verbier, and even though it's a capital, it's still off the beaten path for most visitors. The stone streets of the Vieille Ville (Old Town) are flanked with cafes and restaurants.

ESSENTIALS
GETTING THERE   Sion lies on the major rail lines that connect Milan and Turin (via the Simplon Tunnel) with Geneva and Paris. Trains arrive from both directions every day. Call (𝒞 **0900-300-300** (no area code) for **rail schedules.**

If you're driving, head east from Martigny, and from Visp go west, on E2.

VISITOR INFORMATION   The **Sion Tourist Information Office** is on place de la Planta ((𝒞 **027/327-77-27**). It's open July 15 to August 15, Monday to Friday 8:30am to 6pm, Saturday 10am to 4pm; off season Monday to Friday 8:30am to noon and 2 to 5:30pm, Saturday 9am to noon. During high season the office is also open Sunday 9am to noon.

SEEING THE SIGHTS
Château de Tourbillon ((𝒞 **027/606-47-45**) is perched on a steep rock on a hill overlooking the northern periphery of the town. It's the broodingly impressive ruin of a medieval stronghold built by a 13th-century bishop to defend Sion against the House of Savoy. Destroyed by a fire in 1788, it has never been reconstructed, but you can still make out the remains of a keep, watchtower, and chapel. There's a **panoramic view** ★ of the Rhône Valley from its base, which sits at an elevation of 645m (2,116 ft.). Admission is free.

Atop the town's other steep hill are the deeply weathered walls of an unusual Gothic church, the **Eglise-Fortresse de Valère** ★ (also known as the Château de Valère), whose foundations were built as a fortress by the ancient Romans. In much better shape than the previously mentioned castle, the three-aisle basilica dates from the 12th and 13th centuries. It contains 17th-century choir stalls and what has been called "the oldest playable organ in the world," dating from the 14th century.

Valère Museum ★, in the Eglise-Fortresse de Valère ((𝒞 **027/606-47-10**), is in the former residence of the cathedral chapter and is now the cantonal museum of history and ethnography. It contains fine works of medieval religious art, ancient arms and armor, uniforms, Roman and Gothic chests, and interesting ethnological collections. Both the museum and the fortified church that contains it are open Tuesday to Sunday from 10am to noon and 2 to 6pm (to 5pm Oct–Apr). Admission to both the church and museum costs 7F ($5.75) for adults and 4.50F ($3.70) for children 12 and under. A family pass costs 15F ($12). *Note:* There's a steep uphill climb between the parking lot and the church.

Back in town, the **Hôtel de Ville (town hall),** rue du Grand-Pont, whose inner chambers cannot be visited, has a facade embellished with 17th-century doors and columns. The foundations were laid by the ancient Romans in A.D. 377. On Sion's main street, rue du Grand-Pont, is an **astronomical clock.**

Northeast of the Hôtel de Ville is the **Cathédrale Notre-Dame-du-Glarier,** 13, rue de la Cathédrale (© **027/322-80-66**). It was reconstructed in the 15th century, although the original **Romanesque belfry** ⊛ remains, dating from the 11th and 13th centuries. Inside, look for the triptych in gilded wood, called *The Tree of Jesse.*

Although Sion has the monuments mentioned above, you can connect more intimately with regional life by taking an organized **wine-tasting excursion** (the tourist office—see above—will provide details). A long marked **footpath,** the most impressive walk in the area, is called *le chemin du vignoble,* and it passes through vineyards on the outskirts of the city. Our favorite vintner is the **Varone Vineyard,** a *centre de dégustation* at 30, av. Grand-Champsec (© **027/203-56-83**), across the river. It is open Monday from 2 to 6:30pm, Tuesday to Friday 10am to noon and 2 to 6:30pm, and Saturday 10am to noon and 2 to 5pm. Before beginning your hike, pick up the makings of a picnic at **Co-op City,** place du Midi, right off avenue de la Gare.

WHERE TO STAY

Hôtel Castel   Modern and boxy, this government-rated three-star hotel is at the edge of the road to Simplon at the northeast edge of town. Built in 1968, it was recently renovated. The small rooms have modern furniture and soundproof windows, and each comes with a good bed and tidy bathroom. Many units have views of the jagged cliffs that support the medieval château.

36, rue du Scex, CH-1950 Sion. © 027/322-91-71. Fax 027/322-57-24. www.hotel-castel.ch. 30 units. 125F–155F ($103–$127) double; 165F–185F ($135–$152) triple. Rates include buffet breakfast. AE, DC, V. Free parking. **Amenities:** Restaurant. *In room:* TV.

Hôtel du Rhône   This cinder-block hotel allows you to escape the traffic congestion of the Old City, lying at its outer border. The small rooms are furnished with angular contemporary furniture and full bathrooms. In spite of its no-frills atmosphere, the hotel is the best place to stay in town.

10, rue du Scex, CH-1950 Sion. © 800/780-7234 in the U.S. or 027/322-82-91. Fax 027/323-11-88. www.bestwestern. ch/durhonesion. 45 units. 170F–190F ($139–$156) double. Children 12 and under stay free in parent's room. Rates include buffet breakfast. AE, DC, MC, V. Free parking. **Amenities:** Restaurant; bar; limited room service; laundry service. *In room:* TV, minibar, hair dryer.

WHERE TO DINE

Caves de Touts-Vents *(Finds* VALAISIAN   This restaurant occupies several levels of a 13th-century cellar, whose vaultings were originally built to store wine. You descend a steep flight of stairs to reach the first room, much of which is devoted to a well-stocked bar. Claustrophobics may elect to go no farther. The lack of windows, the ancient stones, the flickering candles, and the effect of the wine work together to make the room cozy. The specialties—and good-tasting ones at that—include tagliatelle with salmon, mushrooms in puff pastry, calves' liver with shallots, and, of course, fondue and raclette.

16, rue des Châteaux. © 027/322-46-84. Reservations recommended. Main courses 9F–30F ($7.40–$25); raclette 29F ($24); fondue 20F–25F ($16–$21). AE, MC, V. Restaurant daily 7–10:30pm. Cafe and bar Tues–Sat 5pm–midnight. Closed mid-July to Aug.

Le Jardin Gourmand ✹✹✹ VAUDOISE   Established in 1996, this is the town's finest restaurant. Set near the railway station, it occupies a trio of rooms outfitted in Louis XVI furniture, with complicated wooden ceilings, floors of Carrara marble, and a glassed-in winter garden that's air-conditioned in summer. If you're absolutely committed to cutting costs, you may opt to dine in the cafe-style brasserie near the entrance, where lunchtime fixed-price menus are rock-bottom inexpensive. It's much more appealing, however, to pass into the inner sanctum, where the owner and chef, Pascal Fantoli, prepares food equivalent to what you'd expect from a culinary citadel in Lausanne or Geneva. Examples include a crawfish- and scallop-studded couscous infused with saffron and served with an aromatic court bouillon, a salad of wild greens with quail meat and foie gras, baby turbot with an anisette-flavored cream sauce, strips of filet of lamb with Provençal-derived aioli (garlic mayonnaise), and a particularly succulent dessert with frozen nougat, almonds, caramel, and rum sauce.

22, av. de la Gare. ✆ **027/323-23-10.** Reservations recommended. Main courses 13F–32F ($11–$26); fixed-price lunch 69F ($57); fixed-price dinner 80F–98F ($66–$80). AE, DC, MC, V. Mon–Sat 11:30am–2pm and 7–10pm. Closed 4 weeks in July–Aug.

L'enclos de Valère ✹✹ FRENCH   It's sometimes unnerving to drive a car up the steep and narrow street leading to this restaurant, but once you reach it, you'll find a site loaded with charm and one of the best-regarded restaurants in Sion. Located near the edge of the gardens that surround the Eglise-Fortresse de Valère, the restaurant is small and intimate, with an outdoor dining area. The dining room has a regional decor, with flagstone floors and a beamed ceiling. The menu changes monthly and may include lamb with garlic and thyme; crawfish salad; filets of perch with white-butter sauce; magret of duckling with raspberry-vinegar sauce; and an "assiette Clos de Valèrie" loaded with dried meats, pâtés, shredded duck meat, and salads. Dessert may include a slice of lemon tart or a crème brûlée.

18, rue des Châteaux. ✆ **027/323-32-30.** www.enclosdevalere.ch. Reservations recommended. Main courses 16F–43F ($13–$35); fixed-price menus 65F ($53), 78F ($64), and 92F ($75). DC, MC, V. Daily 9am–midnight (till 6pm on Sun). Closed Jan–Feb 15 and Mon in Sept and Oct.

Supersaxo ✹ FRENCH/SWISS   This particularly appealing restaurant, outfitted with a modernized decor vaguely inspired by Louis XV architecture, lies within a sheltered, pedestrian-only passageway in the heart of Sion. Inside, you'll find a cosmopolitan staff that prepares a seasonal menu filled with culinary nuances and rare delicacies. The dishes are likely to include a roasted and stuffed rabbit, grilled filet of veal, filet of beef stuffed with foie gras and truffles, and tender roasted rack of alpine lamb. Any of these might be preceded with carpaccio or foie gras. Desserts are appropriately rich and tempting; service is suitably attentive.

In the Passage Supersaxo, between rue de la Lausanne and rue de Couthey. ✆ **027/323-85-50.** Reservations recommended. Main courses 24F–55F ($20–$45); fixed-price menus 92F–115F ($75–$94). MC, V. Mon–Sat noon–2:30pm and 7–9:30pm.

3 Crans-Montana ✹✹

14km (9 miles) N of Sierre; 21km (13 miles) E of Sion; 158km (99 miles) E of Geneva

Crans and Montana-Vermala, at 1,494m (4,900 ft.), are twin ski resorts; both are modern and fashionable and long associated with an upscale Italian clientele. Set on a handsome plateau where the air is said to be "lighter than champagne," they enjoy excellent snowfall and views as far as the Rhône valley. Crans, whose hotel construction began in 1912, is composed for the most part of colonies of apartments and hotels, many in the half-timbered mountain style. Montana, clustered around the shores of Lac Grenon, is the older section, begun in 1892. Connected to them both, at a slightly lower altitude, is Aminona, still an infant resort but rising rapidly.

Note that the lack of street names in many cases is confusing, although restaurants and hotels often have directional signs. It seems that all the residents want to erase the distinctions between Crans and Montana, as the resort has become virtually one over the years.

ESSENTIALS

GETTING THERE   From Geneva, take a direct train to Sierre; call ℂ **0900-300-300** for **rail information.** At Sierre, change to a funicular or bus, each of which charges around 13F ($11) per person each way to Crans-Montana. Call the **Crans-Montana Service des Buses et Funiculaires** (ℂ **027/481-33-55**) for departure times.

A postal bus from Sion makes the run up the mountain to Crans-Montana.

If you're driving, the resorts are accessible by good roads from Sion or the market town of Sierre. From Sion, take E2 east to Sierre; from here, follow the signs up the winding mountain road until you reach Crans-Montana.

VISITOR INFORMATION   Not all thoroughfares have street names; to find establishments that lie off the street plans, you should look for directional signs. The **Tourist Information Office** is at Immeuble Scandia, in Crans (ℂ **027/485-08-00**). In Montana an equivalent organization is on avenue de la Gare (ℂ **027/485-04-04**). It's open Monday to Friday from 8:30am to noon and 2 to 5:30pm, and Saturday from 9am to noon. During high season it's open till 6:30pm Monday to Friday, Saturday 9:30am to noon and 2 to 4pm, and Sunday 9am to noon.

FUN IN THE OUTDOORS

Neither resort limits its allure to wintertime diversions. During the summer Montana tends to focus on spa cures and general health and well-being, and Crans transforms itself into a golf center. Nearby facilities include the 18-hole Plan-Bramois course, on the western outskirts of town, and the 9-hole Jack Nicklaus (formerly known as the Xires) course, on the resort's southern perimeter. For golf information, call ℂ **027/481-121-68.** The Omega European Masters, held at Crans each year in September, draws top golfers from all over the world. Tennis, hiking, and mountain climbing are the main summer sports at Crans-Montana; others include horseback riding, hiking, and fishing. Winter sports include skating, ski-bobbing, and ice-hockey matches. Skiing is available year-round.

There's a spectacular ascent to **Point Plaine-Morte** 𝕮𝕮, at nearly 3,000m (9,840 ft.); but even at such a great height, there are still runs suitable for novice skiers. To get here, take the gondola from Montana-Barzettes to the east of Montana, stopping at Les Violettes first. There's a restaurant at Plaine-Morte.

Cry d'Err, which looms north of the resort, rises to 2,264m (7,426 ft.) and has a large restaurant and a sunbathing terrace. To get here, take the Grand Signal gondola from Montana or the Crans-Cry d'Err gondola from Crans.

Piste Nationale is known for its steep, narrow runs, which attract many skiers. **Mount Tubang,** especially its La Toula run, is another slope only for the advanced skier.

All-inclusive ski passes that provide access to all the cable cars and chairlifts in the Crans-Montana district cost 103F ($84) for 2 days and 262F ($215) for 6 days. Children between the ages of 6 and 15 are charged 62F ($51) for 2 days and 166F ($136) for 6 days. A passport-size photo is required for anyone who wants to buy a ski pass.

SHOPPING

The crisp air and the dozens of outdoor diversions here might inspire purchases of sporting equipment rather than kitschy souvenirs. The accessories and paraphernalia you'll need to do anything in the Alps will jump out at you from virtually every local shop. Two of the best, however, are **Alex Sports,** rue du Prado, in Crans (© **027/481-40-61;** www.alexsports.ch); and **Ski Rinaldo,** route de Rawyl, in Montana (© **027/481-89-17;** www.ski-rinaldo.ch).

WHERE TO STAY
VERY EXPENSIVE
Grand Hôtel du Golf ✸✸✸   This government-rated five-star hotel, a 5-minute walk from the center of Crans, is on an 18-hole golf course, where in winter you can practice cross-country skiing. The hotel, however, does not operate the golf course. The landmark hotel in Crans, the Grand was constructed by British golfers in 1907 and has been run by the same family since World War I. From the bedrooms facing south, you can enjoy views of the Alps and of the Rhône Valley. The ample guest rooms have tidy bathrooms attached. The hotel attracts not only sports people but also the "genteel" crowd who don't like to exert themselves too much.

CH-3963 Crans. © 027/485-42-42. Fax 027/485-42-43. www.grand-hotel-du-golf.ch. 88 units. Winter and July 20–Sept 8 307F–680F ($252–$558) double, 790F ($648) suite for 2; off season 535F–680F ($439–$558) double, 1,240F ($1,017) suite for 2. Rates include half board. AE, DC, MC, V. Free parking. Closed Apr 15–May and end of Sept to mid-Dec. **Amenities:** 2 restaurants; bar; indoor pool; spa; sauna; salon; 24-hr. room service; massage; babysitting; laundry service. *In room:* TV, dataport, minibar, hair dryer.

EXPENSIVE
Aïda-Castel ✸✸   Known for its Valaisian decor, this government-rated four-star hotel is composed of two separate chalet-style buildings united during a series of massive renovations in the early 1990s. They lie on either side of the hotel's driveway, connected by a quiet passageway that passes above the underground piano bar. Set midway between Montana and Crans, near the flashier Hôtel Crans-Ambassador, it offers spacious bedrooms with lots of exposed wood and small seating areas that give the fleeting impression that the rooms are equivalent to small suites. Most accommodations have private balconies, and each comes with a clean bathroom. This is one of the few hotels of Crans-Montana that remains open the entire year.

CH-3962 Montana-Crans. © 027/485-41-11. Fax 027/481-70-62. www.aida-castel.ch. 61 units. Winter 310F–400F ($254–$328) double; summer 200F–350F ($164–$287) double. Rates include breakfast. Half board 40F ($33) extra. Free parking. AE, DC, MC, V. **Amenities:** 3 restaurants; bar; indoor pool; sauna; limited room service; laundry service. *In room:* TV, dataport, minibar, hair dryer.

Hôtel Alpina & Savoy ✸   This is the oldest hotel in Crans, built in 1912. Owned by three generations of the Mudry family, it has been frequently modernized and expanded. The hotel remains consciously unfashionable but venerable, lying a short walk from the departure point for the Cry d'Err gondola. The bedrooms come in different shapes and sizes, but each is exceedingly comfortable with alpine decor, excellent plumbing, and a tidy bathroom.

Route touristique de Crans, CH-3963 Crans. © 027/485-09-00. Fax 027/485-09-99. www.alpina-savoy.ch. 45 units. Winter 200F–290F ($164–$238) double, 240F–310F ($197–$254) suite; summer 140F–220F ($115–$180) double, 240F–310F ($197–$254) suite. Rates include breakfast. Half board 40F ($33) per person extra. AE, DC, MC, V. Parking 20F ($16). Closed Apr 15 to mid-June and Sept 15 to mid-Dec. **Amenities:** Restaurant; piano bar; indoor pool; saunas; limited room service; laundry service/valet. *In room:* TV, minibar.

Hôtel Crans-Ambassador ☆☆ Lying between the twin resorts of Crans and Montana, this is a stylized château built in the 1970s with a contemporary roofline that resembles three connected alpine peaks. It's only a short walk uphill from Lake Grenon and a nearby sports center. The staff members are conscious of their roles as emissaries of one of Crans-Montana's most prestigious hotels. From the bedrooms and public areas, guests have a view over the Alps and Rhône Valley. Despite the iconoclastic architecture of the exterior, the midsize bedrooms are conservatively modern, each with a balcony or terrace. In the summer you'll enjoy the public outdoor terrace brimming with flowers. There are two ski lifts about 91m (298 ft.) from the hotel, Grand Signal and Cry d'Err, as well as the end of one of the ski runs. The hotel has the most complicated rate schedule in Crans; make sure you check in with your accountant.

CH-3962 Montana. ☎ 027/485-48-48. Fax 027/485-48-49. www.crans-ambassador.ch. 72 units. 240F–410F ($197–$336) double; 430F–720F ($353–$590) suite for 2. Half board 60F ($49). Rates include buffet breakfast. AE, DC, MC, V. Parking 15F ($12). Closed mid Nov to mid-Dec. **Amenities:** Restaurant; bar; indoor pool; health club; steam bath; limited room service; babysitting; laundry service. *In room:* TV, dataport, minibar, hair dryer, iron, safe.

MODERATE
Hôtel de la Forêt *Value* This is one of the better bargains in the area. A hotel of one kind or another has stood on this site, about half a mile east of Montana's center, since the turn of the 20th century. Skiers appreciate the hotel's proximity to the slopes—only 180m (590 ft.) from the cable car of Les Violettes-Plaine Morte. Alain and Serge Morard throw weekly raclette parties for their guests. The midsize bedrooms facing south have balconies and some barely perceptible noise from the road; those rooms facing north don't have balconies and get less sun but are quiet and offer views of the forest. Each unit comes with an efficiently organized bathroom

CH-3962 Montana. ☎ 027/480-21-31. Fax 027/481-31-20. www.delaforet.ch. 60 units. Winter 195F ($160) double; summer 125F ($103) double. Rates include half board. MC, V. Parking 15F ($12). Closed mid-Apr to June 1 and mid-Oct to mid-Dec. **Amenities:** Restaurant; bar; indoor pool; sauna; limited room service; laundry service. *In room:* TV, hair dryer, safe.

INEXPENSIVE
Hôtel des Mélèzes *Finds* If you're looking for relative isolation, you'll like this place about half a mile from the town's commercial district in a forest of pines that the French call *mélèzes*. Built in 1959, the hotel is a solid, well-recommended, government-rated three-star choice run with a personal touch. Marie-Louise Lamon offers well-furnished and comfortable, though small, alpine rooms with balconies, plus private bathrooms with shower. The hotel has one of the most appealing sun terraces and greenhouse-style dining rooms in town. Breakfast is served outdoors in the summer, near the 7th hole of an 18-hole golf course.

CH-3963 Crans. ☎ 027/483-18-12. Fax 027/483-16-08. 20 units. 138F–178F ($113–$146) double. Rates include buffet breakfast. MC, V. Free parking. Closed Apr–June 20 and Sept 15–Dec 20. **Amenities:** Restaurant; bar; golf course. *In room:* TV, minibar, hair dryer.

WHERE TO DINE
EXPENSIVE
Le Cervin/La Bergerie ☆ SWISS/VALAIS Set in a meadow above the twin resorts, this red-shuttered, barnlike restaurant offers two different sections, both simply decorated. The more formal Le Cervin, on the street level, is a well-upholstered *maison bourgeoise* with lots of emphasis on the nuances of gastronomy. Here the French and Swiss specialties are likely to include salmon steak with fresh mushrooms, tournedos

with onions, and salads studded with quail eggs and foie gras. La Bergerie, in the building's basement, features *la cuisine valaisanne* and platters of raclettes, fondues, grilled steaks, salads, and brochettes. The daily buffet in the brasserie is especially appealing.

Quartier Vermala, Crans. ℂ 027/481-21-80. Reservations required in the evening. Le Cervin main courses 32F–64F ($26–$52); fixed-price menu 80F–110F ($66–$90). La Bergerie platters 27F–36F ($22–$30). AE, DC, DISC, MC, V. Daily noon–2:30pm and 7:30–10pm. Closed Mon–Tues mid-Apr to mid-June and mid-Oct to mid-Dec.

Restaurant de la Côte 🐾🐾 FRENCH   The best restaurant in the district lies in isolated and panoramic splendor in an alpine house whose facade is surprisingly modest. Inside, there's an aperitif lounge and a modernly decorated space for up to 50 well-dressed diners at a time. The restaurant's location, 3.2km (2 miles) from Sierre and 12km (7½ miles) from Montana, guarantees that you'll need your car (or a taxi) to reach it. As you gaze over faraway vineyards and valleys below, you can enjoy such smooth and perfectly flavored dishes as a gelée of foie gras with braised sweetbreads and a compote of Granny Smith apples, roast wild duck on a bed of juniper berries, and in season, a lightly larded haunch of rabbit stuffed with sage. Desserts are suitably delectable, and service is discreet and polite.

Corin-sur-Sierre. ℂ 027/455-13-51. Reservations recommended. Main courses 33F–60F ($27–$49); fixed-price menu 42F–80F ($34–$66) lunch, 80F–112F ($66–$92) dinner. MC, V. Wed–Sun noon–2pm and 6:30–9:30pm. Closed 3 weeks in June.

MODERATE
Auberge de la Diligence *Value* VALAIS/LEBANESE   This relatively inexpensive alpine tavern is on the highway beside the road leading in from Sierre. It specializes in flavor-filled combinations of cuisine from both the Valais and faraway Lebanon, whose spices and succulent flavors are much appreciated in the cold alpine air. The outdoor terrace is popular on fine days, and there's ample parking nearby. Dishes include couscous and fondues, grilled fish and steaks, well-spiced kabobs of chicken and lamb, and a succulent platter of Lebanese appetizers.

The hotel housing the tavern maintains nine bedrooms upstairs, five with a bathroom and all with TV and phone. Each has a balcony and, although they're larger than you might have expected, they come with almost no amenities or extra services. That fact contributes to their reasonable value at 130F ($107) for a room with a bathroom, and 120F ($98) for a room with shared facilities. Rates include breakfast. Both the hotel and its restaurant are open year-round.

Quartier La Combaz, CH-3963 Crans-Montana. ℂ 027/485-99-85. Fax 027/485-99-88. Reservations recommended in the evening. Main courses 16F–56F ($13–$46). AE, DC, MC, V. Restaurant daily 11:30am–2pm and 7–9:30pm. Cafe daily 8am–11:30pm.

Le Pavillon 🐾 SWISS   Graced with a delightful lakeside locale—a verdant setting near the Migros grocery store in the lowlands of "downtown" Montana—and an expansive terrace, Le Pavillon is popular in both winter and summer. You can drop in for snacks and drinks at any time; at mealtimes, the chef presents a *cuisine du marché,* featuring fresh ingredients from the marketplace. Perfectly prepared menu items are likely to include grilled filet of lamb with Provençal sauce, magret of duckling with orange sauce, filet of beef with green peppercorns, a savory version of fondue *chinoise,* and trout and perch from nearby lakes. Dessert includes a sorbet *valaisan,* flavored with apricots and locally distilled apricot liqueur.

Montana. ℂ 027/481-24-69. Reservations recommended. Main courses 22F–44F ($18–$36). AE, DC, MC, V. Daily noon–2pm and 7–10pm. Closed Mon–Tues in Apr–May and Oct, and 2–3 weeks in Nov (dates vary).

CRANS-MONTANA AFTER DARK

Here's how the night scene works in the twin playgrounds of Montana and Crans: Head for a pub both before and after dinner. Suitably rowdy choices with a bit of flair and humor include **Amadeus Pub,** in the Olympic Hotel, rue Louis-Antille, in Montana (© 027/481-24-95); and the woodsy and British-looking **George & Dragon,** rue du Grand-Place, in Crans (© 027/481-54-96). After your obligatory pints of beer, which cost around 6F ($4.90) each, head off to any of the resort's discos, preferably after midnight. The best of them is **l'Absolut Club,** rue Centrale, in Crans (© 027/481-65-96). The cover is around 20F ($16), which includes the first drink, and both mingle—in ways that can be a lot of fun—electronic dance music with bouts of folkloric evergreen.

4 Zermatt ★★★ & the Matterhorn ★★★

66km (41 miles) SE of Sierre; 48km (30 miles) SW of Brig; 242km (151 miles) E of Geneva

Zermatt, 1,594m (5,228 ft.) above sea level, is a small village at the base of the Matterhorn. It made its debut as a hiking and hill-climbing resort more than 150 years ago when it was discovered by English tourists. World attention was turned on the **Matterhorn** in the 1860s, when Edward Whymper, the English explorer and mountaineer, made a series of attempts to ascend it. Approaching the Matterhorn from the Italian side, he tried six times to climb it and failed. Then, on July 14, 1865, after changing his strategy and approaching the mountain from the Swiss side (using Zermatt as his departure point), he succeeded, and—accompanied by two of his guides—became the first person to reach the summit of the Matterhorn. During the process, however, four climbers in his team had fallen to their deaths.

Three days later, an Italian guide, Jean-Antoine Carrel, spurred on by the acclaim of Whymper's feat, successfully made the climb from the Italian side. Since then, the Matterhorn (known as Mont Cervin to the French-speaking Swiss) still lures mountain climbers, although only a few of them attempt to reach its summit. Two of the most memorable hikes are the climb up to the **Mettelhorn** (3,300m/10,824 ft.) and the hike up to the **Matterhorn Hut,** a few thousand feet below the wind-blasted cliffs that surround the summit.

Zermatt is a world-renowned resort with many luxurious accommodations and dozens of fashionable boutiques. You can walk from one end of the town to the other in about 15 minutes, which is handy because no cars are allowed on the local streets. The town does, however, have one of the best networks of alpine cable cars, gondolas, and cog railways in Switzerland—36 of them operating in the winter and 21 in the summer. In the peak season it's mobbed with hundreds of tourists.

Because more snow falls on Zermatt than on many other winter resort in Europe, high-altitude skiing—especially at the Théodul Pass—continues throughout the spring and early summer. As for winter skiing, skiers can choose between wide, gentle slopes and difficult runs only for world-class champion skiers. Zermatt's **ski school** (© 027/966-24-66) offers certified instruction and mountain guides.

From Zermatt, you can take one of the grandest and most scenic train rides in Europe. The **Glacier Express** might be the slowest express train in the world, taking 7½ hours to pass through southeastern Switzerland, but it's the most panoramic. A stunning feat of mountain engineering, the train begins its daily run in Zermatt, heading for the resort of St. Moritz in the Engadine. Along the way it crosses 291 bridges and goes through 91 tunnels. Windows on the train are designed to take in these stunning mountain panoramas. There's also a dining car on board. Make advance reservations by calling **Rail Europe** at © **877/257-2887,** or see their website at www.raileurope.com.

ESSENTIALS

GETTING THERE Take a train to Visp or Brig, where you can transfer to a narrow-gauge train to Zermatt. Departures are every 20 minutes daily between 6am and 11:30pm. It's about a 4-hour trip from Geneva. For Swiss **rail information,** call © **0900-300-300.**

In addition, buses run from Visp and Brig to Täsch hourly, which is the departure point for the cog railway that ascends frequently to Zermatt. Call the tourist office (see below) for more information.

If you're driving, head to Täsch, 4.8km (3 miles) from Zermatt, and park your car in an open lot or a garage. A rail shuttle in the center of the village will then take you to the resort for 15F ($12) per person round-trip.

VISITOR INFORMATION The **Zermatt Tourist Office** is on Bahnhofplatz (© **027/966-81-00;** www.zermatt.ch) and is open mid-June to mid-October, Monday to Saturday from 8:30am to 6pm and Sunday from 9:30am to noon and 4 to 7pm; otherwise Monday to Saturday 8:30am to noon and 1:30 to 6pm.

Only a few of Zermatt's streets, notably Bahnhofstrasse, have names—most don't. To find your way around, you can rely on the dozens of signs pointing the way to the various hotels and restaurants at the resort.

SEEING THE SIGHTS

There are many diversions in Zermatt, including a popular curling center, with eight rinks, each equipped with precision-crafted curling stones. There are also two natural ice-skating rinks, unusual shops, and a variety of bars and restaurants.

You may also pay a visit to the **Alpine Museum** (© **027/967-41-00**), which details Whymper's race to climb the Matterhorn. Exhibits include climbing equipment, relief models of the great mountain, and artifacts discovered near Zermatt from prehistoric and Roman times. The museum is open June to October daily from 10am to noon and 4 to 6pm; December to May, Sunday to Friday 4:30 to 6:30pm (closed in Nov). Admission costs 6F ($4.90) for adults, 2F ($1.65) for children ages 6 to 16, and is free for children 5 and under. To find the museum, get on Hauptstrasse and find the Hotel Mount Cervin. Across from it is the train station; the museum is in back.

SKIING & HIKING

There are a number of ski-lift passes sold in various combinations, but there isn't much savings regardless of the plan you select. A 2-day pass covering all the lifts in the Zermatt area costs 154F ($126), while day passes cost 78F ($64). The one break that ski-pass holders get is free rides on the ski bus linking all ski areas. To purchase tickets, visit the tourist office (see "Essentials," above).

GORNERGRAT 🎿🎿🎿 Gornergrat is perched at a lofty altitude of 3,099m (10,165 ft.). To get here, take a cogwheel train, the highest open-air railway in Europe, to its terminus. En route, you'll stop at **Riffelberg,** which offers a panoramic view of both the Matterhorn and Mount Rosa. The complete ride from Zermatt to Gornergrat is 63F ($52) round-trip. At Gornergrat an observatory looks out on the bleak expanses of the Gorner glacier and over the heights of the Dom, which, at nearly 4,572m (14,996 ft.), is the highest mountain entirely within Switzerland.

At Gornergrat you can take a cable car to other elevations. A two-stage cable car reaches a point near the top of the **Stockhorn,** at 3,407m (11,175 ft.); the cost is an additional 27F ($22) round-trip from Gornergrat.

BLAUHERD–UNTER ROTHORN 🎿🎿   To get to Blauherd–Unter Rothorn, take a cog railway through a tunnel from Zermatt to the alpine meadows of Sunegga, and then transfer to a cable car. After changing cable cars at Blauherd (which offers many hiking and skiing options of its own), you'll continue by cable car to the flat, rocky summit of the Unter Rothorn, where possibilities for alpine rambles or ski descents abound.

SCHWARZSEE-THEODUL   To reach Zermatt's third major ski area, take a cable car from Zermatt to **Furi-Schweigmatten** (usually abbreviated to Furi). Here you'll find a variety of cross-country skiing and hiking trails, and downhill skiing even in midsummer across the Théodul Pass and the border into Italy. In the winter you can continue downhill on skis to the Italian ski resort of Breuil-Cervinia for lunch, on the opposite side of the Matterhorn from Zermatt. At Furi a cable car carries you downhill to the calm waters of Schwarzsee (Black Lake) at 2,584m (8,476 ft.). Here the **Schwarzseehotel** (✆ **027/967-22-63**) offers vistas plus lunch or a drink on its terrace. Some skiers depart from Schwarzsee for another series of lonely but spectacular downhill runs. The round-trip excursion from Zermatt via Furi to Schwarzsee costs 35F ($29).

KLEIN MATTERHORN 🎿🎿🎿   To reach the "Little Matterhorn" from Furi, you must take two additional cable cars (the first of which will transfer at an alpine junction named Trockenersteg) before reaching an elevator that will carry you up to one of the highest mountain terraces in the world (3,760m/12,332 ft.). If the sky is clear, you'll be able to see both the French and the Italian Alps and breathe a rarefied air usually reserved for the hardiest of alpine climbers. The excursion to Klein Matterhorn from Zermatt costs 75F ($62) round-trip.

SHOPPING

Zermatt's critics accuse it of combining a hard-nosed commercialism, shrewdly calculating the value of every snowflake, with a less harsh obsession with Swiss folklore. Consequently, the town's main shopping thoroughfare, **Bahnhofstrasse,** contains branches of stores you might have expected only in much larger cities, with an emphasis on luxury goods, alpine souvenirs, and sporting goods. Ski and mountaineering equipment here tends to be state-of-the-art. Stores selling the stuff appear virtually everywhere, but worthwhile examples include **Slalom Sport,** Steinmatt (close to the village church; ✆ **027/966-23-66;** www.slalom-sport.ch). Well-recommended competitors, both on Bahnhofstrasse near the Gornergrat cable car, include **Glacier Sport** (✆ **027/967-27-19**) and **Bayard Sport** (✆ **027/966-49-50**).

Local souvenirs in Zermatt include everything from the genuinely artful to the hopelessly kitschy. One of the biggest outlets is **Haus der Geschenke (House of Presents),** on Bahnhofstrasse near the Gornergrat railway station (✆ **027/967-30-51**). A nearby competitor, **WEGA,** on Bahnhofplatz (✆ **027/967-21-66**), is just as folkloric. As an antidote to all the folk souvenirs, some visitors make it a point to search out more universal, or international, forms of art at one of the several art galleries. At the **Galerie Capricorn,** Bahnhofstrasse, near the village church (✆ **027/967-19-41**), you'll find oil paintings, watercolors, lithographs, and engravings, as well as inexpensive posters.

Snow and ice aren't the only things that sparkle in Zermatt, so if you're susceptible to impulse purchases of jewelry, be aware that there are a lot of shops to avoid. One of the most visible is **Bijouterie Schindler,** Bahnhofstrasse 5 (© **027/967-11-18**), which stockpiles both Swiss watches and gemstones.

WHERE TO STAY

Zermatt has something for most budgets. It contains more than 120 hotels and guest-houses, plus a growing array of private apartments and condominiums. Some hotels make arrangements to meet clients at the cog-railway station if you inform them in advance of your arrival.

VERY EXPENSIVE

Grand Hotel Zermatterhof ✶✶✶   This white-walled 1879 hotel, Zermatt's grandest resort, pointedly refuses to imitate a chalet. Rated five stars by the Swiss government, it's more plush and comfortable than anything in town. The bedrooms are paneled and well upholstered, with vivid colors. Alpine-style furnishings add a warm, cozy ambience, and each room is equipped with deluxe beds, plus marble and tile bathrooms boasting dual basins, robes, and heated towel racks. In summer a carriage awaits guests at the rail station at Täsch.

Bahnhofstrasse, CH-3920 Zermatt. © **027/966-66-00.** Fax 027/967-66-99. www.zermatt.ch/zermatterhof. 84 units. Winter 640F–900F ($525–$738) double, 1,020F–1,890F ($836–$1,550) suite; off season 430F–700F ($353–$574) double, 740F–1,500F ($607–$1,230) suite. Rates include half board. AE, DC, MC, V. Closed Oct 10–Nov 28. **Amenities:** 2 restaurants; 2 bars; outdoor pool; health club; Jacuzzi; sauna; steam bath; children's playroom; 24-hr. room service; massage; babysitting; laundry service/dry cleaning. *In room:* TV, dataport, minibar, coffeemaker, hair dryer, safe, Jacuzzi (in some).

Riffelalp Resort 222 ✶✶ *Finds*   Set within a 20-minute cog-railway ride north of Zermatt, this resort sits on sloping terrain midway up the mountain, in the midst of some of the region's most venerated skiing. It originated in 1884, when ancestors of the present owners (the Seiler family) erected a Victorian-style summer-only hotel, which was eventually damaged in a disastrous fire in 1961. Since then, the original building (the "Nostalgia wing") has been repaired and enlarged with a modern annex ("The Chalet"). Each accommodation comes with a midsize bathroom. This government-rated five-star resort offers quick access to the region's spectacular hiking, skiing, and views. The Gornergrat cable car will carry you even higher into the Alps (all the way to the Stockhorn) if you want more altitude, or down into Zermatt if you're looking for a rowdy good time in the town's bars, discos, or restaurants.

Riffelalp, 3920 Zermatt. © **027/966-05-55.** Fax 027/966-05-50. www.riffelalp.com. 72 units. Winter 760F–1,050F ($623–$861) double, 860F–1,200F ($705–$984) suite; summer 495F–550F ($406–$451) double, 620F–675F ($508–$554) suite. AE, DC, MC, V. Closed mid-Oct to mid-Dec and mid-Apr to mid-June. From Zermatt, take the Gornergrat cable car to its halfway point, Riffelalp. **Amenities:** 2 restaurants (1 with an outdoor terrace); wine bar w/piano music; indoor swimming pool; health club w/sauna; room service (7am–11pm); child-care facilities; 2 bowling alleys; in-house movie theater; billiard room. *In room:* TV, dataport, minibar.

Seiler Mont Cervin ✶✶✶   This has remained one of Zermatt's leading hotels since it was established in 1872. The rooms are often sunny and spacious, with fine craftsmanship. Units in the old quarter are more old-fashioned and still preferred by traditionalists. Accommodations in the newest wing have a restrained classic decor, and some are decorated in regional stucco along with hand-carved blond-wood pieces. All but nine units have tub/shower combinations; the remaining nine have only a shower. You and your bags will be picked up at the rail station by a horse-drawn sleigh in the winter or by an old-fashioned horse-drawn carriage in the summer.

Bahnhofstrasse 31, CH-3920 Zermatt. © **800/223-6800** in the U.S. and Canada or 027/966-88-88. Fax 027/967-28-78. www.seiler-hotels.ch. 133 units. Winter 740F–970F ($607–$795) double, from 1,200F ($984) suite; summer 530F–870F ($435–$713) double, from 750F ($615) suite. Rates include half board. AE, DC, MC, V. Closed mid-Apr to mid-June and mid-Oct to end of Nov. **Amenities:** 2 restaurants; bar; indoor pool; fitness center; steam bath; sauna; salon; limited room service; massage; babysitting; laundry service. *In room:* TV, dataport, minibar, hair dryer, safe, Jacuzzi (in some).

EXPENSIVE

Hotel Butterfly   This Best Western hotel lies under a peaked roof, with large windows and flower boxes. The Alps loom in the distance. The interior is warm and cozy, with arched windows, Oriental rugs, and knotty-pine furniture. Mrs. Gunda Woischnig offers small to midsize rooms with balconies facing south, all of them renovated in the late 1990s. The well-stocked hotel bar serves as an intimate rendezvous point, and buffet breakfast is served.

CH-3920 Zermatt. © **027/966-41-66.** Fax 027/966-41-65. www.hotelbutterflyzermatt.com. 40 units. Winter 270F–340F ($221–$279) double; summer 240F–270F ($197–$221) double. Rates include buffet breakfast. Half board 25F ($21) per person extra. AE, DC, MC, V. Closed Apr 20–May 20 and Oct 20–Dec 20. **Amenities:** Restaurant; bar; fitness center; steam bath; sauna; limited room service; laundry service. *In room:* TV, minibar, hair dryer, safe.

Hotel Riffelberg *Kids*   Set in an alpine meadow 2,460m (8,069 ft.) above sea level, a 90-minute trek or a 30-minute cog-railway ride from Zermatt, this isolated hotel sits amid natural splendor in the shadow of the Matterhorn. Built in 1853 by a local clergyman and purchased by the city of Zermatt in 1873, it has served ever since as a well-maintained hotel and restaurant, with the kind of views that restore health to bodies and minds. Because of its altitude, the area gets 8 full hours of sunlight in December, and even more in midsummer. Skiing between December and April, thanks to the nearby Gornergrat cableway, is excellent. Despite several recent renovations, the Riffelberg retains a simple alpine decor in its comfortable but small bedrooms. Round-trip transit from Zermatt on the cog railway costs 50F ($41) per person, and the last train from Zermatt departs at 6pm. The Riffelsee is not far from the train stop; an ibex colony lives nearby as well.

CH-3920 Zermatt-Umgebung. © **027/966-65-00.** Fax 027/966-65-05. www.matterhorn-group.ch. 29 units. Winter 310F–370F ($254–$303) double, 620F–740F ($508–$607) quad; summer 280F ($230) double, 490F ($402) quad. Rates include half board. AE, DC, MC, V. Closed Apr 15–June 20 and Oct 18–Dec 20. **Amenities:** 2 restaurants; bar; Jacuzzi; sauna; children's facilities; limited room service; laundry service. *In room:* TV, minibar, safe.

Hotel Walliserhof *Kids Finds*   Originally a Valaisian farmhouse, this hotel is one of the most successful conversions in town. It enjoys much German patronage, ever since the German newspaper *Bunte* named it "Swiss hotel of the year" a few years back. Renovations have made it worthy of a four-star government rating. In the center of town, it is easy to spot with its red shutters and balconies. It offers a large terrace out front, and inside you'll find stone fireplaces, thick walls, masonry columns, and flagstone floors. The midsize carpeted bedrooms have wooden furniture and good beds, plus neat bathrooms.

Bahnhofstrasse, CH-3920 Zermatt. © **027/966-65-55.** Fax 027/967-65-50. www.reconline.ch/walliserhof. 30 units. Winter 390F–420F ($320–$344) double, 400F–480F ($328–$394) suite; summer 270F–310F ($221–$254) double, 360F–400F ($295–$328) suite. Rates include breakfast. Half board 20F ($16) per person extra. AE, MC, V. **Amenities:** 2 restaurants; bar; limited room service; babysitting (on request); laundry service. *In room:* TV, minibar, hair dryer, safe.

Romantik Hotel Julen *Kids*   Across the river from Zermatt's historic cemetery, this hotel (ca. 1937), with its weathered balconies, is Zermatt's most romantic. The midsize bedrooms are furnished in mountain-resort style with carved pine beds and ceramic-tile bathrooms. Try for one on the south side—they have balconies with views of the Matterhorn. The main dining room features French cuisine and has an ornate ceiling and paneled walls. In addition, the Schaferstube offers more informal fare in a setting of pine wood, ceiling beams, and the inevitable cowbells. The hotel has installed an entire spa, and on the third floor is a "dreamshower" (you select what you want, from warm tropical to ice-cold glacier).

CH-3920 Zermatt. ⓒ **027/966-76-00.** Fax 027/966-76-76. www.zermatt.ch/julen. 32 units. Winter 454F–524F ($372–$430) double, 580F–694F ($476–$569) suite; summer 299F–388F ($245–$318) double, 342F–568F ($280F–$466) suite. Rates include half board. AE, DC, MC, V. **Amenities:** 2 restaurants; bar; indoor pool; health club; spa w/sauna; steam bath; limited room service; babysitting; laundry service. *In room:* TV, minibar, hair dryer, safe.

Schlosshotel Tenne ⓖ

The chiseled stonework and baroque-style stepped roofs, coupled with the Art Nouveau decor of its bedrooms and public rooms, make this hotel a welcome change from the many chalet-style hotels that surround it. Comfort and service are the keynote here, and you live well in alpine surroundings, with stunning views in most directions. Beds are exceedingly comfortable, and the private tiled bathrooms are of a good size. Each of its junior suites contains a whirlpool bathtub and a separate sitting room with fireplace. All south-facing rooms have private balconies.

CH-3920 Zermatt. ⓒ **027/966-44-00.** Fax 027/966-44-05. www.schlosshotel-tenne.ch. 38 units. Winter 300F–340F ($246–$279) double, 340F–400F ($279–$328) junior suite for 2; summer 200F–240F ($164–$197) double, 260F–320F ($213–$262) junior suite for 2. Rates include half board. AE, MC, V. Closed mid-Oct to mid-Dec. **Amenities:** Restaurant; bar; fitness center; steam bath; sauna; limited room service; laundry service, all nonsmoking rooms. *In room:* TV, dataport, hair dryer, Jacuzzi.

Seiler Hotel Monte Rosa ⓖ

According to Edward Whymper, the Englishman who conquered the Matterhorn, this is the best hotel at Zermatt. Of course, he made that pronouncement back in 1865. Monte Rosa has long since lost that position but still holds its own beautifully as one of the most welcoming and traditional hotels in the Valais. Located on the main street, the Monte Rosa has stone posts, lintels, and red shutters around its windows. The lounges have parquet floors, thick rugs, and crackling fireplaces; the antique armchairs are beautifully upholstered in stripes and patterns. The midsize to spacious bedrooms, decorated with Victorian prints and cabinetry, are among the most comfortable in Zermatt. Rooms facing south are the most desirable, the most expensive, and the hardest to come by. Each unit comes with a good-size, immaculately kept private bathroom.

Bahnhofstrasse 80, CH-3920 Zermatt. ⓒ **800/223-6800** in the U.S. or 027/966-03-33. Fax 027/966-03-30. www.seiler-hotels.ch. 47 units. Winter 320F–435F ($262–$357) double, 510F–590F ($418–$484) suite; summer 245F–365F ($201–$299) double, 500F–510F ($410–$418) suite. Rates include breakfast. Half board 100F ($82) extra. AE, DC, MC, V. Closed Apr 18–June 24 and Oct 24–Dec 17. **Amenities:** Restaurant; bar; use of nearby pool and fitness center; limited room service; babysitting; laundry service/dry cleaning. *In room:* TV, dataport, minibar, hair dryer, safe.

MODERATE

Hotel Antika ⓖ

Set behind an attractive chalet facade, each of the bedrooms of this hotel opens onto its own covered loggia with flower boxes and wooden trim. Making use of wood furnishings, rooms have an alpine charm and cozy comfort, with excellent beds and most often mountain views. The interior is accented with Oriental carpets and a partial sheathing of weathered planks. A large garden behind the hotel is great for quiet contemplation of the Matterhorn.

CH-3920 Zermatt. ⓒ **027/967-21-51.** Fax 027/967-57-83. www.antika.ch. 28 units. Winter 106F–245F ($87–$201) double; summer 90F–172F ($74–$141) double. Rates include buffet breakfast. AE, DC, MC, V. Closed May 5–June 10 and Oct 7–Nov 11. **Amenities:** Restaurant; Jacuzzi; sauna; limited room service. *In room:* TV, hair dryer.

Hotel Darioli ⓖ

This five-story, balconied hotel is on the main street near the train station. Built in 1964, the hotel was completely overhauled in 1979 and has been often renovated since. It's one of the few hotels in Zermatt to remain open all year, although its restaurant closes in November. This is one of the best government-rated three-star hotels in town; many guests prefer it to some hotels with higher ratings. The reception area is upstairs. The hotel has Oriental rugs and an attractive wooden bar. The Darioli family offers comfortable midsize rooms with regional furniture, usually painted in vivid colors with stenciled floral patterns. Most of the rooms have private bathrooms. One of the most consistently popular restaurants in Zermatt, Le Gitan (see "Where to Dine," below), is on this hotel's street level.

Bahnhofstrasse, CH-3920 Zermatt. © 027/967-27-48. Fax 027/967-12-37. www.darioli.ch. 22 units, 18 with bathroom. Winter 150F–240F ($123–$197) double; summer 120F–196F ($98–$161) double. Rates include buffet breakfast. AE, MC, V. **Amenities:** 2 restaurants; 2 bars; limited room service; laundry service. *In room:* TV (in some).

Hotel Post ⓐ *(Finds*   Built in 1880 and extensively rebuilt in the 1950s when American-born Karl Ivarsson and his family acquired it, this hotel is better known for its sprawling restaurant and nightlife facilities than for its bedrooms. There's a definite Anglo influence here, not only from the Americans attracted to the place but the increasing numbers of Brits as well. The small to midsize bedrooms have unusual floor plans, deliberately mismatched pieces of antique furniture, modern plumbing, and in some cases a TV. By no means should you assume that the Hotel Post falls into the predictable mold of the typical Swiss hotel. Its clients tend to be the most iconoclastic in Zermatt, and have included many of the great names in British rock 'n' roll, including David Bowie. Fittingly, the Post's labyrinth of nightlife facilities are the loudest, the most irreverent, and the most fun in Zermatt.

Bahnhofstrasse, CH-3920 Zermatt. © **027/967-19-32.** Fax 027/967-41-14. www.hotelpost.ch. 21 units. Winter 206F–292F ($169–$239) double; 328F–360F ($269–$295) deluxe double; summer 152F–234F ($125–$192) double, 234F–266F ($192–$218) deluxe double. Rates include buffet breakfast. AE, DC, MC, V. **Amenities:** 3 restaurants; 3 bars; sauna; limited room service; babysitting; laundry service; disco. *In room:* TV, dataport, hair dryer.

INEXPENSIVE

Hotel Alphubel *(Value*   Located near the train station, this is a large chalet with a solid stone foundation and curved stairs leading to the entrance. The Julen family named it after a local mountaintop. The small rooms are decorated in a functional, modern style with tub-equipped bathrooms. The restaurant is open for half-board guests only and serves good, moderately priced dishes.

CH-3920 Zermatt. © **027/967-30-03.** Fax 027/967-66-84. www.zermatt.ch/alphubel. 30 units. 136F–154F ($112–$126) double. Rates include breakfast. AE, MC, V. Closed Oct to the end of Nov. **Amenities:** Restaurant; bar; sauna. *In room:* TV, hair dryer.

Hotel Tannenhof *(Value*   The hotel is located in the center of the village, just a 3-minute walk from the train station and lying just off the Bahnhofstrasse (follow the signposts onto a pathway). The atmosphere is rustic and the rooms are simple and a bit small, but the place fills up quickly in winter. The hotel has simple alpine furnishings, including good beds, along with thick, cozy rugs.

Bahnhofstrasse, CH-3920 Zermatt. © **027/967-31-88.** Fax 027/967-21-73. www.rhone.ch/tannenhof. 23 units, 14 with bathroom. 100F–130F ($82–$107) double without bathroom; 120F–150F ($98–$123) double with bathroom. Rates include breakfast. AE, DC, MC, V. Closed Oct–Dec 15. **Amenities:** Lounge; laundry service.

Hotel Weisshorn   Convenient for frugal travelers arriving at the train station, this is a bargain in this otherwise high-priced resort area. However, if you're planning a winter visit, make reservations as far in advance as possible, as the hotel fills up quickly. You don't get luxury here but are provided with alpine comfort in a setting of low-paneled ceilings and winding staircases. The place is snug and cozy as the blizzards rage outside. The bedrooms are small but adequate, with plush comforters and, in some cases, small balconies.

Bahnhofstrasse, CH-3920 Zermatt. © 027/967-11-12. Fax 027/967-38-39. www.hotelweisshorn.ch. 17 units. 110F–140F ($90–$115) double; 150F–165F ($123–$135) triple; 180F ($148) family room. Rates include continental breakfast. MC, V. **Amenities:** Restaurant. *In room:* TV.

WHERE TO DINE
EXPENSIVE

Alex Grill ⊛ SWISS   This stylish basement restaurant is decorated with carved paneling, leaded windows, flagstone floors, bright upholstery, and rich accessories. The chefs concoct appetizing dishes based on regional and Swiss recipes prepared with market-fresh ingredients. As an appetizer, try a platter of three kinds of smoked fish or fresh Atlantic oysters. The main courses include grilled lobster, grilled salmon scallop, and giant shrimp with a chive-flavored cream sauce. The meat dishes include veal kidneys in mustard sauce, grilled rack of lamb, chicken breast filled with a salmon-and-herb mousse, and a variety of game in season.

In the Hotel Alex. © 027/966-70-70. Reservations recommended. Main courses 40F–62F ($33–$51); fixed-price menus 70F–80F ($57–$66). AE, MC, V. Daily 7–9:30pm. Closed May to mid-June and mid-Oct to mid-Nov.

The Grill Room/The Stübli ⊛ ITALIAN/SWISS   In what was originally built as a farmhouse, in the heart of town, these restaurants—unlike many of their competitors—remain open every day throughout the year. The Grill Room is the more elegant of the two, serving French, German, and Italian fare. There's an especially elegant collection of hors d'oeuvres, including smoked salmon, and main courses, such as veal cutlets and brook trout with almonds or veal piccata with risotto. The commendable regional dishes are filled with rich, subtle flavors. The less formal Stübli serves basically the same menu but concentrates on alpine Swiss specialties, such as fondues, raclettes, and grilled meats, in a cozy setting.

In the Hotel Walliserhof, Bahnhofstrasse. © 027/966-65-55. Reservations recommended. Main courses 22F–47F ($18–$39). AE, DC, MC, V. Daily 11am–2pm and 7–11pm.

Le Gitan ⊛ SWISS   This is neither the most formal restaurant in town nor the most glamorous. Despite that, reservations during the winter ski season are sometimes booked a week in advance, and virtually everyone in town seems to pick Le Gitan as their favorite restaurant. Set on the street level of a well-managed three-star hotel, the interior is very cozy, with an open fireplace and room for no more than 50 diners. With a wide selection of Swiss and regional specialties available, the array of grilled meats is the house specialty. The grilled beef, veal, game, and pork dishes are all richly garnished and impressively presented. Of special note is an excellent *gigot d'agneau* (lamb) with garlic, and a selection of savory fondues served in the bistro in front of the restaurant.

In the Hotel Darioli, Bahnhofstrasse. © 027/968-19-40. Reservations required. Main courses 19F–45F ($16–$37). AE, MC, V. Daily 6:30–10pm.

Schlosshotel Tenne ⊛ SWISS/INTERNATIONAL   In the lobby level of the previously recommended hotel of the same name, this duplex restaurant includes an upper wraparound gallery and a ceiling fresco covered with a representation of the zodiac. The kitchen continues to steer a steady course between rich, regional specialties and the subtler flavors of an international repertoire. Ingredients are first-rate, and the restaurant is known for its grill specialties. The menu may include herb-flavored shrimp soup, whole-meal noodles, roast salmon in a white-wine sauce, or rack of lamb from the grill. For dessert, try cherries flambé with a honey parfait.

In the Schlosshotel Tenne. ☎ 027/967-44-00. Reservations required in winter. Main courses 18F–60F ($15–$49). AE, MC, V. Daily 7–9:30pm. Closed mid-Oct to mid-Dec.

MODERATE

Arvenstube SWISS/INTERNATIONAL   A tempting variety of international and Swiss dishes is served in this paneled dining room with a corner bar. The chefs here continue to please visitors year after year with their skill. As an appetizer, try the *assiette valaisanne,* a plate of air-dried meats from the Grisons. Other specialties include *riz Casimir* (a curry rice dish), tournedos in a savory-mustard sauce, and sliced veal in a mushroom-cream sauce. These dishes are often served with rösti (Swiss hash browns). Trout with almonds is another favorite.

In the Hotel Pollux, Bahnhofstrasse. ☎ 027/966-40-00. Reservations recommended. Main courses 18F–65F ($15–$53). AE, DC, MC, V. Daily 11:30am–2pm and 6–9pm. Closed 2 or 3 weeks in Nov.

Findlerhof ✸✸ *Finds* SWISS/ITALIAN   The Findlerhof is the best mountain restaurant near Zermatt. Despite its remote location—in the small hamlet of Findeln, on a steep mountainside—the place is very popular. It has a sun terrace and a roof terrace facing the Matterhorn. Your hosts are Franz and Heidi Schwery, who offer such delights as meat and salmon carpaccio, salads laced with salmon and scampi, and excellent pasta dishes.

Findeln. ☎ 027/967-25-88. Reservations required. Main courses 16F–38F ($13–$31); fixed-price menu 24F–37F ($20–$30). No credit cards. Daily 9am–6pm. Take the Sunnegga chairlift to the 1st stop, then hike across the fields; leave your skis in the snow and head down the steep, winding pathway, past the plastic palm trees.

Grillroom Stockhorn ✸ SWISS   This is one of the few restaurants of Zermatt not located in a hotel, and it's one of the two or three best dining rooms in town. A fireplace extends into the dining room of this elegant chalet owned by Emil Julen. The decor includes an alpine wedding chest and regional chairs, as well as travertine floors, heavy beams, varnished pine, earth-tone accents, and stained stucco walls. The savory, rib-sticking specialties include raclette, piccata with spaghetti, fondue bourguignon, and grilled meats. Chocolate fondue is recommended for dessert. There's also a bar.

Riedstrasse. ☎ 027/967-17-47. Reservations required. Main courses 22F–43F ($18–$35). AE, MC, V. Daily 11:30am–1pm and 6:30–10pm. Closed May to mid-June and Oct to mid-Nov.

Portofino Grill INTERNATIONAL   Decorated in tones of marine blue with lots of highly varnished wood, this is the most elegant of the several dining choices in the Hotel Post. A fresh antipasto buffet is laid out in what used to be a boat, and the cuisine—which some visitors consider a welcome change from a constant diet of Swiss alpine food—features seafood and Italian choices. Menu items include a selection of home-made pastas with savory sauces, and freshly prepared veal, poultry, and meat dishes. Many diners opt for a before- or after-dinner drink in the Boathouse Bar. Crafted from the cabin of a once-glamorous three-masted schooner, it seats only a dozen drinkers in cozy, knee-rubbing proximity. The spillover from the main bar moves into what's affectionately known as "The Disaster Room," where photos of the 20th century's greatest marine disasters are prominently displayed.

In the Hotel Post. ☎ 027/967-19-32. Reservations recommended. Main courses 16F–38F ($13–$31). AE, DC, MC, V. Dec–Apr daily 7–11pm. Closed Easter–Nov.

Schäferstübli SWISS   This moderately priced restaurant offers atmospheric dining amid plank-covered walls, heavy beams, flickering candles, and leaded-glass windows. If you're not already a convert of Swiss cuisine, you may easily become one after a meal here. The house specialty is lamb, served in a variety of styles. You can also order grilled veal and beef dishes, traditionally prepared. The restaurant is part of the Romantik Hotel Julen but has its own separate entrance.

In the Romantik Hotel Julen. ℰ **027/967-76-05.** Reservations required. Main courses 14F–35F ($11–$29); lamb fondues 37F ($30) per person; cheese fondues 20F ($16) per person; all-you-can-eat raclette 33F ($27) per person; fixed-price meal 37F ($30). AE, DC, MC, V. Daily 6–9:30pm. Closed May and 2 weeks in Nov.

INEXPENSIVE

Walliserkanne SWISS/ITALIAN   This rustic family restaurant is 2 minutes from the Zermatt train station. Walliserkanne is divided into three main dining rooms and a second restaurant in the basement. The elegant rooms are large and feature paintings by local artists on the walls. The restaurant offers a delectable menu of Italian dishes such as antipasto *misto della casa* (variety of Italian starters), carpaccio *d'agnello con rucola e parmigiano* (thin slices of raw lamb served with arugula and Parmesan), or *vitello tonnato* (slices of roast veal with tuna fish sauce). Pizzas and pastas round out the succulent fare. The menu also offers a wide choice of desserts.

32 Bahnhofstrasse. ℰ **027/966-46-10.** Reservations recommended. Main courses 17F–53F ($14–$43). AE, MC, V. Daily 10am–midnight.

ZERMATT AFTER DARK

Zermatt is known for its après-ski activities, which include tea dances, restaurants, bars, nightclubs, and discos. It has more nightclubs than any other resort in the Valais.

AN ENTERTAINMENT COMPLEX

Hotel Post (ℰ **027/967-19-31;** see "Where to Stay," earlier in this chapter), where everybody shows up after recovering from Elsie's Irish coffee (see below), has a virtual monopoly on nightlife in Zermatt. The owner, Karl Ivarsson, an American, has gradually expanded it into one of the most complete entertainment complexes in Zermatt, with a number of restaurants and nightspots under one roof. Photographs of former guests, including famous athletes and models, are displayed under glass at the reception desk. On the way to the restaurant, in the basement, you'll pass a series of murals telling the story of a lonely tourist looking for love in Zermatt.

Take your pick of the various venues, including the **Jazz Bar,** open December to Easter and 1 month in summer. In winter they import a different band every year, although there's only a piano player in summer. The **Broken Bar,** located in the basement, is where the most hardened ski bums listen to hard rock music at very high volumes, drink heavily, and generally raise hell. **Le Village** is the most interesting disco in Zermatt, built in a 19th-century alpine barn, with Edwardian palms, leather couches, candles, and bentwood chairs. David Bowie has performed here. For hunger pangs, head for the **Brown Cow** at street level, a rustic room with 19th-century farm implements hanging from the ceiling. The menu includes hamburgers, goulash soup, sandwiches, and salads. **The Spaghetti Factory** is also open year-round, until midnight.

THE BAR SCENE

Elsie's Place, at Kirchplatz (ℰ **027/967-24-31**), is a small house, dating from 1879, that packs in a large crowd around 6pm. It's comfortable, sedate, and bourgeois. Skiers show up for hot chocolate or Elsie's famous Irish coffee (15F/$12). The house is on the main street, near the Zermatterhof Hotel. During the day the menu includes ham and eggs, hot dogs, and even escargots. They also serve caviar and oysters (a special luxury in this area). The cafe is open in the winter daily from 11am to 2am and in the summer daily from 4pm to 2am.

One of the most animated and energetic bars is **Grampy's Pub,** Bahnhofstrasse (© **027/967-77-88**), across from the Post Hotel, a pub and disco favored by the resort's army of off-duty waiters, bartenders, chambermaids, and ski instructors. A roughly equivalent competitor is the **Papparia Pub** (© **027/967-40-40**), near the Hotel Julen, where live music produced by Swiss folk and North American country-and-western bands gets your blood pumping.

Hotels that contain relatively animated pubs include the Hotel Bristol, the Schlosshotel Tenne, and the Hotel Excelsior. The least pretentious of the lot is the **Kegelstube ("Bowling Alley Bar")** in the Hotel Bristol (© **027/966-33-80**), where the resort's only bowling alley adds visual distraction to the large bar area. Upstairs, the more formal **Bristol Bar** has a dance floor, a fireplace, and a view of the attached restaurant. The Alex Schlosshotel Tenne's most appealing after-dark spot is the **Bar Tenne** (© **027/967-18-01**), whose Art Nouveau decor is a welcome change from the relentless emphasis on Swiss chalets everywhere else. Here, near a bar that resembles an ambulatory in a monastery, and a DJ booth that might have been a church pulpit, you can relax on comfortable sofas or dance beneath the klieg lights of a circular dance floor. In the Hotel Excelsior (© **027/967-30-17**), you can head for the sometimes rowdy and garrulous **Ex-Bar** or seek refuge in the somewhat calmer, somewhat more upscale, winter-only **Luna Bar,** which is shielded from the noise nearby by thick doors and masonry walls.

Hotel Schwyzerhof (© **027/967-67-67**), with its restaurant, and the **Hotel Simi** (© **027/966-46-00**), with its Dancing Simi, both combine a regime of Swiss folklore and oompah music with alpine warmth, a busy bar area, platters of food, and—in the case of the Hotel Simi—some emphasis on disco. You'll find a rough approximation of big-city, urban life in the form of the **Scotch Corner Bar,** in the Hotel Aristella (© **027/967-20-41**). You can always grab a beer and a shot or two of schnapps in the cozy setting of the Hotel Walliserhof's **Stübli** (© **027/966-65-55**).

10

Lausanne & Lake Geneva

For decades, visitors have sought the scenic wonders of Lake Geneva (Lac Léman) in the southwestern corner of Switzerland. Native son Jean-Jacques Rousseau popularized the lake among the Romantics, and Lord Byron and Shelley both made pilgrimages here.

Formed by the Rhône, Lac Léman is the largest lake in central Europe. It consists of a Grand Lac to the east and a Petit Lac to the west, near Geneva (for a description of Geneva and its environs, see chapter 11). The lake covers 582 sq. km (225 sq. miles); more than half belongs to Switzerland, the rest to France. The French own most of the southern shore, except for Geneva in the west and the Valais in the east; the Swiss hold the entire northern shore, which forms a large arc. The water is limpid blue, except where the muddy Rhône empties into it.

Famous people who chose to live on the lake's shores have included the historian Edward Gibbon; writers Honoré de Balzac, George Eliot, and André Gide; composers Richard Wagner and Franz Liszt; the aviator Charles Lindbergh; and actors Charlie Chaplin, Yul Brynner, Audrey Hepburn, James Mason, Noel Coward, William Holden, David Niven, and Sophia Loren (many of whom went here originally for tax reasons but liked the area so much that they stayed on until their deaths). Some of these actors, such as Chaplin and Hepburn, adopted Switzerland as their permanent home and were buried here.

Since 1823 steamer trips have been the most popular way to tour the lake. Nearly all the cities, hamlets, and towns along the lake have schedules posted at the landing quays, and service usually runs from Easter to October. If possible, though, we recommend touring by car or bus so that you can stop and visit sights along the way. Railways also run along both shores. Our exploration will begin with Lausanne.

1 Lausanne ★★

66km (41 miles) NE of Geneva; 214km (134 miles) SW of Zurich

Lausanne, whose 130,000 inhabitants make it the second-largest city on Lake Geneva and the fifth-largest in Switzerland, is built on three hills overlooking the lake, called Lac Léman by the city's inhabitants. The upper and lower towns are connected by a small metro (subway).

Lausanne has been inhabited since the Stone Age (it was the ancient Roman town of Lousanna). In 1803 the canton of Vaud, of which Lausanne is the capital, became the 19th to join the Swiss Confederation.

For centuries Lausanne has been a favorite spot for exiles and expatriates, attracting, among others, deposed monarchs. Lausanne flourished particularly in the Age of Enlightenment, when it was associated with Rousseau and Voltaire, two of the leading writers in the 18th century. Even today the city is cited by many French-speaking Swiss as the place they would most like to live because of its low-key elegance and sense of grace. Regrettably, it's no longer a center of the intellectual or artistic elite. Voltaire and the likes have given way to water-skiers, swimmers, and "Sunday sailors," most of whom have never heard of Rousseau, much less read him. Even so, Lausanne retains an aesthetic charm and a cultural tradition—today it's the headquarters of the International Olympic Committee.

ESSENTIALS

GETTING THERE   Lausanne doesn't have an airport, so most visitors fly to Cointrin Airport in Geneva (see chapter 11) and then travel on to Lausanne. The train from Geneva leaves for Lausanne every 20 minutes and the trip takes 45 minutes. Call ℂ **0900/300-300** for **train** schedules.

In addition, between late May and late September, a lake steamer cruises several times a day in both directions between Geneva and Saint-Gingolph, Lausanne, Vevey, Montreux, and Nyon. Sailing time from Geneva is about 3½ hours. Round-trip transit from Geneva costs 75F ($62) in first class and 55F ($45) in second class, with 50% discounts for children 16 and under. For information, contact the **Compagnie Générale de Navigation (CGN),** 17, av. de Rhodanie (ℂ **0848-811-848**).

If you're driving, Lausanne is connected by freeway (N1) to Geneva. The Great Saint Bernard road tunnel is 113km (70 miles) to the southeast, reached along E2, which becomes E21 during your final approach.

VISITOR INFORMATION   The **Office du Tourisme et des Congrès,** 2, av. de Rhodanie (ℂ **021/613-73-21** or 021/613-73-73; www.lausanne-tourisme.ch), is open Easter to mid-October daily from 8am to 5pm, Saturday 9am to 6pm, and Sunday 9am to noon and 1 to 6pm; off season, Monday to Friday 8am to 5pm and Saturday 8am to noon and 1 to 5pm.

CITY LAYOUT

Lausanne is spread out along the shore of Lake Geneva, surrounded by suburbs. There are two sections in particular that attract the most visitors—the **Upper Town (Haute Ville),** which is the old part of the city, and the **Lower Town (Basse Ville),** or **Ouchy;** the two sections are connected by a small subway (metro).

HAUTE VILLE *🏛🏛*   Lausanne's Upper Town still evokes the Middle Ages—a night watchman calls out the hours from 10pm to 2am from atop the cathedral's belfry. A visit to the Haute Ville takes about 2 hours and is best done on foot. In fact, walking through the old town of Lausanne is one of its major attractions. It's easy to get lost— and that's part of the fun. This area is north of the railroad station; you can reach it by going along rue du Petit-Chêne. The focal point of the Upper Town, and the shopping and business heart of Lausanne, is **place Saint-François.** The Church of St. François, from the 13th century, is all that remains of an old Franciscan friary. Today the square is filled with office blocks and the main post office; regrettably, La Grotte, the villa with the terrace on which Edward Gibbon completed *The History of the Decline and Fall of the Roman Empire* in 1787, was torn down in 1896 to make room for the post office. While vehicles are permitted south of the church, the area to the north is a pedestrian-only zone; it has more than 2km (1¼ miles) of streets, including **rue de Bourg,** northeast of the church, the best street for shopping. Rue de Bourg leads to the large, bustling rue Caroline, which winds north to **Pont des Bessières,**

one of the three bridges erected at the turn of the 20th century to connect the three hills on which Lausanne was built. From the bridge, you'll see the Haute Ville on your right, with the 13th-century **cathedral of Lausanne,** opening onto place de la Cathédrale. From the square, rue du Cité-de-Vant goes north to the 14th-century **Château Saint-Marie,** on place du Château—once the home of bishops and now containing the offices of the canton administration.

From here, avenue de l'Université leads to **place de la Riponne,** with the **Palais de Rumine** on its east side. From place de la Riponne, rue Pierre-Viret leads to the **Escaliers du Marché,** a covered stairway dating back to the Middle Ages. You can also take rue Madeleine from the place de la Riponne, continuing south to place de la Palud. On the side of place de la Palud is the 17th-century **Hôtel de Ville (town hall).**

South of place de la Palud is rue du Pont, which turns into rue Saint-François (after crossing rue Centrale). Nearby, at **place du Flon,** you can catch the subway to Ouchy. Place du Flon, with its cafes and bars, has become a favorite evening hangout.

OUCHY 𝒜𝒜   Ouchy, once a sleepy fishing hamlet, is now the port and hotel resort area of Lausanne. The lakefront of Lausanne consists of shady quays and tropical plants spread across a lakefront district of about half a mile. The **Château d'Ouchy** stands on place de la Navigation; from here, place du Port adjoins immediately on the east. **Quai de Belgique** and **quai d'Ouchy** are lakefront promenades bursting with greenery and offering the best views of the lake.

GETTING AROUND

BY METRO   To avoid the crawling pace of the city's trams, take the metro. The trip between the heart of the Haute Ville and Ouchy takes 6 minutes. Departures are every 7½ minutes Monday to Friday from 6:15am to 11:45pm. During off-hours and on weekends and holidays, trains run every 15 minutes. A one-way ride from the town center to Ouchy costs 2.50F ($2.05); a 24-hour ticket sells for 7.20F ($5.90).

BY BUS & TRAM   The TL (Lausanne Public Transport Company) has a well-designed network of trams and buses whose routes complement the city's subway line. The tram or bus fare is 2.50F ($2.05), regardless of the distance, for a single trip completed within 60 minutes on lines 1 to 50 of the TL urban network on the Lausanne-Ouchy metro.

You can purchase or stamp your tickets at the automatic machines installed at most stops, or just ask the driver. (A surcharge is collected if you get your ticket from the driver at a stop that has a machine.) A 1-day ticket for unlimited rides costs 7.20F ($5.90) for adults, 3.75F ($3.10) for children.

BY TAXI   Lausanne contains dozens of taxi stands, where you'll usually find a line. Alternatively, you can telephone **Taxibus** (✆ 0800/800-312) or **Taxiphone** (✆ 0800/801-802) for a cab. The meter starts at 7.50F ($6.15); each kilometer traveled adds 3F ($2.45) during daylight hours in town, or 3.50F ($2.85) in town on weekends or at night between 8pm and 6am. For trips outside the town limits, each kilometer traveled costs 4F ($3.30), regardless of the time of day. The first 10 kilograms (22 lb.) of luggage are free, with 1F (80¢) charged for every suitcase thereafter.

BY CAR   If you drive to Lausanne or rent a car here, wearing seat belts is required, and children 11 and under are not allowed to ride in the front seat. In Lausanne there are four types of parking zones: a white zone, in which parking is free and unlimited; a red zone and a blue zone, in which parking is free but variously limited (15 hr. in the red zone and 90 min. in the blue zone); and a fourth zone with parking meters. To park, you must display a parking disk on the dashboard of your car; parking disks are free and can be obtained at police stations, automobile clubs, and most gas stations.

BY BIKE   You can rent bikes at the baggage-forwarding counter of the **railroad station** (✆ 0900-300-300). It's open daily from 6:50am to 7:50pm. The cost is 20F ($16) per day. Bikes can be transported by train from Lausanne to any of the region's outlying districts (or anywhere in Switzerland) for an extra fee.

BY BOAT   To rent boats or *pédalos* (pedal boats), try various rental kiosks at Ouchy and Parc Bourget at Vidy. One of the best of these is **Ste. C. Barke,** place du Vieux-Port, Lausanne-Ouchy (✆ 021/616-08-44).

To France by Lake Steamer

With its scenic beauty, it's hard to beat Switzerland. But for a change of pace, you can visit **Evian-les-Bains** in France. It lies on one of the southern shores of Lake Geneva and is the leading spa resort in eastern France, its lakeside promenade fashionable since the 19th century. Bottled Evian is, of course, one of the great French table waters.

Lake steamers to Evian are operated by **CGN (Compagnie Générale de Navigation; ✆ 021/614-62-22; www.cgn.ch).** They depart from the lakefront quays of Lausanne every hour in summer (May 20–Sept 17), and about three times per day in the dead of winter. Transit takes only 35 minutes each way. Once you get to Evian, you can wander, lunch, and kibitz on your own, as there are no guided tours available. Round-trip cost of passage from Lausanne to Evian is 30F ($25) in second class or 40F ($33) in first class. Note that the midsummer departures that leave either city around noon (there's usually a 12:30pm departure from Lausanne) offer more comprehensive restaurant service than what's available at other times, when there's just a snack bar operational.

ON FOOT   This is the only way to see the old Upper Town effectively. Afterward, you can take the subway to Ouchy and resume your walk along the lakefront quays. Lausanne's civic authorities conduct a **guided walking tour** of their city, lasting 1 to 2 hours, Monday through Saturday. Departure is from place de la Palud, adjacent to the city hall, at 10am and 3pm. The cost is 15F ($12) for adults, 7.50F ($6.15) for seniors and students, and free for children. For more information, call the city's tourist office (see "Essentials," above).

SEEING THE SIGHTS

The **cathedral of Lausanne,** place de la Cathédrale, is the focal point of the Upper Town and one of the finest medieval churches in Switzerland. North of the cathedral, at the end of the Upper Town, is the **Château Saint-Marie.** It was built of brick and stone in the 14th and early 15th centuries. Powerful bishops lived here until they were replaced by the Bernese bailiffs, who turned Lausanne into a virtual colony of Bern. Today the château is used for the canton's administrative offices.

In the center of town is **place de la Palud.** Located on the square is the **Hôtel de Ville (town hall),** which has a 17th-century Renaissance facade; it was completely restored in the late 1970s. Today it's the headquarters of the Communal Council. Also on the square is the **Fountain of Justice,** dating from 1726. A clock with animated historical scenes presents a drama daily every hour on the hour from 9am to 7pm. A traditional market is held here Wednesday and Saturday. To visit the cathedral, take the **Escaliers du Marché,** a covered flight of medieval stairs on one side of the square.

North of place de la Palud is **place de la Riponne,** where you can visit the Italianate **Palais de Rumine,** built in 1906. It contains several museums, a university founded in 1537, and the university and cantonal library with some 700,000 volumes.

On the east side of town, **Mon Repos Park** contains landscaped gardens and the **Empire Villa,** where Voltaire performed his work *Zaïre* for a group of friends. The

Tribunal Fédéral is in the northern area of the park; it was constructed in the 1920s and today houses Switzerland's highest court.

To the north, the **Signal de Sauvabelin,** known popularly as *le signal,* rises above the town. At 637m (2,089 ft.), it has a restaurant and a belvedere opening onto Lake Geneva, with the Fribourg Alps in the distance. It's a 20-minute hike from town.

Ouchy is the lakeside resort and bustling port of Lausanne. Its tree-shaded quays have flower gardens that are nearly half a mile long. The small harbor contains a 700-boat marina, and the Savoy Alps are visible on the opposite shore. The **Château d'Ouchy** is now a hotel and restaurant. The Allies, Greece, and Turkey signed a peace treaty here in 1923. The 13th-century keep is still standing. In the **Hôtel d'Angleterre,** formerly the Auberge de l'Ancre, is a plaque commemorating the stay of Lord Byron, who wrote *The Prisoner of Chillon* here. In the **Beau-Rivage,** the Treaty of Lausanne was ratified in 1923; it settled the final reparations disputes after World War I.

THE TOP ATTRACTIONS

Cathedrale de Lausanne 🕮🕮 One of the most beautiful Gothic structures in Europe, the cathedral stands 150m (492 ft.) above Lake Geneva. Construction began in 1175; in 1275 the church was consecrated by Pope Gregory X. While in Lausanne, the pope met Rudolph of Hapsburg, emperor of Germany and the Holy Roman Empire. The doors and facade of the cathedral are luxuriously ornamented with sculptures and bas-reliefs. The architect Eugène Viollet-le-Duc began a restoration of the cathedral in the 19th century—and it's still going on! The interior is relatively austere except for some 13th-century choir stalls; the rose window also dates from the 13th century. The cathedral has two towers, with an observation deck 225 steps up one of the towers.

Place de la Cathédrale. ✆ 021/316-71-61. Free admission to cathedral; tower 2F ($1.65). Apr–Sept Mon–Fri 8am–6:30pm, Sat 8:30am–6pm, Sun 2–7pm; Oct–Mar Mon–Fri 7:30am–6pm, Sat 8:30am–5pm, Sun 2–5:30pm. Visits not permitted Sun morning during services. Bus: 7 or 16.

Château de Beaulieu et Musée de l'Art Brut 🕮 Located on the northwestern side of town, this château dates from 1756 and was once occupied by Madame de Staël. The museum displays what the artist Jean Dubuffet called *art brut* in the 1940s. This curious mélange of artwork was collected by the painter from prisoners, the mentally ill, and the criminally insane. It's like a bizarre twilight zone of art, often dubbed "psychopathological," especially the art by schizophrenics. Dubuffet despised the pretentiousness of the avant-garde art scene around him, and as a form of protest decided to begin this collection of the works of "nonartists," many of whom he found superior to the more established artists of his day.

11, av. des Bergières. ✆ 021/647-54-35. Admission 6F ($4.90) adults, 4F ($3.30) seniors, students, and children. Tues–Fri 11am–noon and 2–6pm; Sat–Sun 11am–6pm. Bus: 2 to Beaulieu.

Musée Cantonal des Beaux-Arts (Cantonal Museum of Fine Arts) The chief city museum is devoted to the works of artists who painted in western Switzerland from the 18th to the 19th centuries. This complex also houses the Geological Museum, the Museum of Paleontology, the Archaeological and Historical Museum, and the Zoological Museum.

In the Palais de Rumine, 6, place de la Riponne. ✆ 021/316-34-45. Admission 6F ($4.90) adults, 4F ($3.30) students and seniors, free for children 16 and under. Tues–Wed 11am–6pm; Thurs 11am–8pm; Fri–Sun 11am–5pm. Bus: 5, 6, or 8.

Musée Historique de Lausanne/Ancien-Evêché A bishop's palace until the early 15th century, the Ancien-Evêché has a 13th-century fortified tower and a collection of historical studies of Old Lausanne. You can see a 23-sq.-m (248-sq.-ft.) scale model depicting the old city as it was in the 17th century.

4, place de la Cathédrale. ✆ 021/331-03-53. Admission 5F ($4.10) adults, 2.50F ($2.05) seniors, free for students and children 16 and under. Tues–Thurs 11am–6pm; Fri–Sun 11am–5pm. Bus: 7 or 16.

Musée Romain de Lausanne-Vidy   At Vidy, west of Ouchy, lying off the Lausanne-Maladière exit from N1/E25, is one of the more intriguing Roman museums of Switzerland. This museum of antiquities is filled with findings from excavations at the site of Lousonna, a Roman settlement that lasted from about the 15th century B.C. into the 4th century A.D. Once a private home, this place now shows Roman treasures—everything from votive figures to ancient coins, even the tools of daily life, right down to the pins that held up those togas. Guided tours of nearby archaeological digs are conducted on the last Sunday of every month for another 3F ($2.45).

24, chemin du Bois-de-Vaus. ✆ 021/625-10-84. Admission 4F ($3.30). Tues and Thurs–Sun 11am–6pm; Wed 11am–8pm.

Olympic Museum   Seeing that the Comité International Olympique has been installed in Lausanne since 1915, the city decided in 1993 to open a museum recalling the history of the games since ancient Greece. The largest information center for the Olympic movement in the world, it's a tribute to the union of sport, art, and culture, with a coin and stamp collection, an Olympic Study Center, a library, an information center, and a video library recalling some of the games' most historic moments. There's even a scattering of artifacts commemorating the sporting triumphs of South America's Aztec empire. Advanced audiovisual, computer, and robotic technology allows visitors to share in the great feats and the emotions of the athletes. An Olympic flame burns alongside a column that lists the venues where the games have been held.

1, quai d'Ouchy. ✆ 021/621-65-11. www.olympic.org. Admission 14F ($11) adults, 9F ($7.40) seniors and students, 7F ($5.75) children 10–18, free for children 9 and under, 34F ($28) family ticket. May–Sept daily 9am–6pm (till 8pm Thurs); Oct–Apr Tues–Sun 9am–6pm. Closed Jan 1 and Dec 25. Take bus no. 8 from the center of Lausanne or the metro from the rail station to Ouchy, then walk for 15 min. with the lake on your right, passing the Beau-Rivage Place Hotel en route.

THE ACTIVE VACATION PLANNER

The Lausanne tourist office (see "Essentials," above) can tell you the best places to **jog** in and around the city. Vita Parcours trails, broken up by various stops for exercising, are found at Vidy, at Chalet-à-Gobet, and above Pully, the last lying between Lausanne and Montreux. The tourist office will also advise about the best transportation connections to reach starting points, and provide maps showing their various locations.

Following in the footsteps of such celebrities as the late Charlie Chaplin, you can go **hiking**—some call it strolling—through vineyard and château country along the north shore of Lake Geneva. Literally millions have been here before you. Not only the Lausanne tourist office but various town and village offices will advise you of the best itineraries and supply detailed maps to guide you on your way. If you enjoy planning this sort of thing even before your arrival in the Vaud, consider contacting the **Association Vaudoise de Tourisme Pédestre (Vaudois Association of Trekkers and Hill Climbers),** 23, Grand St-Jean, CH-1003 Lausanne (✆ 021/323-10-84).

For more vertiginous and higher-altitude adventures, you can take **mountain wilderness trails** cutting into the Alps Vaudoises. You can explore the canyons and heavily wooded areas around Château-d'Oex, or the alpine meadows above Villars.

A Dramatic Ascent to Les Diablerets

For a high-alpine view of Switzerland's highest heights, consider a day trip from Lausanne to the high-alpine village of **Les Diablerets,** which is rather confusingly designated as the geographical and spiritual centerpiece of a high-altitude and rocky **Les Diablerets region** . To reach Les Diablerets, visitors take a conventional train from Lausanne to the town of Aigle—a 30-minute relatively high-speed ride, priced at 30F ($25) per person round-trip. In Aigle they transfer onto a relatively slow narrow-gauge train that carries them to the village of Les Diablerets—a 46-minute ride priced at 24F ($20) per person round-trip.

In Diablerets you can wander around the alpine village, site of about 10 hotels, including two in the government-rated four-star category. There's an attempt to maintain old-fashioned aesthetics in this town, and it does have some alpine charm. Diablerets "Village" is the centerpiece of three distinct regions: the D'Ifenau ski region, the Le Meilleret ski region (which funnels into yet another ski region known as the Villarf region), and the Glacier region ("Les Diablerets Glacier 3000"). It's also the site of a 7.2km (4½-mile) bobsled ride (*piste de luge*) that's among the most thrilling (terrifying?) in the region.

After visiting "Les Diablerets Village," you can return to Lausanne or continue on to see the **Glacier des Diablerets** at 2,997m (9,830 ft.). In winter a free minibus hauls you to the door of most of the hotels in Les Diablerets Village. Then continue to the base of one of Switzerland's newest (inaugurated in 1999) cable cars at Col du Pillon, which will carry you on to the Glacier des Diablerets. The minibuses take 15 minutes for the ride. In summer there are no free minibuses: instead, you'll board any of five daily departures aboard a Swiss Postal Bus for the 15-minute ride to the base of the cable car at Col du Pillon, and pay 12F ($9.85) per person each way. Or if you want to walk through the village, it will take you about 90 minutes from the railway station to the base of the cable car.

Once you reach Col du Pillon, departures on the cable car to the glacier are continuous between 8:30 and 9am (depending on the season), ending at between 4 and 5:30pm (depending on the season). The 15-minute uphill ride (very steep, very dramatic) requires one change of car at a midway point up the mountain. The cost is 54F ($44) per person round-trip. For **cable car information** and confirmation that the car is running, call © **024/492-33-77** (the cashier) or 024/492-28-14 (the administration).

The summit is the site of a futuristic-looking aerie designed by Mario Botta, resembling an angular Inca temple or a spacecraft, depending on your point of view. Inside, there are two eateries (a self-service restaurant and a more formal sit-down restaurant); and the departure point for winter skiing (Dec to mid-Apr), summer skiing (late June to late July), and lots of hiking trails on or near the edges of the glaciers. There's also a "snow-bus" excursion, priced at 12F ($9.85) for a 30-minute outing, in a vehicle with very big snow tires and big windows. There might be a group of husky dogs on-site practicing dog sledding, Alaskan-style, but this is unpredictable and iffy. The entire site, including the cable car, is closed during May for annual maintenance.

SHOPPING

Shoppers in Lausanne tend to be much more concerned with the commercialized glamour of Paris than with kitschy mountain souvenirs. That being the case, you'll find lots of emphasis on high-profile outfits such as luggage and leather maker **Louis Vuitton,** 30, rue de Bourg (© **021/312-76-60**); or haute jeweler **Cartier,** 6, rue de Bourg (© **021/320-55-44**).

But if handmade souvenirs from the Vaud region appeal to you, head for **Heidi's Shop,** 22, rue du Petit-Chêne (© **021/311-16-89**). For artifacts with deeper patinas that sell for a lot more money, check out the art and antiques at two intriguing, relentlessly upscale antiques shops: **Antiquités R.S.,** 17, av. de la Gare (© **079/210-45-61**), and **Galerie du Château,** 2, place du Tunnel (© **021/647-21-42**); both specialize in 18th- and 19th-century furniture. A worthy competitor, with a greater emphasis on paintings and sculpture, is **Galerie de la Belle Fontaine,** 9-13, rue Cheneau-de-Bourg (© **021/323-47-87**). The biggest and best bookstore in Lausanne is **Librairie Payot,** 4, place Pepinet (© **021/341-33-31**), which carries English-language titles. The biggest jeweler in Lausanne, with a well-established international recommendation, is **Bucherer,** 5, place St-François (© **021/312-36-12**). Competitors, especially for Swiss watches, include **Roman Mayer,** 12, place St-François (© **021/312-23-16**), which has good buys in Omega watches, and **Junod,** 8, place St-François (© **021/312-27-45**), carrying Blancpain watches among others.

The major tobacco outlet is **Besson,** 22, rue de Bourg (© **021/312-67-88**), known for its Davidoff cigars. The best Swiss-made linen, including embroidered handkerchiefs, is sold at **Langenthal,** 8, rue de Bourg (© **021/323-44-02**). Some 19km (12 miles) west of Lausanne, about 20 antiques dealers have assembled a widely divergent trove of antique (and in some cases, merely old) furniture and art objects called **Château Allaman** (© **021/808-82-39**), in the hamlet of Aubonne. Hours are erratic, varying widely with the season and the whims of each dealer, so an advance phone call is strongly recommended.

WHERE TO STAY

The luxury and elegance of the top hotels in Lausanne have made the city a favorite destination of the wealthy. In the summer space is tight, so try to make a reservation. Trade fairs and conventions also keep the better hotels booked. The annual International Tourism Fair is in March. The tourist office can help you find a hotel. If you want to stay directly on the lake, we recommend a hotel in Ouchy.

VERY EXPENSIVE

Beau-Rivage Palace ✦✦✦   One of the leading hotels in the world, the Beau-Rivage Palace is surrounded by 4 hectares (10 acres) of lush gardens, with cedar, begonia, and sculptures. Built in 1861 and extended in 1908, the hotel has been renovated with respect for its original period architecture. The hotel is among the last bastions of formal Europe, attracting both aristocrats and *la grande bourgeoisie,* but not forgetting the demands of the world's business travelers. In the tradition of the grand hotels of yesterday, rooms come in a wide range of styles. The less desirable are somewhat sparsely furnished and open onto the parking area, while the more luxurious have Oriental carpeting, wing chairs, and private balconies overlooking Lake Geneva. The hotel is air-conditioned through an ingenious system using water pumped from nearby Lake Geneva.

One of the hotel's restaurants, La Rotonde, offers a panoramic view of lakes and mountains. The Café Beau-Rivage is recommended separately (see "Where to Dine," below).

17-19, place du Port, CH-1006 Lausanne-Ouchy. ✆ 800/223-6800 in the U.S. or 021/613-33-33. Fax 021/613-33-34. www.brp.ch. 169 units. 470F–780F ($385–$640) double; from 3,500F ($1,625) suite. AE, DC, MC, V. Parking 20F ($13). Metro: Ouchy. **Amenities:** 3 restaurants; 2 bars; 2 pools; tennis courts; fitness center; salon; 24-hr. room service; babysitting; laundry service/dry cleaning. *In room:* A/C, TV, dataport, minibar, hair dryer, iron, safe, Jacuzzi in 8 suites.

Lausanne Palace 🏨🏨🏨   The "Palace" is as grand and elegant a hotel as you'll find anywhere in Europe. The columns, plaster details, and marble floors date from the 19th century; the public rooms are decorated with tapestries, crystal chandeliers, and gilded rococo furniture. The hotel, in the center of Lausanne, offers a grand view of Lake Geneva and the Savoy Mountains. Many of the rooms reflect the hotel's turn-of-the-20th-century style; others are in a more contemporary mode. The best units have Empire reproductions, and some even have marble fireplaces. The front rooms open onto urban streets; the accommodations to the rear face the lake, and most have private balconies. All come with luxurious marble bathrooms.

7-9, rue du Grand-Chêne, CH-1002 Lausanne. ✆ 800/223-6800 in the U.S. or 021/331-31-31. Fax 021/323-25-71. www.lausanne-palace.ch. 150 units. 450F–680F ($369–$558) double; 900F–1,760F ($738–$1,443) suite. AE, DC, MC, V. Parking 20F ($13). Bus: 7 or 16. **Amenities:** 3 restaurants; 2 bars; pool; health club; sauna; Turkish bath; business center; 24-hr. room service; babysitting; laundry service/dry cleaning; nonsmoking rooms; rooms for guests w/limited mobility. *In room:* TV, dataport, minibar, hair dryer, safe, trouser press.

EXPENSIVE

Hotel Angleterre & Résidence 🏨   At the edge of Lake Geneva, a trio of elegant villas from the 18th and 19th centuries combine to form this little hotel on the Ouchy waterfront, standing next to the most luxurious Beau-Rivage. The famous Beau-Rivage hotel in fact owns La Residence, but this hotel is less expensive and even closer to the water. Many guests who can afford the grander palace actually prefer to stay here. There are intimate and cozy touches, including a lounge with a fireplace, Oriental rugs, chintz curtains, and dining in summer on a deck that stretches toward the water. One part of the hotel, L'Angleterre, housed Lord Byron when he was writing *The Prisoner of Chillon.*

15, place du Port, CH-1006 Lausanne. ✆ 021/613-34-34. Fax 021/613-34-35. www.angleterre-residence.ch. 60 units. 390F–430F ($320–$353) double; 430F–480F ($353–$394) junior suite. AE, DC, MC, V. Free parking. **Amenities:** 2 restaurants; bar; indoor pool; exercise room; sauna. *In room:* A/C, TV, minibar, hair dryer, safe.

Hôtel de la Paix 🏨   Opened in 1910, this is a landmark and has seen a lot of changes in the past decades, including recent renovations. With its elaborate balconies and loggias, many with wrought-iron details, the hotel retains its original facade, although the interior has been vastly renewed. In the heart of the city, it faces the lake and the Alps beyond, and is convenient for shopping in the Old Town. A favorite with business clients, it offers completely modern midsize bedrooms, either opening onto the lake or, less desirably, onto one of the city's urban landscapes. About one-quarter of the bedrooms are refurbished every year.

5, av. Benjamin-Constant, CH-1002 Lausanne. ✆ 800/528-1234 in the U.S. and Canada or 021/310-71-71. Fax 021/ 310-71-72. www.hoteldelapaix.net. 109 units. 370F–470F ($303–$385) double; 525F–990F ($431–$812) suite. Rates include buffet breakfast. AE, DC, MC, V. Parking 28F ($23). Dogs welcome with 20F ($16) fee. Metro: St-François. **Amenities:** 2 restaurants; bar; business center; limited room service; babysitting; laundry service/dry cleaning. *In room:* TV, minibar, hair dryer, safe.

Le Château d'Ouchy 🏨   Built around 1900, this first-rate hotel uses a medieval (12th-c.) tower as its core. The château housed countless travelers throughout the 20th century. Many of its die-hard fans consider it the best location in all of Lausanne, across from the flower-bedecked pedestrian walkway of the lakefront. Its once-forti-fied tower, ideal for a honeymoon, is capped with a black-and-red-tile roof and sur-rounded by wings, dungeons, Renaissance-style gables, and Romanesque arches—all crafted from gray stone. Massive renovations have upgraded the restaurants and pub-lic areas. Your opinion of this relic will depend almost entirely on what room you're booked into. Some are faded and in need of renovations; others are exquisite. Request to see the rooms before checking in, if possible. All units come with good-size bath-rooms. If you're in a romantic mood and would like to stay in a castle, and if you aren't too demanding about your modern comforts, this is certainly the most nostalgic and evocative choice in town.

2, place du Port, CH-1006 Lausanne-Ouchy. © **021/616-74-51.** Fax 021/617-51-37. www.chateaudouchy.ch. 39 units. 165F–300F ($135–$246). AE, DC, MC, V. Free parking. Metro: Ouchy. **Amenities:** 2 restaurants; bar; limited room service; babysitting; laundry service/dry cleaning. *In room:* TV, minibar, hair dryer, safe.

MODERATE

Hôtel Agora ✧   Set just 274m (899 ft.) from the railroad station, this is a govern-ment-rated four-star, six-story hotel that opened in 1987 after a total renovation of an older hotel on the site. The look is startlingly unique to Lausanne. Locals often com-pare its architecture, with a facade of sculpted marble, to a spaceship. "ET has landed," wrote one columnist. The small to midsize bedrooms are comfortable and contain modern furniture and firm beds. Amenities include soundproof windows. The accom-modations often have a futuristic aura, in glowing silver or glittering metallic.

9, av. du Rond-Point, CH-1006 Lausanne. © **021/617-12-11.** Fax 021/616-26-05. www.fhotels.ch. 82 units. 207F–257F ($170–$211) double; 262F ($215) junior suite. AE, DC, MC, V. Free parking. Bus: 1, 3, or 5. **Amenities:** Car rental; room service (8am–8pm); laundry service/dry cleaning. *In room:* A/C, TV, dataport, minibar, hair dryer.

Hôtel Carlton   In the summer, awnings decorate the arched windows of this white Mediterranean-style four-story villa with a red-tile roof, located in a park near the lake. Built in 1909, it offers soundproof, midsize bedrooms that are comfortable, with modern decor. Try, if possible, for a room with a balcony, although they don't open onto the lake.

4, av. de Cour, CH-1007 Lausanne. © **021/613-07-07.** Fax 021/613-07-10. 44 units. 175F–245F ($144–$201) dou-ble; 445F–455F ($365–$373) junior suite. Rates include buffet breakfast. AE, MC, V. Free parking. Bus: 2 or 5. **Ameni-ties:** Restaurant; bar; 24-hr. room service; laundry service/dry cleaning. *In room:* TV, minibar, hair dryer.

Hôtel Continental *(Value*   Opposite the main rail station, this hotel is ideally located for both business travelers and visitors. A modern, first-class hotel, it is also conven-ient to the shopping area. While it doesn't have the grand style of some of the palaces recommended, it is most affordable and up-to-date in its amenities. Bedrooms are midsize to spacious, each with an efficiently organized private bathroom.

2, place de la Gare, CH-1001 Lausanne. © **021/321-88-00.** Fax 021/321-88-01. www.hotelcontinental.ch. 120 units. 295F ($242) double; 420F ($344) junior suite. Rates include buffet breakfast. AE, DC, MC. **Amenities:** 2 restaurants; bar; limited room service; laundry service, nonsmoking rooms. *In room:* TV, dataport, minibar, hair dryer, safe.

INEXPENSIVE

Hôtel Aulac *(Value*   This lakefront Ouchy hotel has a baroque yellow facade with white trim and a three-story Renaissance porch flanked by two elaborate columns. Originally built around the turn of the 20th century, this up-to-date hotel has been recently renovated. The mansard roof is inlaid with tiles in a geometric design and topped with a tall Victorian clock tower. Sailboats bob in the lake nearby. The hotel is, in fact, the least expensive accommodation right on the water in Lausanne. It is hardly the best, and most of its bedrooms rarely rise above a standard motel offering. The standardized accommodations are somewhat tacky and battered but reasonably comfortable and are priced at the lower end of the scale below. Request a room with a lake view and balcony. In spite of its drawbacks, this hotel is a favorite and is often heavily booked because of its location.

4, place de la Navigation, CH-1000 Lausanne-Ouchy. ℂ **021/613-15-00.** Fax 021/613-15-15. www.aulac.ch. 84 units. 200F–260F ($164–$213) double. Rates include continental breakfast. AE, DC, MC, V. Metro: Ouchy. **Amenities:** Restaurant; limited room service; laundry service/dry cleaning. *In room:* TV, dataport, minibar.

Hôtel Elite ✶ (Finds   The large, illuminated sign on the front lawn obscures the neo-classical details of this white, five-story hotel with balconies and a flat roof. You'll find this midcity location just uphill from the rail terminal. Even though it's right in the heart of things, this small hotel provides a tranquil atmosphere. Originally built at the turn of the 20th century, it's been operated by the same family since 1938. Fruit trees and a garden add the grace note, and some of the bedrooms are air-conditioned. One room has a kitchenette, and all units contain midsize bathrooms. Fourth-floor units open onto lakeside views, and nonsmoking rooms are available.

1, av. Sainte-Luce, CH-1003 Lausanne. ℂ **021/320-23-61.** Fax 021/320-39-63. www.elite-lausanne.ch. 33 units. 170F–230F ($139–$189) double. Rates include buffet breakfast. AE, DC, MC, V. Bus: 1, 3, or 5. **Amenities:** Car-rental desk; tour desk; dry cleaning; nonsmoking rooms. *In room:* A/C (in some), TV, minibar, hair dryer, safe.

Minotel AlaGare   A government-rated three-star stucco hotel a block from the rail station, this building dates from the turn of the 20th century but has been recently renovated. Access to the hotel is via a pedestrians-only street in the town center, but any resident can drive up to the front door of the hotel and deposit luggage. In summer flowers bloom in the window boxes of the hotel, adding an inviting touch. The interior has pine paneling stained in several different tones. The well-maintained bedrooms have sleek modern styling and are generally small.

14, rue du Simplon, CH-1006 Lausanne. ℂ **021/617-92-52.** Fax 021/617-92-55. www.alagare.com. 45 units. 160F–250F ($131–$205) double. Children under 12 stay free in parent's room. Rates include buffet breakfast. AE, DC, MC, V. Bus: 1, 3, or 5. Closed Dec 29–Jan 2. **Amenities:** Restaurant (closed Sun); lounge; nonsmoking rooms. *In room:* TV, dataport, coffeemaker.

Minotel Crystal   Within walking distance of the Palais de Beaulieu, a congress center, this hotel is often the favorite of visiting business clients. Monsieur and Madame Fiora welcome guests to their location on a quiet pedestrian street. The bedrooms are standardized, with tidy bathrooms. There's an underground parking facility a short walk from the hotel.

5, rue Chaucrau, CH-1003 Lausanne. ℂ **021/320-28-31.** Fax 021/320-04-46. www.minotel.com. 40 units. 210F–215F ($172–$176) double; 255F–320F ($209–$262) triple; 350F ($287) suite. AE, DC, MC, V. Parking 20F ($16). Bus: 1 or 5. **Amenities:** Restaurant; bar; laundry service/dry cleaning; nonsmoking rooms. *In room:* TV, dataport, minibar, hair dryer, safe.

WHERE TO DINE

Lausanne offers a wide range of restaurants where you can find the specialties of Switzerland and the Vaud, as well as those of France, Greece, Italy, and China. Typical Swiss food is served in the Upper Town.

Try the Geneva lake fish, omble chevalier. Trout and perch from the lake are also popular; in autumn many restaurants feature game dishes.

EXPENSIVE

Café Beau-Rivage ✵ SWISS   This grand and elegant restaurant is in a lakeside pavilion, the dining room resembling a Paris cafe, with mirrors, pillars, bay windows, and a flowery terrace. Typical tasty dishes, made only with the freshest ingredients, include steak tartare, *marmite de pêcheur* (casserole of fish), fricassee of chicken flavored with vinegar and tarragon, and tagliatelle with seafood. Sumptuous desserts can be ordered from the trolley. After 7:30pm, the place becomes an enjoyable piano bar. The cafe is open for coffee, tea, pastries, and a lighter menu Monday to Friday from 11am to 1am and Saturday and Sunday from 9am to 1am.

In the Beau-Rivage Palace, 18, place du Général-Guisan, Ouchy. ✆ 021/613-33-33. Reservations recommended. Main courses 32F–52F ($26–$43); fixed-price dinner 70F ($57). AE, DC, MC, V. Daily 11:30am–1am. Metro: Ouchy.

La Grappe d'Or ✵✵✵ SWISS   Philippe Rochat may reign in the suburbs, but in Lausanne proper the domain of Angelika and Peter Baermann is the most sought-after citadel of food and drink. This formal French restaurant has received multiple awards from both Swiss and French gastronome societies. The cuisine doesn't religiously adhere to yesterday, but makes its own creative statement. The atmosphere is that of a rotisserie, and some of the most discriminating palates from all over the surrounding area come here to partake of the chef's latest imaginative effort. Menus change with the seasons, and the meats are excellent, as is roebuck (in season). The seafood part of the menu is likely to include scampi, red mullet, or sea bass with fennel. Every dish is prepared with care and based on the most carefully selected ingredients.

3, rue Cheneau-de-Bourg. ✆ 021/323-07-60. Reservations required. Main courses 28F–50F ($23–$41); fixed-price lunch 58F–78F ($48–$64); fixed-price dinner 128F–178F ($105–$146). AE, DC, MC, V. Mon–Fri noon–2:15pm and 7–10pm; Sat 7–10:30pm. Bus: 7 or 16.

La Petite Grappe/Il Grappolino d'Oro ✵ *Value* SWISS   La Grappe d'Or (see above) is the most famed eatery within the city limits of Lausanne. The good news is that you can enjoy the same high-quality food here, but for less money. Oliver, the son of the founding father Peter Baermann, has opened this more informal restaurant a short walk away. It has the same quality of food, although the service and the dress are more casual. Like its parent, La Petite Grappe adjusts its menu to take advantage of the best of any season, ranging from fresh asparagus in the spring to game in the autumn. The lake-fish dishes are excellent. Try the monkfish with olive juice for example, or saddle of veal with lentils. Cardons, a delectable cousin of the artichoke, are also served when available.

15, rue Cheneau-de-Bourg. ✆ 021/311-84-22. Reservations required. Main courses 28F–50F ($23–$41); fixed-price menu 48F ($39) at lunch, 78F–100F ($64–$82) at dinner. AE, MC, V. Mon–Sat noon–2pm and 7–10pm. Bus: 7 or 16.

MODERATE

Buffet de la Gare CFF SWISS/FRENCH   Inside Lausanne's main rail station, the brasserie is large and bustling, while the restaurant offers a secluded series of cubbyholes and nooks and more upscale service. There's little difference in price between the brasserie and the restaurant. Many find the brasserie more fun, the restaurant more sedate. Good-tasting dishes available at both include vol-au-vent with mushrooms, filets of sole "Uncle Charles," poached turbot in hollandaise sauce, veal sausages, and mignons of pork in cream sauce.

In the train station, 11, place de la Gare. ✆ 021/311-49-00. Reservations recommended in the restaurant only. Main courses 25F–59F ($21–$48); fixed-price menu 30F ($25). MC, V. Restaurant daily 7am–midnight. Brasserie daily 11am–midnight. Bus: 1, 3, or 5.

Le Jardin d'Asie ✿ CHINESE/JAPANESE/MALAYSIAN   The finest Asian restaurant in Lausanne, Le Jardin celebrates the cuisine of China, Japan, and to a lesser degree, Malaysia. The setting is a pale-green-and-pink representation of a garden, with enough space between tables to permit the broadly international clientele discreet conversations. Menu items include a choice of foods from the major culinary traditions of China, as well as sushi, sashimi, and *teppanyaki* (Japanese cuisine prepared by a uniformed chef in front of your table). There's even a choice of Malay dishes, including shrimp or chicken in peanut sauce and beignets of shrimp.

7, av. du Théâtre. ✆ 021/323-74-84. Reservations recommended. Main courses 22F–34F ($18–$28); fixed-price Chinese menu 45F ($37); fixed-price Japanese menu 45F ($37). AE, DC, MC, V. Mon–Sat 11:45am–2pm and 7–10pm. Bus: 7 or 16.

Pinte Besson ✿ *(Finds* SWISS/VAUD   This is a tiny restaurant with a smoke-stained vault of hand-chiseled masonry dating from 1780. It's celebrated locally for its cheese fondues, cheese on toast, and seasonal specialties, along with dried alpine beef. Beef or horse steak is grilled and served on a slate stone. There are sidewalk tables in summer, and benches are placed outside on sunny days.

4, rue de l'Ale. ✆ 021/312-72-27. Reservations recommended. Main courses 18F–37F ($15–$30). MC, V. Mon–Fri noon–2pm and 6pm–midnight; Sat–Sun noon–2pm. Closed Aug. Bus: 1 or 9.

NEARBY DINING

Auberge du Raisin ✿✿ SWISS/FRENCH   It's set in its ways, and its staff is a bit rigid, but despite these minor drawbacks, a stopover at this verdant Relais & Châteaux property will offer impeccable food and insight into upscale, *grand bourgeois* life within French-speaking Switzerland. Set on 13th-century foundations, in the center of the town of Cully, it's most famous for its restaurant, where delicate flavorings are a hallmark of chef Adolfo Blokbergen. Within a setting accented with antique paneling and an elegant sense of alpine rusticity, you can order such classic dishes as steamed supreme of pigeon with truffles, a cold consommé of lobster with fresh tarragon, ravioli stuffed with scallops and served with a caviar-enriched champagne sauce, and a poached filet mignon of veal with summer vegetables. Although a full complement of European wines is offered, ask for a Swiss vintage, particularly one from the surrounding region.

Nine comfortable, somewhat frilly-looking bedrooms are on-site (350F/$287 double; 490F–580F/$402–$476 suite). Rates include breakfast.

1, place de l'Hôtel de Ville, CH-1096 Cully. ✆ 021/799-21-31. Fax 021/799-25-01. www.relaischateaux.com/raisin. Reservations required. Main courses 35F–60F ($29–$49); fixed-price dinner 89F–198F ($73–$162). AE, DC, MC, V. Mon–Sat noon–2pm and 6–10pm. From Lausanne, take Rte. Cantonale, which borders the edge of the lake, following the signs to Vevey, then turn off to follow the signs to Cully.

Hotel de Ville – Philippe Rochat ✿✿✿ SWISS/FRENCH   For years, Philippe Rochat followed dutifully in the footsteps of the founder (Frédy Girardet) of this legendary restaurant, quietly helping the grand patriarch of French cuisine prepare the thousands of upscale platters that contributed to this establishment's fame. Since 1996 and the retirement of his mentor, Switzerland's culinary patriarch, Rochat has taken over, doing a masterful job of keeping Girardet's legend alive while simultaneously updating the menu with some creations of his own. The venue for this minidrama, which has been avidly watched by gastronomes throughout the region, is within the solid stone walls of what was originally conceived in 1929 as Crissier's Town Hall (Hôtel de Ville). He prepares succulent meals for tables of culinary aficionados who sometimes make reservations many months in advance. Specialties change frequently, according to the availability of ingredients and the inspiration of Rochat himself. Recent successes have included a ragout of fresh quail with young vegetables, crawfish in caviar butter, duckling from the wetlands around Nantes cooked pink and prepared with Brouilly wine, preserved duckling in lemon and spices, and glazed sweetbreads with wild mushrooms. The cheese trolley that's wheeled around after the main course is absolutely spectacular.

In the Hotel de Ville, 1, rue d'Yverdon, Crissier. ☎ 021/634-05-05. www.relaischateaux.com/hoteldeville. Reservations essential. Main courses 57F–115F ($47–$94); fixed-price menu 240F–270F ($197–$221). Tues–Sat noon–2pm and 7–9pm. Closed 3 weeks in Aug and 2 weeks Dec–Jan.

LAUSANNE AFTER DARK

Few other cities in Switzerland manage to remain as cosmopolitan but relentlessly conservative as Lausanne. Consequently, you'll find lots to do, often with a Gallic insouciance, after dark. You may begin your evening hanging out in any of the cafes and bars ringing the **Espace Flon,** a cluster of restaurants and shops at place Flon. Lots of hideaways, frequented by strollers of all ages, will be here to tempt you, but one of the most appealing is **Le Grand Café,** esplanade de Mont-Benon (☎ 021/320-40-30). Here, in an American-inspired space that contains some of the glitter and razzmatazz of a Planet Hollywood (with which it's not connected), you can meet a cross section of virtually every night owl in town.

Attractive and popular discos include **Le Mad,** route de Genève (☎ 021/340-69-69), where the fads and preoccupations of nocturnal Paris filter quickly in from the west via an under-30 crowd.

Ouchy White Horse Pub, 66, av. d'Ouchy (☎ 021/616-75-75), draws the crowds at night, who in summer enjoy the terrace with views of the water. Beer is on tap, and a range of tapas and burgers are sold. It's the most authentic pub atmosphere in town.

Lausanne is also a city of culture. With Geneva it shares the Orchestre de la Suisse Romande and also occasionally hosts the legendary ballet company of Maurice Béjart. The local tourist office will advise on what's available at the time of your visit. Most performances of major cultural impact take place at the **Théâtre-Municipal Lausanne,** avenue du Theatre (☎ 021/310-16-00). **Beaulieu,** at 10, av. des Bergières (☎ 021/643-21-11), is also a venue for dance concerts, operas, and orchestral music presentations. Tickets can be purchased at **Billetel,** which has various locations throughout Lausanne. For more information, contact the Théâtre-Municipal Lausanne.

2 Morges ⟨★⟩

11km (7 miles) W of Lausanne; 26km (16 miles) E of Geneva

Set against a backdrop of the Savoy Alps, the small town of Morges on Lac Léman is headquarters for the region's vineyards. Its port was built on an ancient site inhabited by prehistoric lake dwellers. Because of its elegant lakeside setting, and because of its stellar hotels and restaurants, this is one of the premier stopovers along Lake Geneva. If she were still around, longtime resident Audrey Hepburn would confirm that. Today Morges is a favorite stop for a chic set of international yachters.

ESSENTIALS

GETTING THERE Trains run almost every 30 minutes throughout the day between Geneva and Lausanne, and most of them stop at Morges. For **rail information,** call ☎ 0900/300-300.

Bus no. 57 runs from Lausanne to Morges. Call ✆ **0900/300-300** for **bus schedules.** One-way transit costs 20F ($16) from Geneva and 2.40F ($1.95) from Lausanne. If you're driving from Lausanne, head west toward Geneva along N1.

In addition, between late May and September, several lake steamers stop at Morges every day on their way between Geneva and Lausanne; depending on their schedule, some require a boat change at Yvoire. For information, contact the **CGN (Compagnie Générale de Navigation),** 17, av. de Rhodanie, in Lausanne (✆ **0848/811-848;** www.cgn.ch), or **Jardin Anglais,** in Geneva (✆ **021/614-62-00**).

VISITOR INFORMATION   The **Morges Tourist Information Office,** on rue du Château (✆ **021/801-32-33**), is open year-round from Monday to Saturday 9:30am to noon and 2:30 to 6pm.

SEEING THE SIGHTS

Baron Louis of Savoy built the **Castle of Morges** in 1286 to defend himself against the bishopric of Lausanne. The imposing bastion, which originally had a moat, was the residence of a Bernese bailiff from 1536 to 1798. It eventually passed to the canton of Vaud, which used it as an arsenal. Today it contains the **Vaud Military Museum (Musée Militaire Vaudois)** (✆ **021/804-85-56**). The weapons and uniforms on display date from the late 15th century to modern times. The museum is open February to June and September to mid-December, Tuesday to Friday from 10am to noon and 1:30 to 5pm and on Saturday, Sunday, and holidays from 10am to 5pm; in July and August, Tuesday to Friday from 10am to 5pm. Admission is 7F ($5.75).

Musée Alexis Forel ✮, in a 15th-century patrician house at 54, Grand-Rue (✆ **021/801-26-47**), contains a collection of engravings, 17th- and 18th-century furniture, 18th-century silver and glassware, ancient ceramics, and antique dolls—all exhibited in an intimate setting of a former private home. The museum is open Tuesday to Sunday from 2 to 5:30pm. Admission is 6F ($4.90) for adults, free for children.

The town's newest, and in many ways most interesting, museum is the **Pavillon Audrey Hepburn** ✮, chemin des Plantées, in the neighboring hamlet of Tolochenaz (✆ **021/803-64-64**), 1.6km (1 mile) east of Morges. Take the TPM bus no. 2 to reach it or else enjoy the walk. It occupies what was originally built in the 1950s as a wood-sided schoolhouse, set within sight of the stone-sided chalet that Audrey Hepburn occupied on and off again for the last 40 years of her life. Although you can't visit the chalet itself (it's occupied by her son, Sean Ferrer), the one-room schoolhouse offers testimony to a life that incorporated Hollywood stardom with hard, long hours as an ambassador for UNICEF, replete with photos and testimonials from well-wishers throughout the world. Frankly, the scope of the actress-humanitarian's life (born in Brussels in 1929, raised in the Netherlands and England, died in Switzerland in 1993) is broader than many of her movie fans ever realized. Within a very short walk, you can visit Ms. Hepburn's grave in the village cemetery (Cimitière de Tolochenaz). The museum is open year-round Tuesday to Sunday from 1:30 to 5:30pm. Entrance costs 10F ($8.20) for adults and 5F ($4.10) for seniors and children 6 to 18.

If the day is sunny, you can take one of the most lovely **bike rides** in western Switzerland beginning at Morges train station, where you can rent a bike for 30F ($25) a day. The tourist office (see above) will provide a map and help you plot your route. The trail leads from Morges to the village of Lully and goes via Bussy and Ballens to Biere. This takes you through some of the most scenic of Lake Geneva vineyards. From Biere you continue down a small valley to Begnins and then Fechy, the latter a panoramic lookout point. Eventually you reach Aubonne, where you can take a second-class road via Lavigny, Villars-sous-Yens, and Lully back to Morges. The 56km (35-mile) trip takes about 5½ hours.

WHERE TO STAY & DINE

La Fleur du Lac ★★ SWISS/FRENCH   Many residents of Geneva make weekend excursions to taste the unusual and imaginative food served at this beautiful restaurant on the quay beside the lake. Famous specialties include Lake Geneva perch plus imported seafood. The menu, which changes with the seasons, includes an unusual version of medallions of foie gras served with pistachio nuts and a sweet-and-sour sauce inspired by Asia, filet of lake perch with butter sauce and tartar sauce, rosettes of roast lamb with turnips and a butter-enhanced tarragon sauce, and poached supreme of turbot with wine/herb sauce and shellfish. Dessert might be a "fantasy of coconut." More than 250 domestic and foreign wines are available. There's an outdoor terrace facing the lake. A small bistro offers specialties of the day costing 25F ($16) and up. The bus from Lausanne stops in back of the hotel.

The establishment also rents 30 rooms, and no two are alike. All units face south, with a view across the lake to the French Alps and snowcapped Mont Blanc. Most of the rooms have large balconies or terraces, along with phones, TVs, and such amenities as combination tubs/showers, hair dryers, and trouser presses. For room and breakfast, doubles cost 240F to 260F ($197–$213). One suite—for one to four guests—rents for 450F ($369).

Quai Igor-Stravinsky, 70, rte. de Lausanne, CH-1110 Morges. ✆ **021/811-58-11.** Fax 021/811-58-88. www.fleur-du-lac.ch. Reservations required. Main courses 38F–64F ($31–$52); fixed-price lunch 58F ($48), fixed-price dinner 70F ($57). AE, DC, MC, V. Daily 11:30am–2pm and 6:30–10pm. Bus: 57 from Lausanne.

Restaurant de l'Union FRENCH   Set between two historic and central streets of Morges's Old Town, this well-recommended, appealingly old-fashioned restaurant offers well-prepared cuisine that's neither expensive nor pretentious. Prepared by members of the von Kaenel family, the food choices include a succulent version of fricassee of chanterelles. The best beef selection is *tournedos vaudois,* which is grilled on a hot stone set directly atop your table. Also look for an unusual version of horse meat with sweet peppers (a favorite with the lunch crowd eager for a quick platter of very traditional food), and grilled filet of lamb with rosemary. Everybody's favorite dessert is an idiosyncratic and very popular version of *tarte à la raisinée,* which combines the texture of a flan with that of a pastry.

The restaurant is in a hotel that contains 14 simple bedrooms, all with private bathroom, TV, and phone. With breakfast included, doubles cost 180F ($148).

In the Hôtel de Savoie, 7, Grand-Rue, CH-1110 Morges. ✆ **021/801-21-55.** www.hotelsavoie.ch. Reservations recommended. Main courses 19F–42F ($16–$34); fixed-price menu 28F–78F ($23–$64). MC, V. Mon–Sat 11:30am–2:30pm and 6:30–11pm.

3 Nyon ★

22km (14 miles) E of Geneva; 27km (17 miles) SW of Lausanne

Unhurried and peaceful, Nyon has been a popular lakefront resort since the Victorian era; masses of flowers decorate its waterfront quays. In Roman times Julius Caesar used the settlement here as a military outpost for his soldiers. Between 1781 and 1813, Nyon was famous for its delicate, almost translucent porcelain.

A major stopover on the lake-steamer route, Nyon is ideal for walks. You can, in fact, take a walk around the town walls known as **Promenade des Vieilles Murailles.** The walk goes along the 19th-century town walls until the promenade broadens into the **Esplanade des Marronniers,** from which the most stunning panorama unfolds. You can also wander around at leisure, enjoying the flower-filled park and quays bordering the yachting harbor.

ESSENTIALS

GETTING THERE   Nyon lies directly on the rail lines that connect Geneva with Lausanne. Trains depart from both those larger cities for Nyon every 30 minutes throughout the day. Call © **0900/300-300** for **train schedules.**

Nyon is connected by bus to a handful of other French-speaking towns to its northwest, few of which have railway junctions of their own. There are also bus connections from Nyon's railway station to Geneva several times throughout the day. Despite these buses, most travelers arrive in Nyon by train. For bus schedules, contact the tourist office (see below).

If you're driving, head west from Lausanne, or east from Geneva, along N1.

In addition, there are a handful of lake steamers that travel in summer (May–Sept) between Geneva and Lausanne, stopping briefly in Nyon. Trip time by boat from Lausanne to Nyon is 2½ hours. For information and reservations, contact **CGN (Compagnie Général de Navigation),** 17 av. de Rhodanie, in Lausanne (© **0848-811-848;** www.cgn.ch).

VISITOR INFORMATION   The **Nyon Tourist Information Office,** at 7, av. Viollier (© **022/361-62-61**), is open May 29 to September 20, Monday to Friday from 8:30am to noon and 2 to 5:30pm, and Saturday and Sunday from 9:30am to noon and 1 to 6pm; off season Monday to Friday from 8:30am to noon and 2 to 5:30pm.

SEEING THE SIGHTS

For an adventure off the beaten path, you can rent a **bike** for 30F ($25) at the Nyon rail station and cycle to Céligny, lying midway between Coppet and Nyon. You can go all the way to Coppet in 10km (6 miles) by heading south. But spend what time you can at **Céligny,** one of the most enchanting of all lakeside villages.

Richard Burton called Céligny home during the last years of his life. A small port here is filled with yachts and grassy lawns ideal for sunbathing. In fact, the swimming here is the best along the lake. Later you can wander over to the village cemetery to visit the grave of the great actor and former resident. Elizabeth Taylor has told friends that she has purchased the plot next to the man she married and divorced twice.

Musée du Léman, 8, quai Louis-Bonnard (© **022/361-09-49**), is devoted exclusively to the geography, history, marine culture, arts, and ethnography of Lake Geneva. It also contains three large aquariums, plus flora and fauna of the largest lake of western Europe.

Musée Romain, rue Maupertuis (© **022/361-75-91**), displays specimens of Roman architecture, as well as Roman statuary, inscriptions, mosaics, crafts, amphorae, glasswork, and coins. The basilica, which stands at one end of the forum of the Roman colony (Colonia Julia Equestris), was a public building for justice and commerce.

Entrance to either museum costs 8F ($6.55) for adults, 5F ($4.10) for children and students. Both museums maintain the same hours: April to October, Tuesday to Sunday from 10am to noon and 2 to 6pm (open Mon in July–Aug); November to March, Tuesday to Sunday from 2 to 6pm.

WHERE TO STAY

The **Rôtisserie du XVI Siècle,** listed in "Where to Dine," below, also has rooms for rent.

Hôtel Beau-Rivage 👍   This hotel is your best bet. Sections of this hotel were built in 1481, when an inn stood on the site welcoming pilgrims and merchants. Most of the building seen today, however, dates from around 1900. Cozy and old-fashioned, the Beau-Rivage, 7 minutes from the railroad station, was built directly on the quays in the heart of the Old Town. Sweeping views of the lake are available from any of the hotel's many balconies. The public rooms have been tastefully modernized in a summertime motif, which includes a series of brightly colored modern paintings. The midsize bedrooms are traditionally furnished, some with four-posters

49, rue de Rive, CH-1260 Nyon. © 022/365-41-41. Fax 022/365-41-65. www.hotel-beau-rivage-nyon.ch. 50 units. 240F–380F ($197–$312) double; from 480F ($312) suite. Rates include buffet breakfast. AE, DC, MC, V. Free parking outside, 20F ($16) in garage. **Amenities:** Restaurant; bar; limited room service; laundry service. *In room:* TV, dataport, minibar, hair dryer.

WHERE TO DINE

Rôtisserie du XVI Siècle 👍 *Finds* SWISS   This is a charming old inn with good food and affordable bedrooms. The building that gives this establishment its name was constructed during the 16th century on ancient Roman foundations. After a disastrous fire in the early 1990s, this place reopened as a simple, unpretentious restaurant. The delightful cuisine may include filets of perch sautéed with almonds, an array of grilled meats, and salads. The most popular offering is a two-course *menu du jour,* which includes an appetizer and a well-stocked main course, which changes daily. The most prevalent specialties are game hen with rosemary and entrecôte XVI Siècle, a hefty chunk of beefsteak seasoned with local herbs and served with matchstick potatoes. This is not a site for *grande gastronomie*—instead, the food is straightforward, generous in its portions, and geared to popular tastes.

The establishment also offers 19 simple but pleasantly furnished bedrooms, 13 with private bathroom. Doubles without bathroom rent for 150F ($123), going up to 175F ($144) with bathroom.

Place du Marché, CH-1260 Nyon. © 022/994-88-00. Reservations recommended. Main courses 20F–40F ($16–$33). AE, MC, V. Mon–Sat 11:30am–2pm and 6:30–10pm.

4 Vevey 👍

18km (11 miles) E of Lausanne; 6km (4 miles) NW of Montreux

Home of Nestlé chocolate, the resort of Vevey has been popular with British visitors since the 19th century. It's at the foot of Mount Pélerin, which you can ascend by funicular. The town, dating from Roman times, was built at the mouth of the Veveyse River and is the center of the Lavaux vineyards. In the Middle Ages it was known as an important trading post on the route from Piedmont, in Italy, to Burgundy, in France.

Rousseau's descriptions of his "sentimental rambles" in the lake district lured the first Romantic visitors. In time, English and Russian aristocrats selected the sheltered Swiss Riviera for long winter sojourns. Famous exiles to the area have included the English regicide Edmund Ludlow, the French painter Gustave Courbet, the Polish pianist Ignace Paderewski, and the Polish novelist Henryk Sienkiewicz.

As former visitors Henry James, Oskar Kokoschka, and even Dostoyevsky could tell you, Vevey is a great town for walks, especially Old Town, with its interesting restaurants, bars, and shops. You can no longer see Graham Greene or Victor Hugo on the streets, but you'll still find much that is rewarding. Stop in at the tourist office and pick up a free brochure, *On the Trail of Hemingway,* that will direct you to not only the former residences of Papa but places frequented by dozens of celebrities.

ESSENTIALS

GETTING THERE   Vevey lies on the major rail link between Lausanne and (via the Simplon Tunnel) the great cities of northern Italy. Dozens of trains stop here every day. Trip time from Lausanne is 15 minutes and the round-trip fare costs around 20F ($16). Call the tourist office (see below) for more information.

If you're driving from Lausanne, head south along N9; from Montreux, drive northwest on N9 along the edge of the lake.

Daily from May through mid-October, about half a dozen lake steamers transit the length of Lake Geneva, stopping at Lausanne, Vevey, Geneva, and several other cities along the way. Travel time to Vevey from Geneva is almost 5 hours; from Lausanne, about 1 hour. For information, contact the **CGN (Compagnie Générale de Navigation),** 17, av. de Rhodanie, Lausanne (𝄐 **0848-811-848;** www.cgn.ch).

VISITOR INFORMATION   The **Vevey Tourist Office,** 29, Grand-Place (𝄐 **021/ 922-20-20**), is open June to mid-September daily from 9am to 6pm; the rest of the year, Monday to Friday 9am to noon and 1:30 to 6pm and Saturday 9am to 4pm.

SEEING THE SIGHTS

Begin by exploring the **Grand-Place,** a mammoth market plaza, the town's nerve center and largest parking lot, facing Lac Léman. The corn exchange on the north dates from the early 19th century. As you walk in this area and along the quay, you'll enjoy views of the Savoy Alps.

For a slice of local life, head for the **Café de La Clef,** 1, rue du Théâtre (𝄐 **021/ 921-22-45**), where Jean Jacques Rousseau stayed in 1730. This is the landmark cafe of Vevey, and over the years it's seen a parade of who's who from Oona Chaplin to Le Corbusier. As you drink your libation, you can enjoy views of the pillared marketplace out front. The decor is dowdy and unfashionable, just how the habitués like it. If you're around at lunchtime, drop in for local Swiss specialties including lake fish such as perch or even a fondue in winter.

Church of St. Martin, boulevard St-Martin (no phone), dating from the 10th century, is on a belvedere overlooking the resort. It has a large rectangular tower with four turrets, and there's a good view of Vevey from the tower. Its interior has a dusty-looking collection of excavations that, along with the church itself, are always open.

A statue by John Doubleday on the new **square Chaplin,** quai Perdonnet, commemorates the area's most illustrious former resident, Charlie Chaplin. Chaplin moved here from the United States in 1952 with his young wife, Oona O'Neill, in part to escape accusations of Communist sympathies. Except for brief interludes, he remained in Vevey until his death in 1977. When he died, he was considered a popular, unpretentious (and fabulously wealthy) local citizen. The life-size statue erected in his honor represents the little tramp in baggy pants—the character Chaplin made famous—gazing out at his favorite view of Lake Geneva and the Alps in the distance.

Chaplin actually lived in the little village of **Corsier,** above Vevey, which dates from the 2nd century. Its church is thought to have been established by the Abbey of St.

Maurice; inside you can see some 15th-century paintings. Villagers dedicated a park to their famous resident. Although the stately villa he occupied cannot be visited, the comedian is buried in the cemetery (Cimetière de Corsier), a 3-minute walk downhill from the village. Bus nos. 11 and 12 goes from Vevey to Corsier.

Musée de l'Alimentarium   Established in the 1980s with funds derived mostly from the charitable foundations associated with the Nestlé organization, this museum celebrates the development of foodstuffs around the world. Set near the statue of Chaplin, it's the most interactive museum in Vevey, containing lots of buttons that children (and adults) can push to release odors of sizzling foods, activate dioramas and computerized exhibitions, and begin film clips that show the preoccupation of the human race with its own survival.

Quai Perdonnet. ☏ **021/924-41-11.** Admission 10F ($8.20) adults, 8F ($6.55) students and seniors, free for children 16 and under. Year-round Tues–Sun 10am–6pm.

Musée du Vieux-Vevey   This stately château contains two museums: the Musée Historique du Vieux-Vevey and the Musée de la Confrérie de la Vigneron (Winemakers Museum). Exhibits include 18th-century antiques and mementos of the vintners' trade, wrought-iron work, arms, pewter, tools, and some of the paraphernalia associated with the region's wine festivals. Paintings by local artists are also displayed, as well as ancient and medieval artifacts once excavated from the area around Vevey.

2, rue du Château. ☏ **021/921-07-22.** Admission 5F ($4.10) adults; 4F ($3.30) students, seniors, and children 15 and under. Mar–Oct Tues–Sun 10:30am–noon and 2–5:30pm; Nov–Feb Tues–Sun 2–5pm.

Musée Jenisch   This museum was founded at the end of the 19th century, created from a bequest by Fanny Jenisch of Hamburg, who with her husband had made their home in Vevey. Today the museum houses the Fine Arts Museum (Musée des Beaux-Arts) and the Museum of Prints (Cabinet Cantonal des Estampes). The collection is rich in paintings by Swiss artists, and features representative works of Bissier and other artists.

2, av. de la Gare. ☏ **021/921-34-01.** Admission 12F ($9.85) adults, 10F ($8.20) seniors, 6F ($4.90) students, free for children 16 and under. Mar–Oct Tues–Sun 11am–5:30pm; Nov–Feb Tues–Sun 2–5:30pm.

Musée Suisse de l'Appareil Photographique (Swiss Camera Museum)   The only museum of its kind in Switzerland, this five-story celebration of the printed image contains examples of the machines that recorded human history from the earliest daguerreotypes to the present. The uppermost floor is devoted to a changing exposition of modern photographic art, but for aficionados of photography, the fascination here is the amazing range of cameras from the 1920s to today.

6, rue des Anciens-Fossés. ☏ **021/925-21-40.** Admission 8F ($6.55) adults, 6F ($4.90) students, seniors, and children 15 and under. Mar–Oct Tues–Sun 11am–5:30pm; Nov–Feb Tues–Sun 2–5:30pm.

WHERE TO STAY

Best Western Hôtel du Lac ☞   This well-established hotel, affiliated with Vevey's more expensive Hôtel des Trois Couronnes (see below), is popular because of its lakeside view and its distinct sense of old-fashioned charm. A government-rated four-star choice, it was built in 1864 but has been renovated bit by bit ever since. It has a swimming pool and a flower-studded lakeside terrace. Appropriate for a relaxing vacation beside the lake, the hotel is mostly patronized by foreign, especially British, visitors. If you read Anita Brookner's novel *Hôtel du Lac,* you may expect a grander place. Brookner took poetic license in describing its formality and refinement. Some bedrooms are better than others. Many have been updated with contemporary styling;

others, however, are comfortable but vaguely dowdy, languishing back in a bygone era. The hotel restaurant, Le Chenaie, deserves its excellent reputation for Swiss and French specialties.

1, rue d'Italie, CH-1800 Vevey. Ⓒ **800/780-7234** in the U.S. or 021/921-10-41. Fax 021/921-75-08. www.bestwestern.ch. 56 units. 260F–480F ($213–$394) double. Rates include buffet breakfast. AE, DC, MC, V. Free parking outdoors, 15F ($12) in garage. **Amenities:** 2 restaurants; outdoor pool; health club; 24-hr. room service; laundry service. *In room:* TV, dataport, minibar, hair dryer, iron, safe.

Hôtel des Négociants   Built close to Vevey's main square in 1974, this government-rated two-star, four-story, brick-sided hotel does a thriving business in its street-level brasserie. The members of the Bertholet family are your hosts, working hard to carefully maintain the hotel when they're not catering to hungry guests in their dining room. The small guest rooms are functionally furnished but well maintained, each outfitted with a small bathroom.

27, rue du Conseil, CH-1800 Vevey. Ⓒ **021/922-70-11.** Fax 021/921-34-24. www.hotelnegociants.ch. 23 units. 130F–150F ($107–$123) double. MC, V. **Amenities:** Restaurant. *In room:* TV, dataport.

Hôtel des Trois Couronnes 🟊🟊🟊   This leading hotel is famous as the setting of Henry James's first popular success, *Daisy Miller;* the film version, by the director Peter Bogdanovich, was also made here. The Daisy Millers still arrive today, although perhaps not as innocent as the subject of James's novella. It's located in the center of town, in a white-stucco-and-gray-stone building with noble details. Built in 1842, it still remains the grande dame, as it's so often called, of Vevey hotels. Rated five stars by the government, it has been progressively renovated over the years. The lobby has an elegant gallery with white balustrades three floors tall. The midsize to spacious rooms retain their 19th-century charm, the more expensive units with attractive antiques. Each of the accommodations comes with a luxurious private bathroom.

49, rue d'Italie, CH-1800 Vevey. Ⓒ **800/223-5652** in the U.S. or 021/923-32-00. Fax 021/923-33-99. www.hoteltrois couronnes.ch. 55 units. 380F–480F ($312–$394) double; 910F–1,100F ($592–$715) suite. AE, DC, MC, V. **Amenities:** Restaurant; 24-hr. room service; laundry service. *In room:* TV, dataport, minibar, hair dryer, safe.

ON THE OUTSKIRTS

Le Mirador-Kempinski 🟊🟊🟊   Evocative of an elegant manor house, Le Mirador is one of the grandest spas in western Switzerland. Lying 400m (1,312 ft.) above Lake Geneva in the heart of Swiss wine county on Mont-Pélerin, 13km (8 miles) north of Vevey, the hotel is composed of a four-story chalet and an equally luxurious balconied annex. This retreat is deluxe living in grand style, with luxurious furnishings and fine paintings. Although a favorite venue for conferences, the resort is also ideal for the spa devotee, drawn to such treatments as cellular therapy. There is no better example in Switzerland of a 21st-century resort than Le Mirador.

5, chemin du Mirador, CH-1801 Mont-Pélerin. Ⓒ 021/925-11-11. Fax 021/925-11-12. www.mirador.ch. 80 units. 380F–790F ($312–$648) double; 890F–4600F ($730–$3772) suite. Rates include breakfast. AE, DC, MC, V. **Amenities:** 3 restaurants; bar; indoor/outdoor pool; health club; elegant spa; business center. *In room:* TV, dataport, minibar, hair dryer, safe, trouser press.

WHERE TO DINE

La Pinte de l'Hôtel de Ville SWISS   *Pinte* is old French for "bistro," but in this case it suggests an extremely simple eatery where folks often come to drink instead of eat. It's very unpretentious and small. This landmark cafe overlooks the trees and cobblestones of an old square across from the city hall, and outside tables are available in fair weather. The food is simple but good. Appetizers include *assiette valaisanne* (air-dried

beef); typical main courses are steak maison, steak with mushroom sauce, and couscous. It also offers sandwiches and three kinds of fondue.

19, rue de l'Hôtel-de-Ville. ✆ **021/921-78-80.** Reservations recommended. Main courses 16F–30F ($13–$25). MC,
V. Mon–Fri 11:30am–2pm and 6–10pm; Sat–Sun 8am–7pm. Cafe snacks Mon–Sat 7am–midnight.

Restaurant Denis Martin "Le Château" ★★ CONTINENTAL One of the
most spectacular restaurants of Vevey occupies the street level of the town's oldest
building—a baronial villa built in 1599. Inside, a pair of dining rooms offer soaring
vaults composed of stone, contemporary accessories, and a noteworthy collection of
modern sculpture by well-known Swiss artist André Raboud. During clement weather
a flower-studded outdoor terrace offers sweeping views over lawns and the nearby
lake. Menu items change frequently, according to the inspiration of chef and owner
Denis Martin, but two representative, consistently excellent specialties include duck
liver served with apple chutney and spice bread; and line-caught sea bass with basil-
flavored olive oil and sweet peppers. If you prefer to leave the composition of your
meal to the experts, consider one of the fixed-price menus, the most elaborate of
which is composed of 15 artfully presented minicourses.

2, rue de Château, on the street level of the Musée Historique de Vieux Vevey. ✆ **021/921-12-10.** Reservations
required. Main courses 48F–98F ($39–$80); fixed-price menus 160F–210F ($131–$172). AE, DC, MC, V. Tues–Sat
noon–2pm and 7–10pm. Closed Dec 23–Jan 15.

Restaurant du Raisin ★ LYONNAIS/VAUDOIS This is the center of gastron-
omy. An inn has flourished on this site since the 1880s. The real glamour of the place
lies one floor above street level, in a room lined with a changing roster of paintings by
local artists. Here, an intensely cultivated cuisine based on modernized Lyonnais and
Vaudois dishes is served using only fresh and seasonal ingredients. The best examples
include a bouquet of wild greens studded with freshwater crawfish, fava beans, and
vinaigrette; an upscale stew of lobster with artichoke hearts, fresh nasturtiums, and
black truffles; and sea bass with fried zucchini flowers and ratatouille-flavored butter.
Dessert may be a frozen soufflé enhanced with herbed liqueur (La Grande Gruyère)
from the nearby mountains.

Despite the allure of the upstairs restaurant, don't overlook the charm of the street-
level brasserie, a site that wins many office workers' votes for a preferred lunch stop.
Menu items here are cheap, cheerful, and flavorful, and include such platters as
deboned filets of perch, veal kidneys with mustard sauce, duck breast in orange sauce,
and roasted pig's trotters with lentils and sausages.

3, Grand-Place. ✆ **021/921-10-28.** Reservations recommended in restaurant, not necessary in brasserie. Restaurant
main courses 42F–60F ($34–$49); fixed-price menu 55F–85F ($45–$70). Brasserie fixed-price menu 27F–50F
($22–$41); platters 16F–41F ($13–$34). AE, DC, MC, V. Restaurant Tues–Sun 11:30am–2:30pm; Tues–Sat 6:30–10pm.
Brasserie daily 11am–2:30pm and 6:30–10:30pm.

Taverne du Château ★ SWISS Built in 1681, this large stucco building is a lot
more elegant today than when it was originally constructed as a farmer's grange. One
of the most elaborately gentrified buildings in town, it has a large carved beam extending out over one of the top-floor windows. A pulley was attached to the beam to transport supplies to the upper floors. Over the pavement hangs a wrought-iron and gilt
sign with a picture of a horse and two men fighting. Many of the menu items focus
on seafood, served in well-prepared, intensely rehearsed ways. The menu might
include such mouthwatering specialties as a sauté of freshwater crawfish with tomatoes and parsley, sea wolf with basil and sweet-pepper sauce, warm sautéed duck liver,

a gâteau of pigeon, an aromatic rack of lamb with herbs of Provence, and chicken supreme cooked in a pinot noir sauce. In autumn the menu features many game dishes. For many gastronomes, this restaurant is a required stopover along Lake Geneva.

43, rue d'Italie. ℂ **021/921-12-10**. Reservations required. Main courses 35F–65F ($29–$53); fixed-price menu 75F–130F ($62–$107). AE, DC, MC, V. Tues–Sat 11am–3pm and 6:30pm–midnight. Closed Sept 1–15.

VEVEY AFTER DARK

At the columned marketplace in the center of town, **Café de La Clef Chez Manu,** 1, rue de Théâtre (ℂ **021/921-22-45**), was made famous in 1730 when Jean-Jacques Rousseau used to hang out here. As for decor, the place looks lost in a time capsule back somewhere in the early part of the 20th century, but it remains Vevey's enduring favorite as a worthy hangout at all times of the day or night. The place fills up for lunch with locals devouring such dishes as perch from lake Geneva. The other much frequented spot is **Les Temps Modernes,** 6B, rue des Deux Gares (ℂ **021/922-34-39**), both a restaurant and a club. It's the French name for *Modern Times,* one of the most famous films made by Vevey's most famous resident, the late Charlie Chaplin. This club attracts the most diverse group of patrons, from skiers to bankers. With its junky furniture, the club occupies a warehouselike building. If you stay for dinner, the food is excellent, although many visitors come here to enjoy live music performances—everything from hot salsa nights to concert jazz. Sometimes there's no cover unless the performers are well known, at which time a 25F ($21) cover is imposed. Closed in July and August.

5 Montreux ★★

3km (2 miles) E of Vevey; 24km (15 miles) E of Lausanne; 100km (62 miles) E of Geneva

The chief resort of the Swiss Riviera, Montreux rises in the shape of an amphitheater from the shores of Lac Léman. An Edwardian town with a distinct French accent, it has long been a refuge for expatriates, including the novelist Vladimir Nabokov. Known for its balmy climate, it sports a profusion of Mediterranean vegetation, which grows lushly in the town's many lakeside parks. The mountains at the town's back protect it from the winds of winter, allowing fruit trees, cypresses, magnolias, bay trees, almonds, and even palms to flourish.

The city has expanded greatly from its original 19th-century core, incorporating several former villages along the shoreline. One of these, Clarens, was used by Rousseau as the setting for his epistolary novel *La nouvelle Héloïse.* The resort enjoyed its heyday in the years just before World War I, when it had only 85 hotel beds. It hosted such distinguished visitors as Tolstoy, Flaubert, Dostoyevsky, and Ruskin. In recent times the town has revived, and today about three-fourths of the resort's 20,000 inhabitants are engaged in some touristic capacity or another.

Though the resort is favored year-round, it's most densely crowded in summertime, when traffic clogs most of the streets.

ESSENTIALS

GETTING THERE   Montreux not only lies on the famous *Orient Express* line linking Paris to Milan, but it's also connected to the link between Geneva and the Simplon Tunnel. Dozens of trains stop at Montreux every day headed in both directions. The most famous is the *Train Panoramique,* a big-windowed train with a transparent roof that links Montreux to Interlaken. Passengers who take this conveyance often continue, after a change of train, on to Lucerne in a conventional railway car. For bookings, contact **M.O.B. (Société Montreux-Oberland-Bernois),** Gare de Montreux (© **021/989-81-90**). For more Swiss **rail information,** dial © **0900/300-300.**

If you're driving, Montreux sits in the middle of a network of superhighways linking Germany, France, and Italy with Switzerland. The divider of the traffic coming from Germany via Bern is just outside Montreux. From that vantage point, you can go either east or west across Switzerland.

In addition, Montreux is one of the stops on the east-west steamer route between Villeneuve and Geneva. Travel by lake steamer from Lausanne is about 1 hour, or about 3 hours from Geneva. Most boats depart between May and September, with limited service throughout the rest of the year. For information and bookings, contact **CGN (Compagnie Générale de Navigation)** in Lausanne (© **0848/811-848;** www.cgn.ch).

VISITOR INFORMATION   The **Montreux Convention & Tourist Information Office,** rue du Théâtre (© **021/962-84-84;** www.montreuxtourism.ch), is opposite the boat-landing pier. Throughout the year it's open daily from 9am to 6pm.

SEEING THE SIGHTS

Explore the old houses and crooked streets of Old Montreux. Later, stroll along the quayside promenade by the lake. The only way to discover the charms of far-flung and widely scattered Montreux is by using up a lot of shoe leather.

The most impressive castle in Switzerland, the **Château of Chillon** 🏰🏰 (© **021/966-89-10**) is on the lake 3.2km (2 miles) south of Montreux. To reach it, you can ride trolley bus no. 1 for 2.60F ($1.70) each way. But for many the most enthralling way to reach Chillon from Montreux is to walk along the scenery-studded 3km (2-mile) lake path. It's the grandest promenade you can take in Montreux. Most of the castle dates from the 13th century, but its oldest section is thought to be 1,000 years old. The castle was built by Peter II of Savoy and is one of the best-preserved, and most frequently photographed, medieval castles of Europe. So-called sorcerers were tried and tortured here. The most famous prisoner, François Bonivard, was described by Byron in *The Prisoner of Chillon.* Bonivard was the prior of St. Victori in Geneva, and when he supported Geneva's independence in 1532, the Catholic duke of Savoy chained him in the dungeon until 1536, when he was released by the Bernese.

The château is open April to September daily from 9am to 6pm; March and October daily from 9:30am to 5pm; November to February daily from 10am to 4pm. It's closed Christmas and New Year's. Admission costs 10F ($8.20) for adults, 5F ($4.10) for children 6 to 16; it's free for children 5 and under.

Rochers-de-Naye 🏰🏰🏰 at 2,042m (6,698 ft.) is one of the most popular tours along Lake Geneva. From Montreux, a cogwheel train takes visitors in less than an hour up to Rochers-de-Naye. The train ascends the slopes over Lac Léman, passing **Glion,** a little resort on a rocky crag almost suspended between lake and mountains. You come to **Caux** at 1,097m (3,598 ft.), lying on a natural balcony overhanging the blue bowl of the lake. Finally, the peak of Rochers-de-Naye rises high in the Vaudois Alps. In the distance you can see the Savoy Alps, including Mont Blanc and the Jura Alps. At the end is an alpine flower garden, the loftiest in Europe. The train departs from the railway station of Montreux every hour during the day, beginning at 7:30am, with the last departure between 5:30 and 7pm, depending on the season. The travel time, each way, to Caux is 20 minutes. The round-trip fare between Montreux and

Montreux Jazz Festival

One of the biggest musical bashes in Europe occurs at the internationally known **Montreux Jazz Festival** (© 021/966-44-44; www.montreuxjazz.com), beginning the first week of July and running for 2 weeks. Everyone from Bob Dylan to B. B. King is likely to show up for the music and festivities. Ticket prices are high. You pay from 65F to 135F ($53–$111) for each individual ticket. The tourist office in Montreux provides advance information and even sells tickets. Tickets for many events, especially the top ones, often sell out early. If you show up and can't get a ticket, you can still enjoy "Jazz Off," some 500 hours of admission-free open-air concerts, often staged by new or wannabe talent throughout the city. The tourist office keeps a schedule, but much of the fun is spontaneous.

Rochers-de-Naye is 38F ($31). Holders of Swiss Rail passes or Eurail passes pay half price. Call (© **021/989-81-00**) for more information.

Villeneuve, the little port town at the end of the lake, is where Lord Byron wrote *The Prisoner of Chillon* in 1816. Mahatma Gandhi visited Romain Rolland when the French novelist and pacifist lived here. The town and its surrounding countryside have been painted by many artists, including Oskar Kokoschka, who once lived here. Villeneuve is a 25-minute walk from the Château of Chillon, which is visible from virtually every point in the village.

WHERE TO STAY

Many of the leading hotels of Montreux have greatly improved in recent years. Unfortunately, good budget accommodations are lacking. Hotels are superexpensive. If you want to stay in the area more cheaply, seek lodgings in Vevey.

EXPENSIVE

Grand Hôtel Excelsior 🕂🕂   A renowned Montreux landmark since 1903, this government-rated five-star lakeside hotel offers quiet opulence and discreet personal service. The elegant marble foyer has marquetry, a hushed sense of restraint, and Queen Anne antiques. The charm of this hotel is enhanced by oil paintings and baroque sculpture. The luxurious rooms are spacious, and all have lakefront balconies. Each comes with a combination tub/shower except for 11 units, which have just showers.

21, rue Bon-Port, CH-1820 Montreux. © 021/966-57-57. Fax 021/966-57-58. www.hotelexcelsiormontreux.com. 70 units. 480F ($394) double; from 1,100F ($902) suite for 2. Rates include buffet breakfast. Half board 55F ($45) extra. AE, DC, MC, V. Parking 15F ($12). Bus: 1. **Amenities:** 2 restaurants; bar; indoor pool; fitness center; sauna; salon; limited room service; massage; babysitting; laundry service/dry cleaning. *In room:* TV, dataport, minibar, hair dryer, safe.

Hôtel Eden au Lac 🕂🕂   The lingering nostalgia and beautiful restoration of this hotel evoke scenes from the movie *Death in Venice,* based on a work by Thomas Mann. It's a favorite hotel in Montreux, and it's less expensive than the Palace. Situated on the lakeside promenade, it has a grand 19th-century style and a facade that resembles an Art Nouveau wedding cake. The pink-and-white neobaroque Gatsby Bar has stained-glass windows, and there's a garden terrace with magnolias. The owners offer well-appointed, spacious rooms. The junior and senior suites are among the most opulent in Montreux.

11, rue du Théâtre, CH-1820 Montreux. ☎ **021/966-08-00.** Fax 021/966-09-00. www.edenmontreux.ch. 110 units. 390F–470F ($320–$385) double; 620F–780F ($508–$640) suite for 2. Rates include continental breakfast. AE, DC, MC, V. Parking 25F ($21). Bus: 1. Closed mid-Dec to end of Jan. **Amenities:** 3 restaurants; bar; outdoor pool; fitness center; 24-hr. room service; laundry service/dry cleaning. *In room:* TV, dataport, minibar, hair dryer.

Hotel Victoria ⭐⭐   This Relais & Châteaux opens onto views of mountains and lakefront and is surrounded by extensive, manicured grounds. It truly lives up to Lake Geneva's reputation as an idyllic retreat for hedonists. Expect a lot of pampering at this mansion dating from 1869. Noel Coward, the playwright, stayed here some 4 decades ago and raved about it in letters sent back to his theatrical friends in London. Following in Coward's footsteps, the Victoria has witnessed a parade of other celebrities, even royalty. "We try to make our guests feel at home," the owner, Toni Mittermair, told us, and in that stated goal he succeeds admirably. The most desirable bedrooms open onto a private balcony overlooking the lake. All the accommodations are good, however, with well-chosen furnishings, fine art, and luxurious bathrooms.

Rte. de Caux, CH-1823 Glion sur Montreux. ☎ **021/962-82-82.** Fax 021/962-82-92. www.victoria-glion.ch. 50 units. 270F–350F ($221–$287) double; 520F–600F ($426–$492) junior suite. AE, DC, MC, V. **Amenities:** Restaurant; bar; indoor pool; tennis court; small gym; sauna. *In room:* TV, dataport, minibar, hair dryer, safe.

Le Montreux Palace ⭐⭐⭐   Facing the lake, this is an opulent palace that was built in 1906. Despite being the largest hotel in Montreux, a monument visible from miles away, frequent renovations have retained its embellished ceilings, parquet floors, and crystal chandeliers. Once a favorite of Russian czars, it later attracted Vladimir Nabokov—the author of *Lolita,* among other works—who spent long periods of creative time here. Architectural charm abounds—one room has an arched ceiling with an Art Nouveau stained-glass skylight ringed with statues of cupids and demigods. Each of the comfortably old-fashioned bedrooms, many quite spacious, has French doors and a balcony. The rooms in the rear, however, open onto the mountain and not the lake. All units come with luxurious marble bathrooms. In all, the place is elegant, bemused, blasé, and very historic. The Amrita Wellness Spa here is one of the finest in this part of the world, with 10 womblike salons with waterfalls and stone floors. Treatments range from an Indian head massage to Turkish scrubs.

100, Grand'Rue, CH-1820 Montreux. ☎ **021/962-12-12.** Fax 021/962-17-17. www.montreux-palace.com. 235 units. 500F–700F ($410–$574) double; from 960F ($787) suite. AE, DC, MC, V. Parking 30F ($25). Bus: 1. **Amenities:** 2 restaurants; 2 bars; indoor pool; nearby golf course; tennis courts; exercise room; spa; Jacuzzi; sauna; 24-hr. room service; massage; laundry service. *In room:* A/C, TV, dataport, minibar, coffeemaker, hair dryer, iron.

Royal Plaza ⭐⭐   This is the most architecturally avant-garde hotel in Montreux. Designed in a semifuturistic style in 1982, it rises eight floors above an enviable position beside the lake, amid gardens and pedestrian walkways accented with shrubs, lawns, and trees. Because of the slope of the hillside on which the hotel is built, the lobby is set on the hotel's third floor, but few visitors realize that until they begin to explore the hotel a bit. Most of the spacious rooms face the lake and are designed in a sleek modern decor that would suit any five-star hotel in the world. All the accommodations contain luxurious bathrooms.

97, Grand'Rue, CH-1820 Montreux. ☎ **800/327-0200** in the U.S. or 021/962-50-50. Fax 021/962-51-51. www.royal plaza.ch. 147 units. 295F–635F ($242–$521) double; 595F–2,100F ($488–$1,722) suite. AE, DC, MC, V. Underground parking 25F ($21). Bus: 1. **Amenities:** 3 restaurants; 2 bars; indoor pool; fitness center; sauna; car rental; 24-hr. room service; laundry service; nonsmoking rooms. *In room:* A/C, TV, dataport, minibar, hair dryer, iron, safe.

MODERATE

Grand Hôtel Suisse et Majestic 🐾   This opulent landmark, originally built in 1870 and renovated frequently since then, is in the heart of Old Montreux, beside the lake. Take one of the three elevators past the *trompe l'oeil* murals to the Art Nouveau lobby on the top floor. From here you'll have access to a terrace with classical statuary and a panoramic view. Comfort and subdued elegance are the keys to the success of this hotel. Most of the spacious rooms have an updated Belle Epoque decor, each equipped with a luxurious bathroom. The average unit is priced at the lower end of the scale below.

43, av. des Alps, CH-1820 Montreux. ✆ **021/966-33-33.** Fax 021/966-33-00. www.suisse-majestic.ch. 135 units. 190F–460F ($156–$377) double; 470F–800F ($385–$656) suite. Rates include buffet breakfast. AE, DC, MC, V. Bus: 1. **Amenities:** 2 restaurants; bar; car-rental desk; limited room service; laundry service/dry cleaning. *In room:* TV, minibar, hair dryer.

INEXPENSIVE

Auberge des Planches   This off-white building, originally erected in 1800, became a hotel in 1992. In a quiet neighborhood, 5 minutes from the center of town, this has become a popular spot for those on a short stay in Montreux. The rooms are small with a slight Mexican decor and are clean and comfortable. All rooms have private bathrooms with shower. There is an in-house restaurant that serves Mexican food for reasonable prices.

2, rue du Temple, CH-1820 Montreux. ✆ **021/963-49-73.** Fax 021/963-23-11. 36 units. Summer 150F–170F ($123–$139) double; winter 140F–160F ($115–$131) double. AE, DC, MC, V. **Amenities:** Restaurant; bar. *In room:* TV, dataport, hair dryer.

ON THE OUTSKIRTS

Villa Kruger 🐾🐾 *Finds*   This is a real discovery and the most offbeat living choice in the area. In the leafy suburb of Clarens, 1km (½ mile) north of Montreux, the villa was erected in 1874 as a vacation retreat for Paul Kruger, then president of South Africa. Today it is a boutique hotel of charm and grace, although admittedly overly decorated, a whirlpool of fringes, swags, furbelows, and the like along with gilt mirrors, candelabra, Persian rugs, and antiques. You feel like you're staying at the home of your very rich aunt, not at a hotel. This luxury guesthouse lies on the shores of Lake Geneva in a superb setting. The guest rooms consist of three twins and one single, and all have private bathrooms. South African wines are served with a cuisine called "Haute Karoo," a region of South Africa often compared to Provence.

Villas Dubochet 17, CH 1815 Clarens-Montreux. ✆ **021/964-74-72.** Fax 021/964-74-39. 4 units. 415F–520F ($340–$426) double. AE, MC, V. Rates include breakfast. **Amenities:** Restaurant. *In room:* TV.

WHERE TO DINE

VERY EXPENSIVE

Le Pont de Brent 🐾🐾🐾 FRENCH/SWISS   The district's finest and best-known restaurant is in a turn-of-the-20th-century house near a historic bridge in the hamlet of Brent. Gérald Rabaey, the owner and chef, prepares a frequently changing array of seafood, including a soup made with mussels and leeks, Breton lobster with zucchini in a tarragon-flavored cream sauce, rabbit in mustard sauce, and roast pigeon with herbs. Succulent versions of trout, turbot, and sea bass are also featured, along with fresh mushrooms and the best fruits of any season. We could heap praise upon praise on this restaurant and still not do it justice. It is the grandest choice for dining along Lake Geneva. The combination of flavors is inspired. Inventiveness and solid technique reign supreme here. After a meal here you will proclaim you've arrived in paradise as you kidnap the chef to take him home.

In Brent. © 021/964-52-30. Reservations required. Fixed-price menus 200F–240F ($164–$197). MC, V. Tues–Sat noon–2pm and 7–9:30pm. Closed 3 weeks in midsummer and 2 weeks Dec–Jan. From Montreux, follow the signs to Blonary-Brent, driving 3km (2 miles) northwest of the city.

L'Ermitage ⚐⚐⚐ FRENCH/SWISS   Set in Montreux's lakefront suburb of Clarens, this restaurant occupies the dignified premises of a *maison bourgeoise* built in the late 19th century and surrounded with a spacious park. The celebrated chef, Etienne Krebs, owns the place along with his charming wife, Isabelle, who handles the dining room, which has welcomed everyone from the president of Switzerland to Quincy Jones. You'll dine in one of three rattan-filled rooms painted "the colors of water and sun" or on a terrace overlooking the lake. Menu items change with the seasons but always reflect fresh ingredients. Palate-pleasing examples include a casserole of foie gras with celery; filet of fera (a fish from the nearby lake) with capers and artichoke hearts; a salad of baby crawfish in an emulsion of tomatoes and olive oil; rosettes of roast lamb with aromatic alpine herbs; and a supreme thigh of wild duckling in a sheathing of mashed potatoes with a sauté of exotic mushrooms.

The site also maintains four rooms priced at 180F to 300F ($148–$246) and three suites priced at 330F to 420F ($271–$344), with breakfast included. Each has rattan furniture and is individually decorated with taste and flair.

75, rue du Lac, CH-1815 Clarens. © 021/964-44-11. Fax 021/964-70-02. Reservations recommended. Main courses 54F–70F ($44–$57); fixed-price meals 75F–167F ($62–$137). AE, DC, MC, V. Daily 11:30am–2pm and 7–10pm. Closed Sun–Mon Oct–Apr and Dec 21–Jan 21. Drive .8km (½ mile) east of Montreux, following the lakefront road and signs pointing to Vevey.

EXPENSIVE

La Vieille Ferme ⚐ SWISS/INTERNATIONAL   This old stone-walled house is in the village of Chailly, in a building dating from the 13th century when it functioned as a munitions warehouse for local monks and later as a farmhouse. As such, it's one of the oldest buildings in the region. Accompanying your meal will be regional background music, which is performed almost every night. Yvan Mabillard is clearly a master chef, as revealed by his offering of succulent beef dishes, aromatic alpine lamb, chicken, rabbit, frogs' legs, tender veal, lake perch, trout, crawfish, and a velvety goose liver made into a terrine. The menu also includes gratiné of shrimp or grilled beef, and fondue bourguignon and cheese fondue. The chef grills fresh fish and meat better than anyone else in the area. The arrival of large tour groups may interrupt your intimate dinner.

40, rue de Bourg, Chailly-sur-Montreux. © 021/964-64-65. Reservations required. Main courses 30F–55F ($25–$45); fixed-price menu 35F–45F ($29–$37) at lunch, 65F ($53) at dinner. AE, MC, V. Wed–Sun noon–2:30pm and 7–10pm. Closed July. From Montreux, follow the signs to autoroute N1; then just before you reach the autoroute, follow the signs to Chailly-Village, a total of 3km (2½ miles) north of Montreux.

Les Magnolias ⚐ RHONE/PROVENÇAL   Despite its role as the showcase restaurant in one of the most elegant Beaux Arts hotels in Montreux, this is not a particularly expensive establishment—at least by Swiss standards. You'll reach it by passing through the hotel's marble lobby, but once you're inside you'll notice a subtle nautical decor in the comfortable bar off to one side, and an emphasis on the culinary traditions of the Rhône Valley. Menu items change with the season and may include delectable deep-fried zucchini flowers with a *mousseline* of sea wolf, a standard version of *pissaladière niçoise* (a kind of Provençal quiche), filets of perch or sole meunière, and a divine roasted salmon garnished with duck liver and herbs.

In the Grand Hôtel Excelsior, 21, rue Bon-Port. (©) 021/966-57-57. Reservations recommended. Main courses 30F–40F ($25–$33); fixed-price lunch 45F ($37); fixed-price dinner 60F ($49). AE, DC, MC, V. Daily noon–2pm and 7–10pm. Bus: 1.

MODERATE

Restaurant Chinois Wing Wah *(Kids)* CANTONESE   Hearty portions of well-prepared Chinese food and relatively reasonable prices attract many families to this scarlet-and-gold dining room. The owner, originally from Hong Kong, prepares lacquered duck, twice-grilled beef, spicy shrimp, diced chicken with hot peppers, crispy roast chicken, and curried shrimp. The restaurant's name translates as "happiness."

42, Grand-Rue. (©) 021/963-34-47. Reservations required. Main courses 29F–38F ($19–$25); fixed-price lunch 17F–30F ($11–$19), fixed-price dinner 50F–80F ($33–$52). AE, DC, MC, V. Daily 11:30am–2:30pm and 6:30–10:30pm. Bus: 1.

INEXPENSIVE

Caveau des Vignerons SWISS   At the corner of rue di Marché, this is a tavern that has long been a local favorite. A traditional Swiss cuisine is served in a candlelit cave that is elegantly decorated with wood paneling. In this unusual atmosphere, you can order some of the best-tasting dishes in town, all reasonably priced. True devotees flock here for the horse meat, which you can cook yourself at the table, although those from other cultures might prefer to stick to one of the delectable Swiss specialties instead. The Cave turns out some of the best cheese and meat fondues in town. You can also look for the constantly changing daily specials, and finish your selection with one of the creamy desserts.

30, rue Industrielle. (©) 021/963-25-70. Reservations recommended. Main courses 20F–50F ($16–$41). AE, DC, MC, V. Mon–Fri 9am–midnight; Sat 3pm–midnight. Bus: 1.

MONTREUX AFTER DARK

The major action spins around the **Casino de Montreux,** 9, rue du Théâtre (© 021/962-83-83), but don't expect a casino where fortunes are made and lost, or even a particularly impressive architectural monument. The casino here has almost no architectural interest, set in a dull modern building in the heart of town near the lake. Despite that, it can provide some nightlife diversion in an otherwise rather dull town. About 200 slot machines shake, rattle, and roll, along with a handful of roulette tables. There is a small disco open nightly till 4am.

   Harry's New York Bar, in Le Montreux Palace, 100, Grand-Rue (© 021/962-12-12), is the most convivial watering hole and the first Harry's to be established in Switzerland. There's a Harry's Bar in many European cities today, but this particular example—managed by one of the grandest hotels of Montreux—won't remind you of any of them. Once the home of an auto showroom, it underwent an elegant transformation with the installation of rich paneling and touches of brass and leather. The bartenders—a well-trained crew hailing from almost everywhere—mix cocktails the old-fashioned way (shaken, not stirred). Most clients come here to drink, but if you're hungry, they serve light but elegant meals.

   Other hot spots after dark include **Caesar's,** 515, Grand-Rue (© 021/963-75-59), known for its lakeside terrace dances and occasional cabaret; and **Pussycat Club,** 100, Grand-Rue (© 021/963-34-44), a good place to go dancing. There's even a DJ and—get this—a sushi bar.

Geneva

If it's a toss-up between Geneva and the larger city of Zurich (and you have time for only one stopover), make it Geneva. Many patriotic French feel this French-speaking city of elegance and charm should belong in France. It does indeed sit on the doorstep of France. But in some respects Geneva is international, belonging to the world with its 250 international organizations based here, the most important being as the European headquarters for the United Nations, the World Health Organization, and the International Red Cross.

It's the most orderly and serene of all major European cities (or sterile in the view of those who'd like more local color, nightlife, and excitement).

Because of its ideological and geographic isolation from Switzerland, Geneva appears almost like one of those old European "city states." Locals used to burn books here by Rousseau until Voltaire arrived and set them straight. Those romantics Shelley and Byron came here seeking inspiration from the surrounding mountains, but Lenin failed to convert anyone to communism.

As one local and very wealthy lady told us, "Geneva is one of the few places on the planet I can walk around in my white sable without fear I'll be hit by a rotten tomato by an animal rights fanatic, or else have it stolen from me by some poor wretched down and out." She actually said that.

Geneva is located in the Rhône Valley at the southwestern corner of Lake Geneva (or Lac Léman, in French), between the Jura Mountains and the Alps. It's the capital of the canton of Geneva, the second-smallest canton in the Swiss Confederation.

Switzerland's second-largest city has an idyllic setting on one of the biggest alpine lakes and within view of the pinnacle of Mont Blanc. Filled with parks and promenades, the city becomes a virtual garden in summer. It's also one of the healthiest cities in the world thanks to prevailing north winds that blow away all air pollution.

Surrounded by French territory, Geneva is connected to Switzerland only by the lake and a narrow corridor. The city's strong French influence shows in its mansard roofs, iron balconies, sidewalk cafes, and French signs.

1 Orientation

ARRIVING

BY PLANE The **Geneva-Cointrin Airport** (© 022/717-71-11; www.gva.ch), although busy, is quite compact and easily negotiated. **Swiss International Air Lines** (© 877/359-7947 from the U.S.; www.swiss.com) serves Geneva more frequently than any other airline and offers the best local connections, connecting Geneva with Lugano, Zurich, and Bern, plus flying in from several European capitals. Other international airlines flying into Geneva include **Air France** (© 800/237-2747 from the

U.S.; www.airfrance.com), with 10 flights daily from Paris; and **British Airways** (© **022/710-61-00;** www.britishairways.com), with 14 daily flights from London.

To get into the center of Geneva, there's a train station linked to the air terminal with trains leaving about every 8 to 20 minutes from 5:25am to 12:25am for the 7-minute trip; the one-way fare is 9F ($7.40) in first class and 5.40F ($4.45) in second class. A taxi into town will cost between 30F and 40F ($25 and $33), or you can take bus no. 10 for 12F ($9.85).

BY TRAIN Geneva's CFF (Chemins de Fer Fédéraux) train station in the town center is **Gare Cornavin,** place Cornavin (© **0900/300-300** for ticket information). A small tourist office branch is at the train station.

Note: When the Lausanne-Geneva railroad line was extended to Cointrin Airport, a second "main" railroad station was built here with both long-distance and intercity trains. To avoid having to make the trip back to the center from the airport, be sure you get off the train at the Cornavin station.

BY CAR From Lausanne, head southwest on N1 to the very end of southwestern Switzerland.

BY LAKE STEAMER There are frequent daily arrivals by Swiss lake steamer year-round from Montreux, Vevey, and Lausanne (you can use your Eurailpass for the trip). If you're staying in the Left Bank (Old Town), get off at the Jardin Anglais stop in Geneva; Mont Blanc and Pâquis are the two Right Bank stops. For more information, call © **0848/811-848** or visit www.cgn.ch.

VISITOR INFORMATION

Geneva's tourist office, the **Office du Tourisme de Genève,** is located at 18, rue du Mont-Blanc (© **022/909-70-00;** www.geneve-tourisme.ch), and is open daily year-round from 9am to 6pm. The staff provides information about the city, and can also arrange hotel reservations both in Geneva and throughout Switzerland, and refer you to other establishments specializing in car and motorcycle rentals and excursion bookings. They can also give you details about audio-guided visits to the Old Town.

CITY LAYOUT

Geneva is a perfect city to explore on foot. It's divided by Lake Geneva (Lac Léman) and the Rhône River into two sections: the Right Bank and the Left Bank. In addition to taking our walking tour of the highlights (see "Attractions," later in this chapter), you may rent an audio-guided tour in English from the tourist office (see above) for 10F ($8.20). This tour covers more than two dozen highlights in the Old Town, and comes complete with cassette, player, and map. Its estimated duration is 2 hours. A 50F ($41) deposit is collected prior to your receipt of a cassette player.

RIVE GAUCHE (LEFT BANK) This compact and colorful area is the oldest section of the city. Here you'll find Old Town, some major shopping streets, the famous Flower Clock, the university, and several important museums.

Grand-Rue is the well-preserved main street of Old Town. It's flanked by many houses dating from the 15th and 18th centuries. The street winds uphill from the ponts de l'Ile; at place Bel-Air it becomes rue de la Cité, then Grand-Rue, and finally rue de l'Hôtel-de-Ville. Eventually it reaches **place du Bourg-de-Four**—one of the most historic squares of Geneva (Rousseau was born in a simple house at no. 40).

South of this street is **promenade des Bastions,** a greenbelt area overlooking the Arve, with a monument to the Reformation. Directly to the west, in the northern corner of promenade des Bastions, is **place Neuve,** which is the finest square in Geneva.

From place Neuve, you can take rue de la Corraterie, which was once surrounded by the city wall, to the Rhône and the **ponts de l'Ile.** On this bridge is the **Tour-de-l'Ile,** what's left of the 13th-century bishops' castle.

On the shore of Lake Geneva is the **Jardin Anglais (English Garden)** with its Flower Clock and, farther out, the **Parc La Grange** and the nearby **Parc des Eaux-Vives.**

RIVE DROITE (RIGHT BANK)   You can cross to the other side of the Rhône on any of several bridges, including pont du Mont-Blanc, pont de la Machine, pont des Bergues, and ponts de l'Ile. The Right Bank is home to Gare Cornavin, the major international organizations, and several attractive parks.

Place St-Gervais is in the St-Gervais district; this has been the area for jewelers and watchmakers since the 18th century.

Along the northern shore of Lake Geneva is **quai du Président-Wilson,** named for the U.S. president who helped found the League of Nations.

The Right Bank is surrounded by parks, from the tree-shaded promenades along the Rhône to the **Parc de la Perle du Lac, Parc Barton,** and **Parc Mon-Repos** on the outskirts.

FINDING AN ADDRESS   In a system developed during the Middle Ages, all Swiss cities begin their street-numbering system with the lowest numbers closest to the old center of town. The numbers increase the farther out from Old Town you go. Even numbers are on one side of a street; odd numbers are on the other side.

MAPS   The tourist office (see above) presents visitors with a detailed and easy-to-follow free map of Geneva.

NEIGHBORHOODS IN BRIEF

Rues Basses   Rues Basses (translated either as "low streets" or figuratively as "lower town") is found between Old Town and the south bank of the Rhône. It's the major commercial and shopping district of Geneva. Its major street is rue du Rhône, although rue de la Confédération and rue du Marché are also important arteries.

Old Town (Vieille Ville)   At an altitude of 398m (1,305 ft.), Old Town is the most history-rich section of Geneva. This is Left Bank Geneva, with its narrow streets, flower-bedecked fountains, and architectural blends of Gothic, Renaissance, and 18th-century features. The twin towers of the Cathedral of St. Pierre dominate Old Town, whose geographical and spiritual center is place du Bourg-de-Four.

The Promenades of Geneva   These streets almost constitute a "neighborhood" in themselves. This section of quays along both Lake Geneva and the Rhône is best experienced by walking. One of the most scenic walks is from the Parc des Eaux-Vives on the Left Bank to the Parc de Mon-Repos on the Right Bank. Along the way is a clear view of Geneva's most famous and visible monument, the Jet d'Eau. Set a few inches above the surface of the lake, this fountain spurts a plume of shimmering water 138m (453 ft.) into the air. Except during special circumstances, such as the arrival of a foreign head of state, it operates only between March and October.

2 Getting Around

Walking is the cheapest, most practical form of transportation in Geneva. It's also the most advantageous from a tourist's point of view. For the city's quaint Old Town, tree-shaded promenades line the lake, and you can browse many chic shops walking leisurely about Geneva. Savor the measured tempo of life here that makes this city particularly alluring to the foreign visitor.

Nevertheless, if speed is the object, you may avail yourself of the public transportation system, which is reasonably priced and as dependable as a Swiss watch.

BY PUBLIC TRANSPORTATION

Most of Geneva's public tram and bus lines begin at the central place Cornavin in front of the main railroad station. From here, you can take bus F or 8 to the Palais des Nations. Local buses and trams operate daily from 5am to midnight, and you can purchase a ticket from a vending machine before you board. If you don't understand, instructions are given in English. **Transport Publics Genevois** (© **0900/022-021;** www.tpg.ch), next to the tourist office in Gare Cornavin, offers free maps of local bus routings. Trips that stay within zone 10, enveloping most of Geneva, cost 3F ($2.45), and unlimited use of all zones costs 10F ($8.20) for 1 day.

BY TAXI

The meter on whatever cab you take in Geneva will automatically begin calculating your fare at 5.80F ($4.75), and then add between 2.40F ($1.95) and 3F ($2.45) for every kilometer you travel, depending on the time of day or night. The fare from the airport to the center of town ranges from 30F to 40F ($25–$33). No tipping is required, and extra baggage may cost 1F ($.80). To call for a **taxi,** call © **0800/ 801-234** or 0800/801-802.

BY CAR

Driving is not recommended because parking is too difficult and the many one-way streets make navigation complicated. However, should you wish to rent a car and tour Lake Geneva (see chapter 10), you'll find many car-rental companies represented in the arrivals hall of the airport or in the center of the city. Major car-rental companies in Geneva include **Avis,** 44, rue de Lausanne (© **022/731-90-00,** or at the airport 022/929-03-38); **Budget,** at the airport (© **022/717-86-75**); **Hertz,** at the airport (© **022/798-22-02**); and **Europcar,** 37 rue de Lausanne (© **022/909-69-90**).

BY BIKE

Touring the city by bicycle isn't particularly practical because of the steep cobblestone streets, speeding cars, and general congestion. However, you might want to consider renting a bike for touring the countryside around Geneva. The major rental outlet is at the baggage desk at **Gare Cornavin** (© **022/791-02-50**), where city bikes cost 29F ($24) and mountain bikes rent for 40F ($33).

Another major outlet, charging from 7F to 25F ($5.75–$21) per day, depending on the degree of sophistication of the bicycle, is **Genève Roule,** 17, place Montbrillant (© **022/740-13-43**).

FAST FACTS: Geneva

Babysitters A list of agencies is available at the tourist office. Most middle- and upper-bracket hotels will also secure an English-speaking babysitter for you, or you can call **Chaperones Rouges** (✆ 022/304-04-86), an organization associated with the Red Cross responsible for teaching young girls about child-care rituals. Some students make themselves available for babysitting in either a private home or a hotel room; the service is particularly pertinent for sick children.

Bookstore One of the largest in Geneva is the well-stocked **Payot,** 5, rue Chantepoulet (✆ 022/731-89-50), with a good selection of books in French, German, and English.

Business Hours Most banks are open Monday to Friday from 8:30am to 4:30pm (until 5:30pm Wed). Most offices are open Monday to Friday from 8am to noon and 2 to 6pm, although this can vary. It's always best to call first.

Car Rentals See "By Car," above.

Consulates If you lose your passport or have other business with your home government, go to your nation's consulate: **United States,** 7, rue Versonnex (✆ 022/840-51-61); **Australia,** 2, chemin des Fins (✆ 022/799-91-00); **Canada,** 5, av. de L'Areana (✆ 022/919-92-00); **New Zealand,** 2, chemin des Fins (✆ 022/929-03-50); the **United Kingdom,** 37-39, rue de Vermont (✆ 022/918-24-00).

Currency Exchange In a city devoted to banking and the exchange of international currencies, you'll find dozens of places to exchange money in Geneva. Three of the most visible outlets, however, are run by **UBS-SA,** one of the country's largest banking conglomerates. You'll find a branch at the **Gare Cornavin,** 12 place Cornavin (✆ 022/375-33-47), that's open Monday to Friday from 8:30am to 4:30pm; a branch at the **Cointrin Airport** (✆ 022/918-26-34) that's open Monday to Friday from 8:30am to 4:30pm; and a downtown branch at 2, rue de la Confederation (✆ 022/375-75-75) that's open Monday to Friday from 8am to 4pm. The branches in the airport and in the railway station also house "money-automats"—you receive an equivalent amount of Swiss francs for every $20, $50, or $100 bill you insert into the machine.

Dentist English-speaking dentists are available at one of the *cliniques dentaires* at 5, chemin de Malombré (✆ 022/346-64-44), open daily from 8am to 7pm.

Doctor If you become ill and want to consult a doctor, including one who will travel to your hotel, call ✆ 022/322-20-20; or arrange an appointment with an English-speaking doctor at the **Hôpital Cantonal,** 24, rue Micheli-du-Crest (✆ 022/372-33-11).

Drugstores Each night a different set of four drugstores stays open either till 9 or 11pm. Call ✆ 144 or 111 to find out which drugstore will be open. One of the world's biggest drugstores, **Pharmacie Principale,** in Confédération-Centre, 8, rue de la Confédération (✆ 022/318-66-60), offers everything from medicine to clothing, perfumes, optical equipment, cameras, and photo supplies. It's open daily from 9am to 9pm.

Emergencies In an emergency, dial ✆ 117 for the police, ✆ 144 for an ambulance, or ✆ 118 to report a fire.

Eyeglasses You can go to **Visi-Lab** in the Confédération-Centre, 8, rue de la Confédération (☎ **022/318-66-80**).

Hospitals A prime choice for medical aid is the **Geneva University Hospital, 24,** rue Micheli-du-Crest (☎ **022/372-60-19**; www.hug-ge.ch). Most physicians speak English and German but are unlikely to be available on Thursday afternoons.

Library The **American Library,** at 3, rue de Monthoux (☎ **022/732-80-97**), has a subscription service open to those looking for a wide variety of the latest books in English. A month's membership, the minimum allowable, costs 30F ($25). A refundable deposit of 70F ($57) is required before you can borrow your first book.

Lost Property Go to the **Service Cantonal des Objets Trouvés,** 5, rue des Glacis-de-Rive (☎ **022/327-60-00**), open Monday to Friday from 7:30am to 4pm.

Luggage Storage/Lockers Luggage can be stored and lockers rented at the main railroad station, **Gare Cornavin,** place Cornavin (☎ **0900/022-021**).

Newspapers/Magazines Newspapers in Geneva are printed in French, but the latest copies of the *International Herald Tribune, USA Today,* the *New York Times,* and the *Washington Post* are available at most newsstands and in large hotel newsstand kiosks. And if you're planning on moving to Geneva, or spending more than a month here, consider acquiring a copy of the *Guide to English-Speaking Geneva,* which is available free at the American Library (see above) or from the city's premier English-language bookshop, **The ELM (English Language Media),** 5, rue Versonnex (☎ **022/736-09-45**).

Police In an emergency, call ☎ **117**. For nonemergency matters, call ☎ **022/327-41-11**.

Post Office There's a limited **Office de Poste** at Gare Cornavin, 16, rue des Gares (☎ **022/739-21-11**), open Monday to Friday from 6am to 10:45pm, Saturday from 6am to 8pm, and Sunday from noon to 8pm. A better bet is the city's main post office, **Bureau de Poste Montbrillant,** rue des Gares (☎ **022/739-24-58**), which offers a full range of telephone, telegraph, and mail-related services Monday to Friday from 8am to 10:45pm, Saturday 8am to 10pm, and Sunday noon to 8pm.

Restrooms You'll find public facilities at all rail and air terminals and on main squares. Otherwise, you can patronize those in cafes and other commercial establishments such as department stores.

Safety Geneva is one of the safest cities in the world, but that doesn't mean you shouldn't take the usual precautions when traveling anywhere. Protect your valuables. Car thefts have been on the rise. High-class prostitutes and confidence swindlers proliferate in Geneva to prey on the well-heeled.

Shoe Repairs An outlet of **Mr. Minit** is located in the Metro-Shopping arcade, 30, rue du Mont-Blanc (☎ **022/732-42-59**). Most repairs can be performed while you wait.

Taxes There is no special city tax, other than the 6.5% value-added tax (VAT) attached to all goods and services throughout Switzerland.

Telegrams/Telex/Fax Virtually every post office in Geneva maintains a handful of *tele-cabines* where you can pay cash for a phone call to anywhere in the world, but the densest concentration of these phones lies within the main railway station,

Gare Cornavin, place Cornavin (it's open 24 hr. a day). Within less than a block, you'll find additional phones in the **Office de Poste Montbrillant** (Cornavin Dépôt), 16, rue des Gares (© **022/739-24-58**), which is open Monday to Friday from 8am to 8pm and Sunday from noon to 8pm. Either site can send telegrams or faxes for you.

Tipping Most restaurants and hotels, even taxis, add a service charge of 10% to 15% to your bill, so no further tipping is necessary unless you want to reward someone for a special service.

Transit Information For **train information,** call © 0900/022-021 from anywhere in Switzerland. Contact the **airport** at © 022/717-71-11. For **bus information** Monday to Friday from 8am to 9pm, dial © 022/308-33-11; for information on Saturday and Sunday, call © 022/308-34-34.

Useful Telephone Numbers For general telephone directory information, call © 111; for the time, © 161; for the weather, © 162.

3 Where to Stay

A truly world-class city, Geneva has lots of hotels, most of which are clustered around the railway terminal or stretched along the lakefront. But be warned—Geneva hosts a number of international conferences and conventions, so many of its hotels are booked months in advance. And while it does incorporate dozens of expensive hotels in all different architectural styles (from the antique to the supermodern), it doesn't have very many intimate, family-run inns.

Note: Unless indicated otherwise, all rooms in hotels we've recommended below have a private bathroom.

ON THE RIGHT BANK
VERY EXPENSIVE

Four Seasons Hôtel des Bergues *₲₲₲*   After being conglomerated into the luxury Canadian company Four Seasons, a massive renovation downsized 122 rooms to 103 even more spacious rooms in 2005. The elegant, four-story hotel—designated a historic monument by the Swiss—once catered to the monarchs of Europe. Today it's a favorite with the international business community, diplomats, and members of European society. It has long been ranked by *Institutional Investor* as one of the world's top hotels. The hotel's impressive guest list has included Jean Cocteau, the duke of Edinburgh, the queen of Spain, Edward VIII, the queen of Hawaii, and Emperor Franz Joseph and Empress Elizabeth ("Sissi") of Austria. Grandly memorable from its centrally located position at the edge of the Rhône, the hotel also hosted many meetings of the League of Nations. During World War II it was known as the "hotel of the Allies," having played host to so many Allied leaders.

The hotel's public rooms are lavish. The bedrooms have Directoire and Louis Philippe furnishings. Accommodations ranked superior on the Bel Étage floor are the finest choices here, although all units are beautifully appointed. Lake-view rooms are more expensive. The hotel shelters two of the classiest dining rooms in Geneva: Le Pavillon and L'Amphitryon.

Where to Stay in Geneva

Lac Léman

Woodrow Wilson

26

25

24

Quai du Mont-Blanc

Jacquet

Rue Plantamour

23

22

21

20

19

Jet d'Eau

Rade de
Genève

Pont du-
Mont-Blanc

ILE
ROUSSEAU

Pont des
Bergues

JARDIN
ANGLAIS

Quai Général Guisan

17

RIVE
GAUCHE

Rue du Rhône

18

RUES BASSES

les Rues Basses

VIEILLE VILLE
(OLD TOWN)

Cathédral
St-Pierre

Grand Rue

la Corraterie

15

R. de la Croix Rouge

Place
Neuve

Dufour

Favon

Promenade
des Bastions

Université

R. de Candolle

PLAINE DE
PLAINPALAIS

Rd-pt. de
Plainpalais

du Mail

Henri Dunant

Boulevard du Pont d'Arve

R. de Carouge

R. Prévost-Martin

LA CLUSE

Bd. de la Cluse

Quai Gustave Ador

FRONTENEX

PARC DES
EAUX-VIVES

Quai Gustave Ador

PARC
LA GRANGE

Plateau de Frontenex

Avenue W. Favre

MONTCHOISY

Rue des Eaux-Vives

Rue du 31 Décembre

Rue des Vollandes

Rue de Montchoisy

Route de Frontenex

Chemin Frank Thomas

Chemin Av. Rosemont

Route de Chêne

Ch. de la Petite Boissière

Promenade Martin

Av. de l'Armandier

R. de la Marie

Av. Pictet De Rochemont

Rue Agasse

Rue de la Terassière

R. Lachenal

16

Rue Hodler

Pl. Em.
Guyenot

Route de Malagnou

R. De Rive

rd.-pt
de Rive

R. de l'Hôtel de Ville

R. de la Fontaine

Bd. Jacques Dalcroze

Boulevard Helvétique

Ch. Galland

Bd. des Tranchées

Rue de

l'Athenée

Rue de l'Athenée

Cours ses Bastions

Place Ed.
Claparède

Philosophes

Rue St. Léger

Avenue Peschier

Avenue Bertrand

FLORISSANT

Route de Florissant

PARC
A. BERTRAND

Chemin Rieu

Avenue Louis Aubert

CHAMPEL

Avenue de Miremont

Avenue de Champel

Rue A. Lombard

Av. Calas

Train Station

Lac Léman

Jardin Anglais

1/5 mile

0

0

200 meters

N

311

33, quai des Bergues, CH-1211 Genève. © **022/908-70-00.** Fax 022/908-70-90. www.hotelsbergues.com. 103 units. 725F–1,025F ($595–$841) double; from 3,475F ($2,850) suite. AE, DC, MC, V. Parking 38F ($31). Bus: 7. **Amenities:** 2 restaurants; bar; lounge; exercise room; sauna; 24-hr. room service; babysitting; laundry service/dry cleaning; nonsmoking rooms. *In room:* A/C, TV, dataport, minibar, hair dryer, safe.

Hôtel Beau-Rivage ✿✿✿   This grand old landmark 1865 hotel, which has counted Richard Wagner and Sarah Bernhardt among its guests, receives our highest recommendation for its traditional Victorian charm and impeccable service. However, you'll pay—and pay dearly—for the privilege of staying here or at its rival, the even grander Le Richemond (see below). Its colorful history has included the auction of the jewels of the late duchess of Windsor; and after World War I, the treaty creating the Republic of Czechoslovakia was signed here. The most tragic event in its history, however, was the assassination of Empress Elisabeth of Austria, who was stabbed in 1898 by the anarchist Luigi Lucheni as she was leaving the hotel on her way to a lake steamer. To this day, history buffs rent the pale-blue Empress Suite.

The hotel was built by Jean-Jacques Mayer, who came from Stuttgart. Its most striking feature is the open, five-story lobby. The hotel also became the first in Europe to install elevators. Today it's run by the founder's great-grandson, with the help of an enthusiastic staff. The rooms are individually furnished and frequently redecorated. All front rooms have views of the Right Bank. Accommodations are categorized by size, "romantic" rooms being more spacious, and "classical" rooms being medium in size. Some of the romantic units contain frescoes. Each also has a roomy private bathroom, clad in marble or tile, with robes and deluxe toiletries.

13, quai du Mont-Blanc, CH-1201 Genève. © **022/716-66-66.** Fax 022/716-60-60. www.beau-rivage.ch. 93 units. 620F–1,400F ($508–$1,148) double; from 1,900F ($1,558) suite. AE, DC, MC, V. Parking 40F ($33). Bus: 1. **Amenities:** 2 restaurants; bar; 24-hr. room service; babysitting; laundry service/dry cleaning; nonsmoking rooms. *In room:* A/C, TV, dataport, minibar, hair dryer.

Hôtel d'Angleterre ✿   This boutique hotel is the smallest of the grand palace hotels that line the edge of the lake, beside the waterfront promenade of Geneva. Set behind a stately looking facade that was originally erected in 1872, it has successfully competed with larger and equally grand hotels as the hotel of choice for visiting celebrities. In the early 1900s, the king of Belgium was accused of stashing a mistress inside this venerable hotel, and in the late 1990s, Michael Jackson spent 2½ months lodged in one of the suites with some of his children dangling out the windows. Bedrooms are outfitted in tasteful renditions of either Louis XV or like something you'd have expected in a British country house, with flower-patterned chintzes and deep upholsteries. Rooms have been systematically overhauled, several per year, keeping everything spiffy and up-to-date. Especially appealing is the street-level bar area, where a safari-inspired decor mixes what you might have expected in a country house in England but in this case, with a scattering of antique trunks (which double as tables), animal hides-cum-upholsteries, and a sense of colonial adventure.

17, quai du Mont-Blanc, CH-1201 Genève. © **022/906-55-55.** Fax 022/906-55-56. www.dangleterrehotel.com. 45 units. 520F–920F ($426–$754) double; from 990F ($812) suite. AE, DC, MC, V. Parking 29F ($24) extra. Bus: 1. **Amenities:** Restaurant; bar; fitness center; sauna; 24-hr. room service; massage; babysitting; laundry service/dry cleaning; nonsmoking rooms. *In room:* A/C, TV, dataport, minibar, hair dryer, safe.

Hôtel de la Paix ✿✿   In terms of opulence, it's a notch down from the Beau-Rivage, but since its prices are less expensive and it's a lot less pretentious, many clients seek it out for those reasons. Although not in the ultratop tier, it's grand and glamorous, and after a complete overhaul, it's better than it's ever been. Royalty from

Liechtenstein, Monaco, and the Netherlands, as well as international dignitaries and celebrities such as the guitarist Andrés Segovia, have stayed in this 1865 hotel directly on the lake. Designed by an Italian architect and built of stone from Meillerie, the building belonged to the kingdom of Sardinia for a long time. The main salon is a double-tiered arched extravaganza, with marble columns, elaborate Corinthian capitals, and a balustraded loggia overlooking a massive crystal chandelier. Rooms are traditionally furnished and often quite roomy, with antiques intermixed with well-chosen modern pieces. The marble and tile bathrooms are luxuriously equipped. This hotel is a member of the Concorde Hotel group.

11, quai du Mont-Blanc, CH-1201 Genève. ℂ 800/223-6800 in the U.S. or 022/909-60-00. Fax 022/909-60-01. www.hoteldelapaix.ch. 91 units. 600F–800F ($492–$656) double; from 1,500F ($1,230) suite. AE, DC, MC, V. Parking 40F ($33). Bus: 6, 8, 10, or 15. **Amenities:** Restaurant; bar; limited room service; babysitting; laundry service/dry cleaning; nonsmoking rooms. *In room:* A/C, TV, dataport, minibar, hair dryer, safe.

Hôtel Président Wilson ★★★
It's named for Woodrow Wilson and the president's ill-fated attempt to get the United States to join the League of Nations. Located across a busy boulevard from the lakefront, a 5-minute drive (or a brisk walk) from the center of town, this modern hotel is sometimes mistaken for the diplomatic headquarters of some international agency. In 1994 it launched an ambitious expansion program, with the addition of a new wing and a total renovation inside and out. Minor refurbishments and improvements have continued every year since. The guest rooms and suites are furnished with classic European styling, with extensive use of wood and rich fabrics. Luxury extras are all in place, with bidets, robes, marble bathrooms, full-length mirrors, dual basins, and elegant carpeting. Windows open onto views of Lake Geneva and Mont Blanc. Despite the good intentions of the staff, an anonymity prevails. One of the galleries displays the hotel's collection of 17th-century Gobelin tapestries.

47, quai du Président-Wilson, CH-1211 Genève. ℂ 022/906-66-66. Fax 022/906-66-67. www.hotelpwilson.com. 255 units. 580F–1,110F ($476–$910) double; from 1,950F ($1,599) suite. AE, DC, MC, V. Parking 30F ($25). Bus: 1. **Amenities:** 3 restaurants; 2 bars; indoor pool; fitness center; spa; Jacuzzi; sauna; 24-hr. room service; massage; babysitting; laundry service/dry cleaning; nonsmoking floor. *In room:* A/C, TV, dataport, minibar, hair dryer, safe.

Le Palace Hilton Geneva ★
Located at the edge of the lake, this is the largest deluxe hotel in Switzerland, and one of the best in the Hilton chain. Depending on your taste, the hotel is either stylish and glossy or a bit anonymous. All the rooms are custom-designed, with beautiful wood, fabrics, and artwork, and are equipped with spacious marble bathrooms and oversize beds. The rooms overlooking the lake and the town are higher-priced; those opening onto a quiet courtyard cost less. The hotel has a gourmet restaurant, Le Cygne, one of the best in Geneva (see "Where to Dine," later in this chapter), and an elegant Asian restaurant, Le Tsé-Yang.

19, quai du Mont-Blanc, CH-1211 Genève. ℂ 800/445-8667 in the U.S. and Canada or 022/908-90-81. Fax 022/908-90-90. www.geneva.hilton.com. 410 units. 505F–790F ($414–$648) double; from 1,200F ($984) suite. AE, DC, MC, V. Bus: 1. **Amenities:** 4 restaurants; 3 bars; indoor pool; fitness center; car rental; salon; 24-hr. room service; massage; babysitting; laundry service/dry cleaning; nonsmoking rooms; rooms for guests w/limited mobility. *In room:* A/C, TV, dataport, minibar, hair dryer.

Le Richemond ★★★
When you win the $327-million lottery sweepstakes, check in here. Le Richemond, which counts some of the world's most prominent people among its guests, is the greatest hotel in Geneva. When Michael Jackson checked in, he was following in the footsteps of the famous and infamous of yesteryear, including

Colette, Miró, Chagall, and Swiss resident Charlie Chaplin. Erected in 1875, the neo-classical, travertine building has wrought-iron balustrades and is situated near the lake, across from a small park. In the 19th century it was an unpretentious guesthouse, but the hotel has been transformed under the direction of the Armleder family, who have run it since the day it opened. Its public rooms look like a museum, with dozens of valuable engravings and an array of furniture dating from the days of Louis XII. Accommodations range from the most spacious in the city to medium in size; nearly half of the units here are suites, attracting all of Europe, plus international CEOs. This is true Grand Hotel living, with elegant fabrics, tasteful upholstery, and luxurious beds, plus spacious marble bathrooms with robes and a basket of expensive toiletries. Before attempting to book a room here, check its status, as it is expected to be closed for a large part of 2006 for a major face-lift.

Jardin Brunswick, CH-1201 Genève. ✆ 022/715-70-00. Fax 022/715-70-01. www.roccofortehotels.ch. 98 units. 480F–890F ($394–$730) double; from 1,470F ($1,205) suite. AE, DC, MC, V. Parking 50F ($41). Bus: 1. **Amenities:** 2 restaurants; bar; fitness center; salon; 24-hr. room service; babysitting; laundry service/dry cleaning. *In room:* A/C, TV, dataport, minibar, hair dryer.

EXPENSIVE

Hôtel Cornavin ⓕ ⓚ*ids*   Few other hotels in Geneva have been as radically reno-vated, and as frequently, as this government-rated four-star contender that stands adja-cent to the railway station. Originally built in 1932, with a bland and neutral-looking facade that overlooks the bustle of Geneva's most commercial square, it was height-ened in 1998 with the addition of a ninth floor that capped the original structure. That, coupled with a frequent overhaul of each of the already existing bedrooms, pro-duced an efficient, well-managed, business-conscious hotel. Each of the bedrooms is outfitted in pastel tones and a sense of contemporary warmth. Each is soundproof against the noise of the nearby traffic, and contains a neatly kept bathroom. More than a dozen spacious triples and half a dozen doubles with interconnecting doors make this a family favorite.

23, bd. James-Fazy, CH-1201 Genève. ✆ 022/716-12-12. Fax 022/716-12-00. 169 units. 437F ($358) double. Rates include buffet breakfast. AE, DC, MC, V. **Amenities:** Bar; limited room service; laundry service/dry cleaning; nonsmok-ing rooms. *In room:* A/C, TV, dataport, minibar, hair dryer.

Hôtel du Midi   Ideally situated on a tree-lined square near the center of Geneva, this salmon-colored, eight-story hotel reminds most visitors of an apartment building. The reception area is at street level. The windows are double-glazed to keep out the noise, and there's wall-to-wall carpeting in every room. The bedrooms contain such accessories as warming racks for towels. Bedrooms are medium in size and, although not spectacular, are exceedingly well maintained. Bathrooms are a bit cramped, but with adequate shelf space. The Hôtel du Midi manages to remain comfortable in spite of the somewhat plain appearance.

4, place Chevelu, CH-1201 Genève. ✆ 022/544-15-00. Fax 022/544-15-20. www.hotel-du-midi.ch. 90 units. 350F–450F ($287–$369) double. AE, DC, MC, V. Parking 18F ($15). **Amenities:** Restaurant; bar; lounge; limited room serv-ice; laundry service/dry cleaning. *In room:* A/C, TV, minibar, hair dryer, safe.

Hôtel Grand-Pré ⓕ ⓚ*ids*   Set between the center of town and the airport, this mod-ern, six-story, government-rated four-star hotel is convenient and efficient. Rooms are standardized but comfortable, most outfitted with contemporary, comfortable furniture. Everything has been completely renovated, including the fifth-floor breakfast room and the lobby-level bar. Based on management whims and occupancy rates, discounts are sometimes granted on Friday and Saturday nights. The hotel quotes special terms for families, depending on their size, and families with kids especially appreciate the refrigerator in each room.

35, rue du Grand-Pré, CH-1202 Genève. ✆ **022/918-11-11.** Fax 022/734-76-91. www.swissqualityhotels.com. 90 units. 350F ($287) double; 700F ($574) suite. Rates include continental breakfast. AE, DC, MC, V. Parking 20F ($16). **Amenities:** Bar; breakfast room; limited room service; laundry service/dry cleaning; nonsmoking rooms. *In room:* A/C, TV, dataport, minibar, hair dryer.

Le Warwick ✫ *Kids*   This contemporary hotel, located across from the train station, is a strong choice, built during the 1970s and owned and operated by a Hong Kong chain with headquarters in Paris. The abstractly modern lobby contains sweeping staircases, loggias, balconies, marble floors, and Oriental rugs. The refurbished, soundproof bedrooms are often sunny, boldly patterned, and comfortable, with marble bathrooms. Le Warwick allows children up to 12 years of age to stay free in their parent's room. Its brasserie is open for light meals and snacks all day long.

14, rue de Lausanne, CH-1201 Genève. ✆ **800/203-3232** in the U.S. and Canada or 022/716-80-00. Fax 022/716-80-01. www.warwickgeneva.com. 167 units. 450F ($369) double; 700F ($574) suite. Children 12 and under stay free in parent's room. AE, DC, MC, V. Parking 18F ($15). **Amenities:** 2 restaurants; bar; limited room service; babysitting; laundry service/dry cleaning; nonsmoking rooms. *In room:* A/C, TV, dataport, minibar, hair dryer.

MODERATE

Best Western Strasbourg & Univers ✫   Set close to the railway station on a dead-end street that is tranquil, this building was originally constructed around 1900 by a nostalgic entrepreneur originally from Strasbourg. Over the years many different renovations both outside and inside have kept it looking fresh and new. Some of the bedrooms have wooden surfaces and pastel colors; others are comfortably and traditionally conservative. The bedrooms, as befits a turn-of-the-20th-century hotel, range from spacious (usually on the lower floors) to a bit cramped. Each bedroom has fine linens, plus compact bathrooms with tile and decent plumbing.

10, rue Pradier, CH-1201 Genève. ✆ **800/528-1234** in the U.S. or 022/906-58-00. Fax 022/738-42-08. www.strasbourg-geneva.ch. 51 units. 250F–270F ($205–$221) double; 400F–500F ($328–$410) suite. Rates include continental breakfast. AE, DC, MC, V. Bus: 1, 2, 3, 4, 8, 12, 13, or 44. **Amenities:** Lounge; laundry service/dry cleaning. *In room:* TV, dataport, minibar, hair dryer, iron/board, safe, beverage maker.

Hôtel Edelweiss   This brown-and-white, eight-story hotel towers above its neighbors near quai du Président-Wilson. Inside, it has a rustic decor that contrasts with its modern exterior. The bedrooms are cozy and furnished with pine-wood furniture crafted in a country-Swiss style. Even though in the heart of Geneva, you get provincial comfort here. Bedrooms are medium in size with sitting areas and desk space. Bathrooms, although small and plain, are neatly kept. Built in the early 1960s, the hotel is frequently spruced up.

2, place de la Navigation, CH-1201 Genève. ✆ **022/544-51-51.** Fax 022/544-51-99. www.manotel.com/edelweiss. 42 units. 330F ($271) double. Rates include buffet breakfast. AE, DC, MC, V. Bus: 1. **Amenities:** Restaurant; bar; lounge; 24-hr. room service; babysitting; laundry service/dry cleaning. *In room:* A/C, TV, minibar, hair dryer, safe.

Novotel Genève Centre *Value*   One of the most consistently reliable government-rated four-star hotels in Geneva's commercial center is this comfortable, standardized member of a France-based chain. It was originally built in the 1970s as a five-star Ramada, and consequently bedrooms are bigger than what you'd expect at a usual Novotel. From the street, you'll step down into a stylish-looking, marble-trimmed lobby, then head upstairs to larger-than-expected, comfortably standardized bed-rooms, each with a writing table favored by business travelers, and a sofa that can be transformed into an additional bed.

19, rue de Zurich, CH-1201 Genève. ⓒ 022/909-90-00. Fax 022/909-90-01. 206 units. 200F–240F ($164–$197) double; from 1,110F ($910) suite. AE, DC, MC, V. Bus: 1 or 5. **Amenities:** Restaurant; bar; 24-hr. room service; laundry service/dry cleaning; nonsmoking rooms. *In room:* A/C, TV, dataport, minibar, hair dryer, safe.

INEXPENSIVE

Hôtel Bel'Espérance *(Value)*   At the gateway to Old Town, close to the lake, this is a decent budget hotel managed by the Salvation Army. It's no bare-bones hotel: It has well-furnished, good-size bedrooms, accompanied by private showers or bathrooms. Many rooms are suitable for up to four beds, and the most desirable units open onto a private balcony with a view of the Cathédrale de St-Pierre. A homey, warm atmosphere prevails.

1, rue de la Vallée, CH-1204 Genève. ⓒ 022/818-37-37. Fax 022/818-37-73. www.hotel-bel-esperance.ch. 40 units. 150F–190F ($123–$156) double; 180F–200F ($148–$164) triple. Rates include breakfast. AE, DC, MC, V. Bus: 8. **Amenities:** Breakfast room; laundry room. *In room:* TV.

Hôtel Bernina   Set directly across from Gare Cornavin, this is an old-fashioned but worthy hotel with a reputation for fair prices and relatively comfortable accommodations. Don't expect luxury. There's a Sputnik-era severity to the lobby, with furniture like what you'd expect in an airport waiting lounge, and a blasé, not particularly responsive staff. Rooms are high-ceilinged and sunny, albeit somewhat battered, but they are clean, filled with angular modern furniture, and soundproof against the noise of the traffic outside. A Pizza Hut (under separate management) is on the ground floor of the hotel, and the restaurant congestion of the railway station is just across the square.

22, place Cornavin, CH-1211 Genève. ⓒ 022/908-49-50. Fax 022/908-49-51. www.bernina-geneve.ch. 80 units. 150F–220F ($123–$180) double. Rates include breakfast. AE, DC, MC, V. Bus: 10. **Amenities:** Pizzeria; limited room service. *In room:* TV, safe.

Hôtel des Tourelles *(Value)*   Named after the twin towers that flank the edges of its turn-of-the-20th-century facade, this stone-sided, government-rated two-star hotel offers good value in simple, straightforward rooms that are made more palatable by high ceilings, small refrigerators, and, in some cases, balconies overlooking the Rhône and its quays. Some of the bedrooms have decorative marble fireplaces dating from the year of the hotel's construction. The staff is helpful and, in some cases, charming. Units come equipped with tidy bathrooms containing showers. Breakfast is the only meal served. The only drawback to this place involves traffic noise from the busy riverside avenues adjacent to the hotel, but shutting the double-glazed windows helps muffle most of it.

2, bd. James-Fazy, CH-1201 Genève. ⓒ 022/732-44-23. Fax 022/732-76-20. www.destourelles.ch. 23 units. 150F ($123) double. Rates include buffet breakfast. AE, DC, MC, V. **Amenities:** Lounge; laundry service. *In room:* TV, fridge, hair dryer, beverage maker.

Hôtel International & Terminus *(Kids)*   This hotel lies across the street from the main entrance of Geneva's railway station and has been directed by three generations of the Cottier family. Originally built in 1900, it has been radically upgraded, with pairs of smaller rooms reconfigured into larger units especially good for families. Rated three stars by the local tourist board, the hotel offers exceedingly good value. The small to spacious bedrooms are fitted with first-rate furnishings and the maintenance level is high. Bathrooms seem to have been added as an afterthought, in areas not designed for them, and are a bit cramped with shower stalls. The restaurant, La Veranda, serves some of the most reasonable meals in Geneva, and keeps the pizza ovens cauldron hot.

20, rue des Alpes, CH-1201 Genève. © **022/906-97-77.** Fax 022/906-97-78. www.international-terminus.ch. 60 units. 95F–180F ($78–$148) double. Rates include continental breakfast. AE, DC, MC, V. **Amenities:** Restaurant; lounge. *In room:* TV, minibar, safe.

Hôtel Lido   This durable choice 2 blocks from the rail station was built in 1963 and has been completely renovated several times since. This is a simple, government-rated two-star hotel with few if any frills—it's recommended for its bargain price. The small rooms are furnished in a no-nonsense functional style. All rooms come equipped with neatly kept bathrooms with tub/shower combinations. The hotel has five floors with an elevator.

8, rue de Chantepoulet, CH-1201, Genève. © **022/731-55-30.** Fax 022/731-65-01. www.hotel-lido.ch. 31 units. 150F ($123) double. Rates include continental breakfast. AE, DC, MC, V. **Amenities:** Breakfast room; laundry service. *In room:* TV.

Hôtel Moderne   Near the railroad station and the lake, this is a seven-story, rectangular, white structure, with a low-lying, glassed-in extension containing the breakfast room. The public rooms are modern, with Nordic furniture and abstract angles and curves. The bedrooms, each with soundproof windows, have standardized furnishings and are clean, modern, and often sunny. You'll wish the bathrooms had more room to spread out your stuff, though you'll appreciate the tidy maintenance, up-to-date plumbing, and clean showers. The hotel's restaurant serves only breakfast, but there's an Italian restaurant under separate management in the same building.

1, rue de Berne, CH-1201 Genève. © **022/732-81-00.** Fax 022/738-26-58. www.hotelmoderne.ch. 55 units. 210F ($172) double. Rates include buffet breakfast. AE, DC, MC, V. Bus: 10. **Amenities:** Restaurant; breakfast room; limited room service; babysitting; laundry service/dry cleaning. *In room:* TV, dataport, minibar.

Hôtel St-Gervais   One of the simplest hotels we recommend in this guide, this place is inside an old-fashioned, vaguely nondescript building in Geneva's medieval core, a 3-minute walk from Gare Cornavin. Although it has quirky idiosyncrasies that appeal to architects and historic renovators, some guests have expressed annoyance at having to navigate their way to the upper floors with a lot of luggage. Fortunately, there's a cramped elevator on-site, but other than that, the place is minimalist but comfortable, with an emphasis on durable, functionalist furniture. You get routine rooms here, and well-worn but still comfortable beds. As for plumbing, you most often have to settle for a sink, although the hotel maintains an adequate number of hallway bathrooms, which are kept very tidy. Rooms with private bathrooms are also well maintained and come equipped with tub/shower combinations.

20, rue des Corps-Saints, CH-1201 Genève. © and fax **022/732-45-72.** www.stgervais-geneva.ch. 26 units, 2 with bathroom. 85F ($70) double without bathroom, 115F ($94) double with bathroom. Breakfast included. AE, DC, MC, V. **Amenities:** Bar.

ON THE LEFT BANK
VERY EXPENSIVE
Swissôtel Métropole Genève 🌟🌟🌟   Originally constructed around 1850, this is an imposing neoclassical building, which was used during World War II for the storage of prisoner-of-war records by the International Red Cross. Today, set between rue du Rhône and the Jardin Anglais, it offers views of Lake Geneva and the noisy quayside

traffic from its larger rooms, and comfortably conservative bedrooms accented with wood paneling. Rooms are quite palatial, with luxurious beds and marble bathrooms equipped with deep tubs, robes, toiletries, and bidets.

34, quai Général-Guisan, CH-1204 Genève. © 022/318-32-00. Fax 022/318-33-00. www.swissotel.com. 127 units. 720F–850F ($590–$697) double; from 1,250F ($1,025) suite. AE, DC, MC, V. Parking 37F ($30). **Amenities:** 2 restaurants; piano bar; limited room service; massage; babysitting; laundry service/dry cleaning; nonsmoking rooms. *In room:* A/C, TV, dataport, minibar, hair dryer, iron/board, safe, beverage maker.

EXPENSIVE

Hôtel de la Cigogne 🟊🟊🟊   Personalized and charming, this is our favorite Left Bank hotel, a chic, glamorous retreat for the discerning. This deluxe hotel was rebuilt after years of dilapidation and turned into an offbeat Relais & Châteaux that showcases designer and decorator talent. Combined with an adjoining building, the old hotel and its mate have the renovated facades of the original 18th- and 19th-century structures. With three sheltered courtyards overlooking a flowering plaza, this is one of the most tranquil hotels in Geneva. The bedrooms contain handmade mattresses, luxurious bathrooms, and bed linens embroidered with the hotel's coat of arms. Each bedroom is furnished differently, ranging from 1930s movie-mogul style to the "baron and baroness at their country place." Some units have working fireplaces.

17, place Longemalle, CH-1204 Genève. © 022/818-40-40. Fax 022/818-40-50. www.cigogne.ch. 52 units. 455F–570F ($373–$467) double; 790F–890F ($648–$730) suite. Rates include continental breakfast. AE, DC, MC, V. Parking 27F ($22). **Amenities:** Restaurant; 24-hr. room service; babysitting; laundry service/dry cleaning; nonsmoking rooms. *In room:* A/C, TV, dataport, minibar, hair dryer, safe.

Les Armures 🟊🟊   Surpassed only by La Cigogne, this is one of the most elegant and prestigious hotels on Geneva's Left Bank. Positioned a few steps from both the cathedral and the medieval Maison Tavel, it utterly lacks the late-19th-century grandeur of its government-rated five-star competitors across the river, on the north bank of the Rhône. Instead, you'll find a labyrinth of narrow corridors, and architectural gemstones that include beamed (and sometimes frescoed) ceilings and carefully preserved remnants of the building's origins in the 17th century. Each unit is different from its neighbors, usually with exposed brick or stone, and each alternates modern plumbing with richly detailed tile work in its bathrooms. This is not a blockbuster Belle Epoque hotel. The ambience here is cozy and well upholstered, with an ostentation that's subtle and based for the most part on the building's sense of quirky antique charm.

1, rue du Puits-Saint-Pierre, CH-1204 Genève. © 022/310-91-72. Fax 022/310-98-46. www.hotel-les-armures.ch. 28 units. 520F–545F ($426–$447) double; 670F ($549) suite. Continental breakfast included. Extra bed 90F ($74). AE, DC, MC, V. **Amenities:** Restaurant; bar; limited room service; babysitting; laundry service/dry cleaning; nonsmoking rooms. *In room:* A/C, TV, dataport, minibar, hair dryer, safe.

MODERATE

Hotel Tiffany 🟊 *Value*   This little charmer of a Belle Epoque boutique hotel lies on a Left Bank street 3 blocks south of the river and about a 12-minute stroll from the center and the lake. Although it can hardly match the style and glamour of the lakeside palaces, it is attractive in its modest way with everything from stained glass to Art Nouveau bed frames. In its category, it offers some of the most reasonable prices in Geneva, especially considering its style. Rising five floors, it has such touches as leather-clad armchairs and a summertime sidewalk cafe. Bedrooms are midsize with lots of extras, including soundproofing and spacious bathrooms. We prefer the rooms in the "attic," with their beams, rooftop vistas, and sloping walls.

1, rue des Marbriers, CH-1204 Genève. © 022/708-16-16. Fax 022/708-16-17. www.hotel-tiffany.ch. 46 units. 340F–420F ($279–$344) double; from 490F ($402) suite. Rates include buffet breakfast. AE, DC, MC, V. **Amenities:** Restaurant; limited room service; massage; laundry service/dry cleaning. *In room:* A/C, TV, dataport, minibar, hair dryer, safe.

INEXPENSIVE

Hôtel Central   Set on the fifth, sixth, and seventh floors of a prominent building erected in 1924, this hotel has been a haven for cost-conscious visitors to Geneva since 1928. You'll find a very modern format, with a minimalist interior, on a street lined with banks and upscale shops. You'll register in the sixth-floor reception area, containing carved antiques from Bali. (The establishment's Danish-born owner used to manage a five-star hotel there.) Know in advance that the smallest rooms have two-tiered bunk beds, toilets in alcoves off the hallway, and very little space. The more expensive rooms are bigger and more comfortable. All rooms are equipped with a shower and sink. Be alert that the reception staff is available only from 7am to 9pm, so if you're planning on a late-night check-in, make prior arrangements. Breakfast is served in the bedrooms.

2, rue de la Rôtisserie, CH-1204 Genève. © 022/818-81-00. Fax 022/818-81-01. www.hotelcentral.ch. 32 units, 28 with private toilet. 90F ($74) double without toilet; 105F–145F ($86–$119) double with toilet; 205F ($168) suite. Rates include breakfast. AE, DC, MC, V. Bus: 12. **Amenities:** Limited room service. *In room:* TV, dataport.

AT NEARBY BELLEVUE

Hôtel La Réserve 🏵🏵🏵   Elegant and discreet, this prestigious government-rated five-star hotel was built at the edge of the lake in 1973 and enlarged in the mid-1980s. Because local codes wouldn't allow any structure higher than three stories, it was patterned in a vaguely neoclassical style after the many private villas that ring the lake. Set behind white walls and under a red-tile roof, it nestles within 3.2 landscaped hectares (8 acres) that explode into bloom every year with thousands of tulips. It's a 12-minute drive north of Geneva's center, beside the road leading to Lausanne, and it has a setting carefully engineered for maximum peace, quiet, and (very upscale) contemplative rest. The public areas are filled with unusual art (much of it Chinese) and a mixture of conservative modern and Asian furniture. The spacious guest rooms are luxurious, with such extras as soundproofing, fax machines, and large tile or marble bathrooms. Their Chinese restaurant, Tsé-Fung, has the best Asian food in all of Geneva (see "Where to Dine," below).

301, rte. de Lausanne, CH-1293 Bellevue-Genève. © 022/959-59-59. Fax 022/959-59-60. www.lareserve.ch. 102 units. 400F–990F ($328–$812) double; from 890F ($730) suite. AE, DC, MC, V. Free parking. **Amenities:** 2 restaurants; bar; indoor pool; 3 tennis courts; fitness center; spa; sauna; salon; 24-hr. room service; massage; babysitting; laundry service/dry cleaning; nonsmoking rooms. *In room:* A/C, TV, dataport, minibar, hair dryer, safe, Jacuzzi (in suites).

4 Where to Dine

Geneva is one of the gastronomic centers of Europe, with an unmistakable French influence. Genevans today take their dining seriously, and practice fine eating with consummate flair and style. Meals are frequently long, drawn-out affairs.

Naturally, Geneva serves all the typically Swiss dishes, such as filets of perch from Lake Geneva and fricassee of pork. In season many of its restaurants offer cardoon, which is similar to an artichoke and is usually served gratiné. By all means, try the Genevese sausage *longeole*. *Omble chevalier* comes from Lac Léman and is like a grayling, although some compare it to salmon.

Where to Dine in Geneva

Lac Léman

FRONTENEX

Rampe de Cologny
Quai Cologny
Route de Vandœuvres

Plateau de Frontenex

Route de Frontenex

Woodrow Wilson
12
Rue Plantamour
Rue du Mont-Blanc
13
14

PARC DES
EAUX-VIVES

Quai Gustave Ador

PARC
LA GRANGE

Chemin Frank Thomas

Jet d'Eau
26

Av. Rosemont

Avenue W. Favre

MONTCHOISY

Rade de
Genève

Rue des Eaux-Vives
Rue de Montchoisy
Rue des Vollandes
Route de Frontenex

Route de Chêne

Ch. de la Petite Boissière

Quai Gustave Ador
Rue du 31 Décembre

Av. de l'Amandolier
Promenade Martin

Pont du-
Mont-Blanc

R. de la Marie

Av. Pictet De Rochemont

JARDIN
ANGLAIS

ont des
ergues

ILE
ROUSSEAU

Quai Général Guisan

RIVE
GAUCHE

Rue de la Terassière

Rue Agasse

Rue du Rhône
22   23   24
16
R. De Rive   rd-pt
de Rive

25

RUES BASSES

Rue Hodler

R. Lachenal

Route de Malagnou

Chemin Rieu

les Rues Basses

21

VIELLE VILLE
(OLD TOWN)
18

Cathédral
St-Pierre
17   19
Grand Rue

R. de l'Hotel de Ville
20

Pl. Em.
Guyenot

Ch. Galland

FLORISSANT

oratoire

R. de la Croix Rouge

Rue Jacques Dalcroze
Boulevard Helvétique

Bd. des Tranchées

Route de Florissant

Place
Neuve

Promenade
des Bastions

Dufour

Université

R. de Candolle   Rue St. Léger

Cours ses Bastions

Rue de
l'Athenée

Rue de l'Athenée

Avenue Bertrand

PARC
A. BERTRAND.

Avenue Louis Aubert

avory

AINE DE
AINPALAIS

Rd-pt. de
Plainpalais

Philosophes

Place Ed.
Claparède

Avenue Peschier

Henri Dunant

Rue A. Lombard

CHAMPEL

Mail

Boulevard du Pont d'Arve

R. de Carouge

Bd. de la Cluse

R. Prevost-Martin

Avenue de Champel

Avenue de Miremont

LA CLUSE

Av. Calas

Train Station

Cheese is also a staple on the Genevese table, including such Swiss varieties as *tomme* and Gruyère, plus, in season, *vacherin* from the Joux Valley. Naturally, everything will taste better with the Perlan (white wine) and Gamay (red wine) from Geneva's own vineyards.

ON THE RIGHT BANK
VERY EXPENSIVE

Le Chat-Botté ✿✿✿ FRENCH   This grand restaurant is in one of the fanciest hotels in Geneva. Suitably decorated with tapestries, sculpture, and rich upholstery, with a polite and correct staff, it serves some of the best food in the city. There are some critics who consider it among the best restaurants of Europe. If the weather is right, you can dine on the flower-bedecked terrace, overlooking the Jet d'Eau. The meals are expensive but worth the price. The cuisine, although inspired by French classics, is definitely contemporary. Typical starters include delectable zucchini flowers stuffed with vegetables and essence of tomato; and lobster salad with eggplant "caviar," olive oil, and fresh herbs. Some of the most enticing items on the menu we've sampled include carpaccio with black olives and Parmesan cheese, poached wing of skate in an herb-flavored sauce, and oven-roasted Sisteron lamb with stuffed vegetables. The chef's best-known dish is a delicate filet of perch from Lake Geneva, which is sautéed until it's golden. Finish with one of the day's freshly made desserts, perhaps iced truffles in a nougatine casket.

In the Hôtel Beau-Rivage, 13, quai du Mont-Blanc. ✆ 022/716-69-20. Reservations highly recommended. Main courses 39F–85F ($32–$70). Fixed-price menus 60F–180F ($49–$148). AE, DC, MC, V. Daily noon–2pm and 7–9:45pm. Bus: 1.

Le Cygne ✿✿✿ FRENCH   This restaurant is among the best in Geneva, with a decor of lacquered wood, beige and dark-orange velvet, and best of all, an exceptional view over the Geneva harbor to the Alps. It offers a refined cuisine with impeccable service. Plushly comfortable, Le Cygne is a showcase for the culinary skills of its outstanding chef, Philippe Jourdin. The menu changes four times a year and may offer such delightful choices as terrine of blackened chicken in a crawfish and anis-flavored aspic, served with a marinade of mushrooms in walnut oil; an earthy fish soup; smoked filet of sea bass sauced with a truffle-flavored vinaigrette; roast lamb with coriander and tomatoes stuffed with moussaka; and grilled filet of rabbit served with foie gras on a fondue of onions perfumed with fresh thyme. Five elaborate trolleys, each laden with a different roster of treats, combine to create one of the most spectacular—perhaps *the* most spectacular—arrays of desserts served in Switzerland.

In Le Palace Hilton Geneva, 19, quai du Mont-Blanc. ✆ 022/908-90-85. Reservations highly recommended. Main courses 40F–55F ($33–$45); fixed-price lunch 57F–94F ($47–$77); fixed-price dinner 94F–159F ($77–$130). AE, DC, MC, V. Mon–Fri noon–11pm. Closed 2 weeks in Aug. Bus: 1.

Le Neptune ✿✿✿ FRENCH   At one of Geneva's finest restaurants, the decor is intimate, intensely floral, and graced with an enormous fresco displaying an inside view of Neptune's kingdom. Although the kitchen closes on the weekend, during the week it entertains some of the most discerning palates in Geneva. The menu changes based on market conditions, but you're likely to be offered such dishes as herbed vichyssoise with hazelnut oil and a dollop of foie gras, crawfish salad with a barnacle-flavored vinaigrette, cassoulet of oysters seasoned with algae-flavored butter sauce, Atlantic sea bass roasted in a salt crust with thyme, filets of John Dory with a sauce made from whipped butter, and sea-urchin roe served with seafood-flavored pasta. If you're not in the mood for fish, you may enjoy such dishes as rack of Scottish lamb in puff pastry with spices and gray partridge roasted "en casserole" with autumn herbs.

In the Hôtel Mandarin Oriental du Rhône, 1, quai Turrettini. ℂ 022/909-00-06. Reservations required. Main courses 34F–41F ($28–$34); fixed-price lunch 72F ($59); fixed-price dinner 78F–140F ($64–$115). AE, DC, MC, V. Mon–Fri noon–2pm and 7:30–10pm. Closed 3 weeks in Aug and 2 weeks from mid-Dec to early Jan.

EXPENSIVE

La Mère Royaume ⊛ FRENCH   This is one of the oldest restaurants in Geneva, established around the turn of the 20th century and graced with wooden paneling and stained-glass windows. The restaurant is named after a heroine who, in 1602, poured boiling stew over a Savoyard soldier's head and then cracked his skull with the kettle. With an antecedent like that, you'd expect some of the heartiest fare in Geneva, but instead the restaurant offers delicately cooked French specialties, such as *omble cheva-lier*—that delicate white fish from Lake Geneva—and a version of trout that has been pronounced divine. Try such tempting specialties as sea wolf in puff pastry, tender rack of lamb flavored with fresh tarragon, and in the autumn, savory game dishes such as venison and pheasant. The brasserie serves fondues, raclettes, filet of sole, shrimp with garlic, and some winning terrines.

9, rue des Corps-Saints. ℂ 022/732-70-08. Reservations required. Brasserie main courses 20F–37F ($16–$30); fixed-price menu 45F–50F ($37–$41). Restaurant main courses 32F–55F ($26–$45); fixed-price menu 57F–108F ($47–$89). AE, DC, MC, V. Mon–Fri noon–2pm; Mon–Sat 7–10:30pm. Bus: 4, 6, or 7.

La Perle du Lac ⊛ SWISS   Situated in a single-story pavilion owned by the city, this is the only restaurant in Geneva that's not separated from the waters of the lake by a stream of traffic. It's set beneath the venerable trees of Mon Repos Park, not far from the United Nations complex. Although the candlelit interior is lovely, you may want to reserve a table on the outdoor terrace in warm weather. A talented French chef prepares a marvelous mousseline of sweetbreads and mushrooms. Other specialties, each delectable, include line-caught, grilled sea wolf with fresh fennel and olive oil, and braised strips of fera (freshwater lake fish) flavored with saffron. Pigeon breast is another fine choice, served with duck liver and fresh apricots. Ravioli appears in an unusual version stuffed with fresh watercress. The sorbets—ask for a mixture—are superb. Year after year meticulous cooking and the use of only the finest and freshest ingredients make this not only a satisfying choice but an eternal favorite.

128, rue de Lausanne. ℂ 022/731-79-35. www.laperledulac.ch. Reservations required. Main courses 48F–60F ($39–$49); fixed-price menu 83F–115F ($68–$94). AE, DC, MC, V. Tues–Sun noon–2pm and 7:30–10pm. Closed Dec 22–Jan 25. Bus: 4 or 44.

MODERATE

Chez Jacky ⊛ *Finds* SWISS   This provincial bistro should be better known, although it already attracts everyone from grandmothers to young skiers en route to Verbier. It's the domain of Jacky Gruber, an exceptional chef from Valais. There's sub-tlety in Monsieur Gruber's cooking that suggests the influence of his mentor, Frédy Giradet, hailed as Switzerland's greatest chef before his recent retirement. You may begin with Chinese cabbage and mussels and continue with filet of turbot roasted with thyme or perhaps beautifully prepared pink duck on a bed of spinach with a con-fit of onions. Be prepared to wait for each course. The chef tirelessly seeks the most select produce for his imaginative and innovative dishes, and he continues to dazzle his regular clients year after year, winning new converts as well.

11, rue Jacques-Necker. ℂ 022/732-86-80. Reservations recommended. Main courses 46F–48F ($38–$39); fixed-price lunch 48F ($39); fixed-price dinner 60F–90F ($49–$74). AE, DC, MC, V. Mon–Fri 11am–2pm and 6:30–11pm. Closed 1st week of Jan and 3 weeks in Aug. Bus: 5, 10, or 44.

Le Boeuf Rouge LYONNAIS   Few other restaurants in Geneva's center work so hard to bring you an authentic version of the brasserie-style cuisine of Lyon. As such, you'll find such dishes as Lyonnais sausage with scalloped potatoes, chateaubriand in red-wine sauce, blood sausage, and quenelles of pikeperch—any of which might be preceded by a delectable version of onion soup or green salad with croutons and bacon. The decor is appealingly kitschy, complete with lots of Art Nouveau posters and late-19th-century ceramics. The staff here is brusque but kind.

17, rue Alfred-Vincent (corner of rue Paquis). ℂ 022/732-75-37. Reservations recommended. Main courses 32F–52F ($26–$43); fixed-price lunch 37F ($30); fixed-price dinner 48F–55F ($39–$45). AE, DC, MC, V. Mon–Fri noon–2pm and 7–10:30pm; Sat 7–10pm. Bus: 1.

Patara 𝒾𝒾 THAI   This is the most elegant and prestigious Thai restaurant in Geneva, occupying a street-level premises within the Hôtel Beau-Rivage, and a position immediately adjacent to Le Chat Botté, one of the most elegant restaurants in town. Within a decor of teak woodcarvings, Thai paintings, and soothing colors of blue-green, an impeccably dressed, mostly Thai staff will serve flavor-filled examples of the best of their country's cuisine. The best menu items include braised chicken in green curry with coconut milk; steamed sea bass in lime sauce; giant prawns with garlic and cilantro; and pan-fried filet of gilthead in a spicy basil sauce. There's also an interesting selection of food (asparagus and shiitake mushrooms in oyster sauce) for vegetarians. Dessert may include warm papaya pie with ginger-flavored ice cream.

In the Hôtel Beau-Rivage, 13, quai du Mont-Blanc. ℂ 022/731-55-66. Reservations recommended. Main courses 22F–48F ($18–$39); fixed-price menu (minimum 2 diners) 90F ($74) per person. AE, DC, MC, V. Mon–Fri noon–3pm; daily 7pm–midnight. Bus: 1.

INEXPENSIVE
Jeck's Place 𝒾 PAN-ASIAN   Near the Gare Cornavin, this place is a delight. It's like taking a culinary trip to Southeast Asia, with stopovers in such places as China, Malaysia, Thailand, and India. Escaping from the traffic outside, you enter a warm and friendly enclave, where Jeck Tan of Singapore will greet you. The cuisine of Asian specialties provides temptation with every order, the trays of delicacies brought out by waitresses in sarongs. The specialties of the day will be seasoned with delicate blends of spices, notably lemon grass and curry but also chile and ganlaga (from the ginger family). It's not the dull beef sauté, for example, but a medley of delight in a sauce flavored with cloves, curry, cinnamon, coconut milk, and lemon grass. We often make a meal of the appetizers alone, including homemade steamed dumplings stuffed with a blend of pork and vegetables flavored with coriander. The house specialty, and our favorite dish, is Jeck's chicken in green curry. Another exotic treat is a delicate whiting spread with spicy lemon-grass sauce grilled on banana leaves.

14, rue de Neuchâtel. ℂ 022/731-3303. Reservations recommended. Main courses 23F–36F ($19–$30); special lunch platter 15F ($12). AE, DC, MC, V. Mon–Fri 11:30am–2pm; daily 6:30–10pm. Bus: 4, 5, or 9.

ON THE LEFT BANK
MODERATE
Brasserie de l'Hotel de Ville 𝒾 (Finds) SWISS   This is one of the most deliberately archaic-looking restaurants in Geneva, with a reputation that dates from 1764 and a

clientele that prefers that absolutely nothing changes in either its old-fashioned decor or its choice of dishes. In spite of its look, it's rather hip and popular with the Genevois, as well as a growing number of arts-industry hipsters and affluent members of the bourgeoisie, who appreciate the place for its old-fashioned charm. Within a dining room loaded with antique or semiantique kitsch, you'll be joined by antiques dealers and clients from the local antiques shops. The menu is more sophisticated and better than ever. Try the filets of freshwater lake perch meunière. Sometimes the prized fish of Lake Geneva, *omble,* is also served in a butter sauce. One old-fashioned dish remains on the menu, Longeole du val d'Arve (traditional Geneva-style sausages flavored with cumin). You can also order such delights as rack of lamb flavored with herbs of Provence, along with a seasonal focus on asparagus, mushrooms, and game dishes. We always like to launch ourselves with a fresh dandelion salad with medallions of sautéed duck liver.

19, Grand-Rue. Ⓒ 022/311-70-30. Reservations recommended. Main courses 37F–52F ($30–$43); fixed-price menus 60F–109F ($49–$89). AE, DC, MC, V. Daily 11:30am–11:30pm. Bus: 17.

Brasserie Lipp SWISS   This bustling restaurant is named after the famous Parisian brasserie, and when you enter, especially at lunch, you'll think you've been transported to Paris. Waiters in black jackets with long white aprons are constantly rushing about with platters of food, here on the ground floor of a modern shopping complex. The menu contains a sampling of French bistro dishes. Like its Parisian namesake, the Geneva Lipp specializes in several versions of charcuterie. You can also order three kinds of *pot-au-feu* and such classic dishes as a Toulousian cassoulet with *confit de canard* (duckling). The fresh oysters are among the best in the city. These dishes will not dazzle you with subtle nuances, and service is a bit frantic, but it appeals to all lovers of the old-fashioned French brasserie.

In Confédération-Centre, 8, rue de la Confédération. Ⓒ 022/311-10-11. Reservations recommended. Main courses 23F–52F ($19–$43); *plats du jour* 25F ($21) lunch only; fixed-price menus 60F–80F ($49–$66). AE, DC, MC, V. Daily 11:45am–12:15am. Bus: 12.

Café du Centre *Kids* SWISS/CONTINENTAL   This cafe is usually hysterically busy, and permeated with a kind of brusque anonymity. But despite its drawbacks, this remains very much an Old Geneva institution, established in 1871. Part of its charm comes from a location that's separated from the traffic-clogged quays by a clock tower of chiseled stone, and by dozens of flower stalls. Despite the thousands of cups of coffee and glasses of beer served here, it's more akin to a restaurant that serves drinks than a cafe that offers food. During nice weather, most of the business takes place outdoors on a terrace opening onto the square, while the rest of the year, business moves inside into a pair of street-level rooms whose nostalgic decor may remind you of an old-fashioned brasserie in Lyon. A thick, multilingual menu offers food items such as excellent versions of fresh fish as well as Wiener schnitzel, a savory version of onglet of beef, and pepper steak. Café du Centre offers an English-language menu of some 140 items—surely one of those will please your kids.

5, place du Molard. Ⓒ 022/311-85-86. Reservations recommended. Main courses 40F–55F ($33–$45); fixed-price *assiette du jour* 23F ($19) at lunch Mon–Fri only. AE, DC, MC, V. Daily 7am–midnight. Tram: 12.

Café International INTERNATIONAL   Many of the architectural details that were originally installed in this brasserie a century ago are still in place, within a cozy, charmingly battered environment that retains its Belle Epoque sense of style. On Bordeaux-colored banquettes, surrounded with varnished paneling, mirrors, and touches

of brass, you can enjoy honest and soothing dishes that include a "tataki" (small platter) of raw marinated salmon with sesame oil; a well-seasoned stew *(pot-au-feu)* of
meat and vegetables pressed into a cold terrine and sliced; codfish roasted with thyme;
and filet steak served with a sauce *marchand de vin,* crafted from red wine and herbs;
and an excellent version of roasted lamb. Dessert may include chocolate cake layered
with chocolate mousse.

2, rue Bovy-Lysberg, place du Cirque.✆ 022/807-11-99. Reservations recommended. Main courses 23F–38F
($19–$31); fixed-price menu 38F ($31). AE, DC, MC, V. Mon–Fri noon–2:30pm and 7–10pm; Sat–Sun 11:30am–10pm.
Closed 1st 2 weeks of Aug. Tram: 13.

La Coupole SWISS   This is a true brasserie—far more elegant than its Parisian
namesake. The place is more popular at noon, especially with shoppers and office
workers, than it is at night. Fanciful and fun, it's dotted with grandfather clocks, a
bronze Venus, Edwardian palms, and comfortable banquettes. The menu is limited
but well selected; the *cuisine du marché* (fare with local and seasonal ingredients) is a
delight, although many patrons stick to the standard old red-meat bistro specials such
as the inevitable entrecôte.

116, rue du Rhône. ✆ 022/787-50-10. Reservations recommended. Main courses 32F–46F ($26–$38); fixed-price
menu 40F–45F ($33–$37). AE, DC, MC, V. Mon–Sat 11:30am–2:30pm and 7:30pm–12:30am. Bus: 2, 9, or 22. Tram: 12.

La Favola ☆ TUSCAN/ITALIAN   Don't expect anything large or standardized if
you opt for a meal in this supremely ethnic, Tuscan-style restaurant. It's the best Italian restaurant in Geneva, and its most devoted habitués hail it as the best restaurant
in Geneva, period. Set a few steps from the Cathédrale de St-Pierre, it contains only
two cramped dining rooms; the family-managed staff would be a lot more comfortable speaking Italian dialect than the clipped versions of French you're likely to hear
in most other restaurants in Geneva. The menu is small and short but choice, varying
with the availability of ingredients and the seasons. Look for such delightful dishes as
carpaccio of beef; *vitello tonnato* (paper-thin veal with a tuna sauce); lobster salad;
potato salad with cèpe mushrooms; such pastas as fresh ravioli with either eggplant or
bolet mushrooms; and a luscious version of tortellini stuffed with ricotta, meat juices,
red wine, and herbs. Meat and fish vary daily. Don't even think of coming here on
weekends, as the place is locked tight. It contains seating for only 34 diners at a time,
so advance reservations are key.

15, rue Calvin. ✆ 022/311-74-37. Reservations required. Main courses 45F–60F ($37–$49). AE, MC, V. Mon–Fri
noon–2pm and 7:15–10pm. Closed 2 weeks in July–Aug and 1 week at Christmas. Tram: 12.

Les Armures ☆ *Kids* SWISS   In spite of the government-rated five-star elegance of
the hotel that contains this restaurant, it is surprisingly unpretentious and affordable.
Dining is possible on three different floors. The lower you go, the more animated the
scene becomes. This stone building is located on a cobblestone street across from a
medieval arsenal in one of the most colorful neighborhoods of the Old Town. The
building was constructed in the 16th century, and this place has thrived as one of the
most atmospheric restaurants since its founding in 1957. The three different fondues
offered are the best in Geneva. Many Swiss children make an entire meal out of rösti
(Swiss-style hash browns). Other specialties include raclette and several pizza and pasta
dishes. The winter-only sauerkraut garni is also a savory meal—made with several
types of sausage and pork. In fact, the staff still remembers the day in January 1994
when Bill Clinton dropped in to sample their sauerkraut during a break in political

negotiations. Pastas and hamburgers round out the menu here, which should make any child's palate happy.

1, rue des Puits-St-Pierre. (✆ **022/310-91-72.** Main courses 21F–49F ($17–$40); fixed-price menu 50F ($41). AE, DC, MC, V. Mon–Fri 8am–midnight; Sat–Sun 11am–midnight. Bus: 3 or 5.

Restaurant de la Cigogne 🎕🎕 CONTINENTAL This is one of the most appealing and best-staffed restaurants on Geneva's Left Bank, with a growing clientele and a growing reputation for excellence. Classified as a member of the prestigious Relais & Châteaux group, it's housed within an opulently paneled ground-floor room of the also-recommended hotel. Cosseted, discreetly elegant, and cozy, with impeccable service, it offers a full bar, a spectacular wine list, and well-groomed cuisine. At lunch the venue is a bit more businesslike and rapid, segueing into a more relaxed and leisurely venue at dinner. Menu items reflect whatever ingredients are in season at the time of your arrival, but are likely to include, among others, a superb ravioli of shrimp with a brunoise (finely diced) of vegetables and a mousseline sauce; turbot prepared *façon grand-mère;* and a delectable cordon bleu of veal stuffed with foie gras and truffles, served with a galette of polenta with Parmesan and asparagus. Desserts are rolled around aboard a spectacular-looking trolley.

In the Hôtel de la Cigogne, 17, place Longemalle. (✆ **022/818-40-40.** Reservations recommended. Main courses 47F–60F ($39–$49); fixed-price lunch 62F–110F ($51–$90); fixed-price dinner 115F ($94). AE, DC, MC, V. Daily noon–2pm and 7–10pm. Closed Sat–Sun during July–Aug. Bus: 6 or 9.

Restaurant Edelweiss 🎕*Kids* SWISS This is the most famous folkloric, alpine-style restaurant in Geneva. It's set within the cellar of the also-recommended Hôtel Edelweiss, an establishment that carries the alpine chalet theme into its bedrooms, and whose restaurant is the most artfully rustic within its neighborhood. Tables are lined up cozily under a very high ceiling that showcases the flagstone columns, the fluegelhorns, the cowbells, and the live folkloric bands that oompah-pah their way throughout the dinner hour. Rib-sticking menu items include six kinds of fondues, raclettes, roasted lamb chops with herbs, Zurich-style sliced veal in cream sauce, and several kinds of fish. If you have children, this may be a particularly worthy choice because of the visual and folkloric distraction that add to the experience of dining here.

In the Hôtel Edelweiss, 2, place de la Navigation. (✆ **022/544-51-51.** Reservations recommended. Main courses 29F–48F ($24–$39); fixed-price menu 60F ($49); children's platters 15F ($12) each. AE, DC, MC, V. Daily 7–10:30pm. Bus: 1.

Roberto ITALIAN One of the most appealing Italian restaurants in Geneva occupies a relatively formal-looking dining room that's sheathed with wood paneling, mirrors, and a series of contemporary paintings by the restaurant's owner, Roberto Carugati. There's more here, however, than just artwork, as the food is delectable, flavored with the kind of Mediterranean sunshine that you'd expect from a midsummer trip to Italy. Menu items include such succulent pastas as tortellini with chopped veal and a cream sauce; filets of turbot with béarnaise sauce; and scampi served with tarragon. Especially sought-after are the house versions of saltimbocca (veal with ham), *osso buco* (braised veal shanks), and *crespelle ai quattro formaggi* (Italian crepes with four kinds of cheeses).

10, rue Pierre-Fatio. (✆ **022/311-80-33.** Reservations recommended. Main courses 28F–55F ($23–$45). AE, MC, V. Mon–Sat noon–2pm; Mon–Fri 7:15–10pm. Bus: 8, 9, or 12.

INEXPENSIVE

Au Pied de Cochon ★ *Finds* LYONNAIS/SWISS   Named after a restaurant at Les Halles in Paris, this is the best place to go in Geneva for hearty Lyonnais fare if you don't mind the smoke and the noise. The setting is *fin de siècle,* with a staff dressed entirely in black and white. The bistro maintains its Lyonnais antecedents, which every Francophile knows are the most illustrious for fine brasserie-style food. A lot of young people, artists, and local workers dine here, as well as lawyers from the Palais de Justice across the way. The cooking is as grandmother used to prepare it, provided she came from the Lyon area. Naturally, the namesake *pieds de cochon* (pigs' feet) is included on the menu, along with tender alpine lamb, grilled anguillettes, and tripe.

4, place du Bourg-de-Four. ✆ 022/310-47-97. www.pied-de-cochon.ch. Reservations recommended. Main courses 32F–42F ($26–$34). AE, DC, MC, V. Daily 7:30am–2:30pm and 6:30pm–midnight. Closed Sun June–Aug. Bus: 2 or 7. Tram: 12.

L'Aïoli *Finds* PROVENÇAL   Named after the famous garlic sauce of Provence, this popular neighborhood restaurant stands opposite Le Corbusier's Maison de Verre. Something of a local secret, it offers personalized service and some of the finest Provençal cooking in town. Marius Anthoine, the owner, who hails from the Valais, founded the restaurant in 1987. An evening meal includes an appetizer, first plate, main dish, cheese, dessert, coffee, and wine (you can spend more by ordering a la carte). Among the featured dishes are lamb gigot, frogs' legs Provençal, and scampi Provençal. Monsieur Anthoine also makes a delectable *pot-au-feu* as well as beef ragout. Look for the daily specials, such as a savory, Provence-derived lamb stew called *gardiane camarguaise.*

6, rue Adrien-Lachenal. ✆ 022/736-79-71. http://aioli.pagesjaunes.ch/home.aspx. Reservations not required. Main courses 24F–32F ($20–$26); menu dégustation 79F ($65). AE, DC, MC, V. Mon–Fri 11am–2:30pm and 7–10:30pm. Closed Aug. Bus: 1 or 6. Tram: 12.

Le Lyrique SWISS   Le Lyrique contains both a formal restaurant and a brasserie. The restaurant opened in 1981 but was cleverly patterned on turn-of-the-20th-century models. It bustles with urban vitality and is very tuned to the arts and business lives of Geneva. Normally the restaurant is completely closed on Saturday and Sunday unless there's a special presentation at the Grand Théâtre de Genève, just a short distance away (in that event, the restaurant remains open). The brasserie, which has a terrace, is open all day but serves hot meals only during the hours mentioned below. In the restaurant you can try such carefully prepared dishes as filet of sea wolf with grapefruit, a roulade of rabbit with pasta maison, and tagliatelle with scampi. In the brasserie, menu items include chicken supreme with ravioli and leeks, and an *assiette Lyrique,* a meal in itself that combines four vegetarian and fish dishes—tartare of salmon, tartare of vegetables, terrine of vegetables, and eggplant "caviar."

12, bd. du Théâtre. ✆ 022/328-00-95. Reservations recommended. Restaurant main courses 29F–47F ($24–$39); fixed-price menu 55F–70F ($45–$57). Brasserie main courses 27F–35F ($22–$29); fixed-price menu 42F–54F ($34–$44). AE, MC, V. Mon–Fri noon–2pm and 6:30–10pm. Bus: 2 or 22.

Nô Sushi *Value* JAPANESE   Popular, hip, and mobbed every day at lunchtime, this is a large, high-ceilinged space devoted to a labyrinth of countertops that merge into the most bemused and whimsical Japanese restaurant in town. It would probably remind you of an old-fashioned luncheonette, except for a winding conveyer belt that exposes everything that's listed on the menu to the view of its clients. This is the only automated sushi bar in Switzerland, and as such, adds an eccentric and trend-con-scious flair to a neighborhood that's better known for its relative conservatism. You'll know how much something costs by the color of the platter that contains it. You'll pluck everything except the miso soup, which is carried to your seat by a waitress, directly from the moving conveyer belt. Hot foods remain hot thanks to a candle flick-ering beneath. Sushi (with rice) and sashimi (without rice) choices include mullet, calamari, octopus, salmon, and tuna. There are also teriyaki dishes, tempura, and a medley of rice and noodle dishes, any of which you can combine into a full meal.

Confédération Centre, 8, rue de la Confédération. © 022/810-39-73. Reservations not necessary. Sushi, sashimi, rolls, and small platters 10F–15F ($8.20–$12). AE, MC, V. Mon–Thurs 11:30am–midnight; Fri–Sat 11:30am–1am. Bus: 12.

Pizzeria da Paolo ITALIAN/PIZZAS   Bustling, friendly, and completely unpre-tentious, this simple pizzeria offers more than 20 kinds of pizzas in a cozy, wood-sheathed setting close to the water jet that's the very symbol of Geneva. If pizzas aren't your thing (the house specialty is a Pizza Paolo, made from spinach and cheese), there is also a full complement of chicken parmigiana, stuffed and roasted turkey, fresh sal-ads, ham dishes, and fresh fish. Don't expect glamour, just good value and some fill-ing and very tasty Italian food.

3, rue du Lac. © 022/736-30-49. Reservations recommended. Pizzas 18F–25F ($15–$21); main-course platters 25F–50F ($21–$41). AE, DC, MC, V. Daily 11:45am–2pm and 6:45–11pm. Tram: 12.

Taverne de la Madeleine *Value* SWISS   Robust, unpretentious, and known for its no-nonsense approach to serving well-prepared, cost-conscious food, this restaurant—one of the oldest in Geneva—is set against the old city wall beside the Eglise de la Madeleine. The building is a century old, and the restaurant itself was established more than 80 years ago. If you're having difficulty finding the address, just circle the church, and the old three-story house will be on the corner of rue des Barrières. Inside are bistro tables, red cafe chairs, and a brusquely efficient staff catering to the lunchtime business crowd. The establishment is operated by a philanthropic organi-zation that forbids the consumption of alcohol (alcohol-free beer is available). You can order a variety of well-prepared dishes. Specials include four types of pasta, vegetarian sandwiches, and such hearty fare as a big plate of osso buco with *pommes frites* (Bel-gian fries). Menu items also include an *émincé* of Indian-style chicken with curry sauce and rice and piccata of turkey Milanese with tomato sauce and spaghetti. The kitchen also prides itself on its filet of lake perch prepared meunière style or Vevey style with exotic mushrooms.

20, rue Toutes-Ames. © 022/310-60-70. Reservations recommended. Main courses 18F–30F ($15–$25); *plat du jour* 17F ($14). MC, V. Sept–June Mon–Fri 7:30am–6:30pm (last food order at 4pm), Sat 9am–4:30pm (last food order at 2:30pm); July–Aug Tues–Sat 7:30am–9pm. Bus: 2. Tram: 12.

AT NEARBY BELLEVUE

Tsé-Fung ✶✶ CHINESE   Tsé-Fung is one of the best Chinese restaurants in Switzerland. The specialties are Pekinese, Szechuan, Cantonese, and even Mongolian, including marmite mongole, lacquered duck, and steamed fish with Chinese mush-rooms. The restaurant continues to elicit adoration and salivation from its many devo-tees, often Asians who are frequently in Geneva on business. The chefs are so skilled here that their meals might be called seductive. The healthy, clean, crisp flavors of each dish keep this restaurant an ongoing leader in its specialty niche. The restaurant is off the road to Lausanne at the Hôtel La Réserve (see "Where to Stay," earlier in this chapter) and has a terrace by the swimming pool. There's also a bar.

In the Hôtel La Réserve, 301, rte. de Lausanne. ℂ 022/959-58-88. Reservations required. Main courses 55F–145F ($45–$119); fixed-price menu 70F–110F ($57–$90). AE, DC, MC, V. Daily noon–2:30pm and 7–11pm.

AT CAROUGE

A l'Olivier de Provençe ✖ *Finds* FRENCH   Set in Carouge, this Provençal restaurant offers some of the best dining on Geneva's perimeter. Though open throughout the year, it's especially popular in warm weather, when patrons can dine on its tree-shaded terrace. The savory dishes include flambéed versions of *loup de mer* (sea bass), ragout of scampi, entrecôtes, *soupe de poisson,* and fresh salmon with sorrel. In autumn the restaurant is especially known for its game dishes, such as pheasant, rabbit, pigeon, and venison. A platter of guinea fowl appears in two different versions, both a supreme and a chartreuse of guinea with thighs, each served with fresh morels. In all, this is a good, bourgeois restaurant if you don't mind the slight excursion south of the city.

13, rue Jacques-Dalphin, Carouge. ℂ 022/342-04-50. Reservations required. Main courses 39F–52F ($32–$43); fixed-price menus 73F–90F ($60–$74) and 103F ($84). AE, V. Mon–Fri noon–2pm and Mon–Sat 7–10:15pm. Closed Sat July–Aug. Tram: 12.

Le Dix Vins FRENCH   When the owner of this place closed down a more opulent restaurant next door, and focused all his attentions on this upscale and elegant bistro instead, he opted for an artfully ungrammatical name (Le Dix Vins) for the way it sticks in the mind of anyone who speaks a bit of French. It's one of the more charming, and hipper, addresses within this suburb of Geneva, set close to the Place du Marché in the heart of Carouge. Expect a clientele of business workers at lunchtime, and somewhat more intimate groups of friends and companions after dark. Menu items are unapologetically French and traditional, with such comfort-inducing selections as a fricassee of calamari in the style of Provence; a tartare of salmon with citrus-flavored ginger; filet of beef prepared with syrah wine sauce; and a filet of duckling with lemon-lime sauce. René Fracheboud, who seems to be at the epicenter of most of the artists and playwrights living in Carouge, is the hardworking owner.

29, rue Jacques-Dalphin, Carouge. ℂ 022/342-40-10. Reservations recommended. Main courses 30F–40F ($25–$33). AE, DC, MC, V. Mon–Fri noon–2pm and 7–10pm. Closed 3 weeks in Aug. Tram: 12.

AT AIRE-LE-LIGNON

La Taverne du Valais ✖ *Finds* SWISS   This is the best and most appealing grill-style restaurant in the Geneva area. Loaded with alpine charm and rusticity, it lies in a quiet suburb about 6.5km (4 miles) southwest of central Geneva, surrounded with dining terraces and grape arbors. About 90% of the diners here opt for a charcoal brazier that's deposited directly atop your table, and upon which you'll grill whatever you order from the kitchen. The staff will bring out impeccably manicured portions of turkey, lamb, chicken, duck, fish, and/or calamari. A very fresh combination of them all is particularly succulent. With your main course come trays laden with a copious assortment of garnishes that include fruit chutneys, mustards, and tartar sauce; and sauces made from curry, paprika, basil, pimento, ginger, parsley, garlic, and red wine. Hardworking members of the Impala family are your hosts. This place has been a landmark, both for its ambience and its coziness, since 1967.

4, chemin des Sellières, Aire-Le Lignon. ℂ 022/796-23-23. Main courses 40F–45F ($33–$37). AE, MC, V. Wed–Sun noon–2pm; Tues–Sun 7–10pm. Bus: 7, 18, or 27.

AT PENEY-DESSUS

Domaine de Châteauvieux ✦✦✦ INTERNATIONAL   This is one of the finest and most prestigious restaurants in and around Geneva—a city that's known for fine dining. Solid, respectable, and conservative, with a reputation for wining and dining some of the most visible politicians in Europe and the Middle East, it's housed in what was originally built as a *depence* (annex) of a château that was destroyed when the rancor of the French revolution spilled across the border into the canton of Geneva. Expect elegant table settings, impeccable service, a view that overlooks rolling hills and orderly rows of vineyards, and a cuisine conceived by culinary star Philippe Chevrier. During clement weather, tables spill out onto two separate terraces, each accented with candles and flowerpots. Menu items are upscale and endlessly fussed over. You dine in grand style on top-quality ingredients. Nothing is ordinary here. Take pumpkin soup, studded with toasted pumpkin seeds and sautéed bits of veal sweetbreads. The exquisitely tasty wild gray partridge is served on a bed of buttery cabbage and bacon bits, with a sauce like liquid foie gras. The grilled Breton lobster is so tender it provokes admiration, and the line-caught sea bass is superbly prepared.

At Peney-Dessus, 3km (1¾ miles) south of the hamlet of Satigny, 15km (9½ miles) from Geneva. ⓒ 022/753-15-11. Reservations recommended. Main courses 80F–140F ($66–$115); fixed-price lunch 84F ($69) (available any day except Sat); fixed-price lunches and dinners 175F–210F ($144–$172). AE, DC, MC, V. Tues–Sat noon–3pm and 7–10pm. Closed mid-Dec–mid-Jan. Access: From the railway station at Satigny, call the restaurant, and they'll send a van to pick you up.

AT PETIT-SACONNEX

Café du Soleil SWISS   Built in the 1880s in a traditional, all-wood format, on foundations that were at least 300 years old at the time, this is a charming, intensely folkloric dining hideaway that residents of Geneva sometimes make a detour to find. It lies in the center of the hamlet of Petit-Saconnex, about 5km (3 miles) north of Geneva, close to the French border and what functioned for many years as a tollbooth (Fermey Voltaire) that monitored traffic between France and the canton of Geneva. Choose between the wood-paneled street-level dining room and a stone-lined cellar with fewer tables. Your meal may be best started with a Malakoff, a deep-fried *"delice au fromage"* composed of eggs, beer, flour, and cheese, pungent with a sense of the high Alps. Main courses include fondues, some of them spiked with a dose of garlic, brought to your table in a bubbling pot; brochettes of herbed chicken; pave, sirloin, and rump steaks; any of which taste wonderful with any of the establishment's very fresh salads. The setting is antique-looking, appealingly battered, and rustic, accented with solid wooden tables and wooden chairs.

Place du Petit-Saconnex, Petit-Saconnex. ⓒ 022/733-34-17. Reservations recommended. Main courses 19F–25F ($16–$21). No credit cards. Daily 11am–2:30pm; Mon–Sat 6:30–11pm; Sun 6–10pm. Bus: 3.

5 Attractions

You can see most of Geneva on foot. The best way to familiarize yourself with the city, however, is by taking a walking tour, which covers all the major sights.

SUGGESTED GENEVA ITINERARIES

If You Have 1 Day   Begin the day by viewing the spectacular water fountain, the Jet d'Eau, and the Flower Clock in the **Jardin Anglais.** Then take a cruise of **Lake Geneva** on a steamer. Return in the early afternoon and explore the Left Bank's **Old Town.** Have dinner at a restaurant on place du Bourg-de-Four.

Geneva Attractions

Lac Léman

FRONTENEX

PARC DES
EAUX-VIVES

PARC
LA GRANGE

MONTCHOISY

Avenue W. Favre

Plateau de Frontenex

Ch. Av. Rosemont

Chemin Frank Thomas

Rade de
Genève

Pont du
Mont-Blanc

JARDIN
ANGLAIS

RIVE
GAUCHE

RUES BASSES
les Rues Basses

VIELLE VILLE
(OLD TOWN)

Place
Neuve

Promenade
des Bastions

Université

Rd-pt. de Plainpalais
PLAINE DE
PLAINPALAIS

Mail

Woodrow Wilson

Rue Plantamour

Quai du Mont-Blanc

Jaquet

ILE
ROUSSEAU

Pont des
Bergues

Quai Général Guisan

Quai du Rhône

rd.-pt
de Rive

R. De Rive

R. la Fontaine

Grand Rue

Corraterie

R. de la Croix Rouge

Dufour

Favon

Henri Dunant

R. de Candolle

Rue St. Léger

Rue de

Cours ses Bastions

Philosophes

Place Ed.
Claparède

Rue A. Lombard

Boulevard du Pont d'Arve

R. de Carouge

R. Prévost-Martin

Bd. de la Cluse

LA CLUSE

Quai Cologny

Rampe de Cologny

Route de Vandœuvres

Quai Gustave Ador

Rue des Eaux-Vives

Rue des Eaux-Vives

Rue de Montchoisy

Rue des Vollandes

Rue du 31 Décembre

R. de la Mairie

Av. Pictet De Rochemont

Route de Frontenex

Route de Frontenex

Route de Chêne

Ch. de la Petite Boissière

Av. de l'Amandolier

Promenade Martin

Rue Agasse

Rue de la Terassière

R. Lachenal

Pl. Em.
Guyenot

Rue Hodler

Bd. Jacques Dalcroze

Boulevard Helvétique

Ch. Galland

Bd. des Tranchées

R. de l'Hôtel de Ville

Rue de Ville

Route de Malagnou

Chemin Rieu

FLORISSANT

Route de Florissant

Avenue Bertrand

PARC
A. BERTRAND

Avenue Louis Aubert

Rue de l'Athénée

Bd. l'Athénée

Avenue Peschier

CHAMPEL

Avenue de Miremont

Avenue de Champel

Av. Calas

Rue de la Clusette

10
11
12 13
14
5
16
7
17
18 19 20 21 22
23
24
25
26
27
28
29

RIVE
GAUCHE

Train Station

If You Have 2 Days Spend the first day as above. On the second day, visit some of the most important **museums** of Geneva, each completely different. It'll take a full day of sightseeing to absorb the most important: the Musée d'Art et d'Histoire, the Musée International de la Croix-Rouge et du Croissant-Rouge (Red Cross Museum), and the Palais des Nations.

If You Have 3 Days Spend the first 2 days as outlined above. On your third day, take our walking tour of Geneva (see later in this chapter) in the morning, and in the afternoon go on one of the organized excursions to the Alps, including **Mont Blanc,** for a panoramic view.

If You Have 4 Days Spend the first 3 days as suggested above. By now you're an old hand at finding your way around Geneva, and you can use your last days for excursions. While still based in Geneva, take a lake steamer to **Lausanne** (see chapter 10). You'll have time to explore its Old Town and walk its lakeside quays at Ouchy before returning to Geneva in the evening.

If You Have 5 Days Spend days 1 to 4 as above. On the fifth day, take a lake steamer to **Montreux** (see chapter 10). After visiting this lakeside resort, take a trip outside the town to see the **Château de Chillon,** immortalized by Lord Byron.

THE TOP ATTRACTIONS

In addition to the sites listed below, Geneva's other top attractions—all premier sights—are the **Jet d'Eau,** the famous fountain that has virtually become the city's symbol; the **Flower Clock,** in the Jardin Anglais, with 6,500 flowers; and **Old Town,** the oldest part of the city. All these sights, and more, are detailed in our walking tour, later in this chapter.

Musée Ariana 𝄢𝄢 Located to the west of the Palais des Nations, the Italian Renaissance building was constructed by Gustave Revilliod, the 19th-century Genevese patron who began the collection. Today it's one of the top porcelain, glass, and pottery museums in Europe. Here you'll see Sèvres, Delft faïence, and Meissen porcelain, as well as pieces from Japan and China. It's also the headquarters of the International Academy of Ceramics.

10, av. de la Paix. ℂ 022/418-54-50. Free admission to the permanent collection; temporary exhibitions 5F ($4.10) adults, free for children under 18. Wed–Mon 10am–5pm. Bus: 8 or F.

MAMCO (Musée d'Art et Contemporain) 𝄢 Some 20 years in the making, Geneva's first modern art museum opened in 1994 in a former factory building. This prestigious showcase displays a vast collection of European and American art covering the last 4 decades. Out of some 1,000 works of art owned by the museum, only 300 are permanently on display. This space is packed with all the big names—Frankenthaler, Stela, Segal, and others. Some 150 sq. m (about 1,600 sq. ft.) of space is set aside for exhibitions that change three times a year.

10, rue des Vieux-Grenadiers. ℂ 022/320-61-22. Admission 8F ($6.55) adults, 6F ($4.90) students, free for children 17 and under. Tues–Fri noon–6pm; Sat–Sun 11am–6pm. Bus: 1 or 32.

Musée d'Art et d'Histoire 𝄢𝄢 At Geneva's most important museum, displays include prehistoric relics, Greek vases, medieval stained glass, 12th-century armor, Swiss timepieces, Flemish and Italian paintings, and Switzerland's largest collection of Egyptian art. The Etruscan pottery and medieval furniture are both impressive. A

1444 altarpiece by Konrad Witz depicts the "miraculous" draft of fishes. Many galleries also contain works by such artists as Rodin, Renoir, Hodler, Vallotton, Le Corbusier, Picasso, Chagall, Corot, Monet, and Pissarro.

2, rue Charles-Galland (between bd. Jacques-Dalcroze and bd. Helvétique). ℂ **022/418-26-00.** Free admission to permanent collections, 5F ($4.10) temporary exhibitions. Tues–Sun 10am–5pm. Bus: 1, 3, 5, 8, or 17.

Musée International de la Croix-Rouge et du Croissant-Rouge (International Red Cross and Red Crescent Museum) ℱ

Here you can experience the legendary past of the Red Cross in the city where it started; it's across from the visitors' entrance to the European headquarters of the United Nations. The dramatic story from 1863 to the present is revealed through displays of rare documents and photographs, films, multiscreen slide shows, and cycloramas. You're taken from the battlefields of Europe to the plains of Africa to see the Red Cross in action. When Henry Dunant founded the Red Cross in Geneva in 1863, he needed a recognizable symbol to suggest neutrality. The Swiss flag (a white cross on a red field), with the colors reversed, ended up providing the perfect symbol for one of the world's greatest humanitarian movements.

17, av. de la Paix. ℂ **022/748-95-25.** www.micr.org. Admission 10F ($8.20) adults, 5F ($4.10) students, seniors, and children 12 to 16. Wed–Mon 10am–5pm. Bus: 8, F, V, or Z.

MORE ATTRACTIONS
MUSEUMS

The Baur Collections ℱ   This is Switzerland's largest collection of Far Eastern art. The collections, housed in a 19th-century mansion with a garden, constitute a private exhibit of artworks from China (dating from the 10th–19th c.) and Japan (17th–20th c.). On display are ceramics, jade, lacquer, ivories, and delicate sword fittings.

8, rue Munier-Romilly. ℂ **022/346-17-29.** Admission 5F ($4.10) adults, free for children. Tues–Sun 2–6pm. Bus: 1 or 8.

Fondation Martin Bodmer   Martin Bodmer's library had long been a place for reflection and research. It was his inspiration and consultation room where he would study the work of great men and women. Upon his death in 1971, Bodmer left behind a collection of more than 160,000 books, manuscripts, autographs, and artworks depicting 3,000 years of world culture. Including in the display are early handwritten texts of Homer, illuminated manuscripts of the Bible, a manuscript of Grimm's Fairy Tales, and a 15th-century version of the Nibelungenlied. The exhibition also has the first printed versions of Cervantes' *Don Quixote,* Newton's *Principa Mathematica,* Goethe's *Faust,* Chaucer's *Canterbury Tales,* James Joyce's *Ulysses,* and works from Dante Alighieri and William Shakespeare.

19-21, rte. de Guignard, Cologny. ℂ **022/707-44-33.** www.fondationbodmer.org. Admission 8F ($6.55) adults, 5F ($4.10) for children and seniors. Tues–Sun 2–6pm. Closed 2 weeks in May. Bus: 33 or A.

Maison Tavel ℱ   Constructed in 1303 and partially rebuilt after a fire in 1334, this is the city's oldest house. The building has undergone several transformations over the centuries before opening as a museum in 1986. The front wall is typical 17th century, with gray paint, white joints, and stone sculpted heads. The house contains a courtyard with a staircase, a 13th-century cellar, and a back garden. The museum exhibits historical collections from Geneva dating from the Middle Ages to the mid–19th century. The Magnin relief in the attic is outstanding, as is the copper-and-zinc model of Geneva in 1850, which is accompanied by a light-and-tape commentary. Objects of

> **Fun Fact** **Did You Know?**
>
> - Geneva didn't enter the Helvetic Confederation until as late as 1815.
> - Jean-Jacques Rousseau was born in Geneva in 1712, and his archrival, Voltaire, lived here from 1755 to 1759.
> - During the Dark Ages, the kings of Burgundy made Geneva their capital.
> - John Calvin, the reformer, settled in Geneva in 1536, turning it into the "Rome of the Protestants."
> - Napoleon slept in the Old Town on May 9, 1800, and Geneva remained part of France until December 31, 1813.
> - Geneva's annual Escalade celebration still commemorates a victory over the duke of Savoy's troops in 1602.
> - Villa Montalegre in Cologny, outside Geneva, was the birthplace of the horror story *Frankenstein*.

daily use are displayed in the old living quarters. Postcards, books, slides, and small guidebooks are available at the bookstand.

6, rue du Puits-St-Pierre. ✆ 022/418-37-00. Free admission to permanent collection, 3F ($2.45) temporary expositions. Tues–Sun 10am–5pm. Bus: 3, 5, or 17.

Musée Barbier-Mueller   No one would expect a middle-class orphan, raised by a governess, to be one of the greatest art collectors of all time, but that is exactly what Josef Mueller (1887–1977) did. By the age of 31, Mueller had seven works by Cézanne, five by Matisse, five by Renoir, and a healthy assortment of Picassos and Braques, all of which are on display. However, the real heart of his collection are the primitive pieces from Africa, the East Indies, Oceania, the early Americas, tribal Asia, and the prehistoric phases of Greece, Italy, and Japan. Mueller's daughter Monique, a historian, married another art collector, Jean Paul Barbier, who added his discoveries to that of his father-in-law's and together the pair created the Musée Barbier-Mueller.

10, rue Jean-Calvin. ✆ 022/312-02-70. www.barbier-mueller.ch. Admission 5F ($4.10) adults, 3F ($2.45) students and seniors, free for children under 12. Daily 11am–5pm. Bus: 2, 7, 12, 16, or 17.

Palais des Nations ✿✿   The former home of the defunct League of Nations is the present headquarters of the United Nations in Europe, lying 1.6km (1 mile) north of Mont Blanc Bridge. The complex of buildings is the second largest in Europe after Versailles. Tours, conducted in English, last about an hour. They depart from the visitors' entrance opposite the Red Cross building. To join the tour, you'll need to show your passport. The monumental compound was constructed between 1929 and 1936. The highlights of the tour include the Assembly Hall, with a balcony made entirely of marble and lofty bays looking out over the Court of Honor. You are shown the Council Chamber, the home of the Conference on Disarmament with its allegorical murals by José Maria Sert, an artist from Catalonia. A Philatelic Museum offers collections of stamps relating to the League of Nations, along with a wide selection of philatelic publications from around the world, and a League of Nations Museum documents the history of the precursor to the United Nations.

Parc de l'Ariana, 14, av. de la Paix. (C) 022/917-12-34. Admission 10F ($8.20) adults, 8F ($6.55) students, 5F ($4.10) children 6–17. July–Aug daily 10am–5pm; Apr–June and Sept–Oct daily 10am–noon and 2–4pm; Nov–Mar Mon–Fri 10am–noon and 2–4pm. Bus: 5, 8, 11, 14, 18, F, V, or Z.

Patek Philippe Museum Watch-lovers flock to here from all over the world to see one of the best collections of timepieces in existence. There are two collections that are permanently on display here—the Antiques Collection and the Patek Philippe Collection. Founded in 1839, the Patek Philippe company, of course, is one of the most venerated watchmakers in the world. The Antiques Collection contains a wide array of Genevese, Swiss, and European watches from the 16th to 19th centuries. A good portion of the pieces are historically significant to the history of horology. An audiovisual, multilingual presentation accompanies this collection. The Patek Philippe display showcases the more than 160 years that the company has been in business.

7, rue de Vieux Grenadiers. (C) 022/807-09-10. Free admission but donations welcome. Tues–Fri 2–5pm; Sat 10am–5pm. Bus: 1 or 4. Tram: 12 or 13.

RELIGIOUS MONUMENTS

The **Old Town** (*), or Vieille Ville, on the Left Bank, is dominated by the **Cathédrale de St-Pierre** (*), cour St-Pierre ((C) 022/311-75-74), which was built in the 12th and 13th centuries and partially reconstructed in the 15th century. Recent excavations have disclosed that a Christian sanctuary was here as early as A.D. 400. In 1536 the people of Geneva gathered in the cloister of St. Pierre's and voted to make the cathedral Protestant. The church, which has been heavily renovated over the years, has a modern organ with 6,000 pipes. The northern tower was reconstructed at the end of the 19th century, with a metal steeple erected between the two stone towers. If you don't mind the 145 steps, you can climb to the top of the north tower for a panoramic view of the city, its lake, the Alps, and the Jura Mountains.

To enter the St. Pierre archaeological site, called **Site Archéologique de St-Pierre,** go through the entrance in cour St-Pierre, at the right-hand corner of the cathedral steps. The underground passageway extends under the present cathedral and the High Gothic (early 15th c.) **Chapelle des Macchabées,** which adjoins the southwestern corner of the church. The chapel was restored during World War II, after having been used as a storage room following the Reformation. Excavations of the chapel have revealed baptisteries, a crypt, the foundations of several cathedrals, the bishop's palace, 4th-century mosaics, sculptures, and geological strata.

The cathedral and the chapel are open June to September daily from 9am to 7pm; March to May and in October daily 9am to noon and 2 to 6pm; in January, February, November, and December daily 9am to noon and 2 to 3pm. There is no admission charge to visit the cathedral, although donations are welcome; tower admission is 3F ($2.45). Sunday service is held in the cathedral at 10am, and an hour of organ music is presented on Saturday at 6pm from June to September. The archaeological site is open June to September daily from 11am to 5pm; October to May, Tuesday to Sunday from 2 to 5pm; the admission charge is 5F ($4.10) for adults, 3F ($2.45) for students and seniors. Take bus no. 2, 7, 12, or 36.

Next door to the cathedral is a Gothic church where Calvin preached, known as the **Temple de l'Auditoire,** or Calvin Auditorium. It was restored in 1959 in time for Calvin's 450th anniversary.

PARKS, GARDENS & SQUARES

If you walk heading north along the quays, you'll arrive at some of the lushest parks in Geneva. **Parc Mon-Repos** 🎡🎡 is off avenue de France and **La Perle du Lac** is off rue de Lausanne. Directly to the right is the **Jardin Botanique (Botanical Garden),** which was established in 1902. It has an alpine garden, a little zoo, greenhouses, and exhibitions, and can be visited free from April to October daily from 8am to 7:30pm; November to March daily from 9:30am to 5pm.

You can take a boat to the other side of Lake Geneva and get off at quai Gustave-Ador. From there you can explore two more lakeside parks—**Parc la Grange,** which has the most extravagant rose garden in Switzerland (especially in June), and next to it, the **Parc des Eaux-Vives.**

When you leave the Botanical Garden on the Left Bank, you can head west, along avenue de la Paix, about 1.5km (1 mile) north from the Pont du Mont-Blanc, to the Palais des Nations in the **Parc de l'Ariana.**

LES PAQUIS DISTRICT 🎡🎡

One of Geneva's most animated and elegant districts, **Les Pâquis** faces the harbor from the Right Bank of Lake Geneva. To reach it, head north along quai des Bergues, which leads into quai du Mont-Blanc. On your left, at the intersection of quai du Mont-Blanc and Gare Routière, stands the **Brunswick Monument,** the tomb of Charles II of Brunswick, who died in Geneva in 1873. The duke left his fortune to the city with the provision that it build a monument to him. Geneva accepted the fortune and modeled the tomb after the Scaglieri tombs in Verona.

Les Pâquis is a sector of cozy bistros, nightclubs, ateliers, elegant boutiques, and banks. The word *pâquis* comes from the Latin *pascuum,* meaning "pasture." The cows that grazed here are long gone, but from about A.D. 1330 the district consisted of a vast expanse of fields, pastures, and wastelands. It was far from the heart of the city and its protective ditches, and exposed to the permanent danger of invasion.

From the 14th century, as the city developed a stronger defense system, this unincorporated territory became safer, and more and more people made homes here. In

---

Frommer's Favorite Geneva Experiences

Wine Tasting in the Countryside   Winding your way through the rolling vineyards just outside Geneva makes for an enjoyable day's outing. Many of the best Swiss wines never leave the country, and grapes grow on slopes overlooking Lake Geneva and the Rhône. Pick up a brochure called *Discover Geneva and Its Vineyards* from the tourist office and set out.

Sailing Lake Geneva   The crescent-shaped lake, called Lac Léman locally, gives Geneva a resortlike ambience, stretching for 72km (45 miles). In the summer it's alive with activity: sailing, rowing, canoeing, water-skiing, and more.

Wandering through Old Town   Geneva's Vieille Ville has been called "Europe's best-kept secret." Exploring its ancient streets brings you to art galleries, antiques shops, booksellers, and tiny bistros. Follow the Grande-Rue, where Jean-Jacques Rousseau was born, and wander back into time.

the 15th century the Pâquis was home to potters and fisher folk, and eventually homes and small industries began to take root.

In 1831 the French writer Chateaubriand settled at the **Hôtel des Etrangers,** 22, rue des Pâquis. From 1851 on, development was fairly rapid, with the construction of **quai du Mont-Blanc** and of the **Rotonde,** the English church. An American church was also constructed, and in 1857 **quais Pâquis** and **Eaux-Vives** were erected. Construction on the Cornavin railway station began the following year. The **Pont du Mont-Blanc** was erected in 1862. Soon, the lake promenade, the façade des Pâquis, and quai du Mont-Blanc became fashionable.

In 1873 construction began on the **Hôtel National** (Palais Wilson); from 1925 to 1936 it would house the first secretariat of the League of Nations. The Kursaal was built between 1874 and 1879. One of the most infamous events in the history of the area was the assassination of Empress Elisabeth of Austria, in 1898, at the landing stage facing the duke of Brunswick's mausoleum.

After wandering through the district with no particular fixed itinerary, visitors may tour Lake Geneva in a lake steamer. Steamers leave from quai du Mont-Blanc.

ESPECIALLY FOR KIDS

Geneva is a city with many attractions of interest to the younger set. The following are perhaps the coolest of the cool:

Visiting the **Musée International de la Croix-Rouge et du Croissant-Rouge (Red Cross Museum)** is like attending an adventure movie, as kids are enraptured by the sweep and drama of this heroic organization, which has always been near the "core of the action."

One of the best natural-history museums of Europe, the **Musée d'Historie Naturelle** delights children with its tropical birds, mammals, and exotic reptiles.

Jet d'Eau and the **Flower Clock** are exciting introductions for children. After viewing both of them, parents can take their kids for a tour by steamer on Lake Geneva.

FOR THE LITERARY ENTHUSIAST

At 25, rue des Délices, you'll find the house—now the **Institut et Musée Voltaire** (**© 022/344-71-33**)—where Voltaire lived from 1755 to 1760 and from time to time after that up to 1765; he wrote part of *Candide* here. The museum displays furniture, manuscripts, letters, and portraits, as well as a terra-cotta model of the famous seated Voltaire by Houdon. The museum is open Monday to Saturday from 2 to 5pm, and admission is free. Take bus no. 6, 7, 11, 26, or 27.

WALKING TOUR	GENEVA'S QUAYS & OLD TOWN

Start:	Jet d'Eau.
Finish:	Place du Bourg-de-Four.
Time:	2 hours.
Best Times:	Any sunny day.
Worst Times:	Rush hours, Monday to Friday from 8 to 9am and 5 to 6pm.

Along the Quays   If, like most tourists, you arrive in the summer, you may begin your discovery of the city with a long promenade along the quays of Geneva. The one sight you can't miss is the:

❶ Jet d'Eau

In the quai Gustave-Ador, this famous fountain is the trademark of the city. Visible for miles, from April to September it throws water 138m (453 ft.) into the air above the lake. The Genevese call the fountain the *jeddo*. It dates from 1891 but was improved in 1951. Many cities have sent engineers to Geneva to study the workings of the fountain, although it remains a carefully guarded state secret. The fountain pumps 132 gallons of water per second into the air.

Once you've seen the fountain, you'll be ready to explore the quays, with their gardens and ancient buildings. The aquatic population consists of seagulls, ducks, and swans. A fleet of small boats, called *mouettes genevoises,* shuttles visitors from one quay to another from spring until autumn.

Lying directly off quai du Général-Guisan is another Geneva landmark, the:

❷ Flower Clock

In the Jardin Anglais (English Garden), the clock's face is made of carefully landscaped beds of flowers, and it keeps perfect time! The Jardin Anglais is at the foot of the Mont Blanc Bridge, which spans the river at the point where the Rhône leaves Lake Geneva. The bridge was rebuilt in 1969.

Cross Pont du Mont-Blanc and turn left (south) along quai des Bergues on the Right Bank of Geneva until you come to the next bridge, called Pont des Bergues. If you cross this bridge, you'll come to:

❸ Ile Rousseau

A statue of the philosopher sculpted by Pradier in 1834 greets you here. The island, which was Rousseau's stomping grounds and the site of many of his reveries, is now home to ducks, swans, grebes, and other aquatic fowl. Situated in the middle of the Rhône, it was once a bulwark of Geneva's river defenses.

Return to quai des Bergues and continue to walk left along the quay until you reach place St-Gervais to:

❹ Tour-de-l'Ile

A château was built here in 1219, although the tower is all that remains today. The château had been used as a prison

and place of execution by the counts of Savoy. A wall plaque commemorates a visit by Caesar in 58 B.C. Once the fortified core of the Old Town, it bears some similarities to Paris's Ile de la Cité. You can also explore the old markets, which often exhibit the works of contemporary Genevese artists.

The walking tour of the quays is particularly good for children because the sights are outside and easily understandable. If the children get tired, however, you can take them to quai du Mont-Blanc, where they can board *le mini-train de Genève.* This 40-minute excursion will take them along the major parks and quays of Geneva. Departures March to October are daily every 45 minutes from 10am to 11pm. Adults pay a fare of 7.90F ($6.50) and children are charged 4.90F ($4).

Through Old Town At this point, you'll be on the doorway of Geneva's Old Town or Vieille Ville, set on the cultural Left Bank. The district is one of the most remarkable in Switzerland.

After leaving the Tour-de-l'Ile, you can continue across the Rhône until you reach place Bel-Air, on the Left Bank. From here, head south for a short distance along rue de la Monnaie, which quickly becomes rue de la Cité. When that street changes its name to rue de la Tertasse, continue south along this street until you reach:

❺ Place Neuve

This is the cultural heart of Geneva. The square has a statue of General Dufour, who was a cofounder of the Red Cross. Monuments on this square include the Grand Théâtre and the Conservatory of Music. The Grand Théâtre (opera house) was built in 1874 (see "Geneva After Dark," later in this chapter). The conservatory dates from 1858.

Also on the square is the:

❻ Musée Rath

The museum, place Neuve (© 022/418-33-40), has temporary exhibitions of paintings and sculpture. It's open Tuesday

start here

Lake Geneva

JARDIN ANGLAIS

rond-point Rive

carrefour de Rive

pont du Mont-Blanc

pont des Bergues

pont de la Machine

place du Port

place du Lac

place du Rhône

place Bel-Air

place de Hollande

place Grenus

place St-Gervais

place du Bourg-de-Four

PROMENADE DES BASTIONS

finish here

quai Gustave Ador
rue du Lac
rue des Pierres-du-Niton
rue Muzy
rue de la Scie
rue de la Mairie
rue des Eaux-Vives
rue H. Blanvalet
av. de Frontenex
rue du Parc
la Terrassière
rue de la Terrassière
rue Versonnex
rue du Rhône
Duchosal
bd. Helvétique
cours de Rive
bd. Helvétique
rue Pierre-Fatio
rue d'Aoste
rue de Rive
rue Pierre-Fatio
rue F. Hodler
bd. J. Dalcroze
rue du Rhône
rue d'Italie
rue Estienne
rue du Prince
rue du Port
quai Général Guisan
rue de la Croix-d'Or
rue de Vieux-Collège
rue de la Fontaine
rue Vallée
rue Verdaine
rue Chaud
ron-niers
rue Neuve-du-Molard
rue Céard
rue Madeleine
rue de la Croix-Rouge
rue de l'Hôtel-de-Ville
rue du Rhône
place du Lac
rue du Marché
rue de la Rôtisserie
rue Calvin
rue Puits St-Pierre
J. Soleil-Levant
rue Fusterie
rue de la Confédération
rue du Commerce
rue Bezanson
quai l'Ile
Rhône
rue des quai
Moulins
Moulins
Grand Rue
rue des Granges
rue Bémont
rampe de la Treille
rue de la Croix-Rouge
rue de la Cité
rue Corraterie
rue Diday
bd. du Théâtre
rue de Hollande
rue Winkelried
quai des Bergues
rue Kléberg
rue du Cendrier
rue Rousseau
rue Grenus
rue Coutance
rue de Cornavin
rue des Etuves
rue des Granges

pont du Mont-Blanc

Hugues

1/10 mile
0
100 metres
0

1. Jet d'Eau
2. Flower Clock
3. Ile Rousseau
4. Tour-de-l'Ile
5. Place Neuve
6. Musée Rath
7. Monument de la Réformation
   Le Café-Restaurant Papon
8. Hôtel-de-Ville
9. The Arsenal
10. Place du Bourg-de-Four

GENEVA
Walking Tour Area

and Thursday to Sunday from 10am to 5pm, Wednesday from noon to 9pm, and costs 9F ($7.40) for adults, 5F ($4.10) for students, and is free for children under 18. The museum can be reached by tram no. 12 or 13, and bus no. 3, 4, 5, 11, or 12.

From place Neuve, continue southeast along rue de la Croix-Rouge until you come to the:

⑦ Monument de la Réformation

The Reformation Monument was built in 1917 along a 16th-century rampart, beneath the walls of the Old Town on promenade des Bastions. The monument, which is 91m (298 ft.) long, represents John Knox, Calvin, Théodore de Bèze, and Guillaume Farel—the four Genevese reformers. Other statues include Cromwell, the Pilgrim Fathers, and, on either end, Luther and Zwingli.

Retrace your footsteps along rue de la Croix-Rouge until you return to place Neuve. From the square, take a sharp right and follow ramp de la Treille, which becomes rue Henri-Fazy, where you can:

TAKE A BREAK
One of the oldest and most venerated cafes of Geneva, **Le Café-Restaurant Papon,** 1, rue Henri-Fazy (✆ **022/311-54-28**), lies near the Tour Baudet in the vicinity of the Hôtel-de-Ville. A restaurant, creperie, tearoom, and cafe, it has been entertaining drinkers and diners under its vaulted ceilings since the 17th century.

Turn right at rue de l'Hôtel-de-Ville and you'll approach the:

⑧ Hôtel-de-Ville (town hall)

The Hôtel-de-Ville is a short walk from the cathedral and dates from the 16th and 17th centuries. Its Baudet Tower was constructed in 1455. The building, which has a cobblestone ramp instead of a staircase, has witnessed some of the city's most important diplomatic events. The Red Cross originated here in 1864.

Across from the town hall is:

⑨ The Arsenal

This arcaded structure dates from 1634. In the courtyard of the building is a cannon that was cast in 1683.

Continue along rue de l'Hôtel-de-Ville until you reach:

⑩ Place du Bourg-de-Four

This spot was first a Roman forum and later a medieval town square. The Palais de Justice here was built in 1707, but it has housed courts of law only since 1860. While you're in this area, you'll come across a fountain, many antiquaries' shops, and art galleries.

ORGANIZED TOURS
BUS & TRAM TOURS

If you're new in Geneva and want an easy-to-digest breakdown of the way the city is divided into various neighborhoods and districts, consider a tram tour. Departing from the south bank's Place du Rhône (May–Sept only), red-painted, open-sided trolley cars meander through neighborhoods that include the city's medieval center, the glossy shopping districts, and the hotel and museum-studded precincts of the river's north bank. Trams depart at 45-minute intervals every day between 9:15am and 6:45pm, last about 35 minutes, and cost 8.90F ($7.30) for adults and 5.90F ($4.85) for children. For more information, contact **STT Trains Tours S.A.,** 36 bd. St-Georges (✆ **022/781-04-04**).

A 2-hour City Tour is operated daily all year by **Key Tours S.A.,** 7, rue des Alpes, square du Mont-Blanc (© **022/731-41-40**). The tour starts from the Gare Routière, the bus station at place Dorcière, near the Key Tours office. From November to March the tour is offered only once a day at 2pm, but from April to October two tours leave daily at 10am and 2pm.

A bus will drive you through the city to see the monuments, landmarks, and lake promenades. In the Old Town you can take a walk down to the Bastions Park and the Reformation Wall. After a tour through the International Center, where you'll be shown the headquarters of the International Red Cross, the bus returns to its starting place. Adults pay 39F ($32) and children 4 to 12 accompanied by an adult are charged 18F ($15), while children 3 and under go free.

BOAT TOURS

The cold, clear waters of Lac Léman have attracted visitors for many generations. If you're interested in cruising on these waters (which never freeze, even in winter), at least two companies offer worthwhile tours. Your best bet involves determining how extensive you want your tour to be, and then selecting one whose duration corresponds to your schedule.

Regardless of which you select (see below), you'll enjoy sweeping waterside views of the ringing hills, bucolic calm, and some of the most famous vineyards in Switzerland, many of which seem to roll down to the historic waters. Because of bad weather and low visibility in winter, cruises only run between April and late October, and in some cases, only between May and September.

Two separate companies offer cruises along the lake. The smaller of the two, **Mouettes Genevoises Navigation,** 8 quai du Mont-Blanc (© **022/732-47-47;** www.swiss boat.com), specializes in small-scale boats carrying only about 100 passengers at a time. Each features some kind of guided (prerecorded) commentary, in French and English, throughout. An easy promenade that features the landscapes and bird life along the uppermost regions of the river Rhône draining the lake is the company's 2¾ hour-long **Tour du Rhône (Rhône River Tour).** The trip originates at quai des Moulins, adjacent to Geneva's Pont de l'Ile, and travels downstream for about 14km (9 miles) to the Barrage de Verbois (Verbois Dam) and back. From May to September, departures are Wednesday, Saturday, and Sunday at 10am and 2:15pm. It costs 15F ($12) for adults and 10F ($8.20) for children 4 to 12; it's free for children under 4. The same company also offers 1¼-hour tours (four times a day) and 2-hour tours (twice a day) out onto the lake. The longer tour includes a prerecorded commentary on the celebrity residences and ecology of the lake en route. These tours cost 12F ($9.85) for the shorter tour and 22F ($18) for the longer tour. No stops are made en route.

Mouettes Genevoises Navigation's largest competitor, **CGN (Compagnie Générale de Navigation),** quai du Mont-Blanc (© **0848/811-848;** www.cgn.ch), offers roughly equivalent tours, in this case between May and September, that last an hour, departing six to seven times a day (depending on the season) from the company's piers along quai du Mont-Blanc. Known as "Les Belles Rives Genevoises," they charge 12F ($9.85) for adults and 6F ($4.90) for children 6 to 16; children 5 and under ride free. Tours include prerecorded commentaries and are, frankly, about as long in duration as many short-term visitors to the city really want.

Although its hour-long cruises are popular, CGN devotes most of its time, energy, and money to hauling boatloads of commuters and sightseers between the ports that line the perimeter of the lake. They're conducted aboard larger craft that resemble seagoing ferryboats, and the experience is usually more workaday than the short cruises described above. None includes guided commentary. Despite that, many visitors appreciate the silence and the fact that CGN's larger boats each contains an attractive brasserie with uniformed waiters, starched linen, fixed-price menus at 35F ($29) each, and affordably priced *assiettes du jour* (plates of the day). You can ask the sales staff at CGN to configure almost any tour along the lake that appeals to you, incorporating half-day stopovers and/or overnights in towns like Nyon, Lausanne, Vevey, Montreux, Evian, Yvoire, and Thonon. Barring that, you can sign up for either of the prepackaged experiences (*grands et petits* tours of the lake) as described below. In most cases, CGN vessels depart from the piers beside quai du Mont-Blanc, but whenever the schedule warrants it, the departure moves 182m (597 ft.) away, to the piers in the nearby Jardin Anglais.

The most comprehensive ride requires a full day: the **Tour du Grand Lac.** It departs every morning at 9am, pulls for very brief interludes into about half a dozen ports en route, and returns to Geneva that night at 8:45pm. A 2-hour stopover in Montreux, plus a leisurely lunch onboard, is included as part of the experience. The round-trip circuit costs 55F to 73F ($45–$60) for adults and 37F to 55F ($30–$45) for ages 6 to 25; it's free for children 5 and under. A more recommendable, and more practical, tour is **Le Tour du Petit Lac,** which incorporates only the lower portion of the lake, including stops at Nyon (in Switzerland) and Yvoire (in France), and lasts for about half a day. It departs from quai du Mont-Blanc every afternoon at 3pm. The round-trip cost is from 35F to 48F ($29–$39), depending on where you opt to sit in the boat (the upper level is more expensive).

CGN also offers a tour that combines a lake cruise and a visit to the Château de Chillon with a return by train back to Geneva. Between June and September, a boat leaves from the Mont Blanc pier daily at 9:15am, arriving in Chillon at 2:15pm. During July and August an additional boat departs from the Jardin Anglais pier at 10:30am, arriving in Chillon around 3:50pm. Participants can visit the castle before taking a train or bus from the small station at Chillon to Montreux, and then transfer to one of the hourly trains from Montreux back to Geneva. Some visitors opt to dally in Montreux a while, perhaps remaining for lunch or dinner. The cost for the full round-trip excursion is 54F ($44) in second class and 73F ($60) in first class. For **more information,** call 🕾 **0848/811-848.**

A TOUR TO MONT BLANC ✶✶✶

If you have time, we highly recommend a Mont Blanc excursion, which is an all-day trip to Chamonix by bus and a cable-car ride to the summit of the Aiguille du Midi (3,783m/12,408 ft.). The tour leaves Geneva at 8:30am and returns at 6pm daily. Buses leave from the bus station (Gare Routière). You must take your passport with you.

Other mechanized ascents that are part of this tour are to Vallée Blanche by télé-cabin, an extension of the Aiguille du Midi climb, from April to October; to Mer de Glâce via electric rack railway to the edge of the glacier, from which you may descend to the ice grotto (the climb is not available in the winter); and to Le Brevent, an ascent by cable car to a rocky belvedere at 2,370m (7,900 ft.), facing the Mont Blanc range. Lunch is included.

An English-speaking guide will accompany your bus tour. **Key Tours S.A.,** 7, rue des Alpes (place du Mont-Blanc; Case Postale 1745), CH-1211 Genève (🕾 **022/731-41-40**), operator of the excursions, requires a minimum of eight people per trip. Tours range from 240F ($197), including a ride up the mountain.

6 The Active Vacation Planner

Like most cities in health-conscious Switzerland, Geneva has many sports facilities. However, locals often pursue activities outside the city. They're more interested in following their own personal sports programs than they are in spectator sports, except for soccer, which is played in various stadiums. (Matches are announced in the tourist office's monthly "List of Events.")

The big spectator event of the year, the world's most important **lake regatta** is known as the **Bol d'Or** and takes place sometime in June (the Swiss National Tourist Office abroad will provide exact dates), attracting approximately 600 sailboats and more than 3,500 competitors. The lake is virtually covered with white sails. It takes 7 hours for the luckiest to sail from one end to the other—and more than 24 hours for the unluckiest. But participants from all over the world swear it's worth trying.

BIKING   Cyclists consider the Geneva countryside a paradise. What could be better than a ride through forest, vineyard, and cornfield? The most passionate bikers climb Bernex's hill or cross the border into France (bring a passport). See "Getting Around," earlier in this chapter, for details about renting a bike.

GOLF   The best course is **Golf Club de Genève,** 7, rte. de la Capite at Cologny (© 022/707-48-00), which is an 18-hole course open March to December, Tuesday to Sunday from 8:30am to 12:30pm and 2 to 6pm. Greens fees are 150F ($123) for 18 holes. This is a private course but often allows nonmembers to play, preferably those associated with golf courses in their home countries. Always call about admission before heading here, however. There is also an on-site pro shop.

HEALTH CLUB   **Silhouette Health & Fitness,** 4, rue Thalberg (© 022/732-77-40), is the most comprehensive, best-equipped, and most sociable health club in Geneva. Set very close to the grand hotels (Hotel de la Paix, Hotel Beau-Rivage, Hotel Richemond) of the Right Bank, it welcomes temporary visitors to the city for a fee of 20F to 27F ($16–$22), depending on the day of the week and time of day you arrive. Expect everything from aerobics to free weights, with every other kind of health and exercise machine as well. It's open Monday to Friday from 9am to 9pm, Saturday and Sunday 10am to 5pm.

JOGGING   In addition to the many trails that have been laid out in the parks, you can also jog along the quays and the lakeshore beaches. The best places for jogging are Parc Bertrand, Parc des Eaux-Vives, and Parc Mon-Repos.

SAILING   This is the most popular sport in Geneva. All along the quays in the summer, you'll find kiosks offering sailboats for rent.

SKIING   In the winter the people of Geneva flock to the resorts of the Haute Savoie in France, notably Chamonix and Megève. Each resort is about an hour's drive from Geneva. The smaller, lesser-known French resort of Flaine is even closer to Geneva. In Switzerland itself, the place nearest Geneva where there's good skiing is the Glacier of Les Diablerets or the resort of Champéry.

SWIMMING   In summer swimmers usually head for the beaches along the lake. The most popular of these is **Geneva Beach (Genève Plage),** Port Noir (© 022/736-24-82), where you can swim from 10am to 8pm for 7F ($4.55).

TENNIS   Tennis somehow seems more invigorating in the sunshine and sometimes-brisk mountain air near the French Alps. An option for tennis in Geneva is the courts at **Le New Sporting Club,** 47, rte. de Collex (© 022/774-15-14).

7 Shopping

From boutiques to department stores, Geneva is a shopper's dream come true. The city, of course, is known for its watches and jewelry, but it's also a good place to buy embroidered blouses, music boxes from the Jura region, cuckoo clocks from German Switzerland, cigars from Havana (not allowed into the United States), chocolate, Swiss Army knives, and many other items.

Geneva practically invented the wristwatch. In fact, watchmaking in the city dates from the 16th century. Be sure to avoid purchasing a Swiss watch in one of the souvenir stores. If jewelers are legitimate, they'll display a symbol of the Geneva Association of Watchmakers and Jewelers. Here, more than in any other Swiss city perhaps, you should be able to find all the best brands, including Vacheron & Constantin, Longines, Omega, and Blancpain, to name just a few. Sometimes there are discounts on such items as cameras. Most salespeople you'll encounter speak English and are very helpful.

A shopping spree may begin at **place du Molard,** once the harbor of Geneva before the water receded. Merchants from all over Europe used to bring their wares to trade fairs here in the days before merchants immigrated to richer markets in Lyon.

If you walk along rue du Rhône and are put off by the prices, go 1 block south to rue du Marché, which in various sections becomes rue de la Croix-d'Or and rue de Rive, and is sometimes referred to by locals as "la rue du Tram" because of the many trolleys that run along its length. Don't be afraid to comparison-shop in Geneva—many stores jack up prices for visitors.

Store hours vary in Geneva. Most stores are open Monday to Friday 8am to 6:30pm and Saturday from 8am to 5pm.

ANTIQUES

Ernest Schmitt and Co. Antiquities   This store beautifully displays English furniture in the ground-floor rooms of an 18th-century private house. Much of the furniture is from the 18th and 19th centuries, much of it English, and there's also a wide display of antique silver from the same era. Be sure to ask the owner to take you across the cobblestone courtyard to see the other showrooms. 3, rue de l'Hôtel-de-Ville. ✆ **022/310-35-40.**

AUCTIONS

The city has some of the world's most famous auction houses, with sales taking place mostly in May and November. During these periods, myriad social events accompany the auctions. Moreover, the city is an important center for the world art market and hosts prominent art and antiques dealers. Details and venues of sales appear in the tourist office's monthly "List of Events."

Antiquorum   This is the largest repository of antique timepieces in the world, with a reputation that's known to connoisseurs throughout the world. Virtually all of its inventory consists of antique jewelry and antique watches—a sure attraction in this city. Almost everything is sold at auction, rather than over the counter. The array of watches includes some of the most historically important watches in the world. 2, rue du Mont-Blanc. ✆ **022/909-28-50.**

Christie's   Geneva has always attracted some of the wealthiest tourists in the world, and to satisfy their craving for world-class art and antiques, they often attend the showcases and auctions of Christie's Auction House. Along with its leading competitor,

Sotheby's (see below), it's one of the most glamorous art and antiques emporia in Europe. 8, place de la Taconnerie. ✆ 022/319-17-66.

Sotheby's If there's a rare medieval triptych for sale, or a unique collection of 18th-century silver, it's likely to be auctioned at Sotheby's. Rivaled in glamour only by the company's branches in Paris and London, the Geneva branch offers an insight into some of the most unusual art and art buyers in town. 13, quai du Mont-Blanc. ✆ 022/908-48-00.

CHINA

Aux Arts du Feu Founded in 1897, this waterside store sells fine crystal, porcelain, china, silver, and decorative objects from around the world. 18, quai du Général-Guisan. ✆ 022/311-35-21.

CHOCOLATES

Confiserie Rohr The aroma from this chocolate store practically pulls you in off the street. Among other specialties, you'll find chocolate-covered truffles, "gold" bars with hazelnuts, and *poubelles au chocolat* (chocolate "garbage pails"). Another store is at 42, rue du Rhône. 3, place du Molard. ✆ 022/311-63-03. www.chocolats-rohr.ch.

CLOTHING

Addison This is the best menswear store within the sprawling, multilevel shopping mall known as the Confédération Centre. Inside, you'll find salesmen who tend to remember many of their former clients, a sense of personalized intimacy, and enough suits and blazers to outfit any of the well-tailored business meetings of Geneva. Confédération Centre, rue du Marché at place Bel-Air. ✆ 022/312-32-50.

Anita Smaga Its garments are as expensive as they are elegant, and its clientele includes some of the best-heeled women in the world. The look is grand chic couture (and haute couture), but, depending on your taste, there might be an accessory or two appealing to your sense of whimsy. 51, rue du Rhône. ✆ 022/310-26-55.

Chanel Whatever a woman's taste in clothes, and whatever her age, there's nothing that makes her look better than Chanel. Despite the passage of time, the look can usually be identified at a glance, and remains dear to the hearts of stylishly mature women everywhere. This branch in the heart of Geneva's most glamorous shopping district keeps the tradition alive. 43, rue du Rhône. ✆ 022/311-08-62.

DEPARTMENT STORES

Bon Genie Located on place du Molard, this department store sells mostly high-fashion women's clothing. Its storefront windows display art objects from local museums alongside designer clothes. There's also a limited selection of men's clothing, as well as furniture, cosmetics, and perfumes. 34, rue du Marché. ✆ 022/818-11-11.

Magazine zum Globus This is one of the largest department stores in Geneva, with many boutique-style departments that flourish inside and a self-image that's firmly patterned after the upscale Galeries Lafayette in Paris. Expect glamour, lots of upbeat cheerfulness, and departments devoted separately to travel bureaus, an agency selling theater tickets, a hairdresser, newspaper kiosks, and a bistro and sandwich shop/cafe. 48, rue du Rhône. ✆ 022/319-50-50.

GIFTS

Come Prima Our favorite Geneva shop benefits from a spectacular array of gift and leather items, as organized by a hardworking entrepreneur (Myriam Krieger-Demetriadès) whose personality permeates every aspect of the place. Officially, she runs a boutique loaded with top-quality leather bags and carry-alls, as well as one-of-a-kind wooden puzzles. There are also teddy bears from Germany, folk-style cushions embroidered in Hungary, hyperstylish umbrellas, and classically tasteful table decorations. 17, rue de la Cité (place Bémont). ℂ 022/310-77-79.

JEWELRY/WATCHES

Bucherer Located opposite the Mont Blanc Bridge, this chrome-and-crystal store sells deluxe watches and diamonds. The store offers such name brands as Rolex, Piaget, Ebel, Baume & Mercier, Omega, Tissot, Rado, and Swatch. The carpeted third floor is filled with relatively inexpensive watches. You'll also find a large selection of cuckoo clocks, music boxes, embroideries, and souvenirs, as well as porcelain pill boxes and other gift items. 45, rue du Rhône. ℂ 022/319-62-66. www.bucherer.com.

Gübelin Jewelers Dating from 1854, this family-run establishment is known mainly for its brand-name watches, although it also sells beautiful precious stones and jewelry in 18-karat gold. You'll see two perpetual-motion clocks in the windows, giving chronological as well as astrological time, with fanciful enamel notations of the different time zones. You can also buy reasonably priced gifts, such as pen and pencil sets. 1, place du Molard. ℂ 022/310-86-55.

LEATHER

Hermès Like all Hermès boutiques, this store sells purses, leather accessories, diaries, jewelry, watches, ready-to-wear clothing, furs, and, naturally, the famous Hermès scarf, priced at 370F ($303) each, and tie. Everything is beautifully handcrafted. 43, rue du Rhône. ℂ 022/819-07-19.

LINENS

Leinen Langenthal Established over a century ago, this store boasts an enviable reputation for good-quality merchandise and a showroom on the city's most prestigious shopping street, across from the Union des Banques Suisses. Merchandise includes napery, towels, bed linens, and "table suites," some of it embroidered by hand in the Swiss lace center of St. Gallen. 13, rue du Rhône. ℂ 022/310-65-10.

PICTURE FRAMES

Berndt Pierre *(Finds* Never judge a picture by its frame? That's not entirely true, according to this purveyor of antique frames, any of which could suitably adorn that old-master portrait you happened to pick up on your prior trip to Geneva. The store's buyers cull the auction houses of Europe for their inventory of antique lacquered, gilded, painted, carved, or silvered frames. Most frames range in price from 2,500F to 10,000F ($2,050–$8,200), although some simple unpretentious ones cost 125F ($103). Some of the frames at this shop are new but carefully distressed to look as antique as possible, and sell for a lot less money. 34-36, Grand-Rue. ℂ 022/311-74-85.

SHOES

Bruno Magli This is one of the best-stocked shoe stores in Geneva, with an elegant variety of Italian shoes, purses, and accessories. Shoes for both women and men are scattered over one floor, modeled in many ways on the outfit's Fifth Avenue showroom in New York City. 47, rue du Rhône. ℂ 022/311-53-77.

The Land of Time

August 8, 1535 The Protestant Reformation arrives in Geneva. A mob forcibly evicts the Catholic archbishop who, in his haste, forgets his watch. Today it's a prime exhibit in Geneva's watch-and-clock museum.

1541 In the wake of the Reformation, French-born Jean Calvin introduces the Protestant work ethic and welcomes exiled Protestant craftsmen from throughout Europe. Many are watchmakers and jewelers. Alas, ostentatious jewelry is outlawed in the tightly controlled new community, and jewelers' efforts must be funneled somewhere. No zealot ever claimed that a watch wasn't an essential part of any God-fearing man's wardrobe, so the ban against jewelry formed the base of what would eventually become the premier watchmaking center in the world.

1601 A watchmaker's guild enforces rules that regulate the industry. Obligations include public prayers before each assembly of the guild, and that each watch be signed or marked as the work of a specific craftsperson.

1707 A Swiss is appointed watchmaker to the court of the Chinese emperor K'ang-Hi in Peking. Swiss compatriots fan out across the globe, creating markets in places such as the Ottoman court in Istanbul, where business booms with baubles destined for the sultan's harem.

Around 1750 Julien Le Roy, celebrated Paris-based watchmaker to the king of France, complains bitterly that the watchmakers of Geneva are flooding southern France with "their accursed watches."

1780 Most of Geneva's St. Gervais district, behind the present-day Grand Hôtel des Bergues, and 5,000 employees are devoted to the town's biggest industry, watchmaking. The town's most expensive real-estate rentals are always on the fifth and sixth floors of cramped and narrow town houses, where the light is brightest. The neighborhood's most famous child? Jean-Jacques Rousseau, whose father trained him in Plutarch and the Roman classics by night and made watches by day.

1880 Gustav Flaubert, the greatest novelist of 19th-century France, compiles a list of pithy sayings *(Idées Réçues)*. His definition of "pocket watch" was "suitable only if it was made in Geneva."

Today Thousands of technical developments and a rigorous attention to quality have made Switzerland the leading watchmaker in the world, a title it has held for more than 400 years. Although Hong Kong and Japan produce greater numbers of watches today, Switzerland produces the greatest number of upscale watches and the most complicated watches, and receives an estimated 55% of all funds worldwide spent on consumer purchases of watches. In the 1990s Switzerland produced 98 million watches and watch movements worth $5.3 billion (U.S.) at wholesale. You can buy everything from watches worth a millionaire's ransom to "fun watches," "disposal watches," watches designed for deep-sea diving or parachute jumping, all kinds of chronometers and measuring devices, and—newest of all—eco-watches crafted from recycled aluminum cans.

SILVER

Au Vieux Canon   Its specialty is antique English silver, most of it crafted during the 19th and early 20th centuries, and most of it culled from estate sales held throughout the United Kingdom. Also look for 19th-century Viennese bronzes, depicting everything from Europe's great composers to whimsical nymphs waving garlands of flowers. Granted, you might be able to buy an equivalent item for less money if you haul it back from London, but the inventory is elegant and the setting is appropriately opulent. 40, Grand-Rue. (☎ 022/310-57-58. www.vieux-canon.ch.

TOBACCO

Davidoff   This is the most famous tobacco store in the world, with the best cigars you'll find in Europe. This is the place where the Davidoff retail empire all began. For many years, this was the business headquarters of Zino and Marthe Davidoff, White Russian émigrés who arrived in Switzerland in 1911. When they were in their 60s, with the help of a marketing expert (Dr. Schneider) from Basel, they eventually spearheaded a chain of upscale cigar stores that now extends throughout Europe and the Americas. 2, rue de Rive. (☎ 022/310-90-41. www.davidoff.com.

TOYS

Jouets Weber *(Kids)*   This member of a worldwide chain has been selling children's toys and adults' pastimes for at least 150 years from a location at the corner of rue de la Fontaine. Everything, from computer toys to simple playthings carved from wood by craftspeople in the Alps and Asia, is available. Adults appreciate such *jeux de société* (parlor games) as Pictionnari, priced at 60F ($39), which will improve both your social skills and your French-language vocabulary. 12, rue de la Croix-d'Or. (☎ 022/310-42-55.

8 Geneva After Dark

Geneva has more nightlife than any other city in Switzerland. Most activity centers around **place du Bourg-de-Four,** a stagecoach stop during the 19th century. In the Old Town there are lots of outdoor cafes in the summer.

For a listing of nightlife and cultural activities, free copies of the bilingual monthly *Genève Le Guide* (www.le-guide.ch) are distributed at hotel desks and tourist information centers.

THE PERFORMING ARTS

Geneva has always attracted the culturally sophisticated, including Byron, Jean-Baptiste, Corot, Victor Hugo, Balzac, George Sand, and Franz Liszt. Ernst Ansermet founded Geneva's great **Orchestre de la Suisse Romande,** whose frequent concerts entertain music lovers at **Victoria Hall.** For opera there's the 1,500-seat **Grand Théâtre,** which welcomes Béjart, the Bolshoi, and other ballet companies, in addition to having a company of its own.

For a preview of events at the time of your visit, pick up a copy of the monthly "List of Events" issued by the tourist office.

Grand Théâtre de Genève   Modeled on the Paris Opéra, this building was opened in 1879. It burned down in 1951 and was subsequently rebuilt in the same style, except for the modern auditorium, which has a seating capacity of 1,488. From September to July, its resident orchestra and dance company presents eight operas and two ballets, but many other outside companies stage recitals and chamber-music concerts. Place Neuve. ⓒ 022/418-31-30. www.geneveopera.ch. Tickets 31F–181F ($25–$148) for opera, 24F–130F ($20–$107) for ballet.

Victoria Hall   This 1,866-seat hall is the home of the celebrated Orchestre de la Suisse Romande, although it will be closed for part of 2006 for renovations. This is Geneva's most famous musical institution, whose interpretations have been heard throughout the world. For 50 years it was conducted by Ernst Ansermet and, through this maestro, had close associations with Igor Stravinsky. Be aware that, from mid-May through the end of 2006, the hall is closed for renovations. 14, rue du Général-Dufour. ⓒ 022/418-35-00. www.osr.ch. Tickets 10F–105F ($8.20–$86).

THE CLUB & MUSIC SCENE

Au Chat Noir *(Finds)*   In the suburb of Carouge, this is a venue for funk, rock, salsa, jazz, and some good old New Orleans blues. It's crowded on weekends but the club will take reservations. Live music is presented nightly at 9pm (10pm Fri–Sat). After a few drinks you begin to fear that the car suspended from the ceiling might fall in on you. Open Monday to Thursday from 6pm to 4am, Friday 6pm to 5am, Saturday 8pm to 5am, and Sunday 8pm to 4am. 13, rue Vautier, Carouge. ⓒ 022/343-49-98. Cover 16F–20F ($13–$16).

Club 58   This private club does allow nonmembers to enter, although men are required to wear jackets. It has become increasingly popular with people from the developing world, many of whom have settled more or less permanently in Geneva. Occasionally the club presents some top names in show business. Drinks in the club cost 19F–27F ($16–$22). Club 58 is mainly a disco, but it has a restaurant attached. Club opens daily at 7:30pm; restaurant opens at 8pm. 15, Glacis-de-Rive. ⓒ 022/735-15-15. Cover 7F–17F ($5.75–$14).

Griffin's Club   Griffin's is the chic choice in Geneva. Technically it's private—you may or may not get in, depending on the mood of the management at the time of your visit. If you're "correctly dressed" and "correctly behaved," you have a good chance, more likely Monday to Thursday. The popularity of nightclubs comes and goes, but the collection of celebrities who have traipsed here reads like a who's who from the tabloids. Jackets are required for men. The decor is red and black, with lots of live plants and large paintings in the restaurant where main courses are priced at 35F to 60F ($29–$49). Restaurant opens nightly 8pm until at least 3 or 4am. Disco open from 11pm to 5am. In July and August the entire premises are closed every Sunday and Monday. 36, bd. Helvétique. ⓒ 022/735-12-18.

Le Dancing de la Coupole   In one of the downtown area's most popular brasseries, La Coupole, this disco and dance hall focuses most intently on retro music of the 1960s. Whiskey begins at 16F ($13), beer at 9.50F ($7.80). Open Tuesday to Saturday from 5pm to 2am. 116, rue du Rhône. ⓒ 022/787-50-12.

L'Interdit   Hip and well organized, with just the slightest trace of cynicism, this is a well-known pickup bar where a gentleman who's looking for female companionship will probably find it. Security is tight, and the clientele is affluent (or at least it does a realistic imitation of appearing to be so) and international. There's a prominent bar area, a dance floor, and a decorative theme that includes cavorting nymphs, satyrs, and references to ancient Greece and Rome. Open nightly 10:30pm to 5am. 18, quai du Seujet. ⓒ 022/738-90-91. Cover 23F ($19), including 1st drink.

Velvet   Within its genre, this is a safe and well-recommended nightclub, especially popular with visitors, but it isn't for the timid. Unless you're an unusually brazen woman or firmly attached to an attentive male escort, it's more appropriate for men: It's very heterosexual, very permissive, and loaded with working women waiting for a visitor to buy them a drink. In most instances, its tawdrier aspects are rather artfully concealed, although that's a tall order for a place where, beginning around 11pm, as many as 32 topless international beauties begin strutting their stuff in a nonstop, informally choreographed spectacle that continues till around 5am. Despite the unadulterated promiscuity of the place, it lacks the artistic flair of Crazy Horse or Moulin Rouge in Paris. There's a restaurant and a disco on the premises, as well as a master/mistress of ceremonies who gives shape and form to the cabaret. Drinks begin at 20F ($16), but usually average around 25F ($21) each. Open nightly 10pm to 5am. Restaurant closed Sunday, but not the cabaret and bar. 7, rue du Jeu-de-l'Arc. ℭ 022/735-00-00. No cover Sun–Thurs, 12F ($9.85) Fri–Sat.

THE BAR SCENE

Most bars in Geneva close at 1:30 or 2am.

Le Francis Bar   This fashionable bar, often a venue for the *le tout Genève* or "cream of the crop" of Geneva, becomes an attractive piano bar in the evening. Whiskey with soda ranges from 19F to 26F ($16–$21). Live piano music begins at 10pm. 8, bd. Helvétique. ℭ 022/346-32-52.

Le Jardin *(finds)*   Although technically functioning as the aperitif bar for the adjacent restaurant, this place is an attractive option in its own right. Naturally, it attracts a chic and sometimes stuffy crowd, ranging from Texas ranchers to Zurich bankers to glamorous women in $50,000 furs. The Napoleon III decor includes crystal chandeliers and velvet chairs. In the Hôtel Richemond, Jardin Brunswick. ℭ 022/715-77-20.

Mr. Pickwick Pub *(Value)*   This pub serves simple, English-style meals, but most patrons come here to drink. The paneled rooms are filled in the evening with a young crowd, who enjoy the dim lighting and American music. The place gets very crowded and can be fun. Irish coffee is a specialty, but most visitors order beer. Because so many United Nations employees hang out here, this pub is sometimes called the "Tower of Babble." 80, rue de Lausanne (corner of rue Rothschild). ℭ 022/731-67-97.

THE GAY & LESBIAN SCENE

Geneva's gay switchboard is **Dialogai,** 11-13, rue de la Navigation (ℭ **022/906-40-40**). It provides multilingual information and advice to anyone who calls. On the basement level are a library, a cafe and bar, and meeting rooms for Wednesday-night dinners and Sunday-morning brunches. The organization publishes a free list of the gay bars in Geneva and French-speaking Switzerland, and is the best access to the male homosexual network of Geneva. It schedules discussion groups for gay youths and gay seniors, and it also offers support groups for people who are HIV positive.

   Le Kid, 99, bd. Carl-Vogt (ℭ **022/320-44-96**), is a popular gay-oriented cafe and restaurant specializing in vegetarian cuisine. In the university area, it is open all day. **Le Pretexte,** 9, rue du Prince (ℭ **022/310-14-28**), has a dance floor and two bars, plus a trio of areas with different themes, including Italian, Baroque, and Asian. It is the most visible gay disco in town. Big and highly visible within a commercial street on the lake's southern shore, it closes whimsically whenever there isn't enough biz, and—other than every Friday and Saturday—it has erratic hours.

9 Easy Excursions from Geneva

There are many attractions in the region around Geneva. Several of the most popular places—at least around the lake—have been covered in chapter 10, "Lausanne & Lake Geneva." Refer to that chapter for highlights around the lake itself. This section will deal with the attractions that are closest to Geneva.

MONT SALEVE 𝄞

The limestone ridge of Mont Salève (House Mountain) is 6.4km (4 miles) south of Geneva, in France. Its peak is at 1,200m (3,936 ft.), but you'll need a passport to get near it. If you have a car, you can take a road that goes up the mountain, which is popular with rock climbers. Bus no. 8 will take you to Veyrier-Douane, on the French border, where there's a passport and Customs control. A 6-minute cable-car ride will take you to a height of 1,125m (3,690 ft.) on Mont Salève. From there, you'll have a panoramic sweep of the Valley of the Arve, with Geneva and Mont Blanc in the background.

CAROUGE 𝄞

Carouge, a suburb of Geneva, is a historic European town. It dates from the 18th century, when it was built by the king of Sardinia to rival Geneva. Architects from Turin supplied the Piedmontese charm. At the Congress of Vienna, in 1815, Carouge was annexed to the canton of Geneva. Once Carouge was the playground of smugglers and gold washers who panned for the precious metal in the Arve. The Genevese themselves—at least those who wanted to escape from the puritanical city—came here in search of decadence.

Switzerland now considers Carouge a national landmark because of its architecture. It can be reached from Geneva by tram no. 11 from the center. Begin your exploration in the Market Square, with its old fountain, plane trees, and markets. A Roman stone was imbedded in the Church of the Holy Cross. As you walk around, you'll pass the court of the count of Veyrier's palace, dating from 1783; place du Temple, with a fountain from 1857; and a Louis XVI carved door at 18, rue St-Victor.

COLOGNY

Byron and Shelley both lived in the residential suburb of Cologny, where they met at the Villa Diodati in 1816. Fourteen kilometers (9 miles) northeast of Geneva, the suburb is served by both bus A and bus no. 33 from the city. The view of the lake and the city is especially good from the "Byron Stone" on chemin de Ruth (Ruth's Path) leading to the Byron fields.

The best time to go to Cologny is in the afternoon (Tues–Sun 2–6pm), when you can visit the **Bodmeriana Library,** 19-21, rte. du Guignard (✆ **022/707-44-33**), a foundation established by a Zurich millionaire named Martin Bodmer. Get off at the Cologny-Temple stop (bus A) or the Croisée de Cologny stop (bus no. 33) and view the private collection, which contains first editions, rare manuscripts such as the most ancient St. John's Gospel, and various other forms of art (sculpture, painting, and the like). Admission is 8F ($6.55) for adults, 5F ($4.10) for students and seniors, and free for ages 15 and under.

COPPET

Located 15km (9 miles) north of Geneva in the canton of Vaud, this little town on the western shore of Lake Geneva is one of the most interesting destinations in the region.

From Geneva's main station take the train on the Lancy Pont-Rouge–Genève–Coppet line for a 20-minute ride to the Château de Coppet in Coppet. Tickets cost 10F ($6.50) round-trip. If you're driving, head north from Geneva along Route 2.

Château de Coppet ☞ (© 022/776-10-28) attracted some of the greatest minds of the 18th and 19th centuries. The château, which sits on a hill beside the lake, between Lausanne and Geneva, was purchased in 1784 by Jacques Necker, the rich and powerful finance minister of Louis XVI. His daughter was Madame de Staël, a great French woman of letters, who was eventually sent into exile for her opposition to Napoleon. The château is still owned by Necker's descendants. The museum contains some mementos of Madame de Staël. From April through October, the château is open daily from 2 to 6pm (July–Aug also open daily 10am–noon). It's closed between November and March. Admission costs 8F ($6.55) for adults and 6F ($4.90) for students, seniors, and children 6 to 16. It's free for children 5 and under.

A noteworthy local hotel, an elegant place with only 14 units and a well-recommended restaurant, is the **Hôtel du Lac,** 51, Grand-Rue, CH-1296 Coppet (© **022/ 776-15-21**).

Lucerne & Central Switzerland

Lucerne (*Luzern* in German) and its lake lie in the heart of Switzerland, where the tops of the mountains are covered with eternal snow and their sides flanked with glaciers. We're in William Tell country now, where the seeds that led to the Swiss Confederation were sown. It was near Brunnen, in the meadow of Rutli, that the Everlasting League of 1315 was created.

Despite the presence of many small resorts in the neighborhood, Lucerne is the district's largest and busiest city. The lake that nurtures it is the fourth largest in Switzerland, 39km (24 miles) long and (at its broadest) 3km (2 miles) wide. Geologists refer to it as the terminal basin for the nearby glaciers. The lake is known in German as Vierwaldstättersee and in French as the Lac des Quatre Cantons. Either way, it's the lake of the four cantons: Lucerne, Uri, Unterwalden, and Schwyz (from which Switzerland derives its name).

Lucerne and its lake are among the most popular tourist destinations in all of Europe. Paddle-steamers service the many cable cars and lidos (beaches) set at the edge of the water, providing sweeping views of mountains with names like Pilatus and Rigi along the way. The region is rich in panoramas, folklore, and sports such as tobogganing, skiing, hill climbing, ice-skating, and curling. The irregular geography of the brusquely vertical limestone and granite outcroppings make the shoreline one of the most romantic sites in Switzerland.

1 Lucerne ★★★

50km (31 miles) S of Zurich; 90km (56 miles) E of Bern

Lucerne is a tourist favorite partly because it embodies the storybook image of a Swiss town. Located at the north end of the lake, the city abounds in narrow cobblestone streets, slender spires and turrets, covered bridges, frescoed houses, and fountains. Its residents are quick to tell you that you're "never very far from the snow"—Mounts Rigi and Pilatus form the southern gate to the city, and the snowcapped Alps loom in the distance.

Lucerne's strategic gateway to the south and the rich markets of Italy lie between Rigi and Pilatus. The city's history has always been tied to the St. Gotthard Pass. During the 13th century, the routes leading to it were simple mule paths. By 1820 the road had been widened enough to allow the easy passage of carriages. By 1882 Lucerne had a railway tunnel. Once a satellite vassal of the Hapsburgs, in 1332 Lucerne became the first city to join the Swiss Confederation. Unlike Geneva and Zurich, Lucerne did not support the Reformation and has always remained a stronghold of Catholicism.

The city is a renowned cultural center. Richard Wagner spent several of his most productive years in Tribschen, on the outskirts of Lucerne (there's a Wagner museum here). Arturo Toscanini was a founder of the Lucerne International Festival of Music, one of the most important musical events in Europe, which takes place annually in August and September.

The residents of Lucerne are a sports-oriented people. Every summer there are international rowing regattas on Rotsee. Swimmers go to the lido (lake beach) and golfers head for the 18-hole golf course on the outskirts. Other sports include tennis, hiking, and mountaineering. Residents seem especially fond of horse races, and there are plenty of international horse-jumping contests.

You'll find Lucerne at its best on Tuesday and Saturday mornings, when it becomes a lively market town. The markets are sheltered by stately arcades on both banks of the Reuss River.

ESSENTIALS

GETTING THERE   Lucerne lies at the junction of four major rail lines, which connect it by fast train with every other major city of Switzerland. Travel time from Bern on one of the many express trains is 90 minutes; from Zurich, 50 minutes. Call © **157-22-22** (no area code) for **rail schedules.**

If you're driving from Bern, take Route 10 north and east. From Zurich head south and west along E41, turning southwest and following the signs at the junction with N14.

VISITOR INFORMATION   The **Lucerne Tourist Office** is at Frankenstrasse 1 (© **041/227-17-17**). It's open in summer, Monday to Friday from 8:30am to 6pm, Saturday from 9am to 5pm, and Sunday from 9am to 1pm. During winter, hours are Monday to Friday 8:30am to noon and 2 to 5pm and Saturday 9am to 1pm.

CITY LAYOUT

Most arrivals are at the railroad station, on **Bahnhofplatz,** where trains pull in from Zurich and other parts of Switzerland. This train depot is on the south bank of the Reuss River.

If you cross a bridge from the station square, you'll be on the north bank at **Schwanenplatz (Swan Square),** which is the center of Lucerne. Also on the north bank of the Reuss is **Altstadt (Old Town),** containing many burghers' houses with oriel windows and old squares with fountains. The only way to explore this area is on foot.

Kapellgasse is a major shopping street that leads to the **Kornmarkt (Corn Market)** where you'll find the Altes Rathaus (Old Town Hall), dating from 1602. To the west of the Kornmarkt is the **Weinmarkt (Wine Market),** a lovely old square with a much-photographed fountain.

The Kursaal, a casino-and-restaurant complex, stands at Kurplatz on **Nationalquai,** the major quay of Lucerne facing the lake.

From Kurplatz, Löwenstrasse leads to **Löwenplatz,** site of the Panorama, a famed canvas depicting the retreat of the French army during the Franco-Prussian War (1870–71). Nearby stands the even-more-famous Löwendenkmal (Lion Monument), the town's best-known monument.

GETTING AROUND

Lucerne has an efficient network of local buses, one ride on which costs from 1.70F to 5.60F ($1.40–$4.60), depending on the distance you ride. Buy your tickets at automatic vending machines before you board. A ticket that's valid for 3 days costs 8F ($6.55); a ticket valid for a full week goes for 30F ($25). For more information about **bus routes** within Lucerne, call © **041/369-65-65.**

Bikes can be rented at the railway station for 30F ($25) per day June to September between 7am and 7:45pm daily; October to May Monday to Saturday 7am to 7:45pm, Sunday 9:30am to 7pm. A bike trip along the north shore of Lake Lucerne can be one of the scenic highlights of a visit to central Switzerland. This trip can easily absorb a whole day (take along a picnic lunch). The tourist office will provide a map and you can set off from the Lucerne train station heading for St. Niklausen and Kastanienbaum in the direction of Tribschen. If you have time, visit the Richard Wagner Museum. The most beautiful stretch is along the lake to Winkel-Horw beach, where you can go for a brisk lake swim if the temperature is right. The duration of this 13km (8-mile) ride, including the return to Lucerne, should take about 1½ hours.

SEEING THE SIGHTS

The best panoramas are the views from one of Lucerne's nine lookout towers. Part of the old fortifications erected along the north side of the medieval sector, they were all built in a different style between 1350 and 1408. At twilight they stand in dramatic silhouette against the sky. The nine towers are known as the **Museggturme,** but you can climb only three of them. Admission is free, and they're open only from May until the beginning of October from noon to 8pm daily. You can also take a short walk on the old outer wall of the city.

Although our only walking tour (see below) is for the independent traveler, guided walking tours are also available; see the tourist office (see "Visitor Information," above) for more details. These tours cost around 16F ($13). In summer tours depart Monday to Saturday (except holidays) at 9:45am; in winter tours are conducted only Wednesday and Saturday at 9:45am.

SPECIAL EVENTS

The **Lucerne Festival of Music** is held from the second week of August to the second week of September. For more information, contact the International Festival of Music, which also sponsors the **Easter Festival Lucerne,** another popular event (© **041/210-30-80;** http://e.lucernefestival.ch). There's also a **summer night festival** in mid-August with fireworks, music, and festivities along the lake, as well as an annual **Carnival** before Ash Wednesday.

WALKING TOUR	LUCERNE

Start:	Schwanenplatz.
Finish:	Kurplatz.
Time:	2½ hours.
Best Times:	Any sunny day.
Worst Times:	Rush hours, Monday to Friday from 8 to 9am and 5 to 6pm.

The best way to see Lucerne is on foot, going along its lakeside quays, across its old squares, and through the streets of its old town.

Start in the heart of Lucerne at:

❶ Schwanenplatz

Translated as Swan Square, it lies on the north bank of the Reuss River and is reached by crossing the bridge, the Seebrücke, from Bahnhofplatz on the south bank, site of the train station.

Adjoining the square on the west is:

❷ Kapellplatz

This is the site of St. Peter's Church. The church, the oldest in Lucerne, was built in 1178. In the center of the square is a fountain commemorating Carnival revelry in Lucerne.

From here, continue west along a major shopping street, Kapellgasse, until you reach the:

❸ Kornmarkt

This is the old Grain Exchange or "Corn Market," which is today the site of the:

❹ Altes Rathaus (Old Town Hall)

A Renaissance building from 1602, the town hall has impressive masonry, a tremendous roof, and a tall rectangular tower. The tower is a good vantage point from which to survey the crowded market scene on Tuesday and Saturday mornings.

To the left of the town hall is the:

❺ Am-Rhyn-Haus

This 17th-century building houses a Picasso collection (described below). The town house is entered at Furrengasse 21.

After leaving the museum, follow Rathausquai east toward Schwanenplatz again, but only to cross the:

❻ Kapellbrücke (Chapel Bridge)

The symbol of Lucerne, this covered wooden footbridge can be used to cross the Reuss River, leading to the south bank. Built in 1333, the bridge is 170m (558 ft.) long and crosses the river diagonally. It's one of the best-preserved wooden bridges in Switzerland, used originally for defense. There's also an octagonal Wasserturm (Water Tower), used variously as a prison, a torture chamber, and an archive. The bridge was always known for its 122 paintings that hung from its arched roof. Some of them were done in 1599 by Heinrich Wagmann, illustrating the daily activities and dress of the people. The bridge was damaged in a fire in 1993 and two-thirds of the original paintings were destroyed or severely damaged. Lucerne city officials

directed that copies be made. After a $2.1-million reconstruction, this landmark bridge was reopened in the spring of 1994.

You emerge onto Bahnhofstrasse; you can continue right (west) until you see the next covered bridge across the Reuss, the:

❼ Spreuerbrücke (Mills Bridge)

Built in 1407 and restored in the 19th century, this wooden bridge spans an arm of the Reuss. Its gables are painted with the Dance of Death, a mural by Kaspar Meglinger dating from the 17th century. The mural commemorates a plague that swept through the city.

Cross the bridge and take a sharp right to reach:

❽ Mühlenplatz (Mills Square)

This square dates from the 16th century. This was the old site of Lucerne markets.

From Mühlenplatz, walk down Kramgasse (to the east) to reach the:

❾ Weinmarkt (Wine Market)

Here you'll find a lovely old square with a fountain, west of Kornmarkt. Long ago the mystery play *Confraternity of the Crown of Thorns* was performed here. Among the colorful old dwellings on the square is the Müllersche Apotheke, a "drugstore" from 1530.

Directly northeast of the Weinmarkt lies:

❿ Hirschenplatz (Stag Square)

Another landmark square of Lucerne, it's filled with restored buildings, many of them with painted facades and wrought-iron signs. In 1779 Goethe stayed at the Goldener Adler, which is located here.

From Hirschenplatz, head east along Weggisgasse, which opens eventually onto Falkenplatz. From Falkenplatz, continue east along Hertensteinstrasse until you come to Löwenplatz. This is the site of:

⓫ Panorama

Panorama is one of the largest canvases in Europe, covering 1,009 sq. m (10,861 sq. ft.) and curving in a circle around a central platform. Painted in 1889 by Edouard

Walking Tour: Lucerne

finish here

start here

Lake Lucerne/Vierwaldstättersee

SWITZERLAND

Zurich
Lucerne
Basel
Bern
Geneva

Bahnhof-platz

Seebrücke

Kapellbrücke

Reussbrücke

Löwen-platz

Hofkirche

Bahnhof

Reuss

Historisches Museum

Château Gütsch

	Castle
	Church
	Train Station

1 Schwanenplatz
2 Kapellplatz
3 Kornmarkt
4 Altes Rathaus
  (Old Town Hall)
5 Am-Rhyn-Haus
6 Kapellbrücke
  (Chapel Bridge)
7 Spreuerbrücke
  (Mills Bridge)
8 Mühlenplatz
  (Mills Square)
9 Weinmarkt
  (Wine Market)
10 Hirschenplatz
  (Stag Square)
11 Panorama
12 Löwendenkmal
  (Lion Monument)
13 Kursaal
14 Hofkirche
  (Collegiate Church
  of St. Leodegar)
15 Kurplatz

100 yards
100 metres

Castres and contained in a round building that was designed especially for it, it depicts the bloody retreat of the French army into Switzerland during the Franco-Prussian War.

The next stop on this tour is not immediately visible from Löwenplatz but requires a brief detour north along Denkmalstrasse. Within about a block of Löwenplatz, high above your head you'll see one of the most famous statues in Switzerland, the:

⑫ Löwendenkmal (Lion Monument)

Carved in deep relief into the sandstone cliff above the town, the monument is an allegorical reference to the bravery of the Swiss Guards who died in the Tuileries of Paris in 1792 trying to save the life and honor of Marie Antoinette. During his grand tour of Europe, Mark Twain called the Dying Lion of Lucerne "the saddest and most poignant piece of rock in the world." Designed by the great Danish sculptor Bertel Thorvaldsen, the statue was dedicated in 1821.

Retrace your steps back to Löwenplatz, then head south along Löwenstrasse all the way to the lake and Kurplatz, a few steps east of Schwanenplatz, the site of the:

⑬ Kursaal

This spot is a casino-and-restaurant complex on Kurplatz on Nationalquai.

Above Nationalquai, view the twin towers of the Catholic:

⑭ Hofkirche (Collegiate Church of St. Leodegar)

Named after the patron saint of Lucerne, this is the most important church in the city. There was once a monastery at this site, but the present Gothic-Renaissance building dates from the 17th century. The interior has rich wrought-iron work, carvings, and a famous organ from 1640, with 4,950 pipes. Concerts are presented in the summer. The church also has a beautiful courtyard with arcades.

A good way to end the tour, you are now standing at:

⑮ Kurplatz

From here you can take in the best view of the lake from its northern rim. You can also take steamers from this area to visit various resorts along the lake. The view from here encompasses not only the lake but also the Alps from Rigi to Pilatus. The quays are lined with trees, hotels, and shops, ideal for exploring on foot. At the end of the promenade is the lido (beach), called Lucerne's "Riviera."

OTHER ATTRACTIONS

The Bourbaki Panorama   This is the world's best replica of a 19th-century bloodbath that reinforced Switzerland's role as a neutral (nonaligned) power, and that provided the first testing ground for the then-fledging Red Cross. It commemorates an incident in the Franco-Prussian War (1870–71) when the defeated French forces of General Charles Bourbaki (1816–97) fled out of France into Switzerland to avoid annihilation by the Germans. In Switzerland the starving, diseased, and disorganized French forces were disarmed by the Swiss army, then welcomed into homes throughout Switzerland for rest and recuperation from the brutal winter. Today the event is hailed as one of the finest acts of humanitarian courage in Swiss history, and celebrated in the form of this circular painting, completed in 1881, of the bloody battlefield. Originally conceived as a Barnum & Bailey–style tourist attraction in the 19th-century, the site was converted into an auto repair shop in 1925, and the painting was "shortened" in two separate incidents that ultimately removed about 3.6m (12 ft.) of gray sky from the top of the wraparound panorama. Between 1996 and 2003, the site was rebuilt, the painting cleaned, and the museum opened, with recorded narration, as a celebration of a genuinely bizarre but evocative interlude in European history. Be prepared for the recorded sounds of gunshots and cannons, dying men and horses, and a mournful but stirring account of wartime follies and heroism.

Löwenplatz 11. ℂ 041/412-30-30. www.bourbakipanorama.ch. Admission 8F ($6.55) adults, 7F ($5.75) seniors and students, 5F ($4.10) children 6–16, free for children under 6. Daily 9am–6pm. Tram: 1.

Gletschergarten (Glacier Garden)   This so-called glacier garden has 32 "potholes" that were worn into the sandstone bed of an Iron Age glacier, during the era when ice covered the surface of Lake Lucerne. Discovered and cleared of their debris in 1872, the holes measure up to 9m (30 ft.) wide and almost as deep. A museum at the site contains a famous 18th-century relief map of the Alps, prehistoric remains of plant and animal life, and a Swiss homeland museum. A 12-minute film is also shown to visitors.

Denkmalstrasse 4. ℂ 041/410-43-40. www.gletschergarten.ch. Admission 10F ($8.20) adults, 8.50F ($6.95) children, free for children under 6. Apr–Oct daily 9am–6pm; Nov–Mar daily 10am–5pm. Closed Feb 28. Bus: 1.

Historisches Museum Luzern (Museum of Swiss History)   Originally conceived as an arsenal for the storage of weapons in the 1560s, this building was reconfigured as a showplace for medieval and Renaissance art and sculptures in 1983. Adjacent to the surging river that flows through the center of town, this museum celebrates the arts and crafts that emerged from central Switzerland between around 1600 and 1900. One of the museum's centerpieces is the Gothic-style stone monument that once dominated the Wienerplatz, in the town center. (What you'll see there today is a copy.) Thanks to the solid wooden staircase that spirals its way around it, you'll get a close-up view of the stone-carved knights and cherubs that grace its pinnacle—a view that previously was visible only to birds. Other exhibits trace the development of Lucerne beginning around 1300. The top floor of the museum is reserved for special (i.e., temporary) exhibits, including an overview of the way 20th-century Swiss cartoons treat medieval and mystical themes.

Pfistergasse 24. ℂ 041/228-54-24. www.hmluzern.ch. Admission free; special exhibitions 10F ($8.20) adults, 8F ($6.55) seniors, free for children under 16. Tues–Sun 10am–5pm. Bus: 2.

Kunstmuseum (Fine Arts Museum)   The Fine Arts Museum includes many paintings by Swiss artists dating from the 16th century to the present. Ferdinand Hodler (1835–1918) is among those represented, as well as Dufy and Utrillo. The museum also presents changing exhibits of modern-day Swiss and international art. For information about current exhibitions and events, consult the daily press or ask at the tourist office.

Europaplatz 1. ℂ 041/226-78-00. www.kunstmuseumluzern.ch. Admission 10F–16F ($8.20–$13) adults, 8F–12F ($6.55–$9.85) seniors; 4F–7F ($3.30–$5.75) children. Tues and Fri–Sat 10am–5pm; Wed–Thurs 10am–8pm.

Neues Kunstmuseum (Modern Art Museum) ⋆   In the Kultur und Kongress Zentrum (KKZ) (Culture and Convention Center), this museum is the creation of Jean Nouvel, the most famous architect of France. In a setting near the rail station, he has created a futuristic environment for the display of mainly temporary exhibits, most of them avant-garde. There is also a permanent collection of works (which are rotated), ranging from the 15th to the 20th centuries.

The museum, in spite of a kind of neutrality, is nonetheless impressive in its architecture, especially when windows open onto panoramic vistas of urban space. In addition to a vast area to display art dramatically, there is also an art library with special literature and a spectacular terrace with views of the lake and the cityscape. Notices of the nature of temporary exhibitions are posted at the tourist office (see above).

Europaplatz 1. (*C*) **041/226-78-00.** www.kunstmuseumluzern.ch. Admission 10F–16F ($8.20–$13) adults, 4F–7F ($3.30–$5.75) students and children. Tues and Thurs–Sun 10am–5pm; Wed 10am–8pm.

Picasso Museum *☞* A small but choice collection of the works of Pablo Picasso is displayed on three levels, and includes paintings, drawings, original prints, sculpture, and ceramics from the last 20 years of the artist's life. The collection was a gift from Siegfried and Angela Rosengart, who presented the city of Lucerne on its 800th anniversary with eight masterpieces by Picasso, one for each century. Outstanding works include *Woman and Dog Playing* (1953), *Woman Dressing Her Hair* (1954), *The Studio* (1955), *Rembrandtesque Figure and Cupid* (1969), and a sculpture, *Woman with a Hat* (1961). The building, Am-Rhyn-Haus, was finished in 1618 in the Renaissance style by Walthard Am-Rhyn, mayor of Lucerne. It belonged to his descendants until 1946, when it became the property of the city.

In addition, the museum also displays some 200 of the most memorable photographs of David Douglas Duncan, one of the world's great photographers, who became famous for his combat photography of World War II for *Life* magazine. He also took countless photographs of Picasso.

Furrengasse 21. (*C*) **041/410-35-33.** Admission 8F ($6.55) adults, 5F ($4.10) children. Nov–Mar daily 11am–1pm and 2–4pm; Apr–Oct daily 10am–6pm. Bus: 1.

Richard Wagner Museum Wagner lived here from 1866 to 1872 and composed several works, including *Die Meistersinger.* Located about 3km (2 miles) from the city in the suburb of Tribschen, the museum contains some original scores and memorabilia, including letters and pictures. There's an exhibit of antique musical instruments in the summer.

Wagnerweg 27, Tribschen. (*C*) **041/360-23-70.** Admission 8F ($6.55) adults, 5F ($4.10) children. Daily 10am–noon and 2–5pm. Closed Nov 15–Feb. In summer motorboats leave every hour from in front of the railroad station (rail passes are valid for this trip). Bus: 6, 7, or 8 to Wartegg.

Verkehrshaus der Schweiz (Swiss Transport Museum) *☞☞☞* This museum is the best of its kind in Europe and very popular with foreign visitors. It's located beyond the Haldenstrasse cable-car station, lying more than a mile northeast of the center and accessible via bus. All forms of transportation, old and new, are on display, including railway cars, airplanes, automobiles, ships, and spaceships. Also on display is the oldest steamboat in the country, the Riga, built in 1847. The most popular exhibition is a scale model of a Swiss railway crossing the Gotthard Pass (a dozen trains move simultaneously). The museum has recently opened many new attractions, including new rail exhibits and an adventure ride called the Gotthard Tunnel Show.

The Longines Planetarium is at the eastern end of the complex. Here you can experience the constellations, a solar and lunar eclipse, and simulated space travel. Also attached to the transport museum is the Hans Erni House, containing artwork by this well-known native son. The museum has an IMAX theater as well.

Lidostrasse 5. (*C*) **041/370-44-44.** Admission 24F ($20) adults, 22F ($18) students and seniors, 12F ($9.85) children; IMAX/Museum combo tickets 32F ($26) adults, 32F ($26) students and seniors, 21F ($17) children. Apr–Oct daily 10am–6pm; Nov–Mar daily 10am–5pm. Bus: 6 or 8.

NEARBY ATTRACTIONS

There are dozens of half-day and full-day excursions from Lucerne—so many that we recommend you allow at least 5 days to see the city and its environs. There are several points of interest around Lake Lucerne. Most of them can be reached by paddle-steamer along the lake. While en route, you can enjoy a panoramic view of the water and mountains. Lake Lucerne (Vierwaldstättersee) winds its way 39km (24 miles) into the alpine ranges of the heart of Switzerland. Many excursions can be combined with a trip to the top of a mountain by cable car or funicular. Summer is the peak season.

Schiffahrtsgesellschaft Vierwaldstättersee (Lake Lucerne Navigation Co.; ✆ 041/367-67-67; www.lakelucerne.ch) operates a flotilla of lake steamers that chug across the surface of Lake Lucerne, much to the delight of sightseers, who appreciate the steep mountains rising on all sides. Round-trip passage from Lucerne to the lake's most distant point, Flüelen (a 4-hr. round-trip) costs 70F ($57) in first class, 48F ($39) in second class, and departs from the quays opposite the Hauptbahnhof in Lucerne. In midsummer departures begin at 9:15am and continue every hour or so throughout the day. Wherever you decide to disembark en route, find out the departure time of the last boat back to Lucerne. Usually, the last boat from Flüelen departs before 4:20pm. All boats have a restaurant, or at least a cafeteria, onboard.

The **William Tell Express** offers an opportunity to see regions of German- and Italian-speaking Switzerland in one full-day excursion. Between May 12 and October 24, it transports participants, as part of a 6-hour travel experience, from Lucerne, via Lugano, to Locarno. Begin with a 3-hour boat ride from Lucerne to the lakeside hamlet of Flüelen, then hop aboard a special train for a continuation of the trip across some of the most jagged and precipitous mountain scenery in the world. Seats in the first-class compartments have wider windows and skylights, while those in the less comfortable second-class cars are slightly less panoramic. A three-course meal, served aboard the lake steamer during the first part of the journey, is included in the one-way (Lucerne to Locarno) price of 85F ($70) in first class and 80F ($66) in second class. Reservations, preferably several days in advance, are vital. To make them, and get more information, call ✆ 041/367-67-67. If you opt for a round-trip ticket from Lucerne to Locarno and then back to Lucerne, we advise spending at least 1 night in the Ticino before returning back to Lucerne. Round-trip tickets (Lucerne-Locarno-Lucerne) cost 215F ($176) in first class and 130F ($107) in second.

SHOPPING

Few other cities in Switzerland rely as heavily on the tourist trade as Lucerne, so consequently, you'll be faced with a barrage of mercantilism at virtually every street corner. Most obvious of the "heavy artillery" involves sales of wristwatches and folk handicrafts. The biggest jeweler in town is **Bucherer,** Schwanenplatz 5 (✆ 041/369-77-00), whose sprawling displays of luxury goods are rivaled only by the showrooms of **Gübelin,** Schweizenhofquai (✆ 041/429-15-15). Less consciously upscale, and more folkloric in their orientation, are the town's main outlets for handicrafts. These include **Casa Grande,** Kapellgasse 24 (✆ 041/418-60-60); **Schmid-Linder,** Denkmalstrasse 9 (✆ 041/410-43-46); and **Leinen,** Weinmarkt 19 (✆ 041/410-44-33), which inventories clothing for men and women that will evoke Heidi, her grandfather, and her goatherd, Peter. Embroideries and linens for dining rooms and bedrooms are the offerings at **Sturzenneger,** Schwanenplatz 7 (✆ 041/410-19-58). Some of the pieces come from Switzerland's embroidery center of St. Gallen, others from less evocative factories in the Far East, but many are of heirloom quality.

Souvenirs of your trip to Lucerne are a lot less expensive, and a lot more workaday, at either of the town's two mass-market department stores. They are **Manor, Nordmann & Co.,** Weggisgasse 5 (✆ 041/419-76-99); and **EPA,** Rössligasse 20 (✆ 041/410-19-77). Both sell housewares, clothing, school supplies, and anything you'd need to run a home. They also have a limited collection of Swiss souvenirs. More upscale, and more specifically geared to clothing for men, women, and children, is **Globus,** Pilatusstrasse 4 (© **041/227-07-07**).

Hofstetter & Berney, Schweizerhofquai 6 (© **041/410-31-06**), features a well-rounded collection of music boxes. The staff will tell you about the differences in tones and the complexities of sounds produced by the various instruments, all of which are made in Switzerland and which contain varying numbers of musical notes. Some of them might reproduce strains from Pachelbel's Canon, others a replica of the "Austrian National Anthem."

Confiserie H & M Kurmann, Bahnhofstrasse 7 (© **041/210-19-187**), is the most distinguished pastry-and-chocolate shop in Lucerne. Many of the residents of Lucerne remember this shop from their childhoods, when its pastries and chocolates might have been served as part of their birthday parties. Today it's one of the few deeply entrenched big-name pastry makers in Switzerland that hasn't set up additional branches in other parts of the country. Everything is, as you'd expect, highly caloric and highly tempting.

The richly nuanced architecture of the city itself is the backdrop for the outdoor **fruit and vegetable market,** conducted during spring, summer, and autumn from both banks of the river every Tuesday and Saturday from 8am to around 1pm. Between May and October, Lucerne hosts a rowdy, somewhat disorganized **flea market** where the contents of estate sales and whatever anyone discovered in their grandmother's attic is displayed along either side of Untere Burgerstrasse. And the first Saturday of every month throughout the year, during daylight hours, artisans and craftspeople from throughout the region congregate at the **Weinmarkt** to display and sell their wares.

WHERE TO STAY

Lucerne is one of the most visited cities of Switzerland, with a wide range of hotels. But they're mostly expensive and moderate; there's a shortage of good budget hotels. Reservations are very important in the summer, when hordes of Europeans and North Americans pour into this town.

VERY EXPENSIVE

Grand Hotel National ✦✦✦ This is a monumental landmark and the former home base of Cesar Ritz. It's the most appealing hotel in Lucerne, much less stiff than the more famous but somewhat chilly Switzerland. Built "in the style of the French kings," this legend among Swiss hotels has a huge facade of gray stone, with a mansard roof and dozens of gables. Constructed in 1870, when visitors were just beginning to discover Lake Lucerne, it looks like a wing of the château at Versailles. Guests have included monarchs and diplomats from all over Europe. Between 1977 and 1980, the owner reconstructed this grand palace and installed modern conveniences. The main lobby is stately and elegant, one of the grandest in Lucerne. The predictably varied bedrooms are among the most comfortable and luxurious in the city, with thick carpets and old-fashioned charm, often with a four-poster canopied bed. Many have private balconies with a view of the lake. The bathrooms are opulent in white marble.

Haldenstrasse 4, CH-6002 Luzern. © **041/419-09-09.** Fax 041/419-09-10. www.national-luzern.ch. 40 units. 345F–490F ($283–$402) double; 720F–980F ($590–$804) suite. AE, DC, MC, V. Parking 35F ($29). Bus: 6 or 8. **Amenities:** 3 restaurants; bar; indoor pool; sauna; limited room service; massage; babysitting; laundry service/dry cleaning. *In room:* TV, minibar, hair dryer, safe.

Schweizerhof Luzern *⋐ (Overrated* Although it has its admirers, this hotel is formal and opulent but a bit stiff. In our view, Grand Hotel National is just as elegant and a lot more appealing. Nonetheless, the Schweizerhof remains a longtime favorite of many travelers ever since it opened in 1844. The Hauser family has owned this 19th-century "palace" since 1861 and reopened it again in 1999 following extensive remodeling and renovations. It has extended a welcome to such former guests as Napoleon III, Leo Tolstoy, Richard Wagner, and Mark Twain. It consists of three symmetrical white buildings connected by arched passageways lining the lake for at least 2 blocks; one of the buildings is rented as office space. The lobby has pink marble columns and pilasters and a cream-colored ceiling with plaster details. The Belle Epoque–style bedrooms are spacious and well furnished, and have well-maintained bathrooms. Try for a room, if possible, with a view of Lake Lucerne and the surrounding alpine range.

Schweizerhofquai 3, CH-6002 Luzern. ℂ **041/410-04-10.** Fax 041/410-29-71. www.schweizerhof-luzern.ch. 107 units. Apr–Oct 400F–550F ($328–$451) double, 600F–840F ($492–$689) suite; Nov–Mar 310F–420F ($254–$344) double, 500F–710F ($410–$582) suite. AE, DC, MC, V. Parking 25F ($21) in garage. Bus: 1 or 24. **Amenities:** 2 restaurants; bar; 24-hr. room service; babysitting; laundry service/dry cleaning; nonsmoking rooms; rooms for guests w/limited mobility. *In room:* A/C, TV, dataport, minibar, hair dryer, safe.

EXPENSIVE

Art Deco Hotel Montana *⋐⋐* This is one of the best government-rated four-star hotels in central Switzerland. This neoclassic hotel was originally built in 1911 as a private villa high on a hillside overlooking the lake. In the 1960s a modern extension was added with cozy bedrooms, most of which offer views. A private funicular, departing from a point near the edge of the lake, carries clients of the hotel or its restaurants uphill to the hotel's entrance. The interior public rooms would please your Victorian great-great-grandmother, with their old-fashioned appeal of Oriental rugs, swag curtains, brocaded antique chairs and settees, and polished paneling, along with a good infusion of Art Deco styling. The bedrooms, however, are modernized, although with traditional styling, and are comfortable with firm beds and neatly kept bathrooms.

Adligenswilerstrasse 22, CH-6002 Luzern. ℂ **0800-55-23-44** in the U.S. or 041/419-00-00. Fax 041/419-00-01. www.hotel-montana.ch. 62 units. Apr–Oct 320F–440F ($262–$361) double, from 550F ($451) junior suite; off season 310F–380F ($254–$312) double, from 450F ($369) junior suite. Rates include buffet breakfast. AE, DC, MC, V. Free parking. Bus: 6 or 8. **Amenities:** Restaurant; bar; limited room service; babysitting; laundry service/dry cleaning; nonsmoking rooms; rooms for guests w/limited mobility. *In room:* TV, dataport, minibar, hair dryer.

Best Western Premier Hotel Des Balances *⋐* This tranquil government-rated four-star hotel, directly on the Reuss River, also faces the most colorful square in town, an 8-minute walk from the rail station. The elaborate gray-stone building has lots of curlicue wrought-iron balconies; the interior has high ceilings and Oriental rugs. Following massive renovations to both its interior and its facade, the hotel has emerged as one of the finest in its price range in Lucerne. Your room, likely to be decorated in soothing pastels with a freshly tiled bathroom, will open either onto a picture-postcard view of the river or (if in the rear) the historic Weinmarkt. If you're seeking a room in Altstadt, make it the Balances. Guests are permitted to drive to the hotel even though it lies in a pedestrian zone.

There's a great view of the city from the popular riverside cafe. The hotel restaurant, Rotes Gatter, is recommended separately (see "Where to Dine," later in this section).

Weinmarkt, CH-6000 Luzern. ℂ **800/780-7234** in the U.S. and Canada or 041/418-28-28. Fax 041/418-28-38. www.balances.ch. 60 units. Apr–Oct 370F–405F ($303–$332) double, 560F ($459) suite; off season 290F–330F

($238–$271) double, 450F ($369) suite. Rates include buffet breakfast. AE, DC, MC, V. Parking 25F ($21). Bus: 1. **Amenities:** Restaurant; bar; lounge; limited room service; babysitting; laundry service/dry cleaning; nonsmoking rooms. *In room:* TV, dataport, minibar, hair dryer, safe.

The Hotel ★★★ *Finds*   In a panoramic setting in the center of the city, this is a luxurious boutique hotel, the most exclusive in Lucerne. Famed French architect Jean Nouvele designed it. Although familiar to London, this type of urban boutique hotel is new to Switzerland. Called simply "The Hotel," it is luxury personified, yet there is an artful simplicity to it. From the custom-designed furnishings in wood and steel to the luscious, avant-garde cinema scenes on the guest-room ceilings, every aspect of the hotel reflects Nouvele's unique touch. Some two dozen studios and suites are spread across the seven-story building. Preferred are five corner junior suites with park views on both sides. Other options include garden and park luxe suites with patio, and luxe studios with park views. Nouvele achieves his dream of "combining spirituality with elegance into a timeless design—not a matter of decor but of lifestyle."

The bathrooms are among the most luxurious in Lucerne, sexy and cool, and bamboo lovers can book a deluxe suite with a private patio planted with this exotic species—you can shower in a bamboo jungle.

French tradition with Asian refinement are reflected in the cuisine of the stylish Bam Bou restaurant.

Sempacherstrasse 14, CH-6002 Lucerne. © **041/226-86-86**. Fax 041/226-86-90. www.the-hotel.ch. 25 units. 350F–480F ($287–$394) double; from 540F ($443) suite. AE, DC, MC, V. **Amenities:** Restaurant; bar; 24-hr. room service; babysitting; laundry service/dry cleaning; rooms for guests w/limited mobility. *In room:* A/C, TV, dataport, minibar, hair dryer, safe.

Hotel Hermitage ★ *Finds*   In 1990 a run-down older hotel was demolished and in its place arose this modern lakeside building with its own private beach. The Hermitage's pink-painted walls contain spacious doubles and junior suites. Each unit has a lakefront view, a private balcony, and a tastefully modern decor featuring rattan furniture. All units also contain neatly kept bathrooms. Set in a flowering suburb 4km (2½ miles) east of the center of Lucerne, the hotel (rated four stars by the Swiss government) has a cafe-terrace beside the water.

Seeburgstrasse 72, CH-6006 Luzern-Seeburg. © **041/375-81-81**. Fax 041/375-81-82. www.hotel-hermitage.ch. 50 units. May–Oct 380F ($312) double, 410F ($336) junior suite; Nov–Apr 270F ($221) double, 310F ($254) junior suite. Rates include continental breakfast. AE, DC, MC, V. Free parking. Bus: 24. **Amenities:** 2 restaurants; bar; lounge; tennis court; limited room service; laundry service/dry cleaning. *In room:* TV, dataport, minibar, hair dryer, safe.

Hotel Monopol ★   Built in 1898, this grand hotel has a carved limestone facade, wrought-iron balconies, half columns, and elaborately detailed windows. Its central location is convenient for the rail station or the lake. The midsize rooms are individually furnished; some are modern and others have paneling, alcove beds, and chalet chairs. All come equipped with tidy bathrooms.

Pilatusstrasse 1, CH-6002 Luzern. © **041/226-43-43**. Fax 041/226-43-44. www.hotel-monopol.com. 73 units. Apr–Oct 340F ($279) double; Nov–Mar 270F ($221) double. Rates include buffet breakfast. AE, DC, MC, V. Bus: 1. **Amenities:** Restaurant; bar; limited room service; babysitting; laundry service/dry cleaning; rooms for guests w/limited mobility. *In room:* TV, minibar, hair dryer.

MODERATE
Grand Hotel Europe   A neoclassical pediment graces the white facade of this 19th-century hotel lying 1.5km (1 mile) east of the center on the north shore of the lake. There's a row of awnings sheltering the public rooms, which face a garden. The salons

contain large tapestries, Oriental rugs, and comfortable couches and chairs. Most of the rooms are spacious and well furnished, each with a firm bed and well-maintained plumbing. All units have neatly kept bathrooms.

Haldenstrasse 59, CH-6002 Luzern. ℂ **041/370-00-11.** Fax 041/370-10-31. www.europe-luzern.ch. 174 units. 300F–400F ($246–$328) double. Rates include buffet breakfast. AE, DC, MC, V. Free parking. Closed Nov–Mar. Bus: 2. **Amenities:** Restaurant; bar; limited room service; babysitting; laundry service/dry cleaning; rooms for guests w/limited mobility. *In room:* TV, dataport, hair dryer, safe.

Hotel Astoria ⓡ

This first-class modern hotel boasts prominent horizontal rows of windows and a desirable location in the center of Lucerne, a 5-minute walk from the lake. The hotel is often patronized by business travelers and groups drawn to its modern, streamlined, and no-nonsense atmosphere. Well maintained and well respected, this hotel was built in three separate phases: Its main core dates from 1957, and in the mid-1970s and again in 1998, two separate enlargements were added to the hotel's (quieter and calmer) back side. On-site is a hugely popular and trendy club and disco on the upper floor called The Penthouse. The subdued interior of the hotel is decorated with furniture and accessories evocative of Thailand. Each of the well-furnished rooms has a firm bed and a clean bathroom.

Pilatusstrasse 29, CH-6003 Luzern. ℂ **041/226-88-88.** Fax 041/210-42-62. www.astoria-luzern.ch. 180 units. 200F–340F ($164–$279) double; 230F–370F ($189–$303) suite. Rates include buffet breakfast. AE, DC, MC, V. **Amenities:** 3 restaurants; 2 bars; nightclub; limited room service; babysitting; laundry service/dry cleaning; rooms for guests w/limited mobility. *In room:* TV, dataport, hair dryer.

Hotel des Alpes

Set in Lucerne's historic core, this hotel lies in the pedestrian zone. It was originally built around 1740 as an inn for travelers. Today, behind a tall and narrow facade with restrained baroque detailing, the beneficiary of a radical overhaul, it continues to welcome visitors into its premises. Although the public rooms retain their old-fashioned charm, most of the midsize bedrooms have been streamlined and filled with vinyl and laminated pieces in the roadside-motel tradition. Rooms in the rear open onto Altstadt, and those on the upper floors sometimes have views over the low skyline of Lucerne. All of the units contain neatly kept bathrooms.

Though parking is not available on the premises, guests can leave their cars across the river at the railway station, a 5-minute walk from the hotel.

Furrengasse 3, CH-6004 Luzern. ℂ **041/410-58-25.** Fax 041/410-74-51. www.desalpes-luzern.ch. 45 units. Apr–Oct 190F–276F ($156–$226) double; Nov–Mar 160F–234F ($131–$192) double. Rates include continental breakfast. AE, DC, MC, V. Bus: 1, 2, 6, 7, or 8. **Amenities:** 2 restaurants; limited room service; laundry service/dry cleaning. *In room:* TV, dataport, minibar.

Hotel Krone

Despite the lushly baroque facade of this middle-bracket hotel, its bedrooms are simple, well organized, and contemporary looking. This is the result of a radical renovation in the early 1990s that ripped apart the interior of the five-story building. The Hotel Krone is solidly positioned on one of the city's most charming medieval squares, in a neighborhood that shows off Lucerne's architectural personality. Bedrooms in back are slightly bigger than those overlooking the Weinmarkt in front, which have better views and a more intense sense of history. Each unit comes with a neatly kept private bathroom; the third floor is for nonsmoking guests. Don't expect a deeply entrenched sense of luxury, or even a particularly large or opulent-looking lobby: In this case, the space was devoted instead to accommodations. No alcohol is served within the hotel, but there are plenty of bars and restaurants within a short walk.

Weinmarkt 12, CH-6004 Luzern. ℭ 800/528-1234 in the U.S. or 041/419-44-00. Fax 041/419-44-90. www.bestwestern. ch/kroneluzern. 25 units. 200F–440F ($164–$361) double. Rates include breakfast. AE, DC, MC, V. Bus: 1 or 2. **Amenities:** Restaurant; laundry service/dry cleaning; nonsmoking rooms; rooms for guests w/limited mobility. *In room:* TV, dataport, minibar, hair dryer, safe.

Hotel Schiller ⟨⟨

Although it's surrounded by other antique buildings near the railway station, the Schiller stands out with its 19th-century details and colorful awnings above the entrance. It's favored by business travelers who want to be in the commercial center of town, close to the railway station. The interior has many fine touches, including an ample use of white marble. Each midsize room in this comfortable hotel is different; the most modern are on the fifth and sixth floors, while the more traditional fill the lower levels. The front rooms can be noisy at times. Many nonresidents patronize the hotel's drinking and eating facilities.

Pilatusstrasse 15, CH-6002 Luzern. ℭ 041/226-87-87. Fax 041/227-87-90. www.schiller-luzern.ch. 80 units. Apr–Oct 300F–320F ($246–$262) double, 350F ($287) suite; Nov–Mar 200F ($164) double, 220F ($180) suite. Rates include buffet breakfast. AE, DC, MC, V. Bus: 1. **Amenities:** 2 restaurants; 2 bars; babysitting; laundry service/dry cleaning. *In room:* TV, dataport, hair dryer, safe.

Hotel Zum Rebstock ⟨⟨ *Finds*

This is a historic landmark. The foundations of this hotel date from the 12th century, when the site, west of the Hofkirche and south of the Panorama, was the setting for a monastery. Surrounded by vineyards, the half-timbered building has green shutters with a brown-tile roof. In 1443 it was the headquarters of the winegrowers' guild; later it was used as a recruitment center for the Swiss mercenaries who came from this region. The rooms are small but cozily comfortable, each outfitted in a different color and decorative motif. All units contain well-maintained bathrooms. The inn offers two restaurants serving both Swiss regional dishes and international platters.

Sankt-Leodegar-Platz 3, CH-6004 Luzern. ℭ 041/410-35-81. Fax 041/410-39-17. www.hereweare.ch. 30 units. 260F–295F ($213–$242) double. Rates include buffet breakfast. AE, DC, MC, V. Parking 16F ($10). Bus: 1, 2, or 7. **Amenities:** 3 restaurants; bar; limited room service; laundry service/dry cleaning. *In room:* TV, dataport, minibar, hair dryer, safe.

Magic Hotel

Centrally located in Luzern, this hotel offers unique and often amusingly decorated bedrooms. Each room and suite is individually decorated so that no two rooms are alike and you can choose one that fits your personality and taste. The Angel Suite has a Victorian-era elegance, while the Lotus Room utilizes Asian influences and art. Some of the rooms go a little over the top with the decor, such as the tacky Egyptian Suite, which has a large mural of a pharaoh and his two servants over the bed. The Pirate Suite is over the top in a fun way, with the bed in the shape of a ship and a statue of a pirate. Kids would enjoy both rooms but adults might find them a bit tawdry. Rooms with a more tasteful decor are the Swiss Chalet and the Lion-Heart Suite.

Brandgässli 1. CH-6004 Luzern. ℭ 041/417-12-20. Fax 041/417-12-21. www.magic-hotel.ch. 8 units. 200F–290F ($164–$238) double; 290F–350F ($238–$287) suite. AE, DC, MC, V. **Amenities:** Restaurant (lunch and breakfast only); laundry service; nonsmoking rooms. *In room:* TV, dataport, minibar, safe.

Romantik Hotel Wilden Mann ⟨⟨⟨⟨

This is the best choice for the nostalgia buff. Around 1900 a local entrepreneur, operating from the core of an early-16th-century tavern, began slowly but systematically buying up the historic real estate around him. The result you'll see today incorporates seven antique houses—the oldest dating from 1517—into a well-orchestrated whole. Inside, a confusing but charming labyrinth of hallways, many accented with exposed stone and beams, and, in some cases, with artfully old-fashioned paneling, lead to the cozy bedrooms. All rooms are well maintained and have neatly kept bathrooms. Here, warm colors and a sense of yesteryear combine with modern extras for winning four-star comforts.

Even if you don't stay here, consider a meal in the artfully rustic dining room (see "Where to Dine," below).

Bahnhofstrasse 30, CH-6007 Luzern. ✆ **041/210-16-66.** Fax 041/210-16-29. www.wilden-mann.ch. 50 units. May–Oct 335F–380F ($275–$312) double, 430F ($353) junior suite; Nov–Apr 265F–300F ($217–$246) double, 340F ($279) junior suite. Rates include breakfast. AE, DC, MC, V. Bus: 2. **Amenities:** 3 restaurants; limited room service; babysitting; laundry service/dry cleaning; nonsmoking rooms. *In room:* TV, dataport, minibar, hair dryer.

INEXPENSIVE

Hotel Alpha   This severe-looking, white-fronted building is a 10-minute walk from the city center and rail station, near Pilatusplatz. Renovated many times since its original construction, it's one of the simplest hotels in town, offering well-scrubbed but small bedrooms with few extras and modest furnishings, although the mattresses are firm. Those units containing private bathrooms are in most cases equipped with tub/shower combinations. On the premises are two lounges, each with a TV set and a collection of newspapers.

Zähringerstrasse 24, CH-6003 Luzern. ✆ **041/240-42-80.** Fax 041/240-91-31. 66 units, 10 with bathroom. 105F ($86) double without bathroom, 128F ($105) double with bathroom; 135F ($111) triple without bathroom; 170F ($139) quad without bathroom. Rates include buffet breakfast. AE, MC, V. Bus: 1 or 2 to Pilatusplatz. **Amenities:** Breakfast room; bike rental; nonsmoking rooms. *In room:* No phone.

Pension Panorama *(Value*   One of the better bargains in Lucerne, this angular, four-story hotel, built in the 1970s, is on a hill with a sweeping view of the lake and mountains. It's a 10-minute walk from the center of the Old Town. The small rooms are reasonably comfortable and well maintained, although simply and functionally furnished. There's a communal bathroom with tub/shower combination for every four bedrooms. Only breakfast is served, but there's a kitchen for guests to prepare snacks.

Kapuzinerweg 9, CH-6006 Luzern. ✆ **041/420-67-01.** Fax 041/420-67-30. www.pensionpanorama.com. 13 units, 1 with bathroom. 70F–90F ($57–$74) double without bathroom; 120F ($98) double with bathroom. Rates include continental breakfast. MC, V. Free parking. Bus: 4 or 5 to Felsberg. **Amenities:** Breakfast room; nonsmoking rooms. *In room:* TV, no phone.

Pension Villa Maria *(⊀* *(Finds*   Set in a charming garden near the north shore of the lake, this family-run villa was built in 1955 and is today owned by members of the Winkler family. Part of the experience is the welcome they offer in this chalet-inspired private home with comfortably cluttered public rooms decorated in shades of red, gold, and pink. The rooms—all doubles—are clean, spacious, and comfortable with excellent beds. The establishment is located about half a mile from the center of Lucerne.

Haldenstrasse 36, CH-6002 Luzern. ✆ and fax **041/370-21-19.** 10 units, 4 with bathroom. 130F ($107) double without bathroom, 160F ($131) double with bathroom. Additional bed in room 35F ($23) extra. Rates include buffet breakfast. AE, MC, V. Free parking. Closed Nov–Feb. Bus: 6. **Amenities:** Breakfast room; limited room service; babysitting; nonsmoking rooms. *In room:* Dataport (in some), hair dryer.

Tourist Hotel   This budget hotel with a sage-green facade stands beside the river, a 10-minute walk from the train station. The hotel attracts young people and families to its rooms. Nine conventional units can accommodate up to four beds, and communal dormitory-style rooms are also available that contain between 4 and 10 beds each, usually stacked as bunk beds. The furnishings are in a basic, functional modern style. Many of the rooms open onto a view of the river and the faraway mountains of Pilatus and Titlis. Rooms with private bathrooms have clean quarters and mostly contain tub/shower combinations. All units have hot and cold running water. There's a dining room as well as a lounge on the premises. Because the hotel lies in a pedestrian zone, it's hard to find parking.

St. Karliquai 12, CH-6004 Luzern. ⓒ 041/410-24-74. Fax 041/410-84-14. www.touristhotel.ch. 40 units, 8 with bathroom; 28 dormitory beds. 80F–112F ($66–$92) double without bathroom, 100F–160F ($82–$131) double with bathroom; 114F–138F ($93–$113) triple without bathroom, 150F–200F ($123–$164) triple with bathroom; 140F–180F ($115–$148) quad without bathroom, 180F–240F ($148–$197) quad with bathroom; 33F–40F ($27–$33) dorm bed. Those with ISIC card get a 5%–10% discount. Rates include buffet breakfast. AE, MC, V. Bus: 2 or 9. **Amenities:** Breakfast room; lounge; self-service laundry. *In room:* TV, no phone.

Zum Weissen Kreuz Parts of this antique inn date from the 1400s, and although a complete renovation of the premises modernized everything, the site still exudes a nostalgic sense of yesteryear. The small bedrooms are scattered over five floors connected by an elevator, and in some cases a scattering of old-fashioned, turn-of-the-20th-century furnishings can be found. All units have tidily kept bathrooms equipped with shower stalls. Its location near the Picasso Museum and the Kornmarkt adds to its appeal. Behind its white-fronted exterior lies the unpretentious Al Forno restaurant and pizzeria. *Warning:* Don't look for the entrance of this hotel on Furrengasse, as it's positioned on the side street, Badergasse.

Furrengasse 19 (entrance on Badergasse), CH-6004 Luzern. ⓒ 041/418-82-20. Fax 041/418-82-30. www.hotel-wkreuz.ch. 22 units. 130F–195F ($107–$160) double. Rates include breakfast. AE, DC, MC, V. Bus: 1, 4, or 5. **Amenities:** Restaurant; lounge; nonsmoking rooms. *In room:* TV, dataport.

WHERE TO DINE

Lucerne has some of the finest restaurants in Switzerland, in a wide range of prices, so don't confine yourself to your hotel at mealtime.

EXPENSIVE

China Restaurant Li-Tai-Pe ⽊ BEIJING/CHINESE This long-standing Chinese restaurant was founded in 1965 by "grande dame" Margaret Chi Tsun, whose late husband was once an aide to General Chiang Kai-shek. Margaret Chi Tsun is assisted by her daughter, Greta Chi, a modern-day businesswoman with ties to the New World and to Hong Kong. Although fickle fame has passed on, it's still here and serving many of the same excellent dishes it always did. Located on a narrow street in the Old Town, the restaurant has two levels and is decorated with Asian artifacts and somber lighting. Many sweet-and-sour dishes are offered, such as codfish, pork, or crispy chicken. Two especially good dishes are chicken Kung Bao (made with peanuts and chile) and stewed beef with crispy rice. *Boaling* are dumplings with different fillings, a choice appetizer. You may also begin with egg-blossom soup, to be followed by beef with tomatoes or chicken with green peppers.

Furrengasse 14. ⓒ 041/410-10-23. Reservations recommended. Main courses 25F–35F ($21–$29); fixed-price lunch 25F ($21); fixed-price dinner 45F–52F ($37–$43). AE, DC, MC, V. Daily noon–2pm and 6–11pm. Bus: 1 or 2.

Old Swiss House ⽊ SWISS/FRENCH This half-timbered building near the Lion Monument is one of the most photographed attractions in the area. This crowd-pleaser—often filled with groups—is a mandatory stopover on a dining tour of Lucerne and has been since it started attracting a horde of British visitors in 1859. To its credit, it has endured and outlasted everything else, with the food remaining good. The restaurant is decorated in 17th-century style, with porcelain and antique glass, hand-carved oak doors, wooden stairways, leaded- and stained-glass windows with heraldic panes from 1575, antique silver, and old pewter. There are also original oil paintings throughout the house. Perhaps the most outstanding item of the entire collection is a handmade porcelain stove from 1636, in the Knight's Room. The house has a long bar near the entry, private banquet rooms upstairs, and a dining room downstairs. In fair weather you can have lunch on the terrace. There's a city parking lot 180m (590 ft.) away. Waitresses wear regional dress and speak several languages.

One of the dishes this place does best is an elegant version of Wiener schnitzel—a bestseller here for more than 40 years—that's pan-fried aboard a trolley that's wheeled alongside your table. Freshwater fish (fera, omble chevalier, pikeperch) from the nearby lake are excellent too, as well as turbot meunière, filet of beef stroganoff, calves' liver, roasted rack of baby lamb from Scotland, and sliced veal in cream sauce.

Löwenplatz 4. ⓒ **041/410-61-71.** Reservations recommended. Main courses 18F–58F ($15–$48) lunch, 34F–56F ($28–$46) dinner; fixed-price lunch 44F ($36); fixed-price dinner 70F ($57). AE, DC, MC, V. Tues–Sun 9am–12:30am. Closed 3 weeks in Feb. Bus: 1.

Stadtkeller ⓐ SWISS   This is a crowd pleaser. Although there's been an inn in the cellar of Lucerne's town hall since 1685, none of its earlier versions has placed such a heavy emphasis on Swiss folklore. In a cavernous cellar lined with antique accessories, you can enjoy hearty alpine meals whose flavors are enhanced by doses of folk music, which begins at 12:15pm at lunch and at 8pm during dinner. Depending on your tastes, you'll find the experience harmless or just a bit corny, although many visitors consider it the Swiss equivalent of a beer hall in Munich. The most economical way to enjoy the place is simply to order a half liter of beer, with a supplemental charge that's imposed whenever music is playing. But to really get into the experience, consider the heaping platters of smoked pork with sauerkraut, pork or veal sausages with rösti, several kinds of schnitzel with mushrooms, or roulade of beef with new potatoes. Folk music is featured only from March to October.

Sternenplatz 3. ⓒ **041/410-47-33.** Reservations recommended. Main courses 45F–50F ($37–$41); fixed-price lunch 50F ($41); fixed-price dinner 64F ($52). Music surcharge 10F ($8.20) for lunch or dinner imposed on a la carte meals and drinkers only. AE, MC, V. Apr–Oct daily noon–2pm and 8–10pm; Nov–Mar Tues–Sat noon–1:30pm and 7:30–10:15pm.

MODERATE

Hofstube ⓐ SWISS/FRENCH   This flourishing restaurant is in the Hotel Zum Rebstock, next to a building used as a guildhall for Lucerne winegrowers in the Middle Ages. The 1920s-style entrance hall is filled with valuable Art Deco pieces. This is a historic Swiss-style restaurant, with two different dining rooms, both folkloric and charming. The older is the Hofstube; the slightly newer dining area is the Hofegge, which is the site of an elaborate Sunday brunch from 7am to 3pm. Beyond the dining area is a large, illuminated courtyard, where additional tables are set up on warm summer nights. The menu, a classic blend of Swiss and French traditions, usually includes an impressive array of terrines, delicious lake trout, suckling veal with spinach, filet of pork and beef in a cognac sauce, and veal and sultanas in puff pastry.

In the Hotel Zum Rebstock, Sankt-Leodegar-Platz 3. ⓒ **041/410-35-81.** Reservations recommended. Main courses 17F–39F ($14–$32). AE, DC, MC, V. Mon–Sat 7am–midnight; Sun 8am–midnight. Bus: 1, 2, 5, or 7.

La Bonne Cave *(Finds* SWISS/ITALIAN At least some of the charm of this place involves its emphasis on wine, rather than on beer, as is the case with many of its nearby competitors. Set under the medieval stone vaulting of a building in the Old Town, directly beside the river, it offers more than 140 vintages of wine—many of them Swiss, French, or Italian, displayed on wooden racks above a cobble-covered floor. You can always select a bottle from the wine shop here, which will be uncorked in the restaurant and served without any supplemental fees, at prices less than you might have expected in a grander restaurant. But if you want as broad-based an exposure to as many wines as possible, consider several glasses of different vintages. Wine is king but the kitchen also turns out plates of good-tasting food. Menu items include platters of either Italian antipasti or an assortment of Swiss cheese; shrimp marinated in olive oil; *vitello tonnato,* beefsteak tartare; and platters of air-dried alpine beef.

Rathausquai 1. © **041/410-45-16.** Reservations not necessary. Salads 11F ($9); main courses 15F–25F ($12–$21); wines 7F–10F ($5.75–$8.20) per glass. AE, MC, V. Bar and wine shop daily 10am–midnight; food daily 10am–10:30pm.

Rotes Gatter *(★★* SWISS/INTERNATIONAL At this previously recommended hotel in Altstadt, opening onto the historic Weinmarkt, is one of the city's exceptional restaurants. The building housing it was the town jail back in 1369, but it was converted into a restaurant in 1519. Its terrace, with a view of the river Reuss, is one of the most hotly contested seats in town on a balmy summer night. Its refined nouvelle-inspired cuisine attracts both locals and visitors.

The decor is a stylish combination of medieval masonry, 19th-century wrought iron, and postmodern, hi-tech lighting. Try such tempting dishes as freshwater crabs grilled with feta cheese and marinated herbs; filets of pikeperch with olive oil and artichoke hearts; roasted rabbit stuffed with chanterelles and basil; Sisteron lamb in puff pastry with olive oil and thyme juices; and breast of chicken stuffed with shrimp and dill, on a bed of marinated sweet peppers.

In the Hotel des Balances, Weinmarkt. © **041/418-28-28.** Reservations recommended. Main courses 32F–52F ($26–$43); fixed-price dinner 75F–91F ($62–$75). AE, DC, MC, V. Daily 11:30am–1:30pm and 6–10pm.

Wilden Mann Stübe/Burgerstübe *★* SWISS/CONTINENTAL The Burgerstübe, the older of the two dining rooms, dates from at least 1517. Set on the ground floor of the Romantik Hotel, both dining rooms have carefully maintained paneling and antique touches that include coffered ceilings painted with the coats of arms of each of Lucerne's leading families. The restaurant is smoke-free. The food items are rich and succulent, often inspired by the tastes of old Switzerland. Examples include Wildermann pastete, crafted from filet of beef cooked in its own juices and encased in puff pastry; Küglipastete, a shank of veal in a cream sauce with mushrooms in a puff-pastry cone with peas and carrots; hashed Zurich-style veal served with rösti; and breast of veal cooked "Luzern style," with a cream-based kidney sauce. More conventional menu items include chateaubriands, steaks, and roast rack of lamb with rosemary sauce. In midsummer seating expands onto a flowering outdoor terrace overlooking one of the Old Town's historic squares.

In the Romantik Hotel Wilden Mann, Bahnhofstrasse 30. © **041/210-16-66.** Reservations recommended. Main courses 19F–55F ($16–$45); fixed-price lunch 60F ($49); fixed-price dinner 80F ($66). AE, DC, MC, V. Daily 10:30am–11pm (limited menu 2–6pm and after 10pm). Closed 2 weeks in July. Bus: 2.

INEXPENSIVE

Rathaus Brauerei Restaurant *(Finds* SWISS   This is one of the few establishments in Lucerne that brews its beer on-site. They usually include at least four, whose individual characteristics vary according to the season, but which will usually feature the most popular brand, Rathaus Bier, a blond lager that's available year-round; as well as wheat beer; a dark beer known as *dunkel;* and the heaviest, darkest, and strongest of all, *bok.* You'll find the place under the arcades of the riverfront promenade, close to the northern terminus of the city's well-known covered bridge, immediately beneath the exhibitions of the Picasso Museum. You can dine in the open air, or head inside to a series of medieval vaults that shelter the polished copper of the fermentation vats. Menu items reflect the savory, hearty dishes that seem to go well with beer, including schnitzels, lamb steak, Swiss sausage (of veal or pork), and grilled chicken breast filets, as well as deep-fried pikeperch.

Unter den Egg 2. (C) **041/410-52-57.** Reservations not necessary. Main courses 16F–40F ($13–$33); beer 4F–8F ($3.30–$6.55). AE, DC, MC, V. Apr–Sept daily 9am–12:30am; Oct–Mar daily 12:30pm–12:30am.

Restaurant Fritschi *(Value* SWISS/INTERNATIONAL   There's absolutely nothing pretentious about this beer hall/brasserie, where clients have been soaking up suds and enjoying filling platters of traditional food since 1602. The building that contains it has an outrageously colorful replica of a medieval fresco on its facade, and an interior pair of dining rooms, one of which contains a bar, and both of which are sheathed in richly intricate marquetry. Menu items—all familiar to your Swiss great-grand-mother—include four kinds of pork schnitzel; entrecôte of beef; sliced veal with a mushroom-flavored cream sauce; sliced veal with morels; and ostrich steak. There is also a selection of fondues, any of which seem to taste better during cold weather.

Sternenplatz 5. (C) **041/410-16-15.** Reservations recommended. Main courses 24F–43F ($20–$35). MC, V. Daily 11am–11pm. Bus: 1 or 2.

Schiffrestaurant Wilhelm Tell SWISS   Built in 1908, this lake cruiser (*Schiff* is German for "ship") sailed boatloads of happy passengers from one end of Lake Lucerne to the other. After it was replaced by newer ships in the late 1960s, it was transformed into a floating restaurant in 1972. Now permanently moored at one of the quays, it's usually ringed with a colony of swans, which feed off the scraps thrown overboard. Drinks and snacks are served on outdoor cafe tables in the bow area, where you can have a beer or coffee throughout the day. A formal restaurant is found under the low ceiling of the aft section, where fine food is served with alert attention. The ship's engine, brightly polished and set behind glass, is on display as a work of industrial art. The well-chosen menu may include excellently prepared filets of perch or sole prepared seaman's style, chopped chicken breast with smoked ham and bits of apple in a calvados sauce with rösti, and flavorful grills of succulent veal and beef.

Landungsbrücke 9. (C) **041/410-23-30.** Reservations recommended. Main courses 22F ($18); fixed-price lunch 20F–23F ($16–$19). AE, MC, V. Daily 10am–midnight. Closed Jan–Feb. Bus: 2.

Vinotek Opus *(Finds* CONTINENTAL/MEDITERRANEAN   Set within a pair of interconnected medieval buildings, one side of which opens onto views of the river, this wine bar rocks and rolls in one of the most irreverent formats in town. It's understood that you'll come here for at least one glass (and perhaps several) of the Swiss and foreign wines served. You can also order platters of Serrano-style smoked ham, Italian soft cheese marinated in olive oil with garlic, *vitello tonnato,* a tartare of smoked salmon, and gazpacho studded with smoked mussels. There are even some experimental dishes such as Asian lasagna "Shanghai" (with Asian vegetables, shiitake mushrooms, snow peas, tofu, and soy sprouts), or red snapper in red curry sauce, as well as more mainstream platters such as fried perch filets or roulades of rabbit filet. The cellar contains more than 650 types of wine. Sprawling and convivial, the place offers seating in two dining rooms, at tables beside two different bars, and a wide terrace beside the river overlooking the Old Town.

Bahnhofstrasse 16. (*C*) **041/226-41-41.** Reservations not necessary. Platters 22F–36F ($18–$30); wine 8F–16F ($6.55–$13) per glass. AE, MC, V. Bars daily 8:30am–midnight; kitchen Sun–Thurs 11:30am–11:30pm, Fri–Sat 11:30am–12:30am.

Wirtshaus Galliker ✿ SWISS   Generous portions of unpretentious, well-prepared food are served amid a rustic decor and an often-rowdy atmosphere of fun-loving Luzerners out for a night of gluttonous drinking and smoking. The house itself was first mentioned in documents in 1681. Back then it was a private residence, but it became a restaurant in 1800 and was purchased in 1856 by the Galliker family, whose members still run it. They're especially proud of their small garden in back with space for 28 diners. The waitresses, some of whom may look like your Swiss-German grandmother if you had one, keep the suds and the regional fare flowing. The cuisine is a sort of Lucerne soul food, everything from tripe in white-wine sauce to calf's head, with sweetbreads from nearly all barnyard animals. Farm-style bratwurst seasoned with caraway seeds is consumed along with chunky bread in mass quantities. Less esoteric favorites include beef Stroganoff and thinly sliced calves' liver sautéed in butter with herbs and served with rösti. Fruity desserts are a summer favorite. If you're sharing a table, it's polite to wish your fellow diners *guten appetit.*

Schützenstrasse 1. (*C*) **041/241-10-02.** Reservations required. Main courses 24F–53F ($20–$43). AE, DC, MC, V. Tues–Sat 9:30am–midnight. Closed last 2 weeks of July and 2 weeks in Aug. Bus: 2.

LUCERNE AFTER DARK

The most sophisticated entertainment is found at **Vegas,** the lavishly redecorated new casino at the Grand Casino Luzern, Haldenstrasse 6 ((*C*) **041/418-56-56**). You can try your luck at 140 slot machines. Poker, roulette, and black jack are also available. On the second floor, you can indulge in a few rounds of boule. Other options here include strip shows at the Red Rose Night Club/Cabaret, and folklore shows in Le Chalet, with traditional music, dances, and costumes, as well as yodeling, alphorn (a large horn) playing, and flag throwing.

On a more cultural note, if you speak German, you can enjoy performances at the **Stadttheater,** Theaterstrasse 2 ((*C*) **041/210-33-63**). Directly on the lake on the rail station side of town, it's the home of Luzern's major theater group. Operas in their original language are also staged here. The Allgemeine Musikgesellschaft Luzern is the local resident orchestra, presenting performances at the **Kunsthaus,** Frohburgstrasse 6, from October to June, or at the Kultur und Kongress Zentrum (see below). For more information, call (*C*) **041/210-50-50.**

In the late 1990s the city of Lucerne inaugurated one of the most dramatically modern, large-scale buildings in central Switzerland, the **Kultur und Kongress Zentrum (KKZ),** Europaplatz 1 ((*C*) **041/226-77-77**), as a glittering showcase to corporate conventions and the performing arts. Poised behind the railway station in starkly modern contrast to the spires and alpine architecture of the rest of Lucerne, its controversial shape may remind newcomers of an enchanted "music box" that glitters with acres of glass and metal panels in shades of forest green, dark blue, and red. It was designed with a spectacular copper-sheathed roof by noted Parisian architect Jean Nouvele. Its auditoriums have some of the best acoustics in central Europe, thanks to rotating panels behind the stage. Expect heavy use of this site for classical, rock, and heavy-metal concerts. (For ticket information about the concerts that will be presented here, check out the posters in front of the building, or call the concert hall itself at © **0848/800-800** or 0900/552-225.) There's also a snack bar and cafe on the premises.

If you like Swiss folkloric presentations, head for the **Stadtkeller,** Sternenplatz (© **041/410-47-33**), which has good food and presents a program of traditional Swiss entertainment, complete with alphorns, cowbells, national costumes, flag throwing, and yodeling. Presentations take place March to October daily from 8 to 10:30pm.

Other episodes of Swiss folklore can be experienced aboard the **Night Boat Luzern,** Seestrasse 106 (© **041/319-49-78**), a cruiser that departs from Pier 6 in front of Lucerne's railway station. It operates every night, business permitting, between May and September, departing at 8:45pm and returning at 10:15pm. Advance reservations are required. In most cases, members of a folk musical group perform onboard, and there's also a restaurant serving Swiss alpine food. If you opt for the cruise with dinner, the combined cost is around 88F ($72). The boat ride without dinner costs 55F ($45). There is also a happy hour cruise for 38F ($31).

The Altstadt (Old Town) always brims with pubs and cafes, of which **Mr. Pickwick's Pub,** Rathausquai 6 (© **041/410-59-27**), is the most authentic looking and the most popular British pub in Lucerne, with a sudsy, woodsy-looking decor that's awash with Brits, beer, and anyone else who simply wants to toss back a pint or two from a riverfront location near the northern end of the Old Town's covered bridge. It generally stays open nightly until 1am, which is very late by the standards of Lucerne.

If you're tired of yodeling and want south-of-the-border spice, head for **Cucaracha,** Pilatusstrasse 15 (© **041/226-87-87**), for a night of nachos, burritos, and Coronas. Many hotels have more subdued bars, especially the **National,** Haldenstrasse 4 (© **041/419-09-09**), which has a glossy American-type bar, and the **Palace Hotel,** Haldenstrasse 10 (© **041/416-16-16**), which has one American-style bar. The most ultracool place in Lucerne is **The Lounge Bar** of The Hotel, Sempacherstrasse 14 (© **041/226-86-86**).

P-1 the Bar, on the top floor of the Hotel Monopol, Pilatusstrasse 1 (© **041/220-13-15**), is our favorite nightclub in Lucerne. We say that partly because it's crowded with the kinds of hip and available people you can talk to, and partly because it boasts one of the most dramatic physical settings of any nightclub in Switzerland. To reach it, you'll wait in line on the lobby level of the hotel, a Belle Epoque beauty that sits across the plaza from the railway station. An attendant will funnel clients, in elevator-size blocks, into a lift that will haul you to a point beneath the hotel's ornate copper-sheathed cupola. Here, recently released dance music, three bars, and a pair of outdoor terraces combine to create an instant party ambience that virtually everyone finds invigorating. By all means, climb to the club's highest point for open-air views of Lucerne that are among the best in the city. Incidentally, this nightclub's name (P1) derives from a simplification of its address (Pilatusstrasse 1).

The Loft, Haldenstrase 2 (© **041/410-92-44**), is a serious contender for the title of the most hip and with-it nightclub in a town that's loaded with worthy competition. Music is a sophisticated blend of whatever you might have expected in London or Los Angeles, and the crowd is young and beautiful. The decor includes at least two bar areas and a balcony that overlooks a high-tech dance floor ringed with free-standing candelabrum, whose candles seem to flicker in rhythm to the music. There is a cover charge of 10F to 15F ($6.50–$9.75).

The terrace of the **Penthouse Bar** at the Hotel Astoria, Pilatusstrasse 29 (© **041/226-88-88**), offers a panoramic view over the rooftops of the city and the dramatic mountainscape beyond. Large sofas are an invitation to linger. On weekends live DJs keep everybody in a party mood. Also at the same hotel is the **Pravda Dance Club,** one of the city's best venues for meeting other young people. Exotic drinks in a romantic Kasbah-like setting can be ordered at the **Casablanca Bar** at the Hotel Schiller, Pilatusstrasse 15 (© **041/226-87-87**).

Heaven, Burgerstrasse 21 (© **041/210-41-43**), is Lucerne's only gay bar, and as such, it attracts people (mostly men) from many of the hamlets of central Switzerland. Don't expect too much—the venue can be glum, and overall you'll get a sense that most of the clients would rather be partying in say, Hamburg or Berlin. You might be happiest here if you define the place as a distinctive but low-energy local pub where most of the clients happen to be gay, German-speaking, and Swiss.

EASY EXCURSIONS FROM LUCERNE

Lake Lucerne is known for its scenery and the many old-world villages along its shores. Many poets have praised the area's beauty. You may be lucky enough to stay in a hotel room that commands a view of the lake.

Lake steamers and mountain railways can get you to most points of interest around Lake Lucerne. Boat cruises are free if you have a Eurail or InterRail pass. Mountain railways can whisk you to elevations of 3,000m (9,840 ft.) or more in a very short time. Our first adventure will be a major mountain excursion to Mount Pilatus, a 2,100m (6,888-ft.) summit overlooking Lucerne.

MOUNT PILATUS ✦✦✦

Pilatus-Kulm is located 15km (9 miles) south of Lucerne. Its German name derives from an old legend: During medieval times, it's said, the city fathers of Lucerne banned travel up the mountain because they thought that its slopes were haunted by the ghost of Pontius Pilate; they feared that Pilate would be angered by intrusive visitors and cause violent storms. For many years after the ban was finally lifted, only a few souls were brave enough to climb the mountain. Queen Victoria made the trip in 1868. Today the ascent to Pilatus is one of the most popular excursions in Switzerland.

Between May and November, weather permitting, the cog railway operates between Alpnachstad, at the edge of the lake, and the very top of Mount Pilatus. From the quays of Lucerne, take a lake steamer for a scenic 90-minute boat ride to Alpnachstad. If you have a rail pass, remember that it will be valid on this steamer.

At Alpnachstad, transfer to the electric cog railway, which runs at a 48% gradient—the steepest cogwheel railway in the world. Departures are every 45 minutes daily from 8:50am to 4:30pm May to September only. At Pilatus-Kulm you can get out and enjoy the view. There are two mountain hotels and a belvedere offering views of Lake Lucerne and many of the mountains around it. For the descent from Mount Pilatus, some visitors prefer to take a pair of cable cars—first a large cabin-style téléphérique, then a small gondola. The cable cars end at Kriens, a suburb of Lucerne. Here you can take bus no. 1, which will carry you into the heart of Lucerne. The round-trip fare on the cog railway and cable car is 80F ($66), 50% off for children under 16.

A similar excursion to Pilatus is possible in the winter, but because the cog railway is buried in snow, you must alter your plans. You'll have to ascend and descend by cable car, which many visitors find exhilarating. From the center of Lucerne, take bus no. 1 from the Bahnhof to the outlying suburb of Kriens. At Kriens, transfer to a cable car that glides over meadows and forests to the village of Fräkmüntegg, 1,380m (4,526 ft.) above sea level. The trip takes half an hour. At Fräkmüntegg, switch to another cable car, this one much more steeply inclined than the first. A stunning feat of advanced engineering, it swings above gorges and cliffs to the very peak of Mount Pilatus (Pilatus-Kulm). Unlike the cog railways, these cable cars operate year-round. The round-trip ride by cable car from Kriens to Fräkmüntegg costs 38F ($31). *Insider tip:* Visit Pilatus early in the day. Clouds and fog sometimes move in after the noon hour and mask the magnificent view from the top of this mountain peak. You can be fooled by a clear view at the bottom of Pilatus, only to reach the top later to be engulfed in the clouds.

For information, consult the staff at the city's tourist office or call © **041/329-11-11.** They're well informed about these excursions, as are the desk personnel at most of Lucerne's hotels.

RIGI ★★★

For another panoramic view from a hilltop belvedere, go to Rigi, 15 miles east of Lucerne. The view from Rigi is different from that atop Mount Pilatus, so if you see both, you won't be replicating your experience. Pilatus offers the more panoramic vista, but the view from Rigi is more beautiful. By most accounts, Rigi (1,680m/5,510 ft.) is the most famous mountain view in the country. However, you may be disappointed if the weather's not clear. Rigi is called the "island mountain" because it appears to be surrounded by the waters of lakes Lucerne, Zug, and Lauerz. It's accessible by two cog railways and a cableway.

Adventurous visitors making the "grand tour" in the 19th century spent the night at Rigi-Kulm to see the sun rise over the Alps. Victor Hugo called it "an incredible horizon . . . that chaos of absurd exaggerations and scary diminutions." Later, Mark Twain also climbed to the top to see the sun rise across the Alps. But he was so exhausted, as he relates in *A Tramp Abroad,* that he collapsed into sleep, from which he didn't wake until sunset. Not realizing that he had slept all day, he at first recoiled in horror, believing that the sun had switched its direction and was actually rising in the west. This experience continues to be one of nature's loveliest offerings in all of Europe. For those wanting to partake of the tradition, many hotels are perched on the mountainside.

You can travel to the mountain by taking a 55-minute trip by lake steamer from Lucerne to Vitznau, a small resort on the northern shore of the lake. The rack railway from Vitznau to Rigi-Kulm was the first cog railway in Europe, built in 1871. You can also approach the mountain from Arth-Goldau, which is on the southern shore of Zug Lake. The Arth-Goldau cog railway to Rigi-Kulm opened in 1876. The maximum gradient is 21%. Both cog railways cost 60F ($49) for the round-trip. It's possible to go up one way and come down the other if you want to see both sides of the mountain. The trip from Vitznau takes 40 minutes and the trip from Arth-Goldau lasts 35 minutes. There are a dozen departures a day in season. An alternative ascent is strongly advocated by the local tourist office. Begin at the quays in Lucerne, and take a lake steamer to Vitznau. From here, after a stroll through the town, go to the top of Rigi-Kulm by cog railway and admire the view from the top. Then descend halfway down

Impressions

We were soon tramping leisurely up the leafy mulepath, and then the talk began to flow, as usual. It was twelve o'clock noon, and a breezy, cloudless day; the ascent was gradual, and the glimpses from under the curtaining boughs, of blue water, and tiny sail boats, and beetling cliffs, were as charming as glimpses of dreamland.

—Mark Twain, on "Climbing the Rigi"

the mountain via the same cog railway, getting off midway at Rigi Kaltbad. Here you'll switch to the Rigi Seilbahn cable car, which will carry you the rest of the way downhill, a 15-minute downhill walk from the hamlet of Wiggis. You can begin this trip daily between 8am and around 2pm, which is the last reasonable departure time, if you want to see the sights and return to Lucerne before dark. The tourist office or a staff member at the phone number listed below will recite the available times of departures. Many visitors, however, find that the most convenient departure time from Lucerne is at 8:32am and again at 10:32am. For more information about anything to do with ascents of Mount Rigi, call the **Lucerne Tourist office** at © **041/227-17-17.** The ascents described in this section are possible only from March to October.

DIETSCHIBERG ᏒᏒ

The best view of Lucerne and its lake can be enjoyed from Dietschiberg, at 619m (2,030 ft.). Board the cable car on Haldenstrasse in Lucerne. The trip takes about half an hour. You can also see Pilatus and Rigi from a belvedere platform.

GUTSCH

One sweeping panorama of the region that's easily accessible from the center of Lucerne (and doesn't involve a full day's excursion) is the mountain plateau of Gütsch, 514m (1,686 ft.) above sea level. Board a short funicular on Baselstrasse for the 10-minute ride. At the top is a belvedere platform beside the Hotel Château Gütsch, which takes in the city, the lake, and the snowcapped Alps. The funicular departs in both directions every 10 minutes throughout the year, beginning at 8:30am and terminating every night at midnight. Every day from 12:45 to 1:15pm, there's a 30-minute lunch break for the operators. The ride costs 6F ($4.90) one-way. For more information, call the **Château Gütsch** (© **041/249-41-00**).

MOUNT TITLIS ᏒᏒ

Mount Titlis, which is visited as an excursion from the little resort of Engelberg, is the highest point from which you can get a view over central Switzerland. The summit is always covered by snow and ice; there's an "ice cave," in addition to a glacier trail. The view from the belvedere, at 2,970m (9,742 ft.), takes in the Jungfrau and the Matterhorn, as well as Zurich and Basel on a clear day. There's a summer ski run with a ski lift. There are also two restaurants: the **Panorama Restaurant Titlis** (© **041/639-50-88**), at 3,000m (9,840 ft.), and the **Gletscher–Restaurant Stand** (© **041/639-50-85**), at 2,412m (7,911 ft.).

To get to the summit, you take a funicular and three cable cars. The last stage of the cable-car trip is the most spectacular, as you're taken right over the glacier. Visitors with respiratory problems may want to forgo this trip because of the thinness of the air at such elevations. The terminal at the summit (which is referred to in some timetables as Kleintitlis, or Little Titlis) has an observation lounge and a large sun terrace.

To get to Titlis from Lucerne's Bahnhof, drive or take a train to Engelberg; the round-trip costs 79F ($65). Then to reach the summit, take the cable cars that run daily beginning at 8:30am, with the last one back at 4:20pm. In winter skiers use this connection to get to the higher slopes. For more information and schedules, call *C* **041/639-50-50** or 041/639-50-61.

2 Bürgenstock (★(★

16km (10 miles) SE of Lucerne

The most luxurious resort in the region, Bürgenstock is situated above Lake Lucerne on a 10km (6-mile) limestone ridge. The late Audrey Hepburn, Sophia Loren, and many other movie stars have lived here, swelling the resort's international reputation for glamour. Bürgenstock is lower in altitude than other resorts in the region, reaching only 492m (1,614 ft.) on its northern side; the southern edge of town gently slopes through fertile pastureland to the Stans Valley.

ESSENTIALS

GETTING THERE   About a dozen trains make the 40-minute trip from Lucerne to Kehrsiten-Bürgenstock every day. From Kehrsiten-Bürgenstock, you transfer to a steeply ascending cog railway (its gradient is 45%) that departs every 25 to 45 minutes throughout the day for the 7-minute ascent to Bürgenstock. Call *C* **0900/300-300** for **rail schedules.**

In the summer frequent **lake steamers** (*C* **041/367-67-67**) leave from the quays in the center of Lucerne, taking 30 minutes to reach the pier at Kehrsiten. From here, passengers transfer to the cog railway.

Because the road to Bürgenstock is winding and treacherous, it's better to go via the lake steamer or train as outlined above. However, if you insist on driving, head south from Lucerne on N8 to Stansstad and, from here, take a steep and narrow, often-dangerous road east for 5km (3 miles) until you reach Bürgenstock.

VISITOR INFORMATION   There are no street names, so follow hotel directional signs. The **Bürgenstock Tourist Office** (*C* **041/612-99-15**) is open daily from 8am to 6pm.

EXPLORING THE AREA

When in Bürgenstock you can forget about museums and a lot of man-made attractions. What you do is walk and walk and absorb the mountain panoramas. One of the great walks of central Switzerland, the **Bürgenstock–Felsenweg trail,** begins here. Allow about 2½ hours for the walk from Bürgenstock high above Lake Lucerne to the village of Ennetbürgen.

Begin at the upper funicular station at Bürgenstock, heading east past the Palace Hotel. Then turn left and strike out. Along the way you'll be treated to stunning views of Lake Lucerne and even Pilatus.

At the **Hammetschwand Lift** you can interrupt your walk to enjoy a ride on the highest free-standing lift in Europe. You're taken to a lookout point 1,127m (3,697 ft.) above sea level, where the view stretches all the way to the Swiss Alps to the south. Afterward you enter a series of short tunnels and pass the historic chapel of St. Jost, erected in 1733 as the tomb of a hermit from the Middle Ages. Heading down the slopes, you eventually reach the village of Ennetbürgen, with its ferry dock, where you can board vessels to take you to other towns along Lake Lucerne.

WHERE TO STAY & DINE

Bürgenstock Hotels 🐵🐵🐵   This is one of the most exclusive hotels in Europe, and also the largest privately owned hotel complex in Switzerland. Set in a 4.8-hectare (12-acre) private park, it consists of three separate buildings: the Grand Hotel (opened in 1873), the Palace Hotel (opened in 1904), and the Park Hotel (opened in 1888 but demolished and rebuilt in a plush, modern style in 1991). The public rooms of each of the three hotels abound in art treasures, including works by Rubens, Van Dyck, Tintoretto, and Brueghel. The furniture is worthy of a modern-day Versailles, and many different fireplaces throw off a welcoming glow. The bedrooms are traditionally furnished, spacious for the most part, and well maintained with luxurious appointments. All units have very well-kept bathrooms. In the summer a battalion of gardeners keeps the grounds immaculate and flowering.

Ch-6363 Bürgenstock. 📞 800/874-4002 in the U.S. or 041/612-90-10. Fax 041/612-90-11. www.buergenstock-hotels.ch. 183 units. Grand and Palace hotels 220F–470F ($180–$385) double. Park Hotel 320F–660F ($262–$541) double; 390F–730F ($320–$599) suite. Rates include buffet breakfast. AE, DC, MC, V. Free parking. **Amenities:** 5 restaurants; 4 bars; 2 pools (1 indoor, 1 outdoor heated pool); 9-hole golf course; 2 tennis courts; health spa; 2 saunas; limited room service; massage; babysitting; laundry service/dry cleaning; nonsmoking rooms; rooms for guests w/limited mobility. *In room:* TV, minibar, hair dryer, safe.

Hotel Fürigen   Located on a wooded hillside high above the lake, this resort hotel has white walls and a red-tile roof with gables and towers. Completely renovated in 1991, it offers midsize, comfortable bedrooms with excellent beds and good views. All rooms also come equipped with tidy bathrooms. The hotel operates two restaurants on the lake, one serving Greek dishes, the other Italian.

CH-6363 Bürgenstock. 📞 041/618-69-69. Fax 041/618-69-00. www.hotel-fuerigen.ch. 84 units. 240F–290F ($197–$238) double; 360F ($295) suite. Rates include buffet breakfast. AE, DC, MC, V. Free parking. **Amenities:** 2 restaurants; lounge; bar; fitness center; limited room service; babysitting; laundry service/dry cleaning; rooms for guests w/limited mobility. *In room:* TV, dataport, hair dryer, safe, solarium.

Waldhotel Bürgenstock *Value*   This is a far more affordable and democratically priced hotel than the Bürgenstock Hotel's bastion of luxury accommodations. There has been a hotel at this site since 1895. The present modern building was constructed after the previous hotel burned in 1958. The new version has an elegantly paneled lounge, an elevator, and a narrow terrace with a view of the snowy mountains. Most of the spacious rooms have balconies, all have firm beds, and those with private bathrooms are for the most part equipped with tub/shower combinations. The hotel is accessible by a single-lane road that winds through an alpine meadow dotted with huts and 19th-century chalets.

The Waldhotel also offers a less expensive alternative to dining at the Bürgenstock Hotels.

CH-6363 Bürgenstock. 📞 041/611-03-83. Fax 041/610-64-66. www.waldhotel-buergenstock.ch. 55 units, 4 without bathroom. 244F–260F ($200–$213) double with or without bathroom. Rates include continental breakfast. MC, V. Free parking. Closed Dec 27–Jan 3. **Amenities:** Restaurant; indoor heated pool; health club; sauna; steam room; limited room service; babysitting; laundry service/dry cleaning; rooms for guests w/limited mobility. *In room:* TV, minibar, hair dryer, safe.

3 Weggis ★★

30km (19 miles) E of Lucerne

The lakeside resort of Weggis is on the sunny side of Mount Rigi, one of three holiday centers (Vitznau and Gersau are the others) that offer the kind of mild climate found in favored parts of Italy. Weggis and the other resorts are about an hour's walk or a 5-minute drive apart. Well-tended garden promenades stretch for several miles along the lakeshore. Mark Twain stayed here in 1897.

Of the three resorts, Weggis is the most preferred. It's usually the first port of call for steamers from Lucerne and is also easily accessible from the international St. Gotthard railway line, although it's not on the main traffic route.

Many excursions are possible from early spring to late autumn. You can take the aerial cableway up to Rigi-Kaltbad (1,427m/4,681 ft.), a mountain health resort behind Weggis. This is great walking country, not only on the promenade quays but also on the slopes of the Rigi, which are planted with vines. Even some almost tropical species of vegetation grow here. In addition, mountain transport links Weggis with the Rigi Railways.

ESSENTIALS

GETTING THERE   Several **lake steamers** (© 041/367-67-67) depart from the quays of Lucerne for Weggis every day, requiring about 45 minutes for the transfer. Once you reach Weggis, a local bus run by the village transports you (in the summertime only) from the lakefront to the upper reaches of the town.

Though Weggis is not directly accessible by rail, the railway junction of Kussnacht lies 9.6km (6 miles) from Weggis. From Kussnacht, buses depart for the 10- to 13-minute ride to Weggis.

If you're driving from Lucerne, drive east on Route 2, along the northern rim of Lake Lucerne, cutting south on Route 2b at the signposted turnoff to Weggis.

VISITOR INFORMATION   The **Weggis Tourist Office** (© 041/390-11-55) is open Monday to Friday from 8am to 6pm, Saturday and Sunday 9am to 2:30pm. (Off season the office remains closed on weekends.) If you'd like to go biking along the banks of Lake Lucerne, you can stop in here and rent a bike for the day for 18F ($15).

WHERE TO STAY & DINE

Hotel Albana ★   This hotel is outclassed only by the Beau-Rivage (see below). The Hotel Albana was built in the Art Nouveau style in 1896 and has been run by the Wolf family since 1910. One of the public rooms, with a grand piano and a 3m (10-ft.) Meissen ceramic stove, looks almost baronial. Heavy brass chandeliers hang from the frescoed ceiling, and large rococo mirrors reflect the wood paneling. The midsize bedrooms are modernized with excellent beds. Many have good views of the nearby lake. The best food at the resort is served in the Panorama Restaurant, which has large windows and a terrace above the lake. The decor of the hotel's Jazz Bar was inspired by Matisse; on some nights it offers live music.

CH-6353 Weggis. © 041/390-21-41. Fax 041/390-29-59. www.albana-weggis.ch. 56 units. 250F–360F ($205–$295) double. Half board 48F–58F ($39–$48) extra. Rates include buffet breakfast. AE, DC, MC, V. Closed Dec 15–Jan 15. **Amenities:** Restaurant; bar; 2 lounges; sauna; bike rental; limited room service; babysitting; laundry service/dry cleaning; rooms for guests w/limited mobility. *In room:* TV, dataport, minibar, hair dryer, safe.

Hotel Beau-Rivage ★★   One of the attractions of this 1908 hotel is its expanse of manicured lawn, which reaches down to the lake near the boat landing. The view of the mountains from here is exhilarating. The symmetrical hotel has a series of wrought-iron balconies, and the traditional and spacious rooms are comfortably furnished with wood, brass, and pastel shades. Comfortable bedrooms open onto panoramic lake and mountain views.

CH-6353 Weggis. ⓒ 041/392-79-00. Fax 041/390-19-81. www.beaurivage-weggis.ch. 41 units. 216F–418F ($177–$343) double. Half board 50F ($41) extra. Rates include continental breakfast. AE, DC, MC, V. Free parking. Closed late Oct to Mar. **Amenities:** Restaurant; bar; pool; limited room service; laundry service/dry cleaning; nonsmoking rooms. *In room:* TV, dataport, minibar, hair dryer, safe, robes.

Hotel Central am See　This old-fashioned resort hotel, built with six large gables and many smaller ones, stands on a shady peninsula with a swimming pool near the lake. Constructed in 1912, it offers an interior with traditional furniture and an elevator carrying clients to the well-maintained, rather stark bedrooms, most of which offer a view of the lake and mountains. All units come equipped with tidy bathrooms containing showers. The hotel has a greenhouse-style restaurant, the Winter Garden, overlooking the lake.

CH-6353 Weggis. ⓒ **041/392-09-09.** Fax 041/392-09-00. www.central-am-see.ch. 35 units. Oct to mid-May 180F–250F ($148–$205) double; mid-May to Sept 180F–270F ($148–$221) double. Rates include buffet breakfast. AE, DC, MC, V. Parking 7F ($4.55). Closed Nov 1–Jan 15. **Amenities:** 2 restaurants; bar; outdoor heated pool; bike rental; limited room service; babysitting; laundry service/dry cleaning. *In room:* TV, dataport, minibar (in some), hair dryer.

Hotel Rössli *Value*　Completely renovated, this century-old hotel with elaborate shingles occupies the most desirable lakefront position at the center of the resort town, facing a tranquil square with flowers, statues, and a fountain. The hotel has ornate wood balustrades and russet-colored shutters. The interior is modern, with a decor of wrought iron, wicker chairs, and hanging lamps. The Nölly family offers pleasant midsize rooms with attractive furniture and neatly kept bathrooms. You'll also find a sidewalk cafe in front.

CH-6353 Weggis. ⓒ **041/392-27-27.** Fax 041/390-27-26. www.wellness-roessli.ch. 65 units. 180F–260F ($148–$213) double. Half board 30F ($25) extra. Rates include buffet breakfast. AE, DC, MC, V. Free parking. Closed Nov–Mar. **Amenities:** Restaurant; lounge; nonsmoking rooms. *In room:* TV, dataport, coffeemaker, hair dryer, safe.

4 Vitznau ⓐ

26km (16 miles) E of Lucerne; 4km (2½ miles) SE of Weggis

Vitznau is located on a different bay of Lake Lucerne, at the foot of the Rigi. At 439m (1,440 ft.), it offers an alpine panorama that's mirrored in the lake. It's an hour's drive from Zurich.

　　Sports vacations are especially popular in Vitznau from April to October. Facilities include swimming in the lake, indoor and outdoor pools, and tennis courts. There are also many inviting hiking trails—ideal for long walks—in the meadows, woodlands, and mountains.

　　The Vitznau-Rigi railway starts at Vitznau along the shores of Lake Lucerne, on the south side of Mount Rigi. The railway terminates at Kulm peak, after passing through the mountain stations of Rigi-Kaltbad-First, Rigi Staffelhöhe, and Rigi Staffel. In the summer old-fashioned steam trains travel on this stretch of electric rack-and-pinion railway. Pause to enjoy the beauty of the resort before heading up to the mountain. Departures are every 30 minutes.

ESSENTIALS

GETTING THERE   The only rail line servicing Vitznau is a local alpine train connecting it to such panoramic points as Rigi-Kulm and Rigi-Kaltbad. Call ℂ **0900/ 300-300** for **rail schedules.**

Buses depart for Vitznau from the Küssnacht railway station, which is reached from Lucerne by train every hour, requiring about 45 minutes, including a stopover in Weggis. Some of the buses continue to Gersau, where there's a connection to Brunne. For **bus schedules** and information, call ℂ **041/367-67-67.**

Ferries depart for Vitznau from the quays of Lucerne every hour in summer and about every 2 hours in winter. The trip takes about 1 hour. Call ℂ **041/367-67-67** for more information.

If you're driving, the resort is reached by first passing through Weggis (see section 3, above), then continuing along Route 2b south to Vitznau, a very short drive along the lake.

VISITOR INFORMATION   The **Vitznau Tourist Board,** in the town center (ℂ **041/398-00-35;** www.vitznau.ch), is open November to Easter, Monday to Friday from 8:30am to noon and 1 to 6:30pm, Saturday 9am to 5pm, and Sunday 9am to noon. From Easter to June and September to October, hours are Monday to Friday 8:30am to noon and 1 to 6:30pm, Saturday 9am to noon. During July and August the office is open Monday to Friday 8:30am to 6:30pm, Saturday 9am to 5pm, and Sunday 9am to noon.

EXPLORING THE AREA

If you'd like to enjoy the pleasures of the lake itself, both paddleboats and motorboats are available for rent at **Anker Travel,** Zihlstrasse (ℂ **041/397-17-07**). It's also possible to swim in the bay here, although the temperatures are a mite chilly for those from sunnier climes.

If you're biking down from Vitznau, you can tour the entire right bank of the lake by **Route 2,** which runs all the way to Altdorf (see section 6, below).

WHERE TO STAY & DINE

Hotel Rigi   Although the service from the staff may leave you as cold as an alpine lake, this is a clean and decent place that can be recommended for its economy. About a block from the boat-landing dock, the hotel is a century-old monument within the town center, although rooms have been kept fairly up-to-date. Units come in a variety of shapes and sizes and are comfortable, with firm beds and good maintenance. Opt, if available, for one of the corner bedrooms that open onto their own private balconies

---

Finds An Idyllic Swimming Hole

To escape from the crowds along Lake Lucerne, we'll let you in on a secret: At the very southeastern tip of Lake Lucerne is the narrow and splendid inlet lake, the **Urnersee,** which attracts fewer visitors than the resorts along Lake Lucerne even though it's no less majestic or beautiful. In fact, this is the more remote, the wildest, and the loveliest part of the whole of Lake Lucerne. A natural rock obelisk, called **Schillerstein,** rises some 25m (82 ft.) out of the Urnersee, and is dedicated to Friedrich von Schiller, the author of _Wilhelm Tell._

---

and a view of the lake. Don't expect many in-room amenities outside of a telephone and private bathrooms.

Seestrasse, CH-6354 Vitznau. © 041/397-21-21. Fax 041/397-18-25. www.rigi-vitznau.ch. 35 units. 120F–190F ($98–$156) double. Rates include breakfast. AE, DC, MC, V. **Amenities:** Restaurant; bar; lounge; limited room service; laundry service/dry cleaning. *In room:* TV, dataport, minibar (in some), hair dryer.

Park Hotel Vitznau ★★★　One of the most elegant waterside havens along the Lucerne Riviera, this Belle Epoque hotel offers lavish living. It was designed by architect Karl Koller and built in 1902 at the foot of Mount Rigi. A wing added in 1985 maintains the spirit of the original "fairy-tale castle." Today's hotel grew out of a simple 1866 B&B that once attracted such wanderers as Mark Twain and Victor Hugo. The spacious bedrooms have been completely renovated, with marble-clad bathrooms and such thoughtful extras as heated towel racks. The bathtubs with showers have been dubbed "pharaonic." English chintz, both in draperies and upholstery, give the rooms a summery look. Try for one of the seven or so lake-view rooms on the first floor in the older section, each of which has a sprawling lakefront terrace. Room nos. 121 and 123, with particularly large terraces, are most frequently requested. Ceilings within the hotel's public areas are particularly high and grand, each a decorative throwback to the late-19th-century age of hotel design. There's also a sun terrace with parasols. The a la carte restaurant, Quatre Cantons, with a lakeside terrace, is one of the finest French restaurants in Switzerland.

Kantonstrasse, CH-6354 Vitznau. © 041/399-60-60. Fax 041/399-60-70. www.parkhotel-vitznau.ch. 112 units. 530F–750F ($435–$615) double; from 880F ($722) suite. Rates include buffet breakfast. AE, DC, MC, V. Parking 20F ($16). Closed Oct 5–Apr 21. **Amenities:** 3 restaurants; bar; indoor pool; 2 tennis courts; health club; sauna; free bikes; 24-hr. room service; babysitting; laundry service/dry cleaning; water-skiing; rooms for guests w/limited mobility. *In room:* TV, dataport, minibar (in some), hair dryer.

5 Brunnen ★★

45km (28 miles) SE of Lucerne

Brunnen is a popular vacation resort in the canton of Schwyz. It's located at the foot of Fronalpstock, in a beautiful inlet at the southern end of Lake Lucerne, where you find the Urnersee (or Lake Uri), one of the most beautiful lake sites in Switzerland. There's a fine view of the two lakes and the Alps from the quays. The resort is about an hour's drive from Zurich's Kloten International Airport.

ESSENTIALS
GETTING THERE　Some of the local trains running between Zurich and Lugano or Locarno in Switzerland's deep south stop in Brunnen, although some require changes in such towns as Goschenen. Call © 0900/300-300 (no area code) for **rail schedules.**

A miniarmada of buses commutes dozens of times every day from Schwyz to both the waterfront and the railroad station at Brunnen, requiring only about 12 minutes for the one-way passage. Other buses travel from Brunnen to the beginning of the cable car that ascends to Morschach. For **bus schedules** and information, call © 041/390-11-33.

Several lake steamers depart from the quays of Lucerne for Brunnen throughout the day, with more frequent service scheduled during midsummer. Travel time from Lucerne to Brunnen ranges from 2 to 2½ hours. For more information, call © 041/367-67-67.

The Legend of William Tell

One of the most famous names in Swiss history, linked with that country's struggle for liberty, concerned a William Tell, who may never have existed. But to the Swiss he is very real, the father who with his crossbow hit the apple that the tyrannical Austrian bailiff of Uri, Gessler, had placed on the head of his son.

When Gessler allegedly asked Tell why he had brought a second arrow, Tell told him he intended it for Gessler if he had hit his son instead of the apple. Furious, Gessler had Tell dragged to his boat at the northwestern shore of Lake Lucerne. A storm came up and Gessler released Tell from his fetters, hoping that his strong arms could save the boat party. Tell escaped and waited on the shore near Gessler's castle. When Gessler arrived, Tell hit him with an arrow straight through the heart. Or so the story goes.

First found in a ballad, the tale dates from at least before 1474. Over the years various authors have smoothed away inconsistencies and rounded out the tale. But it was Schiller's play in 1804 that gave the tale worldwide renown.

Alleged proofs of the actual existence of a William Tell break down hopelessly upon scholarly examination. For example, entries in the parish registers are forgeries. One document that alleged that 114 men in 1338 had been "personally acquainted" with Tell didn't surface until 1759—no doubt a fake.

Tellskapelle (the Tell Chapel) stands today as a monument to the legend, lying at the Lake of the Four Cantons between Sisikon and Flüelen.

From Lucerne, drive to the resorts of Weggis and Vitznau (see sections 3 and 4, earlier in this chapter), then continue southeast along Route 2b until you reach Brunnen.

VISITOR INFORMATION The **Brunnen Tourist Office,** Bahnhofstrasse 32 (© **041/825-00-41**), is open Monday to Friday from 8:30am to 6pm and Saturday and Sunday from 9am to 3pm.

EXPLORING THE AREA

What you do here is walk along the shady **lakeside quays** 🕸🕸, among the country's most scenic parts, taking in views of the wild and remote lake, the Urnersee. The views of the lake from the quays are stunning, taking in the awesome Uri-Rotstock, twin peaks with a small glacier.

The area around Brunnen—so beloved by Hans Christian Andersen—is the cradle of the Confederation and abounds in reminders of the country's history, including archives in Schwyz where the Confederation documents are displayed, and the Federal Chapel in Brunnen.

This is also William Tell country. Around the year 1250, several families left Raron in the Valais and crossed the Alps to establish new homes in desolate Schächental/Uri. Records confirm that the Tell family helped found the settlement. According to folk legend, William Tell was the hero of a decisive battle in 1315 and reportedly died in 1350. Historians, however, have no proof of these events.

Nevertheless, the Swiss honor the man who shot an apple off the head of his brave young son with a bow and arrow in a test of prowess. Many visitors travel to Sisikon, just south of Brunnen, to see the **Tell Chapel,** which was restored in 1881. The chapel contains records from the early 16th century and paintings by Stückelberg.

NEARBY ATTRACTIONS   Brunnen is the starting point of **Axenstrasse,** the stunning panoramic road—a masterpiece of engineering—leading south to the St. Gotthard Pass. It goes along the rim of Lake Uri (Urnersee), in and out of subterranean passageways and galleries carved out of the mountain. Brunnen is also a base for excursions by ship, mountain railway, bus, and train to points around Lake Lucerne.

WHERE TO STAY & DINE

Hotel Bellevue   Built in the 1800s and completely renovated many times since, this baroque hotel at the edge of the lake offers cozy, old-fashioned comfort. Werner Achermann and his family offer well-maintained rooms, most with carpeting and all with well-maintained bathrooms. The hotel also has a sun terrace.

Axenstrasse 2, CH-6440 Brunnen. ℂ **041/820-13-18.** Fax 041/820-38-89. www.bellevue-brunnen.ch. 48 units. 160F–240F ($131–$197) double. Half board 30F ($25) per person extra. Rates include buffet breakfast. AE, DC, MC, V. Free outdoor parking; 10F ($8.20) garage. Closed Nov–Apr. **Amenities:** Restaurant; lounge; laundry service/dry cleaning; rooms for guests w/limited mobility. *In room:* TV, dataport, minibar, hair dryer.

Seehotel Waldstätterhof 🏵🏵   One of the few government-rated five-star hotels opening onto the lake, the Waldstätterhof offers old-style comfort. The symmetrical white building has a mansard roof and a series of balconies overlooking the lake. Plenty of modern comforts have been installed since the hotel opened in 1870. Each of the well-furnished and spacious rooms offers a well-maintained bathroom. The public rooms are grand and the dining room has fanciful chandeliers. The grounds are well kept and free of traffic and include a private beach on the lake. There's also a terrace restaurant, a less-formal dining room, and a rotisserie. The Lake Lucerne steamers stop nearby, and the Schiller Memorial Stone can be seen on the opposite shore of the lake. The hotel is open year-round.

Waldstätterquai 6, CH-6440 Brunnen. ℂ **041/825-06-06.** Fax 041/825-06-00. www.waldstaetterhof.ch. 104 units. 220F–430F ($180–$353) double; 590F–710F ($484–$582) suite. Half board 50F ($41) extra. Rates include buffet breakfast. AE, DC, MC, V. Free parking outside; 20F ($16) garage. **Amenities:** 2 restaurants; bar; tennis court; health club; sauna; limited room service; babysitting; laundry service/dry cleaning. *In room:* TV, dataport, minibar, hair dryer, safe.

6 Altdorf

54km (34 miles) SE of Lucerne

Altdorf is the town where the William Tell legend is said to have taken place. A statue of the Swiss national hero stands in the main square. The key to the St. Gotthard Pass, Altdorf is north of the Alps and 3km (2 miles) south of where the Reuss River flows into the Urnersee. It's the capital of the canton of Uri and the starting point of the road over the Klausen Pass. The most scenic way to get to Altdorf from Lucerne is to ride a lake steamer to Flüelen and transfer to a bus. The total trip takes about 3 hours. Call the tourist office (see below) for more information.

ESSENTIALS

GETTING THERE   Several daily trains make the 27-minute trip to Altdorf from the region's biggest railway junction, Arth-Goldau, on their way south to Chiasso and eventually Milan. Call ℂ **0900/300-300** for **rail schedules.**

The bus routes coming into Altdorf connect the town with mountain hamlets, which usually have no railway junctions of their own. In the summer a handful of buses connect it with Zurich's Hauptbahnhof, sometimes with a transfer in Flüelen. Travel time from Zurich is about 1½ hours. For bus schedules and information, call © **041/618-85-55.**

If you're driving from Brunnen on Lake Lucerne, continue south along N4.

VISITOR INFORMATION   The **Altdorf Tourist Office** (© **041/872-04-50**) is open Monday to Saturday from 9 to 11:30am and Monday to Friday 1:30 to 5:30pm.

SEEING THE SIGHTS

The famous **William Tell statue** is in front of the early-19th-century town hall and a tower dating from the Middle Ages. The monument was created by Richard Kissling in 1895; it was this image, engraved on a postage stamp, that became familiar to people all over the globe.

Altdorf is set in a scenic area of central Switzerland that makes for good biking. You can rent a bike at the train station (© **041/870-10-08**). You can also rent mountain bikes and motorbikes at **Mototreff,** Flüelerstrasse 20 (© **041/870-97-37**). Armed with a good map from the tourist office, set out on your adventure.

NEARBY ATTRACTIONS   The road to the Klausen Pass leads to **Bürglen,** one of the oldest hamlets in Uri. Snowdrifts block the pass from October to May. Bürglen, according to legend, was the birthplace of William Tell. The **Tell Museum,** Hauptstrasse (© **041/870-41-55**), contains documents and mementos relating to the early history of Switzerland. The museum is in a Romanesque tower adjacent to the parish church. It's open April to June and September and October daily from 10 to 11:30am and 1:30 to 5pm; in July and August daily from 9:30am to 5:30pm. Admission is 4F ($3.30) for adults, 2F ($1.65) for children 16 and under.

WHERE TO STAY & DINE

Goldener Schlüssel (Value)   The best of the lot is this five-story, government-rated three-star hotel in the center of town. A historic inn dating from the 19th century, it faces a tiny medieval plaza and is distinguished by a wrought-iron sign bearing a golden key (*goldener Schlüssel*). The hotel's accessories include a handful of original paintings. The bedrooms are cozy and comfortably furnished and those units with bathrooms have clean showering facilities.

The hotel's well-reputed restaurant serves a cuisine based on all-Swiss recipes and local ingredients.

Schützengasse 9, CH-6460 Altdorf. © 041/871-10-02. Fax 041/870-11-67. 25 units, 18 with bathroom. 120F–135F ($98–$111) double without bathroom; 180F–218F ($148–$179) double with bathroom; 310F ($254) suite. Half board 50F ($41) per person extra. Rates include buffet breakfast. AE, DC, MC, V. Free parking. **Amenities:** Restaurant; lounge; gym, Jacuzzi; sauna; limited room service. *In room:* TV, minibar, hair dryer.

Hotel Bahnhof (Finds)   Anna Niederberger and her family own this small, well-established tourist hotel that resembles a private house, with a modern addition in front. Built in 1880, it still retains many of its old-fashioned and somewhat quirky architectural details. It has dated furniture, and each room has a sink. The accommodations are small but pleasantly paneled and comfortable, with good beds.

CH-6460 Altdorf. © 041/870-10-32. Fax 041/870-99-32. www.bahnhof-altdorf.ch. 15 units, none with bathroom. 90F ($74) double. Rates include continental breakfast. No credit cards. Free parking. **Amenities:** Restaurant; lounge; nonsmoking rooms. *In room:* No phone.

7 Amsteg

14km (9 miles) S of Altdorf; 6.4km (4 miles) S of Erstfeld

This traditional stop on the St. Gotthard route is a good base for walks and mountain excursions. Amsteg is at the mouth of the Maderanertal. In the distance you can see a tall viaduct, which holds the tracks of the St. Gotthard railway.

ESSENTIALS

GETTING THERE   Train service was discontinued to the rarely used Amsteg railway station several years ago, so railway passengers headed for Amsteg get off at the hamlet of Erstfeld. From here, the Swiss railway system operates shuttle service, by bus, at hourly intervals throughout the day for the price of 4F ($2.60) per person each way. For information on both the **railway** and the **shuttle,** call © **0900/300-300.**

VISITOR INFORMATION   Amsteg does not have a tourist office. The tourist office (© **044/872-04-50**) of Altdorf, just north of Amsteg, is open Monday to Saturday 9 to 11:30am and Monday to Friday from 1:30 to 5:30pm.

WHERE TO STAY & DINE

Hotel Stern und Post ⭒   This is the most colorful and atmospheric hotel in Amsteg. It has been managed since 1734 by members of the Tresch family, who established it as part of their administration of the local branch of the then-private Swiss Postal system. After 1850, when the Swiss Postal system became a branch of the national government, the family maintained this hotel in addition to nearby lodgings for more than 400 horses, most of which were used for hauling mail and supplies over the nearby Gotthard Pass. Today, under the administration of Elizabeth Tresch, this hotel retains many of its ornate 19th-century antiques, moldings, doors, and decorative accessories. Some of the bedrooms are furnished with Victorian-style beds and lots of gingerbread, with high ceilings and nostalgic reminders of another era. Rooms containing private bathrooms have well-equipped facilities; there are only sinks with running water in those without. Public areas, discreetly modernized and enlarged and—in newer wings—pierced with panoramic windows, have gray-green walls and reminders of the hotel's earliest origins. The in-house restaurant, which seats up to 40 guests, will spoil you with a plentiful cuisine and well-chosen wines from their private cellar.

CH-6474 Amsteg. © **041/883-14-40.** Fax 041/883-02-61. www.sternpost.ch. 20 units, 14 with bathroom. 120F–160F ($98–$131) double without bathroom; 130F–250F ($107–$205) double with bathroom. 35F ($29) supplement for half board per person (3 nights' minimum stopover required for half board). Rates include breakfast. AE, DC, MC, V. Parking 8F ($6.55) per night. Closed Jan to mid-Mar. **Amenities:** Restaurant; bar; limited room service; babysitting; laundry service/dry cleaning. *In room:* TV, dataport, hair dryer.

8 Andermatt ⭒

50km (31 miles) SE of Lucerne

At the crossroads of the Alps, Andermatt is a sports center known for its long, sunny days in winter. It's in the Urseren Valley, at the junction of two alpine roads—the St. Gotthard highway and the road to Oberalp and Furka. Visitors flock here for the valley's scenic grandeur, best absorbed by hiking in summer or cross-country skiing in winter.

ESSENTIALS

GETTING THERE   Andermatt lies directly on a secondary rail line connecting Chur with Lucerne, where further connections can be made on express trains to the rest of Switzerland. Travel time from Lucerne is about 1¾ hours. Call ℂ **0900/ 300-300** for **rail schedules.**

Three or four buses travel daily from the bus junction of Airolo to Andermatt. To Airolo, buses funnel in every day from Basel, Lucerne, Zurich, and Lugano, with connections to such other resorts as Brig and Oberwald. For **bus schedules** and information, call ℂ **081/949-20-34.**

If you're driving from Amsteg, continue south along N2.

VISITOR INFORMATION The **Andermatt Tourist Office,** Gotthardstrasse 2 (ℂ **041/887-14-54**), is open Monday to Saturday from 9am to noon and 2 to 5:30pm.

EXPLORING THE AREA

Andermatt is a good base for hikes across the mountain passes, including the St. Gotthard Pass and the Furka Pass. In the winter skiers flock to Gemsstock, Natschen, Oberalp, and Winterhorn. Also in winter the town offers 10 lifts, five cable cars, 21km (13 miles) of cross-country trails open November to May, and 56km (35 miles) of downhill runs. Intermediate to advanced skiers are attracted to the resort. Safety devices help protect against snowdrifts and avalanches. Other sporting facilities include a Swiss Ski School, an ice-skating and curling rink, an indoor swimming pool, and squash courts. Sleigh rides are also offered.

South of Andermatt, the **St. Gotthard Pass** ✿, at 2,109m (6,918 ft.), provides a link between the Grisons and the Valais Alps. It's one of the most stunning and scenic passes in Switzerland, used by merchants and messengers as far back as the early Middle Ages. The road through the pass was built in the 18th and 19th centuries atop a much older footpath; it's still the shortest route between the two watersheds that fall away on either side. A 15km (9-mile) railway tunnel burrows under the peak of the St. Gotthard massif; nearby, the St. Gotthard road tunnel, opened in 1980, is the longest one in the world. There's no toll along the 16km (10-mile) route, which is open year-round. (The road high above it closes during heavy snowfalls.)

If you don't have a car, you can take either the postal bus over the pass or the train through the tunnel. The postal bus leaves from Andermatt and goes to Airolo daily between mid-April and September 21. Departures from Andermatt are at 9:35am and 12:30pm. The last bus back leaves Airolo at 5pm. In winter the pass is closed and postal buses can't get through, but you could take the train to Göschenen and from there continue by train to Airolo. Trains run through the tunnel frequently, the only way for trains to cross this mountain-pass area. For **train information** and schedules, call ℂ **0900/300-300.**

The 32km (20-mile) **Furka Pass Road** ✿✿✿ going from Gletsch to Andermatt takes about 2½ hours and is one of the most scenic rides in Europe. Begin the trip at Gletsch at 174m (571 ft.). As you drive along, you'll have panoramic views of the Rhone Glacier, and both the Bernese and Valais Alps. The pass at 2,392m (7,846 ft.) is the highest shelf of the towering longitudinal furrow, dividing the Swiss Alps from the rail junction at Martigny to the town of Chur. In 1982 a railway tunnel, a stunning feat of modern engineering, opened the pass between the villages of Oberwald and Realp. Going through the barren valley of Garschen and bordering the foothills of Galenstock, a mountain peak, the road comes to the severe Urseren Valley before passing through the villages of Realp, Hospental, and finally Andermatt, where you might want to spend the night.

WHERE TO STAY & DINE

Hotel Aurora   Although this hotel presents a modern and unassuming facade to the world outside, the pleasant and warmly decorated interior and the hands-on management of its owners (the Christen family) make a stay here worthwhile. Built in 1969, it's a well-managed, government-rated three-star hotel, lying at the southern edge of the village, within a 5-minute walk of the town center. Each small room has touches of pine paneling and a neatly kept bathroom.

CH-6490 Andermatt. ℭ **041/887-16-61.** Fax 041/887-00-86. www.aurora-andermatt.ch. 26 units. 120F–150F ($98–$123) double; 156F–177F ($128–$145) triple. Rates include buffet breakfast. AE, MC, V. Free parking. Closed May and Nov. **Amenities:** Restaurant; lounge; bar; sauna; limited room service; laundry service/dry cleaning. *In room:* TV, dataport, hair dryer, safe.

Hotel Drei Könige und Post ⍟   This old and fabled inn still puts up wayfarers. There has been a series of inns at this site since 1234, and Goethe spent the night at one of them in 1775. This family-run hotel has been rebuilt or renovated many times since. There's a cafe terrace in front of this white-walled chalet with buttressed eaves and brown shutters. Regional Swiss dishes are served in the hotel restaurant. The Renner family offers well-furnished paneled rooms, 10 of which have balconies. Rooms range from small to midsize, and each is comfortable with traditional furnishings. All units are equipped with well-maintained bathrooms.

Gotthardstrasse 69, CH-6490 Andermatt. ℭ **041/887-00-01.** Fax 041/887-16-66. www.3koenige.ch. 21 units. 150F–260F ($123–$213) double. Half board 40F ($33). AE, DC, MC, V. Free outdoor parking; 10F ($8.20) garage. Closed Apr 15–May and Nov–Dec 15. **Amenities:** Restaurant; lounge; fitness center; Jacuzzi; sauna; Turkish bath; limited room service; babysitting; laundry service/dry cleaning; nonsmoking rooms; dataport. *In room:* TV, minibar, hair dryer, safe.

13

The Grisons

Of all the Swiss cantons, the Grisons is both the largest and the least developed. Its German name is Graubunden; to the Romansh-speaking population it's Grischun, and the Italians call it Grigioni. Grisons is the French (and English) name, although French is rarely spoken in this canton.

This sparsely settled, easternmost Swiss region is very mountainous and contains 225 sq. km (140 sq. miles) of glaciers. One-fifth of the canton's total area is covered with forests. The region contains the sources of the Rhine and Inn (En in Romansh) rivers, which form the major valleys of the canton. Juf, at nearly 2,100m (6,888 ft.) above sea level, is the highest permanently inhabited village in the Alps. Even the 150 or so valleys of the Grisons lie at high altitudes, between 886m and 1,969m (2,906 ft. and 6,458 ft.), and the region's highest peak, Bernina, reaches 3,986m (13,074 ft.). The alpine scenery here differs from that of other areas of Switzerland in altitude as well as topography—the air is clear and invigorating, which has led to the establishment of many health centers in the Grisons. The height makes it cooler at night, but it enjoys the extra daytime warmth of other southern cantons.

The Grisons was once a territory of Rhaetia, peopled by Celtic tribes in pre-Christian times. In 15 B.C., the Romans conquered the Rhaetians, began colonization, and built alpine roads. The Germanic Franks entered the Roman provinces in the 3rd century and established themselves along the Rhine. They and their successors,

the Ostrogoths, introduced Teutonic influences into the Roman territories they seized, gradually changing the language of the inhabitants to Germanic dialects, especially in the northern regions. As a result, German is spoken today by about half the Grisons population, mainly around Davos and Chur, the capital of the canton. About a sixth of the people of the Grisons—those living in the south—speak the language of their next-door neighbor, Italy.

The people of the upper valleys of the Rhine and the Inn were isolated enough to resist Germanic influences, and today they still cling to their ancestral tongue, Romansh—the language of a third of the Swiss living in the Grisons. Both the dialect spoken in the Engadine (Ladin) and that spoken in the Vorderrhein Valley (Surveltisch) are derived from the Latin of Rhaetia. The centuries have altered it, so that today it sounds rather like Spanish spoken with a German accent. In 1938 Romansh officially became the fourth of the Swiss national languages.

The Grisons was one of the last regions of Switzerland to benefit from busy commerce with the rest of the country. Cars were forbidden on all roads until 1927, and even today it's illegal to drive cars in Arosa after nightfall. This ban on the use of roads helped to popularize the Rhaetian railway, whose narrow-gauge trains cross the region along hairpin turns and through dozens of tunnels. Today this railway, as well as the postal buses that crisscross the district, provide panoramas of a harsh and sometimes-bleak landscape.

The peasants of this canton banded together in 1395 to form the Ligue Grise (Gray League), from which the name Grisons is derived. Two other such leagues were formed in the area to oppose Hapsburg domination. In 1803 the three leagues formed a single canton, which joined the Swiss Confederation. The belief system of the Protestant Reformation, however, was adopted by only part of the canton, and today sections of it remain staunchly Catholic.

Since the 1950s, much of the Grisons has earned its living from tourists, who visit for the skiing and the small villages, as well as the local red and "green" wines (vetliner), the exquisite embroidery, and the hand-woven linens still produced in many mountain homes.

1 Chur ⟨★

122km (76 miles) SE of Zurich; 59km (37 miles) W of Davos

The capital of the Grisons, Chur is the oldest town in Switzerland. According to recent excavations, the area had been inhabited as early as 3000 B.C. The Romans established a settlement in 15 B.C., naming it Curia Rhaetorum. In 450 B.C. a recently Christianized Chur became the see of a bishop. The town still has a bishop, but he no longer has the power of his medieval predecessors, who ruled virtually every aspect of life in Chur until 1526.

Set at an elevation of 586m (1,922 ft.), Chur lies near the head of the Rhine Valley, surrounded by towering mountains. The Plessur River, a tributary of the Rhine, flows through the center of town. Chur is at the natural junction of several of the most important routes from Italy over the alpine passes and as a result incorporates both Italian and Rhaetian influences.

Favored by visitors, who appreciate the wilderness surrounding it, Chur is the largest mercantile center between Zurich and Milan. It's also an important rail center, a terminal for several of the most scenic railway lines in Switzerland: the narrow-gauge rail line to St. Moritz (the Rhätische Bahn), the Chur-Arosa line, the *Glacier Express,* the *Palm Express,* and the *Bernina Express.* You might also go to Splügen, said to have the prettiest mountain-pass village in the area.

Chur also offers a variety of sports facilities. Summer sports include hiking and mountain biking. A pair of swimming pools, both indoor and outdoor, lies within the **Sportanlagen Obere** (✆ **081/254-42-88**), as well as a gymnasium and health club. Access to either of the pools costs 6F ($4.90) for adults and 3F ($2.45) for children ages 6 to 15. (It's free for children 5 and under.) Access to the gym costs 15F ($12) for everyone, but entrance is restricted to persons who can present a membership card from any other gym or health club, presumably as a means of determining that the bearer is familiar with how to exercise in a nondestructive way. In the winter skiers in and around Chur have access to the top 20 ski areas surrounding Chur, some of which reach 2,700m (8,856 ft.) and are only 1½ hours away.

Chur's Old Town is best discovered on foot. The route outlined by the city is the most scenic and most historic. You travel at your own pace, just following in the footsteps of others. In addition, the tourist office (see "Essentials," below) provides German-language guided tours that depart from the tourist office every Wednesday at 2:30pm, but only between April and October. Participation in any of the guided tours costs 8F ($6.55) for adults and 4F ($3.30) for children ages 6 to 16. They're free for children 5 and under.

ESSENTIALS

GETTING THERE   The town is the end of some international lines, such as the standard-gauge railway from Sargans. It's also the starting point for the narrow-gauge line to St. Moritz, known as the Rhätische Bahn. The Chur-Arosa line and the Glacier Express also start here. Chur also has frequent train connections from Zurich. Call ✆ **0900/300-300** for rail schedules.

Chur lies near the terminus of several bus lines, which link its railway facilities with some of the villages scattered throughout the nearby valleys. The two most prominent of these are Davos and St. Moritz, where bus connections can be made to Munich, across the German border. For **bus schedules** and information, call ✆ **081/254-40-60** for questions about buses within the city limits, and 081/256-3166 for buses traveling to or from Chur from points outside the city limits.

If you're driving, Chur is about 90 minutes from Zurich along N3 (later N13), and easily reached by expressway.

VISITOR INFORMATION   The **tourist office** is located at Grabenstrasse 5 (✆ **081/252-18-18**) and is open Monday from 1:30 to 6pm, Tuesday to Friday from 8:30am to noon and 1:30 to 6pm, and Saturday from 9am to noon.

SEEING THE SIGHTS

You'll want to spend as much time as possible in Chur to see the legacies left by the many emperors, kings, armies, and traders who have marched through here. In the medieval sector you'll come across squares with flower-bedecked fountains and narrow streets, along with elegant houses and many towers.

The **cathedral of Chur** ♔, Hof 19 (for information, call the tourist office at ✆ **081/252-18-18**), was built between 1151 and 1282 on an ancient foundation and was renovated extensively in the 19th century. Inside, the high altar displays a 15th-century gilded-wood triptych in the Gothic style, the largest of its kind in Switzerland. Be warned that extensive renovations within the cathedral's interior will restrict access—depending on the work schedule—to various sections of the cathedral. City officials predict a completion sometime during 2007. Until then, many areas of the cathedral, including its treasury, will be closed to the public.

Near the cathedral, the baroque **Bishop's Palace,** which is not open to the public, was built in 1732 and is still the private residence of a bishop. The palace opens onto Hofplatz—site of a Roman fort.

Bündner Kunstmuseum (Fine Arts Museum)   Known as the Villa Planta, this museum, set in a park, displays paintings and sculptures by many well-known Grisons artists. Some of the works are by Giovanni, Segantini, Angelica Kauffmann, Ferdinand Hodler, and Cuno Amiet, as well as by Alberto and Augusto Giacometti. You'll also find works by Ernst Ludwig Kirchner (1880–1938), the German painter and leader of the Brücke school of expressionists.

Bahnhofstrasse 35, at Postplatz. ✆ **081/257-28-68.** Admission 10F ($8.20) adults, 7F ($5.75) students, free for children 16 and under. Tues–Sun 10am–noon; Tues–Wed and Fri–Sun 2–5pm; Thurs 2–8pm.

Rätisches Museum   Loaded with memorabilia from the town's (and the region's) history, this folklore museum is one of the best places in the district for an insight into the harsh climate and agrarian origins of the Grisons.

Hofstrasse 1. ✆ **081/257-28-89.** Admission 6F ($4.90) adults, 4F ($3.30) students, free for children 15 and under. Tues–Sun 10am–noon; Tues–Wed and Fri–Sun 2–5pm; Thurs 2–8pm.

WHERE TO STAY
EXPENSIVE
Romantik Hotel Stern ♔♔   Like most members of the Romantik chain, this historic hotel is filled with authentic antiques. You know you're in for a special experience when you arrive. If notified in advance, the hotel will send a 1933 Buick to pick you up at the rail depot. The outside of the hotel looks like a giant strawberry mousse with white shutters. The interior has pine paneling—some of which dates from 1677—and vaulted or timbered ceilings. The modern and well-maintained bedrooms have 19th-century regional country antiques and are each fitted with a comfortable bathroom. Some have carefully preserved ceiling beams or trusses, many of them very old. In 1948 playwright Berthold Brecht lived here for 5 weeks during the midsummer production of one of his plays at a nearby theater. Special grace notes include a rooftop terrace, a lounge with a fireplace, and lots of memorabilia that evoke rustic and alpine Switzerland.

Reichsgasse 11, CH-7000 Chur. ✆ **081/258-57-57.** Fax 081/258-57-58. www.stern-chur.ch. 58 units. 290F ($238) double. Rates include buffet breakfast. Half board costs 40F ($33) extra per person. AE, DC, MC, V. Free parking outdoors, 16F ($13) inside. **Amenities:** Restaurant; limited room service; laundry service. *In room:* TV, minibar (in some).

MODERATE

Hotel Chur   The Chur lies in the center of town near the Old Town and about a 10-minute walk from the rail station. This imposing neoclassical building with arched windows and fifth-floor gables contains two different dining areas with old-fashioned (but frequently renovated) charm, and comfortable, well-furnished bedrooms, each with a medium-size bathroom.

Welschdörfli 2, CH-7000 Chur. ✆ **081/254-34-00.** Fax 081/254-34-10. www.hotelchur.ch. 54 units. 155F–177F ($127–$145) double. Rates include buffet breakfast. AE, DC, MC, V. Free parking. **Amenities:** 5 different dining areas; bar; limited room service; laundry service. *In room:* TV, dataport, minibar, hair dryer.

Hotel Freieck   Built originally in 1575 and rising seven imposing, fresco-covered stories, this is an old favorite. It has been renovated countless times since. Clinging stubbornly to tradition, the hotel, in the center of town, boasts a facade decorated with drawings of grapevines, a sundial, and two lions. The renovated, well-scrubbed, and midsize bedrooms contain simple furniture and comfortable bathrooms, mainly with shower only. The owners place a lot of emphasis on its dining rooms, which include stucco rooms with massive beams and vaulting as well as a more contemporary-looking, richly paneled modern area.

Reichsgasse 44/50, CH-7002 Chur. ✆ **081/252-17-92.** Fax 081/253-34-19. www.freieck.ch. 37 units. 150F–190F ($98–$124) double. Rates include buffet breakfast. AE, DC, MC, V. Free parking 7pm–8am. **Amenities:** Bar; limited room service; laundry service. *In room:* TV, minibar (in some), hair dryer.

INEXPENSIVE

Hotel Drei Könige ✿   This historic hotel is at the entrance to the Old Town. The building's foundation dates from at least the 14th century. Excavations in the hotel cellar unearthed a collapsed tunnel that had led to the bishop's palace at the opposite end of the old city. Over the years the hotel has welcomed royalty, high-ranking politicians, and world-famous artists. The Drei Könige Hall on the premises used to be part of a monastery and, later, the seat of government.

Except for a handful of budget accommodations without private bathrooms, under the eaves the well-scrubbed midsize rooms have comfortable furniture, including good beds, and the standard amenities such as up-to-date plumbing with an equal mixture of showers or tubs. The hotel has one of the most popular restaurants in town (see "Where to Dine," below).

Reichsgasse 18, CH-7000 Chur. ✆ **081/252-17-58.** Fax 081/252-17-26. www.dreikoenige.com. 40 units, 28 with bathroom. 110F–130F ($90–$107) double without bathroom; 130F–240F ($107–$197) double with bathroom. Rates include continental breakfast. AE, DC, MC, V. Parking 15F ($12). **Amenities:** Restaurant; bar; access to nearby health club and golf course; limited room service; laundry service. *In room:* TV, dataport (in some), minibar, hair dryer, iron.

Hotel Zunfthaus Rebleüten ✿✿   In its way, and thanks to a sophisticated blend of Scottish and Swiss ownership, this is one of the most appealing, and most hip, hotels in town. The venue is a meticulously restored guildhall dating from the 1470s, artfully positioned behind a bubbling fountain on one of the Old Town's most evocative squares. Graced with frescoes and blue-painted shutters on its facade, and staffed inside by a crew of great warmth and humor, it offers clean, well-maintained, and not particularly ostentatious bedrooms, each with simple but well-planned comforts. The coziest of the bedrooms (including nos. 5, 6, 7, 8, and 9) lie on the building's uppermost floor, beneath the sloping eaves. Here, architectural features include views of massive exposed beams and panoramas out over the Old Town.

Pfisterplatz 1, CH-7000 Chur. ℭ **081/257-13-57**. Fax 081/257-13-58. www.rebleuten.ch. 10 units. 140F ($115) double with breakfast; 210F ($172) double with half board. Rates include buffet breakfast. AE, MC, V. **Amenities:** Restaurant with 2 outdoor terraces; bar; laundry service. *In room:* TV, safe.

WHERE TO DINE
EXPENSIVE
Duc de Rohan ✸ SWISS/MEDITERRANEAN   Many Swiss consider this the most posh, most impressive, most formal, and most stately looking restaurant in town—and we concur. Meals are served in Europeanized comfort in the restaurant or on a garden-style outdoor terrace. Drinks are available in the restaurant. Carefully prepared specialties include a variety of seafood dishes and homemade ravioli.

Masanserstrasse 44. ℭ **081/252-10-22**. Reservations recommended. Main courses 20F–45F ($16–$37); fixed-price 3-course menu 103F ($84). AE, DC, MC, V. Mon–Sat 11:30am–2pm and 5:30–9:30pm.

MODERATE
Hotel Stern Restaurant ✸ GRISONS   Jean-Luc Rohner's previously recommended hotel is known for serving some of the most authentic Grisons-inspired recipes in eastern Switzerland. At this historic 1677 hotel, the restaurant is wrapped in time-worn *arvenholz*, a rich wood paneling. Regional wine is served in pewter pitchers and waiters are in folk costumes. This may sound corny, but somehow it works.

When we call the cuisine traditional, we're referring to great-grandmother style. For example, begin with barley soup or air-dried beef on a wooden plate. The rye bread from Puschlav that accompanies most dishes is scented with anise and butter. Lake trout is poached and flavored with Riesling, and vegetarian meals are also prepared. *Bizochels sursilvans* are country-style flour dumplings with bacon and potato pieces, onions, cheese, and melted butter. Dessert may be walnut ice cream with damsons.

Reichsgasse 11. ℭ **081/258-57-57**. Reservations recommended. Main courses 19F–38F ($16–$31); fixed-price lunch 17F–71F ($14–$58); fixed-price dinner 21F–71F ($17–$58). MC, V. Daily 9am–2pm and 5–10pm.

Zunfthaus Rebleuten ✸✸ FRENCH/ITALIAN/SWISS   Originally built as a guildhall in the 1400s, this is one of the most enduring, most charming, and most historic restaurants in Chur. Within a trio of rooms that date from 1483, amid 200-year-old tables and chairs, an antique clock, fireplaces, and ceiling frescoes that evoke alpine Switzerland of long ago, you can benefit from the skill and hard work of the Law family, a Scottish and Swiss managerial team that seems to handle all guests, and all venues, with heroic style. Consider the filets of sole with wild rice; tomato mousse with shrimp; a mixed platter of air-dried beef with mountain sausages; filets of flounder in a potato crust, or roasted breast of goose in a cabbage-and-kirsch sauce. A particularly appealing appetizer is the stuffed trout in a saffron sauce. During clement weather the establishment offers two separate outdoor terraces, each with views out over the town's historic core.

Pfisterplatz. ℭ **081/252-17-13**. Reservations recommended. Main courses 22F–37F ($18–$30); fixed-price menus 20F–35F ($16–$29). AE, DC, MC, V. Mon–Sat 7:30am–midnight; Sun 7:30am–6pm.

INEXPENSIVE
The Weinstube in the Hotel Drei Könige SWISS   Cozy and evocative, this well-patronized dining room, set on the first floor of the previously recommended hotel, is covered with worn paneling, whose nicks and scratches only add to the character of the room. Don't expect haute cuisine here. Instead you get soul-satisfying mountain-style food prepared with honest ingredients handled in an efficient

and straightforward manner. Meals are served amid hunting trophies, collections of medals, and old photographs.

The Weinstube welcomes some of Chur's most prominent citizens. Sometimes the chef prepares a double entrecôte *marchand de vin* or a chateaubriand Henri-IV. You can also order more standard fare, such as *pot-au-feu* (meat stew) and polenta with cheese.

Reichsgasse 18. © 081/252-17-25. Main courses 16F–25F ($13–$21); fixed-price menu 20F ($16). AE, DC, MC, V. Daily 10am–2pm and 5–10pm (last order).

CHUR AFTER DARK

The hot spot in town is **Giger Bar,** Comercialstrasse 23 (© **081/253-75-06**). The Oscar-winning H. R. Giger, a native of Chur and set designer on the movie *Alien,* was responsible for creating this 1980 bar and disco with its Starship *Enterprise* aura. Its biggest competitor for the francs and patronage of the clientele, which ranges in age from 18 to around 60, is the **Safari Beat Club,** Kupfergasse 11 (© **079/418-55-55**). Outfitted like a camp safari movie (faux-leopard skin upholsteries, references to darkest Africa), it attracts some of the most energetic dancers in town, both male and female. Admission costs 12F ($9.85), which usually includes the first drink.

2 Arosa ★★★

30km (19 miles) E of Chur

Arosa, one of the highest of the alpine resorts (1,800m/5,904 ft. above sea level), lies in a sheltered basin above the Schanfigg Valley. The most popular resort in the Grisons after Davos and St. Moritz, it basically consists of one main street (Poststrasse) lined with hotels and shops. Though parts of the village date from the 14th century, the resort has a modern and contemporary look. If St. Moritz is too ultrachic for you, Arosa may be your answer. Both visitors and the hotels that house them tend to be low-key and family-oriented, often favoring ski jackets over dinner jackets. Arosa lures the family trade through such attractions as kindergartens for children.

ESSENTIALS

GETTING THERE Trains connect Chur and Arosa at the rate of one per hour during the day (trip time: 1 hr.). Trains from Zurich take 3 hours to reach Arosa. Call © **0900/300-300** for **rail information** and schedules. Zurich is the nearest airport to Arosa.

If you're driving the 31km (19-mile) drive from Chur in good weather, allow at least an hour, as the road is steep, with hairpin curves. Don't make the drive in icy weather. Instead, take the narrow-gauge railway, which has been in operation since World War I.

VISITOR INFORMATION Poststrasse is the main traffic artery through the center of town; visitors can follow hotel and restaurant directional signs. The tourist office is on Poststrasse (© **081/378-70-20;** www.arosa.ch), and is open Monday to Friday 8am to noon and 1:30 to 6pm, Saturday 9am to 1pm, and Sunday 9am to noon.

GETTING AROUND Every night in Arosa, between midnight and 6am, most cars are forbidden from moving within the resort's center, with the exception of taxis and Night Express buses (see below), which make scheduled runs through the town center, stopping at the parking areas that flank the periphery of the resort. The most consistent of the night buses operates only in wintertime. Known as the **"Night Express"** (call the tourist office for information), it's a minivan service that runs continually from 8pm to 2am between December and April, charging 3F ($2.45) per person per ride anywhere along its trajectory. The vehicles are marked NIGHT EXPRESS and can be stopped for boarding or getting off anywhere along the way.

FUN IN THE GREAT OUTDOORS

Skiing is the big attraction in Arosa, but summer activities and other winter sports, such as tobogganing and horse-drawn sleigh rides on the Arlenwald road, are also popular. Tennis, squash, bowling, and golf can all be played year-round at indoor facilities. Walks can be taken over 60km (37 miles) of easy and varied trails kept open in the winter. In addition, guided walks are conducted from June to October, both in the morning and in the afternoon. The tourist office (see above) will supply details and trail maps. Visits are possible to a chapel from the 1400s, a cheese maker, and a local museum.

Arosa draws an international crowd to its ski slopes, offering 64km (40 miles) of the best ski runs in the Grisons. It also has the Swiss Ski School, which, with 100 instructors, is one of the best ski schools in Switzerland.

Skiing is popular in the Obersee area at the eastern edge of the resort, whose focal point—reached by cable car—is the **Weisshorn** 🐾🐾 (2,611m/8,564 ft.). During the day, cable cars leave for the Weisshorn at the rate of one every 20 minutes. You first make the ascent to the middle station, Larn Mittle, at 1,992m (6,534 ft.), from which there are panoramas of Arosa. From the top station is one of the grandest views in eastern Switzerland, taking in a vast panorama of the Grison Alps. Even Chur can be viewed to the northwest, at the foothills of the Calanda mountain peak.

To the west, skiers take the Hörnli gondola, reaching Hörnligrat (2,454m/8,049 ft.) in about 16 minutes. Drag lifts at Hörnligrat fan out, taking skiers to the top of several different ski slopes.

The **Swiss Ski School** (📞 081/377-11-50) provides skiing lessons for both adults and children, and private ski instruction is available from the **Grison Association of Private Ski Instructors Arosa** (📞 081/377-14-07).

Intermediate, advanced, and professional skiers come to Arosa because of its proximity to the slopes on either side of the valley formed by the Weisshorn and the Hörnli mountains. Access to the 76km (47 miles) of marked downhill runs on either side of the valley is made possible by at least 16 cable cars, some chairlifts, and a network of buses that make frequent runs up and down the valley floor. A ski pass that provides access to all of this costs 104F ($85) for 2 days, 224F ($184) for 5 days, and 239F ($196) for 7 days. The cost for children is 58F ($48) for 2 days, 123F ($101) for 5 days, and 150F ($123) for 7 days. Other passes that allow access to the ski slopes as far away as Davos, Klosters, Flims, and Lax are available, as well as some of the slopes in the Engadine, but only in increments of 90 days at a time.

Arosa offers some of the best horseback riding in eastern Switzerland. Visit the stables at **Fuhrhalterei,** Wierhof (📞 081/377-41-96), which are open throughout the year. The Ritsch family usually has a dozen or so horses on hand, each willing to carry you across scenic local trails for around 32F ($26) per hour. You must call them at least a day in advance to make arrangements. The stables lie just outside the center adjacent to a local campground.

SHOPPING

The best way to get an overview of the diversity of Arosa's shops is to stroll up and down its main street, Poststrasse. If you're looking for equipment or clothing that will keep you competitive in this sports-conscious town, head for **Sprecher Sports,** Poststrasse

(© 081/377-12-06); **Carmena Sport,** Poststrasse (© 081/377-12-05); the winter only **Bananas Sport** (© 081/377-15-51), in the building that houses the departure point for the Weisshorn cable car; or **Schatz Sport,** Poststrasse (© 081/377-18-14), near the Hotel Kulm. If it's Grisons souvenirs you're looking for, head for **Vital,** Poststrasse (© 081/377-12-77). The best bet for a winning mixture of books (mostly in German, but with some in English and French) and Grisons-inspired souvenirs and gift items is **Banker,** Poststrasse (© 081/377-16-90). Other than that, your best bet is to simply wander along either side of the street.

WHERE TO STAY

Most of Arosa's hotels are modern and expensive. In the peak winter season, reservations are imperative. Most hotels in Arosa demand a minimum stay of 7 to 10 days over the Christmas holidays. In the summer it's much easier to find accommodations. Some hotels are on a street plan; others are not. Those that aren't are clearly signposted from the center of town.

VERY EXPENSIVE

Arosa Kulm Hotel 𝕽𝕽𝕽   This government-rated five-star hotel, built in the 1970s, is one of the two leading hotels here, surpassed only by the Tschuggen Grand Hotel (see below). A simple guesthouse stood here in 1882. Surrounded by rushing streams and close to the departure point of one of the cable cars rising into the surrounding mountains, the hotel is large, glamorous, and contemporary, with well-insulated, spacious, and exceedingly comfortable bedrooms plus deluxe bathrooms. The decor combines warm tones with pine-wood paneling. Almost everyone stays here on half board, which is, for the most part, required. At Christmastime prices go even higher than those mentioned below.

CH-7050 Arosa. © 081/378-88-88. Fax 081/378-88-89. www.arosakulm.ch. 142 units. Winter 510F–770F ($418–$631) double, from 930F ($763) suite for 2; off season 170F–190F ($139–$156) double, from 270F ($221) suite for 2. Rates include half board. Parking 20F ($16) extra per night. AE, DC, MC, V. Closed Apr 14–June 13 and Sept 13–Dec 5. **Amenities:** 5 restaurants; 2 bars; indoor swimming pool; golf; tennis courts; exercise room; spa; sauna; biking; kid's club; limited room service; massage; babysitting; laundry service; bowling. *In room:* TV, dataport, minibar, hair dryer, iron, safe.

BelArosa 𝕽 *(Kids)*   This is the pioneer hotel in the trend away from big government-rated five-star hotels. It is an informal, family-style suite inn. The service is highly attentive, the accommodations are of good quality, and there's plenty of atmosphere here as well. Each suite is spacious, with a generous living room with a tile stove—kitchenettes in some. Most of the accommodations also open onto a balcony with a view.

Prätschilstrasse, CH-7050 Arosa. © 081/378-89-99. Fax 081/378-89-89. www.belarosa.ch. 22 units. Winter 400F– 680F ($328–$558) suite; summer 230F–370F ($189–$303) suite. Rates include buffet breakfast. AE, DC, MC, V. **Amenities:** Bar; Jacuzzi; sauna; steam bath; babysitting; laundry service; nonsmoking rooms. *In room:* TV, dataport, kitchenette (in some), fridge.

Tschuggen Grand Hotel 𝕽𝕽𝕽   With its potted palms, distressed tortoise-shell wallpaper, and brass-framed mirrors, this modern high-rise could be in the pages of *Architectural Digest.* It's one of the most glamorous hotels in the Swiss Alps. The hotel looks down over Arosa from a hillside position that emphasizes its modern, rectangular design. No attempts were made to duplicate traditional chalet architecture, and the interior is richly outfitted with some of the most opulent accessories in Arosa. The spacious rooms are handsomely decorated and beautifully kept. Each week there are two *soirées élégantes,* for which evening dress is compulsory. The hotel opens every year around the first of December, with Arosa's traditional ski weeks, and continues until early April.

Sonnenbergstrasse, CH-7050 Arosa. © 081/378-99-99. Fax 081/378-99-90. www.tschuggen.ch. 129 units. 490F–565F ($402–$463) double; from 770F ($631) suite for 2. Rates include buffet breakfast. AE, DC, MC, V. Parking 30F ($25). Half board 40F ($33) extra per person. Closed Apr 3–Dec 2. **Amenities:** 4 restaurants; bar; indoor pool; fitness room; steam bath; sauna; salon; 24-hr. room service; laundry service; bowling alley; kindergarten with nurse. *In room:* TV, dataport, minibar, hair dryer, safe.

EXPENSIVE
Golfhotel Hof Maran ⟨⟩   Set high in an alpine meadow, about 1.6km (a mile) from the center of Arosa, this impressive-looking wood-sided mountain chalet is rustically decorated with beamed ceilings, lots of pine-wood paneling, carpeting in autumnal colors, and comfortable armchairs. Many of the handsomely furnished mid-size bedrooms have balconies for year-round tanning. Accommodations come in varied styles although the overall effect is exceedingly comfortable alpine traditional.

In Maran, Nord CH-7050 Arosa. © 081/378-5151. Fax 081/378-51-00. www.hofmaran.ch. 53 units. Winter 390F–500F ($320–$410) double; summer 270F–340F ($221–$279) double. Rates include breakfast. AE, DC, MC, V. Closed Apr 11–June 14 and Sept 15–Dec 18. **Amenities:** 2 restaurants; bar; 18-hole golf course; 5 tennis courts; saunas; steam room; limited room service; babysitting; laundry service; skating rink. *In room:* TV, dataport, minibar, hair dryer, safe.

Waldhotel-National Hotel ⟨⟩⟨⟩⟨⟩   This sylvan retreat, although not as elegant as the Tschuggen Grand or the Arosa Kulm, is the most tranquil and isolated retreat at the resort. Set in a forest, this generously proportioned building was designed with symmetrical wings extending from a central core. Originally the Waldhotel was a sanatorium and later it became a military hospital, and it still promotes its role as a center for "Fitness and Wellness." In the public rooms, accessories include apricot-colored stencils decorating the arched ceilings, a beautifully carved and embellished booth resembling a church pulpit, and decorative ovens sheathed in ceramic tiles. The mid-size to spacious bedrooms are comfortably and attractively furnished, with price level determined by the view. Rooms facing south open onto a view of Arosa, and those looking north open onto a vast woodland.

CH-7050 Arosa. © 081/378-55-55. Fax 081/378-55-99. www.waldhotel.ch. 93 units. Winter 400F–540F ($328–$443) double, 680F–1,050F ($558–$861) suite for 2; summer 140F–160F ($115–$131) double, 400F–540F ($328–$443) suite for 2. Children 5 and under stay free in parent's room; children 6–12 are charged 50% of the adult rate. Rates include half board. AE, DC, MC, V. Closed Apr 20–June 14 and Sept 14–Dec 5. **Amenities:** Restaurant; indoor pool; gym; limited spa facilities; steam room; limited room service; massage; laundry service. *In room:* TV, minibar, hair dryer, safe.

MODERATE
Hotel Cresta ⟨Value⟩   It's true the hotel is rather functional, but it's far from basic. The bedrooms are bright and spacious, each well furnished with a tiled bathroom. The heated indoor swimming pool comes as a pleasant surprise, as do the view terrace and a garden. Rolf and Romy Jäggi are your hosts with the most. The central location and the affordable prices have made the hotel a favorite among families traveling together. All rooms are twin bedded and handsomely maintained, and the best accommodations are those facing south with their own private balconies. Some of the best accommodations have a sitting area with a third bed for that additional family member.

Talstrasse 57, CH-7050 Arosa. © 081/417-16-16. Fax 081/417-16-85. www.cresta-hotels.ch. 40 units. Winter 280F–300F ($230–$246) double; summer 190F–210F ($156–$172) double. Rates include breakfast. AE, DC, MC, V. Free parking. **Amenities:** Restaurant; indoor pool; sauna; nonsmoking rooms; rooms for guests w/limited mobility. *In room:* TV, minibar, safe.

Hotel Eden ⚜ Hotel Eden, in the center of Arosa, is surrounded by pine trees, near the cable car and ski lift. It has five floors of weathered balconies and sun-streaked planking over white walls. The hotel interior is brightly colored, whimsical, and very comfortable. This is an aggressively marketed hotel with a flair for entertaining non-Swiss clients with or without their children, and a sense of urbanized, big-city hipness. The public rooms have marble floors, Oriental rugs, hanging lamps, and wall-to-wall carpeting. Each of the spacious and comfortably furnished bedrooms has a private bathroom. The rooms with southern exposures have balconies.

CH-7050 Arosa. 𝄞 **081/378-71-00.** Fax 081/378-71-01. www.edenarosa.ch. 80 units. 210F–350F ($172–$287) standard double; 360F–440F ($295–$361) designer double. Rates include breakfast. AE, DC, MC, V. Parking 15F ($12) per night. Closed Apr–Dec. **Amenities:** 3 restaurants (including a sushi bar); bar; gym; Jacuzzi; sauna; children's playroom; limited room service; massage; babysitting; laundry service; billiards; dataport; disco; skating rink; ski school. *In room:* TV, minibar, hair dryer.

INEXPENSIVE

Arve Central Originally built about a century ago and remodeled many times since then, this hotel is set back from the main street but still very much in the center of the action. It's located only a short walk from the train station. Some of the pleasant bedrooms have balconies crafted from weathered wood and are attractively furnished with a collection of upholstered settees and wooden chalet chairs. The rooms in the rear, however, have no balcony and don't open onto a view. Overall, it provides unpretentious comfort but not a lot of glamour.

Hubelstrasse, CH-7050 Arosa. 𝄞 **081/378-52-52.** Fax 081/378-52-50. www.arve-central.ch. 48 units. Winter 165F–211F ($135–$173) double; off season 104F–139F ($85–$114) double. Rates include half board. AE, DC, MC, V. Parking 10F–14F ($8.20–$11). Closed May. **Amenities:** 2 restaurants; fitness center; Jacuzzi; sauna; limited room service; laundry service. *In room:* TV, minibar, hair dryer.

Hotel Alpina ⚜ *Finds* Finally we've found a hotel in Arosa that looks from the outside like the type of old-fashioned chalet that's always associated with Switzerland. The balconies have hand-carved railings and trim. There's a terraced garden, and near the entrance a Swiss flag flaps in the mountain breeze. Our favorite rooms are up under the eaves. All of the accommodations have been renovated without losing any of their alpine charm, and each comes with a private bathroom. Many have exposed beams whose massive dimensions testify to the antique age of the building. The public rooms are filled with furniture painted in alpine designs, baroque clocks, and traditional chairs and couches.

CH-7050 Arosa. 𝄞 **081/377-16-58.** Fax 081/377-37-52. www.arosa.ch/hotels/alpina. 35 units. Winter 175F ($144) double; summer 145F–180F ($119–$148) double. Rates include half board. AE, DC, MC, V. Free parking outdoors, 12F ($9.85) indoors. Closed late Apr to mid-June and mid-Nov to Dec 6. **Amenities:** Restaurant; bar; laundry service. *In room:* TV, dataport, hair dryer.

Hotel Streiff *Value* A government-rated three-star hotel, this establishment is set at the edge of a forest, a short distance uphill and away from the center of Arosa. Although there's ample use of varnished pine both inside and out, very little attempt was made at this simple place to duplicate the look or feel of a traditional chalet. Trails, cable cars, and chair and ski lifts are all nearby. All of the small to midsize rooms have a well-organized private bathroom. The bedrooms are sensibly but somewhat sparsely furnished with angular modern pieces, a bit bland but comfortable and clean.

CH-7050 Arosa. 𝄞 **081/378-71-71.** Fax 081/378-71-78. www.streiff.ch. 41 units. Winter 157F–197F ($129–$162) double; summer 116F–133F ($95–$109) double. Rates include half board. No credit cards. Closed Apr 15–June 30 and Sept 1–Dec 15. **Amenities:** Restaurant; limited room service. *In room:* TV, dataport, hair dryer, safe.

Vetter *(Value* Centrally located a few steps from the railroad station and the Tschuggen cable car, this boxy-looking, flat-roofed hotel offers glassed-in verandas, open porches, and wooden balconies. The interior is a mix of wrought iron and wood beams, enlivened by pithy bits of wisdom stenciled in German above a masonry fireplace. Everything is well maintained and comfortable. Many of the accommodations lack a private bathroom; the hallway facilities, however, are adequate and well maintained. Furnishings are generally ragtag unless you get one of the time-mellowed antique rooms in wood paneling. Some units open onto views of woodlands; others face the busy street and town center. The rooms without a bathroom are among the best bargains in Arosa in the winter ski season.

CH-7050 Arosa. ℂ **081/377-17-02**. Fax 081/377-49-19. www.arosa.ch/hotels/vetter. 28 units, 15 with bathroom. 150F–180F ($123–$148) double without bathroom; 175F–205F ($144–$168) double with bathroom. Rates include buffet breakfast. No credit cards. Parking 3F ($2.45). Closed Apr 29–Nov 30. **Amenities:** Restaurant; bar; nearby access to indoor pool and squash court; children's playroom; limited room service; laundry service. *In room:* TV, minibar.

WHERE TO DINE

Most guests book into the Arosa resort hotels on a board basis. Nearly all the major restaurants are in hotels—hence the shortage of well-known independent dining spots. However, if you can break away from your hotel for a main meal, you may want to try one of the places below.

Cuculouche MEXICAN/SPANISH Since it was established in the late 1990s, this Mexican/Latino restaurant has captured the hearts and imaginations of many of the young and fun-loving night owls of Arosa. The setting looks less Mexican than you might have expected, with less folkloric and fewer rustic implements, say, in a Tex-Mex emporium in San Antonio. Instead, you'll find walls painted in vivid tones of red, blue, and yellow, some Cuban and South America–derived paintings, and a bar that busily dispenses tequila-based drinks whose party-colored hues might remind you of a sunset in the Yucatán. Menu items include tacos, tortillas, burritos, fajitas, an excellent version of spareribs, and chili. Overall, this place is a welcome antidote from too constant (and too dour) a dose of the Alps, especially during the midwinter chill.

Unterseestrasse. ℂ **081/377-55-05**. Reservations not necessary. Main courses 21F–39F ($17–$32). AE, DC, MC, V. Daily 6–10:30pm. Closed early Oct to Nov and mid-Apr to late June.

Trattoria Toscana ℱ ITALIAN/CONTINENTAL This antique log building belongs to the very upscale Kulm Hotel, which lies nearby and on the opposite side of the street. It takes its true flavor, however, from its charming and extroverted managers, Armando Solaro and Raffaelo Limone. Mr. Solaro worked for several years in Sardinia as the personal chef of the Aga Khan—an experience that helps him understand the demands of his international clientele. The restaurant is a few steps from the inner-Arosa Tschuggen chairlift, near the top of the village. One side of the cozy room overlooks the spectator seats around one of the village's ice-skating rinks. In sunny weather you can dine outside. The *daube de boeuf* specialty is marinated for a full day before it's served with spinach and fresh vegetables. Other Continental specialties, including foie gras and a sophisticated array of fish, are also well prepared. Lunches here are simple and relatively fast-paced affairs, aimed at active people doing active exercise in the great outdoors. Dinners are more languid, more elegant, and more formal, showcasing the talents of the chef and *maître d'hôtel*.

In the Arosa Kulm Hotel, Poststrasse. ℂ **081/378-88-88**. Reservations required. Main courses 17F–42F ($14–$34) lunch; 36F–55F ($30–$45) dinner. AE, DC, MC, V. Dec 4–Apr 15 daily 11:45am–2:30pm and 7–10:30pm. Closed Apr 16–Dec 3.

AROSA AFTER DARK

Don't be confused by the presence in Arosa of a building known as the Spielcasino, within the Kursaal, on Poststrasse. Despite the implications of its name, there's no casino inside—it functions as a somewhat desultory and low-key venue for some shops, restaurants, and bars, having closed its gambling facilities several years ago. One of its highlights is its disco, **Nuts** (℃ **081/377-39-40**), a glossily modern haven for drinkers and dancers that's open every day in midsummer and midwinter between 9:30pm and at least 3am. Entrance costs around 8F ($6.55) per person. Expect a crowd of seasonal visitors ages 18 to 55, some energetic dancing, and a lot of voyeuristic ogling of the attractive and fit bodies that venture onto the dance floor.

The most sophisticated, and most popular, piano bar in Arosa lies on the lobby level of the contemporary-looking Hotel Carmenna (℃ **081/377-17-66**), within a cozy and richly paneled environment that can be a lot of fun. Music usually begins in winter every evening around 5pm, and continues, with breaks, on till around 11pm, with a somewhat lesser exposure during July and August.

Another amusing after-dark choice is the **Kitchen Klub** of the Hotel Eden (℃ **081/378-71-06**), in the center of Arosa. This dance club is inside what functioned, at the turn of the 20th century, as an actual kitchen. The old pots and pans are still there. This place starts to fill up after dinner, and the DJ, sitting on top of old refrigerators, keeps the music lively. Entrance costs 8F ($6.55) per person. It's open every night from 7:30pm, but only in winter, between December and early April. The **Hotel Obersee,** Aussere Poststrasse (℃ **081/377-19-49**), has an attractive restaurant and a warm and convivial bar that from time to time focuses on the music produced by live bands, but because their schedules are erratic, it's best to phone before you head over there.

Close to the railway station is **Gada,** Poststrasse (℃ **081/377-17-66**), a bar and disco whose decor emulates that of an antique chalet. The Post Hotel, on Poststrasse, offers a handful of stubes, a pizzeria, and **The Crazy Club** (℃ **081/378-50-00**), where drinks flow and a cabaret act features attractive women who strip in ways that tease and titillate but rarely get really down and dirty. A sometime competitor, offering cabaret only during midwinter's high season, most nights between 9pm and 3am, is an area known as "the Lounge" in the **Hotel Seehof** (℃ **081/377-15-41**), which is otherwise just a quiet and rather conventional bar. Entrance to both sites is free.

Finally, you can drop in to the bar of the previously recommended restaurant, **Cuculouche,** on Unterseestrasse (℃ **081/377-55-05**), for a sunset-colored cocktail whose ingredients (tequila, mango, strawberries, and more) you might have expected in the Yucatán.

3 Klosters ★★

13km (8 miles) N of Davos; 43km (27 miles) E of Chur; 29km (18 miles) E of Landquart

Life at this 1,200m (3,936-ft.) village in the Prattigau Valley has changed greatly from 1222, when a cloister was founded here. Many visitors prefer the intimacy and hospitality of Klosters to the carnival-like atmosphere of Davos. Unlike some of its neighbors (most notably St. Moritz), Klosters has few unattractive structures. All its buildings are constructed in the chalet style, giving the town a pleasing architectural harmony. Local residents claim that the sport of tobogganing originated here.

The main road to Davos runs through Klosters, and the two resorts have been known to compete aggressively for the tourist franc. Famous past visitors include Sir

Arthur Conan Doyle and Robert Louis Stevenson, who is said to have finished *Treasure Island* here. In the heyday of tax benefits, Klosters became known as "Hollywood on the Rocks." It still attracts an international crowd of movie people. It has also been given a royal seal of approval by the king and queen of Sweden, who visit regularly; but invariably generating more publicity were Prince Charles and the late Princess Diana, who for many years considered it one of their favorite Swiss resorts.

ESSENTIALS

GETTING THERE There are frequent express trains between Zurich and the railway junction at Landquart. From Landquart, connecting trains depart about once an hour for Klosters on secondary rail lines. Call © **0900/300-300** for **rail information** and schedules.

If you're driving from Zurich, head south on the N3 expressway until you reach Landquart, at which point you cut southeast along Route 28.

VISITOR INFORMATION Some roads in the center have street names; others outside the town don't, but establishments can easily be found by following directional signs. The **Klosters Tourist Board,** in the center of town at Alte Bahnhofstrasse 6 (© **081/410-20-20;** www.klosters.ch), is open in the winter Monday to Saturday from 8:30am to noon and 4 to 6pm and Sunday from 9:30 to 11:30am and 3:30 to 6:30pm; and in the summer Monday to Friday 8:30am to noon and 2:30 to 6pm, and Saturday 8:30am to noon and 2:30 to 4pm.

GETTING AROUND A city bus, known locally as either the "Ortsbus" or the "Klosters-Serneus" bus, makes frequent runs from Klosters-Dorf (the railroad station) to the base of the town's ski lifts, passing virtually every building in town along the way. Access to the bus is free for anyone in possession of a "guest card" (which proves your residency within a local hotel or guesthouse) or a ski pass. Otherwise, a ride on the bus costs from 1F (80¢) to 3F ($2.45), depending on how far within the town you ride.

SKIING & OTHER OUTDOOR FUN

Some of the finest downhill skiing in the world is here, with slopes for beginners as well as for the most advanced skiers. A kindergarten will look after the very young while you hit the slopes. The most populous part of Klosters, centered around the railway station, is called **Klosters-Platz (Klosters Square).** A smaller, less populated neighborhood—site of the resort's excellent ski school—lies about a mile to the north and at a slightly lower altitude. Set near the departure point for the Madrisa cable cars, it's known as **Klosters-Dorf (Klosters Village).**

The region contains two principal areas for skiing or hiking, the more popular of which is the **Gotschna-Parsenn.** To reach it, board the Gotschnagrat cable way in Klosters-Platz; the cable car carries more than 50 skiers up to the 2,263m (7,423-ft.) Gotschnagrat elevation. In the peak season, especially around February, expect lines. A series of cable ways, a chairlift, and 18 ski lifts hook up with the Davos-Parsenn skiing areas, where your highest point will be Weissflühgipfel (2,778m/9,112 ft.). The Parsenn area is world-renowned and has some of the longest runs in Europe. It offers more than 14 different cable ways and ski lifts, plus more than 137km (85 miles) of well-kept runs.

The other major area, **Madrisa,** dates from the 1960s. To reach it, you go to Dorf via a bus, which leaves from Klosters-Platz every 10 to 30 minutes, depending on the season. From Dorf, the Klosters-Albeina gondola, a conveyance that's suitable for between one and four occupants at a time, will take you to a height of 1,897m (6,222 ft.). Then, by drag lift, known as the Schaffüggli, you rise to 2,355m (7,724 ft.).

Nontransferable R.E.G.A. (season) tickets are priced according to the number of days you plan to ski. For ski passes for the whole area, refer to "The Active Vacation Planner" in section 4 on Davos, below.

Horse sleighing, curling, and skating are popular sports for those who don't ski. Ask at the tourist office (see "Essentials," above) about the various venues for these activities.

In the summer Klosters is in the center of fine hiking grounds. The Madrisa and Gotschna-Parsenn cable cars will carry you to starting points on both sides of the valley for hikes on well-marked trails through woods and alpine meadows. In Klosters you can also enjoy tennis, squash, mountain biking, and swimming in a heated pool.

SHOPPING

Most of the shops are sports-oriented. One of the best is **Grischa-Sport,** Bahnhofstrasse 12C (**ℂ 081/422-18-55**). Galleries abound but the one that seems the most genuinely devoted to various works of Graubünden artists is **Alexis Art Gallerie,** Talstrasse 1 (**ℂ 081/422-36-37**). For local paintings and Grisons-style souvenirs, visit **Déjà-Vue,** Bahnhofstrasse 7, in Klosters-Platz (**ℂ 081/422-56-54**).

WHERE TO STAY

Some hotels in Klosters are not on street plans, but directional signs point the way from the center.

VERY EXPENSIVE

Hotel Pardenn ✻✻✻   A posh and luxurious resort complex, often host to the rich and famous, this government-rated four-star deluxe hotel offers tradition, comfort, atmosphere, conservatism, and a feeling of graciousness—a winning combination for which you'll pay plenty. The terrace overlooks the well-landscaped lawn. Inside you'll find such architectural touches as a monumental, green-marble, circular staircase, masses of flowers, lots of wooden paneling, and oil paintings. Many of the small to midsize accommodations have pine paneling, while others contain flowery carpets and Louis XV–style armchairs. Try, if possible, for a room with a balcony facing south. The rooms are well accessorized although the bathrooms are often small.

Monbielerstrasse 18, CH-7250 Klosters. ℂ 081/423-20-20. Fax 081/423-20-21. www.pardenn.ch. 64 units. Winter 302F–492F ($248–$403) double, 482F–532F ($395–$436) junior suite; summer 282F–302F ($231–$248) double, 432F ($354) junior suite. Rates include half board. AE, DC, MC, V. Free parking outside, 15F ($12) in a garage. Closed Apr 5–June 20 and Sept 14–Dec 12. **Amenities:** 3 restaurants; piano bar; pool; gym; sauna; salon; limited room service; massage room; laundry service. *In room:* TV, minibar, hair dryer.

Hotel Vereina ✻✻✻   Ultrachic and elegant, this landmark hotel, launched in 1890, has made an amazing comeback in the 21st century, even knocking the Pardenn off its pedestal as the number-one choice in Klosters. The location is a short drive from the village center, the ice-skating rink, and a 9-hole golf course. Guests come here to ski in winter; in summer they can be found sunbathing in the large and well-maintained garden. The two-story hotel is small and offers the most personalized service at the resort. There are more suites than double rooms, each with bathrooms lined in Italian marble. Bedrooms are spacious, each supplied with elegant furnishings, plus your robe and pair of slippers laid out at night. The choice of restaurants guarantees a wide choice of food from the kitchen brigade—in fact, cuisine is one of the reasons for booking here. In winter you'll find us in the cozy bar around the piano. The on-site spa is state-of-the-art.

Hwy. 179, CH-7520 Klosters. © **081/410-27-27.** Fax 081/410-27-28. www.vereinahotel.ch. 25 units. Winter 410F–580F ($336–$476) double, 800F–1,400F ($656–$1,148) suite; summer 260F–375F ($213–$308) double, 450F–810F ($369–$664) suite. Rates include breakfast. AE, DC, MC, V. Free parking. **Amenities:** 3 restaurants; bar; indoor pool; fitness room; spa; sauna; limited room service; babysitting; laundry service; nonsmoking rooms; 1 room for guests w/limited mobility. *In room:* TV, dataport, minibar, safe, beverage maker.

EXPENSIVE

Chesa Grischuna ✭✭✭   This historic *landgasthof* (country inn) in the center of Klosters is the most celebrated of its kind in the whole resort area. Set behind a lavishly decorated facade and rebuilt in 1938 on the foundation of a farmhouse and guesthouse from the 1860s, this six-story hotel has hosted some of the most illustrious personalities of Europe. Since this hotel is on the see-and-be-seen circuit, it can command and get a lot of francs. The small to midsize rooms are for the most part paneled in local pine and fir, and are both elegant and cozy. The overflow from the main house is lodged in a comfortable annex nearby where the rooms are more spacious. The hotel is famous for its chic restaurant.

Bahnhofstrasse 12, CH-7250 Klosters. © **081/422-22-22.** Fax 081/422-22-25. www.chesagrischuna.ch. 25 units. Winter 360F–480F ($295–$394); summer 250F–280F ($205–$230) double. Rates include breakfast. Half board is available in any season for an additional supplement of 45F ($37) per person. AE, DC, MC, V. Free parking. Closed Easter to early July and mid-Oct to mid-Dec. **Amenities:** Restaurant; bar; limited room service; babysitting; laundry service. *In room:* TV, dataport, hair dryer.

Silvretta Park Hotel ✭   Opened in 1990 as a reconstruction of a well-respected hotel that had been in business since the 1870s, this government-rated four-star hotel lies opposite Silvretta Park with its cross-country ski runs and ice rink for skating, hockey, and curling. It's within walking distance of the Gotschna lift connecting the Parsenn skiing area with Klosters. Designed in a stylishly updated evolution and enlargement of a Swiss chalet, with lots of varnished pine, and sophisticated styling, it offers comfortably modern and midsize rooms in a countrified style, each containing an elegant bathroom. Facilities include a balcony or terrace.

CH-7250 Klosters. © **081/423-34-35.** Fax 081/423-34-50. www.silvretta.ch. 101 units. Winter 280F–620F ($230–$508) double, 380F–860F ($312–$705) suite for 2; summer 280F–330F ($230–$271) double, 390F–460F ($320–$377) suite for 2. Rates include half board. AE, DC, MC, V. Indoor parking 10F–18F ($8.20–$15), 5F–10F ($4.10–$8.20) outdoors. Closed Easter to early July and mid-Oct to mid-Dec. **Amenities:** 3 restaurants; bar; indoor pool; fitness center; Jacuzzi; sauna; Turkish bath; salon; limited room service; massage; babysitting; laundry service; disco. *In room:* TV, minibar, hair dryer, safe.

MODERATE

Bad Serneus Kur- und Sporthotel *Value*   This well-managed and cozy government-rated three-star hotel is one of the most visible buildings in Klosters' suburb of Bad Serneus, 6km (3½ miles) north (and downhill) from Klosters. Consequently, despite the fact that the rooms are cozy, well maintained, and comfortable, prices are somewhat lower than in the heart of Klosters. Each unit comes either with private tub or a shower bathroom. When snowfalls are deep, clients can ski here from Klosters; they'll have to take a short bus ride, with their equipment, for access to the resort's ski lifts. Older (it originated as a private farmhouse more than 200 years ago, but with many subsequent enlargements) and solidly built of heavy slabs of wood painted yellow with black shutters, the hotel was enlarged and upgraded in 1987 and contains public rooms with wooden beams, regional-style stenciling, and blazing fireplaces. In summer guests can stroll in nearby flower-filled meadows.

Bad Serneus, CH-7250 Klosters. ℂ 081/422-14-44. Fax 081/422-22-51. www.badserneus.ch. 52 units. Winter 240F–320F ($197–$262) double; summer 160F–250F ($131–$205) double. Rates include half board. AE, MC, V. Closed mid-Apr to mid-May and Oct 20–Dec 20. **Amenities:** Restaurant; indoor pool; sauna; massage facilities; laundry service.

INEXPENSIVE

Hotel-Pension Büel   Built in stages between 1967 and 1986, this is a simple and completely unpretentious government-rated three-star hotel with stucco walls, brown trim, and balconies. Inside, it's clean, well scrubbed, and rustic, with blazing midwinter fireplaces and, in most cases, flagstone floors and knotty-pine ceilings. Rooms are small and basic yet cozily comfortable with tasteful furniture and tidy maintenance. Fifteen units come with private shower, the rest with tubs.

Büel-Weg 1, CH-7252 Klosters-Dorf. ℂ 081/422-26-69. Fax 081/422-49-41. www.hotelbuel.ch. 18 units. Winter 210F–230F ($172–$189) double; summer 180F–190F ($148–$156) double. Rates include half board. AE, MC, V. Parking 4F–8F ($3.30–$6.55). Closed May and Nov. **Amenities:** Restaurant. *In room:* TV.

WHERE TO DINE

Alte Post SWISS/FRENCH   Chef John Ehrat, Jr., pampers the palate with regional specialties in this roadside chalet outside town that's decorated with game trophies and ceramics. In the autumn he prepares carefully selected game and fish dishes with the freshest ingredients, and throughout the year he does marvelously flavorful adaptations of both lamb and fish. Guests dine in the restaurant or the intimate grillroom, where meats are grilled over an open fire. It's a fun, informal place and has long been a celebrity favorite. Guests enjoy such winning fare as smoked trout with juniper, supreme of salmon with pink peppercorns, and fresh mushrooms in a nest of homemade noodles.

Doggilochstrasse 136, Klosters-Aeuja. ℂ 081/422-17-16. Reservations required. Main courses 32F–54F ($26–$44); menu dégustation 93F ($76). AE, DC, MC, V. Wed–Sun 12:30am–3pm and 6–9pm (last order). Closed May and Nov.

Chesa Grischuna 🎯🎯🎯 INTERNATIONAL   This restaurant is so popular that celebrities often book tables a year in advance. Some of its famous patrons have included Truman Capote, Rex Harrison, Audrey Hepburn, the Aga Khan, Winston Churchill, Deborah Kerr, and Queen Juliana of the Netherlands. More recent celebrities have included the author John Irving and a bevy of pop and cinema stars whose names aren't released easily because of security reasons. The restaurant has attractively decorated alpine walls and a scattering of unusual portraits. Part of the reason for its persistent popularity is the warm welcome from the Guler family, and, of course, the food. Specialties prepared with the freshest and best of ingredients include a crepe *suédoise* (Swedish) stuffed with shrimp, chicken livers in puff pastry on a bed of leeks, grilled salmon with white butter and tomato sauce, and rack of lamb. In the summer you can eat outside.

Bahnhofstrasse 12. ℂ 081/422-22-22. Reservations required in winter. Main courses 25F–49F ($20–$40); fixed-price lunch 35F ($29); fixed-price dinner 69F–84F ($57–$69). AE, DC, MC, V. Winter daily 7am–midnight; off season daily 11:30am–2pm and 6:30–10pm. Closed Easter to early July and mid-Oct to mid-Dec.

Hotel Wynegg Restaurant *Finds* SWISS   This restaurant is set on the ground floor of a 20-room hotel built in 1878, and the hotel is noted for its kitchens, partly because of the hard work of the owner, Ruth Guler, the niece of the owner of the prestigious Chesa Grischuna. The hotel came into prominence after Prince Charles chose this modest place for a discreet afternoon drink with the duke of Gloucester, one of his cousins. The restaurant—clean, cozy, and straightforward—offers simple but well-prepared meals, which may include local air-dried beef, hearty soups, entrecôtes, and an especially good veal steak with rösti. The decor is alpine kitsch with cuckoo clocks and checkered tablecloths. Two of the best-recommended dishes here include strips of veal Zurich-style, and a succulent version of calves' liver.

The rooms are strictly no-frills, costing 95F ($78) per person nightly in a double without private bathroom, 125F ($103) per person nightly in a double with private bathroom; all rates include breakfast and dinner. Regrettably, the hotel and its restaurant are open only in wintertime.

Landstrasse 205, CH-7250 Klosters. ℂ **081/422-13-40.** Fax 081/422-41-31. Reservations required. Main courses 35F–45F ($29–$37). AE, MC, V. Daily noon–2pm and 6–10pm. Closed Apr 15–Dec 15.

Walserstube *☆☆☆* SWISS   The Walserstube's Beat Bolliger entertains everybody from celebrities such as Prince Andrew to regular folks, and has been doing so since 1981. The time-worn and alpine-seasoned building materials came in part from an old Grisons farmhouse, and the restaurant and cafe are paneled with this wood. Art objects and antiques are used discreetly throughout the place. The location is right on the main street of town with often-heavy traffic in the peak summer and winter seasons. His cuisine is a winning combination of fresh ingredients and the best culinary skills. As you sit under the restaurant's massive wood beams and alpine carvings, you might begin with a duckling foie gras or a yogurt mousse with seasonal fruit. In season, asparagus is featured and prepared in a variety of elegant ways. The fish is special here, including salmon with onions, a fricassee of lobster, ravioli stuffed with crayfish, and trout grilled and served with ratatouille. You can also order excellent meat dishes, among them Scottish lamb seasoned with thyme.

Although acclaimed as the leading restaurant of Klosters, the Walserhof also offers 14 elegant accommodations. In winter, with breakfast included, charges range from 290F to 370F ($238–$303) in a double. In summer doubles are 240F to 370F ($197–$303).

In the Walserhof Hotel, CH-7250 Klosters-Platz. ℂ **081/410-29-29.** Fax 081/410-29-39. www.walserhof.ch. Reservations required in peak season. Main courses 46F–65F ($38–$53); fixed-price lunch 42F–88F ($34–$72); fixed-price dinner 98F–170F ($80–$139). AE, DC, MC, V. Daily 11:30am–2pm and 6–11pm. Closed late Apr to mid-June and late Oct to early Dec.

KLOSTERS AFTER DARK

One of the most consistently popular nightclubs in Klosters is the **Casa Antica,** Landstrasse 176 (ℂ **081/422-16-21**). Set on the resort's main street, directly across from the Alexis Gallery, it's a rustically (some say indestructibly) decorated bar and disco whose clientele ranges from 18 to 65. Open nightly during both midsummer and midwinter (with less frequent openings, depending on business, in shoulder seasons), it charges a 10F-to-17F ($8.20–$14) per-person entrance fee, which includes the first drink.

4 Davos *☆☆☆*

24km (15 miles) E of Chur; 11km (7 miles) S of Klosters

Along with St. Moritz and Zermatt, Davos has some of the finest sports facilities in the world, as well as a diversified choice of après-ski entertainment. The variety of activities makes it a favorite vacation spot for the chic and wealthy as well as for the hundreds of ordinary folk just out to have a good time in the mountains.

The name Davos (first Tavauns, later Dafaas) entered written history in 1160 in a document in the Episcopal archives of Chur. In 1289 a group of families from the Valais established homes here. In 1649 the town bought its freedom from Austria.

Kirchner: The Tormented Genius

Ernst Ludwig Kirchner was born in Aschaffenburg, Germany, in 1880. He studied architecture in Dresden and in 1905 was a cofounder of an expressionist group, Die Brücke, which was disbanded in 1913. The artist moved to Berlin in 1911, and it was there that his body of work reached its zenith. His highly personal paintings were noted for their sharp, vivid colors, their eroticism, and their psychological tension.

Physically and mentally scarred by his confrontation with Berlin and his experiences in military service, he tried several sanatoriums before deciding on Davos in 1917. First on the Stafelalp, later in the house In den Lärchen, and finally on the Wildboden, he produced a unique body of work. In Nazi Germany in 1936, his paintings were withdrawn from museums and labeled "degenerate art." As a result of the defamation of his character and his oeuvre, he fell into a deep depression that ended in suicide in 1938. His grave and that of his longtime companion, Erna, are located in the Davos forest cemetery.

For a look at this artist and his work, visit the **Davos Kirchner Museum,** Ernst Ludwig Kirchner Platz (© **081/413-22-02;** www.kirchnermuseum.ch). Entrance to the museum is 10F ($8.20) for adults and 8F ($6.55) for seniors and children. From Christmas to Easter and mid-July to September, it's open Tuesday to Sunday from 10am to 6pm; the rest of the year, Tuesday to Sunday from 2 to 6pm.

The two sections, Davos-Platz and Davos-Dorf, were once separate entities, but in the past 25 years or so, construction on the land between the two has served to join them, making Davos today somewhat larger than St. Moritz.

The canton of Davos is the second largest in Switzerland. The high valley that contains it is surrounded by forest-covered mountains that shelter it from rough winds. The area thus has a bracing climate, which has proven ideal for a summer-and-winter resort. Davos first entered the world limelight as a health resort in the 19th century, when Dr. Alexander Spengler prescribed mountain air for his tuberculosis patients. He brought the first summer visitors here in 1860 and the first winter ones 5 years later. There are still several sanatoriums in the area.

Thomas Mann used Davos, at the foot of the Zauberberg (Magic Mountain), as the setting for his famous novel *The Magic Mountain.* He visited the resort when his wife went there briefly in 1913 for her health, seeing it as a symbol of the general malaise that afflicted Europe on the eve of World War I. Robert Louis Stevenson wrote the last seven chapters of *Treasure Island* here between 1881 and 1882, as he, too, tended his consumptive wife. Another writer, Sir Arthur Conan Doyle, engaged in a daring run on skis over the Furka Pass to Arosa. Unfortunately, the much-celebrated villa-hotel where all three writers stayed, Am Stein, contains only private apartments and cannot be visited.

The German painter Ernst Ludwig Kirchner (1880–1938) lived at Davos from 1917 until his death. He was a leading exponent of the expressionist movement.

In addition to being a well-known summer-and-winter vacation resort, Davos is also a health spa, a sports center, and an important venue for international meetings.

Whether you're a hiker, mountain biker, downhill or cross-country skier, hang-glider, or ice-sports fan, Davos is an ideal place. Many nonathletes visit just for the relaxation. There's a wide choice of hotels, restaurants, bars, and discos, plus museums and concert and theater performances.

ESSENTIALS

GETTING THERE   Trains from Zurich usually require a transfer in the provincial railway junction of either Landquart or Filisur, where secondary rail lines continue on to Davos. Throughout the day, trains travel to Davos from both these towns every hour. The nearest airport is Zurich's Kloten, but the trip involves three different trains and two transfers. For information about train schedules, call © **0900/300-300.**

Bus lines connect Chur with Munich, stopping at Davos and several other mountain towns along the way, but they usually require transfers. Call the tourist office (below) for more information.

If you're driving, proceed to Klosters (see section 3, earlier in this chapter), then continue south on Route 28 to Davos.

VISITOR INFORMATION   The **Davos-Dorf Tourist Office** is at Promenade 67 (© **081/415-21-21;** www.davos.ch), and is open Monday to Friday from 8:30am to 6:30pm, with telephone service until 7pm; on Saturday it's open from 9am to 5pm, and on Sunday from 10am to noon and from 3 to 5:30pm.

CITY LAYOUT   The town's two sections, Davos-Platz (1,535m/5,035 ft.) and Davos-Dorf (1,538m/5,045 ft.), are linked by a boulevard flanked by boutiques, shops, hotels, and cafes. This thoroughfare is the famous Promenade, which takes the one-way traffic flow from Dorf to Platz (beware, however, if you're driving, as buses go in both directions). The lower artery, Talstrasse, runs along the railroad tracks, linking the train station in Davos-Platz with the station in Davos-Dorf.

Not all roads in Davos have street names, but there are signs pointing the way to all the hotels and restaurants. Public children's **playgrounds** are found in the Kurpark in Davos-Platz and opposite the lower terminal station of the Parsenn funicular at Davos-Dorf.

GETTING AROUND   Silver-sided buses, many of them plastered with advertisements from seemingly every store in town, run along the major arteries from Davos-Dorf to Davos-Platz, making scheduled stops near all the main hotels and restaurants. In winter the buses depart daily every 10 minutes from 7am to 11:20pm; in summer departures are every 20 minutes. A single ride costs 2.70F ($2.20), but rides are free for anyone who displays a guest card (they're available to anyone staying in one of Davos's hotels or guesthouses).

The postal bus leaves from the Davos-Platz railroad station. Organized excursions are available on the postal buses; for information, go to the nearest post office.

Tips A Free Ride

Any resident of a hotel or guesthouse in Davos showing proof of that occupancy and having paid the room tax can ride on town buses for free.

SEEING THE SIGHTS

Among the old buildings to be seen in Davos-Platz are the parish Church of St. John the Baptist, with a nave dating from 1280 to 1285. The church, now restored, was completed in 1481. It stands east of the train station along Talstrasse. A window in the choir is by Augusto Giacometti. The adjoining Rathaus (town hall) has been extensively restored. Its paneled Grosse Stube (Great Chamber) dates from 1564.

In Davos-Dorf you can visit the 14th-century **Church of St. Theodulus.** At Museumstrasse 1 is the **Altes Pfründhaus** (Old Prebend House), the town's only surviving example of a medieval burgher's domicile, now sheltering a minor local museum, the **Heimatmuseum** (© **081/416-26-66**), which traces the history of the resort town through a collection of objects and documents relating to its past. It's open January to April and June to October on Wednesday, Friday, and Sunday from 3 to 5pm, although special tours can be arranged in other months by contacting the museum or the tourist office. Guided tours cost 100F ($82). Adult admission is 5F ($4.10); children are charged 2F ($1.65).

THE ACTIVE VACATION PLANNER

SKIING   Recreational skiing began here in 1888, but Davos first appeared on the world sports stage in 1899, when a large ice rink was opened for the world figure-skating and the European speed-skating championship competitions. In the same year the Davos-Schatzalp funicular and the Schatzalp toboggan run were inaugurated. Now Davos is one of the best ski regions in the world.

On both sides of the valley, you're faced with five large ski areas, of which the most noted is the **Parsenn-Weissflüh.** Some experts say that this is the finest ski area in Europe. To reach it, take the Parsennbahn (railway) from Davos-Dorf to **Weissflühjoch** (2,622m/8,600 ft.), the gateway to the major ski area, with a huge number of runs in every category; there are a few downhill ski runs leading back to Davos that are suitable for only the most skilled skiers.

From Weissflühjoch, where there's a restaurant, take the cableway to **Weissflühgipfel** ✦✦ (2,778m/9,112 ft.). It takes about 30 minutes transit, via a trio of cable-car stages, from Davos-Dorf. From there you can reach the celebrated Küblis run to the north.

Davos shares its snow with nearby Klosters, where you can also ski, but cable cars and T-bar lift service may keep you happy with the ski opportunities nearer to Davos. Beginners are advised to stick to Rinerhorn or perhaps Pischa, where, if you're graded "intermediate" by your ski-school instructor, you may be directed to the somewhat more challenging slopes at Jakobshorn.

The ski facilities around Davos aren't the most widespread and far-flung in Switzerland, but they nonetheless incorporate enough challenges to keep intermediate and expert skiers engrossed. Most visitors opt for **Davos's Top Ski Pass,** also known as the **Davos/Klosters R.E.G.A. Ski Pass,** which includes access to five different ski regions around Klosters and Davos. Together, they incorporate 322km (200 miles) of marked ski runs, and access to three funiculars, 10 cable cars, four gondolas, and 39 other mechanical conveyances designed to haul you and your equipment uphill. It also includes free rides on the railway cars from Küblis, a nearby hamlet surrounded by snowfields, back uphill to Davos. Adults pay 121F ($99) for a 2-day pass, 210F ($172) for a 4-day pass, and 282F ($231) for a 6-day pass. Children 6 to 16 are granted reductions of around 70% off those rates, and children 5 and under ride free.

OTHER SPORTS   Several winter sports besides skiing are offered here as well. For information on curling, contact the **Davos Curling Club/Davos-Village Curling Club,** Promenade 46, Davos-Platz (© **079/610-24-54**). Two hours of curling, including instruction, cost 35F to 40F ($23–$26) per person.

If you're interested in ice-skating on the **Natureisbahn,** Davos-Platz, the largest natural ice rink in Europe, phone the Davos-Dorf Tourist Office (see "Essentials," above), which manages the rink. Admission costs 6F ($4.90) for adults, 4F ($2.60) for children. Prices are 1F (80¢) less for holders of the Guest Card, which is presented to all hotel guests. The rink is usually open from December to late February, depending on weather conditions. Davos-Platz also has a huge artificial ice rink, and both are open daily from 10am to 4pm, with additional openings every Thursday and Saturday from 8 to 10pm. In addition to this natural ice-skating rink midway between Davos-Platz and Davos-Dorf, there are at least two other ice-skating venues. For any information about ice-skating, contact the tourist office (see above) or www.davos-skating.ch.

Many Davos sports facilities can be used in both the winter and the summer. It has first-class tennis courts, sailing and windsurfing on Lake Davos, swimming, and horseback riding. There's an 18-hole golf course, **Golf Club Davis** (© **081/416-56-34;** www.golfdavos.ch), with a weekday greens fee of 85F ($70) that includes a golf cart; on weekends the fee goes up to 110F ($90). If you're staying in accommodations at Davos, there's a 10F ($8.20) discount. Golf clubs can be rented for an additional 40F ($33) a day. There's also a large indoor ice rink if you want to keep your skills and your skates sharp during the summer months.

Davos has an impressive **Tennis & Squash Center,** on Clavadelerstrasse 2 in Davos-Platz (© **081/413-31-31;** www.indoor-sport.ch), which is open daily from 8am to 10pm. Prices depend on when you play, day or night. Court rental from 5:30 to 10:30pm is 28F ($23) for an indoor or outdoor court in summer or between 42F and 45F ($34–$37) in winter.

Want to go swimming? Call **Hallenbad,** Promenade 99, next to the Kongress (© **081/413-64-63**), for information on either indoor swimming in winter or outdoor swimming in the summer. Adults pay 8F ($6.55) and children 6 to 15 are charged 5F ($4.10), all of which includes changing-room facilities. With use of the mixed sauna included, adults pay 15F ($12).

HIKING & WALKING   Well-marked and -maintained footpaths and mountain trails give access to meadows, pastures, woods, and mountains both close to and far away from Davos. A 451km (280-mile) network of pathways follows brooks, crosses alpine meadows, and leads to remote hamlets, allowing you to explore the side valleys of Sertig, Dischma, and Flüela. Davos mountain railways provide access to five different walking areas and to the most rewarding vantage points around Davos. The tourist office (see "Essentials," above) will supply more details.

SHOPPING

Davos is not obsessed with Swiss folklore but you'll find lots of emphasis on cutting-edge sports equipment and clothing. Check out **Ettinger Sport,** Promenade 153, Davos-Dorf (© **081/410-12-12**), or its less comprehensive counterpart at the opposite end of the resort, **Angerer Sport,** Promenade 49, Davos-Platz (© **081/413-66-72**).

Souvenirs of your stay in the Grisons are most conveniently acquired at **Pfister Holzladen,** Promenade 121A, Davos-Dorf (© **081/416-40-60**), or **Trauffer Souvenirs,** Promenade 78, Davos-Platz (© **081/413-55-78**). **Benetton** sells casual men's

Finds Hiking without Luggage

Three Grisons vacation resorts—Arosa, Lenzerheide-Valbella, and Davos—have joined forces to create a "Hiking without Luggage" program. It's intended for hikers who enjoy walking from one resort to another but don't want to be bothered by luggage. Instead, your luggage is delivered to your next hotel for you, an arrangement made by various hotels. Either a 3-night/4-day or a 6-night/7-day program can be booked. The most popular departure point for this program is Davos, although, if the idea appeals to you, you can hike in the opposite direction from, say, Lenzerheide-Valbella into Davos.

There are two hiking routes between Arosa and Davos to choose from. The easier one is via the Sapün, and the more challenging and loftier route is via the Tritt. Both paths lead to the Strela Pass. You can either take the Schatzalp/Strela mountain railway to get to Davos or continue on foot. The 4-day program, including 3 nights' accommodations with half-board included, is available for 365F to 525F ($299–$431) per person. The 7-day program, including 6 nights accommodations, with half-pension included, costs 605F to 920F ($496–$754) per person. Children from 12 to 16 years old are eligible for a 30% discount, children from 6 to 11 get a 50% discount, and children under 6 stay for free. Included in the price is breakfast, luggage transfer, one ascent or descent in a mountain railway for each day's hike, the relevant maps and route descriptions, and box lunches for most of the days you'll be hiking. The program is available only during the warm-weather months.

For more information, call the **Davos Tourist Office** (✆ **081/415-21-21**).

and women's clothes at Promenade 62, in Davos-Platz (✆ **081/413-49-50**). If you're looking for etchings, oil paintings or watercolors, or lithographs created by artists from the region and from everywhere else as well, head for any of the oft-changing exhibitions at either of the resort's most noteworthy art galleries, **Galerie Iris-Wazzau,** Promenade 72, Davos-Platz (✆ **081/413-31-06**), or **Galerie Eule Art,** Promenade 41, Davos-Platz (✆ **081/413-15-00**).

WHERE TO STAY
IN DAVOS-PLATZ
Very Expensive
Steigenberger Belvédère ✦✦✦   This, the most famous and prestigious hotel in Davos, occupies a light-gray neoclassical building on the main road of Davos-Platz. Originally built around 1875, it was purchased in the 1980s by the Germany-based Steigenberger chain and lavishly upgraded to some of the highest standards in Switzerland. The carefully groomed interior has a series of intricately carved fireplaces, ornate ceilings, a well-polished bar, and both contemporary and Victorian armchairs. Guests have a choice of modern, Belle Epoque, or regionally decorated rooms, many with furniture crafted from a local wood called arvenholz. A few, however, are rather standard in decor. It's worth visiting the pool for the murals even if you don't swim: A Tahitian lagoon with flamingoes and lifelike jungle plants sway in the imaginary breeze, and seem to grow right out of the pool.

Promenade 89, CH-4270 Davos-Platz. (© **800/223-5652** in the U.S. and Canada or 081/415-60-00. Fax 081/415-60-01. www.davos.steigenberger.ch. 131 units. Winter 426F–780F ($349–$640) double, 667F–1,990F ($547–$1,632) suite for 2; summer 308F–352F ($253–$289) double, 386F–970F ($317–$795) suite for 2. Rates include breakfast. Half board 25F ($21) extra per person. AE, DC, MC, V. Indoor parking 25F ($21), free outdoor parking. Closed mid-Apr to mid-June. **Amenities:** 2 restaurants; bar; indoor pool; sauna; 24-hr. room service; massage; babysitting; laundry service. *In room:* TV, minibar, hair dryer, safe.

Expensive

Hotel Europe ⚐ This longtime favorite is near the tourist office and the Schatzalp-Strela funicular. Right in the heart of Davos-Platz, the hotel lies just a few steps from the lifts, a few yards from the ice rink, and only 5 minutes from the golf greens. It was built in 1868, and is thus the oldest of the resort's big hotels. The present building is a flat-roofed, white stucco structure whose exterior detailing has been restored. The formal interior is decorated with Oriental rugs and hunting trophies. Rooms are not at all lavish, with laminated furniture, but they are well equipped with double glazing, tiled bathrooms (generally with tubs), and twin beds. Opt, if possible, for a unit with a balcony facing south.

Promenade 63, CH-7270 Davos-Platz. (© **081/413-59-21.** Fax 081/415-41-11. www.europe-davos.ch. 64 units. Winter 280F–480F ($230–$394) double, 800F–1,080F ($656–$886) junior suite for 2; off season 210F–300F ($172–$246) double, 560F–680F ($459–$558) junior suite for 2. Rates include buffet breakfast. AE, DC, MC, V. Indoor parking 15F ($12), outdoor parking free. Davos bus to stop 10. **Amenities:** 2 restaurants; bar; indoor pool; fitness room; sauna; 24-hr. room service; babysitting; laundry service; on-site casino. *In room:* TV, dataport, minibar, hair dryer.

Kongress Hotel Davos ⚐ Well-designed and efficient, this first-class hotel lies midway between Davos-Dorf and Davos-Platz, about .8km (½ mile) from each. From its premises, you'll enjoy a view of the Landwasser River and snowfields in winter or green Davos mountains in summer. The hotel, which opened in 1982, lies immediately adjacent to the Convention Center, and it's next to the indoor swimming pool complex. Virtually all the sports facilities of Davos are close by. In addition, a public bus stops in front of the hotel for frequent rides to the ski runs. The midsize bedrooms are smartly furnished.

Promenade 94, CH-7270 Davos-Platz. (© **081/417-11-22.** Fax 081/417-11-23. www.hotelkongress.ch. 80 units. Winter 330F–420F ($271–$344) double; off season 250F–290F ($205–$238) double. Rates include breakfast. Half board 30F ($25) per person extra. AE, DC, MC, V. Free parking outdoors; 10F ($8.20) in garage in summer, 12F ($9.85) in winter. Closed mid-Apr to mid-May. Davos bus to stop 10. **Amenities:** Restaurant; bar; sauna; limited room service; laundry service. *In room:* TV, dataport, minibar, hair dryer, safe.

Morosani Posthotel ⚐ Set at the gateway to the Promenade in Davos-Platz, this is a landmark that has been efficiently run for more than a century by the Morosani family. The hotel consists of three buildings connected by a rustically decorated underground tunnel. The cozy lobby has an open fireplace, and bedrooms are spacious.

Promenade 42, CH-7270 Davos-Platz. (© **081/413-74-74.** Fax 081/415-45-01. www.posthotel-davos.ch. 90 units. Winter 350F–520F ($287–$426) double; summer 320F–360F ($262–$295) double. Winter rates include half board; summer rates include breakfast. AE, DC, MC, V. Free parking outdoors, 15F ($12) in garage. Closed mid-Mar to mid-May and Oct 5–Dec 6. Davos bus to stop 9. **Amenities:** Restaurant; bar; indoor pool; sauna; playground; limited room service; babysitting; laundry service. *In room:* TV, minibar, hair dryer.

IN DAVOS-DORF
Very Expensive

Flüela Hotel ⚐ More than 150 years after its opening, this thick-walled, solidly built hotel is still managed by the Gredig family, who focus entirely on winter (not summer) lodgings for their guests. Its unadorned beige facade conceals an elegantly rustic and cozy interior with comfortable and well-furnished bedrooms, each fitted with cozy appointments and state-of-the-art plumbing. Most of the bedrooms are renovated, and substantial improvements have been made to the health club and exercise areas. Overall, it's a cozy, well-managed choice in Davos.

Bahnhofstrasse 5, CH-7260 Davos-Dorf. *©* **081/410-17-17.** Fax 081/410-17-18. www.fluela.ch. 73 units. 410F–820F ($336–$672) double; 720F–910F ($590–$746) suite. Rates include half board. AE, DC, MC, V. Parking 15F ($12). Closed late Apr to late Nov. **Amenities:** 2 restaurants; bar; sauna; Turkish bath; limited room service; massage; babysitting; dry cleaning. *In room:* TV, dataport, minibar, hair dryer, safe.

Moderate

Hotel Dischma *Value* This is a well-recommended government-rated three-star hotel with modern amenities and a location in the heart of Davos-Dorf, near the Parsenn funicular; the Pischa bus stop is about a 5-minute walk away. The small to midsize bedrooms are renovated although still rustic; you don't check in here for style but for value. Nonetheless, there is much comfort, including well-maintained plumbing.

Promenade 128, CH-7260 Davos-Dorf. *©* **081/410-12-50.** Fax 081/416-32-88. www.dischma.ch. 27 units. Winter 226F–270F ($185–$221) double; summer 156F–170F ($128–$139) double. Rates include buffet breakfast. Supplement for half board 25F–35F ($21–$29) extra per person. AE, DC, MC, V. Free parking. Bus to stop 5. **Amenities:** 2 restaurants; 2 bars; limited room service; laundry service. *In room:* TV, minibar, safe, hair dryer.

Parsenn Sporthotel In the heart of Davos-Dorf, across the road from the Parsennbahn, this is a large and substantial Grisons chalet whose facade is covered in intricate stencils. Built in 1907 and enlarged in 1972, it sits beside a large parking lot and near a cluster of gas stations, not far from the base of several ski lifts. The ceilings of the public rooms are beamed or vaulted, sheltering a mountain-rustic decor with few frills but with a sense of genuine old-fashioned charm. The midsize bedrooms are comfortable—some are newer than others—furnished in a pine-wood chalet style. Half of them are equipped only with shower, the rest with a tub/shower combination.

Promenade 152, CH-7260 Davos-Dorf. *©* **081/416-32-32.** Fax 081/416-38-67. www.hotelparsenn.ch. 40 units. Winter 224F–284F ($184–$233) double; 214F–284F ($175–$233) junior suite for 2; summer 150F–160F ($123–$131) double; 180F ($148) junior suite. Rates include breakfast. Half board available for an additional 20F ($13) per person per day. AE, MC, V. **Amenities:** Restaurant; bar. *In room:* TV, hair dryer, safe.

Inexpensive

Hermann Hotel *Value* One of the most reliable cost-conscious hotels in town sits on the main street of Davos-Dorf, near the edge of the town facing Klosters. Originally built about a century ago, it's a four-story building with a flat roof and—at least on the outside—very few of the architectural adornments usually associated with an old-fashioned chalet. Inside, you'll find a cozy, simple decor, a clientele that appreciates the inexpensive half-board supplements, and very simple bedrooms outfitted with lots of varnished pine. Two-thirds of the rooms contain small, shower-only private bathrooms; occupants of the other units will find the corridor bathrooms adequate.

Dorfstrasse 23, CH-7260 Davos-Dorf. *©* **081/416-17-37.** Fax 081/416-35-73. www.hotel-herrmann-davos.ch. 30 units, 20 with bathroom. Winter 150F–190F ($123–$156) double with bathroom, 140F–180F ($115–$148) double without bathroom; summer 130F ($107) double with bathroom, 100F ($82) double without bathroom. Rates include breakfast. Half board 20F ($16) extra per person. Outdoor parking free, indoor parking 10F ($8.20) per night. MC, V. Closed Sept 20–Dec 20 and Easter to late June. **Amenities:** Restaurant (open only to residents on half board); bar.

Hotel Bûnda Modern and well maintained, and set within a short walk from the Davos-Dorf railway station and the lake, this hotel consists of two buildings connected via an underground passageway. Built in 1964 and 1995, they contain cozy, relatively spacious bedrooms, with those in the newer annex looking somewhat more contemporary than their old-fashioned counterparts in the other building. Each unit contains a private shower-only bathroom. Many of the rooms have rustic-looking beamed ceilings, and many open onto private balconies. The in-house restaurant expands during clement weather onto a wooden deck whose view stretches out over the other houses in the neighborhood.

Museumstrasse 4, CH-7260 Davos-Dorf. © **081/417-18-19.** Fax 081/417-18-20. www.buenda.ch. 31 units. Winter 220F–330F ($180–$271) double, with half board included; summer 170F–220F ($139–$180) double, with breakfast included. Supplement for half board in summer 25F ($21) per person. AE, DC, MC, V. Closed mid-Apr to early June. Garage parking 11F ($9). **Amenities:** 2 restaurants (1 reserved for hotel residents); bar; fitness room; steam room; sauna. *In room:* TV, minibar, hair dryer, safe.

IN DAVOS-LARET

Hübli's Landhaus 🐾 *(Finds* Built a century ago as a relay station 5km (3 miles) from the center of Davos, on a traffic-filled highway between Davos and Klosters, Hübli's is one of the region's best little hotels for the money. The dynamic owners put most of their energy into the excellent restaurant (see "Where to Dine," below), although there's a selection of small bedrooms connected to the restaurant by a tunnel. The rooms have earth-tone fabrics and furniture and exposed hardwoods, and are known for their coziness and their vaguely folkloric references. Rooms are equally divided between those with tub bathrooms and those with shower. In the height of midwinter, the hotel provides free transportation to the ski lifts of Davos.

Kantonsstrasse, CH-7265 Davos-Laret. © **081/417-10-10.** Fax 081/417-10-11. www.hublis.ch. 20 units, 14 with bathroom. Winter 242F–296F ($198–$243) double without bathroom, 250F–340F ($205–$279) double with bathroom; summer 150F–162F ($123–$133) double without bathroom, 170F–200F ($139–$164) double with bathroom. Rates include breakfast. Half board 25F ($21) per person extra. AE, DC, MC, V. Free parking. Closed early Apr to late June and Nov–Dec 15. Travel 3.2km/2 miles north of Davos-Dorf along Rte. 28 toward Klosters. **Amenities:** Restaurant; limited room service. *In room:* TV, minibar, hair dryer, safe.

WHERE TO DINE

EXPENSIVE

Bündnerstübli 🐾 SWISS   The walls and the ceiling of this cozy place are covered with local pine, giving it a rustic look. The menu, however, is a lot more sophisticated, and the venue is a lot more worldly, than its mountain veneer would have you believe. Within an undeniably cozy ambience that lies within a 5-minute walk downhill from the center of Davos-Dorf, you can enjoy such glamorous food as smoked carpaccio of venison with duck liver, South African shrimp in a vegetable-flavored vinaigrette, rack of veal stuffed with shrimp, and braised filets of turbot on a bed of truffled leeks.

Dischmastrasse 8, Davos-Dorf. © **081/416-33-93.** Reservations required. Main courses 32F–58F ($26–$48); fixed-price menus 68F–90F ($56–$74). AE, DC, MC, V. Thurs–Tues 11:30am–2pm and 5–11pm. Closed Easter to late June and Nov.

Hübli's Landhaus 🐾🐾🐾 CONTINENTAL   This is the finest and most sophisticated restaurant around Davos, with a reputation throughout Switzerland that draws many clients to its position 5km (3 miles) east of town, beside the highway leading to Klosters. Inside the solid white walls of what was built a century ago as a relay station for the Swiss postal service, you'll find a handful of artfully simple dining rooms and superb cuisine. Felix and Anne-Marie Hübli offer specialties that change with the seasons and the availability of the ingredients. Examples include a terrine of foie gras served with a salad of artichokes, lobster bisque, filet of turbot with lemon-flavored cream sauce, veal chop with chanterelle-flavored cream sauce, and roast duckling with blackberry sauce. Dessert may be a parfait of Peruvian mangoes or perhaps a gratin of fresh summer berries served with passion-fruit sorbet.

Kantonsstrasse, Davos-Laret. *C* **081/417-10-10.** Reservations recommended. Main courses 40F–69F ($33–$57); fixed-price lunch 22F–48F ($18–$39); fixed-price dinner 84F–130F ($69–$107). AE, DC, MC, V. Tues–Sun 11:30am–2pm and 6:30–9:30pm. Closed early Apr to late June, Nov–Dec 15, and at lunch in winter.

Restaurant Pöstli ✰ SWISS   In winter this elegant room usually offers live music from 5 to 5:30pm and from 8:30pm until closing time. In summer live music begins at 6pm and lasts until closing. The restaurant has a bar as well as a more formal seating area. Your choice in tasty platters is extensive—a different fresh fish daily or something classic, such as *Tafelspitz* (boiled beef Viennese-style). Other selections are veal liver with polenta, venison in a hunter's sauce, filet of U.S. beef with mushrooms, and rack of lamb with braised cabbage. Overall, it's a well-managed, cozy restaurant with lots of ambience and flavorful food.

In the Morosani Posthotel, Promenade 42 at Postplatz, Davos-Platz. *C* **081/413-74-74.** Reservations required. Main courses 24F–62F ($20–$51); fixed-price menus 75F–88F ($62–$72). AE, DC, MC, V. Daily 11am–2pm and 6:15pm–1am. Closed mid-Mar to mid-May, Oct 5–Dec 6, and Sun–Mon in summer.

MODERATE

Bistro Gentiana SWISS   Housed in a gold-colored building opposite the Hotel Schweizerhof in the center of town, this restaurant is known for its 10 different types of fondue dishes, as well as for its unusual list of dishes prepared with snails. Unpretentious and bustling, and within a cozy alpine environment, the establishment serves ample portions of air-dried beef and ham, as well as inexpensive daily specials. Its selection of desserts includes local pears in cinnamon syrup, honey-flavored ice cream, and chocolate mousse. Wines are sold by the carafe. Don't overlook the somewhat more formal pair of upstairs dining rooms, whose focal point is a blue-toned painting by the German artist Ernst Ludwig Kirchner, a former resident of Davos.

Promenade 53, Davos-Platz. *C* **081/413-56-48.** Reservations required. Main courses 20F–45F ($16–$37); meat and cheese fondues 25F–45F ($21–$37). AE, DC, MC, V. Daily year-round 11am–11pm. Closed Wed in summer.

DAVOS AFTER DARK

Everybody's favorite late-night den, bar, and disco is the **Bar Rotliechtli,** which somewhat provocatively translates as "Red Light Bar." It's also known as Cava Grischi, near Postplatz, just off the main street of Davos-Platz (*C* **081/414-90-00**). Warm, cozy, cramped, and convivial, it offers a rustic-looking decor of varnished pine and masonry, free entrance, and a bar that caters to all ages and all types of personalities, provided that they're late-nighters looking for interaction with like-minded extroverts. It's open nightly from 8pm till around 2am. Beers cost from 8F ($6.55) each.

14

The Engadine

The Valley of the Inn (or En, as the locals call it in Romansh) stretches for 97km (60 miles), from the Maloja Plateau (1,786m/5,858 ft.) to Finstermünz. All of the villages here except Sils lie at a higher altitude than the plateau. The highest is St. Moritz, at 1,811m (5,940 ft.).

The Engadine is enclosed by great mountain ranges with meadows and forests on the steep hillsides. The villages are built of stone, originally as a protection against the fires that swept the narrow windy valleys. The whitewashed houses in the villages, known for their larders, often have *sgraffito* decorations (designs in plasterwork), with mottoes and heraldic devices. The population is of Rhaeto-Romanic heritage and is mostly Protestant.

From the Maloja Pass, the road runs northeast through the Upper Engadine, where the clear mountain skies and dry, light breezes make the area popular in both summer and winter. Since the 19th century, when the Upper Engadine became fashionable for its "air cure," it has developed into a winter-sports resort, highlighted by St. Moritz.

The two major attractions of the Lower Engadine, where the valley is narrower and more heavily forested, are the mineral springs of Scuol and the Swiss National Park, an 89km (55-mile) wildlife sanctuary.

St. Moritz is the major rail terminus for the valley. For **information** and schedules, call ℂ **0900/300-300.** From here you can make bus or rail links to other villages of the Engadine.

EXPLORING THE REGION BY CAR

The Lower Engadine is reached from Davos over the Flüela Pass (2,345m/7,692 ft.) and the Ofen Pass (2,115m/6,937 ft.). Four major passes lead into the Upper Engadine: Maloja (1,786m/5,858 ft.), Julier (2,248m/7,373 ft.), Albula (2,275m/7,462 ft.), and Bernina (2,286m/7,498 ft.). The upper valley contains several lakes, including that of St. Moritz.

If you have time to drive only one of these passes, and weather conditions are right, make it the **Bernina Pass** 🚗🚗, a 2-hour, 55km (34-mile) drive between St. Moritz and Tirano in Italy. This pass is one of the most spectacular in Europe, and is most often blocked by snow from October to May. Since the pass is not cleared at night, it is best to start out in daytime.

Leaving St. Moritz, on the way toward Pontresina, you'll pass **Muottas Muragl,** from which you can take a funicular to an altitude of 2,414m (7,918 ft.), where you'll be rewarded with the most stunning view of the Upper Engadine Gap. The panorama also takes in a chain of lakes lying between St. Moritz and Maloja. From the top of the station, you can take some of the most dramatic mountain walks in eastern Switzerland, enjoying the alpine flora and fauna.

The road passes by Pontresina, a resort, and continues until the **Chünetta Belvedere** at 2,050m (6,724 ft.). You cannot drive all the way to the top of the belvedere but still have to go 1 hour on foot. At the belvedere the spectacular peaks of the Bernina Massif, including Piz Bernina and Piz Morteratsch, lie before you.

As you continue along, you'll pass another sign, directing you to the **Diavolezza,** another spectacular belvedere at 2,723m (8,931 ft.) that includes a 15-minute journey by cable car. Diavolezza is the starting point of one of the most famous glacier runs in the world. See "Pontresina," later in this chapter, for more information.

After crossing the Bernina Pass, where there are clear views of the Piz Cambrena and its glacier, you come to **Alp Grüm** at 2,058m (6,750 ft.), overlooking the Palü Glacier and the Poschiavo Valley. Going through the resort of Poschiavo you arrive finally at **Tirano** on the downward slope, passing through tobacco fields and vineyards. At Tirano you will have arrived on Italian soil.

THE ENGADINE OUTDOORS

You don't come to this rugged part of Switzerland to stay in your hotel room all day, not with a wilderness out there to explore. After leaving the chic resorts such as St. Moritz, you enter wild, untamed scenery.

Great Express Trains

From Zurich, the *Glacier Express* climbs over the Alps from St. Moritz to Zermatt in the Valais. The *Engadine Express* also goes from Chur through the Swiss National Park into the Lower Engadine. The *Palm Express* from St. Moritz to Lugano is one of the great train rides in the area, going from the snowy alpine peaks and mountain lakes of the Upper Engadine to the subtropical atmosphere of the Lake District near Italy. The scenery along the way is some of the most panoramic in Switzerland. You have a choice of a 1- or 2-day itinerary, the latter involving a hotel night en route. For information and seasonal availability, call Rail Europe at © **877/237-2887.**

For hikers, the **Swiss National Park Service,** Schweizerischer National Park (© **081/856-12-82;** www.nationalpark.ch) maps out a group of panoramic half- or full-day adventures into the choicest and most scenic of its wilderness land holdings. Many of these take you along rugged and often steep mountain trails, so you should be in good shape. All major villages and resorts in the Engadine also offer signposted and well-maintained hiking trails and footpaths. Visit local or regional tourist offices to learn more. All maps and information are available at the Zuoz Tourist Office (see "Essentials" under "S-Chanf & Zuoz," below), where the helpful staff can plan an outdoor itinerary suitable to your specific interests.

For one of the **great walks** in the Engadine, you can take in vistas of four highland lakes at 1,771m (5,809 ft.) above sea level. Even at this high altitude the walk is like traversing the floor of a valley. The walk begins at Maloja and goes for 14km (8½ miles) to the resort of Silvaplana. Allow some 3 to 3½ hours for this alpine stroll. From Maloja, traverse the eastern or southern tier of Lej da Segl. The route is well marked leading you to Segl-Maria, one of the most charming old Romansh villages. Eventually you reach the resort of Silvaplana. As you walk along you'll be following in the footsteps of Nietzsche, who lived in this area and often took this walk "to think."

For serious **mountaineering,** the **Bergsteigerschule La Margna** at Pontresina has a mountaineering school with guided tours. One day of instruction for beginners costs 450F ($369). Call © **081/838-83-33** to arrange for an appointment and to get prices and listings of scheduled climbing trips.

White-water expeditions are possible on the River En, but only between June and September. A half-day's outing where you'll shoot the rapids in a rubber-sided raft is priced at 105F ($86), but cost can vary depending on the options you select. A full day's excursion goes for 170F ($139). For more information about this, contact **Swissraft Engadine** (© **081/911-52-50;** www.swissraft.ch), in Scuol, or any local tourist office within the Engadine.

It's also possible to go **horseback riding** in the Engadine. The best stables are in St. Moritz (see section 3, later in this chapter).

The Engadine is known for its steep, river-eroded canyons, the sides of which rise vertiginously upward on either side. An outfit that can help direct you through some of the steepest of these is **St. Moritz Experience,** via Suot Chesas CH-7512 Champfer (© **081/833-77-14;** www.stmoritz-experience.ch). For 180F ($148) per day from 9am to 5pm, they'll include transportation, use of all equipment, and instruction on how to navigate up and down the edges of canyons and valleys whose microclimates are softer and gentler than those on the windswept upper regions nearby. The same outfit will take you on an 8-hour glacier-and-rock hike for around 120F ($98) per person.

1 S-Chanf & Zuoz ⟨★

48km (30 miles) SE of Davos; 19km (12 miles) NE of St. Moritz

These two Engadine resorts with a combined population of under 2,000 residents offer attractive, and less expensive, alternatives to St. Moritz, located to the southwest.

ESSENTIALS

GETTING THERE   About 17 local trains travel daily from St. Moritz. They arrive first at Zuoz and then continue to S-Chanf, 15 and 20 minutes away, respectively, with one-way tickets priced at 17F and 19F ($14 and $16). For **rail information** and timetables, call ℭ **0900/300-300.**

By car from St. Moritz, drive northeast along Route 27.

VISITOR INFORMATION   The **Zuoz Tourist Office** is in Zuoz on the main street, via Maistra (ℭ **081/854-15-10**). Most of the year, it's open Monday to Friday from 9am to noon and 3 to 6pm. During the low season, it's open Monday to Friday from 3 to 5pm. There's a smaller tourist office in **S-Chanf,** on via Maistra (ℭ **081/ 854-22-55**). We would advise you to contact the office in Zuoz first. For information on transportation by bus between the two villages, contact the tourist office or call ℭ **081/834-90-90.**

EXPLORING THE TOWN
IN ZUOZ

This old-world village, once the chief population center of the Engadine, is located by the Inn River amid alpine meadows and lush forests. Most of the 1,200 inhabitants of Zuoz speak Romansh.

This is the best-preserved village in the Upper Engadine, with the most striking collection of Engadine houses to be found anywhere in the valley. The best-known is the famed **Planta House** (two houses actually), on the **main square** ★★ of the village, with an outdoor staircase and a rococo balustrade. The Planta family, historically important in the region, built most of the spectacular structures in town. This privately owned house cannot be entered by tourists.

Another stop that merits a visit is the **village church.** Inside, look for the severed-bear's-paw theme—a heraldic symbol of the Plantas that also appears on a fountain in the main square. Augusto Giacometti designed some of the church's modern stained-glass windows.

A fledgling summer resort, Zuoz offers a wealth of activities from horseback riding to summer skiing. At 1,722m (5,648 ft.) above sea level, this minor winter-sports center has a **ski school** (ℭ **081/854-11-79**) for beginners, including children, as well as for those more advanced in the sport. The school is only open for business during midwinter. The most experienced skiers will gravitate to the heights of the Piz Kesch region or else journey by train to St. Moritz.

Numerous cross-country tracks lead through Zuoz in all directions, and the village is the finishing point of the Engadine ski marathon. Curling, ice-skating, and sledding are other winter sports pursued here.

IN S-CHANF

At 1,530m (5,018 ft.), this village with a most unusual name is a summer and winter resort at the entrance to the **Swiss National Park** 🖈🖈🖈 . This park, which covers a landmass of 174 sq. km (280 sq. miles), is the only one of its kind in Switzerland. Hunting is strictly forbidden within its precincts, as it is viewed as a nature preserve and shelter for alpine flora and fauna. Entrance to the park is free, and it's popular in midwinter as a cross-country ski zone and in summer as a hiking destination.

WHERE TO STAY & DINE

IN ZUOZ

Posthotel Engiadina 🖈   The most visible and prestigious hotel in Zuoz is a beau-tifully preserved, pink neobaroque structure that was built more than 125 years ago as a lodging for passengers on the Swiss postal routes. Public rooms remain faithful to the style of the original construction, but they've been charmingly updated with murals and all the modern conveniences you'd expect from a government-rated four-star hotel. At least one of the parlors contains antiques, Art Deco chandeliers, and an unusual collection of antique clocks. Bedrooms are more modern than the building's elaborate exterior would suggest. Recently renovated, they're conservative, cozy, and tasteful, with tiled bathrooms equipped mostly with well-maintained tub/shower combinations. The two in-house restaurants produce some of the finest cuisine in the area, specializing in international and regional foods. A glass of ruby vintage Veltliner goes wonderfully with their Engadine sausage.

CH-7524 Zuoz. Ⓒ 081/854-10-21. Fax 081/854-33-03. www.hotelengiadina.ch. 42 units. 190F–319F ($156–$262) double; 294F–348F ($241–$285) junior suite. Rates include breakfast. Half board, if clients remain for a minimum of 3 days, 38F ($31) per person per day. AE, DC, MC, V. Closed Apr–May and mid-Oct to mid-Dec. **Amenities:** 2 restau-rants; bar; indoor pool; tennis court; sauna; limited room service; laundry. *In room:* TV, hair dryer.

IN S-CHANF

Hotel Scaletta *Finds*   Originally built in 1624 as a relay station for passengers and horses struggling over the Engadine passes, this hotel evokes old Europe. It's one of the most immediately recognizable buildings in S-Chanf, thanks to a gray-green antique facade that's accented with sgraffito, on a tiny square a few steps from the vil-lage church. The five rooms in the oldest section are the most charming, thanks to antique paneling, high ceilings, and somewhat larger dimensions. More contempo-rary-looking bedrooms, comfortable and well-maintained but without the patina or antiques of the others, lie within a wing that was added to the original hotel in the late 1980s. All units contain neatly kept bathrooms equipped with showers. The hotel's in-house restaurant serves Swiss cuisine at reasonable prices. This is one of the few hotels in the region, incidentally, that remains open throughout the year.

Via Maistra 52, CH-7525 S-Chanf. Ⓒ 081/854-03-04. Fax 081/884-05-06. www.hotel-scaletta.ch. 20 units. 130F–195F ($107–$160) double. Rates include breakfast. Half board 32F–58F ($26–$48) per person. AE, DC, MC, V. **Amenities:** Restaurant; bar; curling rink. *In room:* TV, minibar, safe.

2 Samedan 🖈 & Celerina 🖈

3km (2 miles) NE of St. Moritz; 5km (3 miles) NW of Pontresina

These twin resorts are virtually at the doorstep of St. Moritz and are sometimes referred to as suburbs of St. Moritz. But that's a somewhat demeaning label, as Samedan and Celerina have individual characters.

Samedan, originally a Roman settlement, survived to become a principal village of the Upper Engadine. Over the years many well-known Swiss families have made their homes here. Seek out the Planta House (the same family that made its mark on Zuoz) and note its large roof and impressive library of Romansh works.

Celerina, a hamlet on the Inn River, has long been overshadowed by its more celebrated neighbors. But for those in search of local color, Celerina (Schlarigna in Romansh) is an ideal choice as a winter or summer resort. Known for its charming Engadine houses, this little village on a sunny plain is sheltered from bitter winds.

ESSENTIALS

GETTING THERE   Almost 20 **trains** depart from St. Moritz every day, stopping 4 minutes later in Celerina and 7 minutes later in Samedan. Trains also run from Chur to Samedan. For information, call © **0900/300-300.**

Buses running from St. Moritz to Lugano are not scheduled to stop at Celerina and Samedan; usually, however, if you let the driver know that you'd like to get off at either point, he'll stop for you. Buses running between Pontresina and St. Moritz (there are two to five buses a day, depending on the season) stop regularly at Samedan.

If you're **driving** from St. Moritz, head northeast along Route 27.

VISITOR INFORMATION   The **Celerina Tourist Office** (© **081/830-00-11**), in the center, is open Monday to Friday from 8:30am to noon and 2 to 6:30pm and Saturday from 10am to noon and 3 to 5pm. It is closed Saturday from October to December and mid-April to mid-June. In the center of Samedan, the **Samedan Tourist Office** (© **081/851-00-60**) is open Monday to Friday from 8:30am to 6pm and Saturday from 9am to noon and 3 to 5:30pm.

EXPLORING THE AREA
IN SAMEDAN

The village (1,548m/5,077 ft.) has its own ski lift and ice-skating rink, plus a ski school. In the summer it's ideal for mountain walks and for climbing. The tourist office will provide maps. Visitors can fish or play tennis and golf. When there's snow, it's possible to take a horse-drawn sleigh to St. Moritz in less than an hour, and all mountain transportation can be reached in a short time.

IN CELERINA

Celerina has an old Romanesque church, **St. John's (San Gian),** with a painted ceiling dating from 1478.

The Cresta run, a mecca for bobsledders, starts from St. Moritz and terminates near Celerina. The village also has ice rinks for curling and skating, a toboggan run, and a ski school. Winter packages for skiing, cross-country, and curling are offered, as well as summer guided mountain-bike tours with a picnic included.

Several interesting **conducted tours** are offered in the summer through the tourist office. An experienced guide will take you on an explorative tour through the Swiss National Park, or you can join a botanical excursion to see alpine flowers in bloom. Strenuous geological and mineralogical tours are also offered, and you can make an exciting journey from the Diavolezza over the glacier to Morteratsch. The latter tour is offered only in the spring and summer.

Celerina (about 1,702m/5,583 ft.) is known for its belvederes and panoramic views. One such view is of **Piz Nair,** at 3,251m (10,663 ft.). To reach it, you can take a cable car from St. Moritz, departing every 20 minutes daily from 8:30am to 5pm. You'll ride from St. Moritz to Corviglia. At Corviglia you board another cable car between Corviglia and Piz Nair. The round-trip passage for this ride is 50F ($41) for adults and 30F ($25) for children. The circular panorama takes in the Bernina summits. For information, call ℂ **081/839-80-15.**

You can also visit **Muottas Muragl** (2,412m/7,911 ft.). From the lower station at Punt Muragle, funicular departures are about every 30 minutes. The round-trip fare is 29F ($24) for adults and 15F ($12) for children. You'll have views of the Upper Engadine Gap, and in the distance you can see the peaks of the Bernina massif. You'll probably see ibex and marmots as you take mountain walks. For information, call ℂ **081/842-83-08.**

WHERE TO STAY
IN SAMEDAN

Hotel Bernina   Built in 1865, the Bernina maintains much of its original grandeur. The entire edifice is painted pale pink, with Italianate detailing over the windows. The comfortable midsize bedrooms are furnished in a rustic Engadine style, with patterned carpeting and big windows. On the premises, guests can enjoy a summer terrace and a private park. Nine units contain only a shower; the rest have a tub/shower combination.

CH-7503 Samedan. ℂ **800/780-7234** in the U.S. and Canada or 081/852-12-12. Fax 081/852-36-06. www.hotel-bernina.ch. 57 units. Winter 287F–375F ($235–$308) double; summer 230F–270F ($189–$221) double. Rates include buffet breakfast. Half board (3-day minimum stay) 50F ($41) per person extra. Children 6–12 are charged 50% of the adult rate; children under 6 stay free in parent's room. AE, DC, MC, V. Free parking outdoors, 15F ($12) in garage. Closed May and Nov. **Amenities:** 2 restaurants; bar; tennis court; sauna; tour desk; limited room service; laundry service; nonsmoking rooms; rooms for guests w/limited mobility. *In room:* TV, minibar, hair dryer.

Hotel Quadratscha ⭐   Somewhat more appealing that the Bernina (see above) thanks to a radical reconstruction and renovation, this hotel was established in 1975 on the site of an Engadine-style private home that was built in the 1870s. During the renovation, the lobby was enlarged, the leisure (health and sports) facilities were improved, and the in-house restaurant, U3 (separately recommended below), was rebuilt using antique paneling and architectural accessories. The bedrooms are outfitted in a cozy alpine style, each with comfortable furnishings and a mountain view.

CH-7503 Samedan. ℂ **081/851-15-15.** Fax 081/851-15-16. www.quadratscha.ch. 26 units. Summer 220F–300F ($180–$246) double, 260F–360F ($213–$295) suite; winter 280F–320F ($230–$262) double, 360F–440F ($295–$361) suite. Rates include breakfast. Half board 30F–40F ($25–$33) extra per person, depending on the season. AE, DC, MC, V. Outdoor parking free, indoor parking 18F ($15). Closed mid-Apr to mid-June and mid-Oct to mid-Dec. **Amenities:** Restaurant; bar; indoor pool; sauna; limited room service; massage; laundry service. *In room:* TV, minibar, hair dryer, safe.

IN CELERINA

Cresta Palace Hotel ⭐⭐   Set within a 5-minute walk from the railway station and the center of Celerina, within a stately looking white-stucco building with green shutters and a pedigree dating to around 1910, this is the most extravagant, most opulent, and most prestigious hotel in town. It's also the highest-rated, granted four stars by the local tourist authorities. Each of the bedrooms was radically upgraded and renovated with contemporary styling and lots of varnished hardwood, plus they offer sweeping views over the mountains nearby. Most contain bright colors, rustic pine-wood furnishings, tiled, good-size bathrooms, and a sense of well-ordered coziness. Many clients here are frequent repeaters, known to the staff and to each other.

Hauptstrasse, CH-7505 Celerina. ℂ **081/836-56-56.** Fax 081/836-56-57. www.crestapalace.ch. 98 units. Winter 320F–510F ($262–$418) double; summer 220F–400F ($180–$328) double. Rates include breakfast. Half board 50F

($41) extra per person. AE, DC, MC, V. Parking 15F ($12) in winter, 10F ($8.20) in summer. Closed Easter to mid-June and Oct 19–Dec 6. **Amenities:** 2 restaurants; bar; indoor pool; 2 tennis courts; gym; sauna; steam room; limited room service; massage; laundry service. *In room:* TV, dataport, minibar, hair dryer, safe.

Hotel Misani *(Value)* This is a cost-conscious and solid hotel that's set behind an ocher-colored facade on the near perimeter of Celerina, a 4-minute walk from the center. Rated three-and-a-half stars by the local government, it was built before 1900 but was radically renovated and frequently renewed since. Originally established 120 years ago, it was enlarged with an annex in the 1970s, then rebuilt to include the annex behind a single, carefully orchestrated facade that incorporated its various elements and outbuildings into a coherent, ocher-fronted whole. Bedrooms are warm, cozy, and contemporary-looking, most with tub/shower combinations. The hotel's restaurant, the Ustaria, is well recommended and well run.

Hauptstrasse, CH-7505 Celerina. *(C)* **081/833-33-14.** Fax 081/833-09-37. www.hotelmisani.ch. 38 units. Summer 150F–290F ($123–$238) double; winter 150F–335F ($123–$275) double; from 460F ($377) suite year-round. Rates include breakfast. AE, DC, MC, V. Parking 8F–10F ($6.55–$8.20) outdoors, 10F–20F ($8.20–$16) indoors. Closed Apr and mid-Oct to late Nov. **Amenities:** 2 restaurants; limited room service; babysitting; laundry service. *In room:* TV in some, phone in most.

WHERE TO DINE

U3 *(G)* ITALIAN This restaurant's paneling and elaborate architectural detailing are remnants of a villa that originally stood on this site in the 1870s. Today a polite staff serves a wide array of well-prepared Italian dishes, most cooked in health-conscious ways with olive oil and an emphasis on fresh vegetables and Mediterranean flavors. You may opt for any of several fresh-made pastas, salads, a "turban" of sole with shrimp, a platter containing three different filet mignons, several kinds of grilled fish and meat, and—in season—venison or quail with truffles. Cuisine is well conceived, flavorful, and well suited to the bracing climate.

In the Hotel Quadratscha, Samedan. *(C)* **081/851-15-15.** Reservations recommended. Main courses 28F–50F ($23–$41). AE, DC, MC, V. Daily 7–10pm. Closed mid-Apr to mid-June and mid-Oct to mid-Dec.

3 St. Moritz *(★★★)*

80km (50 miles) S of Davos; 74km (46 miles) SE of Chur; 202km (126 miles) SE of Zurich

St. Moritz is the *ne plus ultra* of winter glamour—a haven for German and Italian aristocracy and the jet-setters who come in February and March. Long a favorite of movie stars, it also attracts internationally prominent people in politics, the world of finance, and the arts. St. Moritz may well be the most fashionable resort in the world.

Not all its visitors, however, are prestigious. The author Peter Viertel wrote that St. Moritz attracts "the hangers-on of the rich . . . the jewel thieves, the professional backgammon players and general layabouts, as well as the high-class ladies of doubtful virtue (if such a thing still exists)."

On the southern side of the Alps in the Upper Engadine, at an altitude of 1,800m (5,904 ft.), St. Moritz (San Murezza in Romansh) was originally known for its mineral springs, which were discovered, probably by the Celts, some 3,000 years ago. From Roman times through the Middle Ages, visitors came here in the summer to experience the curative powers of the spring waters. The hamlet first appears in written history in an official document referring to the sale of the Upper Engadine by a count to the bishop of Chur in 1138. It was first referred to as a spring by the Swiss-born alchemist and physician known as Paracelsus.

Use of the spring waters was a summer pursuit. It was not until 1834 that the first winter guest stayed in the area. The earliest skiers appeared on the Upper Engadine scene in 1859 (the natives thought they were nutty), and in 1864 a pension owner, Johannes Badrutt, brought a group of English people to St. Moritz to spend the winter, starting what has grown into a flood of tourism.

ESSENTIALS

GETTING THERE   St. Moritz is linked by rail (through a complicated series of tunnels) to the rest of Switzerland via Chur, with other links to such non-Swiss population centers as Milan and Munich. Travel time by train from Chur is 2 hours. St. Moritz is also the end point of the world-famous *Glacier Express,* which links Zermatt, in the southwest, with St. Moritz, in the southeast. For **rail information** and schedules, call ✆ **0900/300-300.**

The *Glacier Express*

The most famous of Switzerland's railway lines, the *Glacier Express* 🏵🏵🏵 connects the highest peaks and glaciers of the southeastern Alps with those of the southwestern Alps. When the train link opened in 1928, the danger of winter blizzards and snowdrifts required that many of the most isolated mountain bridges be dismantled every October and then reassembled the following May. As a result, in the winter trains were rerouted on a lengthy detour through Zurich and northern Switzerland. In 1982 a 13km (8-mile) tunnel was drilled beneath the Furka mountain, and today trains run uninterrupted across the mountains all year long. The route is one of the most spectacular in the world, with 91 viaducts and tunnels and 291 bridges along the way. There's one daily train that runs between the regions in the winter; in summer, with its longer hours of sunlight, there are two and, in rare cases, three trains per day.

The one-way trip from Zermatt to St. Moritz takes 7½ hours and costs 215F ($176) in first class and 129F ($106) in second class. En route, many travelers opt to disembark in the medieval trading city of Chur to spend the night. From Chur, convenient connections can be arranged to Davos and all points east, including many towns in the alpine regions of Austria.

Advance seat reservations are required for the comfortably upholstered coaches with restaurant cars. Note that the Swiss Pass covers the full fare on the *Glacier Express,* but because part of the route is administered by a different organization from the rest of the Swiss Rail network, holders of any travel pass in the Eurailpass family, including Youthpass and Flexipasses, are charged about half the total fare. For more information about fares, call ✆ **877/257-2887.**

For more general information about the journey, contact any Switzerland Tourism, or the **Swiss Center,** 608 Fifth Ave., Suite 202, New York, NY 10020 (✆ **212/757-5944**).

St. Moritz is linked by bus to Chur, Lugano, and Pontresina, each of which is easily reachable via bus connections from Munich. Call the tourist office (see below) for further information.

By car from Zurich, take N3 (later N13) to Chur and, once there, head southwest along Route 3.

VISITOR INFORMATION The St. Moritz tourist office, **Kur- und Verkehrsverein,** via Maistra 12 (© **081/837-33-33;** www.stmoritz.ch), will answer many of the questions a visitor might have. It's open in midsummer and midwinter, Monday to Friday from 9am to 6:30pm, Saturday 9am to 6pm, and Sunday from 4 to 6pm; off season, Monday to Friday from 9am to noon and 2 to 6pm, and Saturday from 9am to noon.

SEEING THE SIGHTS

Engadine Museum ⚘ This museum offers a glimpse of the history of St. Moritz and the Engadine. You'll learn about the sgraffito on Engadine buildings and local styles of architecture, and see a collection of Engadine antiques and regional furniture. The elegantly decorated state room shows how nobility in the area lived. Artifacts from the Bronze Age, when Druids lived in the land, are also on display, including the 3,000-year-old encasement of the spring of Mauritius. St. Moritz stands on a former "mystic place" of the Druids.

Via dal Bagn 39. © **081/833-43-33.** Admission 5F ($4.10) adults, 2.50F ($2.05) children. June–Oct Mon–Fri 9:30am–noon and 2–5pm, Sun 10am–noon; Dec–Apr Sun–Fri 10am–noon, Mon–Fri 2–5pm. Closed May and Nov. Bus: 1.

Segantini Museum Housed here are works by the artist Giovanni Segantini (1858–99), who lived in the Engadine (Maloja) during the last years of his life. The artist is known for his technique termed divisionism; his most important work is a triptych called *Birth, Life, Death,* which is exhibited at the museum, among other important pictures.

Via Somplaz 30. © **081/833-44-54.** Admission 7F ($5.75) adults, 5F ($4.10) students, 3F ($2.45) children 6–16. Tues–Sun 10am–noon and 3–6pm. Closed mid-Oct to Nov and May. Bus: 1.

THE ACTIVE VACATION PLANNER

The tourist office has complete details about the various activities in the area. Although skiing is the premier sport, other winter-sports activities, including curling, ice-skating, tobogganing, bobsledding, and an early form of ice hockey, were enjoyed by most winter visitors in the last part of the 19th century.

SKIING

The world's oldest ski school is at Moritz-Dorf, founded in 1927. A total of five ski complexes encircle St. Moritz, the nearest being Corviglia-Piz Nair, which has some challenging, 1.6km (1-mile) runs back to the base. There's an abundance of snow in winter on 402km (250 miles) of downhill ski runs, 161km (100 miles) of cross-country ski trails, and the Olympic ski-jumping hill.

Corvatsch, at 1,740m (5,707 ft.), is known for its bowl skiing. **Corviglia** has broad runs attracting fledgling and intermediate skiers and is the base for skiing **Piz Nair** ⚘⚘, the highest skiable mountain at 3,251m (10,663 ft.), with a vertical drop of 1,424m (4,671 ft.). Nearby, in Pontresina, a neighbor resort (see the next section), are the steep **Piz Legalb** and **Diavolezza,** with skiing for all levels of experience, including a run over the Morteratsch Glacier. All five mountains can be skied on one lift pass.

The upper Engadine region, of which St. Moritz plays the pivotal role, has 54 mechanical ski lifts, 349km (217 miles) of marked ski slopes, seven ski schools, and an estimated 700 ski instructors who come and go seminomadically from season to season. A general ski pass valid for 1 day costs 57F to 70F ($47–$57) for adults, 38F to 47F ($31–$39) for children 13 to 27, and 19F to 24F ($16–$20) for children 12 and under. Various other ski passes are also sold, including a popular 6-day pass, which costs 265F to 339F ($217–$278) for adults, 178F to 227F ($146–$186) for those ages 13 to 27, and 90F to 115F ($74–$94) for children 12 and under. These rates include unlimited use of all ski lifts and slopes in the Engadine region. Telephone **Engadine Information Center** at © **0900/558-040** for more information about cable cars and ski lifts in the Engadine region.

The groomed and tracked cross-country runs in the Upper Engadine valley include a tame 1.6km (1-mile) loop near the cross-country center; trails are laid out between the valley resorts. A 1.6km (1-mile) segment is lit for night skiing. The Engadine cross-country ski marathon—a 42km (26-mile) run conducted in mid-March every year, is a major event. Instruction in cross-country skiing, available in groups on Monday, Wednesday, and Friday from 11am to 1pm, costs 40F ($33) for one half-day lesson, and 100F ($82) for three half-day lessons. A full day's cross-country excursion, as part of a large group, costs 45F ($29). For more information, contact the **Schweizer Langlaufschule St. Moritz** (© **081/833-62-33**).

HORSEBACK RIDING

Although this is the only riding stable in St. Moritz, **Reithalle,** via Ludains 3 (© **081/833-57-33**), has earned the respect of competitors throughout eastern Switzerland. Set within a 10-minute walk from the center of St. Moritz, it maintains about a half-dozen sturdy horses that are well used to life in the harsh alpine climate. An hour's ride, either in the rink (for beginners) or in the surrounding forests and meadows (for intermediate and advanced riders) costs 60F ($49). Longer promenades tend to be discouraged. Don't overlook horseback riding as a midwinter diversion, as the horses need to be exercised throughout the calendar year. You're likely to cross untrammeled snowfields of pristine beauty, and even take leisurely treks across the surface of a frozen lake. Dress accordingly—the windchill factor for midwinter outings is fierce.

OTHER WINTER SPORTS

Horse racing on the frozen lake of St. Moritz is popular, or you can take rides on the natural-ice bobsled run. There are 30 curling rinks, winter golf played on the frozen lake, and tobogganing on the Cresta run. You can also play tennis and squash indoors.

If you're interested in **curling** but don't know how to do it, you can have a first training session free (40 min.). Individual **curling lessons** thereafter cost 45F ($37) for 45 minutes. Call © **081/833-45-88** for details. The curling rink is the A1 Parc rink on via Maistra.

A bobsled ride costs 210F ($172), but you get your picture taken, a drink, and a certificate in addition to the ride. Bobsled rides occur at the town's **Olympic Bobsled Run** on via Maistra (© **081/830-02-00**). Advance reservations are required.

SUMMER SPORTS

Windsurfing at St. Moritz and on the lakes of nearby resorts, especially Silvaplana, has boomed in popularity. If you're already experienced, rental of equipment for 2 hours costs 40F ($33). If you're a beginner, or if you just want to brush up on your technique, private lessons are available, costing 270F ($221) for 10 lessons. Call **Water Sports Center** in Silvaplana (© **081/828-92-29**) for information. Sailing on the area's 25 lakes is also possible.

The closest golf course lies in Samedan, 7km (4½ miles) down the valley. This is a 5,994m (6,587-yard) par-72 course. Greens fees for a full day are 90F ($74) and club rental is 35F ($29) a day. Golfing is available from the end of May to the beginning of October daily from 7am until 7pm, depending on the weather. In July and August the course often stays open later. Call **Samedan/St. Moritz Golfplatz** (© 081/851-04-66) for more information. There's also a 9-hole course that's part of the Kulm Hotel (© **081/336-82-36**).

For tennis and squash information, consult the **Corviglia Tennis Center** in St. Moritz-Bad (© **081/833-15-00**). Rates for tennis are 28F ($23) per hour outdoors and 32F ($26) per hour indoors during the summer, or 32F to 54F ($26–$44) per hour for winter indoor tennis. Rental of one racquet and balls is 3F ($2.45), and two racquets and balls rent for 5.50F ($4.50). Squash courts run 20F ($16) for 45 minutes in summer and 20F to 30F ($16–$25) for the same period of time in winter. The center is open daily from 9am to 8pm or 11pm depending on the season.

Fishing, in season between May 15 and September 15, requires the purchase of a fishing license, available only to interested parties age 16 or older. A passport and another form of picture identification are required to get a fishing license, which costs 50F ($41) for 1 day or 100F ($82) for 1 week. Equipment and bait are also available. For more information about **fishing** in the area, call © **081/833-67-52.**

SPAS

The spa section of this resort town is called **St. Moritz-Bad,** where you can take mud and carbon-dioxide mineral-water baths, physical therapy, and physiotherapy while you enjoy the stimulating alpine climate in a modern **Health Spa Center (Heilbad Centrun)** Plazza Paracelcus (© **081/833-30-62**), next to the Kempinski Grand Hotel. The spa opened in 1976. From Roman times to now, "taking the waters" has been a popular pursuit for those seeking natural curative treatment for relief from pain and stress. The charge for every treatment at the spa is lower for residents of any of the town's hotels or apartments. Treatments cost 90F ($74) for a 50-minute massage and 40F ($33) for an hour-long soak within a mineral-rich "carbonic bath."

SHOPPING

Most of St. Moritz's shops line either side of the steeply inclined **via Maistra,** and most of the horrendously upscale ones vie with one another for proximity to the town's most spectacularly expensive hotel, **Badrutt's Palace** (© **081/837-10-00**), near the corner of via Serlas. On its premises you'll find boutiques for Gianni Versace, Prada, Jil Sander, Bulgari, and Louis Vuitton, as well as enough upscale shops for watches and jewelry to outfit a prosperous royal court. But if it's well-designed sports equipment you're looking for, or relatively durable clothing that will shelter you from the fierce Engadine weather, head for any of the following shops: **Boom Sports,** via Tegiatscha 5 (© **081/832-22-22**); **Corviglia Sports,** via Maistra 21 (© **081/833-44-77**); and **Ender Sport,** via Maistra 26 (© **081/833-35-36**).

The region produces lots of folkloric crafts that may commemorate your stay in the Engadine. The town's main outlet for all sorts of woodcarvings, including depictions of gnarled native Engadiners in Swiss costumes and some handcrafted furniture, is **Ettlin,** via Rosatsch 7 (© **081/832-17-07**). More broad-based in its folkloric inventories, with ceramics, glassware, textiles, and wrought iron, is the souvenir-and-artifacts shop **Grischuna,** via dal Bagn 54 (© **081/833-42-36**).

The town's largest jeweler, and the one that saturates the high-season market with more advertising campaigns than any other in town, is **Bucherer,** via Maistra 17 (© **081/833-31-03**). Finally, the town's largest emporium for chocolates is **Merkur,** via Serlas 26 (© **081/833-57-26**).

WHERE TO STAY

St. Moritz offers several different types of accommodations, with dozens of hotels, boardinghouses, and chalet-style apartments. But because it's expensive, you may prefer one of several neighboring resorts, such as Pontresina, Silvaplana, S-Chanf, Zuoz, Samedan, or Celerina, all of which are covered in this chapter. The following hotels are in the heart of St. Moritz.

VERY EXPENSIVE

Badrutt's Palace Hotel ✸✸✸   This architectural hodgepodge of mock Gothic has been at the center of St. Moritz society for decades. Society isn't what it was, but today's glitzy and the ritzy still fill its vast precincts—that is, if they can afford the lethal tariffs. However, for those on the winter see-and-be-seen circuit, this flamboyant edifice remains an enduring symbol of wealth, prestige, and conspicuous consumption. Set in the center of town behind a chiseled stone facade and a series of mock-fortified towers, the Palace was built at the turn of the 20th century by Caspar Badrutt. Over the years the chic and famous have come through the doors of the Palace, including the shah of Iran, Greta Garbo, and Aristotle Onassis. Almost no "name" arriving today can match the roster of yesteryear. The hotel's Great Hall soars in Gothic dimensions above twin black-marble fireplaces, clusters of antique furniture, and massive bouquets of flowers. Except for some special suites and spacious doubles, most of the rooms are fairly standardized and "international" in styling. You're paying more for the address than the room if you lodge here.

Via Serlas 27, CH-7500 St. Moritz. © **800/223-6800** in the U.S. and Canada or 081/837-10-00. Fax 081/837-29-99. www.badruttspalace.com. 165 units. Winter 400F–3,100F ($328–$2,542) double, 1,950F–12,000F ($1,599–$9,840) suite; summer 345F–1,150F ($283–$943) double, 1,320F–2,055F ($1,082–$1,685) suite. Rates include breakfast. Half board 100F ($82) extra per person. AE, DC, MC, V. Parking 25F ($21). Closed early Apr to late June and mid-Sept to early Dec. Bus: 1. **Amenities:** 7 restaurants; 4 bars; indoor pool; 4 tennis courts; gym; sauna; 24-hr. room service; babysitting; laundry service/dry cleaning; nonsmoking rooms. *In room:* TV, dataport, minibar, hair dryer, iron, safe.

Carlton Hotel ✸   Owned by the Grand Hotel Tschuggen of Arosa, this is an elaborate, ocher-colored château that was originally built for Nicholas II, the last tsar of Russia, in 1913. With a view of the lake and the mountains, it's one of the loveliest hotels in St. Moritz—luxurious, but without the glitzy consumption of Badrutt's Palace overall. One particularly spectacular sitting room has tall, narrow columns with neoclassical designs and a pair of matching fireplaces. The bedrooms are well furnished and spacious with white marble bathrooms.

Via Badrutt 11, Dorf, CH-7500 St. Moritz. © **081/836-70-00.** Fax 081/836-70-01. www.carlton-stmoritz.ch. 105 units. Winter 590F–1,070F ($484–$877) double, 900F–2,900F ($738–$2,378) suite for 2; summer 420F–520F ($344–$426) double, 600F–1,000F ($492–$820) suite for 2. Rates include half board. AE, DC, MC, V. Parking 30F ($25) in winter, 15F ($12) in summer. Closed Apr 10–June 15 and Sept 28–Dec 10. Bus: 1. **Amenities:** 2 restaurants; bar; indoor pool; health club; sauna; salon; limited room service; massage; babysitting; laundry/dry cleaning. *In room:* TV, dataport, minibar, hair dryer, safe.

Hotel Waldhaus am See ✸✸ *Finds*   Built in 1880 as a tavern, this building was later expanded into a private home by a Swiss industrialist and now resembles a castle. Today it's one of the few buildings in St. Moritz to remain open all year. You can dine in one of three lovely rooms, the largest of which has access to a sheltered sun terrace and views over the lake. Helen and Claudio Bernasconi-Mettier, the hosts, offer comfortably conservative midsize rooms with firm beds and good plumbing. All units contain a private bathroom, mostly with shower only, although some come with combination tub/shower. The most desirable accommodations have views of the lake.

Via Dimlej 6, CH-7500 St. Moritz. (℡ 081/836-60-00. Fax 081/836-60-60. www.waldhaus-am-see.ch. 54 units. Winter 1,230F–1,490F ($1,009–$1,222) double; summer 940F–1,140F ($771–$935) double. Rates include half board. AE, DC, MC, V. Free parking outside, 18F ($15) in garage. **Amenities:** 3 restaurants; bar; sauna; steam bath; massage; laundry/dry cleaning. *In room:* TV, dataport, minibar, hair dryer, safe.

Kempinski Grand Hotel des Bains ♦♦♦ *Kids*

This hotel originated in 1896 as the Grand Hotel des Bains. Sometime in the 1950s, it was reorganized as the Kurthaus Park Hotel, but since December 2002, after being ripped apart and rebuilt by Kempinski, it's the Kempinski Grand Hotel des Bains. Set at the eastern entrance to St. Moritz, adjacent to the ski slopes and ski lifts, it has welcomed the Sultan of Brunei. The decor is very grand hotel with lots of mahogany, brown marble from Sardinia, and local granite from the Engadine. This was the first of only two Kempinskis in Switzerland (the other, newer one, is near Montreux). In contrast to the Kulm Hotel and the Suvretta House (both of which have a distinct and aged clientele, and a passion about formality), it caters to a young-ish, hip, and urban clientele ages 30 to 50. The deluxe citadel offers sumptuous accommodations and living on a very grand scale. It has a casino, two state-of-the-art restaurants, and the best health, fitness, and beauty facilities in the area. Bedrooms are spacious and stylish, each thoughtfully designed and laid out for ultimate comfort, and each coming with a deluxe bathroom with heated floors in winter. The most luxurious living of all are the glamorous spa suites or the tower suites. The cuisine is one of the reasons to book here, with seasonally adjusted menus. Of course, not only can you get top-notch Swiss and international cuisine, but also superb Italian viands, many of the recipes "a secret" of cooks long ago.

CH-7500 St. Moritz. (℡ **081/838-38-38.** Fax 081/838-30-00. www.kempinski-stmoritz.com. 184 units. Winter 560F–1,000F ($459–$820) double, 850F–3,600F ($697–$2,952) suite; summer 415F–565F ($340–$463) double, 790F–2,500F ($648–$2,050) suite. Rates include breakfast. Half board 35F ($29) extra per day. Parking free outdoors, 25F ($21) indoors. AE, DC, MC, V. Closed mid-Apr to mid-June and late Sept to mid-Dec. **Amenities:** 3 restaurants; 3 bars; indoor swimming pool; health club/exercise room; spa w/sauna and steam room; children's play area; 24-hr. room service; babysitting; laundry service/dry cleaning; nonsmoking rooms; casino. *In room:* TV, dataport, minibar, hair dryer, safe.

Kulm Hotel ♦♦♦

We prefer this tranquil bastion of luxury even to the Palace itself. These three elegant buildings, the oldest of which was erected in 1760, were taken over in 1856 by Johannes Badrutt, who was the first to encourage British vacationers to come to the Alps and who went on to establish Badrutt's Palace. In 1878 it became the first building in Switzerland to have electricity, and it was the center of the Olympic Games in 1928 and 1948. Over the years the Kulm has hosted royalty from all over the world, including the kings and queens of industry and entertainment. It still draws a sedate clientele, those who deliberately shun the more ostentatious Badrutt's Palace. The public rooms are beautifully paneled, with vaulted ceilings. The spacious bedrooms are grand classics, with traditional furnishings, generous closet space, and luxury beds; tiled bathrooms have dual marble basins, heated towel racks, and robes. A large part of the city's world-famous bobsled run, the Crest run, and the curling rinks of St. Moritz are on hotel property.

Via Veglia 18, Dorf, CH-7500 St. Moritz. (℡ **800/223-1230** in the U.S. and Canada or 081/836-80-00. Fax 081/836-80-01. www.kulmhotel-stmoritz.ch. 180 units. Winter 610F–990F ($500–$812) double, 1,140F–1,690F

($935–$1,386) suite; summer 265F–395F ($217–$324) double, 750F–990F ($615–$812) suite. Rates include half board. AE, DC, MC, V. Parking 15F ($12) in garage in summer, 25F ($21) in winter. Closed mid-Apr to June and mid-Sept to early Dec. Bus: 1. **Amenities:** 3 restaurants; 2 bars; indoor pool; 9-hole golf course; tennis court; gym; spa center w/sauna; children's playroom; salon; limited room service; massage; laundry; curling rink; ice-skating rink. *In room:* TV, dataport, minibar, hair dryer, safe.

Suvretta House ★★ *Kids*   Set about 1.5km (1 mile) from the resort town, this five-star government-rated hotel is a citadel of subdued elegance and conservative charm. It attracts an established clientele with its grand decor and understated elegance and is slightly more luxurious than Badrutt's Palace, though it doesn't quite reach the lofty peaks of Kulm. The place is so formal that it's off-putting to some visitors. It was built in 1912 on a plateau surrounded by mountains and lakes. Its Edwardian facade has two neomedieval towers and a baroque central gable that has become the hotel's trademark. Except for areas of richly grained oak paneling and Engadine sgraffito, the interior is covered with plaster and pierced with an endless series of vaulted arches. The spacious guest rooms in traditional or alpine style are luxurious without being glitzy. The roomy bathrooms are tiled. It's surrounded with more land than any other hotel in St. Moritz and offers a private ski lift about 90m (295 ft.) from the hotel.

Via Chasellas 1, CH-7500 St. Moritz. ✆ **081/836-36-36.** Fax 081/836-37-37. www.suvrettahouse.ch. 210 units. Winter 640F–1,580F ($525–$1,296) double; summer 480F–1,200F ($394–$984) double. Rates include half board. AE, DC, MC, V. Parking 20F ($16) in winter, 15F ($12) in summer. Closed Apr 12–June 26 and Sept 7–Dec 13. **Amenities:** 2 restaurants; 2 bars; indoor pool; driving range; 3 tennis courts; gym; sauna; children's playground; game room; salon; 24-hr. room service; massage; babysitting; laundry service; curling rinks; ice-skating rink. *In room:* TV, dataport, hair dryer, iron, safe, robe.

EXPENSIVE

Best Western Hotel Albana ★   A hotel was first established here in 1644; the current property has been managed by the Weinmann family since 1971. This is a popular hotel, loaded with folkloric accessories and painted a salmon color with white trim and decorated with regional designs and an occasional hunting trophy. The midsize to spacious bedrooms usually have ceiling beams or elaborate paneling and occasionally a regional armoire. They also contain elegant bathrooms with tub and shower (20 with shower only). There are more hunting trophies in this hotel, scattered through the upstairs hallway and even within the rooms specially designated as a "museum of the hunt," than within any other hotel in the region. Overall, it makes for an interesting display of regional charm and folksiness.

Via Maistra 6, CH-7500 St. Moritz. ✆ **800/780-7234** in the U.S. and Canada or 081/836-61-61. Fax 081/836-61-62. www.albana.ch. 72 units. Winter 340F–590F ($279–$484) double; summer 280F–540F ($230–$443) double. Rates include breakfast. Half board 35F ($29) per person extra. AE, DC, MC, V. Parking 15F ($12) in garage in winter, 10F ($8.20) in summer. Bus: 1. **Amenities:** Restaurant; bar; gym; Jacuzzi; sauna; limited room service; massage; babysitting; laundry; solarium. *In room:* TV, minibar, hair dryer, safe.

Hotel Crystal ★   A short walk from the Corviglia cogwheel train, this large white-painted building looks oddly futuristic compared to the 19th-century structures around it. The interior combines comfortable alpine rusticity of knotty-pine Engadine-style cabinets and ceiling beams with wall-to-wall carpeting and informal furniture. All the midsize bedrooms are accented with either Swiss pine or walnut paneling. A cavernous 350 sq. m (3,767-sq.-ft.) fitness center was added in the basement of the hotel. The lobby and some of the rooms have also been enlarged, although the rustic alpine decor is still intact.

Via Traunter Plazzas 1, CH-7500 St. Moritz. ⓒ **888/989-1768** in the U.S. or 081/836-26-26. Fax 081/836-26-27. www.crystalhotel.ch. 73 units. Winter 360F–560F ($295–$459) double, 570F–1,570F ($467–$1,287) junior suite; summer 270F–350F ($221–$287) double, 430F–630F ($353–$517) junior suite. Rates include breakfast. Half board 40F ($33) extra per person per day. Parking 20F ($16). AE, DC, MC, V. Closed Apr–May and Oct 10–Nov. Bus: 1. **Amenities:** Restaurant; bar; health club; sauna; Turkish baths; limited room service; massage; babysitting; laundry service. *In room:* TV, dataport, minibar, hair dryer, safe.

Hotel Schweizerhof 🟉🟉

This government-rated four-star establishment is still owned by the von Gugelberg-Hoehemer family, and has been since it was built in 1896. In 1906 the German Kaiser Wilhelm II celebrated his 48th birthday party inside this hotel in a lavish ceremony draped with flowers. Staid and traditional, it's well maintained and continues in its upscale tradition. It's a favorite of many clients who prefer its somewhat-dated Victorian overlay to the more obvious five-star hotels in town. It's also one of the few hotels of its size and stature remaining open year-round. The best units are on the fifth floor, which dates from the 1970s. This is where all the suites and the best doubles have views to the south. The least expensive accommodations are those facing north, which also lack tubs. What makes this hotel exceptional is its personal service, along with its array of drinking and dining choices.

Via dal Bagn 54, Dorf, CH-7500 St. Moritz. ⓒ **081/837-07-07.** Fax 081/837-07-00. www.schweizerhofstmoritz.ch. 84 units. Winter 320F–700F ($262–$574) double, 500F–830F ($410–$681) suite; summer 260F–450F ($213–$369) double, 450F–490F ($369–$402) suite. Rates include breakfast. Half board 40F ($33) in summer, per person per day. AE, DC, MC, V. Free parking outdoors, 21F ($17) in garage. Bus: 1. **Amenities:** 2 restaurants; 4 bars; steam bath; sauna; limited room service; massage; laundry service. *In room:* TV, dataport, minibar, hair dryer, safe.

Monopol 🟉🟉

Set above a busy street, this 3-decades-old stucco building offers elegant public rooms furnished with French pieces, oil paintings, and well-polished wood detailing. Half of the usually spacious bedrooms are designed around Louis XV and Louis XVI or rustic furniture, while the other half have been renovated in a modern Swiss style, with lots of wood and updated bathroom fixtures.

Via Maistra 17, Dorf, CH-7500 St. Moritz. ⓒ **081/837-04-04.** Fax 081/837-04-05. www.monopol.ch. 66 units. Winter 340F–560F ($279–$459) double, 480F–790F ($394–$648) suite; summer 270F–370F ($221–$303) double, 380F–470F ($312–$385) suite. Rates include breakfast. Half board 40F ($26) per person per day. AE, DC, MC, V. Closed mid-Apr to mid-May and mid-Oct to Dec 10. Bus: 1. **Amenities:** Restaurant; 2 bars; pool; fitness center and spa; sauna; limited room service; massage; babysitting; laundry service. *In room:* TV, dataport, minibar, hair dryer, safe.

MODERATE

Hotel Eden 🟉

A pleasant hotel whose architecture evokes a Tuscan villa, this establishment was built more than a century ago and has been in the Degiacomi family for some 40 years. It doesn't cost as much as either of its more glamorous neighbors, the Kulm and Badrutt's Palace. The Eden, which opens onto a tiny but charming plaza in the center of town, is filled with pine-wood paneling and family antiques. Each of the simple and modernized midsize bedrooms has tasteful, conservative furniture, and all units come with a midsize private bathroom (some with complete tubs). The hotel dining room is only open to hotel guests.

Via Veglia 12, Dorf, CH-7500 St. Moritz. ⓒ **081/830-81-00.** Fax 081/830-81-01. www.edenstmoritz.ch. 36 units. Winter 330F–390F ($271–$320) double; summer 220F–270F ($180–$221) double. Rates include buffet breakfast. AE, MC, V. Free parking. Closed mid-Apr to mid-June and mid-Oct to mid-Dec. Bus: 1. **Amenities:** Restaurant; limited room service; massage; babysitting; laundry service. *In room:* TV, dataport, hair dryer, iron, safe.

Hotel Languard 🟉🟉 *Finds*

Built more than a century ago as the private home of the owner of the nearby Kulm Hotel, this much-enlarged and -altered property lies just off the main street of town. It's run by a conservative Swiss staff and the Trivella family, who display their family's ski awards (one of their brothers, Roberto, was a champion in 1978) in a glass case by the reception desk. The hotel's pine-paneled interior is well maintained and very inviting, with a breakfast room that overlooks the valley and the lake. Some of the small to midsize rooms have private balconies, and all have private bathrooms, of which all but five have a combination tub/shower.

Via Veglia 14, CH-7500 St. Moritz. ℂ 081/833-31-37. Fax 081/833-45-46. www.languard-stmoritz.ch. 22 units. Winter 245F–485F ($201–$398) double; summer 220F–330F ($180–$271) double. Rates include buffet breakfast. AE, DC, MC, V. Free parking. Closed May and Nov. Bus: 1. **Amenities:** Massage; laundry service. *In room:* TV, dataport, hair dryer, safe.

Hotel National ⚐ Few other hotels in St. Moritz recall conservative mountain-style Switzerland as evocatively, or as rigidly, as this one. Built a century ago, it's also one of the cheapest and least luxurious in town. Other than an occasional refurbishment, very little changes around here. The outside has neoclassical details and wrought-iron balconies, while the interior has a scattering of Oriental rugs, informal furniture, and comfortable but small bedrooms. The family-run hotel is opposite a large indoor swimming pool. Its restaurant serves Swiss and French dishes along with various specialties from the different sections of Italy.

Via de l'Ova Cotschna 1, CH-7500 St. Moritz. ℂ 081/833-32-74. Fax 081/833-32-75. 28 units. Winter 230F–290F ($189–$238) double; summer 190F ($156) double. Rates include breakfast. Half board 30F ($25). AE, MC, V. Closed Apr 15–May and Oct 15–Dec 15. Bus: 1. **Amenities:** Restaurant; pool (nearby). *In room:* No phone.

WHERE TO DINE

Although meals may be included in the cost of your hotel room, you may want to sample the selections at other hotels and restaurants. There are also dozens of fashionable *konditoreien* (coffeehouses).

VERY EXPENSIVE

Chadafo Grill, in the Chesa Veglia ⚐⚐ FRENCH This is one of the most upscale restaurants in a resort that's loaded with almost-comparable equivalents. Owned and operated by the also-recommended Badrutt's Palace Hotel, whose mock-fortified bulk rises a short walk away, it's housed within one of the most historic buildings in St. Moritz, the Engadine-style *Chesa Veglia,* Originally built in 1658 of stone, stucco, and now deeply weathered wood, this antique *chesa* (house) retains much of its original paneling and carving, and a monumental arched entranceway that's often depicted as part of the press and PR for St. Moritz itself. Within its sprawling interior is a labyrinth of rooms (and three separate restaurants) whose decor is entirely composed of architectural remnants from older, since-demolished, houses.

Despite competition from two in-house establishments (see below), the culinary and atmospheric star of this place is the **Chadafo Grill,** where impeccable service blends with an antique decor of high-alpine charm and top-notch cuisine. Expect a whiff of the glamour of faraway Paris coupled with alpine *Gemütlichkeit,* and odors wafting in from the kitchen. Specialities change with the season, but are likely to include chateaubriand, roasted rack of lamb with alpine herbs, shrimp with Pernod sauce, trout meunière, chicken Kiev, terrines of foie gras, and garnishes that include dollops of, among others, caviar.

The same building contains the two other restaurants, including the middle-bracket **Patrizier-Stube,** a casual dining spot serving Swiss and French food daily from 11am to 11pm. Main courses cost from 42F to 65F ($34–$53) each. Less appealing is a simple pizzeria, **The Hayloft,** which serves pizzas, pastas, and grills, but only at dinnertime, winter and summer alike, every day from 6:30 to 11pm. Main courses in The Hayloft cost from 26F to 40F ($21–$33). Overall, we emphasize that the star of the entire complex is the Chadafo Grill.

In the Chesa Veglia, via Veglia 2, Dorf. ℂ 081/837-28-00. Reservations required. Main courses 40F–65F ($33–$53). AE, DC, MC, V. Daily 11:30am–3pm and 6:30pm–midnight. Closed Mid-Apr to late June and early Sept to Dec 1.

Jöhri's Talvo ✿✿✿ ENGADINE/FRENCH   Established in 1992 inside the solid pine-sheathed walls of a 350-year-old Engadine house, this restaurant is St. Moritz's most upscale dining option. It lies in the center of the satellite village of Champfèr, a 10-minute walk from the western periphery of St. Moritz. The much-praised cuisine manages to blend both regional recipes (as filtered by the owner's French training) with the skillful preparation of upscale ingredients. For example, the menu lists different preparations of North Atlantic lobsters and scallops in wine sauce. Our personal favorite is a whole turbot cooked in a salt crust, which is broken open at table side, then served with an array of garnishes and dressings.

Better suited to the cold, high-altitude climate, however, are a range of regional dishes derived from time-honored Engadine traditions. These include *capuns* (spinach-flavored pasta cooked with cold-weather greens in consommé and served with truffles); *puschlav* ("poor man's soup," prepared with consommé and enriched with flour); and lamb raised in nearby meadows prepared with mustard sauce, mountain herbs, and sautéed potatoes. The restaurant's owners, Roland and Brigitte Jöhri, are highly conscientious and devote lots of attention to their unusual cuisine.

Via Gunels 15, Champfèr. ℂ 081/833-44-55. Reservations recommended. Main courses 46F–88F ($38–$72); fixed-price lunch 98F–198F ($80–$162); fixed-price dinner 160F–198F ($131–$162); fixed-price fish menu from 195F ($160). AE, DC, MC, V. Tues–Sun 11am–11pm (closed Tues in summer). Closed Easter to mid-June and Oct 15–Dec 15.

Jorimann's Refugium ✿✿✿ INTERNATIONAL   This is one of the most superb dining choices in the Engadine. Set directly at the edge of St. Moritz's lake, on terrain that slopes gently downhill, this is a posh, stylish, and cozy restaurant that benefits from the management team of Peter Jorimann and his California-educated wife, Jutta Stergner. Within a decor that includes a solid stone floor, wooden paneling, and impeccably laundered napery, you'll enjoy well-prepared cuisine that's artfully served. The chefs offer inventive cooking, beginning perhaps with a terrine of foie gras. One divine platter is pronounced a "variation" of freshwater and saltwater fish. Surely pepper steak never tasted better than it does here, but we were quickly won over by the alpine lamb in a rosemary sauce as well. For something delicate, subtle, and superb, opt for the milk-fed filets of baby veal with an herb-laced risotto.

Via Dim Lej 1. ℂ 081/833-30-00. Reservations required. Fixed-price menus 115F–120F ($94–$98). AE, DC, MC, V. Fri–Tues 11:30am–2pm and 7:30–10:30pm (daily with same hours Dec 20–Jan 7 only).

Nobu JAPANESE   The newest addition to the St. Moritz culinary scene is another outlet of a restaurant that gained fame in Manhattan, where it is still known for incorporating new ingredients into old dishes or retooling traditional recipes. Internationally renowned chef Nobuyuki "Nobu" Matsuhisa has crossed the Atlantic and opened what quickly became the trendiest, and most difficult, reservation in town. In one of chef Matsuhisa's restaurants you never know who could be in the booth next to you. Celebrities such as Gwyneth Paltrow, Gavin Rossdale, Robin Williams, Mark Wahlberg, Nicole Kidman, Barbara Streisand, and Giorgio Armani to name a few have all been spotted chowing down on Nobu's Western-influenced, Japanese culinary creations. However, the Hollywood price tag that comes with the prestige are a direct effect of Matsuhisa flying in many of his ingredients from halfway around the globe.

So what does one of the world's greatest sushi chefs have in store for you? Excellent starters include New Zealand mussels with your choice of Matsuhisa sauces, Toro tartar, tuna takati with Panzu, and squid "pasta" in a garlic sauce. For a main dish we recommend the filet of salmon with teriyaki or Anti-Cucho sauce. Those who can't decide what they want should try the tempura, sashimi, or sushi dinners, which offer a variety of the type of fare they've chosen. Other than the dinners, sushi and tempura are served by the piece, so diners can try each variety on the menu or stick to their favorites. Reservations can be backed up for months at a time in peak season and for weeks in low season, so call far in advance.

In the Badrutt's Palace Hotel. © **081/837-10-00.** Reservations required. Main courses 60F–120F ($49–$98); sushi and tempura 3.60F–12F ($2.95–$9.85) per piece. AE, DC, MC, V. Dec to mid-Apr daily 7:30–11pm. Closed mid-Apr to Nov.

EXPENSIVE

La Marmite ☆☆ SWISS This woodsy lunch establishment is the best high-altitude restaurant in the Grisons. It can be reached only by the Corviglia funicular. The Mathis family offers excellent service and a varied menu. There's also a less expensive cafeteria on the premises that in midwinter is usually crowded with skiers. The region's choicest ingredients turn up in such dishes as creamed venison soup, fresh duck liver with truffles, calves' foot in a truffle sauce, and a bone-warming bouillon—perfect for a cold day—flavored with marrow, vegetables, sherry, and meat.

Corviglia Bergstation. © **081/833-63-55.** Reservations recommended. Main courses 33F–78F ($27–$64). AE, DC, MC, V. Daily 8:30am–6pm. Closed Apr 15–Dec 15.

Landgasthof Meierei ☆☆ SWISS Built a century ago as a relay station for the Swiss postal service, today it houses four dining rooms, which have in days of yore served the shah of Iran, the playboy industrialist Günther Sachs, Picasso, the Aga Khan, and King Farouk of Egypt. Those heady glory days are but a local legend as the place has become solidly bourgeois today. Considering the glamorous clientele that the place has attracted, it serves an earthy and simple menu, ranging from local sausage served with potato salad to veal filets with varied sauces and several fish dishes. Also try the Wiener schnitzel and goulash dishes.

No diner is allowed to drive a car along the difficult-to-navigate service roads that reach the restaurant. You can hire a taxi or a horse-drawn sleigh, the latter costing up to 90F ($74) for four passengers. Our recommendation is that you park your car in the public parking lot near the edge of the lake, just below the Hotel Waldhaus am See, and walk the 20-minute lakeside promenade to the restaurant. The footpath has been carefully paved, and there are only a few slopes to negotiate. Before you set out, it's advisable to phone the restaurant to confirm that it's open.

There are nine cozy alpine rooms rented here costing from 95F to 150F ($78–$123) for a double or from 150F to 190F ($123–$156) for a suite, including breakfast.

Via Dimiej 52. © **081/833-20-60.** Reservations required. Main courses 22F–45F ($18–$37). AE, MC, V. Tues–Sun 10am–2:30pm and 6:30–9:30pm. Closed Apr 15–June 15 and Oct–Dec 15.

Rôtisserie des Chevaliers ☆ FRENCH This exquisitely paneled grillroom, in one of the most historic hotels in St. Moritz, offers a cozy ambience that's especially suited to cold weather. The delectable menu is likely to include terrine and goose liver, grilled sea bass flambé, baby turbot prepared "Marseille style," and a unique stuffed veal à la Hotel Kulm. Dishes are most often based on what's the freshest and best produce available in any given season.

In the Hotel Kulm, via Veglia 18, Dorf. © **081/836-80-00**. Reservations required. Main courses 53F–70F ($43–$57). AE, MC, V. Daily 7pm–midnight. Closed May–Nov. Bus: 1.

MODERATE

Lapin Bleu SWISS/FRENCH/ITALIAN   Half-board guests of the hotel usually dine upstairs in the elegant grillroom, but in many ways we prefer the warm, wood-lined decor and the polite service of the street-level tavern. Specialties from the hearty alpine kitchen include steak tartare with egg; grilled filet steak; chateaubriand with béarnaise sauce, potato croquettes, and vegetables; and fondue bourguignon or *chinoise*. Liver, pork, and several preparations of veal, pasta, and seafood, including lobster, are also served. Many residents of St. Moritz come here to dine, a good sign.

In the Hotel Steffani, Somplatz 1. © **081/836-96-96**. Reservations required in winter. Main courses 24F–55F ($20–$45); fixed-price lunch 38F ($31), fixed-price dinner 55F ($45). AE, DC, MC, V. Daily 11:30am–11:30pm.

Restaurant Acla ✦ *(Finds* SWISS/INTERNATIONAL   Situated in the Hotel Schweizerhof, this "little house on the mountain"—as its name is translated from Romansh—serves Swiss specialties and international dishes in a rustically appealing and rather formal ambience. In summer, during clement lunch hours, the venue moves onto a flowering outdoor terrace called Il Restaurant Giardino. Prices in Il Giardino are slightly lower than those in Acla. Summer specialties include such dishes as filet of perch with tomato crust and olive-oil sauce with grilled zucchini; sautéed guinea fowl breast with summer vegetables and semolina-mushroom slices; and filet of veal with basil-cream sauce, leaf spinach, and fine noodles. In winter main courses include salmon with strips of celery, morels, and truffle sauce, served with early potatoes; cereal risotto with asparagus; grilled zucchini and tomato ragout; or chateaubriand with béarnaise sauce. You can also order classic dishes such as Wiener schnitzel or the famous *Tafelspitz* (the boiled beef of Vienna) served with apple-horseradish and chive sauce, or blinis with caviar and smoked salmon. Trout is from the Inn River.

In the Hotel Schweizerhof, via del Bagn 54, Dorf. © **081/837-07-07**. Reservations recommended. Main courses 35F–40F ($29–$33); fixed-price lunch 22F ($18); fixed-price dinner 60F–65F ($49–$53). AE, DC, MC, V. Daily noon–2pm and 7–9:30pm.

Restaurant Cascade ITALIAN   Next door to the Hotel Steffani, this restaurant offers enticing Italian recipes. With its etched-glass mirrors and bentwood chairs, it's popular with a young, informally dressed crowd for drinks as well as good food. Dishes include carpaccio, gnocchi Piedmont-style, and other dishes, mainly home-made pastas and tender and well-flavored entrecôtes.

Via Somplatz 6, Dorf. © **081/833-02-01**. Reservations required in winter. Main courses 28F–50F ($23–$41). AE, DC, MC, V. June–Nov Wed–Sun 6–11:30pm; Dec–Apr daily 6–11:30pm. Closed May.

Veltliner-Keller SWISS/ITALIAN   It's a cafe and tavern by day, but this venue is at its best for evening dining, when the rustically informal premises welcome many of the town's professional ski-and-see crowd. The menu includes mushroom salads, trout with mushrooms, spaghetti, and a wide selection of meats and fish, along with a savory risotto and many kinds of pasta. Desserts include just about every in-season fruit in Europe. This is a very simple and very ethnic Swiss place, the quintessential local tavern preferred by many of the locals, some of whom are hotel workers.

Via dal Bagn 11. © **081/833-40-09**. Reservations required for dinner. Main courses 22F–44F ($18–$36). AE, DC, MC, V. Daily noon–3pm and 6–11:30pm.

INEXPENSIVE

Hanselmann Originally established in the mid-1800s, this tavern and tearoom has grown to occupy a much-embellished building decorated with sgraffito. Today it's one of the best and most inexpensive places in town for breakfast or lunch. It's owned by Fritz Mutschler, grandson of the original founder. From the German-language breakfast menu, you may choose an omelet, an egg-and-cheese dish, or a country platter piled high with Black Forest ham and Valais rye rolls. Other dishes include Welsh rarebit and smoked salmon with buttered toast. The upstairs restaurant opens at 11:30am. The place is also popular with the après-ski crowd.

Via Maistra 8. ℂ **081/833-38-64.** Reservations accepted only for lunch. Main courses 18F–42F ($15–$34); breakfast 8F–22F ($6.55–$18); fixed-price breakfast 16F ($13); fixed-price lunch 28F ($23). MC, V. Dec 25–Feb and July–Aug daily 7:30am–7pm; Mar–June and Sept–Dec 24 Wed–Mon 7:30am–7pm.

Restaurant Engadina *(Value* SWISS In the direct center of St. Moritz-Dorf, across the street from the town hall, is this old-fashioned family dining room that's uncharacteristic for St. Moritz. You get good value for your money here. Pleasant, comfortable, and simple, it consists of two hunter-style rooms filled with trophies and alpine accents, such as pine-wood tables and paneling. There's even an outdoor wooden deck for drinking and dining if the weather is right. Selections include carpaccio, *petite marmite* (a famous Parisian soup made with lean pieces of meat and vegetable stock), fondues (with cheese or champagne), grilled steaks, goulash, and snails in garlic butter. The food is robust and hearty—no one ever accused the chefs of being too imaginative, but this is the type of chow the locals love.

Piazza da Scuola 2. ℂ **081/833-32-65.** Reservations recommended. Cheese fondue 30F ($25) per person; main courses 38F–43F ($31–$35). AE, DC, MC, V. Winter Mon–Sat 10am–10pm; summer Mon–Sat noon–2pm and 6:30–9:30pm.

Trattoria Bellaval *(Value* ITALIAN/SWISS This is one of our preferred low-cost restaurants in St. Moritz. Set within a century-old hotel near the town center, within a woodsy-looking dining room, it focuses on grilled schnitzels and steaks (both beef and pork) and a dazzling range of pastas that you'll build yourself based on whatever combination of sauce and toppings (21 different kinds), noodles (five different kinds), and sizes (medium, large, and *grande*) you designate. Some of the best antipasti in town in served here, and all the salads are delicious fare and freshly made. You may also check out the daily specials, and vegetarians will take delight in the vegetable lasagna.

In the Hotel Bellaval, via Grevas 55. ℂ **81/833-32-45.** Reservations not necessary. Main courses 11F–24F ($9–$20); fixed-price 2-course menu 26F ($21). AE, DC, MC, V. Daily 11:30am–midnight. Closed Nov.

ST. MORITZ AFTER DARK

Few other resorts are as depressing off season as St. Moritz, where very few of the local entrepreneurs even pretend to be interested in doing business. But as the midwinter and midsummer seasons get underway, you'll find lots of warm cubbyholes in St. Moritz, often in hotels whose bars are inspired by the Romansh sgraffito that's so prevalent in the region. Many are eminently appropriate for a quiet and cozy drink, and some, as noted below, make special efforts to attract drinking and sometimes dancing clients from other hotels.

One of the best examples of this is the **Hotel Schweizerhof,** via dal Bagn 54 (ℂ **081/837-07-07**), where three separate bars provide a labyrinth of nightlife options that range from the subdued to the rowdy. They include the **Muli Bar** (only open in winter), with North American–style country-western music; the **Stübli** (open year-round), which divides its energies between cozy folkloric platters, a resident musician, and foaming steins of beer; and the **Piano Bar** (open in summer and winter but closed mid-Sept to mid-Dec and Easter and mid-Jan), where melodies are tinkled out by visiting pianists from throughout Europe.

Bobby's Pub, in the Caspar Badrutt Shopping Gallery, via dal Bagn 50a (✆ **081/834-42-83**), is everybody's favorite English-style pub, replete with faux Victoriana and beers from throughout Europe, including merry old England. A well-entrenched staple on the nightlife circuit is **Vivai's Disco,** in the Hotel Steffani, via Somplazt 1 (✆ **081/836-96-96**). Here, despite an antique-looking entrance etched in Engadine-style line drawings, the music is contemporary and the decor is intimately lit and modern. Depending on whether there's live music, entrance costs 30F ($25), which usually includes the first drink.

More expensive, and much more posh, are the disco and bar facilities in **Badrutt's Palace Hotel,** via Serlas 27 (✆ **081/837-10-00**). Most visible of these is the **King's Club Disco,** where outsiders can mingle with the rich and famous, or more likely the wannabes, in a mock-medieval decor that reverberates with the sound of recently released dance music. Jackets and ties for men aren't required. Cover is from 35F to 45F ($29–$37), depending on the season and night of the week, and includes the first drink. In winter it's open every night from 10:30pm to 3am. In summer it's open only Friday and Saturday from 10:30pm to 3am. Quieter, somewhat less manic bars and watering holes, all of them relentlessly upscale, are scattered throughout other parts of the hotel as well.

4 Pontresina ⟨★⟨★

6km (4 miles) E of St. Moritz; 85km (53 miles) SE of Chur; 208km (130 miles) SE of Zurich

Pontresina (1,775m/5,822 ft.) doesn't have the fame of St. Moritz, but it offers some of the best hiking and mountaineering in the Engadine. Its long hours of sunshine in the winter, and its access to all the noted ski sites in the greater St. Moritz area, make Pontresina an attractive alternative to the more expensive town. Situated in the Upper Engadine on the road to the Bernina Pass, at the mouth of the Bernina Valley, it's surrounded by larches, stone pines, and the Alps. From Pontresina, you also have views of what's called the "glacier amphitheater" of the Roseg Mountains.

Originally a 19th-century summer resort, Pontresina has become a leading ski resort, known for its famous ski runs, cross-country skiing tracks, and a family-friendly venue that's less expensive and less forbidding than more glamorous St. Moritz. The village today is filled with hotels and shops and has much old Engadine architecture.

ESSENTIALS

GETTING THERE   From Zurich, via Chur, a train arrives in Pontresina every hour throughout the day until 9pm (until 10pm Fri–Sun). There's also a train arriving every hour from St. Moritz. For **train schedules,** call ✆ **0900/300-300** or the railway station in Pontresina (✆ **081/842-63-37**).

In the winter a "sportbus" runs between St. Moritz and Pontresina every 25 minutes daily from 7:30am to midnight (until 2am Fri–Sat). Tickets can be purchased at the post office or directly on the bus. Each way costs 8F ($6.55); for information call the **bus station** in St. Moritz (✆ **081/837-67-63**).

If you're driving from St. Moritz, head northeast along Route 27, then cut southeast at the junction with Route 29.

VISITOR INFORMATION   In lieu of street names, follow hotel or restaurant directional signs. The **Pontresina Tourist Office** (© 081/838-83-00; www.pontresina. com) is open Monday to Friday from 8:30am to noon and 2 to 6pm. During high season it is also open Saturday 9am to noon and 3 to 6pm; Sunday 2 to 6pm.

EXPLORING THE AREA

The Engadine provides a wealth of hiking tours that combine rides on cable cars or gondolas with sometimes strenuous hikes across rocky or, in some cases, glacial terrain. The most spectacular of these is the **Diavolezza tour** ⚐, which reaches a maximum height of 2,723m (8,931 ft.), and which includes views of—and if you opt for it, hikes over—as many as two separate glaciers. To access it, travel by road for 7km (4½ miles) south of Pontresina, following the signs to the Bernina Pass until you reach the lowest station of the Diavolezza cable car, and climb aboard for a head-spinning 15-minute ascent to the top. One-way transit costs 20F ($16) for adults and 10F ($8.20) for children ages 6 to 16; the round-trip cost for adults is 28F ($23) and 14F ($11) for children. If it's winter, you can ski back down to the valley, or—more precariously (and this is only for experts)—you can negotiate down the face of the glacier to the hamlet of Morteratsch. The better bet occurs in summer, when you can take a guided hike along the surface of the glacier as part of a 4- to 5-hour tour that's recommended only for the fit and hardy. (Don't even consider this without the proper equipment, including sturdy boots with rubber treads, sunglasses, sunscreen, and protection against the rain and sometimes howling winds, even during midsummer.) A guide waits for participants every day, from May to September, at the top of the Diavolezza cable car, at noon. Participation in the walking tour costs 30F ($25) for adults, and 15F ($12) for children under 12. For more information about the Diavolezza hiking tour, contact the tourist offices of any of the surrounding towns and villages, including St. Moritz, Silvaplana, and Pontresina, or the **Pontresina Mountaineering School** (Bergsteigerschule Pontresina; © 081/838-83-33).

Another of the region's panoramic aeries, in this case one that's more conveniently reached than the above-recommended Diavolezza, is **Alp Languard,** whose chairlifts will carry you to a height of 2,550m (8,364 ft.). You'll access it from a hillside above the rest of the town that's within walking distance. A one-way ticket costs 15F ($12) and 7F ($5.75) for children 6 to 16, and a round-trip ticket costs 20F ($16) and 10F ($8.20) for children 6 to 16. Ascents are continuous during daylight hours throughout the year. For more information, contact **Sesselbahn Languard** at © 081/842-62-55.

The area's chief attraction is **Muottos Muragl** ⚐⚐⚐, a mountain whose peak is reached by funicular. The excursion begins in Pontresina, where you board a bus that travels 3km (2 miles) downhill in the direction of Samedan, to a final destination at the base of the funicular, Punt Muragl. The funicular ride takes 15 minutes to reach a platform set at 2,414m (7,918 ft.) above sea level. From it you'll see the Upper Engadine Gap, with the mountain ranges of Piz Julier and Piz Rosatsch on either side. If the day is clear, you can also see the lakes between Maloja and St. Moritz. The excursion, including bus rides, costs 24F to 28F ($20–$23) round-trip, but a one-way ticket is available as well, for 15F to 18F ($12–$15) depending on the season. For information in Pontresina, call the tourist information center or inquire at the reception desk of your hotel. For information about the funicular, contact **Standseilbahn Muottos Muragle** at © 081/842-83-08.

WHERE TO STAY
VERY EXPENSIVE
Grand Hotel Kronenhof ⚜⚜⚜   This is the grandest hotel in town and has been run by the same family since the 1850s. Set in the center of the Pontresina, behind iron gates and a circular driveway, the Kronenhof is decorated with Corinthian columns and vaulted, frescoed ceilings. Its oldest section dates from 1848; the impressive details are from 1898 and include such baroque accessories as gilt, baby-pink cherubs, alluring nymphs, dark wood pine, restored murals, and even the original parquet floors. The midsize to spacious bedrooms are renovated as need dictates. Many are individually decorated with traditional Biedermeier pieces; others are in soothing pastels.

CH-7504 Pontresina. ℂ **081/830-30-30.** Fax 081/830-30-31. www.kronenhof.com. 97 units. Winter 280F–885F ($230–$726) double, 930F–1,250F ($763–$1,025) suite; summer 270F–495F ($221–$406) double, 560F–880F ($459–$722) suite. Rates include breakfast. Half board 60F ($49) extra per person. AE, DC, MC, V. Parking 25F ($21). Closed Apr and mid-May and Sept–Dec. **Amenities:** 2 restaurants; bar; 2 pools (1 indoor); 2 tennis courts; fitness area; sauna; steam bath; limited room service; massage; babysitting; laundry service; bowling; ice-skating rink. *In room:* TV, dataport, minibar, hair dryer, safe.

EXPENSIVE
Hotel La Collina & Soldanella ⚜   This establishment is composed of two con-nected hotels, one built just after the turn of the 20th century (the government-rated three-star Soldanella) and the other during the 1970s (the four-star La Collina). Many loyal clients deliberately opt for rooms in the Soldanella, knowing that the facilities of the better-rated La Collina are at their disposal, including La Collina's elegant dining room. Clients for either property register in the lobby of La Collina before heading through a network of hallways and covered passageways to their respective buildings. Regardless of which of the areas you select, bedrooms are comfortable, and the public rooms are cozy and elegant, with Oriental carpets and a scattering of regional antiques.

CH-7504 Pontresina. ℂ **081/838-85-85.** Fax 081/838-85-00. www.collina.ch. 46 units (28 in La Collina, 18 in Sol-danella). In La Collina 320F–410F ($262–$336) double. In Soldanella 290F–330F ($238–$271) double. Rates include half board. AE, DC, MC, V. Free parking outdoors. Closed Apr–May and Oct 10–Dec 20. **Amenities:** Restaurant; lim-ited room service; laundry service. *In room:* TV, dataport, minibar, hair dryer, safe.

Hotel Schweizerhof ⚜   The Schweizerhof is from 1910, but it was so drastically modernized in 1975 that old-time visitors hardly recognize it; much of its roofline (including the towers and turrets) was removed. Yet it remains a huge, comfortable hotel. The midsize rooms are well furnished and comfortable, and the corner bay-win-dowed doubles open onto views to the southwest. All the bathrooms are neatly main-tained, 45 units equipped with tub/shower combinations, the rest with private showers.

CH-7504 Pontresina. ℂ **081/842-01-31.** Fax 081/842-79-88. www.schweizerhofpontresina.ch. 65 units. Winter 242F–392F ($198–$321) double; summer 228F–328F ($187–$269) double. Rates include breakfast. Half board 47F ($39) per person extra. AE, DC, MC, V. Parking 15F ($12). Closed Apr 14–June 14. **Amenities:** Restaurant; bar; exer-cise room; Jacuzzi; sauna; steam bath; limited room service; massage; laundry service. *In room:* TV, dataport, minibar, hair dryer, safe.

MODERATE
Best Western Hotel Bernina ⚡Value   This hotel is not particularly historic, but it offers good value and cozy comfort in an often-forbidding landscape. Recently tiled midsize bathrooms (mainly with combination tub/shower), pine-wood furnishings, and flower prints make the bedrooms inviting after renovation. The most panoramic views are from the corner doubles with private balconies. All rooms have been reno-vated since 2000, each with wood paneling and lots of folkloric touches. The dining

room is decorated with panels of local wood, and the hotel's popular restaurant has excellent a la carte specialties. It's a place where the locals from the ski school meet in the winter.

CH-7504 Pontresina. ℂ **800/780-7234** or 081/852-12-12. Fax 081/852-36-06. www.hotelbernina.ch. 43 units. Summer 200F–250F ($164–$205) double; winter 210F–300F ($172–$246) double. Rates include breakfast. Half board 30F ($25) per person. AE, DC, MC, V. Parking 18F ($15) in winter, 10F ($8.20) in summer. Closed Apr 15–June 1 and Oct to mid-Dec. **Amenities:** 2 restaurants; bar; steam bath; sauna; limited room service; massage; laundry service. *In room:* TV, dataport, minibar, hair dryer, safe.

Hotel Garni Chesa Mulin   The staff goes out of its way to make guests feel welcome in this quiet, centrally located hotel originally built in 1983. The public rooms are filled with plants, which serve to accentuate the wood paneling. The large, airy bedrooms were renovated in 1996, have comfortable furnishings, and in all except for six units, full bathrooms come with tub/shower combinations (the remaining with shower only).

CH-7504 Pontresina. ℂ **081/838-82-00.** Fax 081/838-82-30. www.chesa-mulin.ch. 30 units. Winter 210F–230F ($172–$189) double; summer 185F–198F ($152–$162) double. Rates include buffet breakfast. AE, DC, MC, V. Free parking outside, 15F ($12) in garage nearby. Closed May and Nov. **Amenities:** Solarium; sauna; laundry service. *In room:* TV, minibar, hair dryer, safe.

WHERE TO DINE
EXPENSIVE
Hof Restaurant ⓖ CONTINENTAL/SWISS   One of the most reliable dining rooms in town occupies a stone-floored room whose walls are accented with reproductions of medieval-looking sgraffito and big windows that overlook surrounding landscapes. The menu, geared for the high-altitude, hearty climate outside, features generous portions of regional recipes that reflect the local traditions of both Switzerland and nearby Austria and Italy. Examples include pork filets with lemon sauce; lamb cutlets with balsamic vinegar sauce; carpaccio of veal or beef; air-dried *bundnerfleisch* (a type of beef); different preparations of salmon and trout; and the classic dish of Vienna, *Tafelspitz,* the boiled beef with horseradish sauce. Dessert may include rich chocolate cake or flambéed raspberries with cream.

In the Hotel Schweizerhof. ℂ **081/842-01-31.** Reservations recommended. Main courses 30F–50F ($25–$41); fixed-price menus 53F ($43). AE, DC, MC, V. Daily 11am–11pm. Closed Apr 14–June 14.

Kronenstübli ⓖⓖ SWISS/FRENCH/ITALIAN   The restaurant at the Grand Hotel Kronenhof is one of the most popular spots in town, serving the finest cuisine. It's filled with valuable pieces of brass and pewter; the wood paneling is from the mid–19th century. The cuisine is fresh-flavored, inventive, and prepared with time-tested skill. You may enjoy a "variation of tomatoes with cheese" served with a dollop of basil-flavored sorbet; a medley of marinated salmon and tuna served with mango-flavored vinaigrette and strips of roasted duck meat; and filets of pikeperch in a potato crust, served with cheese sauce and fresh chanterelles. Veal mignon with a foie-gras mousse is especially delightful, or perhaps a supreme of turbot with saffron.

In the Grand Hotel Kronenhof. ℂ **081/842-01-11.** Reservations required. Main courses 40F–68F ($33–$56); fixed-price 5-course menu 120F ($98). AE, DC, MC, V. Daily noon–2pm and 7–10pm. Closed Apr to mid-May and Sept–Dec.

INEXPENSIVE
Stüva SWISS/CONTINENTAL   This restaurant provides intimate, vaulted rooms, where guests gather on snowy nights for classic raclette and fondues. Of course, other

good-tasting fare, such as pastas, fresh trout, steaks, and various schnitzels, are also offered. The service is efficient.

In the Hotel Bernina. (© 081/852-12-12. Reservations recommended. Main courses 20F–28F ($16–$23); fixed-price menu 36F–48F ($30–$39). AE, DC, MC, V. Daily 11am–midnight. Closed Apr 15–June 1 and Oct 3 to mid-Dec.

5 Silvaplana (★

6km (4 miles) SW of St. Moritz

Situated on Lake Silvaplana, in sight of Lake Champfèr, within a 10-minute drive of St. Moritz, the little village of Silvaplana (1,770m/5,806 ft.) is at the foot of Piz Corvatsch (3,401m/11,155 ft.), at the beginning of the Julier Pass.

Built around a late Gothic parish church, whose stone walls were completed in 1491, the hamlet of Silvaplana is one of the most unspoiled resort towns in the Engadine.

ESSENTIALS

GETTING THERE   Silvaplana is not serviced by any railroad. Local residents usually take the bus or drive to the railway station at St. Moritz for most of their transportation needs.

A flotilla of blue-sided Engadine buses make runs every 15 minutes in winter, and every 30 minutes in summer, from the St. Moritz railroad station to the center of Silvaplana at a cost of 2.50F ($2.05) each way. The yellow-sided Palm Express bus also travels through Silvaplana as part of its twice-per-day route from Lugano to St. Moritz. One-way transit from Lugano to St. Moritz costs 65F ($53) each way. For information on either of these forms of buses, contact **Engadine Buses** in St. Moritz at (© **081/834-91-00.**

If you're driving from St. Moritz, head southwest along Route 27 for 10 minutes.

VISITOR INFORMATION   Between October and May the **Silvaplana Tourist Office** (© **081/838-60-00;** www.silvaplana.ch) is open Monday to Friday from 8:30am to noon and 1:30 to 6:30pm, and Saturday from 9am to noon and 4 to 6pm. Between June and September it's open Monday to Friday from 1:30am to 6pm and Saturday from 9am to noon and 4 to 6pm.

EXPLORING THE AREA

Swimming, hill climbing, horseback riding, fishing, and even windsurfing on Lake Silvaplana are available in the summer. A range of cross-country trails and hiking paths are situated around the lake of Silvaplana.

Whether you're a skier, a mountaineer, a nature lover, or just a sightseer, you may want to visit **Corvatsch.** From Silvaplana, go across the narrow neck of water where Lake Champfèr and Lake Silvaplana join and take an aerial cable car at Surlej. In just 15 minutes you'll reach the mountain station, from which you have a view of the lakes, meadows, forests, and villages of the Upper Engadine. From the lookout terrace, you take in a panorama of what appears to be an infinity of mountain peaks, with the giant glacier of the Bernina group seemingly close enough to touch.

From December to May, skiers are presented with nearly 80km (50 miles) of ski runs covered with deep, powdery snow, while in the summer you can ski on the granular ice of the glacier. Ski lifts, the most visible of which is the **Corvatsch Bergbahn** (© **081/838-73-73**), carry skiers to the glacier throughout the year. It charges round-trip fares of 36F ($30) for adults and 18F ($15) for children.

The town's ski school, **Skischule Corvatsch** (✆ **081/828-86-84** for information), which is open only from December to May, charges 85F ($70) per hour for private lessons, or 45F ($37) per person for group lessons that last for a full day.

WHERE TO STAY

Hotel Albana 👫👫   This year-round hotel, a government-rated four-star choice and the best at the small resort town, stands on medieval foundations. Designed with beamed ceilings and a stone fireplace, it also has half-timbered walls and regional stenciling throughout. The midsize bedrooms are modern and inviting. The best accommodations are those with private balconies facing south.

CH-7513 Silvaplana. ✆ **081/828-92-92.** Fax 081/828-81-81. 39 units. Winter 250F–440F ($205–$361) double; summer 250F–340F ($205–$279) double. Rates include buffet breakfast. AE, DC, MC, V. Parking 18F ($15) in garage in winter, 10F ($8.20) in summer. Closed May and Oct 20–Nov 21. **Amenities:** Restaurant; indoor pool; gym; Jacuzzi; sauna; steam bath; concierge; limited room service; laundry service. *In room:* TV, dataport, minibar, hair dryer, safe.

Hotel Julier Palace   In the heart of Silvaplana, this hotel consists of a red-fronted, turn-of-the-20th-century chalet (the Hotel Julier) connected to a smaller, yellow-fronted annex that was added in the 1980s. The bedrooms in the annex are a bit larger than those in the Julier and more modern in their decor. The hotel is family-operated, with a good knowledge of foreign languages and customs. Large areas of both buildings were renovated during the early 1990s. All units come with midsize private bathrooms, mainly with shower only. Most are outfitted with warm colors and often some genuine charm. Most rooms were renovated in 2002.

CH-7513 Silvaplana. ✆ **081/828-96-44.** Fax 081/834-30-03. 35 units. www.julierpalace.com. 140F–240F ($115–$197) double; 700F–1,000F ($574–$820) suite. Rates include buffet breakfast. Half board 30F ($25) per person extra. AE, DC, MC, V. Free parking outdoors, 15F ($12) in garage. **Amenities:** Restaurant; bar; limited room service; laundry service. *In room:* TV, hair dryer, safe.

Hotel Sonne   This is a good government-rated two-star hotel with a sense of bourgeois charm that it takes very, very seriously. In the center of the village, this four-story building is decorated with flower boxes, monochromatic regional designs, and neoclassical details. The rustically modern interior has settees in the salon and old-fashioned wallpaper and paneling in the dining rooms. The small rooms are well maintained and comfortably furnished.

CH-7513 Silvaplana. ✆ **081/828-81-52.** Fax 081/828-80-21. 45 units, 31 with bathroom. Summer 115F ($94) double without bathroom, 170F–205F ($139–$168) double with bathroom; winter 155F ($127) double without bathroom, 205F ($168) double with bathroom. Rates include breakfast. Supplement for half board 40F ($33). 50% reduction for children under 12. Rates include breakfast. AE, DC, MC, V. Free parking. **Amenities:** 2 restaurants; bar (winter only); limited room service; laundry service. *In room:* TV (on request).

WHERE TO DINE

Le Gourmet 👍 SWISS   The dining room in the Hotel Albana is the best choice in Silvaplana. It has a richly appealing decor of wrought iron, heavy timbers, and striped fabrics. The chef prepares such tempting specialties as medallions of pork with grapes and nuts, sweetbreads in an artichoke sauce with a purée of asparagus, filet of lamb with black truffles, and filet of red mullet with saffron and fresh morels.

The hotel also maintains a less glamorous second-floor dining room, the Spunta Grischun, which offers Engadine dishes, at comparable prices costing 30F to 39F ($25–$32).

In the Hotel Albana. ✆ **081/828-92-92.** Reservations recommended. Main courses 30F–40F ($25–$33); fixed-price menu 55F–65F ($45–$53). AE, DC, MC, V. Daily noon–1:30pm and 7:30–10pm. Closed May and Oct 20–Nov 21.

15

Lugano, Locarno & the Ticino

If you don't normally think of palm trees in Switzerland, you haven't seen the Ticino. Also called the Tessin, it's the Swiss Riviera—the retirement fantasy of thousands of Swiss living in the northern cantons. Although Italian is the major language, German and French (as well as English) are also widely spoken.

A visitor could spend at least 2 weeks just touring the valleys of the Ticino. Officially, the canton begins at Airolo (the southern exit of the St. Gotthard Tunnel), but most visitors head for the district's major resorts of Locarno, Lugano, and fast-rising Ascona. Lugano and Locarno share the shores of lakes Lugano and Maggiore with Italy. Relations between Switzerland and Italy, however, weren't always peaceful. The Ticino was basically carved out of the Duchy of Milan by Swiss soldiers and staunchly defended in several bloody battles.

The name of the canton is taken from the Ticino River, a tributary of northern Italy's Po River. The balmy climate produces subtropical vegetation, which thrives in gardens famous throughout Switzerland. The district's weather is almost addictive between March and November, but the rest of the year can be cold and damp.

The proximity of Italy manifests itself in the Ticino's architecture and cuisine. Many buildings are made of stone and are proportioned like structures in Lombardy or Tuscany. Also, in many cases, a trattoria will be owned by a Swiss-German husband and a Swiss-Italian wife, so their cuisine ends up being a concession to each other's culinary traditions.

Sometimes getting to the Ticino is part of the fun. One of the most dramatic ways to arrive is over the **Simplon Pass** 🎔🎔, a journey that stretches from the German-speaking town of Brig in Switzerland and, after crossing the pass, descends to the Italian border town of Domodossola, a distance of some 64km (40 miles). The pass owes its origins to Napoleon, who demanded a low-altitude pass 1,950m (6,396 ft.) above sea level through which artillery could be transported. This pass is often closed between December and early May because of bad road conditions. At those times automobiles are transported onto flatbed trains, which are carried through one of the longest railway tunnels in the world, the Simplon Tunnel. The tunnel stretches for 20km (12 miles). But when the pass is open, it affords one of the most panoramic mountain views in Europe.

Rail passengers can also arrive dramatically by taking the **_Bernina Express_** 🎔🎔🎔, a 4-hour trip that begins in Chur and ends in Tirano, Italy. As you near the town of Chur you will be awed by the rugged peaks around you, but before the end of the journey, as you near the Italian border town of Tirano, you will see palm-lined lakefronts. This is the only express train that crosses the Alps with no tunnels, and, as such, it is one of the steepest railway lines in the world. At Tirano, the end of the rail run from Zurich, you can make easy bus connections on to Lugano. For more information about the _Bernina Express,_ call **Rail Europe** at © 877/257-2887.

1 Bellinzona

22km (14 miles) E of Locarno; 35km (22 miles) N of Lugano; 192km (120 miles) S of Zurich; 416km (260 miles) W of Geneva

The opening of the St. Gotthard Tunnel made this once-remote Swiss town on Italy's side of the Alps very accessible. Bellinzona is known for the beauty of its old city and the nearby hills, as well as for the hospitality of its inhabitants.

Because of its location astride the best of the ancient military and trade routes between Rome and its colonies in the north, the town is believed to be of Roman origin. It was later occupied, along with the rest of the Ticino, by both the Celts and the Ligurians. Records of the town date from A.D. 590. As the strategic key to the passes of St. Gotthard, San Bernardino, and Lucomagno, Bellinzona loomed large in the history of Lombardy. In the 8th century it was owned outright by the bishop of Como, and ownership went back and forth between Como and Milan in the 13th and 14th centuries. By 1798 it had become the capital of its own canton, Bellinzona, in the Swiss Confederation. Five years later it was incorporated into the newly formed canton of the Ticino, where it has remained ever since, serving as the canton's capital.

Saturday morning is a good time to visit here to see the lively outdoor market, between 7 and noon. Peddlers, vendors, country people, artisans, and townsfolk converse in Italian over the wares.

ESSENTIALS

GETTING THERE Bellinzona is the easiest destination to reach in the Ticino. Every train from the north of Switzerland stops here, as Bellinzona lies on the Brussels-Basel-Zurich-Milan international line. Indeed, every day one or another regional or international train stops here about once every 30 minutes. For **rail information** and schedules, call ℂ 0900/300-300.

The nearest airport is at **Lugano-Agno,** 30 minutes from Bellinzona by train.

If you're driving from Zurich, continue along the N2 expressway through the St. Gotthard Tunnel into the Ticino. N2 continues southeast to Bellinzona.

VISITOR INFORMATION The **Bellinzona Tourist Bureau,** Palazzo Civico at Piazza Nosetto (ℂ **091/825-21-31;** www.bellinzonaturismo.ch), is open daily from 9am to 6pm and Saturday 9am to 1pm.

EXPLORING THE AREA

Bellinzona has three castles dating from the 13th to the 15th centuries: the Schwyz, the Unterwald, and the Uri.

Castle of Uri ⊕ (Castelgrande, or San Michele in Italian; ℂ **091/825-81-45**), built in 1280, is the most ancient and the largest castle in town. To reach the castle, take an elevator from piazza del Sole in the town center. In addition to the elevator, there are signposted paths from piazza Collegiata and piazza Nosetto for those who'd like to take one of the most scenic walks in the area. The castle was restored in 1991 with a historical section and a small numismatic museum. The castle contains a restaurant (see "Where to Dine," below), a banquet room, and a congress hall. It's open daily from 10am to 6pm. Admission is 4F ($3.30) for adults; 2F ($1.65) for children, students, and seniors 65 or over.

The most outstanding of the three medieval fortifications is the **Schwyz Castle** ⊕⊕ (Castello di Montebello; ℂ **091/825-13-42**). It has a 13th-century château with a courtyard, as well as several 15th-century additions. Today it's a minor museum of history and

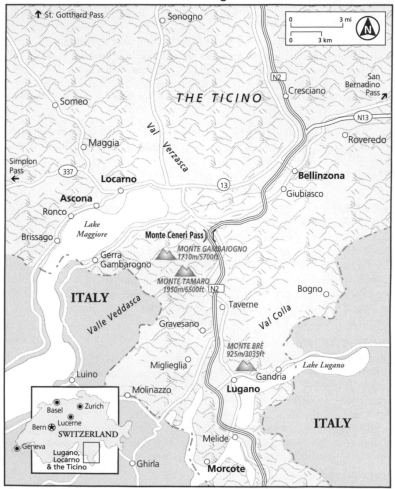

archaeology. To get here by car, start from viale Stazione and follow the steep ramp up to this huge citadel. It's open daily from 10am to 6pm, and admission is 4F ($3.30) for adults; 2F ($1.65) for children, students, and seniors 65 or over.

Castle of Unterwald ✿ (Castello di Sasso Corbaro; ✆ **091/825-59-06**) was built in 1479. It can be reached by the same road that goes up to the Schwyz (see above). The view from the terrace here is the finest in Bellinzona. You'll see not only the lower valley of the Ticino but Lake Maggiore as well. The castle hosts temporary exhibitions. Open only April to October, daily from 10am to 6pm, the castle's admission price is 4F ($3.30) for adults and 2F ($1.65) for children, students, and seniors, depending on the exhibit. A combination ticket to all three castles costs 8F ($6.55) for adults and 4F ($3.30) for children.

Finds **Bellinzona Blues**

In late June hordes from throughout Switzerland gather in Bellinzona for the annual **Blues Festival,** where free concerts are staged in squares. Some of the biggest names in blues have appeared here, and the tourist office (see "Essentials," above) will supply the details, which change every year.

Also worth visiting is the collegiate **Church of Sts. Peter and Stephen,** dating from the 16th century. It's a fine Renaissance structure, with a richly embellished baroque interior. The location is across from Castelgrande.

Guided walking tours of Bellinzona, its Old Town, and its castles are available upon request at the tourist office (see "Essentials," above).

SHOPPING

Pick up a map from the tourist office in the center of the Old Town. A look at the map will direct you to **Villa dei Cedri** (*℗* **091/821-85-20**), Bellinzona's municipally owned art gallery, founded in 1985. The gallery contains private art donated to the city but also mounts temporary exhibitions. In back is an enclosed garden and grounds where the townsfolk grow their own small crop of local merlot, bottles of which are offered for sale in the gallery. It's open Tuesday to Friday from 2 to 6pm, Saturday and Sunday from 11am to 6pm. Admission is 8F ($6.55) for adults; 5F ($4.10) for students, children, and seniors 65 or over.

WHERE TO STAY

Albergo Unione   The best hotel in town is a plain-looking white building with a pink-marble extension with balconies. It's surrounded by gardens, some with fountains. The government-rated three-star hotel offers modernized, midsize rooms with flowered carpets, tiles, firm beds, and up-to-date plumbing, mainly with private showers, although some units also offer bathrooms with tubs.

Via Général Guisan 1, CH-6500 Bellinzona. *℗* **091/825-55-77.** Fax 091/825-94-60. www.hotel-unione.ch. 33 units. 210F ($172) double; 240F ($197) triple. Rates include breakfast. AE, DC, MC, V. Closed Dec 20–Jan 15. **Amenities:** Restaurant; bar; limited room service; laundry service/dry cleaning; nonsmoking rooms. *In room:* TV, dataport, minibar, hair dryer.

WHERE TO DINE

Castelgrande   TICINESE/ITALIAN   Located in the largest and most ancient castle in Bellinzona (see "Exploring the Area," above), this restaurant might be predictably overrun with camera-toting tourists getting off tour buses. But unlike restaurants installed in most European castles, the upstairs dining room here is decidedly upmarket. Downstairs, there's an informal grotto with terrace, which serves less expensive Ticino and Italian dishes, while the more formal upstairs room features gourmet specialties. When dining in this second-level room, men are advised to wear a jacket.

The restaurant is not only the most luxurious in appointments in town, it also serves the best food. The cuisine combines that of the Ticino region with dishes inspired by sunny Italy. Game is a feature, and the wine list is particularly extensive. Try such dishes as pigeon with onions in a sweet-and-sour sauce, or if it's autumn, perfectly cooked quail with porcini mushrooms. The chef's imagination is reflected in such dishes as goose liver accompanied by blueberries. Guests can ask for a table in the cavelike interior or, if the weather is right, for one on the large terrace.

Salita al Castello. ℂ **091/826-23-53.** Reservations recommended. Main courses 19F–54F ($16–$44). AE, DC, MC, V. Tues–Sun noon–2:30pm and 6:30–10pm.

Locanda Orico   ITALIAN/FRENCH   This is one of the best restaurants in the Ticino, serving a refined cuisine based on market-fresh ingredients. The inn lies in a stately town house at the foot of Castelgrande in the center of Bellinzona. The chef, Lorenzo Albrici, was once a student of Frédy Girardet, hailed as one of the greatest chefs of Europe. The fixed-price lunch menu (40F/$26) is the town's great dining bargain. An array of warm and cold appetizers is there to tempt you, ranging from house-marinated salmon in a sweet-and-sour sauce to carpaccio of duck liver flavored with sea salt. Baked shrimp are also a starter, floating in an Andalusian gazpacho. Main courses, which are especially delightful, are filet of freshwater lake perch stuffed with green leafy vegetables and filet of roasted veal with rosemary-flavored butter. For dessert, there is nothing better than a symphony of fresh fruit au gratin, flavored with Grand Marnier. This place represents grand provincial dining at its best.

Via Orico 13. ℂ **091/825-15-18.** Reservations recommended. Main courses 38F–50F ($31–$41). AE, DC, MC, V. Tues–Sat 11:30am–2pm and 6:30–11pm.

2 Locarno ⋆⋆

22km (14 miles) W of Bellinzona; 40km (25 miles) N of Lugano

This ancient town at the north end of **Lake Maggiore** is a vacation resort known for its mild climate. The rich Mediterranean vegetation includes camellias, magnolias, mimosa, wisteria, azaleas, and oleander in the spring. Olives, figs, and pomegranates also flourish in this climate.

Locarno entered world history in 1925 when an international conference held here resulted in a series of agreements known collectively as the Locarno Pact. It was in Locarno that the former enemies of World War I, seeking to reorder the affairs of Europe, committed themselves to a peaceful coexistence. Locarno was chosen over Lucerne, reportedly, because the mistress of the French representative wanted the meeting to be held on Lake Maggiore. The "spirit of Locarno," however, did not last long; within a decade the participants were again arming for war.

If you take the electric railway between Locarno and the Simplon Pass, you'll pass through the Centovalli, named for the hundred valleys that slope toward the river. There are many charming villages on the banks of this river. At Carnedo, in Italy, the railway climbs up to the plateau of Santa Maria Maggiore, a wide, barren, and solitary district that stretches for about 10km (6 miles) at 840m (2,755 ft.) above sea level. A steep descent leads down to the railway junction of Domodossola. This international railway serves as a link between the Gotthard and the Simplon lines. The bridges are technological wonders.

ESSENTIALS

GETTING THERE   The nearest airport is at Lugano (see section 4, later in this chapter), 45 minutes away by train.

The Locarno-Domodossola electric railway links Locarno with the Italian town of Domodossola. From here, you can continue to Brig in the Rhône Valley, through the Simplon Tunnel. Railway lines connect Brig with Lake Geneva and Bern through the Lotschberg Tunnel. Direct trains from Lausanne or Bern take 4 hours to reach Locarno. From the other direction, through the St. Gotthard Tunnel, Locarno is 23km (14 miles) west of Bellinzona by rail. For **rail information** and schedules, call ℂ **0900/300-300.**

Locarno sits atop the bus routes that connect Ascona with Lugano, and they continue on to many different mountain villages to the northeast until arriving at Chur. For more details about bus transportation, call the tourist office (see below).

After driving through the St. Gotthard Tunnel and reaching Bellinzona on the N2 expressway, take Route 13 west to reach Locarno.

VISITOR INFORMATION   The **Locarno Tourist Bureau,** on largo Zorzi (℗ **091/ 791-00-91**), is open March to October, Monday to Friday 9am to 6pm, Saturday 10am to 6pm, and Sunday 10am to 1:30pm and 2:30 to 5pm; November to February, Monday to Friday 9am to 12:30pm and 2 to 6pm.

SEEING THE SIGHTS

Start your walk around town at **piazza Grande,** the main square. On the north side the arcades are filled with shops. You can find antiques, art, Swiss and Italian handicrafts, and high fashion from Milan.

From piazza Grande, follow the curvy via Francesco Rusca to the Old Town. Along the way, you can visit the **Castello Visconti,** piazza Castello 2 (℗ **091/756-31-80**). This structure is all that survives from a late-medieval castle in which the dukes of Milan lived. It was severely damaged in 1518. Today the castle contains a Museum Civico, which displays many Roman artifacts excavated in the area. It's open only April to October, Tuesday to Sunday from 10am to 5pm. Admission is 6F ($4.90).

The most important sight in Locarno is the **Santuario della Madonna del Sasso** ⊛ (℗ **091/743-62-65**), on a wooded crag above the resort in the hamlet of Orselina. Hearty visitors and devout pilgrims can climb to the church, at an elevation of 350m (1,148 ft.). However, we recommend the funicular, which leaves every 15 minutes from 7am to 11pm. The round-trip fare is 6.60F ($5.40) for adults, 3.30F ($2.70) for children. The church was founded in 1480 after a friar, Bartolomeo da Ivrea, reportedly saw a vision of the Virgin. It was reconstructed in 1616. The basilica contains much artwork, including Bramantino's *Flight into Egypt* (1520). In a museum next door to the basilica hang masterpieces by such artists as Raphael. Another masterpiece, painted in 1870, is *Christ Carried to the Sepulcher,* by Antonio Ciseri. This procession scene is most often described as "Caravaggiesque." The stunning **panoramic view** ⊛ can be taken in from the loggia, opening onto the rooftops of Locarno with Lake Maggiore in the distance. The grounds are open March to October daily from 7am to 6:45pm. Today the general public is not admitted at will but arrangements can be made with the friars by calling in advance and booking a reservation to visit.

One of our favorite pastimes is to go **biking** along the way. At the train station (Piazza Stazione; ℗ **091/743-65-64**) you can rent bikes for 30F ($25) per day, with mountain bikes also going for 30F ($25) per day. Bikes can be rented daily from 8am to 7pm.

Fleeing the city (not that you would want to), you can take a postal bus (630) to the village of **Sonogno** in just 1 hour. At the end of the ride, you'll be in the midst of towering peaks in one of the Ticino's most scenic valleys, **Val Verzasca.** After getting off the bus, take the first left and let the yellow signs direct you to **Lavertezzo,** across shaded glens and riverbeds through perfect and bucolic valley scenery. Allow about 3½ hours to go from Sonogno to Lavertezzo. Should you tire at any time, you can take one of the postal buses that run through the valley.

THE GAMBAROGNO RIVIERA ⊛⊛⊛

The Gambarogno Riviera, with its characteristic Ticinese villages, spreads along Lake Maggiore's left shore for about 11km (6½ miles) to the Italian border. It begins at

Contone, at the foot of the Monte Ceneri, and includes part of the Piano di Magadino (plain of Magadino) as well as the wildlife refuge, Bolle di Magadino, in a delta formed by the Ticino River.

The lush vegetation, the green chestnut forests, and the iridescent colors of the lake ranging from azure to emerald green give a uniqueness to this well-preserved region. Thanks to its Mediterranean climate, the annual temperatures average 59°F (15°C). In summer the weather is ideal for all aquatic sports. The Riviera isn't just a lakeshore but a steep mountain sloping up from the lake. On one side it is crowned by Monte Tamaro, at 1,950m (6,396 ft.) above sea level, and on the other by Monte Gambarogno, at 1,710m (5,609 ft.). It is this latter mountain that gives its name to the region. There's a panorama of the Alps from Monte Rosa on the west to the chain of Ticinese Alps on the north.

The region is riddled with some 201km (125 miles) of **footpaths.** The Locarno Tourist Bureau (see "Essentials," above) distributes a map indicating every trail; this map also outlines various itineraries with the time that it takes to cover them.

One path indicated on the map provides access to the whole area, from the mouth of the Ticino River to the village of Magadino, from which the biological cycles of local species can be observed. More than 300 different kinds of birds alone live and nest in this tangle of vegetation. **Ente Turistico del Gambarogno**, via Cantonale, CH-6574 Vira (Gambarogno; © **091/795-18-66**), arranges guided tours of the area in a rowboat but only on Thursday. Open January to May and November and December, Monday to Friday 8am to noon and 2 to 6pm; June, September, and October, Monday to Friday 8am to noon and 2 to 6pm, Saturday 9am to noon; July and August Monday to Friday 8am to 6:30pm, Saturday 9am to noon and 3 to 5pm, and Sunday 9am to noon.

SHOPPING

Most of the merchandise that's for sale in Locarno is practical instead of glittery. There is a cluster of fashionable boutiques along piazza Grande, the centerpiece of the town's shopping district, but overall, shoppers usually do best by wandering through the sprawling spaces of the town's three department stores. These are **Globus,** Largo Zorzi (© **091/756-39-39**), where a worthy collection of local handicrafts and Swiss souvenirs is for sale; the somewhat less upscale but just as comprehensive **Mannore,** Piazza Grande (© **091/756-86-99**); and **Migros,** via Franchini 31 (© **091/756-88-11**). Migros is known in other corners of Switzerland only as an American-style grocery-store chain, but in Locarno the store sells Italian and Swiss food, wine, and specialty goods such as prosciutto, as well as hardware, clothing, souvenirs of the region, and virtually everything else you'd expect in a major department store.

Does your proximity to Italy make you thirsty for the fruits of the grape? Two family-run vineyards lie within 3km (2 miles) of Locarno, and both sell bottles of their products from the premises. They are **Delea,** signposted in the hamlet of Losone, a short drive north of Locarno (© **091/791-08-17**), and **Matasci,** signposted in the hamlet of Tenero (© **091/735-60-11**). Each produces both white and red wines, all of which are for sale.

WHERE TO STAY

Locarno has many good hotels that accommodate travelers on their way to or from Italy. You can also spend a pleasant vacation along the lake here.

EXPENSIVE

Grand Hotel Locarno (*Kids*)   This very grand hotel opened in 1876 to celebrate the inauguration of the St. Gotthard railway line; nearly half a century later it provided accommodations for some of the most important leaders of Europe during the Locarno conference. The hotel sits amid gardens in the middle of town, facing the lake. You get grand comfort here. The salons on the main floor are capped with Belle Epoque frescoes of flowers, cherubs, and mythological figures. The hotel is large, well managed, and comfortable, with the best and most expensive rooms facing the lake. The hotel's activities for children make it a family favorite.

Via Semplone 17, CH-6600 Locarno-Muralto. © 091/743-02-82. Fax 091/743-30-13. www.grand-hotel-locarno.ch. 80 units. 180F–356F ($148–$292) double. Half board 35F ($29) extra. Rates include buffet breakfast. Children under 12 stay free in parent's room. AE, DC, MC, V. Free parking. Closed Nov. **Amenities:** Restaurant; bar; outdoor heated pool; tennis court; children's center; limited room service; babysitting; laundry service/dry cleaning; rooms for guests w/limited mobility. *In room:* TV, dataport, minibar, hair dryer, safe (in some).

Hotel Orselina   Guests enjoy a dramatic view from this peaceful five-story oasis in a suburb north of town, accessible by funicular from Orselina. Situated on a hillside, it resembles a Spanish parador. The lake is visible in the distance. Its sloping lawns, shaded loggias, and many-tiered subtropical gardens may cause you to linger for a month at this tranquil retreat. It's got everything but a lakeside location. The midsize to spacious rooms are well furnished and comfortable, each with a firm French bed and a balcony facing south. Those in the newer wing are more up-to-date, although all the accommodations are warmly inviting.

Via Santuario 10, CH-6600 Orselina-Locarno. © 091/735-73-50. Fax 091/735-73-51. www.orselina.com. 74 units. 356F–466F ($292–$382) double; 508F–620F ($417–$508) suite. Rates include half board. MC, V. Outdoor parking 5F ($4.10), garage parking 8F–12F ($6.55–$9.85). Closed Dec 1–Feb 25. **Amenities:** Restaurant; bar; 2 heated pools (1 indoor); tennis court; health club; Jacuzzi; sauna; children's playground; limited room service; laundry service/dry cleaning; rooms for guests w/limited mobility. *In room:* TV, dataport, minibar, hair dryer, safe (in some).

Hotel Reber au Lac   This elegantly patrician hotel is the grandest resort at Locarno and has been run by the Reber family since it opened in 1886. A genteel favorite, it shuns ostentation for solid, gracious, bourgeois comfort. Spacious gardens surround the hotel, and some of the structure, notably the west wing, has been modernized. Some of the best rooms, those with frontal views of the lake, remain the way things used to be, and one room is available for those with limited mobility. Regardless of your room assignment, each unit is generally spacious and all are well furnished with well-maintained plumbing. A bathing beach and private pier are also on the premises.

Viale Verbano 55, CH-6600 Locarno-Muralto. © 091/735-87-00. Fax 091/735-87-01. www.hotel-reber.ch. 70 units. 290F–510F ($238–$418) double; 510F–610F ($418–$500) suite. Rates include buffet breakfast. Half board 45F ($37) per person extra. AE, DC, MC, V. Parking 11F ($9) in private garage. **Amenities:** 3 restaurants; bar; outdoor heated pool; tennis court; sauna; limited room service; massage; laundry service/dry cleaning; 1 room for guests w/limited mobility; private lakeshore beach. *In room:* TV, dataport, minibar, hair dryer, safe.

Ramada-Treff La Palma au Lac   Dating from the mid-1950s (and looking it), this balconied hotel of six- and seven-story buildings faces the lake and is a particular favorite of clients who were young when Queen Elizabeth was. Sun chairs and chaise longues are set up on the terrace. The updated public rooms are decorated with oil paintings and tapestries and retain their 19th-century grace. The elegantly furnished and spacious bedrooms have an Italian flair, and units with private balconies overlook the lake.

Viale Verbano 29, CH-6600 Locarno-Muralto. © 091/735-36-36. Fax 091/735-36-16. www.ramada-treff.ch. 68 units. 280F–420F ($230–$344) double; 460F–520F ($377–$426) suite. Rates include buffet breakfast. AE, DC, MC, V.

Free parking outside. **Amenities:** 2 restaurants; bar; sauna; limited room service; massage; laundry service/dry cleaning; rooms for guests w/limited mobility. *In room:* TV, dataport, minibar, hair dryer.

MODERATE

Hotel Belvedere ★★ *(Finds)*   Set on a steep hillside in the upper heights of Locarno, this ocher-colored neoclassical hotel is a beautifully landscaped retreat. It was built in 1910 on the foundations of a 300-year-old house. Reopened in 1990 after 4 years of total restoration, it offers modernized comforts and sweeping views of the lake from each of its streamlined and contemporary bedrooms. All but three of its bedrooms have a private balcony, and 20 of the accommodations come with bathrooms with private showers, while the rest have combination tub/showers.

Via ai Monti della Trinità 44, CH-6600 Locarno. © 091/751-03-63. Fax 091/751-52-39. www.belvedere-locarno.ch. 81 units. 260F–346F ($213–$284) double; 330F–420F ($271–$344) suite. Rates include buffet breakfast. Half board 40F ($33) per person extra. AE, DC, MC, V. Parking 13F ($11). Take Locarno's only funicular, departing from via Ramogna near the lakefront, to its 2nd stop (Belvedere), a few steps from the hotel. **Amenities:** 2 restaurants; bar; 2 pools (1 saltwater heated indoor); health club; Jacuzzi; limited room service; massage; laundry service/dry cleaning; nonsmoking rooms; rooms for guests w/limited mobility. *In room:* TV, dataport, minibar, hair dryer, safe.

Remorino Hotel-Garni ★ *(Finds)*   In a secluded residential area a short walk from the center of town, this vastly improved hotel lies only 2 minutes from the lakeside promenade. For almost 3 decades it has been owned by the Kirchlechner-Qualizza family, which now personally directs the management. All the bedrooms have new furnishings along with immaculately maintained bathrooms, 10 of which come only with shower. Try, if possible, for a bedroom facing the lake. The garden is especially inviting, with its Mediterranean plants such as camellia, magnolia, and olive and palm trees.

Via Verbano 29, CH-6648 Minusio-Locarno. © 091/743-10-33. Fax 091/743-74-29. www.remorino.ch. 25 units. 160F–320F ($131–$262) double. Rates include buffet breakfast. AE, V. Free parking outdoors, 12F ($9.85) in garage. Closed Nov–Feb. **Amenities:** Heated outdoor pool; laundry service/dry cleaning; free bikes. *In room:* A/C (in some), TV, dataport, minibar, hair dryer, safe.

Rosa Seegarten *(Value)*   For good value in Locarno, try this old-fashioned, cream-colored hotel on the lake, a 3-minute walk from the train station. Half board is encouraged. Meals are served on a lakeside terrace under a grape arbor. This is the largest terrace in town, capable of seating between 150 and 200 people. All the comfortable but functionally furnished small rooms have a toilet and shower.

Viale Verbano 25, CH-6600 Locarno. © 091/743-87-31. Fax 091/743-50-02. www.rosa-seegarten.ch. 37 units. 200F–300F ($164–$246) double. Rates include buffet breakfast. Half board 35F ($29) per person extra. AE, DC, MC, V. Free parking. Closed Nov–Mar 15. **Amenities:** Restaurant. *In room:* TV, minibar (in some rooms), hair dryer, safe (in some rooms).

INEXPENSIVE

Camelia   Surrounded by a sumptuous garden, this hotel in the Muralto section of Locarno is family run and inviting. Its charm lies in its romantic architecture of the early 20th century. The bedrooms, however, are so modern they look almost functional but are comfortable and well maintained. The food is one good reason to stay here, especially if you like Italian specialties. The staff is also most helpful, arranging bungee jumping, rock climbing, canyoning, and other activities such as helping you rent motorbikes. The hotel also shuttles guests to and from the local train station and the airport.

Via G.G. Nessi 9, CH-6600 Muralto-Locarno. © 091/743-00-21. Fax 091/743-00-22. www.camelia.ch. 41 units. 178F–192F ($146–$157) double. AE, DC, MC, V. **Amenities:** Restaurant; bar; business services; laundry service; 1 room for guests w/limited mobility; nonsmoking rooms. *In room:* TV.

Hotel dell'Angelo *(Finds*   In the center of the action, this hotel at the end of piazza Grande could be a winning choice even if you're not staying here to save money. Reconstructed in 1976, it grew up over the ruins of a building from the late 17th century. Arches on the ground floor and balconies trimmed in iron grace its facade. As with many bargain rooms, the furnishings are sparse—with much use of Formica—but they're clean and comfortable nevertheless. Freshly starched linens and immaculately scrubbed tile, shower-only bathrooms complete with bidets make the rooms more appealing. In contrast to the bedrooms, some of the public lounges are more enticing, with paintings and antiques adding a grace note. The hotel's terrace features views of the town.

Piazza Grande 1, CH-6600 Locarno. ⓒ 091/751-81-75. Fax 091/751-82-56. www.hotel-dell-angelo.ch. 55 units. 110F–210F ($90–$172) double. Rates include buffet breakfast. AE, DC, MC, V. Parking 16F ($13). **Amenities:** Restaurant; bar; reading room. *In room:* TV, dataport, hair dryer, safe.

WHERE TO DINE

Several Locarno restaurants also rent rooms. They're sometimes noisy because of all the restaurant activity going on in the same building, but they are bargains and centrally located. At least you won't have to worry about appointing a designated driver for the evening. Choices include the **Cittadella** and the **Ristorante Zurigo.**

EXPENSIVE

Centenario ✸✸✸ FRENCH/ITALIAN   There is no finer dining in Locarno than that found here, not even in the restaurants of the most deluxe hotels. The dining room, with austere white walls and straight-back chairs, has a simplicity that contrasts with the colorful creations of Gérard Perriard. The menu is based on fresh ingredients from the market. Seasonal specialties—and delightful ones at that—include sea bass with fennel, foie gras of duck with salad, lobster salad in mango sauce, and stuffed lamb in asparagus sauce. For an unusual first course, ask for a cold consommé of quail eggs garnished with caviar.

Lungolago 17, Muralto. ⓒ 091/743-82-22. Reservations required. Main courses 32F–60F ($26–$49); fixed-price menu 58F–130F ($48–$107). AE, DC, MC, V. Tues–Sat noon–2pm and 7–10pm. Closed 3 weeks in Feb and 3 weeks in July.

Restaurant Cittadella ✸ MEDITERRANEAN   Located in the center of the Old Town, this restaurant complex is separated from the narrow cobblestone street by a granite arcade draped with vines. The downstairs trattoria has timbered ceilings, stucco walls, and an informal ambience. Upstairs is a chic enclave of *cuisine moderne* deftly and imaginatively prepared. Specialties include a goose-liver terrine and a salad of large shrimp with nuts and mango. A mixed grill with saltwater and freshwater fish is delicious.

If you don't object to the often-noisy streets of the historic Old Town, you'll find 10 simply furnished bedrooms upstairs renting for 130F to 160F ($107–$131) for a double, including a buffet breakfast.

Via Cittadella 18. ⓒ 091/751-58-85. Fax 091/751-77-59. Reservations required. Restaurant (upstairs) main courses 45F–80F ($37–$66); fixed-price gourmet menu 76F ($62). Trattoria (downstairs) main courses 35F–50F ($29–$41); pizzas 15F–20F ($12–$16). AE, DC, MC, V. Tues–Sun noon–2pm and 7–11pm.

MODERATE

Restaurant La Carbonara SWISS/ITALIAN   There's a well-stocked bar near the entrance of this restaurant, separated from the dining room by a glass partition. The stucco walls are decorated with original paintings and copper pots. Patrons of this restaurant are regaled with full-flavored dishes perfectly prepared. Specialties include veal kidney with grappa and mushrooms, saltimbocca (veal with ham), and a large pasta menu, featuring macaroni with four different types of cheese. Other dishes include *braciola alla pizzaiola* (stuffed beef in a tomato sauce), grilled shrimp, and 15 types of pizza.

Piazza Stazione. (© 091/743-67-14. Reservations not required. Main courses 20F–50F ($16–$41); fixed-price menu 18F–25F ($15–$21). AE, DC, MC, V. Daily 11:30am–midnight.

LOCARNO AFTER DARK

Nightlife in Locarno may not impress you, as it's a lot quieter here than in larger, and more extroverted, Ticino cities such as Lugano. So either haul yourself off to Lugano for the night, or drag out your dinner and have a nightcap in the bar at your hotel. If this idea doesn't particularly appeal to you, you may opt for a stroll along the lakefront, stopping perhaps at the **Café Debarcadero,** lungolago G. Motta (© 091/751-05-55), which stays open every night till midnight. Debarcadero also offers pizzas and pastas for 12F to 18F ($9.85–$15). Another option is the cozy bar in the **Hotel Arcadia,** Lungolago G. Motta (© 091/756-18-18), where potted palms, rattan furniture, and black-and-pink marble flooring evoke a Caribbean hideaway. Piano music sometimes accompanies the liquor.

There's a congenial bar tucked away next to the dining room of the previously recommended **Ristorante La Carbonara** (© 091/743-67-14).

One of the best piano bars is the **Palm'Arte** at the Hotel La Palma au Lac, viale Verbano 29, Locarno-Muralto (© 091/735-36-36).

If you're intrigued with gambling, you may decide to spin the small-stakes wheel of fortune at the town's obscure and rather dull casino, the **Kursaal Locarno,** largo Zorzi (© 091/756-30-30). Open every day of the year but Christmas, from noon to 3am Monday to Thursday and noon to 4am Friday to Sunday, it offers a small bar area, lots of noisy slot machines, and croupiers at blackjack and roulette tables.

3 Ascona ⊙*

4km (2½ miles) SW of Locarno; 42km (26 miles) NW of Lugano

Once a tiny fishing port, Ascona has swiftly developed into a resort to rival nearby Locarno. Located snugly on Lake Maggiore, it has long been a popular rendezvous point for painters, writers, and celebrities. Lenin found the place ideal, as did Isadora Duncan and Carl Jung. Rudolf Steiner, Hermann Hesse, and Paul Klee also lived here. Today Ascona is one of the most popular destinations in the Ticino.

New developments have obscured much of the Old Town cherished by these famous people, but the heart of Ascona is still worth exploring—although you'll use up a lot of shoe leather. It has colorful little shops, art galleries (some good, some of the souvenir variety), and antiques stores.

Because of its mild climate, Ascona has subtropical vegetation. Flowers bloom year-round. Facilities include a golf course, a *lido* (beach), and a *Kursaal* (casino).

ESSENTIALS

GETTING THERE   Ascona has no railway station of its own, so most train passengers disembark at nearby Locarno and transfer to a bus or taxi for the short ride to Ascona. Locarno has good connections to the region's major railway junction of Bellinzona, which has frequent express train connections from Milan and Zurich. For **rail information** and schedules, call © 0900/300-300.

A handful of buses connects Ascona with the railroad junction of Locarno, a short distance to the northeast. The bus ride takes 15 minutes, and departures are every 15 minutes and cost 2.60F ($2.15) one-way. For bus information, call Locarno's tourist office (see "Essentials" in section 2, earlier in this chapter).

If you're driving, continue west from Locarno along Route 13.

The best way for many to get around Ascona and the rim of the lake itself is by bike, which can be rented at **Facchi Claudio,** via Locarno 105 (© **091/791-13-41**). The cost, depending on the bike, ranges from 17F to 20F ($11–$13) per day. Hours are Monday to Saturday from 8:30am to noon and 2:30 to 6pm, Sunday 8:45 to 11:45am only.

VISITOR INFORMATION   The Ascona Tourist Board, in Casa Serondine, piazzetta San Pietro (© **091/791-00-90;** www.ascona.ch), is open mid-March to late October, Monday to Friday 9am to 6pm, Saturday 10am to 6pm, and Sunday 2:30 to 5pm.

SEEING THE SIGHTS

Collegio Pontificio Papio, off via Cappelle, has one of the most beautiful Renaissance courtyards in Switzerland. Dating from 1584, the building has two-story Italianate loggias. The **Chiesa Santa Maria della Misericordia** is part of the cloisters of the Collegio Pontificio Papio. Built at the end of the 14th century, it contains one of the largest late-Gothic frescoes in Switzerland.

Casa Serodine (also called Casa Borrani), which lies off piazza G. Motta, was built in 1620 and has one of the most richly embellished facades of any secular structure in the country.

Museo Comunale d'Arte Moderna, via Borgo 34 (© **091/759-81-40**), has both changing exhibitions of modern art and a permanent collection, the latter including works by Klee and Utrillo. It is open March to December, Tuesday to Saturday from 10am to noon and 3 to 6pm, and Sunday 4 to 6pm, charging adults 5F ($4.10) and students, seniors, and children 3F ($2.45).

Near the town, **Isole di Brissago** ⊛, off the shore of Lake Maggiore, contains a botanical garden of Mediterranean and subtropical flora. The gardens can be reached by boat not only from the center of Ascona but also from other lakeside locales, including Locarno. Boats depart Ascona daily at 9:30am and run throughout the day, with the last departure from the island back to Ascona at 6pm. The ride takes 10 minutes and costs 13F ($11). Admission to the botanical park is an additional 7F ($5.75).

You can also visit the little village of **Ronco** ⊛⊛ along the corniche road west, an 18km (11-mile) trip. This very Mediterranean-type village is on a slope in one of the most charming settings in all of the Ticino. Erich Maria Remarque, the German author of *All Quiet on the Western Front,* lived here and is buried in the cemetery of the little church.

SHOPPING

Ascona doesn't place much emphasis on the sale of cutesy souvenirs, and as such, you'll have to look hard for shops selling only handicrafts. You'll find postcards and a limited array of smaller, less impressive items imported directly from Italy at newsstands and kiosks in the town's pedestrian zone, which is centered around via Borgo and its offshoots. More prevalent, however, are stylish shops selling luxury goods such as crystal at **Baccarat,** Carrà dei Nasi 22 (© **091/791-21-38**). For upscale, Milan-inspired clothing for women, the best shop is **Jiuditta,** in the Galleria della Carra (© **091/791-20-19**).

More intriguing are any of the town's roster of antiques dealers and art galleries. The town's most appealing antiques store, **Monna Lisa,** via Collegio 6 (© **091/791-45-52**), is managed by Hans-Peter Lehmann and his English/Irish wife, Liz. Inside, you'll find a worthy collection of china, silver, paintings, and furniture.

WHERE TO STAY

Bus no. 31 from Locarno services the hotels listed below.

VERY EXPENSIVE

Albergo Casa Berno ★★ *Finds*   Built into a hillside on a forest road above the town, this deluxe hotel with several balconied wings is a gem of a retreat. Its good-size rooms are comfortably furnished—some of them with elegant Louis XVI–style chairs. Each room has a concrete balcony with a southern exposure, and all are equipped with beautifully maintained bathrooms. The view extends from Bellinzona (see section 1, earlier in this chapter) to the Islands of Brissago.

Via G. Madonna, CH-6612 Ascona. © 091/791-32-32. Fax 091/792-11-14. www.casaberno.ch. 62 units. 424F–502F ($348–$412) double; 576F ($472) junior suite. Rates include half board. AE, DC, MC. V. Free parking. Closed late Oct to Mar. **Amenities:** Restaurant; bar; outdoor heated pool; sauna; limited room service; massage; babysitting; laundry service/dry cleaning. *In room:* TV, dataport, minibar, hair dryer.

Castello del Sole ★★★   The grandest hotel in Ascona is surrounded by an 8-hectare (20-acre) park and green meadows. This peaceful haven is near the Maggia River, at the point where it flows into Lake Maggiore. It has the atmosphere of a private estate, 2km (1½ miles) from the center of town. There's an antique palazzo with many courtyards. The spacious public rooms have vaulted ceilings, granite columns, and marble terraces, with one room available for those with limited mobility. The rooms, which come in various shapes and sizes, have balconies and beautiful furniture, along with deluxe bathrooms. The suites are in a building east of the main hotel. Located nearby is the 18-hole golf course Locarno.

Via Muraccio 142, CH-6612 Ascona. © 091/791-02-02. Fax 091/792-11-18. www.relaischateaux.com/castellosole. 85 units. 540F–700F ($443–$574) double; 780F–940F ($640–$771) junior suite; 1,600F ($1,312) deluxe suite. Rates include continental breakfast. Half board 50F ($41) per person extra. AE, DC, MC, V. Free parking. **Amenities:** 2 restaurants; 2 pools (1 heated indoor); golf course nearby; 7 tennis courts; fitness center; spa; sauna; salon; 24-hr. room service; babysitting; massage; laundry service/dry cleaning; 1 room for guests w/limited mobility. *In room:* TV, dataport, minibar, hair dryer, safe.

Hotel Ascolago ★   This is a large concrete-block hotel with an angular facade and a roofline inspired by a Chinese pagoda. It's ideally located in the center of town, in a park with flowers and sculpture. A portico by the entrance looks as if it was designed by Le Corbusier. Many of the spacious bedrooms have been upgraded and are fairly stylish, decorated with subtle pastels and rosewood pieces, while others linger in the stuffy, fussy mode. Each room, however, is comfortable, with rows of awning-shaded balconies opening onto views of the garden and the lake.

Via Albarelle, CH-6612 Ascona. © 091/791-20-55. Fax 091/791-42-26. www.ascolago.ch. 18 units. 280F–460F ($230–$377) double. Rates include half board. MC, V. Free parking. Closed Nov 15–Dec 15. **Amenities:** Restaurant; bar; 2 heated pools (1 indoor); sauna; windsurfing equipment; 24-hr. room service; laundry service/dry cleaning; sailing school; nonsmoking rooms; 1 room for guests w/limited mobility. *In room:* TV, dataport (in 2 rooms), minibar, hair dryer.

Relais & Châteaux Hotel Giardino ★★★   Although this atmospheric Mediterranean villa is one of four government-rated five-star hotels in Ascona, it's the most romantically appealing. Set about .4km (¼ mile) from the heart of town, connected by an antique shuttle bus that makes hourly runs back and forth, this glamorous, Mediterranean-style villa was built on a large plot of land in 1986. Today its structure incorporates Portuguese and Italian tile work, Veronese marble, antique Swiss panels imported from very old *Weinstubes* in Zurich, and some of the most sophisticated interior decor in the region. The spacious bedrooms are cozy and plushly accessorized. Most alluring of all is the lavish garden *(il giardino)*, whose illuminated lily pond is covered with a moveable stage for the entertainment, which is sometimes provided after 8pm.

Via Segnale 10, CH-6612 Ascona. Ⓒ **091/785-88-88**. Fax 091/785-88-99. www.giardino.ch. 77 units. 600F–730F ($492–$599) double; 735F–965F ($603–$791) suite. Rates include buffet breakfast. AE, DC, MC, V. Free parking. Closed mid-Nov to Mar. **Amenities:** 2 restaurants; bar; outdoor pool; health club and spa w/Jacuzzi, sauna, steam bath; 24-hr. room service; babysitting; laundry serviced/dry cleaning; nonsmoking rooms; rooms for guests w/limited mobility. *In room:* TV, dataport, minibar, hair dryer, safe.

EXPENSIVE

Hotel Sasso Boretto 🔆   The entire balconied structure of this hotel seems to be set on top of concrete columns. Glass windows frame the ground floor, which is surrounded by redbrick terraces and Mediterranean trees. Most of the bedrooms (20 are nonsmoking) are decorated in warm, monochromatic tones of brown and beige. The larger ones show Italian flair; the smaller ones are less dramatic but cozy and comfortable nonetheless, with well-maintained bathrooms.

Via Locarno 45, CH-6612 Ascona. Ⓒ **091/791-71-15**. Fax 091/786-99-00. www.sassoboretto.com. 50 units. 220F–360F ($180–$295) double. Rates include continental breakfast. Half board 40F ($33) per person extra. AE, DC, MC, V. Parking 15F ($12). Closed Jan 5–Mar 19. **Amenities:** 2 restaurants; bar; indoor heated pool; health club; sauna; 24-hr. room service; laundry service/dry cleaning; nonsmoking rooms. *In room:* A/C (in some), TV, minibar, hair dryer.

Seeschloss-Castello 🔆🔆 *(Finds)*   This gem will appeal to romantics. The tower was built in 1250 by a countess of Milan from the Ghiriglioni family. It served as the fortified dwelling of the family, which eventually controlled most of the navigation on the lake. Today palms and palmettos surround the flagstone terrace leading to the stone entryway. Pull the wrought-iron bell handle for assistance. The lobby is filled with antiques, and the spacious rooms are well maintained and comfortable, with private bathrooms with shower or combination tub/shower. The best rooms—certainly the most romantic—are those in the tower. These are ideal for both honeymooners and off-the-record weekenders.

Piazza G. Motta, CH-6612 Ascona. Ⓒ **091/791-01-61**. Fax 091/791-18-04. www.castello-seeschloss.ch. 46 units. 248F–328F ($203–$269) double; 348F–568F ($285–$466) double in the tower. Rates include buffet breakfast. Half board 38F ($31) per person extra. AE, DC, MC, V. Free parking outdoors, 19F ($16) in garage. Closed Nov to mid-Mar. **Amenities:** Restaurant; bar; outdoor heated pool; limited room service; laundry service/dry cleaning; nonsmoking rooms. *In room:* TV, dataport, minibar, hair dryer.

MODERATE

Albergo Elvezia au Lac   This hotel lies in the heart of the resort town with a cobblestone terrace facing the lake and an indoor dining room just behind it. The upper-story terrace is ringed with vines. Each room, ranging from small to medium, is priced according to its panorama over the lake and whether it has a balcony or terrace looking inward to the city. All units come with a private bathroom with shower, some containing bathtubs as well.

Piazza G. Motta 15, CH-6612 Ascona. Ⓒ **091/791-15-14**. Fax 091/791-00-03. www.hotel-elvezia.ch. 20 units. 176F–246F ($144–$202) double. Rates include continental breakfast. AE, DC, MC, V. Parking 12F ($9.85). Closed Nov–Feb. **Amenities:** Restaurant; limited room service; laundry service. *In room:* TV, minibar.

Hotel la Perla   This white-walled hotel is located in a residential area away from the lake. Its small rooms have balconies with a good view of the mountains, and each comes with private bathroom. Note that there are three extra double rooms separated from the hotel with private bathrooms, but without balconies, costing 150F to 180F ($123–$148).

Via Collina 14, CH-6612 Ascona. ℂ **091/791-35-77**. Fax 091/791-79-62. www.laperla.ch. 50 units. 190F–220F ($156–$180) double. Rates include buffet breakfast. AE, DC, MC, V. Parking 7F ($5.75). **Amenities:** Restaurant; outdoor heated pool; breakfast-only room service; laundry service; nonsmoking rooms. *In room:* TV, dataport, minibar, safe.

Tamaro du Lac ⚘ *Finds*   A welcome is painted in Latin above the huge arch leading into the flagstone reception hall of the original core of this gracious lakefront hotel, which was formerly an abbey. Farther on is a sky-lit central courtyard, with vines growing over the massive vaults of the arcade surrounding it. In the early 1990s a comfortable, very quiet annex was added a few steps from the main building. The owners have decorated the interior with antiques and some romantic artifacts. The bedrooms, although lacking great style, are comfortably furnished and extremely well maintained, each with a private shower (some with tubs).

Piazza G. Motta 35, CH-6612 Ascona. ℂ **091/785-48-48**. Fax 091/791-29-28. www.hotel-tamaro.ch. 51 units, 41 with bathroom, in main building; 10 units, all with bathroom, in annex. 180F–290F ($148–$238) double with bathroom; 130F–150F ($107–$123) double without bathroom. Rates include breakfast. Half board 33F ($27) per person extra. AE, DC, MC, V. Parking 11F ($9) in private garage, 9F ($7.40) in private parking outside. Closed Nov 15–Mar. **Amenities:** Restaurant; limited room service; laundry service/dry cleaning; nonsmoking rooms; rooms for guests w/limited mobility. *In room:* A/C (in some), TV, minibar, hair dryer, safe.

WHERE TO DINE

The harbor of Ascona is lined with many restaurants. Most guests dine outside during the summer, by the lake. There are also many fine restaurants on the cobblestone streets of the Old Town.

EXPENSIVE

Al Pontile ITALIAN/FRENCH   Many of the restaurants along the quays look alike and have similar menus, but the decor here, with a darkly rustic interior and hanging straw lamps, seems a little warmer and more intimate than elsewhere. The food is better too. The menu might include quail with risotto, *osso buco,* and saltimbocca (veal with ham), in addition to a variety of good pasta dishes. Fish dishes include scampi, sole, and salmon. For dessert, we recommend one of the homemade pies.

Longalago G. Motta 31. ℂ **091/791-46-04**. Reservations not required. Main courses 35F–45F ($29–$37); fixed-price menu 72F–79F ($59–$65). AE, MC, V. Daily 6–9:30pm.

Aphrodite/Hostaria Giardino ⚘⚘⚘ FRENCH/ITALIAN   These two restaurants are in the most desirable deluxe hotel in Ascona, about .4km (¼ mile) from the center of town. Aphrodite, the more elegant and formal, requests that men wear jackets and ties for meals served on a flowering terrace within view of a water garden and plenty of greenery. Menu specialties change every week but include perfectly prepared modern choices, tea-smoked duck breast; wild sea bass with a saffron tomato risotto; or marinated fresh uncooked tuna in lime oil with sautéed vegetables. The chef prepares 16 different fixed-price menus whose composition changes daily, based on the seasonal ingredients available.

The Hostaria Giardino is in a cozy environment reminiscent of a mountain hideaway, with old-fashioned menu items similar to what your Italian-Swiss grandmother might have prepared for you when you were a child. Portions are copious.

In the Relais & Châteaux Hotel Giardino, via Segnale. © **091/791-01-01.** Reservations recommended. Aphrodite main courses 35F–55F ($29–$45); fixed-price menu (only on Sun) 150F ($123). Hostaria Giardino main courses 25F–35F ($21–$29). AE, DC, MC, V. Aphrodite daily 12:30–2pm and 7–9:30pm. Hostaria Giardino Wed–Mon 7–11pm. Closed Nov 16–Mar 10.

Navegna ✦ TICINESE   This is one of the best restaurants in Locarno, both for aesthetic and gastronomic reasons. If the weather permits, we highly recommend that you sit on the beautiful terrace overlooking the lake. The white tablecloths with lace edges add to the delight. If you must sit inside, the sophisticated dining room with its deep browns and soft creams has a lovely view as well—just try to get a seat next to a window. Almost all of the food here is fresh, going from owner Enrico Ravelli's farm straight to chef Marco Meneganti's kitchen. The homemade pasta is delicious, as are the poultry dishes.

Albergo Navegna, which houses Restaurant Navegna, is also a charming hotel, although it is secondary to the restaurant. Double rooms range from 150F to 250F ($123–$205) and have televisions, telephones, minibars (in some), hair dryers (in some), and balconies (in some). Try to get a south-facing room if you decide to stay here because they all have views of the lake.

Via alla Riva 2. © **091/743-22-22.** www.navegna.ch. Reservations recommended. Main courses 32F–44F ($26–$36). MC, V. Daily noon–2pm and 7–9pm. Closed Tues in Sept.

MODERATE

Al Torchio ITALIAN   The first room of this rambling restaurant offers a rustic decor, red candles, and designs painted on the plaster walls. On a warm night you may continue past the American-style salad bar in the back and turn left into the vine-covered courtyard. The well-prepared menu may include rabbit with leeks in beer sauce, filet of lamb, a divine risotto with porcini mushrooms, a winter fondue, and a succulent spaghetti with clams. An especially delectable dish is homemade tagliolini stuffed with pulverized fish and shrimp and served with a tomato sauce flavored with olive oil and fresh herbs. For dessert, try the *gelato misto* (a mixed selection of ice cream) or a sorbet with vodka. There's a garden-style piano bar in a summery courtyard.

Contrada Maggiore 1. © **091/791-71-26.** Reservations recommended. Main courses 18F–38F ($15–$31); fixed-price menu 35F–59F ($29–$48). AE, MC, V. Daily noon–2pm and 6–10pm. Closed Tues in winter.

Ristorante Borromeo ✦ SWISS/ITALIAN   Dating from around 1350, this former monastery and Catholic school is one of the most popular restaurants in the region, noted for its outdoor terrace. Local residents flock to its three rustic rooms with high ceilings. The kitchen staff is versatile, knowing how to prepare the best of both the Italian and Swiss kitchens. They use very fresh ingredients and don't oversauce. The menu may include risotto Milanese with saffron, a mixed grill, piccata Marsala, trout, scampi, and an especially good *osso buco*. On our recent rounds, we especially enjoyed saltimbocca (veal with ham), served with a potato-based gnocchi.

Via Collegio 16. © **091/791-92-81.** Reservations recommended. Main courses 25F–46F ($21–$38). AE, DC, MC, V. Daily noon–2pm and 6–10pm. Closed Mon July–Aug.

INEXPENSIVE

Osteria Nostrana (Value) PIZZA/PASTA   This is one of the most active harborfront restaurants in Ascona, with sidewalk tables overlooking the lake and its fashionable promenade. The rustically comfortable dining room serves the town's best and most reasonably priced pastas and pizzas. They also feature daily specials, sometimes as many as 15 per day, depending on the season and what's good at the market. The best pasta is the spaghetti *alla carbonara* (with meat sauce), although the linguine *ai fruitti di mare* (with shellfish) is a close runner-up, as is the fusili with heavy cream and ham. For a superb pizza, opt for the Siciliana with anchovies and black olives or the *prosciutto e funghi* (ham and mushrooms).

Piazza Giuseppe Motta. ℂ 091/791-51-58. Reservations not necessary. Pasta and pizzas 15F–25F ($12–$21). AE, DC, MC, V. Summer daily 9am–midnight; winter daily 10am–11:30pm.

ASCONA AFTER DARK

Ascona is quiet and calm, with not nearly as energetic a night scene as, say, nearby Lugano. A likable bar favored by those seeking live music is **Piper,** via Aerodromo 3 (ℂ 091/791-13-74). Finally, an establishment noted for its ability to provide feminine companionship for unaccompanied men is **Happyville,** via Borgo (ℂ 091/791-49-22), where a tiny dance floor is a lot less important than the seductively lit stage. Strip shows are usually presented nightly beginning around 11:30pm.

4 Lugano ★★★

32km (20 miles) S of Bellinzona; 229km (143 miles) S of Zurich

Lugano is a Swiss town with an Italian flavor. The Italian influence is evident in the city's cafes, sunny piazzas, cobblestone streets, and arcades. It's a city designed for walking. You can wander at leisure, exploring its historic old streets.

Lugano is built along the shore of **Lake Lugano** ★★★ , which the Italians call Lake Ceresio. The peaks of San Salvatore and Monte Brè loom on opposite sides of town. The low mountains protect it from cold alpine winds, and the climate is ideal from March to November. As the cultural center of the Ticino, Lugano has attracted many artists and casual visitors.

ESSENTIALS

GETTING THERE   The airline **Swiss,** Aeroporto Lugano (ℂ 0848/852-000), provides air links between Lugano and Zurich. Taxis await visitors at the Lugano airport for the 10-minute ride to the center of Lugano.

Lugano is a major stop along the rail lines that connect Milan with Zurich. As such, trains from all parts of Switzerland arrive throughout the day and night. For **rail information** and schedules, call ℂ 0900/300-300 or call the Lugano rail station at ℂ 091/923-66-91. Rail passengers arrive at the Lugano railroad station, piazzale della Stazione, which is in the center of the city, west of piazza Indipendenza. If your luggage is light, you can walk to many of the hotels; if not, you can take one of the taxis waiting outside the station.

Lugano is linked by bus to dozens of hamlets in the Ticino that lack rail connections. There are also long-range trains that come from Italian cities: Como (trip time: 45 min.), Venice (trip time: 5 hr.), and Milan (trip time: 90 min.).

If you're driving, pass through the St. Gotthard Tunnel and continue south along N2, via Bellinzona, all the way to Lugano.

GETTING AROUND   An explanation of fares and ticket machines can be found in a brochure distributed by the tourist office and the Public Transport Board, **Trasporti Pubblici Luganesi,** via Carducci (ℂ 058/866-72-24).

You must purchase a ticket before boarding a **bus** or a **train.** If you're caught without one, you may have to pay a 55F ($45) fine. You can purchase a 1-day ticket from automatic ticket machines for 5F ($4.10). This ticket allows you unlimited travel for 24 hours from the moment you purchase it. It includes the Funicular Lugano–Main Street SBBM, but not line 12, Lugano-Brè.

For **taxi service,** call ✆ **091/922-88-33.**

The town of Lugano and the lakefront itself are ideal for **bikers.** You can rent a bike at the railway station in Lugano (✆ **051/221-56-42**), at ticket window no. 1. Prices begin at 31F ($25) per day, depending on the type of bicycle.

VISITOR INFORMATION   The **Lugano Tourist Office** is at riva Albertolli 5 (✆ **091/913-32-32;** www.lugano-tourism.ch). It's open Monday to Friday from 9am to 7:30pm, Saturday from 9am to 5:30pm, and Sunday from 10am to 5pm.

CITY LAYOUT   The center of town is **piazza Riforma,** dominated by a neoclassical city hall constructed in 1844. From here you can explore the ancient streets of the Old Town on foot.

Lugano is built along several lakeside quays, of which **riva Albertolli, riva Vincenzo Vela,** and **riva Antonio Caccia** are the most important. They are ideal for long, leisurely walks. They run from piazza Cassarate to piazza Paradiso.

Other major squares of Lugano, also by the lake, are **piazza Riziero Rezzonico** and **piazza Alessandro Manzioni,** the latter with gardens.

The biggest park of Lugano, also opening onto the lake, is the **Parco Civico,** site of the Casino, the Palazzo dei Congressi, and the town's large swimming pool.

Directly east of the center is **Castagnola,** a suburb and site of the Villa Favorita, with its celebrated collection of art.

Towering over Lugano are two hills, **Monte San Salvatore,** at 898m (2,945 ft.), and **Monte Brè,** at 918m (3,011 ft.). They're ideal for full- or half-day excursions.

SEEING THE SIGHTS

The city tourist office (see "Essentials," above) offers a **walking tour** with a guide on Monday at 9:30am, April to October. These free tours depart from the Chiesa degli Angioli at piazza Luini.

IN TOWN

Parco Civico 🏵🏵 is the city park along Lake Lugano. It contains the Palazzo dei Congressi (the convention center), the Casino, and the Villa Ciani art museum. Outdoor concerts are presented in the summer.

Cattedrale di San Lorenzo (St. Lawrence), via Cattedrale, in the Old Town, was originally a Romanesque church. It was reconstructed in the 13th and 14th centuries and overhauled in the 17th and 18th centuries. It has three outstanding Renaissance doorways and a baroque interior. Look for the 16th-century tabernacle at the end of the south aisle; it was designed by the Rodari brothers of Maroggia.

The other important church is the **Chiesa di Santa Maria degli Angeli (Church of St. Mary of the Angels),** piazza Luini, located on the south side of the resort. This church was built at the end of the 15th century and is known throughout the Ticino for its **frescoes** 🏵🏵 by Bernardino Luini, the Lombard painter. His huge fresco *The Crucifixion* dates from 1529. Many critics have compared the beauty of his work to that of Leonardo da Vinci. John Ruskin found an "unstudied sweetness" in Luini's work. The church was occupied by Franciscans until 1848.

NEARBY ATTRACTIONS

The best way to discover the small lakeside villages around Lugano is to rent a bike at the train station (see above) and set off to explore. Arm yourself with a good map from the tourist office and head for the **nature reserve** of Origlio Lake, proceeding to Ponte Capriasca, where you can visit a **parish church** with a copy of Leonardo da Vinci's *Last Supper.* From here you can continue to the villages of **Tesserete** and **Colla** along the left valley side of Cassarate, going through the woods with a marked trail to **Sonvico.** On your way back to Lugano, you'll pass through the idyllic villages of **Dino, Ponte di Valle,** and finally Lugano. In all, the trip takes in about 37km (23 miles) and can be done in about 4 hours.

Swiss Miniature Village *(Kids)*   Small replicas of the major buildings in Switzerland are displayed along a labyrinth of asphalt paths. There's also a miniature of the twin castles in Sion. You can purchase an official guidebook for detailed explanations. This attraction is especially popular with children.

Via Cantonale, Melide-Lugano. © 091/640-10-60. Admission 13F ($11) adults, 7F ($5.75) children 15 and under. Daily 9am–6pm. Closed Nov to mid-Mar. Take a train from Lugano Village.

Villa Favorita *(★★ Finds)*   The much-married and much-divorced—and the very rich—Baron von Thyssen-Bornemisza was a headline-making legend in his day. He was also one of the world's greatest art collectors, his holdings rivaled only by Queen Elizabeth II. The bulk of his collection was sold to launch the Thyssen-Bornemisza Museum in Madrid. In a 17th-century mansion, Villa Favorita has been greatly reduced in scope but what art remains is worth a visit. Paintings are by such figures as Lucien Freud, Edward Hopper, Jackson Pollock, Giorgio de Chirico, and Andrew Wyeth. Even if you don't like art, the gardens are worth a visit, planted with both regional and exotic flora.

Via Rivbera 14, Castagnola. © 091/972-17-41. Admission 10F ($8.20). Easter–Oct Fri–Sun 10am–5pm. Bus: 1.

Villa Heleneum   Lying 4km (2½ miles) northwest of Lugano, this landmark building is along the much-frequented walk to Gandria. It contains the Museum of Extra-European Cultures, which exhibits objects from Oceania, Indonesia, and Africa. The collection was donated by Serge Brignoni, an exponent of the surrealist movement. There's also a center for ethnographic studies, as well as a library annexed to the museum.

Via Cortivo 24, Lugano-Castagnola. © 091/971-73-53. Admission 5F ($4.10) adults, 3F ($2.45) children. Wed–Sun 10am–5pm. Bus: 1.

THE ACTIVE VACATION PLANNER

Watersports are popular in Lugano; you can also bike or play golf and tennis.

BOATING   You can rent rowboats and motorboats along the lakefront.

SAILING   Go to **Circolo Velico,** Lago di Lugano, Foce Cassarate (© **091/972-62-98**), which charges 15F to 20F ($12–$16) per hour or 55F to 100F ($45–$82) for a half day, depending on the size of the boat.

SCUBA   Try **Lugano-Sub,** Riva Paradiso 23 (© **091/994-37-40**).

SWIMMING   The **Lido** (© **091/971-40-41**) is a sandy stretch of beach along the lake. You can also relax on the lawn or eat at the cafeteria on the terrace. Admission to the Lido is 6F ($4.90) for adults, 4F ($3.30) for children 9 to 20, and 1F (80¢) for children 8 and under. Rental of a cabana costs another 6F to 10F ($4.90–$8.20) deposit. The beach is open in the summer daily from 9am to 7:30pm.

In addition, many hotels have heated pools, some with salt water.

WATERSKIING   The **Club Nautico-Lugano,** via Calloni 9 (© **091/649-61-39**), between Lugano and Melide, charges 150F ($123) per hour, instruction included.

WINDSURFING   You can windsurf on the lake at **Club Nautico-Lugano,** via Calloni 9 (© **091/649-61-39**), between Lugano and Melide. The cost is 17F ($14) per hour.

SHOPPING

Its role as capital of Italian-speaking Switzerland almost guarantees that Lugano's selection of merchandise will include a cosmopolitan blend of Teutonic and Mediterranean merchandise. Most of it can be viewed along either side of the resort's main shopping street, **via Nassa.** The richest trove of handicrafts is available at **Bottega dell'Artigiano,** Quartiere Maghetti, Piazza Indipendenza 1 (© **091/922-81-40**). Managed and maintained by the Cooperativa per l'Artigianato Ticinese, a quasi-governmental organization for the promotion of old-fashioned handicrafts, it offers textiles, woodcarvings, pottery, and metalware, most of them made in the Ticino.

You'll find five floors of department-store shopping at everybody's favorite large store, **Manor,** piazza Dante (© **091/912-76-99**). A roughly equivalent department store, with some gift items and more of an emphasis on foodstuffs, groceries, hardware, and housewares, is **Migros,** via Pretorio 15 (© **091/913-72-13**). If you're looking for chocolates and pastries, head for a bakery that many locals remember from their childhood, **Münger,** via Luvini 4 (© **091/985-69-43**).

WHERE TO STAY

Lugano has hotels in all price categories. Many are located in the suburbs of Paradiso, Cassarate, and Castagnola.

VERY EXPENSIVE

Hotel Splendide Royal *金金金*   The splendor of the 19th century is evident in the elegant architecture of this mansard-roofed hotel. Built in 1888, the Splendide Royal has welcomed many famous people (and even a few infamous ones). Maria, queen of Romania; Vittorio Emanuele di Savoia; George H. W. Bush; and Sophia Loren have stayed here. The public rooms are decorated with columns, crystal-and-gilt chandeliers, Venetian furniture, and Oriental rugs. Guests have a choice of bedrooms, either in the flowery rooms of the original landmark wing, where some rooms contain ceiling frescoes, or in the 1983 modern wing, where the decoration is in soft colors and the furnishings in a streamlined beech. The swimming pool is shaped like an oyster, and there's a rock garden.

Riva A. Caccia 7, CH-6900 Lugano. © 091/985-77-11. Fax 091/985-77-22. www.splendide.ch. 96 units. Mar 15–Oct 500F–700F ($410–$574) double, 1,300F ($1,066) suite; Nov–Mar 14 420F–500F ($344–$410) double, 950F ($779) suite. Rates include continental breakfast. Half board 65F ($53) per person extra. AE, DC, MC, V. Free parking outdoors, 30F ($25) in garage. Bus: 1. **Amenities:** Restaurant; bar; indoor heated pool; fitness room; sauna; 24-hr. room service; massage; babysitting; laundry service/dry cleaning; nonsmoking rooms. *In room:* A/C, TV, dataport, minibar, hair dryer, safe.

Principe Leopoldo & Residence *金金金*   This extravagant mansion lies on a panoramic hill site, Collina d'Oro (Golden Hill), in an exclusive neighborhood overlooking the lake. The villa was built in 1868 as the home of Prince Leopold, of Austria's von Hohenzollerns. After World War I it was sold to a Swiss industrialist. In 1986 the villa was transformed into the Ticino's smallest luxury hotel, with an understated Italian style. Today it's our favorite hotel in Lugano. There's a modern addition with a two-story atrium and a cascade of illuminated water. The suites have beige

travertine trim, and each spacious room has a terrace overlooking the lake and the suburb of Paradiso. The hotel has more amenities and services than any other in the
Ticino, including deluxe toiletries, well-lit vanity mirrors, pressing facilities, and even
complimentary shoeshines. The hotel restaurant is one of the finest and most elegant
in the Ticino (see below).

Via Montalbano 5, CH-6900 Lugano. © 091/985-88-55. Fax 091/985-88-25. www.leopoldohotel.com. 77 units.
470F–590F ($385–$484) double; from 1,100F ($902) suite. Rates include buffet breakfast. Children under 12 stay free
in parent's room. AE, DC, MC, V. Parking 25F ($21). **Amenities:** 2 restaurants; bar; 2 outdoor heated pools; 2 tennis
courts; fitness center; Jacuzzi; sauna; concierge; minibus transportation, including airport pickups; business center;
24-hr. room service; massage; babysitting; laundry service/dry cleaning; nonsmoking rooms. *In room:* A/C, TV, dataport, minibar, hair dryer, safe.

EXPENSIVE

Grand Hotel Villa Castagnola au Lac ★★★   The beauty of this ocher, Mediter-
ranean-style villa across the street from the lake is enhanced by its exotic trees and
plants—even banana trees, no less. The public rooms contain marble or parquet
floors; some have large fireplaces in consonance with their baronial decor. Each spacious bedroom is uniquely and luxuriously furnished, decorated tastefully in Mediterranean styling. The manager has instructed his staff to pay attention to even the
smallest detail to make guests feel at home. All rooms open onto views of the lake and
the subtropical park, and all but eight contain a splendid bathroom with tub and
shower (the rest with shower only).

Viale Castagnola 31, CH-6906 Lugano. © 091/973-25-55. Fax 091/973-25-50. www.villacastagnola.com. 93 units.
370F–520F ($303–$426) double; from 770F ($631) suite. Rates include buffet breakfast. Half board 65F ($53) per person extra. AE, DC, MC, V. Free parking outdoors, 10F ($8.20) in garage. Bus: 1. **Amenities:** 2 restaurants; bar; indoor
heated pool; indoor golf; 2 tennis courts; fitness center and spa w/sauna and Turkish bath; watersports rentals; 24-
hr. room service; massage; laundry service/dry cleaning; nonsmoking rooms. *In room:* A/C (in most units), TV, dataport, fridge, hair dryer, iron/board, safe.

Romantik Hotel Ticino ★★ *Finds*   The central courtyard of this former 15th-cen-
tury convent is covered with a glass ceiling for year-round comfort. In front of the narrow hotel is one of the most charming squares in the Old Town. Antique cupboards
and chests are in the stairwell. Each of the small bedrooms is uniquely furnished, usually with 19th-century provincial pieces. They are exceedingly comfortable with well-
maintained plumbing.

Piazza Cioccaro 1, CH-6901 Lugano. © 091/922-77-72. Fax 091/923-62-78. www.romantikhotels.com. 18 units.
390F–490F ($320–$402) double; 680F–790F ($558–$648) suite. Rates include buffet breakfast. AE, DC, MC, V. Parking 25F ($21). Bus: 1 or 2. **Amenities:** Restaurant; bar; limited room service; laundry service/dry cleaning; nonsmok-
ing rooms. *In room:* A/C, TV (on request), dataport, minibar, hair dryer.

MODERATE

Holiday Inn Lugano Centre   This first-class chain hotel was built in 1975 out of
concrete and glass and is today one of the finest hotels on the outskirts of Lugano. The
seven-story high-rise is near the Lugano-Sud exit from the main highway. Many of the
public rooms have red leather accents and wood trim. The showplace salon has
French-style armchairs, Oriental rugs, and large windows with a view of the garden.
The bedrooms are quite comfortable and well equipped.

Via Geretta 15, CH-6902 Lugano-Paradiso. © 091/986-38-38. Fax 091/986-38-39. www.holiday-inn.com/luganocentre.
92 units. 280F–320F ($230–$262) double; from 320F ($262) suite. Half board 48F ($39) per person extra. AE, DC, MC, V.
Free parking outdoors, 15F ($12) in garage. Bus: 1 or 9. **Amenities:** Restaurant; bar; 2 heated pools (1 indoor); health club;
2 saunas; 24-hr. room service; laundry service/dry cleaning; nonsmoking rooms; 1 room for guests w/limited mobility. *In
room:* A/C, TV, dataport, minibar, fridge, hair dryer, iron, trouser press.

Hotel du Lac *Value*   Architecturally bandboxy and lacking style, this hotel nonetheless offers much comfort and good value. Owned by the Kneschaurek family since 1920, it was reconstructed in the early 1960s. Renovated and improved over the years, it enjoys a lakefront location with its own private swimming area in front. All the midsize to spacious bedrooms have been updated with the installation of improved plumbing with combination tub/shower bathrooms. All open onto lakeside vistas; the most desirable accommodations—and the most tranquil—are on the sixth floor.

Riva Paradiso 3, CH-6902 Lugano-Paradiso. (℃ **091/986-47-47.** Fax 091/986-47-48. www.dulac.ch. 53 units. 226F–380F ($185–$312) double; 440F–520F ($361–$426) suite. Rates include buffet breakfast. AE, DC, MC, V. Parking 10F ($8.20). **Amenities:** Restaurant; outdoor heated pool; exercise room; Jacuzzi; sauna; 24-hr. room service; massage; babysitting; laundry service/dry cleaning; nonsmoking rooms. *In room:* TV, dataport, minibar, hair dryer, safe.

INEXPENSIVE
Albergo Domus Garni   This redbrick building with balconies is on the main road from Lugano to Paradiso, about 1.5km (1 mile) from the center of Lugano. The attractive and spacious interior is decorated with potted palms and Oriental rugs. The uncluttered bedrooms have large windows and a lighthearted decor, with an equal mixture of private showers or combination tub/shower bathrooms.

Riva Paradiso 24A, CH-6902 Lugano-Paradiso. (℃ **091/994-34-21.** Fax 091/993-02-69. www.hoteldomus.ch. 30 units, 24 with bathroom. 100F–110F ($82–$90) double without bathroom; 130F–170F ($107–$139) double with bathroom. Rates include buffet breakfast. AE, DC, MC, V. Free parking outdoors, 15F ($12) in garage. Bus: 2. *In room:* TV, minibar, hair dryer (on request), safe.

Carlton Hotel Villa Moritz *Finds*   Peace and quiet are assured at this hotel, as it's located in a park a good distance from the main road. The Wernli-Sigrist family manages several 19th-century buildings clustered near a swimming pool surrounded by flagstones. The hotel also benefits from being on the sunny side of Mount Brè. The bedrooms are comfortably furnished with traditional styling. The public rooms are modern, with stone accents around the bar. Public buses transport guests to the center of Lugano in 10 minutes.

Via Cortivo 9, CH-6976 Lugano-Castagnola. (℃ **091/971-38-12.** Fax 091/971-38-14. www.carlton-villa-moritz.ch. 55 units. 180F–250F ($148–$205) double. Rates include buffet breakfast. AE, MC, V. Parking 12F ($9.85). Closed late Oct to late Mar. Bus: 1. **Amenities:** Restaurant; bar; outdoor heated pool; 24-hr. room service; laundry service/dry cleaning. *In room:* TV.

San Carlo Garni   Modern decor, fully renovated rooms, and low rates have made this a popular spot with visitors. Via Nassa is a great shopping street, located in the heart of the city, so it is easy to get to just about anywhere in Lugano from the hotel. The lakefront is only a block away. The rooms are very small, but they have all the basics and more. The staff is friendly and attentive, happily giving tips about the best places to see and go. There is a breakfast room, but there are only a few tables, so either get up early or have it delivered to your room.

Via Nassa 28, CH-6900 Lugano. (℃ **091/922-71-07.** Fax 091/922-80-22. www.scta.ch. 44 units. 100F–160F ($82–$131) double. AE, DC, V. **Amenities:** Breakfast room; room service (breakfast only); nonsmoking rooms; rooms for guests w/limited mobility. *In room:* TV.

Zurigo   Located nearby to several points of interest, such as parks and the waterfront promenade, this value hotel has become a popular spot in Lugano. Midsize to spacious rooms are modern and brightly furnished. Refurbishing has upgraded the hotel to a new level in spite of the linoleum floors. If you're going when the weather will be warm, know that the more spacious superior accommodations are the only ones equipped with air-conditioning. Any other part of the year, however, standard rooms are just as comfortable. For those looking for some rest and relaxation, the north-facing rooms are quieter most of the time.

Corso Pestalozzi 13, Old Town, CH-6900 Lugano. ℰ **091/923-43-43.** Fax 091/923-92-68. www.hotelzurigo.ch. 40 units. 140F–180F ($115–$148) double. AE, DC, MC, V. **Amenities:** Breakfast room. *In room:* A/C (in some), TV.

WHERE TO DINE
EXPENSIVE
Principe Leopoldo ✮✮✮ INTERNATIONAL   Excellent regional and international cuisine are combined with a luxury setting in three rooms to make award-winning meals. The chef creates memorable dishes here, especially his divine risottos, one made with Gorgonzola and pears, another a green risotto with lobster and fresh herbs. The chef will dazzle you with his steamed sea bass filet with fresh tomatoes or his roasted turbot with Mediterranean "perfumes." We were also dazzled with his saltimbocca of rabbit with fresh mushrooms and his young duck breast roasted with lemon. Some dishes, such as roasted Scottish lamb with fine herbs, are prepared only for two. Hors d'oeuvres are the finest at the resort, everything from a quail salad with peaches and walnuts to lobster medallions on a carpaccio of fennel and oranges. Although the menu is international, it is strongest on Ticinese and Mediterranean dishes. Each tantalizing course comes with superb wines in perfect condition.

In the Villa Principe Leopoldo & Residence, via Montalbano 5. ℰ **091/985-88-55.** Reservations required. Main courses 29F–39F ($24–$32). AE, DC, MC, V. Daily noon–2:30pm and 7–9:30pm.

Ristorante al Portone ✮ SWISS/ITALIAN   If you enjoy Italian-style modern cuisine, head for this sophisticated restaurant managed by chef Roberto and Doris Galizzi. As with all *cuisine moderne,* many of the combinations sound bizarre, but the taste is usually sensational. Large scampi with curry and mango and the sole "in the style of Roberto" are veritable palate pleasers. If you order the most expensive fixed-price menu, you can *lascia fare à Roberto*—leave it up to Roberto, the chef. You'll rarely be disappointed: Roberto is known for putting his own culinary spin on even the most traditional of Italian dishes. The desserts are also exceptional. Regrettably, the restaurant closes in August at the peak of the tourist invasion.

Viale Cassarate 3. ℰ **091/923-55-11.** Reservations required. Main courses 45F–56F ($37–$46); business lunch 58F ($48); fixed-price menu 120F–150F ($98–$123). AE, DC, MC, V. Tues–Sat noon–2pm and 7:30–9:30pm. Closed Jan 1–10 and mid-July to mid-Aug.

Ristorante Santabbondio ✮ *Finds* MEDITERRANEAN   Its amiable, hardworking staff refers to the restaurant as a much-renovated, century-old grotto, but they're using the word to describe a rustic farmhouse (ca. 1862) rather than a cave. It's less than a mile south of Lugano, midway between the town center and the airport. Menu choices are based on a solid and well-intentioned respect for *cuisine du marché,* incorporating a roster of market-fresh specialties that changes every day. In a setting suitable for up to 50 diners at a time, outfitted in Tuscan-made terra-cotta tiles and tones of green and white, you'll enjoy some of the most sophisticated cuisine in the district. Examples include tartare of salmon served with a parfait of tomatoes and shrimp, Scottish grouse roasted in aged balsamic vinegar, scallops in a ginger-flavored orange-and-basil sauce, grilled filets of turbot with capers, and medallions of goat with wine sauce. Martin Dalsass is the well-rehearsed chef.

Via Fomelino 10. ℰ **091/993-23-88.** Reservations recommended. Main courses 35F–59F ($29–$48); fixed-price menu 168F ($138). AE, DC, MC, V. Tues–Fri noon–2:30pm and 7:30–10:30pm; Sat 7:30–11pm. Closed 1st 2 weeks in Jan.

MODERATE

Locanda del Boschetto ⊀ *(Value)* SWISS/ITALIAN   The place doesn't spend much money on decor, other than some rustic alpine wood, and no one puts on airs here. Service is direct in the sort of no-frills trattoria style. Guests can watch the chef cook beef and fish over the glowing coals. He produces a simple but flavor-filled cuisine, which includes a mixed grill of local fish, spaghetti with clam sauce, grilled calves' liver, and several succulent beef dishes. The well-known restaurant is in a wooded area near the highway.

Via Boschetto 8. ⓒ 091/994-24-93. Reservations recommended. Main courses 18F–51F ($15–$42). AE, DC, MC, V. Tues–Sun noon–2pm and 7–10pm. Closed 15 days in Nov. Bus: 1 or 2.

Mövenpick Ristorante Parco Ciani MEDITERRANEAN/INTERNATIONAL Guests select from two distinct dining areas, decorated in soft pastel tones with a bright atmosphere. One of the dining rooms has bentwood armchairs, while the other contains reproductions of Empire-style antiques. Located at the edge of a city park, the concrete block structure has irregular balconies and large windows. The menu is one of the largest in the center of town. The cookery is internationally acceptable rather than creatively innovative. Begin with a minestrone made with fresh vegetables, or sample carpaccio. Many guests, particularly those from south of the border (in Italy) prefer to begin their meal with one of the many pasta dishes, including tagliatelle, spaghetti, pappardelle, tortellini, and even a risotto. One risotto served with artichokes is delectable. The chef wisely allows you to order three different sizes of pasta, depending on your appetite. A salad buffet is offered, and every night at least three vegetarian main courses are featured. Many dishes are made with curry, the fish of the day is often grilled, and for the carnivore, there's an ample selection ranging from veal T-bones to U.S. Angus entrecôtes.

In the Palazzo dei Congressi, piazza Indipendenza. ⓒ **091/923-86-56.** Reservations recommended. Main courses 20F–48F ($16–$39). AE, DC, MC, V. Daily 9am–midnight. Bus: 1, 8, or 9.

Ristorante Orologio ITALIAN/INTERNATIONAL   The Orologio occupies the ground floor of a buff-colored building with restrained detailing and leaded-glass windows. The restaurant has 19th-century French-provincial chairs and an ice chest displaying salads and condiments. Amusing illustrations advertise the dishes—a mermaid draws your attention to the fish courses, although the menu features more meat courses. In September and October there's an emphasis on game and mushroom dishes such as the filet of venison with porcini mushrooms or the platter of venison for two. Pheasant dishes are also well prepared. Of all the restaurants we've recommended in Lugano, this one draws the most mixed reaction. Some locals swear by it and some foreign visitors sound its praise; others would have preferred to be sent elsewhere.

Via Nizzola 2. ⓒ **091/923-23-38.** Reservations recommended. Main courses 30F–55F ($25–$45). AE, DC, MC, V. Mon–Fri 11am–3pm and 7–10:30pm. Closed Aug. Bus: 1 or 2.

INEXPENSIVE

Grotto dei Pescatori ⊀ *(Finds)* ITALIAN   Inaccessible by car, the only way to reach this isolated restaurant is by boat, so consequently a meal here will also involve a scenic cruise along the lake. It's set within a 5-minute walk of the hamlet of Caprino (site of only about five houses) in what was built in the 1920s as a rough-and-ready bar for the region's fishers. Over the years, it has evolved into the full-fledged, endlessly charming hideaway you'll see today. The kitchens here are set within a grotto, with food being hauled out to a lakeside terrace. Many of the day's delectable specials are written on a blackboard. Examples include a succulent version of very fresh lake perch served as simply as possible, with a sage-flavored butter sauce. Other specialties include lake fish prepared *carpione*-style (braised and then cold-marinated in white wine vinegar) and buckwheat polenta with beef braised in red wine.

Caprino. © **091/923-98-67.** Reservations recommended on weekends. Main courses 7F–34F ($5.75–$28). MC, V. May–Sept daily 11am–11pm. From the Imbarco Giardino piers in Lugano's Piazza Riforma, take any of the boats operated by the **Navigazione Lago di Lugano** (© **091/971-52-23**), whose final destination is Gandria, and get off at the Caprino/Grotto dei Pescatori stop. Boats depart at 90-min. intervals and charge 20F ($16) round-trip.

La Tinera ✸ *Value* SWISS/ITALIAN A familiar array of Italian specialties are served at budget prices in this basement trattoria in the center of the historic Old Town. No one bothers to dress up here, as families, often Italian, mingle with visitors for the day, each "tucking in" plenty of the regional fare served in generous portions. Fresh pasta dishes, risotto, and a robust selection of grilled meats are cooked the same as in grandmother's day. No one would want to change a thing. Regional wine is served in ceramic carafes.

Via dei Gorini 2 (off piazza Riforma). © **091/923-52-19.** Reservations not accepted. Main courses 14F–20F ($11–$16). AE, MC, V. Mon–Sat 11:30am–3pm and 5:30–11pm. Bus: 1 or 2. Or walk down via Pessina. Closed last week of July and 1st 3 weeks of Aug.

NEARBY DINING & LODGING
Motto del Gallo ✸✸ *Finds* MEDITERRANEAN For a visual treat, visit this baroque house practically bursting with atmosphere. There's a collection of antiques and the tables are covered with lace. The restaurant is in a 15th-century hamlet that alone is worth the trip—13km (8 miles) from Lugano on the road to Bellinzona. The excellent menu features a selection of homemade pastas, including green tagliolini with scampi. Two types of risotto are offered, one of them cooked delectably in champagne. Fresh fish looms large on the menu, including a selection of "fruits of the sea" gratinée with zabaglione. Main meat dishes are likely to include a veal mignon, veal kidneys cooked with sherry, a mixed medley of meats, or perhaps alpine-style lamb roasted aromatically with fresh herbs. Instead of dessert, such as one of the cold soufflés, many diners prefer to end their meal with a regional cheese of the Ticino. The wine list includes some 500 wines from all over the world.

If you're looking for a romantic place to spend the night, there are three well-maintained suites here, which cost 235F ($193) for two, including breakfast.

CH-6807 Taverne. © **091/945-28-71.** Fax 091/945-27-23. Reservations required. Main courses 29F–49F ($24–$40); business lunch 35F–65F ($29–$53); *menu dégustazione* 120F ($98); *menu gastronomico* 139F ($114). AE, DC, V. Tues–Sat noon–2pm; Mon–Sat 7–10pm. Take the unnumbered bus or local train marked TAVERNE.

LUGANO AFTER DARK
Lugano reigns as the center of the Ticino's nightlife circuit, with options that attract local residents from quieter towns throughout the district. Two of the most obvious options involve visits to either of the two casinos described below.

CASINOS
Casino Lugano This casino features 350 slots, 26 table games, two elegant restaurants, and five bars. Games of chance include American roulette, blackjack, French roulette, Caribbean stud poker, punto banco, poker, and wheel-of-fortune. Entrance is free but visitors must show a passport. Open Sunday to Thursday noon to 3am, Friday and Saturday noon to 4am. Via Stauffacher 1. © **091/973-71-11.**

Casino Municipale   This casino lies on Italian soil, across the lake from Lugano, only 20 minutes away by ferry. The casino is a glittering establishment, filled with an international clientele and such games as blackjack and chemin de fer, along with the inevitable slot machines. Here, in Italy, gambling stakes are unlimited. Oddly, however, despite the casino's location, the currency is Swiss. Patrons must show a passport and men must have a jacket, tie, and shirt on—a policy that's strictly enforced.

The casino is in the village of Campione, which, because of the vagaries of 19th- and 20th-century politics and because of the rugged terrain around it, is completely surrounded by Switzerland. Even its telephone area code is the same as Lugano's. Long ago, the imperial fiefdom of Campione was presented to a Milanese monastery and it has remained Italian ever since. The men of Campione were famous for their stonework, and many buildings in Milan are a testament to their skill. Take a moment to admire their handiwork in some of the local buildings. ID is required for admission. Open daily at 3:30pm–2am. Piazzale Milano 1, Campione, Italy. ℂ 091/640-11-11. Cover 15F ($12).

OTHER NIGHTLIFE OFFERINGS

Other than gambling, you'll find a dense roster of bars and cafes, many of them lining the edges of the historic center's most famous square, piazza Riforma. One of the most interesting is the **Café Olimpia** (ℂ **091/922-74-88**), an elegant stone building with hundreds of chairs set out in front and a focus on live music some evenings. A few steps away is the **Café Tango** (ℂ **091/922-27-01**), more like a bar than a traditional cafe, where an Argentine motif (and recorded music) often attracts clients from everywhere in Europe. If you ever wondered about South American expatriates and where they happened to live in Switzerland, head no farther than the **Mango Club,** piazza Dante 8 (ℂ **091/922-94-38**). Here, almost everybody will know how to salsa and merengue, probably better than you, and with a more convincing grasp of *Español* as it's spoken in Colombia and the Dominican Republic. Originally established in 1995 and now a fixture on the nightlife circuit of the Ticino, it's open every night beginning at 10pm, with many of the guests arriving after 12:30am. Cover, which includes the first drink, costs 12F ($9.85).

Titanic, via Cantonale, pambio-Noranco (ℂ **091/985-60-10**), attracts the young and hip to the largest dance club in the Ticino. The cover charge usually begins at 15F to 20F ($12–$16). Go late. The club lies off the A2 exit for Lugano-Sud.

If strip-tease *artistes* are your thing, consider **Dancing Cécil,** riva Paradiso, in the nearby suburb of Lugarno-Paradiso (ℂ **091/994-97-24**), at the hotel Vittoria. It's open daily from 10pm.

5 Morcote ⭐⭐

11km (7 miles) S of Lugano; 40km (25 miles) S of Bellinzona

Morcote is one of the most idyllic villages of Switzerland. Its arcaded houses and old streets are built on the southern slopes of Monte Arbostora, at 826m (2,709 ft.). Cypresses and vineyards grow on the mountain.

ESSENTIALS

GETTING THERE   Several buses depart from Lugano every day for Morcote (trip time: 30 min.).

Throughout the summer about a dozen boats make the trip every day from Lugano to Morcote, with many intermediary stops along the way. Depending on the schedule, trip time is between 50 minutes and 2 hours. The round-trip boat fare is 28F ($23). In the winter boats continue to run, but on a less frequent schedule.

For bus and boat schedules and information, contact the tourist office (see below). If you're driving from Lugano, head south along Route A4.

VISITOR INFORMATION   Morcote now has its own tourist information office in the center (☎ **091/996-11-20**). Office hours are Tuesday to Sunday from 1 to 5pm and Saturday 10am to noon and 1 to 5pm.

SEEING THE SIGHTS

Chiesa di Madonna del Sasso dates from the 15th century; it was reconstructed later, however, and given a baroque overlay. It has some memorable 16th-century frescoes. A staircase with more than 400 steps leads down to the village and the lake, and the cemetery contains the remains of many famous people.

Scherrer Park (☎ **091/996-21-25**) contains typical Ticino trees and plants, as well as sculpture and architecture. Some of the sculpture is from the Far East. Admission is 7F ($5.75) for adults, 5F ($4.10) students and seniors, 1F (80¢) children 16 and under. It's open March to October daily from 10am to 5pm.

WHERE TO STAY

Carina Carlton 🖈🖈   This hotel has an Italian-style facade, with pink-and-cream trim and lime-green shutters. Such lighthearted contrast of colors also marks the lobby, which is decorated with Oriental rugs. The hotel's several terraces are filled with potted plants and small tables. A structure of whimsical design, it was once owned by the architect Gaspare Fossati (1809–83), a native of Morcote, who was known for his renovations of Saint Sophia in Constantinople (present-day Istanbul). Some of the awards he received from the Ottoman sultan are displayed in the lobby. The Carina Carlton offers midsize bedrooms filled with provincial furniture (some of it antique).

Via Cantonale, CH-6922 Morcote. ☎ **091/996-11-31**. Fax 091/996-19-29. www.carina-morcote.ch. 22 units. 190F–260F ($156–$213) double; 280F–320F ($230–$262) suite. Rates include continental breakfast. Half board 46F ($38) per person extra. AE, DC, MC, V. Closed Oct 19–Mar 6. **Amenities:** Restaurant; outdoor heated pool; limited room service; laundry service/dry cleaning. *In room:* TV, minibar, hair dryer, safe.

WHERE TO DINE

Bellavista 🖈🖈🖈 *Finds* CONTINENTAL/MEDITERRANEAN   On a belvedere towering over Lake Lugano, this is a cozy restaurant of charm and grace. It is clearly the outstanding dining choice of the area, lying in the vineyards of Vico Morcote. The restaurant is housed in two typical Ticinese buildings that date back at least 3 centuries. In summer, terrace dining with a panoramic view is preferred, or, in cooler weather, perhaps you'd like a table in front of the fireplace. The Schwarzer family, your hosts, are demanding in their standards and are accustomed to pleasing some of the most discerning palates in both Switzerland and northern Italy. The menu is spectacular and many dishes come as a surprise—those lobsters flown in are the same type the Bush family enjoys in Maine, for example. The homemade pasta dishes don't get much better than those served here.

You may also consider Bella Vista as a hideaway place to stay. It rents 12 charmingly furnished bedrooms with tub and shower and such amenities as a minibar. Guests can also enjoy the sun terrace and solarium. Doubles rent for 150F to 200F ($123–$164), with suites going for 330F ($215). You can arrive early for a drink at the bar or a walk in the garden.

Strada de Vigh 2, CH-6921 Vico-Morcote. ✆ **091/996-11-43.** Reservations required. Main courses 29F–38F ($24–$31); fixed-price menus 75F ($62), 85F ($70), 95F ($78). AE, DC, MC, V. July–Sept daily 6:30–9:30pm, Tues–Sun noon–1:30pm; Oct–Nov and Feb–June Tues–Sun 6:30–9:30pm, Wed–Sun noon–1:30pm. Closed Dec–Jan. Lies 2km (1¼ miles) south of Melide.

Ristorante della Posta SWISS/ITALIAN   Established in 1863, this restaurant features two terraces staggered back from each other overlooking the lake. It operates from the center of Morcote. Waiters scurry with food-laden trays from the kitchen across the street. The setting is charming, but the traffic makes it somewhat hectic. Delectable specialties include risotto with mushrooms, *osso buco* with polenta, fresh lake fish, and real Italian pizza. Fresh fish is the chef's specialty, and it's most often served grilled. There are also several different preparations of fresh mushrooms offered nightly, and the veal cutlet Milanese is always reliable.

In the Albergo della Posta, via Cantonale. ✆ **091/996-11-27.** Main courses 28F–48F ($23–$39); pizza 12F–19F ($9.85–$16). AE, DC, MC, V. Daily 8am–midnight. Closed Nov to mid-Mar.

Ristorante Panorama ✿✿ INTERNATIONAL   This gourmet temple overlooks the lake with a view of the town of Brusino Arsizio. The restaurant is on the sixth floor of the hotel Olivella au Lac. The restaurant is known for its sublime cuisine, intimate atmosphere, and impeccable service amidst an oasis of lawns, flowers, and elegant terraces. Azaleas, palm trees, and jasmine creepers assault you at every turn in this elegant environment. Fresh products—wholesome whenever possible—are a hallmark of the refined, creative, and deliciously light cuisine, much of it based on healthy ingredients. Chef Leopold Enz frequently changes his menu and adjusts it seasonally. The menu truly depends on his inspiration of the moment, but is likely to include such delights as a goose liver pâté, a delectable scampi risotto, a whole white fish cooked in a foil wrap with tender artichokes, and, a special delight, young chicken baked with dates and apples.

CH-6921 Vico Morcote. ✆ **091/996-10-01.** Reservations required. Main courses 23F–60F ($19–$49). AE, DC, MC, V. Daily 7–10:30pm.

16

Liechtenstein

With a history dating from the 14th century, Liechtenstein is a wonderful land of fairy-tale castles (one inhabited by the reigning prince), chalets decorated with geraniums, Rhine meadows, and small villages high in the Alps.

Separated from Switzerland by the Rhine River, it's one of the smallest independent sovereign states of Europe, along with San Marino in Italy and Andorra in the Pyrenees. The entire country is only about 26km (16 miles) long and 6km (4 miles) wide.

Liechtenstein is famous for its finely engraved postage stamps, which are treasured by collectors the world over. The stamps illustrate the country's religion (predominantly Roman Catholic), monarchy, art, history, landscape, nature, and leisure activities. Stamps provide 25% of the government's income, and new series are introduced all the time. There's a postal museum in Vaduz, the capital of the principality.

Although commonly regarded as remote, Liechtenstein is actually very accessible from eastern Switzerland. A number of good roads link the two countries, and there are no border formalities or Customs stops. There are guards at the Austrian border, but they rarely stamp visitors' passports.

The ideal way to explore Liechtenstein is to wander around. Every village has a network of hiking and walking routes, which the locals themselves put to good use. Marked hiking routes cover 150km (93 miles) in the alpine area and 119km (74 miles) in the valley, which, considering the country's size, takes up a huge chunk of the land space.

Malbun and Steg are ideal starting points for mountain tours, and Gaflei and Planken (the tiniest hamlet in the country) are departure points for the Drei Schwestern area. The tourist office (see below) has a pamphlet outlining the best hiking trails throughout the Unterland (Lower Country), the Oberland (Upper Country), and the alpine region.

Guided half- or full-day tours are arranged every Thursday in summer by the **Liechtenstein Alpine Association.** Routes depend on weather conditions and are published on the Saturday preceding the tour in local newspapers under a column headed "Wanderungen des Liechtensteiner Alpenvereins." For information and registration, contact the guide given in the announcement.

1 About Liechtenstein

ORIENTATION

GEOGRAPHY   The Rhine River forms Liechtenstein's western boundary; the Swiss canton of St. Gallen is on the other bank. To the east is the Austrian province of Vorarlberg, and to the south are the Grisons of Switzerland. Liechtenstein is cradled by the **Drei Schwestern (Three Sisters)** mountains.

Liechtenstein

PEOPLE   About 33,000 citizens live in 11 communes (comparable to Switzerland's cantons). Most—more than 80%—are Roman Catholic and of German ancestry. They enjoy one of the highest standards of living in the world and pay very little in taxes. Unemployment is rare.

The country's prosperity, however, is a relatively recent development. Many old-timers remember the hardships of World War I, when the country was virtually cut off from food supplies because of blockades. The social and economic growth since the end of World War II has exceeded that of any other Western nation. Today Liecht-enstein is one of the most highly industrialized countries in Europe. The industry is hardly noticeable, however, because the factories and workshops are dispersed among orchards, meadows, and woodlands. There are no smokestacks, with their pollution from fumes. One of the industrial specialties is the production of false teeth.

Liechtenstein has a rich cultural life, supported by royal patrons and the coopera-tion of neighboring countries. Though open to foreign influences, through commerce and cultural exchanges as well as through tourism, Liechtenstein maintains its unique national identity by severely restricting citizenship. Any foreigner wishing to become a citizen must first be approved by a majority of the commune he or she intends to live in; then his/her application must be approved by parliament, and then by the monarch. The process is obviously meant to discourage immigration.

LANGUAGE   Most residents of Liechtenstein, who are largely of Austrian origin, speak a German dialect. English is also understood throughout the country.

GOVERNMENT   The Principality of Liechtenstein is a constitutional hereditary monarchy with a unicameral parliament (Diet). The state power is vested in the prince and the people. The prince's powers are passed on through hereditary succession to the throne and are independent of the will of the people. The people also have political power and must work together with the prince, according to the constitution.

Members of the parliament are chosen for 4 years by general elections. The right to vote is universal (women received the right to vote in 1984), secret, and direct. Public referendum is an important right of all citizens. Any law passed by the Diet that is not declared urgent may be put to referendum. The constitution also assures freedom of speech, freedom of the press, and freedom of assembly.

Liechtenstein has a prime minister and four councilors, appointed by the prince for a 4-year term. They act as a link between the prince and the Diet. In 1969 the principality celebrated its 250th anniversary.

Liechtenstein made world headlines in 2003 when its prince, Hans-Adam II, demanded and got sweeping powers in a nationwide referendum. If he weren't granted these powers, he had threatened to move to Austria. Desperate to hold onto their prince, 64.3% of the electorate voted to give him such rights as the power to dismiss governments and approve judicial nominees. The revised constitution also allows the prince to veto laws simply by refusing to sign them within a 6-month period. The prince likened the opposition to "World War II traitors." One supporter, Adriaa Dill, told the press: "The country should be exactly the way the prince wants to have it. It's his country. It has his name on it." Former prime minister Mario Frick said otherwise, claiming the referendum made Liechtenstein "an international laughing stock."

ESSENTIALS

GETTING THERE   The nearest airport is **Kloten International Airport** outside Zurich, about 130km (80 miles) to the west of Vaduz. There is both train and bus transportation into Liechtenstein from Zurich.

Many express trains pass through Liechtenstein, but none stop there. You can take a train from Zurich to Sargans or to Buchs in nearby Switzerland. Call © **0900/300-300** for **rail schedules.** At both Sargans and Buchs, you'll find good bus connections to Vaduz and other communes in Liechtenstein.

If you're driving from Zurich, head southwest along N3 until you reach the junction with N1, then take N1 north to the turnoff for Vaduz.

FAST FACTS: Liechtenstein

Currency The Swiss franc is legal tender in Liechtenstein; the exchange rate is the same as in Switzerland (see "Money" in chapter 2).

Documents Required All travel documents recognized by Swiss authorities are valid in Liechtenstein. However, you'll encounter the formalities of any western European border crossing if you enter through Austria.

Holidays Public holidays are January 1 (New Year's Day), January 6 (Epiphany), February 28 (Mardi Gras), Good Friday, Easter Monday, May 1 (Labor Day), May

25 (Feast of the Ascension), June 5 (Whit Monday), June 15 (Corpus Christi), August 15 (Feast of the Assumption), September 8 (Nativity of Our Lady), November 1 (All Saints' Day), December 8 (Feast of the Immaculate Conception), December 25 (Christmas), and December 26 (Boxing Day).

Information For further information about the principality, contact the **Liechtenstein National Tourist Office**, Städtle 37 (P.O. Box 139), FL-9490 Vaduz, Liechtenstein (© **00423/232-14-43**). This office is open July to August, Monday to Friday from 9am to 5:30pm; and the rest of the year, Monday to Saturday 9am to noon and 1:30 to 5:30pm.

Mail The postage rates are the same as in Switzerland (see "Fast Facts: Switzerland," in chapter 2). But you must, of course, use Liechtenstein stamps.

Medical Needs Doctors and dentists take turns handling emergency calls (the names of those currently available are published in the Sat and Sun newspapers). Your hotel will put you in touch with an English-speaking doctor or dentist. Phone © **144** for an ambulance.

Telephone To call Liechtenstein from the U.S., dial your international prefix (usually **011**), followed by Liechtenstein's country code **00423,** followed by the seven-digit local number. To call Liechtenstein from anywhere in Switzerland or anywhere else in the world, dial whatever international prefix is required at the phone you happen to be using, followed by the country code for Liechtenstein (00423), followed by the seven-digit local number.

2 Vaduz ⋆

130km (80 miles) E of Zurich; 38km (24 miles) E of Chur

Vaduz (pronounced Va-*dootz*) is the capital of the Principality of Liechtenstein. Vineyards surround this little town (pop. about 5,000) at the foot of the royal family's castle. The rural commune, known for its good wines, is also very hospitable and sociable to visitors. The capital is most often visited on a brief stopover—just time enough to buy some of the famous postage stamps and record the visit to this tiny country in your passport. But as the capital of one of the last vestiges of the Holy Roman Empire and the seat of the only German-speaking monarchy in the world, Vaduz merits a closer look—at least to walk its streets and visit some of its museums.

ESSENTIALS

GETTING THERE   See "Essentials" in "About Liechtenstein," above.

VISITOR INFORMATION   The **Vaduz Tourist Office** is at Städtle 37 (© **00423/ 232-14-43**). It's open daily from 9am to noon and 1:30 to 5pm.

SEEING THE SIGHTS

Traffic is allowed one-way on the main street, **Städtle.** Also at the center of Vaduz is the **Rathaus (town hall).** The post office is across the street. Vaduz offers a wide range of sports and entertainment. Facilities include a miniature golf course, tennis courts, and a large swimming pool.

One of the best ways to get around not only Vaduz but other parts of the country itself is to rent a bike or a small motorcycle. Rentals are possible at **Bike Garage,** Triesen 10 (📞 **00423/390-03-90**). The cost is 35F ($29) per day for the average bike.

The prince's castle, **Schloss Vaduz,** dates from the 12th century. The oldest parts are the keep and the buildings on the east side. The castle was burned down by Swiss troops in 1499 and rebuilt at the beginning of the 16th century. It has round bastions at the northeast and southwest corners. Once a bleak and gloomy fortress, the castle is much improved. The interior—not open to the public—contains lavish furnishings, antiques, and priceless artwork. The exterior of the fortress is surely worth seeing. The climb along the wooded footpath takes 20 minutes and starts between the Hotel Real and the Hotel Engel. There's a sweeping vista from the grounds of the castle.

In the upper village, on the road to the castle, is the **Red House.** This was the seat of the vassals of the counts of Werdenberg during the Middle Ages. The house was acquired along with the vineyard by the Monastery of St. Johann in the Toggenburg.

Kunstmuseum Liechtenstein ⓐⓐ   The princes of the House of Liechtenstein have been art collectors since the 17th century. Their treasures were in a palace in Vienna until 1940, when Prince Franz Joseph II decided to display his collection in his own country. The collection occupies two floors of a gallery above the tourist office. The works by Rubens are among the greatest in the world. They include *The Toilet of Venus* and a cycle of nine large paintings illustrating the history of a Roman consul. Many of the pictures on exhibit are reproduced on Liechtenstein's famous stamps. The art collection is the country's most outstanding attraction.

Städtle 37. 📞 00423/235-03-00. www.kunstmuseum.li. Admission 8F ($6.55) adults, 5F ($4.10) students, seniors, and children 6–16, free for children 5 and under. Tues–Sun 10am–5pm; Thurs open till 8pm.

Briefmarkenmuseum (Stamp Museum)   Philatelists and other admirers come from all over the world to see the Liechtenstein stamps. The collection includes the stamps of the Universal Postal Union, printing plates, and postal documents. Liechtenstein's first stamp dates from 1912. The museum was opened in 1930.

Städtle 37. 📞 00423/236-61-05. www.pwz.li. Free admission. Daily 10am–noon and 1–5pm.

SHOPPING

If there's any flash and glitter in Liechtenstein at all, it appears only in very subdued form. You may especially notice this during your shopping excursions, which are best limited to central Vaduz, a neighborhood that can never really escape the sense of being a somewhat overgrown village. An outlet that sells gift items from Liechtenstein, Austria, Italy, and Switzerland is **L'Atelier,** Städtle 36 (📞 **00423/232-46-88**). Its merchandise, as selected by the outfit's longtime owner, Hélène de Marchi, includes lamps, dolls, hand-painted silks, stoneware, pewter, and other handmade objects.

Liechtenstein has been famous since the turn of the 20th century for its rustic and durable pottery, produced in natural-looking colors such as blue, beige, and yellow, in factories that lie within a 10-minute drive of Vaduz. The larger of the principality's two factories for stoneware is **Schaedler Keramik A.G.,** which straddles Hauptstrasse (📞 **00423/373-14-14**), the main street of the hamlet of Nendeln, 8km (5 miles) north of Vaduz. Its only real competitor, at least within the principality, is the somewhat smaller outfit **Haas Kunst Keramik A.G.,** Zollstrasse 70, in the nearby hamlet of Schaan (📞 **00423/232-18-83**). Both firms maintain sales outlets on their premises and present pottery-making demonstrations to anyone who's interested.

The principality's premier outlet for wines produced by vineyards belonging to the prince is the **Hofkellerei des Fürsten Liechtenstein,** Feldstrasse, Vaduz (② **00423/ 232-10-18**). Set in a solid, not particularly imaginative-looking building that's owned by the prince, it stockpiles the fruits of his family's vineyards, most of which are either in the principality or in Lower Austria (Niederösterreich) just across the border. Look for both whites and reds and a somewhat heavy-handed emphasis on the organization's royal connections.

When shopping, don't overlook the Liechtenstinian postal service, which produces more stamps than are ever used to actually mail letters. One of the busiest emporiums in the principality is the bureaucratic-looking kiosk in the main post office, **Postwert Zeichenstelle der Regierung,** Städtle, FL-9490 Vaduz (② **00423/236-64-44**). Here stamps that commemorate Liechtenstein's history, botany, zoology, and achievements are sold to avid collectors, and even to folk who never thought they were collectors.

WHERE TO STAY

Most of Liechtenstein's hotels are in the capital.

VERY EXPENSIVE

Park Hotel Sonnenhof ✿✿✿   The finest hotel in the principality, a Relais & Châteaux, is also among the finest in Europe. Diplomatic receptions are held here frequently. Built in the late 1800s, the hotel has been modernized into a streamlined chalet, with balconies and awnings. The garden is beautiful, and the spacious, elegant rooms are handsomely decorated and furnished with luxury beds and state-of-the-art plumbing, including luxurious tub/shower combinations in all but three (shower only).

Mareestrasse 29, FL-9490 Vaduz, Liechtenstein. ② 00423/232-11-92. Fax 00423/232-00-53. www.sonnenhof.li. 29 units. 380F–500F ($312–$410) double; 500F–600F ($410–$492) junior suite. Rates include buffet breakfast. Half board 75F ($62) per person extra. AE, DC, MC, V. Free parking outdoors, 15F ($12) in garage. **Amenities:** Restaurant; lounge; indoor heated pool; nearby tennis courts; sauna; limited room service; laundry service. *In room:* TV, dataport, minibar, hair dryer, safe.

MODERATE

Gasthof Löwen ✿   Set on the highway within a pleasant and well-cultivated garden, this is the oldest inn (established in 1380) in Liechtenstein. Few others evoke old-fashioned alpine life as effectively as this one, thanks to its antique rooms outfitted with furniture that was originally crafted around 1920, and a clear, clean color scheme of stark white offset with varnished paneling. Bedrooms come in a variety of sizes and shapes, but all are comfortably Middle Europa, with dowdy furniture, soft beds, crisp linens, and plumbing that still works (though often noisily).

Herrengasse 35, FL-9490 Vaduz, Liechtenstein. ② 00423/238-11-44. Fax 00423/238-11-45. www.hotel-loewen.li. 7 units. 265F–335F ($217–$275) double. Rates include buffet breakfast. AE, DC, MC, V. From Vaduz, take the bus marked FELDKIRCH. **Amenities:** Restaurant; piano bar; limited room service; laundry service. *In room:* TV, dataport, minibar, hair dryer, safe.

Hotel Engel   This unassuming and unpretentious small inn lies on the main street of Vaduz, a roadway filled with summer tourist buses. The owners run a welcoming hotel, and many of the rooms have flower-festooned balconies overlooking the action. The midsize rooms have bright colors and newly tiled bathrooms with private shower or tub. The hotel is modern outside and decorated with rustic artifacts inside. It also has the only Chinese restaurant in the country, plus an international restaurant.

Städtle 13, FL-9490 Vaduz, Liechtenstein. © **00423/236-17-17.** Fax 00423/233-11-59. 20 units. 165F–180F ($135–$148) double. Rates include buffet breakfast. AE, DC, MC, V. Free parking. **Amenities:** 2 restaurants; limited room service; rooms for guests w/limited mobility. In room: TV, dataport, minibar.

Hotel Real ⊛⊛   Rich in tradition, this well-maintained hotel is on the main street, below the wooded bluff on which the palace of the prince is built. Although known primarily for its restaurant, it is a superlative choice for its luxurious bedrooms as well. The facade is decorated with flower boxes in the summer. The spacious rooms are well maintained and comfortable and have been renovated in a modern style, with deluxe mattresses and beautifully maintained private bathrooms, equally divided between those with private shower and those with tub/shower combination. The hotel restaurant serves the best food in the principality (see "Where to Dine," below).

Städtle 21, FL-9490 Vaduz, Liechtenstein. © **00423/232-22-22.** Fax 00423/232-08-91. www.hotel-real.li. 13 units. 240F–270F ($197–$221) double; 370F–430F ($303–$353) suite. Rates include buffet breakfast. AE, DC, MC, V. Parking 8F ($6.55). **Amenities:** Restaurant; bar; limited room service; laundry service. In room: TV, dataport, minibar, hair dryer, safe.

INEXPENSIVE
Hotel Garni Landhaus Prausch   Located a 5-minute walk east from the town center, this structure dates from 1917, when it was built as the home of a conservative and prosperous burgher. Today it retains the solid and well-grounded aura of its original function. The public areas are covered with flagstone floors, while the small bedrooms have wall-to-wall carpeting and durable, reliable country-style furnishings, including private bathrooms with showers (some with tubs).

Zollstrasse 16, FL-9490 Nendeln, Liechtenstein. © **00423/235-00-35.** Fax 00423/232-54-86. 20 units. 140F ($115) double. Rates include buffet breakfast. AE, DC, MC, V. Free parking. Closed Oct–Mar. **Amenities:** Dining room; indoor heated pool; whirlpool; Jacuzzi; sauna; nonsmoking rooms. In room: TV, dataport, minibar.

WHERE TO DINE
EXPENSIVE
Restaurant Real ⊛⊛⊛ CONTINENTAL   Members of the royal family are frequent guests here—their castle looms above the restaurant, which is on the main street of Vaduz. Cafe tables and chairs are outside. The dining rooms have paneling and lighting fixtures shaped like grape garlands. You'll appreciate the well-polished ambience of understated prosperity. The chefs are the finest in the principality, working with the very best ingredients, which they fashion into delectable platters with razor-sharp techniques. There is a certain charm and fragrance connected with every dish. The menu may include bouillabaisse, scampi ravioli, a gratin of seafood, *Tafelspitz* (boiled beef), veal piccata, or perhaps a perfectly done Wiener schnitzel.

Städtle 21. © **00423/232-22-22.** Reservations required. Main courses 42F–61F ($34–$50); fixed-price 5-course meal 133F ($109). AE, DC, MC, V. Daily noon–2pm and 6–10pm.

Restaurant Torkel ⊛ *(Finds)* FRENCH   The prince owns this charming country inn on the site of an old wine press. It's in the royal vineyards on the outskirts of town; park your car and follow the signs a short distance to a low-lying building. The cuisine, never accused of being overly imaginative, is satisfying and most filling, a true regional flavor of central Europe. Seasonal specialties are likely to include veal dishes, filet goulash Stroganoff, freshwater fish in Riesling sauce, and "Torkelsteak." Noodle and rösti dishes are also offered. Wine is available from the royal cellars, including a house variety of the local sparkling wine (Sekt). The menu changes every day, offering only what is fresh at the market.

Hintergasse 9. (℗ **00423/232-44-10.** Reservations recommended. Main courses 32F–59F ($26–$48). AE, DC, MC, V. Mon–Fri 11:30am–2:30pm; Mon–Sat 6:30–11:30pm.

INEXPENSIVE

Old Castle Inn GERMAN/AUSTRIAN/SWISS   Locals gather at the long, half-timbered bar to drink and gossip, and German folk music or background pop music is played. You'll be able to see the castle from the leatherette banquettes that surround the wooden tables. Outside is a terrace with a striped canopy and geraniums around the border. The menu is changed daily. There's a good selection of wurst and steak dishes, or you may choose one of the cold dishes or well-stuffed sandwiches. There are different kinds of "schnitzel" available, each platter served with *pommes frites* (Belgian fries) and a salad. The menu also includes such standard fare as minestrone, spaghetti, lasagna, hamburger, and veal liver Venice style.

Aeulestrasse 22. (℗ **00423/232-10-65.** Reservations not required. Main courses 14F–42F ($11–$34). AE, DC, MC, V. Daily 9am–midnight.

VADUZ AFTER DARK

Conservative—and according to its critics, drab—Liechtenstein can't even begin to compete with the nightlife options of larger cities in Switzerland. Your best bet will probably involve retiring early after a nightcap at either your hotel bar or one of the spots mentioned below. Discos aren't really a factor here. Noteworthy bars, however, include the **Vanini Bar,** a youthful, high-energy meeting place in the Hotel Adler, Herrengasse (℗ **00423/232-21-31**); and the **Apero-Bar,** a site associated with the Restaurant Wolff, Städtle (℗ **00423/232-23-21**).

3 The Unterland

Formed by the Rhine Valley, Liechtenstein's Unterland (Lower Country) is at the foot of the Drei Schwestern (Three Sisters) mountains. It contains eight villages along the slopes of the Eschnerberg and five parishes. The landscape is a rugged mix of wooded hills, meadows, and clean brooks. Agricultural and industrial development has not been allowed to damage the environment.

The **Eschnerberg Historical Trail** is an extensive network of footpaths. The Eschnerberg hills were a refuge for prehistoric settlers, offering an islandlike setting in the marshy Rhine Valley. The marshes have since been drained. A hike here is pleasant and informative. You'll learn the history of the people who have lived in this region.

All the villages recommended below are on the postal-bus route from Vaduz. The Vaduz tourist office will provide a map outlining the various routings and transportation connections possible.

SCHELLENBERG

This second-smallest parish in the principality (pop. 577) also has the smallest surface area. It was already settled when the New Stone Age began. Some of the Iron Age artifacts displayed in the National Museum in Vaduz were unearthed here. The Herren (nobles) von Schellenberg built two castles here in the Middle Ages. One of the castles, the **Obere Burg Schellenberg,** has been restored and offers a good view. Schellenberg is a starting point for the Eschnerberg Historical Trail.

MAUREN-SCHAANWALD

These two villages are a mile apart, in a parish covering only 5 sq. km (3 sq. miles). Mauren is one of the most beautiful sights in Liechtenstein. It was called Muron in 1178 and today is known as the "Village of the Seven Hillocks." The remains of Roman baths and a 2nd-century farmhouse or outbuilding have been excavated here. The village is also known for its fine church, dating from 1787. The meadows and woodlands between Mauren and Schaanwald have been designated a bird sanctuary. The preserve contains a conservation pond and a nature trail. The villages are on the Schaan-Feldkirch road leading to Austria.

GAMPRIN-BENDERN

This small parish along the Rhine has picture-postcard charm. The two hamlets on the west spur of Eschnerberg are rich in archaeological discoveries. Excavations have shown that the area was inhabited continuously from about 2500 B.C. to the Roman era. Discoveries around Gamprin have yielded many clues about the culture of the New Stone Age. The remains of a farm and a small church dating from A.D. 55 have been found on the hill on which the **Bendern church** stands today. This church belonged to the Convent of Schanis (St. Gallen) from 809 to 1177 and to the Monastery of St. Luzi (Chur) from 1200 to 1816. After the Reformation, the St. Luzi monks built a larger structure, which included the abbot's quarters.

It was at Bendern's **Kirchhügel** that the men of the lowlands swore loyalty to the prince of Liechtenstein in 1699. It's very scenic and includes a fitness track, a history trail, and a campground. The **Mariengrotte (Mary's Grotto)** at Bendern is the only shrine of its kind in the country.

ESCHEN-NENDELN

Eschen was first mentioned in the Carolingian land registry in 850 under the name Essane, derived from the Celtic word *esca,* meaning "by the water." The water refers to the Esche, a nearby brook. Flint artifacts from the Middle Stone Age, about 5000 B.C., have been found here, and New Stone Age settlements have been excavated at Malanser and Schneller. The upper part of Eschen, **Schönbühl,** is one of the country's most attractive residential areas.

The parish includes the village of **Nendeln,** in which the foundation of a Roman villa and a prehistoric settlement have been discovered. Nendeln lies 5km (3 miles) northeast of Schaan, on Route 16.

Several buildings in the area are worth a visit. The **Pfründhaus** is a prebend structure, where the clergy lived. **Holy Cross Chapel,** on the Rofenberg, was formerly a place of public assembly. The restored **church at Eschen** has the original walls of the old church laid bare. Other churches include **St. Sebastian's Chapel** and the **Rochus Chapel.** Liechtenstein's first industrial enterprise was a **tile factory** founded at Nendeln in 1836. For a century, it was the only industrial plant in the Unterland.

There's a pool in Eschen and a health trail in Nendeln. You can also enjoy the peaceful mountain footpaths of the Eschnerberg trail.

WHERE TO STAY & DINE

Hotel Engel   This is one of two hotels with the same name (see "Where to Stay" in section 2, above) in Liechtenstein, a fact that causes lots of confusion to visitors arriving in the principality for the first time. A 10-minute drive north from Vaduz, near the principality's biggest ceramic factories (recommended separately in "Shopping" in section 2), the hotel has a dark, modern facade and a large, antique wine press in the yard. Seasonal flowers and plants add freshness to the public areas, a fact that appeals to some local residents, who like to congregate in the hotel on Sunday mornings. The midsize bedrooms are simple, durable, and very clean; 10 have a phone and TV. All the units are equipped with a private bathroom with shower (some with tubs).

Churer Strasse 1, FL-9485 Nendeln, Liechtenstein. ⓒ **00423/373-31-31.** Fax 00423/373-12-60. 17 units. 130F–175F ($107–$144) double; 210F ($172) minisuite. Rates include breakfast. AE, DC, MC, V. Closed Dec. **Amenities:** Breakfast room. *In room:* TV (in some), dataport, phone (in some).

4 The Oberland

The Oberland (Upper Country) of Liechtenstein was the former estate of the count of Vaduz. It consists of Vaduz and five parishes or communes: Planken, Schaan, Triesen, Triesenberg, and Balzers. Although the area is in the south of Liechtenstein, it's still known as the Upper Country because of topography. The Unterland (Lower Country), to the north, is filled with meadows and hills gently rising from the Rhine Valley, while the Oberland, from Planken on south, consists of higher country, reaching up to the Liechtenstein Alps.

In the shadow of the Drei Schwestern mountains, the Oberland abounds in woodlands and mountain trails, alpine flowers, and protected animal species. Settlements founded by Swiss immigrants some 700 years ago still retain their ancient traditions. There are plenty of opportunities for recreation throughout the region, but the alpine portion is the best place for winter sports.

All the villages and hamlets discussed below are reached by postal bus from Vaduz. Pick up a map at the tourist office in Vaduz (see "Essentials," earlier in this chapter), where you can also learn about possible routings and schedules.

Planken is the starting point for excursions to the **Drei Schwestern (Three Sisters)** area. From here, you'll have an outstanding panoramic view of the Rhine Valley and the Swiss mountains extending from Pizol to Lake Constance. A chapel here dedicated to St. Joseph contains copies of old masters and a bronze cross by Georg Malin.

SCHAAN

Located on the Arlberg railway line, at the foot of the Drei Schwestern, 3km (2 miles) west of Vaduz, Schaan is the country's main communications center. The Carolingian land registry (ca. A.D. 831) lists Liechtenstein's second-largest parish under the name Scana. Archaeologists have discovered the remains of a Roman fort, two Roman legionnaires' helmets from the 1st century A.D., and an Alemannic decorative shield from the 6th or 7th century. The 12th-century **Romanesque church** is worth a visit.

There's a **sports center** (ⓒ **00423/233-35-25**) near a forest, offering tennis courts, a health center, an indoor swimming pool, public baths, and a children's playground. You can also hike in the mountains.

Theater a Kirchplatz (ⓒ **00423/237-59-69**) is one of the important cultural centers of the region. It presents international artists.

WHERE TO STAY & DINE

Dux Hotel   This Iberian-style country house is very superior for a tourist-class hotel. Built in 1924, it has a large sun terrace and long wrought-iron balconies. The rugged mountains loom in the background, and there are several old oak trees on the lawn. The comfortable, midsize rooms have wood ceilings and modern amenities, including private bathrooms with shower (some with tubs). The recently renovated hotel is accessible to wheelchairs.

Duxweg 31, FL-9494 Schaan, Liechtenstein. ℂ 00423/232-17-27. Fax 00423/232-48-78. 10 units. 120F–143F ($98–$117) double. Rates include buffet breakfast. MC, V. Free parking. Closed Feb and the 1st 3 weeks of Sept. **Amenities:** 3 restaurants; nearby tennis court; sauna; limited room service; laundry service; nonsmoking rooms. *In room:* TV, dataport, minibar.

Hotel Linde *(Value* This is the town's hotel bargain. The semibaroque facade has a single ornate gable and a pumpkin-colored extension. Well-pruned hedges shield the sun terrace from the street traffic. The clean and comfortable, but small, rooms are functionally furnished. The hotel's restaurant (closed on Sun) serves a very limited but reasonably priced menu.

Feldkircherstrasse 1, FL-9494 Schaan, Liechtenstein. ℂ **00423/232-17-04.** Fax 00423/232-09-29. 23 units. 130F–150F ($107–$123) double. Rates include continental breakfast. AE, MC, V. Free parking. Closed Dec 20. **Amenities:** Restaurant; lounge. *In room:* TV, dataport, minibar, hair dryer, safe.

Hotel Sylva im Sax *(Finds* This little chalet in the woods is so inviting that you may want to anchor here for the night and make the easy commute to Vaduz. It's about a block above the main road. A mother and daughter, Friederecke and Sylva Eberle, offer well-furnished rooms and a sauna. The largest room is laid out for business travelers and includes a fax machine and a second telephone. The restaurant serves some of the best food in the area.

Saxgasse 6, FL-9494 Schaan, Liechtenstein. ℂ **00423/232-39-42.** Fax 00423/232-82-47. 12 units. 174F–196F ($143–$161) double. Rates include buffet breakfast. V. Free parking. **Amenities:** Restaurant; bar; sauna; nonsmoking rooms. *In room:* TV, minibar, hair dryer.

Schaanerhof This is a modern hotel with a pink-and-white facade and balconies on several sides. The interior is comfortable and warm, and the bedrooms are well furnished and maintained. The main dining room serves Italian, Austrian, and Asian dishes, with a revolving monthly menu featuring different cuisines of the world.

In der Ballota 3, FL-9494 Schaan, Liechtenstein. ℂ **00423/232-18-77.** Fax 00423/233-16-27. www.schaanerhof.li. 28 units. 320F–380F ($262–$312) double. Rates include buffet breakfast. AE, DC, V. Free parking. Closed Dec 22–Jan 8. **Amenities:** Restaurant; bar; gym; Jacuzzi; sauna; Turkish bath; laundry service; nonsmoking rooms. *In room:* TV, dataport, minibar, hair dryer.

TRIESENBERG

The largest parish of Liechtenstein has stretches of woodland, scrub, farmland, and pasture. High above the Rhine Valley is the village Triesenberg, containing about 2,000 inhabitants, reached by taking a hill road out of Vaduz. The road is filled with steep bends but offers extensive views. The farming community is developing into a center for light industry and tourism.

Triesenberg, like Planken, was settled in the late 13th century by Swiss immigrants from the Valais. Many of the parish residents wear colorful regional garb. Modern materials and methods are used to build the houses, but the style dates from the early 14th century. The influence of the Valais is evident. The restored town hall is elegant.

You can visit the **Heimatmuseum (Valais Heritage Museum),** which traces the culture of these immigrants. Artifacts, including tools, crafts, and furnishings, depict their life, that and a 20-minute slide show in English. The museum (ℂ **00423/262-19-26**) lies at Dorfzentrum, charging an admission of 2F ($1.30). It's open June to August, Tuesday to Friday 1:30 to 5:30pm, Saturday 1:30 to 5pm, and Sunday 2 to 5pm; September to May, Tuesday to Friday 1:30 to 5:30pm, Saturday 1:30 to 5pm.

At 780m (2,558 ft.), Triesenberg is a good base for excursions to the Liechtenstein Alps. Fine highways and well-tended hiking trails lead from Triesenberg to the alpine resorts: Masescha (1,230m/4,034 ft.), Silum (1,500m/4,920 ft.), Gaflei (1,500m/ 4,920 ft.), Malbun (1,575m/5,166 ft.), and Steg (1,380m/4,526 ft.). Steg is on the way to Malbun and features the Valuna-Lopp cross-country skiing center and a ski lift. The .8km (½-mile) Gnalp-Steg tunnel connects the valley with the alpine area.

WHERE TO STAY & DINE

Hotel Kulm   Spring blossoms cascade down the balconies of this centrally located hotel with a pink and light-grained wood facade. It offers a wide view of the valley, with a sidewalk cafe in front. The interior is a mix of rustic and modern styles. The furniture is comfortable in the well-maintained bedrooms, half of which contain a private bathroom with shower, the others with combination tub/shower.

Dorfzentrum, FL-9497 Triesenberg, Liechtenstein. ℭ 00423/237-79-79. Fax 00423/237-79-78. www.hotelkulm.li. 20 units. 127F–170F ($104–$139) double. Rates include buffet breakfast. Half board 33F ($27) per person extra. AE, DC, MC, V. Free parking. **Amenities:** Restaurant; bar; rooms for guests w/limited mobility. *In room:* TV, dataport, hair dryer.

Hotel Restaurant Steg   This well-kept hotel, run by the Lamperts, is north of Triesenberg on the road to Steg. The building is more than 200 years old and has been renovated frequently, most recently in the late 1980s. It's a rather underpublicized and unpretentious choice. The small rooms are simple but generally adequate. In addition to the regular doubles, there are two dormitories, one for 10 occupants, another for 5 occupants. Corridor bathrooms are well maintained and uncrowded.

FL-9497 Steg/Triesenberg, Liechtenstein. ℭ 00423/263-21-46. Fax 00423/263-21-47. 11 units, none with bathroom; 7 dorm beds. 80F ($66) double; 25F ($21) dorm bed. Rates include breakfast. Half board 25F ($21) extra. MC, V. Free parking. Closed Apr 15–May 15 and Nov 15–Dec 15. **Amenities:** Restaurant. *In room:* No phone.

MASESCHA

Hikers and mountaineers prefer this small resort village 3km (2 miles) north of Triesenberg. The hamlet is perched high above the Rhine Valley. You can admire the cliffs, woods, lush meadows, and clear mountain brooks of this alpine world. In the village you should see **Theodul's Chapel,** a restored medieval church.

MALBUN

Fast rising as a winter ski area, Malbun, 15km (9 miles) north of Vaduz, is the center of winter sports in Liechtenstein, with ski lifts, chairlifts, a ski school, and hotels with indoor swimming pools. You can take the chairlift up to the **Bettlerjoch Peak,** at 2,070m (6,790 ft.). The Prince of Wales and Princess Anne learned to ski here many winters ago. In the summer this is an ideal starting point for mountain walks.

WHERE TO STAY & DINE

Alpenhotel 🎿 *Finds*   This is one of the oldest hotels in Malbun, in the same family since 1908. It's filled with charming details, such as chandeliers made from deer antlers. The wooden ceilings are painted with alpine floral designs and the heavy timbers are carved with regional reliefs. Jacob and Elsa Vögeli-Schroth are eager to please. There is a modern annex and a covered swimming pool. The attractive restaurant serves savory food.

Malbun, FL-9497 Triesenberg, Liechtenstein. ℭ 00423/263-11-81. Fax 00423/263-96-46. www.alpenhotel.li. 23 units. 80F–170F ($66–$139) double. Rates include buffet breakfast. Half board 25F ($21) per person extra. AE, DC, MC, V. Free parking. Closed Apr 15–May 15 and Nov to mid-Dec. **Amenities:** Restaurant; indoor heated pool; limited room service; laundry service. *In room:* TV, dataport, minibar.

Hotel Gorfion-Malbun 𝘈 *(Kids)*   This government-rated four-star chalet—the best in town—is near the ski lifts. The timbered lounge has a fireplace and stucco walls decorated with farm implements. The small to midsize rooms are comfortable and well furnished in a modern but not stylish way. The restaurant serves excellent meals in a homelike atmosphere.

Malbun, FL-9497 Triesenberg, Liechtenstein. (✆) **00423/263-29-44.** Fax 00423/263-95-61. www.s-hotels.com. 64 units. Winter 220F–260F ($180–$213) double, 280F ($230) junior suite for 2, 460F ($377) junior suite for 4; summer 160F–200F ($131–$164) double, 220F ($180) junior suite for 2, 340F ($279) junior suite for 4. Rates include buffet breakfast. AE, DC, MC, V. Free parking. Closed Apr 16–May 19 and Oct 16–Dec 19. **Amenities:** Restaurant; bar; indoor heated pool; sauna; steam room; business services; limited room service; laundry service, nonsmoking rooms. *In room:* TV, dataport, minibar, hair dryer.

Appendix

AT THE CROSSROADS OF EUROPE
Despite its "neutral" image, Switzerland has a fascinating history of external and internal conflicts. Its strategic location, at the crossroads of Europe, made it an irresistible object to empire builders from Roman times. There's even evidence that prehistoric tribes struggled to hold tiny settlements along the great Rhône and Rhine rivers.

The first identifiable occupants were the Celts, who entered the alpine regions from the west. The Helvetii, a Celtic tribe, inhabited a portion of the country that became known as Helvetia. The tribe was defeated by Julius Caesar when it tried to move into southern France in 58 B.C. The Romans conquered the resident tribes in 15 B.C., and peaceful colonization continued until A.D. 455 when the barbarians invaded, followed later by the Christians. Charlemagne (742–814) conquered the small states, or cantons, that occupied the area now known as Switzerland and incorporated them into his realm, which later became the Holy Roman Empire. In the years that followed, Switzerland became a battleground for some of the major ruling families of Europe, especially the Houses of Savoy, the Hapsburgs, and the Zähringen.

BIRTH OF THE CONFEDERATION
The Swiss have always guarded their territory jealously. In 1291 an association of three cantons formed the Perpetual Alliance—the nucleus of today's Swiss Confederation. To be rid of the grasping Hapsburgs, the Confederation in 1439 broke free of the Holy Roman Empire. It later signed a treaty with France, a rival power, agreeing to provide France with mercenary troops. This led to Swiss fighting Swiss in the early 16th century. The agreement was ended around 1515, and in 1516 the confederates declared their complete neutrality.

THE REFORMATION The Protestant Reformation created bitter conflicts in Switzerland between those cantons defending papal Catholicism and those embracing the new creed of Protestantism. Ulrich Zwingli, who like Martin Luther had converted from the Catholic faith, led the Swiss Reformation, beginning in 1519. He translated the Bible into Swiss-German and reorganized church rituals. The Protestant movement was spurred by the 1536 arrival in Geneva of John Calvin, who was fleeing Catholic reprisals in France.

Geneva became one of the most rigidly puritanical strongholds of Protestantism in Europe, fervently committed to its self-perceived role as the New Jerusalem. The spread of Calvinism led to the coining of the French term "Huguenot," a corruption of the Swiss word Eidgenosse (confederate).

After Zwingli died in a religiously motivated battle in 1531, the Swiss spirit of compromise came into play and a peace treaty was signed, allowing each region the right to practice its own faith. Today 55% of the Swiss define themselves as Protestant, 43% as Roman Catholic, and 2% as members of other faiths.

Despite the deep divisions within the confederation created by the Reformation, the confederates managed to stay together by adopting a pragmatic approach to their religious and political differences. Such an approach to national issues, based on compromise, remains one of the cornerstones of the Swiss political system. Later, during the Thirty Years' War (1618–48), the Swiss remained neutral while civil wars flared around them.

INDUSTRIALIZATION & POLITICAL CRISES Turning to economic development, Switzerland in the 18th century became the most industrialized nation in Europe. A rapid population growth, however, created social problems, widening the division between the new class of wealth and the rest of the population. Popular uprisings occurred, but it was only after the French Revolution that they had an effect, causing the Swiss Confederation to collapse in 1798.

Under French guardianship, progressives moved to centralize the constitution of the Swiss Republic. This pull toward centralization clashed with the federalist traditions of the semi-independent cantons. In 1803 Napoleon Bonaparte established a confederation with 19 cantons, but when he fell from power, Swiss conservatives revived the old order. Much of the social progress resulting from the Napoleonic period was reversed and the aristocrats had their former privileges restored to them.

The present Swiss boundaries were fixed at the Congress of Vienna in 1814–15. In 1848, a federal constitution was adopted and the capital established at Bern.

The federal state, by centralizing responsibility for such matters as Customs dues and the minting of coins, created conditions favorable to economic progress. The construction of a railway network and the establishment of a banking system also contributed to Switzerland's development. Both facilitated the country's export industry, consisting chiefly of textiles, pharmaceuticals, and precision machinery.

NEUTRALITY THROUGH TWO WORLD WARS During World War I (1914–18), Switzerland maintained its neutrality from the general European conflict but experienced serious social problems at home. As purchasing power fell and unemployment rose dramatically, civil unrest grew. One cause of bitterness was that Swiss men conscripted into the army automatically lost their jobs. In November 1918 workers, dissatisfied with their conditions, called a general strike, the first and only one in Switzerland's history. The strike led to the introduction of proportional representation in elections. In the 1920s a 48-hour workweek was introduced and unemployment insurance was improved.

Dateline

- **15 B.C.** The Romans conquer the Helvetii and other resident alpine tribes.
- **A.D. 455** Barbarian invasions begin.
- **742–814** Charlemagne incorporates much of what is now Switzerland into his enormous empire.
- **1291** Three cantons form the Perpetual Alliance, the germ of today's Swiss Confederation.
- **1439** The confederation breaks free of the Holy Roman Empire (dating from 962).
- **1516** The confederates (Eidgenossen) proclaim their neutrality in Europe's conflicts.
- **1798** The French Revolution brings an invasion of radical forces and ideas, and the old confederation collapses.
- **1803** Napoleon Bonaparte establishes a new 19-canton confederation, with relatively enlightened social policies.
- **1814–15** The Congress of Vienna guarantees the national boundaries and neutrality of Switzerland.

continued

In 1920 Switzerland joined the League of Nations and provided space for the organization's headquarters at Geneva. As a neutral member, however, it exempted itself from any military action that the League might take.

In August 1939, on the eve of World War II (1939–45), Switzerland, fearing an invasion, ordered a mobilization of its defense forces. But an invasion never came, even though Switzerland was surrounded by Germany and its allies. It proved convenient to all the belligerents to have, in the middle of a continent in conflict, a neutral nation through which they could deal with each other. Switzerland was also successful in deterring a Nazi invasion by indicating to Hitler that it was determined to defend itself. It managed to convince Nazi Germany that any invader would pay in blood for every foot of ground gained in Switzerland.

The sense of neutrality remains so strong that even as recently as 1986, the Swiss voted, in a national referendum, against membership in the United Nations. Switzerland, however, did join the United Nations Educational, Scientific, and Cultural Organization, contributing to its Third World development funds.

Switzerland's political isolationism of the postwar years coincided with a period of unprecedented financial and industrial growth. Many social-welfare programs were introduced, unemployment was virtually wiped out, and the country moved into an enviable position of wealth and prosperity.

INTO THE FUTURE   In 1992 the Swiss rejected the opportunities offered by the economic integration of Europe, preferring their traditional isolation and neutrality. A referendum in December 1992 vetoed the government's attempt to seek full membership in the E.U. But the vote was close: 50.3% against and 49.7% in favor.

All six French-speaking cantons backed the plan, while all but one of the German-speaking cantons opposed it. This revealed a rather dangerous split in a multicultural country's aspirations and political hopes. The plan for European integration was favored not only by the government but also by bankers, labor leaders, intellectuals, and most industrialists. However, it was overwhelmingly rejected by the small rural communities that form much of the Swiss landscape.

Fear of a flood of refugees might have made the final decision for many Swiss, who have looked in horror at the onslaught of workers from abroad pouring into Germany and creating disharmony.

In 1996 and 1997, headlines proclaimed Switzerland a banker for Nazi gold. In July 1997 teams from three major U.S. accounting firms moved into 10 Swiss banks to begin an independent

---

- **1848** The Swiss adopt a federal constitution, still in force today; Bern is recognized as the capital.
- **1914** Switzerland declares its neutrality at the outbreak of World War I.
- **1918** Swiss workers stage the only general strike the country has ever known.
- **1920** Switzerland joins the League of Nations, offering space for a headquarters at Geneva.
- **1939** Fearing an invasion by Nazi Germany, the country orders a total mobilization of its air and ground forces.
- **1939–45** Remaining neutral, despite its laundering of Nazi gold, Switzerland becomes a haven for escaping prisoners of war and avoids direct conflicts.
- **1948** Switzerland introduces broad-based social reforms, including the funding of old-age pensions.
- **1986** The Swiss electorate votes against membership in the United Nations.
- **1992** By a close vote, the Swiss reject ties to an economically integrated Europe.
- **1996–97** Critics around the world attack Switzerland's

inquiry into funds that may have belonged to Holocaust victims.

The Clinton administration accused Switzerland of prolonging World War II by acting as banker to Nazi Germany. But authorities in Bern quickly rejected the accusation as "unsupported" and termed Washington's assessment "one-sided." Reeling from these charges, Switzerland faced new accusations that its wartime weapons industry profited from—and favored—Hitler's Germany in arms trading worth millions of dollars.

The Swiss government ordered its banks to preserve any remaining records of their dealings with Nazi Germany. But in January 1997, a Swiss security guard at the Union Bank of Switzerland halted the destruction of documents from the wartime era, including some that appeared to deal with the forced auctions of property in Berlin during the 1930s.

In 1998 three Swiss banks agreed to pay $1.25 billion to Holocaust survivors, hoping to settle the claims of thousands of survivors whose families lost assets in World War II.

In May 2000 Swiss voters by a 67% majority broke with their long-held isolationism and approved agreements with the E.U. that will link this tiny alpine nation more closely with its neighbors such as Austria, Germany, France, and Italy. The government hopes that the bilateral accords will be a first step toward eventual Swiss membership in the union.

In March 2002, and by a slender margin, neutral Switzerland agreed in a countrywide vote to leave behind decades of isolationism and become a member of the United Nations. The referendum passed by a ratio of 54.6% for it and 45.4% against it. The government lobbied hard for Switzerland to shed its go-it-alone stance and become the 190th member of the global body.

Neutral, peace-loving Switzerland a base for Al Qaeda? Impossible, you say. In 2004 the attorney general of Switzerland, Valentin Roschacher, announced that his country has been used as a financial and logistical base by associates of Al Qaeda for plotting terror against the West. Thirteen suspects were arrested, each involved in Islamic "charity" work. The cases are pending.

---

role as a World War II banker for the Nazi war effort.

- **1998** Three Swiss banks agree to a $1.25-billion fund to be distributed among Holocaust victims.
- **2000** Swiss voters agree to closer E.U. link.
- **2002** Swiss abandon isolation to join U.N.
- **2004** Switzerland a "terror waystation" for Al Qaeda

suspects who used the country as a base.

Index

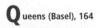

FROMMER'S® COMPLETE TRAVEL GUIDES

Alaska
Amalfi Coast
American Southwest
Amsterdam
Argentina & Chile
Arizona
Atlanta
Australia
Austria
Bahamas
Barcelona
Beijing
Belgium, Holland & Luxembourg
Belize
Bermuda
Boston
Brazil
British Columbia & the Canadian Rockies
Brussels & Bruges
Budapest & the Best of Hungary
Buenos Aires
Calgary
California
Canada
Cancún, Cozumel & the Yucatán
Cape Cod, Nantucket & Martha's Vineyard
Caribbean
Caribbean Ports of Call
Carolinas & Georgia
Chicago
China
Colorado
Costa Rica
Croatia
Cuba
Denmark
Denver, Boulder & Colorado Springs
Edinburgh & Glasgow
England
Europe
Europe by Rail

Florence, Tuscany & Umbria
Florida
France
Germany
Greece
Greek Islands
Hawaii
Hong Kong
Honolulu, Waikiki & Oahu
India
Ireland
Italy
Jamaica
Japan
Kauai
Las Vegas
London
Los Angeles
Los Cabos & Baja
Madrid
Maine Coast
Maryland & Delaware
Maui
Mexico
Montana & Wyoming
Montréal & Québec City
Moscow & St. Petersburg
Munich & the Bavarian Alps
Nashville & Memphis
New England
Newfoundland & Labrador
New Mexico
New Orleans
New York City
New York State
New Zealand
Northern Italy
Norway
Nova Scotia, New Brunswick & Prince Edward Island
Oregon
Paris
Peru

Philadelphia & the Amish Country
Portugal
Prague & the Best of the Czech Republic
Provence & the Riviera
Puerto Rico
Rome
San Antonio & Austin
San Diego
San Francisco
Santa Fe, Taos & Albuquerque
Scandinavia
Scotland
Seattle
Seville, Granada & the Best of Andalusia
Shanghai
Sicily
Singapore & Malaysia
South Africa
South America
South Florida
South Pacific
Southeast Asia
Spain
Sweden
Switzerland
Texas
Thailand
Tokyo
Toronto
Turkey
USA
Utah
Vancouver & Victoria
Vermont, New Hampshire & Maine
Vienna & the Danube Valley
Vietnam
Virgin Islands
Virginia
Walt Disney World® & Orlando
Washington, D.C.
Washington State

FROMMER'S® DOLLAR-A-DAY GUIDES

Australia from $60 a Day
California from $70 a Day
England from $75 a Day
Europe from $85 a Day
Florida from $70 a Day

Hawaii from $80 a Day
Ireland from $90 a Day
Italy from $90 a Day
London from $95 a Day

New York City from $90 a Day
Paris from $95 a Day
San Francisco from $70 a Day
Washington, D.C. from $80 a Day

FROMMER'S® PORTABLE GUIDES

Acapulco, Ixtapa & Zihuatanejo
Amsterdam
Aruba
Australia's Great Barrier Reef
Bahamas
Berlin
Big Island of Hawaii
Boston
California Wine Country
Cancún
Cayman Islands
Charleston
Chicago

Disneyland®
Dominican Republic
Dublin
Florence
Las Vegas
Las Vegas for Non-Gamblers
London
Los Angeles
Maui
Nantucket & Martha's Vineyard
New Orleans
New York City
Paris

Portland
Puerto Rico
Puerto Vallarta, Manzanillo & Guadalajara
Rio de Janeiro
San Diego
San Francisco
Savannah
Vancouver
Venice
Virgin Islands
Washington, D.C.
Whistler

FROMMER'S® CRUISE GUIDES

Alaska Cruises & Ports of Call

Cruises & Ports of Call

European Cruises & Ports of Call

FROMMER'S® DAY BY DAY GUIDES

Amsterdam
Chicago
Florence & Tuscany

London
New York City
Paris

Rome
San Francisco
Venice

FROMMER'S® NATIONAL PARK GUIDES

Algonquin Provincial Park
Banff & Jasper
Grand Canyon

National Parks of the American West
Rocky Mountain
Yellowstone & Grand Teton

Yosemite and Sequoia & Kings
Canyon
Zion & Bryce Canyon

FROMMER'S® MEMORABLE WALKS

Chicago
London

New York
Paris

Rome
San Francisco

FROMMER'S® WITH KIDS GUIDES

Chicago
Hawaii
Las Vegas
London

National Parks
New York City
San Francisco

Toronto
Walt Disney World® & Orlando
Washington, D.C.

SUZY GERSHMAN'S BORN TO SHOP GUIDES

Born to Shop: France
Born to Shop: Hong Kong, Shanghai
& Beijing

Born to Shop: Italy
Born to Shop: London

Born to Shop: New York
Born to Shop: Paris

FROMMER'S® IRREVERENT GUIDES

Amsterdam
Boston
Chicago
Las Vegas
London

Los Angeles
Manhattan
New Orleans
Paris

Rome
San Francisco
Walt Disney World®
Washington, D.C.

FROMMER'S® BEST-LOVED DRIVING TOURS

Austria
Britain
California
France

Germany
Ireland
Italy
New England

Northern Italy
Scotland
Spain
Tuscany & Umbria

THE UNOFFICIAL GUIDES®

Adventure Travel in Alaska
Beyond Disney
California with Kids
Central Italy
Chicago
Cruises
Disneyland®
England
Florida
Florida with Kids

Hawaii
Ireland
Las Vegas
London
Maui
Mexico's Best Beach Resorts
Mini Las Vegas
Mini Mickey
New Orleans
New York City

Paris
San Francisco
South Florida including Miami &
the Keys
Walt Disney World®
Walt Disney World® for
Grown-ups
Walt Disney World® with Kids
Washington, D.C.

SPECIAL-INTEREST TITLES

Athens Past & Present
Cities Ranked & Rated
Frommer's Best Day Trips from London
Frommer's Best RV & Tent Campgrounds
in the U.S.A.

Frommer's Exploring America by RV
Frommer's NYC Free & Dirt Cheap
Frommer's Road Atlas Europe
Frommer's Road Atlas Ireland
Retirement Places Rated

FROMMER'S® PHRASEFINDER DICTIONARY GUIDES

French

Italian

Spanish

THE NEW TRAVELOCITY GUARANTEE

EVERYTHING YOU BOOK WILL BE RIGHT, OR WE'LL WORK WITH OUR TRAVEL PARTNERS TO MAKE IT RIGHT, RIGHT AWAY.

To drive home the point, we're going to use the word "right" in every single sentence.

Let's get right to it. Right to the meat! Only Travelocity guarantees everything about your booking will be right, or we'll work with our travel partners to make it right, right away. Right on!

Here's a picture taken smack dab right in the middle of Antigua, where the guarantee also covers you.

The guarantee covers all but one of the items pictured to the right.

For example, what if the ocean view you booked actually looks out at a downright ugly parking lot? You'd be right to call – we're there for you. And no one in their right mind would be pleased to learn the rental car place has closed and left them stranded. Call Travelocity and we'll help get you back on the right track.

Now, you may be thinking, "Yeah, right, I'm so sure." That's OK; you have the right to remain skeptical. That is until we mention help is always right around the corner. Call us right off the bat, knowing that our customer service reps are there for you 24/7. Righting wrongs. Left and right.

Now if you're guessing there are some things we can't control, like the weather, well you're right. But we can help you with most things – to get all the details in righting,* visit **travelocity.com/guarantee**.

*Sorry, spelling things right is one of the few things not covered under the guarantee.

I'd give my right arm for a guarantee like this, although I'm glad I don't have to.

You'll never roam alone.℠

IF YOU BOOK IT, IT SHOULD BE THERE.

Only Travelocity guarantees it will be, or we'll work
with our travel partners to make it right, right away.
So if you're missing a balcony or anything else you
booked, just call us 24/7 **1-888-TRAVELOCITY**

travelocity
You'll never roam alone